The Dynamics of Opportunity in America

Irwin Kirsch • Henry Braun
Editors

The Dynamics of Opportunity in America

Evidence and Perspectives

Editors
Irwin Kirsch
Educational Testing Service
Princeton, New Jersey, USA

Henry Braun
Lynch School of Education
Boston College
Chestnut Hill, Massachusetts, USA

ISBN 978-3-319-25989-5   ISBN 978-3-319-25991-8   (eBook)
DOI 10.1007/978-3-319-25991-8

Library of Congress Control Number: 2015955136

Springer Cham Heidelberg New York Dordrecht London
© Educational Testing Service 2016

Printed on acid-free paper

Springer International Publishing AG Switzerland is part of Springer Science+Business Media (www.springer.com)

This book is dedicated to our colleague and friend Andy Sum. Andy worked closely with us on the America's Perfect Storm *report and helped to inspire this initiative with his commitment to understanding the factors influencing opportunity in America and his passion for sharing what was learned to inform the public discourse.*

Preface

Opportunity has long played a central role in the American experience. Although the playing field has never been entirely level, most Americans still believe that with hard work, some intelligence, and a little luck, it is possible to make a better life for oneself and one's family. That is, the American Dream is alive and well. This was certainly the case in the decades following World War II, when the American economy grew strongly and, to a reasonable extent, prosperity was shared among all income groups. However, after 1980 things began to change. For one thing, the productivity gains recorded by the economy since then have not been shared equally, resulting in greater inequality in both income and wealth. For another, economic restructuring, due in part to the forces of technology and globalization, has increased the premium to high skills, while those with weaker skills have lost ground in real terms. In addition, policy choices at various levels of government, as well as changing business practices, have generally contributed to the growing divergence in economic outcomes.

One question many are asking is: Does this really matter? In fact, recent data tells us it matters a great deal. There is strong evidence that a family's circumstances are increasingly predictive of the human and social capital that will be accumulated by its children and, consequently, their own prospects as adults. Today, a large proportion of a new birth cohort will grow up in circumstances that will give them a small, if not negligible, chance of following a trajectory that will lead them to a markedly better place than where they started. In other words, the playing field has tilted sharply, making it more difficult for many to have a decent chance of realizing the American Dream. The devastation wrought by the Great Recession of 2007–2009, along with the slow recovery that followed, has only added to the pessimism of the general public regarding the future.

It is in this context that, in 2013, Kurt Landgraf, then President and CEO of Educational Testing Service (ETS), decided, with the full support of the ETS Board of Trustees, to fund an initiative now titled *Opportunity in America*, which builds on a report issued by ETS in 2007 titled *America's Perfect Storm*.[1] That report examined the likely impact of three powerful forces on the prospects for the future. Those forces were (i) wide gaps in literacy and numeracy among both school-age and adult populations, (ii) seismic changes in economic activity and the restructuring of labor markets, and (iii) demographic trends leading to a population that, over a generation, would be somewhat older and much more diverse. The authors argued that, left unchecked, the convergence of these forces would drive the country on a path leading to lower average cognitive skills and greater polarization, economic and otherwise, with grave implications not only for millions of individual lives, but also for society as a whole.

Under the direction of a national advisory panel, this initiative looks more deeply into the dynamics of how human and social capital are developed, along with their growing influence not only on adult outcomes but also on the transmission of opportunity to the next generation. An overarching goal of the initiative is to contribute to public understanding of how these dynamics drive inequality of opportunity where, by opportunity, we mean pathways to the accumulation of human and social capital.

This volume is one of several products planned for the *Opportunity in America* initiative. It contains 13 chapters and an epilogue, written by leaders across a range of fields including education, economics, demography, and political science. They bring a variety of historical, theoretical, and research perspectives to the discussion of inequality of opportunity. As a set, these chapters not only illuminate key aspects of the problem but also offer suggestions of what policies, programs, and/or changes in practices could begin to reverse the trends we are seeing. Written in an engaging style, this volume constitutes an essential foundation for informed discussion and strategic analysis.

* * *

We extend our deep appreciation to those who contributed to the ETS initiative now known as *Opportunity in America*. We especially wish to thank the authors who contributed to the development of this volume and to acknowledge the guidance provided by the members of our National Advisory Panel, whose names appear in the appendix. We enjoyed the opportunity to collaborate with all of them. In addition to Kurt Landgraf, who, with the full backing of the Board of Trustees, provided the funding and support necessary to conduct this phase of the work, we also wish to thank Walt MacDonald, the current president and CEO of ETS, and Ida Lawrence, Senior Vice President for Research and Development, for their continued interest and support of the initiative.

Special thanks also go to our colleagues at ETS for their excellent work on various aspects of the project including contacting and supporting the national advisory panel members and the authors, arranging their travel and contracts, as well as for their planning and supporting the meetings and seminars that were held in Washington, DC, and at Educational Testing Service in Princeton, NJ. These

---

[1] Irwin Kirsch, Kentaro Yamamoto, Henry Braun, and Andrew Sum, *America's Perfect Storm* (Princeton, NJ: Educational Testing Service, 2007).

individuals include Marylou Lennon, Judy Mendez, Anita Sands, and Judy Shahbazian. We also wish to extend our gratitude to Larry Hanover for his careful handling of the review and editing process for each author and to Clara Sue Beym for her watercolor that graces the cover of this volume.

Princeton, NJ, USA   Irwin Kirsch
Chestnut Hill, MA, USA   Henry Braun

Editors' Note

In December 2015, just before this book went to press, the Every Student Succeeds Act, the successor to No Child Left Behind, was passed by Congress and signed by the President. Although it continues some of the testing requirements and disaggregated reporting of NCLB, it severely curtails federal oversight of state accountability systems. We offer this note to provide context when reading certain chapters, written several months earlier, that address NCLB and related issues. For a detailed summary, see http://edworkforce.house.gov/uploadedfiles/joint_esea_conference_framework_short_summary.pdf.

Contents

About the Editors and Contributors

Editors

Irwin Kirsch is Tyler Chair in Large-Scale Assessment and Director of the Center for Global Assessment at Educational Testing Service (ETS). He also serves as Project Director of ETS's *Opportunity in America* initiative.

Henry Braun is Boisi Professor of Education and Public Policy in the Lynch School of Education and Director of the Center for the Study of Testing, Evaluation, and Education Policy at Boston College. He also serves as Project Co-Director of ETS's *Opportunity in America* initiative.

Contributors

Bruce Baker is Professor at the Graduate School of Education at Rutgers University and maintains blogs on school finance and educational policy.

Jared Bernstein is a Senior Fellow at the Center on Budget and Policy Priorities. He previously served as Chief Economist and Economic Adviser to Vice President Joe Biden.

Danielle Farrie is Research Director of the Education Law Center in Newark, New Jersey.

Chrystia Freeland is the Canadian Minister of International Trade and Member of Parliament for University-Rosedale, Toronto, author of *Plutocrats: The Rise of the New Global Super-rich and the Fall of Everyone Else*, and journalist.

Harry J. Holzer is Professor at the McCourt School of Public Policy at Georgetown University and is an Institute Fellow at the American Institutes for Research. He previously served as Chief Economist at the U.S. Department of Labor.

Carl Kaestle is University Professor of Education, History, and Public Policy emeritus at Brown University.

Ishwar Khatiwada is a Labor Economist at the Center for Labor Markets and Policy at Drexel University.

Robert I. Lerman is an Institute Fellow at the Urban Institute, Emeritus Professor of Economics at American University, and a Research Fellow at IZA in Bonn, Germany. He is also the Founder of the American Institute for Innovative Apprenticeship.

Douglas S. Massey is the Henry G. Bryant Professor of Sociology and Public Affairs at Princeton University's Woodrow Wilson School of Public and International Affairs.

Leslie McCall is a Professor in the Department of Sociology and Faculty Fellow at the Institute for Policy Research at Northwestern University.

Jennifer A. O'Day is an Institute Fellow of the American Institutes for Research and is the Founder and Chair of the California Collaborative on District Reform.

Richard V. Reeves is a Senior Fellow in Economic Studies, Co-Director of the Center on Children and Families, and Editor-in-Chief of the Social Mobility Memos blog at the Brookings Institution.

David G. Sciarra is Executive Director of the Education Law Center in Newark, New Jersey.

Timothy M. (Tim) Smeeding is the Arts and Sciences Distinguished Professor of Public Affairs and Economics at the University of Wisconsin-Madison. He was previously Director of the Institute for Research on Poverty at Wisconsin-Madison.

Marshall S. Smith is a Senior Scholar at the Carnegie Foundation for the Advancement of Teaching, a former Dean and Professor at Stanford, and a former Under Secretary and Acting Deputy Secretary at the U.S. Department of Education in the Clinton administration. He is a Fellow of the American Academy of Arts and Sciences and the National Academy of Education.

Andrew M. Sum is Professor Emeritus of Economics at Northeastern University in Boston. He was previously the Director of the Center for Labor Market Studies.

Jonathan Tannen is a Doctoral Candidate in the Urban and Population clusters of the Woodrow Wilson School and the Office of Population Research at Princeton University.

List of Figures

List of Tables

Chapter 1
Introduction: Opportunity in America—Setting the Stage

Henry Braun and Irwin Kirsch

Abstract Opportunity has long been the bedrock of American society. Today, however, the solid foundation that once grounded the lives of millions is fracturing along economic and social lines. Human capital, encompassing a broad set of cognitive and interpersonal skills, has become increasingly important in determining labor market outcomes as the evolving economic landscape, shaped by the interplay of globalization and technology, as well as governmental and business policies, changes who is working and what they are paid. There is now also a tighter link between human and social capital, which is the set of networks, norms, and values that serve to foster development and success. The strengthening of this relationship has contributed to a polarization in the accumulation of human and social capital that translates into distinctly different life outcomes for individuals. This changing landscape also affects the intergenerational transmission of opportunity, with children's circumstances at birth becoming more determinative of their prospects as adults. This introduction sets the stage for the chapters that follow, which offer perspectives on opportunity from fields ranging from education and demography to economics and political science. The authors of these chapters, national leaders in their fields, offer their insights into policies and practices that could help us move forward to improve equality of opportunity and better realize America's values and ideals.

Keywords Opportunity transmission • Skills • Human capital • Social capital • Education funding • Race/ethnicity • Socioeconomic status • Segregation • Labor market • Wages • Unemployment • Family income • Standards-based reform • Apprenticeship • Indicators • American Dream

H. Braun (✉)
Lynch School of Education, Boston College, Chestnut Hill, MA 02467, USA
e-mail: henry.braun@bc.edu

I. Kirsch
Educational Testing Service, Princeton, NJ, USA

© Educational Testing Service 2016
I. Kirsch, H. Braun (eds.), *The Dynamics of Opportunity in America,*
DOI 10.1007/978-3-319-25991-8_1

1

Introduction

Opportunity has long been the bedrock of American society. Although, as a country, we have never fully realized the ideal of opportunity for all, most Americans have believed that with hard work and a little luck it was possible for them to make a better life for themselves and their children. Today the experience of increasing numbers of Americans tells a vastly different story. The solid foundation that once grounded the lives of many is fracturing along economic and social lines.

Our current economic landscape has been shaped by the complex interplay of globalization and technology as well as national and state policies. Many of the resulting changes have been positive. But the technology-driven globalized economy has also had devastating consequences for many American workers. It has changed who is working, where they work, and what they are paid. As a result of increasingly sophisticated technology, millions of jobs have simply disappeared. Assembly line jobs have been replaced by industrial robots, scanners are doing the work of grocery store cashiers, and software has been developed to handle routine administrative jobs formerly performed by bookkeepers and payroll clerks. Other jobs have been shipped overseas to take advantage of low-cost labor. Production jobs associated with apparel manufacturing or the assembly of electronic components, as well as service jobs at help desks and call centers, are just a few examples.

One outcome of this changing economic landscape is that the broad set of skills that constitutes human capital has become increasingly important in determining employment and wages. Critical skill sets extend beyond proficiency in reading, math, and writing to include analytical, technical, problem solving, and communication skills. Rapidly evolving technologies and a job market where the average worker can expect to change jobs multiple times over his or her career have also put demands on individuals to be increasingly nimble and able to learn on their own. In the fast-paced competitive global marketplace, those who can bring higher-level skills and the flexibility to adapt are in demand. Those without such skills are lagging behind.

The growing importance of skills is not confined to the workplace. Many of the everyday tasks required to manage our lives and plan for the future are becoming increasingly complex as well. Whether we are paying bills online, using the Internet to look for a job or complete a class assignment, or taking on responsibilities that were once handled by employers such as selecting a health care plan or managing a retirement account, skills matter more in daily life as well as on the job.

Just as changes in the economic landscape have increased the importance of human capital, changes in the social landscape have affected the ability of individuals to develop positive social capital, or the set of networks, norms, and values that serve to foster development and success. In previous generations, strong social networks and common norms of civic engagement that constitute social capital transcended socioeconomic classes. People tended to vote at similar rates regardless of their education levels; marriage rates were similar in both affluent and disadvantaged communities; and children in most neighborhoods participated in sports and clubs. But over the past generation or two, social capital has become more strongly related to human capital; that is, those with limited human capital are even more disadvantaged because they often lack necessary social capital, and those with more human capital tend to have the networks, norms, and behaviors that provide the most benefit in today's environment.

Educational Testing Service's *Opportunity in America* initiative defines opportunity as pathways to the development of human and social capital. Those pathways may be more or less open for individuals based on the circumstances into which they are born and the trajectory of their lives. The presence or absence of opportunities to develop human and social capital, as well as the choices individuals make to take advantage (or not) of those opportunities, translate into distinctly different life outcomes and, as the generational cycle continues, lead to differential prospects for their children.

This transmission of opportunity from one generation to the next is driven by the dynamics of advantage or disadvantage, with one advantage building upon another for some children, while one disadvantage is compounded by the next for others. The result is diverging destinies that are increasingly defined by circumstances of birth. While birth circumstances have always impacted an individual's life chances, today's children are being born into an America that is increasingly polarized along economic, educational, and social lines, an America where it is harder to make up for early gaps in opportunities to develop human and social capital. This is not in anyone's best interests. It not only impacts this generation and the next, but also the very quality of our society and, ultimately, our democracy.

This volume is an important part of the ETS initiative, which is designed to advance the national conversation about opportunity in America, as it serves as the empirical undergirding for the other parts. The chapters address a number of topics and perspectives ranging from education and demography to economics and political science. The authors shed light on a variety of issues and challenges regarding inequality of opportunity, but they also offer insights into policies and practices that could help us think anew about how to move in a direction that is more in keeping with our national values and ideals.

Of course, it is obvious that a single volume, no matter how rich, cannot hope to capture the full complexity of the current situation. There are multiple forces and policies acting at different levels: supranational, national, regional, and local. Supranational forces like globalization, the accelerating infusion of technology into different workplaces, the increasing power and reach of information and communication technology, and even cultural shifts are not easily tamed at the national level. But other forces are driven by policies adopted by various levels of government. They range from national economic and social welfare policies to state laws governing education funding, collective bargaining and right to work, and local zoning ordinances. These forces interact in complex ways over time that shape trends in opportunity. Moreover, the dynamics play out in systematically different ways depending on location, race/ethnicity, socioeconomic status, and other factors. Thus, we should always bear in mind that oft-cited national averages can conceal more than they reveal and that countervailing policies and interventions must take into account local realities if they are to achieve even a modicum of success.

Description of the Volume

This volume is divided into four parts. Part I comprises Chaps. 2 through 5 and sets a context for understanding opportunity in America. Part II includes Chaps. 6 and 7, each focusing on labor market issues as they relate to opportunity. Chapters 8 through 11 make up Part III and explore the relationship between education and opportunity. Finally, Part IV looks at opportunity through the political lens. It includes Chaps. 12 and 13 as well as a concluding epilogue.

Part I: Understanding Where We Are Today

Chapter 2 by Douglas S. Massey and Jonathan Tannen describes trends in residential segregation by race and income. Through striking contrasts between affluent Whites and poor Blacks with respect to social and economic resources, they highlight the importance of place in determining individuals' life chances. In particular, they note that even today, approximately one-third of Blacks living in metropolitan areas reside in so-called hypersegregated neighborhoods, generally characterized by failing schools, high crime rates, and few possibilities for employment (see also Wilson 2011). Similar trends appear to be developing for Hispanics. Massey and Tannen conclude as they began with the assertion that "residential segregation is the structural linchpin of America's system of racial stratification."

The magisterial Chap. 3 by Carl Kaestle chronicles governmental efforts in education since the mid-19th century, with greater attention to more recent history and the ongoing tension between traditionalists, who favor local control, and those who argue that greater central authority is essential to achieving broader improvement in educational outcomes. From his historical analysis he draws conclusions regarding both the limits of governmental action (at different levels) and the policies that could contribute to greater equity in educational outcomes.

Chapter 4, by Bruce Baker, Danielle Farrie, and David G. Sciarra, tackles the current state of public education finance, with particular reference to the twin goals of equal educational opportunity and educational adequacy. It is commonsensical that districts serving more disadvantaged students require more resources per capita to approach educational equity. In most states that is the case, at least to some degree, but most have also lost ground during and since the Great Recession. Extra resources directed at more poorly funded districts matter, as the authors demonstrate, because they typically result in improvement in factors associated with greater student learning, such as smaller class sizes, more competitive teacher wages, and better instructional support. Inadequate funding continues to plague the drive to provide appropriate resources to those who need them the most.

Chapter 5 by Henry Braun begins by reviewing trends in income inequality over the last four decades, highlighting the increasing gaps, especially since the late 1990s. He argues that greater separation between rungs of the income ladder has implications not only for individuals but also for civil society and the democratic polity. Keeping with the definition of opportunity as pathways to developing human and social capital, Braun proposes a tripartite framework of *Gates, Gaps* and *Gradients* to aid in both understanding and communicating the complex dynamics that shape children's developmental trajectories. He notes that we are experiencing an accelerating accumulation of advantage—or disadvantage—that is leading to an ever-greater divergence in adult outcomes, with clear implications for the prospects of the next generation, and concludes with some reflections on how we can begin to reverse these trends.

Part II: The Labor Market

Chapter 6, by Jared Bernstein, focuses on wages. He reviews wage trends over the last 35 years and offers strong empirical evidence of wage stagnation, or even decline, at all but the highest levels of educational attainment while noting some important differences in the experiences of men and women at comparable educational levels. He then presents a critical examination of the various explanations for the observed wage trends, including skill-biased technological change. He argues that although none of these explanations offer a complete answer, they each offer some insight. Bernstein concludes that the most powerful antidotes to the current situation would be the reduction in labor market slack and the strengthening of labor market institutions and standards. Such changes would be particularly beneficial to workers at the lower end of the income scale. However, given the political gridlock in Washington, a systemic approach to labor market issues is not likely and one can only hope for some piecemeal improvement and policy advances at the state or local levels. Recent success in raising the minimum wage in some cities is an example of such advances.

Chapter 7, by Ishwar Khatiwada and Andrew M. Sum, deals primarily with labor market participation and presents a wealth of relevant data drawn from a number of sources. Arguing that the much-cited unemployment rate gives a grossly incomplete picture of labor market participation, they define *labor underutilization* as the sum of unemployed, underemployed (those who are working part time but cannot obtain full-time work), and hidden unemployed (those who have stopped looking for a job but want to be in the full-time work force), divided by the total civilian labor force.

With that definition, in 2013–2014, the underutilization rates varied from 2.9 % for individuals with master's or higher degrees to 13.9 % for those with neither a high school diploma nor a GED. Although the rates increased for all groups since 1999–2000, the lower the educational attainment, the greater the increase.

Correspondingly, over the same period, employment/population ratios fell dramatically, especially for younger, minority youths. Of course, being underutilized not only affects individual and household income but has implications for the timing of other life milestones such as family formation and establishing a stable residence. They conclude that over the last 15 years or so, the labor market has not only seen a marked increase in inequality related to socioeconomic status but also considerable variation by location and race/ethnicity. They assert that a "full employment" economy would do much to reduce overall underutilization rates as well as the stark inequalities now extant.

Part III: Education and Opportunity

Chapter 8, by Timothy M. (Tim) Smeeding, focuses on early development from conception to entry into kindergarten. Marshalling a wealth of empirical evidence, as well as recent scientific research, he constructs a strong argument for the role of contextual factors in shaping opportunity and the resulting accumulation of human and social capital. These factors comprise family structure and maternal health, family income and wealth, parenting practices, social institutions, and neighborhood characteristics. He employs the term *dynamic complementarity* to describe how the concatenation of advantages (i.e., open gates to opportunity) results in the amplification of their individual effects (compare to Heckman on the virtuous cycle begun by effective early interventions; Heckman and Masterov 2007; Heckman and Mosso 2014). He expresses grave concerns regarding the implications of current trends in inequality of opportunity for intergenerational mobility and, like Braun, offers some policy prescriptions for halting the polarization we are now observing.

In Chap. 9, Jennifer O'Day and Marshall S. Smith address the role of schooling in leveling the playing field of opportunity. They argue that, in many districts across the country, systemic problems, along with discriminatory practices and general dysfunction in many schools, leave millions of disadvantaged students behind. When compounded by a range of neighborhood deficits, including a severe lack of resources, the result is that these students fail to gain the skills they need to realize their legitimate aspirations. Sifting through the history of 50 years of educational reform, the authors distill five key lessons to guide future efforts—efforts that should be systemic and sustained. They propose a high-level, three-pronged strategy to improve educational achievement as well as suggestions on the roles best played by different stakeholders including governments, educators, and communities. Through their elaboration of this strategy they are, in effect, offering a radical updating of the standards-based reform strategy contained in their seminal papers of the early 1990s (Smith and O'Day 1991; O'Day and Smith 1993). The chapter concludes with a review of current developments in education finance and policy in California and speculates on what this might portend for the country as a whole (Kirst 2013).

Chapter 10, by Robert I. Lerman, argues that an expanded, properly supported initiative on apprenticeship would be a powerful and cost-effective strategy to prepare tens of thousands of young adults for technical occupations that lead to middle class wages and benefits. Unlike other countries, notably Germany, the U.S. does not have a good track record with regard to apprenticeships, although Lerman is able to cite some current examples. He argues that a range of robust apprenticeship programs would not only benefit students who would otherwise drop out of high school or graduate with weak skills and no relevant work experience, but also employers who would have access to trained, entry-level employees and the capacity to upgrade their workplace. He concludes with a set of strategies to move the apprenticeship initiative forward, drawing on recent experiences in Great Britain as well as in some states. While recognizing that political and financial obstacles remain, he is guardedly optimistic about the future of the initiative.

In Chap. 11, Harry J. Holzer addresses the problem that too many students from disadvantaged backgrounds, even those who enroll in tertiary education programs, fail to accumulate sufficient human capital to enable them to compete successfully in the job market. The causes are many, including weak preparation in K-12, poor counseling (or none at all), attendance at typically lower resourced institutions (e.g., community colleges), and low completion rates (especially at proprietary institutions), among others. Complementing Lerman's chapter, Holzer's argues that, in view of the variety of needs and challenges, the U.S. must initiate or strengthen a broad range of policies and practices to improve the labor market outcomes for these students. That range encompasses better high school-to-work pathways (e.g., apprenticeships and career technical education), alternative postsecondary options linked to local labor market needs, and substantially higher completion rates at two- and four-year institutions. While acknowledging that the long-term success of any or all of these policies depends in large part on trends in the labor market, he argues that a more coherent and focused public investment strategy is essential to reducing the opportunity gap we now have.

Part IV: Politics and the Road Ahead

Chapter 12 by Leslie McCall offers empirically grounded insights into the public's views on the causes of the present state of inequality of opportunity and economic outcomes, as well as the implications for themselves and their families. She identifies three potential policy responses and explores their relationships both to historic norms and to a range of current conceptions of what would characterize a fair society. The data presented display a general decline in belief in the American Dream. For example, over the period 2001–2012, in response to the question, "How satisfied are you with the opportunity for someone in this nation to get ahead by working hard?", the percentage of the public that responded very or somewhat satisfied declined from 76 to 53 %. In other graphs and tables she further documents this decline, as well as a substantial divergence in views between the general public and those residing comfortably at the top of the income/wealth ladder. She concludes with consideration of a set of linked policy options that are most in line with a majority of the public who, she believes, are less polarized on these issues than their political representatives. What is missing, she argues, is innovative political/economic leadership that, building on local initiatives, could forge a national commitment to shared prosperity that would, over time, reduce class-based advantages in the intergenerational transmission of opportunity.

Chapter 13, by Richard V. Reeves, focuses on indicators, that is, summary statistics or metrics that can be used to describe a current state and, when collected systematically over time, can reveal trends to inform policy makers and other stakeholders. He maintains that if America is to have an "opportunity policy agenda," then "indicators are necessary to guide policy, drive data collection strategies, and measure progress."[1] In this regard, he offers both a short history and a useful taxonomy. He asserts that it is important to have clear policy goals in order for the selected indicators, as well as the investments that must be made in collecting, analyzing, and summarizing the needed data, to be as productive as possible. Reeves offers as one important opportunity-related goal an increase in relative intergenerational income mobility, adducing evidence that such mobility has been relatively flat in the U.S. but particularly "sticky" at the extremes of the income distribution. (The argument for indicators that he puts forward, however, is relevant to any policy goal.) Ideally, Reeves suggests, we should have a dashboard of opportunity indicators, ranging from short term to long term, at various levels of aggregation and based on data collected on regular schedules. Examples are drawn from a number of sources, including the United Kingdom and Colorado.

The last entry is a short epilogue by Chrystia Freeland. In it she maintains that if the U.S. is to be successful in reducing income inequality, it must do so not by a frontal attack on capitalism but by striving to reform market capitalism to move (back) to a model of inclusive prosperity so that national wealth can be more equally shared. In this effort, the support of some of the 1 %, and especially the 0.1 %, is crucial—and she quotes two of that elite group who believe the nation's present course in the distribution of wealth is not sustainable. Although many would argue that the prospect of widespread support for these policies is highly unlikely, she cites a number of instances in the past where America's business elite accepted financial sacrifices for the common good. Perhaps one more such occurrence is not beyond the realm of possibility!

Conclusion

One cannot read the chapters in this volume without developing both a sense of dread and a feeling of hope. It is evident that there are two Americas: one where opportunities abound, adults are able to navigate rough economic seas, and their

---

[1] For an extended treatment of the use of indicators to monitor public policies and public services, see Bird et al. (2005).

children inherit compounding advantages that enable them to thrive in their own right, and the other where opportunities are scarce, adults struggle on a daily basis, and their children inherit compounding disadvantages as a result of the closed gates along their developmental trajectories. Significant and growing gaps across a range of domains not only shape individual lives but also the very fabric of society. Although there are some who remain unfazed by the specter of increasing inequality of opportunity, most express grave concerns about the future if the forces and policies driving us apart remain unchecked. They argue that it is long past time to take constructive action to reverse the effects of these forces and policies.

The rhetoric of the American Dream is not only uplifting but also highly motivating. Across the country, local communities and even whole regions are coming together to understand their present situation and to plan and implement countervailing strategies. The chapters in this volume call out a number of these efforts and offer suggestions for how we can move forward—strategically and tactically—with both efficacy and efficiency. We agree that there is hope but that the scope and pace of action are yet inadequate to the challenge. The modest goal of this volume is to help to catalyze an ongoing national conversation by contributing an accessible and empirically grounded understanding of America's recent past and possible futures. By taking ambitious actions at scale over a long period of time, we believe that it is still possible to avert the bleak future that otherwise lies ahead.

References

Bird, Sheila, David Cox, Vern Farewell, Harvey Goldstein, Tim Holt, and Peter Smith. 2005. Performance indicators: Good, bad, and ugly. *Journal of the Royal Statistical Society* 168(1): 1–27.

Heckman, James J., and Dimitriy V. Masterov. 2007. The productivity argument for investing in young children. *Applied Economic Perspectives and Policy* 29(3): 446–493.

Heckman, James J., and Stefano Mosso. 2014. *The economics of human development and social mobility*, NBER Working Paper 19925. Cambridge, MA: National Bureau of Economic Research.

Kirst, Michael. 2013. *The common core meets state policy: This changes almost everything*, PACE Policy Memorandum. Stanford: Policy Analysis for California Education.

O'Day, Jennifer A., and Marshall Smith. 1993. Systemic reform and educational opportunity. In *Designing coherent education policy: Improving the system*, ed. Susan Fuhrman, 250–312. San Francisco: Jossey-Bass.

Smith, Marshall S., and Jennifer A. O'Day. 1991. Systemic school reform. In *The politics of curriculum and testing, politics of education association yearbook 1990*, ed. Susan Fuhrman and Betty Malen, 233–267. London: Falmer Press.

Wilson, William Julius. 2011. Being poor, Black, and American: The impact of political, economic, and cultural forces. *American Educator* 35(1): 10–46.

Part I
Understanding Where We Are Today

Chapter 2
Segregation, Race, and the Social Worlds of Rich and Poor

Douglas S. Massey and Jonathan Tannen

Abstract Residential segregation has been called the "structural linchpin" of racial stratification in the United States. Recent work has documented the central role it plays in the geographic concentration of poverty among African-Americans as well as the close connection between exposure to concentrated deprivation and limited life chances. Here we review trends in racial segregation and Black poverty to contextualize a broader analysis of trends in the neighborhood circumstances experienced by two groups generally considered to occupy the top and bottom positions in U.S. society: affluent Whites and poor Blacks. The analysis reveals a sharp divergence of social and economic resources available within the social worlds of the two groups. We tie this divergence directly to the residential segregation of African-Americans in the United States, which remains extreme in the nation's largest urban Black communities. In these communities, the neighborhood circumstances of affluent as well as poor African-Americans are systematically compromised.

Keywords Residential segregation • School segregation • Racial segregation • Hypersegregation • Poverty concentration • Poverty • Neighborhood disadvantage • Racial stratification • Geographic mobility

Introduction

Residential segregation has been called the "structural linchpin" of racial stratification in the United States (Pettigrew 1979; Bobo 1989; Bobo and Zubrinsky 1996), and over time its role in the perpetuation of Black disadvantage (and White advantage) has become increasingly clear to social scientists (for a review, see Massey

D.S. Massey (✉)
Henry G. Bryant Professor of Sociology and Public Affairs, Princeton University, Princeton, NJ, USA

J. Tannen
Woodrow Wilson School, Office of Population Research, Princeton University, Princeton, NJ, USA

© Educational Testing Service 2016
I. Kirsch, H. Braun (eds.), *The Dynamics of Opportunity in America*,
DOI 10.1007/978-3-319-25991-8_2

2013). William Julius Wilson (1987) was the first to notice the rising concentration of poverty in Black inner city neighborhoods during the 1980s. Massey (1990) subsequently sought to explain this growing concentration of Black poverty using a simulation to demonstrate how rising rates of Black poverty interact with high levels of Black segregation to concentrate poverty in certain areas and neighborhoods. Massey and Denton (1993) went on to argue that by concentrating poverty, racial segregation created a uniquely harsh and disadvantaged social environment for poor African-Americans and residential circumstances with much fewer advantages for affluent African-Americans compared to Whites of similar social status.

In his analysis of the mathematics underlying Massey's simulation exercise, Quillian (2012) demonstrated that concentrated poverty stemmed not simply from an interaction between Black poverty and Black segregation but was also affected by the level of geographic separation between poor and nonpoor Blacks as well as the degree of segregation between poor Blacks and others who were both nonpoor and non-Black. Given conditions that commonly prevail in metropolitan America, however, Quillian (2012, 370) gave his support to Massey's theoretical argument. When African-Americans are highly segregated, increases in Black poverty are absorbed by a relatively small number of compressed, racially homogeneous neighborhoods, increasing the geographic concentration of poverty in ghetto areas.

Subsequent research has confirmed the close connection between Black segregation and geographically concentrated disadvantage and demonstrated the powerful negative influence of concentrated poverty on individual life chances (Sampson 2012; Massey and Brodmann 2014). Owing primarily to the persistence of racial residential segregation, poor African-Americans experience levels of neighborhood poverty, violence, and social disorder that are rarely, if ever, experienced by the poor of other groups (Peterson and Krivo 2010; Sampson 2012). Moreover, the high exposure of African-Americans to geographically concentrated disadvantage not only persists over the individual life cycle but also is maintained across the generations. Indeed, Sharkey (2013) found that half of all African-Americans nationwide had lived in the poorest quartile of urban neighborhoods for at least two generations, compared to just 7 % of Whites. Whereas in 1968 Otis Dudley Duncan argued that Black socioeconomic disadvantage was transmitted along the lines of race, in the twenty-first century, Sharkey shows how Black disadvantage is increasingly transmitted on the basis of place.

Here we review trends in the degree of Black residential segregation along with rates of Black and White poverty from 1970 to 2010 to assess the structural potential for concentrated poverty and how it has changed over time. We then examine trends in neighborhood conditions experienced by poor Whites and Blacks and compare them to those experienced by affluent Whites and Blacks. Our analysis documents the widening gap between the social worlds inhabited by those at the top and bottom of the U.S. socioeconomic hierarchy and underscores the powerful effect that segregation has in undermining the quality of the neighborhoods even of African-Americans.

Four Decades of Segregation and Poverty

Our analysis draws on census tract data obtained from the decennial censuses of 1970, 1980, 1990, 2000, and 2010 as well as data from the 2008–2012 American Community Surveys for 287 consistently defined Metropolitan Statistical Areas (MSAs; borrowing liberally from a dataset developed by Rugh and Massey 2014). Figure 2.1 shows trends in the degree of Black–White segregation from 1970 to 2010. The values are weighted averages of segregation indices computed for all MSAs, where weights are the proportion of all metropolitan Blacks living in each MSA. The trends thus represent changes in the degree of segregation experienced by the average Black metropolitan resident over time.

We measure segregation using the well-known *index of dissimilarity*, which gives the relative share of two groups that would have to exchange neighborhoods to achieve an even residential distribution (Massey and Denton 1988). We proxy neighborhoods using census tracts, which are small local areas averaging around 4,000 persons defined by the U.S. Census Bureau. In an even residential distribution each tract would replicate the racial composition of the metropolitan area as a whole. For example, if an MSA were 10 % Black and 90 % White, then evenness would be achieved when each tract was 10 % Black and 90 % White, yielding an

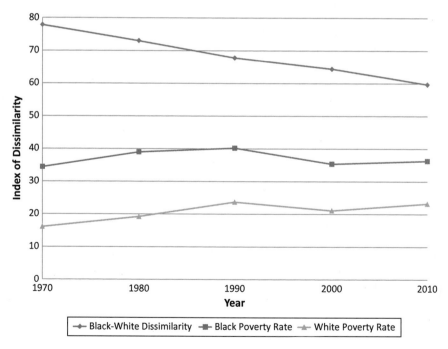

Fig. 2.1 Black-White residential dissimilarity and Black and White poverty rates in metropolitan areas

index value of zero. In general, tract-based dissimilarity indices of 60 or greater are considered to be high, those between 30 and 60 moderate, and those under 30 low.

According to these criteria, average levels of Black-White segregation have remained in the high range throughout the past four decades. Nonetheless, levels of racial segregation *have* displayed a slow but steady decline over time, with the dissimilarity index going from 78 in 1970 to around 60 in 2010, a decline of about five points per decade. Although the trend in Black-White segregation may have been downward on average, Rugh and Massey (2014) found considerable variation across MSAs in the rate of decline. Their statistical analysis revealed that lower levels of Black segregation and more rapid shifts toward integration were predicted by small metropolitan population size, high Black socioeconomic status, low levels of anti-Black prejudice, permissive density zoning in suburbs, the presence of a college or university, larger concentrations of military personnel, and a small Black percentage. In general, therefore, metropolitan areas experiencing a decline in segregation over the past 40 years have been those of small size with a relatively small Black population of high socioeconomic status, with suburban zoning regimes that allow multi-unit housing, and a military base and/or colleges or universities in the metropolitan region. Obviously this profile does not fit the metropolitan areas where most African-Americans live.

Figure 2.1 also shows trends in Black and White poverty from 1970 to 2010. We define poverty as coming from a household within an income of $30,000 or less (the cutoff for receipt of a federal Pell college grant for low-income students). As can be seen, there is little evidence of any downward trend in the level of Black poverty over time. Indeed, the poverty rate *rose* from 34 to 40 % between 1970 and 1990; and although it fell to a rate of 35 during the economic boom of the 1990s by 2010, it had risen back to up 36 %, two points above where it stood in 1970. The rate of White poverty likewise rose between 1970 and 1990, going from 16 to 24 % before dropping back to 21 % in 2000 and then rising back up to 23 % in 2010. For both racial groups, we expect trends in the concentration of poverty generally to follow trends in the rate of poverty (Jargowsky 1997). Thus it should rise during the 1970s and 1980s, fall in the 1990s, and then rise again during the 2000s, though absolute levels of poverty concentration naturally will be much lower for Whites than Blacks.

As already noted, declines in Black-White segregation were quite uneven across regions, with high levels generally persisting in sizable poor Black communities located in the nation's large metropolitan areas. In their analysis of 1980 census data, Massey and Denton (1989) went further to identify a subset of areas in which African-Americans were segregated along multiple geographic dimensions simultaneously, a pattern of intense isolation they labeled hypersegregation. In hypersegregated metropolitan areas, African Americans are highly segregated (index value above 60) on at least four of segregation's five underlying geographic dimensions. Thus African-Americans were not only unevenly distributed across neighborhoods but also experienced high levels of isolation, living in nearly all-Black neighborhoods that were clustered tightly together to form a densely packed community located in and around the city center. In 1980, such areas housed a disproportionate share of all African-Americans. Although a recent analysis by Massey and Tannen (2015) revealed that the number of hypersegregated areas dropped sharply between 1970 and 2010, 34 % of all metropolitan Black residents still lived under conditions of hypersegregation 40 years later, with another 21 % living under conditions of "high" segregation (dissimilarity index above 60).

The top of Fig. 2.2 shows trends in Black-White segregation for the five most racially segregated metropolitan areas as of 2010. These data underscore how limited progress toward racial integration has been in the nation's largest urban Black communities. In MSAs such as Milwaukee, New York, Chicago, Detroit, and Cleveland—places with well-known and long-established Black ghettos—progress toward residential integration has been limited, with dissimilarity indices ranging narrowly between 73 and 80 even in the age of Obama. Among all hypersegregated areas, the average Black-White dissimilarity index fell from 79 in 1970 to 66 in 2010, and their ranks included St. Louis, where Blacks and Whites at present are bitterly divided over the killing of an unarmed Black teenager by a White police officer in the predominantly Black suburb of Ferguson.

Figure 2.2 also shows trends in Black-White dissimilarity among the five least segregated metropolitan areas in 2010. As can be seen, in smaller metropolitan areas with tiny Black populations levels of segregation, the dissimilarity index fell quite rapidly over the past four decades. In Provo, Utah, for example, the index fell from 83 in 1970 to just 18 in 2010. Of course, the Black population of Provo numbered just 4,012 in 2010 and was relatively affluent, not to mention Provo is a college town (home to Brigham Young University). The average dissimilarity index for all five areas went from 66 in 1970 to 19 in 2010, but the average size of the Black

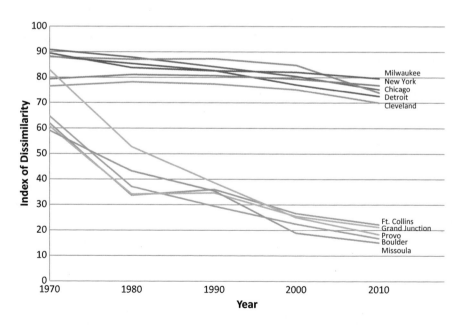

Fig. 2.2 Segregation trends in the most and least segregated metropolitan areas

population was 2,600 and all five areas contained colleges or universities, again not a profile that applies to most Black metropolitan residents.

The link between the degree of Black segregation and the relative size of the Black population reflects changes in White racial attitudes since the civil rights era. In the 1960s, large majorities of White Americans supported racial segregation in principle, agreeing that Whites had a right to keep Blacks out of their neighborhoods and that African-Americans should respect that right. By the 1990s, however, the percentage of Whites expressing this viewpoint had fallen to single digits, and most had adopted a color-blind ideology of equal opportunity for all regardless of race (Schuman et al. 1998).

Despite the collapse of White support for segregation in principle, however, negative racial stereotypes remain firmly rooted in White social cognition and White respondents show little tolerance for associating with very many African-Americans in practice, especially in intimate settings such as neighborhoods and schools. On surveys, as the hypothetical number of Black students or neighbors increases, larger and larger shares of White respondents express discomfort, declaring a reluctance to enter a neighborhood and expressing a desire to leave (Charles 2003, 2006). Even after controlling for a neighborhood's property values, crime rates, and school quality, the likelihood that a White subject would be willing to purchase a home in a neighborhood declines sharply as the percentage of Blacks rises (Emerson et al. 2001).

Under these circumstances, in metropolitan areas with small Black populations, Whites can simultaneously honor their ideological commitment to equal opportunity and satisfy their desire not to share schools or neighborhoods with many Black people. In Provo, for example, the Black percentage is just 0.7 %, so under conditions of complete integration (a Black-White dissimilarity index of zero) each neighborhood would be just 0.7 % Black, which is well within White tolerance limits. In contrast, Milwaukee County is 27 % Black, so complete integration there would yield neighborhoods that were 27 % Black, which is well beyond the comfort level of most Whites—hence the current pattern of high, stubborn levels of segregation in metropolitan areas containing large Black communities but rapid shifts toward integration in areas where few African-Americans actually live.

Nonetheless, patterns of racial segregation did change after the civil rights era. Whereas virtually all metropolitan areas were highly segregated by race in 1970, 40 years later, segregation levels vary widely across metropolitan areas. Indeed, from 1970 to 2010 the standard deviation of Black-White dissimilarities rose from 10.2 to 11.2. At the same time, the standard deviation of Black poverty rates fell from 10.1 to 8.2. With stable means and declining variability in rates of Black poverty but declining means and rising variability with respect to Black segregation, the geographic concentration of Black poverty over time has increasingly come to be determined by inter-metropolitan variation in the degree of Black residential segregation.

Poverty and Privilege in Black and White

Historically, poor African-Americans have been concentrated disproportionately at the bottom of the U.S. socioeconomic distribution while affluent Whites have congregated near the top. As noted earlier, we define poverty as having a household income of $30,000 or lower; for our purposes we define affluence as having a household income of $120,000 or greater. In order to examine shifts in the size of the gap between the top and bottom of American society, therefore, we chart trends in the social and economic characteristics of neighborhoods occupied by the affluent and poor of both races, with dollar amounts expressed in constant 2010 dollars. Figure 2.3 begins the analysis by plotting trends in the proportion of households with incomes of $30,000 or lower in the neighborhoods inhabited by affluent Blacks and poor Blacks, as well as affluent Whites and poor Whites.

Figure 2.3 indicates the degree to which Blacks and Whites at the top and bottom of the income distribution are exposed to poverty within the social worlds defined by their neighborhoods. Obviously poor African-Americans have always experienced a higher concentration of poverty than other groups, and as expected, changes in the degree of poverty concentration closely follow trends in the rate of poverty generally. In 1970 the average poor African-American lived in a neighborhood that was 40 % poor, and this figure increased to 49 % by 1990 before dropping to 44 % in 2000 and then edging back up to 45 % in 2010. Although affluent African-Americans are less exposed to neighborhood poverty than poor Blacks (25 % and

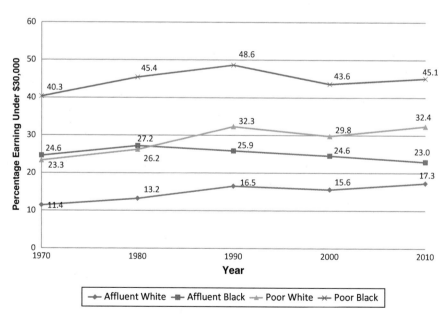

Fig. 2.3 Percentage of households earning less than $30,000 in neighborhoods of metropolitan areas (by various race/income groups)

27 %, respectively), in 1970 and 1980 their exposure to poverty was on a par with levels typically experienced only by poor Whites, whose respective figures stood at 23 and 26 % in the 2 years. In contrast, affluent Whites experienced neighborhood poverty rates of just 11 and 13 %, indicating their privileged status in the American status hierarchy.

As levels of racial segregation moderated after 1980, however, affluent African-Americans began to achieve greater geographic separation from the poor, and the poverty rate in affluent Black neighborhoods dropped from 27 % to 23 % between 1980 and 2010. The degree of concentrated poverty experienced by poor Whites rose, however, in keeping with the overall rise in levels of White poverty, with concentration going from 26 to 32 % over the period. Affluent Whites, of course, continued to experience the least exposure to poverty within their neighborhoods across the four decades, with the degree of poverty concentration rising slowly from 13 to 17 % but always remaining well below the levels observed for other race-class groups.

In summary, as of 2010 we observe a clear hierarchy with respect to neighborhood disadvantage, with poor African-Americans experiencing by far the greatest concentration of poverty (45 %), followed by poor Whites (32 %), affluent Blacks (23 %), and affluent Whites (17 %). This ordering is important because research indicates that the high rate of neighborhood disadvantage commonly experienced by poor Blacks is the principal structural reason for the remarkable lack of socio-economic progress among African-Americans since the end of the civil rights era (Sharkey 2013).

Figure 2.4 continues the analysis by looking at the other end of the spectrum of neighborhood quality, focusing on exposure to neighborhood affluence by examining trends in the percentage of households earning $120,000 or more in neighborhoods occupied by the affluent and poor of both races. In keeping with affluent Whites experiencing the least exposure to poverty, they also display by far the highest exposure to affluence within their social worlds. Although the percentage of affluent households in the neighborhood of the average affluent White person fell slightly from 22 % to 20 % from 1970 to 1980, thereafter the figure steadily rose to reach 30 % in 2010. Once again, affluent African-Americans experienced great difficulty translating their income attainments into improved neighborhood circumstances in 1970, achieving only the concentration of affluence attained by poor Whites, at just under 10 %. As racial segregation moderated over time, however, the concentration of Black affluence steadily rose, until by 2010 the average affluent African-American lived in a neighborhood in which 22 % of the households were also affluent.

Although exposure to affluent households within neighborhoods also rose somewhat for poor Blacks and Whites between 1970 and 2010, the increase was quite modest: the percentage affluent rose from 9 to 13 % for poor Whites and from 4 to 7 % for poor Blacks. In general, then, the range of exposure to affluence, along with the benefits it confers, widened substantially over the decades, as indicated clearly in the figure. Even though affluent African-Americans improved their standing with respect to poor Whites and poor Blacks, however, they by no means caught up to

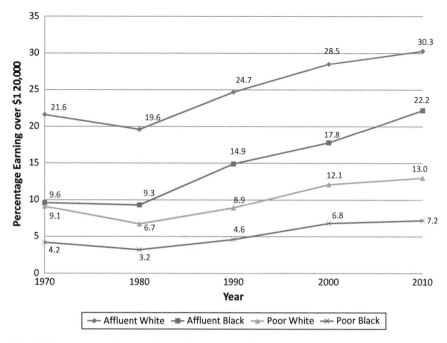

Fig. 2.4 Percentage of households earning more than $120,000 in neighborhoods of metropolitan areas (by various race/income groups)

affluent Whites, replicating the clear hierarchy observed in Fig. 2.3, with affluent Whites on top, followed in order by affluent Blacks, poor Whites, and poor Blacks.

Exposure to affluence within neighborhoods necessarily implies exposure to attributes and characteristics associated with affluence, thus generating a range of benefits for residents. One such attribute is education, and Fig. 2.5 shows the percentage of college graduates within neighborhoods occupied by affluent and poor Blacks and Whites. Holding college degrees confers status and prestige, of course, but college graduates also vote at higher rates to generate more political influence, exhibit lower rates of crime and delinquency, express greater interpersonal tolerance and trust, are more involved in cultural and educational institutions, and generally exhibit healthier lifestyles, thus creating a more salubrious, nurturing, and supportive neighborhood environment.

On this important indicator of neighborhood advantage, we once again observe the familiar pattern of racial and class stratification and a growing spread between race-class segments over time. Again affluent Whites experience the highest exposure to college graduates and poor Blacks experience the least, with affluent Blacks and poor Whites falling in-between. From 1970 to 2010 the percentage of college graduates in affluent White neighborhoods rose from 19 to 44 %, whereas the share rose only from 5 to 19 % in poor Black neighborhoods, widening the gap from 14 to 25 points. As before, affluent Blacks were only able to experience the low levels of exposure to college graduates in 1970; but over time they again improved their

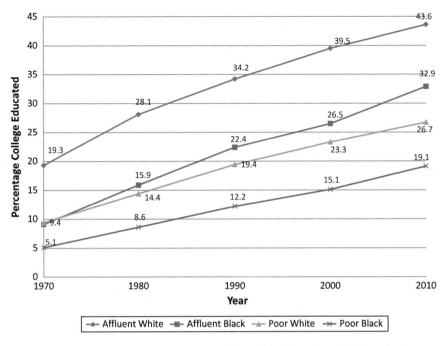

Fig. 2.5 Percentage of individuals 25 and over with a college degree in neighborhoods of metropolitan areas (by various race/income groups)

relative standing. By 2010 the average affluent African-American lived in a neighborhood where 33 % were college graduates, compared to a figure of 27 % for poor Whites. Despite this improvement relative to poor Whites, affluent Blacks still had not closed the gap with affluent Whites, which remained fairly constant from 2000 to 2010.

The final indicator of neighborhood advantage we consider is potential home wealth, which we measure by multiplying median home values within neighborhoods by the proportion of homeowners in the same neighborhoods. The product, plotted in Fig. 2.6, indicates the amount of wealth potentially accessible to the average neighborhood resident in the form of home equity. As can be seen, in 1970 the average affluent White person lived in a neighborhood where potential home wealth stood at $105,000 compared to only $29,000 in the neighborhood of the average poor Black person (figures once again in constant 2010 dollars). Among affluent African-Americans, potential home wealth was only $50,000, a figure even lower than the $56,000 figure for poor Whites.

Over time potential home wealth increased for all race-class groups, but the increase was greatest for affluent Whites, whose potential home wealth stood at $275,000 in 2010. Although affluent African-Americans were again able to improve their standing relative to poor Whites, they were unable to close the gap with affluent Whites. As of 2010, their potential home wealth stood at around $193,000, roughly $82,000 below affluent Whites (compared to a gap of $55,000 in 1970) but

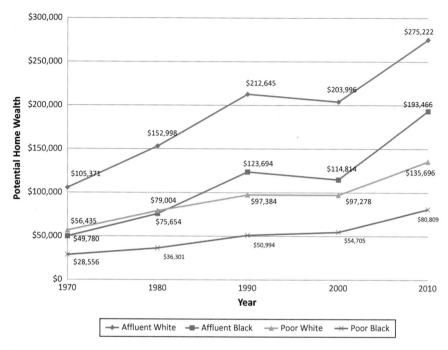

Fig. 2.6 Potential home wealth in neighborhoods of metropolitan areas (by various race/income groups)

nonetheless above the value of $136,000 experienced by poor Whites. As expected, poor African-Americans displayed the least access to potential home wealth, with a figure of just $81,000 in 2010, only 29 % of the potential home wealth accessible to affluent Whites in their neighborhoods.

In addition to the financial cushion provided by access to wealth, home values also translate directly into access to higher quality education given that public schools in the United States are financed mostly by real estate taxes. Thus the 3.4-to-1 differential in potential home wealth between affluent Whites and poor Blacks translates into a comparable differential with respect to school funding, ultimately producing a profound gap in the quality of education available to those at the top and bottom of American society. The connection between racial segregation and stunted educational achievement among Blacks is very well established empirically (Goldsmith 2009; Billings et al. 2012; Rothstein 2004, 2014). The close connection between school segregation and residential segregation is confirmed by the data in Fig. 2.7, which displays the relationship across states between the level of neighborhood segregation (Black-White dissimilarities computed for tracts) and the degree of educational segregation (Black-White dissimilarity between school districts using state-level data obtained from the National Center for Educational Statistics; http://nces.ed.gov/ccd/bat/). As can be seen, residential segregation explains 61 % of the variance in school segregation across states, suggesting that the continued

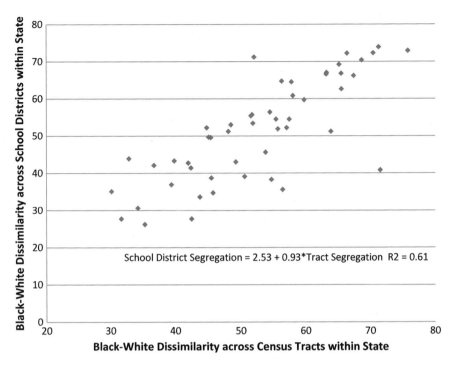

Fig. 2.7 Relationship between racial segregation by neighborhood to racial segregation by school district across states

segregation of African-Americans thus explains much of Black underachievement in the educational realm.

Segregation and the Divergence of Social Worlds

Earlier we explained that geographically concentrated poverty follows directly from two fundamental structural conditions in society: a high rate of minority poverty and a high degree of minority residential segregation, a relation now established both mathematically and empirically. We also noted that although average levels of Black residential segregation have fallen in the past four decades, the declines have been highly uneven and inter-metropolitan variation in the degree of segregation has increased. In contrast, levels of Black poverty have remained fairly stable, on average, and inter-metropolitan variability has decreased. Under these circumstances we would expect to observe a significant positive association between Black-White segregation and the concentration of Black poverty. To the extent that Whites are disproportionately affluent, of course, a high degree of Black-White segregation also tends to concentrate White affluence, as shown in Fig. 2.4. Thus we expect variation in racial residential segregation to substantially affect the size of the gap in

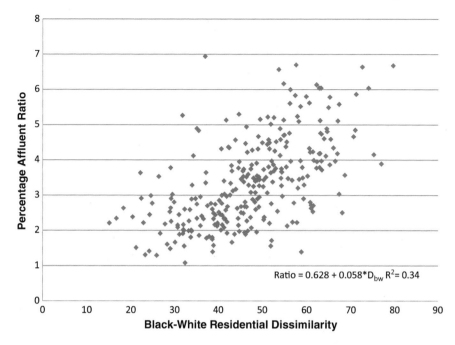

Fig. 2.8 Relationship between racial segregation and gap in percentage affluent between poor Black and affluent White neighborhoods

neighborhood circumstances experienced by poor Blacks and affluent Whites in American society, that is, between the social worlds of the most affluent and poorest segments of the nation.

Figure 2.8 illustrates this relationship through a scatterplot showing the ratio of the average percentage affluent in neighborhoods occupied by affluent Whites (indicating the neighborhood privilege enjoyed by those at the top of American society) to the average percentage affluent in neighborhoods occupied by poor Blacks (indicating the relative lack of neighborhood privilege suffered by the bottom of U.S. society) expressed as a function of the level of Black-White segregation. The diagram reveals an obvious positive relationship, confirming the close connection between segregation and race-class inequality in the United States.

As can be seen, as the degree of racial segregation rises, the gap between affluent White and poor Black neighborhoods with respect to the rate of affluence steadily rises. According to the estimated equation, shifting the Black-White dissimilarity index from 15 to 80 (roughly the observed range of Black-White segregation) would raise the size of the gap from a ratio of 1.5 to 5.3. Although the equation does not control for the many other factors that might be expected to influence the size of the gap between those at the top and bottom of American society, it nonetheless illustrates the degree to which segregation by itself operates to concentrate geographical advantages and disadvantages, as demonstrated analytically by Quillian (2012) and empirically by a growing number of studies (cf. Massey and Denton 1993; Sampson 2012; Sharkey 2013; Massey and Brodmann 2014).

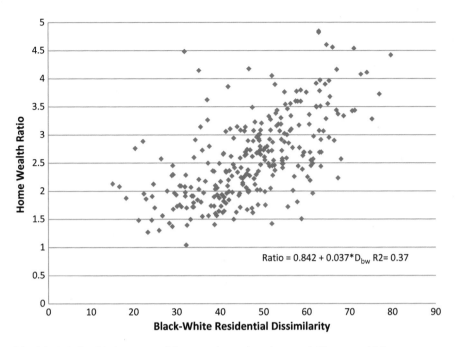

Fig. 2.9 Relationship between racial segregation and gap in potential home wealth between poor Black and affluent White neighborhoods

Figure 2.9 repeats the analysis using the ratio of affluent White to poor Black potential housing wealth to reveal an even stronger relationship between segregation and the gap in neighborhood access to wealth. Shifting levels of Black-White segregation from their minimum to maximum would raise the housing wealth gap from a ratio from 1.4 to 3.8. Black residential segregation thus goes a long way toward explaining the savage neighborhood inequalities in wealth that increasingly separate poor African-Americans from affluent Whites in American society today.

Inequality in Hypersegregated America

Results from the foregoing sections reveal sharply rising disparities in the neighborhood circumstances experienced by those at the bottom and top of the American socioeconomic distribution. Whether we consider exposure to poverty, concentrated affluence, exposure to college graduates, or potential home wealth, the gap in the quality of the social worlds inhabited by affluent Whites and poor Blacks has increased steadily over the past four decades. The gap between affluent Whites and poor Whites has also increased, and although affluent Blacks have gained ground on poor Whites as their neighborhood circumstances have improved, they have not come close to closing the gap with respect to affluent Whites.

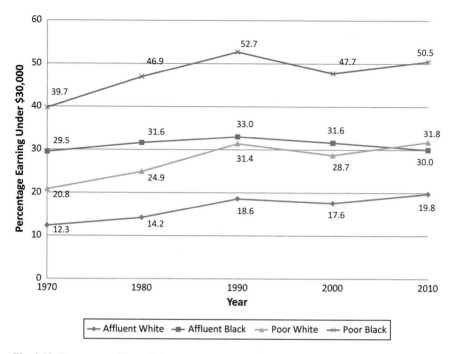

Fig. 2.10 Percentage of households earning less than $30,000 in neighborhoods of hypersegregated metropolitan areas (by various race/income groups)

These results prevail across U.S. metropolitan areas generally, including many that have displayed falling levels of Black-White segregation over the decades and are now characterized by moderate rather than high levels of racial segregation. However, roughly a third of all Black metropolitan residents still lived under conditions of hypersegregation in 2010, and in this section, we consider the changing fortunes of different race-class groups living under conditions of the most extreme form of residential segregation seen in the United States. Figure 2.10 begins the analysis by showing trends in exposure to neighborhood poverty experienced by different race-class groups in the 21 metropolitan areas that were hypersegregated as of 2010.

Although the trends in poverty concentration are similar to those observed across metropolitan areas generally (see Fig. 2.3), in hypersegregated areas the levels of Black poverty concentration are systematically higher. The percentage poor in the neighborhood of the average poor Black resident of a hypersegregated area thus rises from 40 % in 1970 to a peak of 53 % in 1990 before dipping and rising again to stand at 51 % in 2010. In addition, rather than decreasing as in Fig. 2.3, the concentration of poverty experienced by affluent African-Americans hardly changes at all and affluent African-Americans fail to improve their geographic position relative to poor Whites. In 2010 the exposure of affluent Blacks to poverty was 30 % greater in hypersegregated areas compared with all metropolitan areas (30 % compared to

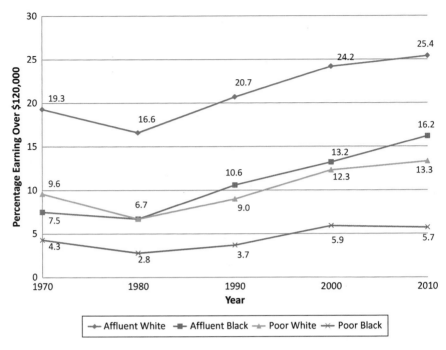

Fig. 2.11 Percentage of households earning more than $120,000 in neighborhoods of hypersegregated metropolitan areas (by various race/income groups)

23 %) and the exposure of poor Blacks to poverty was 12 % greater (50.5 % compared to 45 %). Thus high levels of Black residential segregation severely constrain the ability of affluent Blacks to limit their exposure to poverty and its problems (see Pattillo 2013).

We observe the same pattern of change over time with respect to exposure to affluence, only in reverse, as shown in Fig. 2.11. Under conditions of hypersegregation, both affluent and poor African-Americans experience less exposure to affluence in their neighborhoods relative to those in metropolitan areas generally, and once again affluent Blacks are unable to distance themselves geographically from the neighborhood circumstances experienced by African-Americans across metropolitan areas generally. As of 2010, the average affluent African-American living in a hypersegregated area experienced an affluence rate of just 16 % compared to 22 % for affluent African-Americans across metropolitan areas generally. Under conditions of the most intense segregation, in other words, affluent African-Americans experienced just 73 % of the neighborhood affluence experienced by those in all metropolitan areas.

Figure 2.12 shows trends in neighborhood exposure to college graduates within neighborhoods of hypersegregated metropolitan areas and demonstrates once again how affluent African-Americans are less able to achieve residential contact with this advantaged group under conditions of high residential segregation and are unable to

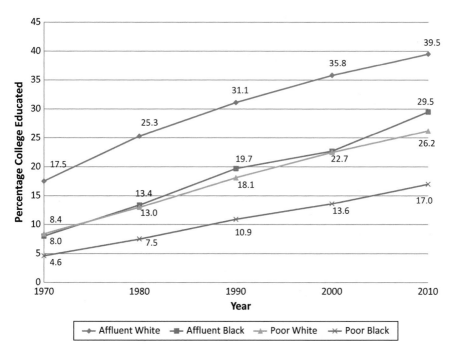

Fig. 2.12 Percentage of individuals 25 and over with a college degree in neighborhoods of hypersegregated metropolitan areas (by various race/income groups)

move much above the geographic position of poor Whites. Whereas the average affluent Black resident lived in a neighborhood where 33 % had graduated from college (compared with 27 % for poor Whites, as shown in Fig. 2.5) when averaged across all metropolitan areas, the average affluent Black person living in a hypersegregated metropolitan area lived in a neighborhood where only 30 % were college graduates (compared with 26 % among poor Whites). Under conditions of hypersegregation, the most affluent African-Americans achieve neighborhood circumstances that are little better than those achieved by poor Whites.

Finally, Fig. 2.13 demonstrates the especially pronounced effect of hypersegregation on potential home wealth. Not only do poor and affluent African-Americans in hypersegregated metropolitan areas experience less access to housing wealth than those in all metropolitan areas, but the shortfalls are quite dramatic. As of 2010, the typical affluent African-American lived in a neighborhood with $193,000 in potential home wealth when averaged across all metropolitan areas, but only $123,000 when averaged across hypersegregated areas (see Fig. 2.6). Among poor African-Americans, potential home wealth averaged $81,000 across all metropolitan but only $62,000 in hypersegregated areas. Thus hypersegregation reduced access to home wealth by 23 % for poor Blacks and 37 % for affluent Blacks.

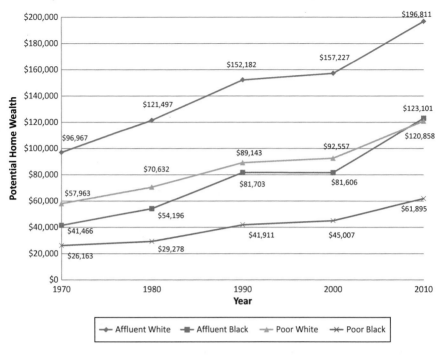

Fig. 2.13 Potential home wealth in neighborhoods of hypersegregated metropolitan areas (by various race/income groups)

Conclusion

In any metropolitan area, resources are unevenly distributed in space, and in order to gain full access to opportunities in society, people must be free to move. In the United States, especially, geographic mobility has always been part and parcel of economic mobility (Park 1926). As members of different ethnic groups have moved upward economically, they have sought to translate their economic gains into improved neighborhood circumstances, gaining access to better schools, lower crime rates, more supportive peer groups, lower insurance rates, and higher home values (Massey and Denton 1985). By moving up the residential ladder, they put themselves and their children in a better position to achieve additional socioeconomic mobility.

For African-Americans, however, the translation of economic mobility into residential mobility and improved neighborhood conditions has historically been thwarted by segregation and the prejudice and discrimination that create and maintain it (Massey and Denton 1993). Owing to the combination of high segregation and high poverty, the concentration of poverty in Black neighborhoods has persisted and in many ways deepened over the decades. As a result, a large share of African-Americans has become "stuck in place," passing place disadvantage and its deleterious effects from generation to generation (Sharkey 2013). Although poor African-Americans actually move quite frequently, each move simply replicates the status quo of place disadvantage (Sampson 2012).

Our findings here reveal both continuity and change with respect to racial residential segregation in the United States. Whereas racial segregation was universal across metropolitan areas in 1970, by 2010 it had declined in many areas, particularly those of lesser size with smaller and more affluent Black populations, more permissive density zoning, and lower levels of racial prejudice. Although Whites no longer supported segregation in principle, they remained concerned about its implications in practice and expressed reluctance to live in neighborhoods with more than a small share of African-Americans, leading to rapid desegregation in many metropolitan areas but persistently high segregation in the nation's largest Black communities, with hypersegregation prevailing in 21 metropolitan areas containing around a third of Black metropolitan residents.

In this context, segregation has emerged as a major structural determinant of exposure to neighborhood advantage and disadvantage in American society. Whether we consider the concentration of poverty, access to affluence, exposure to college graduates, or potential home wealth, the differential in neighborhood quality between those at the top and bottom of the American social hierarchy has steadily widened over the past four decades, and as of 2010 the size of this gap was substantially determined by the degree of Black-White segregation prevailing in different metropolitan areas. The higher the level of racial segregation in an area, the greater the inequality in the social worlds defined by circumstances within affluent White and poor Black neighborhoods; the greater the level of racial segregation across neighborhoods, the greater the degree of segregation within schools.

Our focused analysis of neighborhood trends in hypersegregated areas further demonstrated the power of segregation not only to compromise the neighborhood circumstances of poor African-Americans but also to limit the ability of affluent Black residents to improve their geographic position in urban society. Although affluent African-Americans were unable to close the gap with affluent Whites in terms of exposure to affluence, education, and wealth over the past four decades, across metropolitan areas they were able to improve their geographic situation relative to poor Whites. In hypersegregated areas, however, this was not the case. Not only was the quality of neighborhoods inhabited by affluent Blacks lower in absolute terms compared to their affluent counterparts across metropolitan areas generally, but also their neighborhood circumstances improved little relative to those experienced by the very poorest of Whites. These findings confirm what social scientists have long known: Residential segregation continues to be the structural linchpin in America's system of racial stratification.

Beyond its role in creating and perpetuating the Black urban underclass, recent evidence suggests the pernicious effects of persistent, high segregation need our focus because they are likely not limited to just one group. It may be spreading to Hispanics as well. Although Massey and Denton (1989) failed to identify any metropolitan area in which Hispanics were hypersegregated in 1980, by 2000 Wilkes and Iceland (2004) found that the two largest Hispanic communities—New York and Los Angeles—had both become hypersegregated, and according to Rugh and Massey (2014), Hispanic segregation is generated by the same factors that segregate African-Americans. In addition, a large share of Hispanics are undocumented and lack any social, economic, or civil right in the United States, and Hall and Stringfield (2014) find that Hispanic-White segregation rises as the estimated prevalence of undocumented migrants in the population increases. In the United States, therefore, we may be gravitating to a new racial order with Whites (and possibly Asians, given their educational income and levels) occupying privileged social worlds at the top of the socioeconomic hierarchy and Blacks and Hispanics inhabiting positions of concentrated disadvantage at the bottom.

References

Billings, Stephen B., David J. Deming, and Jonah E. Rockoff. 2012. *School segregation, educational attainment and crime: Evidence from the end of busing in Charlotte-Mecklenburg* (NBER Working Paper 18487). Cambridge, MA: National Bureau of Economic Research.

Bobo, Lawrence D. 1989. Keeping the linchpin in place: Testing the multiple sources of opposition to residential integration. *International Review of Social Psychology* 2: 305–323.

Bobo, Lawrence, and Camille L. Zubrinsky. 1996. Attitudes on residential integration: Perceived status differences, mere in-group preference, or racial prejudice? *Social Forces* 74(3): 883–909.

Charles, Camille Z. 2003. The dynamics of racial residential segregation. *Annual Review of Sociology* 29: 167–207.

Charles, Camille Z. 2006. *Won't you be my neighbor? Race, class and residence in Los Angeles.* New York: Russell Sage Foundation.

Duncan, Otis D. 1968. Inheritance of poverty or inheritance of race? In *Understanding poverty*, ed. Daniel P. Moynihan, 85–110. New York: Basic Books.

Emerson, Michael O., George Yancey, and Karen J. Chai. 2001. Does race matter in residential segregation? Exploring the preferences of White Americans. *American Sociological Review* 66(6): 922–935.

Goldsmith, Pat Rubio. 2009. Schools or neighborhoods or both? Race and ethnic segregation and educational attainment. *Social Forces* 87(4): 1913–1942.

Hall, Matthew, and Jonathan Stringfield. 2014. Undocumented migration and the residential segregation of Mexicans in new destinations. *Social Science Research*. doi:10.1016/j.ssresearch.2014.03.009.

Jargowsky, Paul A. 1997. *Poverty and place: Ghettos, barrios, and the American city.* New York: Russell Sage Foundation.

Massey, Douglas S. 1990. American apartheid: Segregation and the making of the underclass. *American Journal of Sociology* 95: 1153–1188.

Massey, Douglas S. 2013. Inheritance of poverty or inheritance of place? The emerging consensus on neighborhoods and stratification. *Contemporary Sociology* 42: 690–697.

Massey, Douglas S., and Stefanie Brodmann. 2014. *Spheres of influence: The social ecology of racial and class inequality.* New York: Russell Sage Foundation.

Massey, Douglas S., and Nancy A. Denton. 1985. Spatial assimilation as a socioeconomic outcome. *American Sociological Review* 50: 94–105.

Massey, Douglas S., and Nancy A. Denton. 1988. The dimensions of residential segregation. *Social Forces* 67: 281–315.

Massey, Douglas S., and Nancy A. Denton. 1989. Hypersegregation in U.S. metropolitan areas: Black and Hispanic segregation along five dimensions. *Demography* 26: 373–393.

Massey, Douglas S., and Nancy A. Denton. 1993. *American apartheid: Segregation and the making of the underclass.* Cambridge, MA: Harvard University Press.

Massey, Douglas S., and Jonathan Tannen. 2015. A research note on trends in Black hypersegregation. *Demography* 52: 1025–1034.

Park, Robert. 1926. The urban community as a spatial pattern and a moral order. In *The urban community*, ed. Ernest W. Burgess and Robert E. Park, 3–18. Chicago: University of Chicago Press.

Pattillo, Mary. 2013. *Black picket fences: Privilege and peril among the Black middle class*, 2nd ed. Chicago: University of Chicago Press.

Peterson, Ruth D., and Lauren J. Krivo. 2010. *Divergent social worlds: Neighborhood crime and the racial-spatial divide.* New York: Russell Sage Foundation.

Pettigrew, Thomas. 1979. Racial change and social policy. *Annals of the American Academy of Political and Social Science* 441: 114–131.

Quillian, Lincoln. 2012. Segregation and poverty concentration: The role of three segregations. *American Sociological Review* 77(3): 354–379.

Rothstein, Richard. 2004. *Class and schools: Using social, economic, and educational reform to close the Black-White achievement gap.* Washington, DC/New York: Economic Policy Institute and/Teachers College Press.

Rothstein, Richard. 2014. The racial achievement gap, segregated schools, and segregated neighborhoods—A constitutional insult. *Race and social problems* 6, doi:10.1007/s12552-014-9134-1.

Rugh, Jacob S., and Douglas S. Massey. 2014. Segregation in Post-Civil Rights America: Stalled integration or end of the segregated century? *The DuBois Review: Social Science Research on Race* 11(2): 202–232.

Sampson, Robert J. 2012. *Great American city: Chicago and the enduring neighborhood effect.* Chicago: University of Chicago Press.

Schuman, Howard, Charlotte Steeh, Lawrence D. Bobo, and Maria Krysan. 1998. *Racial attitudes in America: Trends and interpretations.* Cambridge: Harvard University Press.

Sharkey, Patrick. 2013. *Stuck in place: Urban neighborhoods and the end of progress toward racial equality.* Chicago: University of Chicago Press.

Wilkes, Rima, and John Iceland. 2004. Hypersegregation in the twenty-first century: An update and analysis. *Demography* 41(1): 23–36.

Wilson, William Julius. 1987. *The truly disadvantaged: The inner city, the underclass, and public policy.* Chicago: University of Chicago Press.

Chapter 3
Federalism and Inequality in Education: What Can History Tell Us?

Carl Kaestle

Abstract This chapter assesses the history of government efforts in the United States to enhance opportunity in education and to suggest lessons from the past. We focus primarily on federal policy, keeping in mind that solutions must depend upon successfully blending the resources and prerogatives of the federal government, the states, and local school districts. This chapter takes a chronological look, starting at free public education's onset to provide a foundation for the problems of inequality we face today. It then moves through the expanding federal role in the post-World War II years, followed by the battles over desegregation and the focus on providing resources to disadvantaged students. It then discusses standards-based reform, with a focus on how we arrived at the No Child Left Behind law and the issues surrounding the Common Core. Title I of the Elementary and Secondary Education Act, which targets impoverished students, is reviewed in detail. The lack of connection between Title I assignments and family income level, as well as lack of connection between Title I assignment and performance on the National Assessment of Academic Progress (NAEP), renders research results inconclusive in judging Title I's effects, but given that NAEP does show increasing average scores for Black and Hispanic students as well as declining gaps between those groups and White students, the evidence is sufficient that the program should be continued and improved. The chapter concludes by drawing some generalizations about the federalist governance system and its relation to educational equity and offers suggestions on ways to move forward, including changes regarding Title I and the federal role in education.

Keywords Federal policy • Education • Achievement gap • Desegregation • Standards-based reform • Elementary and Secondary Education Act (ESEA) • Title I • No Child Left Behind (NCLB) • Common Core • School finance • *Brown v. Board of Education* • Civil Rights Act • English language learners • Bilingual education • Disabilities • Special education • Discrimination against women

C. Kaestle (✉)
Department of Education, History, and Public Policy,
Brown University, Providence, RI 02912, USA

© Educational Testing Service 2016
I. Kirsch, H. Braun (eds.), *The Dynamics of Opportunity in America*,
DOI 10.1007/978-3-319-25991-8_3

Introduction

This chapter assesses the history of government efforts in the United States to enhance opportunity in education and to suggest lessons from the past. We focus primarily on federal policy, keeping in mind that solutions must depend upon successfully blending the resources and prerogatives of the federal government, the states, and local school districts. Of course, initiatives do not always stem from the federal government. Sometimes the states are the innovators and become models for federal education initiatives. Also, the landscape is complicated because members of the executive, legislative, or judicial branches at each level can initiate action, sometimes opposing one another. Federalism is not simply a system of congenially shared responsibilities.

In fact, shared governance in education policy arouses the alter egos of federalism: centralism and localism. Localists believe that governance and authority should be largely local because decisions made close to home are more efficient, more responsive, and more democratic. They believe that centralized decisions are inefficient and intrusive. Centralists believe that some values are best initiated by the federal government, that the central government should promote practices that serve our notions of civil rights, sound education, and national priorities.

This chapter takes a chronological look, starting at the onset of free public education. It then moves through the expanding federal role in the post-World War II years, followed by the battles over desegregation and the focus on providing resources to disadvantaged students. It then discusses standards-based reform, with a focus on how we arrived at the No Child Left Behind law and the issues surrounding the Common Core. Following the chronology, I end by evaluating the outcomes of these reform efforts and offering suggestions on ways to move forward.

Throughout the chapter, the overriding strand of thought is examination of equal opportunity through these various periods, including equity in how resources are devoted to the poor and other populations as well as removing barriers such as segregation. The theme of developing a meritocracy has been a long-existing theme in America as well, increasingly so beginning in the 1950s. Overall quality of education, not just equality, is discussed in latter sections as well as it has entered the fray via standards-based reform and the focus on improving education at all schools for all students, not just closing achievement gaps.

In discussing inequalities in educational achievement, we should keep in mind a few thoughts. First, there are various types of inequities—in students' health, housing, income, and parents' education. Also, achievement gaps across race-ethnic and income groups are very resilient. To reduce them, it is logical to reach beyond the schools to think about educational disadvantage in terms of these inequities. Furthermore, if we measure success by our standards for equity today, in truth all past efforts will come up short; our concepts of inclusiveness today are much broader than before. Lastly, data for such comparisons were nonexistent until recent decades. Thus, when we say that the National Defense Education Act of 1958 "worked," we do not mean that scores rose in science. More often the evidence is in photographs of children smiling in front of test tubes. In 1963, Francis Keppel, John Kennedy's new commissioner of education, complained to a friend that the Office of Education did not have a single scrap of data on learning outcomes. Although Senator Robert Kennedy insisted that the Elementary and Secondary Education Act (ESEA) of 1965 require accountability through testing academic achievement, it took the federal government over 20 years to implement Kennedy's mandate effectively.[1]

Development of Free and Public Schools Through the Progressive Era

The Creation of Free Public School Systems, 1840–1860

We begin with the states' creation of free school systems in the 1840s, building upon local efforts. Traditional educational historians argued that the fountainhead of our public schools was the district school in small-town colonial New England. But that claim is inflated as some New England towns did not establish schools, and barriers existed from the outset. In towns with public schools, girls faced shorter sessions and lower expectations and were banned from the grammar schools and colleges. Most children of color were excluded at all levels, left unlettered, or taught by their parents. Children from poorer White families faced the barrier of "continuation school"—a part of the school year that wasn't free.

The "common school" reformers of the 1840s reacted to some of these limitations. They wanted to attract as many students as possible into a single system, not just to equalize opportunity but for social stability through state-sponsored moral education and mutual understanding across class lines. Many wealthy families declined the invitation, but in general the common school reformers in the Northeast and the new Northwest gained their main objectives by 1860: free schooling supported by local property taxes, the consolidation of small districts into town systems, and some state-sponsored teacher training (Kaestle 1983).

This was not simply a top-down state initiative. Enrollments were increasing in the early nineteenth century before the common school movement. This was partly because of an increase in girls' education and partly because states encouraged towns to organize school districts and levy taxes for schools. In addition to these local initiatives and state actions, many states had access to funds that derived from federal lands. Nonetheless, until the mid-twentieth century, the lion's share of the funds for free public education was from local property taxes (Goldin and Katz 2008; Kaestle and Vinovskis 1980).

---

[1] For the accountability amendment by Robert Kennedy, and Francis Keppel's efforts to develop more reliable assessments, see Kaestle (Forthcoming). For an effort to reach back to earlier decades and estimate changes in students' reading ability, see Kaestle and Stedman (1987).

The establishment of free public schools across the Northeast and the Midwest improved equality of opportunity in education. Enrollments, daily attendance, and the length of the school year increased. Of course, the remaining barriers for people of color, children with disabilities, and women are striking from today's perspective. Increased opportunity also did not immediately result in closer-to-equal amounts of education received by working-class children.

Two other factors led to unequal outcomes. First, school attendance was not mandatory, so bias existed due to working-class families reacting to their economic realities and their family culture, with children and teens working instead of attending class (Kaestle and Vinovskis 1980, 82–99). Second, unequal resources across districts meant different school quality and length of school year. Funding schools through local property taxes is one of the most abjectly unequal aspects of public education in the United States. It is still with us today, and rare among nations.

1865–1895: Expansion and Professionalization

In the period of 1865–1895, public schooling underwent more expansion and professionalization. Urban school systems acquired professional superintendents and became the model for well-run schooling. Testing, long before the IQ vogue, served superintendents as a way to monitor quality among teachers and schools. Teacher training began in newly developed "normal schools" and shorter-term "teachers institutes." The effect on educational opportunity is not easy to quantify, but enrollments, attendance, and length of school year continued their upward trajectory. Toward the end of this period, public high schools outnumbered private academies but were still predominantly the preserve of middle class students, the children of professionals, shopkeepers, engineers, office workers, accountants, skilled craftsmen, and others (on testing, see Reese 2013; on the expansion of elementary education, and information on academies, see Goldin and Katz 2008, 129–62).

The 'Progressive' Era: Redefining Equal Opportunity

Local reformers praised their high schools as the "keystone of the arch," or the "capstone" of a "perfect system." Reformers praised these new secondary schools as an institution of meritocracy, free and open to all. High school students were predominantly female (about 60 %) in the late nineteenth century, though the increasing restriction of child labor in the manufacturing sector meant that more working-class boys stayed in school as the new century unfolded. The percentage of 14- to 17-year-olds in school grew from 11 % in 1900 to 32 % in 1920 and became the modal experience at 51 % in 1930 (Simon and Grant 1970; on the development of high school, see Reese 1995; Krug 1964; Rury 2005, 84–89).

As the proportion of youth in high schools increased, it became apparent that not all students were preparing to go to college. This generated a great deal of thought about what curricula were appropriate for students with different educational and occupational futures. These discussions occurred in an era when theorists of human behavior were placing great emphasis on heredity, when racism was increasing in social relations, and an imperialist foreign policy thrust the United States into the development of colonies. Standardized student testing moved from its mid-nineteenth-century roots to its hereditarian embrace with IQ tests, all putting a genetic hue on the emerging version of meritocracy (see Reese 2013; Kaestle 2012, 93).

Educators talked about "hand minded" and "brain minded" children and their different needs. In an explicit revision of equal opportunity, they developed different curricula for different children. Reflecting a growing conviction among educators, Stanford's Ellwood Cubberley (1909, 57) declared that people should reject the "exceedingly democratic idea that all are equal, and that our society is devoid of classes."

Many saw the creation of collegiate, general, vocational, and commercial tracks as steps forward for democracy: These different curricula would augment equal opportunity by providing an appropriate high school education for everybody. This was the era of corporate capitalism; in this context, democracy required not only participation and citizens' education but also expertise, science, and efficiency. Whatever the merits of this new concept of equal opportunity—and we should not think it merely as a hypocritical justification for inequality—it was compromised by biased predictions of students' futures, too often arising from their race, gender, ethnicity, and social class.

Expanding the Federal Role in Education (World War II to the Space Race)

The Postwar Years

Before 1950 the federal government played a minimal role in elementary, secondary, and higher education. It had partially funded the early development of public schools in the states through land grants in the early nineteenth century, and it had expanded opportunity for college attendance by creating land-grant colleges in the late nineteenth century. It had also given modest support for the differentiation of curriculum through its vocational education grants beginning in the early twentieth century. For the most part, however, education funding and policy were almost entirely in the hands of the states and local districts. The federal share of local school budgets in 1950 was, on average, 2.9 %.

Congress made its first foray into federal education funding in 1941 with the enactment of what would be called "impact aid," which compensated communities that saw an influx of schoolchildren amid the swift expansion of tax-exempt military facilities. But the key major war-related federal activity in education was the Servicemen's Rehabilitation Act (1944), which provided educational support, housing loans, rehabilitation training, and other benefits to military personnel returning home after World War II. The principal beneficiaries of this "GI Bill" were White males, because many of its programs and program officers were biased against Black GIs and because the numbers of servicewomen were a tiny percentage of all returning veterans. For White males, however, it provided substantial opportunities in college or other education. It also helped to double the number of college graduates in the decade following 1945 (see Bound and Turner 2002, 784–815; Turner and Bound 2003.)

Liberal Congress members and the National Education Association lobbied for federal aid, not for programs targeted at particular educational goals but for construction, teacher salaries, or simply for spending at the discretion of local school boards. Their bills, however, were routinely defeated in the 1940s and 1950s, as they also were in the 1920s and 1930s. Opponents included southern segregationist Democrats, who feared that federal aid would be used to press for integration; Roman Catholic representatives, who supported their churches' position against federal aid to public schools; and conservative Republicans, who opposed federal aid as something intrusive and foreign-inspired. This effective Congressional alliance was dubbed the "3 R's" of localism in education policy: race, religion, and "Reds."

It should be recognized, however, that not all opposition to federal aid was simply motivated by these negatives. The positive image of local control was shared by President Eisenhower, his friend James Conant—the most respected education reformer of the 1950s—and many local leaders. They saw local control as a spur to citizens' participation and support for public education, as well as a more efficient, responsive, and democratic form of governance. Unfortunately, those who championed local control of schools, either consciously or unconsciously, also favored inequality as well, not only because of racial segregation but because of vast disparities of per-pupil expenditures in districts with different property wealth.

Education, the Space Race, and Meritocracy

We have seen that at the secondary level educators had already established a notion of meritocracy in the early twentieth century, long before the advent of the SATs, which were designed to promote that goal. It was grounded in achievement testing, teachers' reports, guidance counselors' decisions, and the differentiated curricula of the "comprehensive American high school." By the early 1950s, many critics of the public schools focused on the weak version of Progressive education known as "Life Adjustment," which focused on practical tasks for the large middle group of students who were neither in the higher academic tracks nor in vocational education.[2] This criticism took the high road of equality, demanding the same academic curriculum for all, but it had little effect on school practice. The professional devotion to Life Adjustment was substantial, from school district offices to the federal Office of Education. The idea that meritocracy meant different curricula for differently able students, a legacy of the Progressive Era, was deeply embedded in the schools.

Meanwhile the American science and technology community was growing anxious about academic learning in the schools as a matter of national security and national competition. The brief public scare following the launch of Sputnik into space by the Russians in 1957 energized these concerns. Through skillful politicking by the bill's handlers and some concessions to Catholic educators, the National Defense Education Act (NDEA) was passed the following year. It was not designed to equalize opportunity but to raise the academic quality of schoolwork in the sciences, mathematics, and foreign languages, especially for the most academically talented students. By turning attention away from the utilitarian Life Adjustment curriculum, however, it may have had some positive effect across a range of high school students. On the other hand, the grants required a 50 % match by the local district, suggesting that wealthier districts were more likely to apply for NDEA grants, thus reinforcing inequality (on the passage of NDEA, see Urban 2010).

Historian David Gamson has argued that the NDEA was supported by educators around the nation not just because everyone was alarmed by the launch of Sputnik but because the programs of the NDEA were easily compatible with the aims and programs in the field. This was a startling interpretation at first, because journalists at the time and many historians since have emphasized that Sputnik shocked the schools into rethinking their flabby "progressive" curricula and introducing more academically rigorous courses in math, science, and languages. This is a half-truth. The other half is that several of the underlying assumptions and intentions were legacies of the Progressive era, when educators had invented the multiple-curricula high school, with an emphasis on testing and guidance, all of which was revived and advocated in 1959 by Conant's popular book, *The American High School Today*, the bible of the "comprehensive" high school (see Gamson 2007).

The NDEA was more important to the federal role in education than it was to expanding educational opportunity. There had been no federal grant programs generally open to all public schools except for vocational education. NDEA prevailed over a storm of opposition about the perils of federal aid to education, succeeding politically for several reasons. It abandoned the goal of the professional education organizations to get "general" aid with no requirements attached. NDEA was a "categorical" bill, like vocational education. It prescribed which subject areas were eligible for support. It specified the need for language labs. It supported area studies in higher education and instruction in languages generally not taught in the United States.

---

[2] The most widely debated assault was from Arthur Bestor, a historian at the University of Illinois, in his *Educational Wastelands: The Retreat from Learning in Our Schools* (1953). See Kaestle (1990).

Congress was more receptive to this kind of bill. In contrast to general school aid, it gave the impression of accountability: dollars paid for programs established. It honored the state education agencies, which received the money and monitored the programs. Flexibility was great; accountability was slim. It also proved flexible. When advocates for history, English, home economics, and other subjects complained, Congress broadened NDEA in subsequent reauthorizations. Gradually, NDEA took on somewhat more of the look of general aid.

NDEA was a breakthrough politically, but it did not expand much in subsequent reauthorizations. It was popular with local school administrators, but the big professional lobby groups resumed their crusade for federal aid that would be more general and more generous. More importantly, by the mid-1960s, NDEA was overshadowed by the seemingly sudden shift of priorities between 1958 and 1964, when the Johnson administration was developing the next big education bill. It was focused not on the most academically talented children in the nation but on the most disadvantaged. The ESEA bill of 1965 became the ongoing omnibus education bill (Peterson 1983, 60, 70–76, 132).

Desegregation

Brown v. Board of Education of 1954 would prove the launching pad for wide-ranging changes in America even though shifts in school segregation patterns would prove glacial at the outset. The more activist period on desegregation dovetailed with Lyndon Johnson's adoption of a "War on Poverty" a decade after *Brown,* starting with the Civil Rights Act of 1964 and setting the stage for ESEA's Title I program in 1965, which targeted impoverished students but also worked against segregation.

The Role of ESEA in Desegregation

Johnson's sudden shift toward poverty was inspired by his ambition to achieve a domestic agenda surpassing his idol, President Franklin Roosevelt. It is an intriguing connection. Roosevelt's New Deal was constructed in the face of a collapsed economy, while Johnson's Great Society programs were made possible politically by a buoyant economy that raised all boats, as James Patterson (1996) has argued.

Although Johnson's advisers warned him they could not discern much support for poverty reform, there were some harbingers of concern for the disadvantaged. There was a flurry of attention to Michael Harrington's book, *The Other America: Poverty in the United States* (1962). Also, although the *Brown* decision on racial integration had languished in the court system for 10 years, it would prove to be a constitutional lodestone. More important was the rise to leadership of Martin Luther King and the escalation of the civil rights movement.

The two most important legislative initiatives that applied to education on these two themes were Title VI of the Civil Rights Act of 1964, which forbade discrimination in any federally funded program, and ESEA's Title I, which was enacted the next year and provided funds for compensatory reading and math education in schools with a high percentage of families below the poverty level. Although the principal aim of Title I was to improve academic achievement of low-performing students in high-poverty schools, it was also used in tandem with Title VI to pressure school districts to eradicate racial segregation. The federal government threatened to withhold Title I funding from districts found to be deliberately segregating their students. The long-delayed desegregation effort now became the most coercive intervention of the federal government into state and local systems in our history (on the passage of ESEA, see Sundquist 1968 along with Eidenberg and Morey 1969; on the Civil Rights Act, see Orfield 1969; Graham 1990).

Federal Action to Desegregate K-12 Education in the South

It is well known that very little action was taken to implement the *Brown* decision between 1954 and 1964. In order to achieve a unanimous decision, Earl Warren wrote vaguely (and famously) that the Court expected that desegregation would occur with "all deliberate speed." The second *Brown* decision, in 1955, addressed the implementation of desegregation. The Court left enforcement in the hands of the federal district courts in the South. Many southern states and some southern courts willfully misinterpreted the *Brown* decision to require only that they would have to wipe laws that sanctioned segregation off the books. As other court decisions moved away from that minimalist interpretation, other southern school districts contrived procedures they called "freedom of choice." It combined elaborate bureaucratic delays with illegal intimidation of African-Americans who asked to enroll their children at White schools (on the massive resistance period, see Barley 1997; Webb 2005; Patterson 2001).

Following the passage of the Civil Rights Act, every school district in the country, North and South, was required to file an affidavit with the Office of Education stating either that no segregation was occurring in its schools or describing a plan to discontinue such segregation. The main targets of the Office of Education were school systems in the 21 states that had mandatory or optional legalized segregation, most of which were in the Old South and border states.

More than 10 years after the *Brown* decision, there were virtually no Black students attending schools with White students in the Old South. Some federal judges supported desegregating districts, but increasingly they did not. Court orders were issued requiring desegregation, but the wheels of justice moved slowly. On the executive side, some federal officers also delayed and compromised, but increasingly, federal civil rights officers supported efforts to desegregate. Johnson kept his distance from the issue but issued occasional statements of support for the effort. President Richard Nixon tried to go slow to protect his "southern strategy" for reelection by opposing busing for desegregation. But the machinery of federal enforcement, after more than a decade of inaction, was geared up to enforce the *Brown* decision by 1968 when the Supreme Court declared in *Green v. Kent Co., Va.* that "freedom of choice" systems would not be allowed if they did not result in actual integration.[3]

A profound transformation like school desegregation needed the combined efforts of the judiciary, the executive branch, and Congress. None of those branches took up the cause for the first decade. Under Johnson, the weak link was Congress, with its potent coalition of southern segregationists and conservative Republican. By the end of the first Nixon administration (1972) and into the Ford administration, both the White House and the Congress were ambivalent or resistant to desegregation, in particular to busing. Nonetheless, major gains were made in the South in the years between 1968 and 1974, driven partly by some key Supreme Court decisions, the efforts of local plaintiffs and civil rights organizations, and the widespread opinion in favor of integration among staff lawyers at the civil rights offices in the Department of Health, Education, and Welfare (HEW) and the Justice Department.

Although the courts were not very effective at implementation, they played an important role in clarifying issues and supporting the authority of the executive branch. The Supreme Court's declaration against "freedom of choice" plans was one turning point, as was its 1973 decision in *Swann v. Charlotte-Mecklenburg* (North Carolina), which insisted that busing was an appropriate remedy and was mandatory if other methods were inadequate.[4] At this point, many resistant southern districts threw in the towel and opted for at least a nominal level of integration. These Court decisions accelerated the most dramatic change in the entire federal desegregation initiative: the abrupt decrease in the percentage of African-American students in the Deep South and border states who were attending schools that were 90–100 % Black. That may not capture the essence of the ideal of integration, but it was the government's chief aim, and after almost 20 years of resistance, it happened quite rapidly. In 1968, the percentage of African-Americans in the South attending overwhelmingly Black schools was 77.8 %, and by 1972, it had dropped to 24.7 %. Comparable figures for the shift from 1968 to 1972 for the other regions were as follows (Clotfelter 2004):

- Border states: 60.2–54.7 %
- West: 50.8–42.7 %
- Midwest: 58.0–57.4 %
- Northeast: 42.7–46.9 %

---

[3] Green v. County School Board of New Kent County (North Carolina), 391 U.S. 430 (1968).

[4] Swann v. Charlotte-Mecklenburg Board of Education (North Carolina) 402 U.S. 1 (April 20, 1971); see also Douglas 1995; Wilkinson 1979.

Obstacles in the North

Federal efforts to desegregate school systems in the North (and West) came later and were less successful. The Office of Education, as early as 1965, began investigating four selected cities (Boston, Chicago, San Francisco, and Chester, PA) where citizens' groups had documented school board policies that contributed to segregation, beyond the impact of housing segregation. They argued that they could address the issue in the North on the basis of the Civil Rights Act, even though the states involved did not have laws sanctioning segregation. Title VI simply says that no program receiving federal funds could discriminate on the basis of race, color, or national origin.

Commissioner Frank Keppel, acting on the directions of the assistant HEW secretary for civil rights (with whom he disagreed), pressed the matter with the Chicago school board, enraging Mayor Richard Daley. Politics trumped the Constitution. Daley cried "local control" and reminded Johnson that he had delivered Illinois' Democratic vote for him. Keppel lost his job as commissioner. When Keppel's replacement, Harold Howe, proved to be equally energetic on desegregation, some former supporters of desegregation in the Congress became frustrated; they thought that the executive branch was becoming overly aggressive. Together with southern segregationists, they pressured HEW to "centralize" all civil rights matters across the department, removing Howe from the enforcement of desegregation. But despite new people in charge, the policy slowly moved forward in the South and, in a minor way, the North (an essential revision of the usual narrative about Keppel's Chicago debacle is Miech (n.d.); see also Kaestle (Forthcoming)).

Although northern school systems were more segregated than those in the South by the 1970s, four factors militated strongly against desegregation in the North: first, public and judicial confusion about what the term "de facto segregation" meant; second, demographic trends that made it logistically difficult for a district with a high proportion of non-White students to effectively desegregate its schools; third, Congressional and public weariness of the coercive tactics required to move recalcitrant districts toward integration; and fourth, the rising opinion of American citizens—including many African-Americans—that busing for integration was wrong. This opinion was reinforced by a shift among the Black civil rights leaders in the generation after Martin Luther King, who eschewed integration in favor of better resources in their community's schools.

As to the first barrier, many journalists and some jurists kept alive the distinction that Southern desegregation was de jure (enacted in law and therefore unconstitutional), while Northern desegregation was de facto, existing mostly due to housing patterns and thus out of reach of the *Brown* decision. Of course, the housing segregation itself was the result of pervasive discrimination by landlords of rental dwellings, real estate people, and developers, as well as by government agencies condoning "red-lining" and other discriminatory practices. Decisions within the education policy sector were also grossly discriminatory. Districts deepened segregation through their choice of new construction sites, determining bus routes, drawing attendance boundaries, and granting transfer rights.

In the early days of activism at the Office of Education, federal officials relied upon the Civil Rights Act to attack segregation in states not covered by the *Brown* decision. These efforts preceded by a few years the Supreme Court's important decision in *Keyes v. Denver* (1973). That case built upon the language and reasoning of various lower court judges who had declared that northern segregation caused by the decisions of local school boards was not de facto segregation but clearly de jure segregation and thus failed the test of the 14th Amendment's Equal Protection Clause just as clearly as the laws that were struck down in the *Brown* decision. *Keyes* cemented this understanding of northern segregation among the judiciary, though many people continued to argue that northern segregation was different and beyond legal remedy (Kaestle Forthcoming).

The second barrier to northern segregation was the rising percentage of students of color in large cities like Detroit and Newark. As long as desegregation enforcement was restricted to single school systems rather than metropolitan areas, heavily White suburbs escaped involvement in the desegregation of cities that were predominantly non-White. Absent a metropolitan strategy, the prospect of busing children of color around the city to integrate them with a small number of White children was neither logistically nor educationally reasonable.

That restriction was given the imprimatur of the Supreme Court in the Detroit case *Milliken v. Bradley* in 1974, which declared the suburbs not culpable. *Milliken* provided a tiny loophole to allow for metropolitan solutions, and there were subsequently a few such desegregation agreements reached voluntarily or with court encouragement, but *Milliken* generally proved an effective barrier to desegregating large urban systems.[5] Thus, when federal courts generally recognized that northern segregation due to local policy decisions was de jure segregation, the Supreme Court declared that school boards in governmentally separate suburbs could not be held responsible for segregation in the central cities they surrounded.

In the 1980s and 1990s, the Supreme Court would demand clear evidence of intent on the part of northern school boards accused of deliberate segregation. Without such evidence, they lifted court supervision of those systems.

The third barrier to effective federal action on northern segregation was growing public weariness with the conflict and a shift of opinion about its merits. In 1972, according to a *Newsweek* poll, 58 % of White southerners favored racial integration, but 74 % opposed busing to achieve such integration. In the North it was 68 % in favor of integration and 68 % opposed to busing. When the question was framed as busing for integration "outside of local neighborhoods" in a Gallup poll of the early 1970s, only 9 % of African-Americans supported it.[6]

---

[5] Milliken v. Bradley, 418 U.S. 717 (1974). Also see Baugh 2011. The best book on the decline in desegregation efforts is Orfield and Eaton (1996).

[6] The percentage for Whites is from *Newsweek* (March 6, 1972). The African-American results from a Gallup poll are reported in Frum (2000, 252).

Indeed, for some African-Americans, it was not simply an opposition to busing but disillusionment with integration itself and the feeling that it was the wrong solution. The generation of civil rights leaders that succeeded King included some prominent figures who questioned the proposition that the way to improve Black children's education was to have them go to school with White children. The Student Nonviolent Coordinating Committee expelled its White members and adopted a policy of Black Power. Floyd McKissick, director of the Congress of Racial Equality, sent his children to integrated schools in Washington, D.C., where they had "pages torn out of books, water thrown on them in the dead of winter, ink down the front of their dresses."[7]

Other African-Americans came to think it was demeaning for policy officials to imply that their children could not learn well unless they were in school with Whites. This position dovetailed with the movement toward Black Power. Historian Jack Dougherty found that when Black leaders in Milwaukee pressed hard for desegregation, the federal government had not yet decided what to do about northern segregation and was unresponsive. By the time federal officials focused on Milwaukee desegregation, they faced a divided Black community. Many Blacks had defected from integration to community control (Dougherty 2004).

Assessing the Success of Desegregation

Effects on School Composition These shifts in the early and mid-1970s did not quash the ongoing desegregation suits and investigations of the North and South. There was a certain momentum behind the 10 years of activism. Many civil rights officers in the Office of Education and the Justice Department still pressed on, notably David Tatel, director of HEW's Office of Civil Rights (OCR), in the late 1970s. But in the 1980s and 1990s the landscape had very much changed. A more conservative court removed court supervision of several cities despite continuing racial segregation, which the Court deemed to have not been caused by school board policies. The Court made it more difficult to document intentional discrimination and took the position that court supervision was not intended to go on indefinitely.[8] The public and their representatives grew weary of the segregation battles. The proportion of children of color increased in urban school systems, and public policy drifted toward compensatory education and improving inner-city schools. President Ronald Reagan wanted to see less federal civil rights enforcement, and he succeeded.

The extent of desegregation in the regions of the United States, and the turning points of trends, can be seen in Table 3.1. The Northeast was hardly affected by the

---

[7] Quoted on CORE's website, "Floyd B. McKissick: 2nd National Director of CORE," http://www.core-online.org/History/mckissick.htm

[8] Missouri v. Jenkins 495 U.S. 33 (1990); Dowell v. Board of Education of Oklahoma City Public Schools 498 U.S. 23 (1991); Freeman v. Pitts 503 U.S. 467 (1992).

Table 3.1 Trends in desegregation, 1950–2000: percentage of Black students in 90–100 % non-White schools, by region

Region	1950[a]	1960[b]	1968	1972	1976	1980	1989	1999	2000
Northeast	–	40.0	42.7	46.9	51.4	48.7	49.8	50.2	51.2
Border	100	59.0	60.2	54.7	42.5	37.0	33.7	39.7	39.6
South	100	100	77.8	24.7	22.4	23.0	26.0	31.1	30.9
Midwest	53.0	56.0	58.0	57.4	51.1	43.6	40.1	45.0	46.3
West	–	27.0	50.8	42.7	36.3	33.7	26.7	29.9	29.5
U.S.	–	–	64.3	38.7	35.9	33.2	33.8	37.4	37.4

Source: *After Brown: The Rise and Retreat of School Desegregation* by Clotfelter, Charles T. Reproduced with permission of Princeton University Press in the format Book via Copyright Clearance Center
For updated figures, see Orfield et al. 2014
[a]Extrapolated from 1950–1954
[b]Extrapolated from 1960–1964

efforts of the federal government and other pressures to desegregate. The border states responded to the *Brown* decision rather substantially before the big push came from the federal government; by 1960, 59 % were in schools with 90 % or more non-White students. The states of the Deep South responded in two batches. Some districts went along fairly quickly in the mid-1960s, reducing the absolute segregation down to a situation where 77.8 % of the South's Black students were still in strongly segregated schools in 1968. In the next four years, due to the efforts of civil rights workers in both the waning years of the Johnson administration and the first Nixon administration, they dramatically reduced segregation, to the point that only 24.7 % of southern Black students were in 90 % to 100 % non-White schools. The Midwest and particularly the West reduced the percentage of Black students in strongly segregated schools, more than in the Northeast, perhaps because they were so much less urbanized and had relatively fewer large ghettos of African-Americans. (The figures here do not tell us about the expanding Hispanic population in the West and its relationship to racial isolation vis-à-vis Whites and Blacks.) Whatever the subtleties in the process, the West and the South had the lowest percentage of Blacks in schools with 90 % to 100 % minorities.

If we look at a different criterion, the percent of Black students who were enrolled in schools that had 50–100 % non-White students, the regional differences are less stark. In all five regions, somewhere between 67 % to 78 % of all African-American students were in majority non-White schools. The trends from 1980 to 2000 show modest increases in segregation on both measures considered here. Work on school resegregation since 2000 supports the trend toward greater isolation.[9]

In general, federal and state litigators have attempted to desegregate schools by working around housing segregation, urging busing, modified attendance boundaries,

---

[9]The data on Black students in majority non-White schools is also from Clotfelter (2004, Table 2.1, 56). Studies of resegregation since 2000 include Reardon et al. (2012, 533–47). On racial isolation more generally, see Massey et al. (2009).

fair transfer policies, and other tactics. They achieved very substantial results in formal desegregation of schools in the Deep South and the border states. But by the time the courts had delegitimized the myth of de facto school segregation and federal officials moved to desegregate the cities of the North, the *Milliken* decision (1974) exempted the all-White suburbs of Detroit from responsibility for segregation in the city. This withdrew the essential tool that school integrationists needed. Furthermore, as Charles Clotfelter (2004) notes, in these latter years, White parents still retained multiple strategies to avoid integration by moving to suburbs, sending their children to private schools, or enrolling them in public schools whose tracking systems isolated the races, all of which were legal. Combating these counter-tactics was beyond the reach of the legal repertoire developed in the school desegregation initiative. In the face of these realities, the Supreme Court retreated from racial integration and the public turned away from the struggles to desegregate. The campaign in the North was lost.

The historical balance sheet on desegregation has assets and deficits. It repudiated legally segregated schools, expanded the definition of "legal" to cover the policy actions of local officials, and achieved its formal goal in the Deep South and border states. More children went to schools that included both Blacks and Whites. Despite very widespread resegregation over the past 40 years, we shall never return to the 100 %, school-by-school segregation that the South and border states had in 1955. But it is not as clear a victory as the eradication of separate railroad cars or other public facilities. With schooling and housing, the facts on the ground display continuing, profound segregation, some of it still due to discrimination, some to economic status, some to choices made by Whites and people of color.

Effects on Students The *Brown* decision was the Magna Carta of desegregation. The decision was cited in other cases involving other venues of public life. For many people *Brown* was the irreversible application of the Equal Protection Clause to deliberate segregation in American public life. But what were the consequences for the children who were integrated? In 2004, Clotfelter summarized his and others' research on some complex questions about the effects of integration. Increases in Black students' academic achievement were certainly not an automatic product of integration. Research has documented only modest improvements in Black achievement in reading correlated with desegregation, and only scattered increases in math. On the other hand, desegregation did not typically lower scores for White students, a common anxiety among White people reluctant to have their children integrated with Black students (Ibid., 187).

Many people hoped that increased interracial contact would foster understanding and tolerance. Clotfelter reports that when schools are thoroughly desegregated— with real opportunities for students of different races to take the same classes, participate in clubs and sports together, and collaborate on projects—desegregation has often correlated with students making more friends across racial lines and expressing more tolerant views than students in other schools. But schools desegregated only through formal means left resistant Whites with many mechanisms for resegregation internally.

Some self-reported attitudes about race showed more tolerance and engagement between 1975 and 2000 despite *increased* school segregation. Nationally there was an increase in the percentage who said they did "a lot" with students of other races, from about 33 % to 42 % for Black students and from 15 % to 31 % for White students, without controlling for the racial composition of their schools. Similarly, the percentage of high school students who said that if they had children, it would be desirable if those children would have friends of another race, increased from about 36 % to 41 % for Whites, and about 43 % to 48 % for Black students. These modest rises seem contrary to the increases in segregation and in any case could not demonstrate a causal effect stemming from desegregation. If these findings are technically valid, these more tolerant attitudes may simply illustrate that society—schools, media, and parents—had on average taught more children the propriety of such attitudes, all the while putting up with, or consciously supporting, more segregation (Ibid., 182).

All of these findings are "squishy." There is some evidence that integration done well—without resegregating students internally and providing a climate favorable for multiracial contact—can affect tolerant racial attitudes. Stated conversely, when Whites are segregated—school by school, within classrooms, by school tracking policies or by parents seeking private school attendance in predominantly White schools—school segregation is playing handmaiden to residential segregation in the United States. Together they have severe negative economic, social, and political consequences for African-Americans and other people of color. Racial isolation is also a deficit for Whites.

Some integrationists believe that school segregation is simply an offense to the Constitution and an indignity to those segregated, whatever the measurable results. But the consequences of *Brown* at the ground level suggest a pyrrhic victory. Today, our society blends pervasive segregation with a belief that the legal issues are settled and thus nothing can be done about it. To those who believed in the promise of *Brown*, this is not just frustrating but tragic. Gary Orfield, a tireless advocate of integration, said in 1996 that our society was "sleepwalking back to *Plessy versus Ferguson*," the 1896 Supreme Court case that sanctioned segregation while promising equality that was never given (Orfield and Eaton 1996, Chap. 12, 331). In sum, *Brown* and the desegregation campaign that followed 10 years later banned legally sanctioned discrimination and—through great effort—reduced actual segregation in the South and border states and in scattered areas across the North, Midwest, and West.

The Challenges of Title I: The Early Years

Several factors augured ill for the success of ESEA's Title I in improving the performance of poor students despite its enduring success politically over the decades. First, the alleviation of poverty was not a strong policy priority for the average American citizen or school superintendent. Also, there was little knowledge at the federal level or within the state and local levels about how to improve the academic achievement of these children. Congress spent the bulk of its attention debating how Title I money would be allocated, not how educators could improve poor children's education.

But Congress also did not devote much money to it. The Great Society programs were many in number and light on budgets. Johnson's War on Poverty was a big idea, but most of its programs were in the Office of Economic Opportunity, whose advocates fought hard to keep these programs experimental and small at first. HEW persuaded the President to locate ESEA in the Office of Education, but Congress did not give the resources needed to do the job. Advocates' hopes that budget appropriations would increase after the first year were confounded by the expansion of the Vietnam War.

Congress not only appropriated too little money but spread it across too many districts. Initially the entitlement was calculated by the number of students from families below $2000 in family income or receiving state welfare. The latter was a concession to big states like New York, whose welfare payments exceeded $2000. However, when those numbers were tallied, that figure was multiplied by a factor reflecting the existing per-pupil costs on average in the individual state, an inducement to get the support of richer states that spent higher amounts per child on education. Meanwhile, the initial definitions of poverty income levels were increased in order to make more attendance areas eligible. Soon, almost half the school districts in the country had some Title I schools. Liberal Democrats in future years would react to this by introducing "concentration grants," which allocated extra funds to the districts with the highest proportion of poverty families. Still, the redistributive effect of Title I was modest.

Title I also foundered because many districts felt little commitment to the stated purpose—to improve the education of children in poverty. They simply violated the law and used the funds for many nonapproved purposes. Scandals emerged within a year. Ruby Martin, former OCR director, and Phyllis McClure, of the NAACP's Legal Defense Fund, documented districts in which Title I funds were used to pay teachers and buy supplies that had nothing to do with Title I programs. Title I funds paid for disposal of sewage, renting an administration building, purchasing a heating system, buying buses for regular school runs, and constructing an instructional television studio for all students (Martin and McClure 1969, 6, 9–11, 13, 14, 21, 29).[10]

Gradually, the government brought such blatant violations of rules under control, but more subtle problems existed. Some schools used the funds only to bring the expenditures for poor children up on average from the existing unequal levels to those of more affluent children within a district. Federal officials found this "comparability" problem difficult to define and monitor. Other schools used Title I funds to replace local or state funds even though federal officials emphasized that Title I funds must "supplement" local amounts spent on these children, not "supplant" those local funds. Another knotty problem has been documented by economists:

---

[10] Thanks to David K. Cohen and Susan L. Moffitt for providing me with a copy of this report.

Adding funds in a given year may seem like an advantage to the Title I programs, but those gains were often offset by subsequent reductions in local taxes for education (Gordon 2004; Cascio, Gordon, and Reber 2013).

It was virtually impossible for the federal government to ascertain whether the funds were reaching the stated goal, which was not just to spend the money on poor children but reduce achievement gaps between rich and poor. Few states had regular statewide achievement tests, and there was an intense phobia against developing federal tests. People widely believed that federal tests would drive curriculum, which was the prerogative of localities and the states. Senator Robert Kennedy insisted upon an accountability clause in Title I because he believed that schools had no idea how to accomplish its goals. However, that clause only required districts to devise whatever tests they wished to use and report them annually to the state, a provision that was inadequate on the face of it and was, in any case, widely ignored.[11] As we shall see, important reforms were made in education legislation, and in Title I in particular, in the 1970s and 1980s.

New Equity Issues Emerge in the 1970s

Four important equity issues emerged in the 1970s—an effort to have the federal government encourage equalization of local-per pupil expenditures, which emanated from the Nixon White House and a Presidential Commission—and three others initiated by members of Congress working with citizens advocacy groups: improving opportunities for English language learners, women, and children with disabilities.

Nixon Seeks to Equalize Expenditures

Before moving ahead to the 1980s, it is worth looking at the issue of school finance reform, which blossomed as an issue early in the Nixon administration. Several different forces led to the establishment of a presidential task force on school finance. The administration had become interested in equalizing resources across districts, partly because they were so unequal but also because the administration had become committed to the improvement of inner-city schools as an alternative to extensive busing for desegregation.

The California Supreme Court had issued a decision requiring equalization of school resources in that state, but the school board in San Antonio, Texas, was

---

[11] On the debates and passage of ESEA, see Sundquist (1968) and Eidenberg and Morey (1969). For critical perspectives on its weaknesses, see Jeffrey (1978), and especially Cohen and Moffitt (2009), which emphasizes the paucity of educational resources at all levels and the loose policy levers in the federal system of educational governance.

challenging such equalization just as the President's Commission on School Finance began its work. In its final report, the commission recommended a shift to full funding of education by the state. Districts would be allowed to raise up to 10 % of the state allocation as a supplement and retain all authority over the spending of the district's entire allocation. In allocating money to districts, the state would consider criteria that included "differentials based on educational need, such as the increased costs of educating the handicapped and disadvantaged." The federal government would offer grants to states as an incentive for states to gradually shift to full state funding of schools and to "more nearly equalize resources among the States for elementary and secondary education."

The commission urged states to help local communities to offer early childhood education to children over 4 years old, and it urged state and local officials to reorganize districts to balance resources and favor a diversity of racial and economic background. The national interest, said the commission, included concentrating funds for low-income children, emergency school assistance for districts developing a more heterogeneous student body, and revenue sharing to states for special education (President's Commission on School Finance 1972).

Some of these goals had been around for some years, but the most radical and central policy shift, to full state funding, found no takers in the Congress. And in the *Rodríguez v. San Antonio* decision, the Supreme Court (in a 5–4 majority) declared that the San Antonio Board of Education had not violated students' rights under the Equal Protection Clause of the 14th Amendment. Equal expenditures in education, they said, was not a constitutional right. That did not preclude states or the federal government from taking steps to equalize per pupil resources voluntarily, but it put a halt to claims that the U.S. Constitution required it. The establishment of this barrier led many civil rights attorneys to pursue suits calling for equalization of resources within individual states, no longer arguing on the basis of the U.S. Constitution but on the explicit or implied rights of students based on state constitutions and laws. For this important and complex story, see Chap. 4.

Bilingual Education

The history of bilingual education is complex, with mixtures of tolerance and opposition, all the way back to British colonial America. Most states, however, gradually suppressed instruction in the native languages of English language learners. The League of United Latin American Citizens preached an assimilationist message but also promoted Hispanic cultural affairs and, more importantly, argued against the segregation and inferior treatment of Hispanic students from the 1920s through the 1960s. Indeed, the federal court decision in *Méndez* (1946) disallowed segregation of Spanish-speaking students. Loopholes allowing segregation for "educational" reasons kept this declaration from meaningful implementation, but it was widely considered as a precedent for the *Brown* decision. By the late 1960s bilingual education and desegregation became the twin aims of Hispanic activists. Senator Ralph

Yarborough of Texas introduced a small, optional program to support English language learners. It became Title VII of the reauthorized ESEA in 1968. It passed without much support from Johnson, who did not like his fellow Texan and was preoccupied with the heavy financial burden of the Vietnam War.

These small beginnings for bilingual education coincided with the rise of the Chicano Movement, emanating mostly from the Southwest. Unlike earlier Mexican-American school reformers who focused on segregation and poor facilities, the Chicano organizations supported cultural reform of the school curriculum and the proud advancement of Chicano identity in all aspects of life. In strikes and protests in 1968 and later, Chicano leaders, including many high school students, demanded more bilingual teachers, more Hispanic counselors, and more respect for Chicano culture.

These ideas had some hold in Anglo politicians' circles. President John F. Kennedy's Committee on Equal Employment Opportunity released a report in 1963 declaring that the schools should have a curriculum that would "reflect Spanish as well as American traditions, and should hire teachers in both cultures." When the Nixon administration took office in 1969, he supported bilingual education, partly because he saw Hispanic votes in the offing, partly because he enjoyed supporting something that Johnson had not supported, and partly because he wanted to be seen as an innovator. OCR Director Stanley Pottinger was more liberal than Nixon was on most issues, and he sensed a green light on bilingual education. He issued a startling memo in 1970 arguing that because Title VI of the Civil Rights Act banned discrimination in any federal program, including discrimination against students on the basis of national origin, it actually required a curriculum that reflected students' language and culture. Pottinger did not have the resources to enforce such an opinion, and he did not insist that bilingual education per se was required. Still, the OCR memo sent a strong federal message (Pottinger 1970; on Hispanic struggles for more treatment, see Moreno 1999; San Miguel 1987; 2004; Strum 2010; Davies 2007, Chap. 6).

By now bilingual education was being advocated around the country. A strong bill passed in Massachusetts, and in the courts, a case called *Lau v. Nichols* was testing the language rights of non-English speaking students in San Francisco. Upon reaching the Supreme Court, the justices, in a unanimous decision, based their endorsement of students' language rights on the Civil Rights Act and Pottinger's memorandum. They declared "there is no equality of treatment merely by providing students with the same facilities, textbooks, teachers and curriculum" because "students who do not understand English are effectively foreclosed from any meaningful education." Like Pottinger's memo, the Court decision (1974) did not require bilingual education but insisted that all school systems had a responsibility to accommodate the learning needs of English language learners. However, when OCR issued a set of strong guidelines called the "Lau Remedies," the following summer, bilingual education was strongly favored.[12]

---

[12] Lau v. Nichols 414 U.S. 563 (1974); U.S. Department of Health, Education, and Welfare, Office of Civil Rights 1975, Appendix B.

This preference for bilingual education reflected Congressional action in the Bilingual Education Act of 1974. Spearheaded by Ted Kennedy and Alan Cranston in the Senate, it endorsed the primacy of bilingual education with a bilingual-bicultural approach. This was the apex of the reigning but fragile view of language rights and cultural pluralism. By the end of the decade, scores of dissenting reports and opinions had been registered.

The lasting effect of the Bilingual Education Act of 1974 was to confirm that accommodating students' English language learning was now mandatory. It also implied that bilingual education was not just a preferred but a necessary response to *Lau*. Finally, the act provided substantially more support for technical assistance and grants for research and development ($68 million, about 10 times that of the Bilingual Act of 1968) (Schneider 1976; Stewner-Manzanares 1988).

Although bilingual education remained the predominant pedagogy for meeting English learners' language needs, there was a surge of negative criticism in the late 1970s and the 1980s. Many critics did not agree that bilingual education was superior to other techniques. Others launched philosophical salvos against accommodating the languages of non-English speakers. Some researchers pointed out the problems in "transitional" bilingual programs, which required subtle judgments about when a student should be transferred to regular English-speaking classes. In some cases, bilingual programs became isolated, and some children stayed in them longer than was effective for gaining content knowledge.

In the 1980s, a conservative President Reagan and a mixed Congress passed various bilingual education laws that prescribed what percentage of programs had to be bilingual and how many could be allowed through other pedagogies. The road beyond 1992 was mixed. Bilingual education had many critics but survived except in a few states that passed anti-bilingual legislation.

Many authorities in the 1970s argued that equal opportunity would not be achieved unless children, Hispanic and those of other national origins, could see their cultures reflected in the schools' curriculum. Though some Hispanic commentators have criticized bilingual programs, many others still believe in the ideal of bilingual-bicultural education in a pluralistic school environment. That hope was politically fragile, but there is no doubt that many public schools installed bilingual education programs, and some introduced a more pluralistic curriculum. The bilingual education movement, however flawed in some eyes, did move us in a more equal direction. A federal program that began modestly, with a small grants program, became obligatory by a sweeping but ambiguous Supreme Court decision.

Title IX Bars Discrimination Against Women

A second problem that received heightened attention in the 1970s was discrimination against women. Title IX of the 1972 Education Amendments forbade such discrimination in all federally funded education programs. Its effect in education was to add women to the list of groups already protected by the Civil Rights Act, which banned discrimination on the basis of race, ethnicity, or national origin.

Title IX received no opposition from the Nixon White House and enjoyed bipartisan support in the Congress. Some have thought that its quiet acceptance is mysterious, because it promised numerous changes in the traditional practices of schools and colleges. There were several reasons for this relatively easy passage. The women's movement, despite some setbacks, had laid the groundwork for wide publicity and considerable support for women's rights by 1971. The Congress and the White House were focusing their most energetic debates on busing for desegregation. After the bill's passage as the Education Amendments of 1972, when more politicians realized the implications of the law, there was much debate surrounding the drafting of regulations that would bring the brief language of Title IX to life. Most attention was focused on college admissions and school and college athletics. Compromises were made on undergraduate admissions, including exemption for single-sex colleges and on other matters, with HEW Secretary Caspar Weinberger in charge.

The regulations did not appear until 1975. When they appeared, OCR was understaffed and ill prepared to respond to complaints. Education Commissioner Terrel Bell fretted privately about the impact of Title IX enforcement on local control. Weinberger was succeeded by Forrest David Mathews, who disliked bureaucracy and was opposed to a strong federal policy role in education. Thus the implementation of Title IX had barely begun when the administration of Democrat Jimmy Carter began in January 1977. Tatel, the OCR director, furthered the implementation of Title IX along with ongoing desegregation work. However, federal civil rights enforcement declined under the Reagan administration (Salomone 1986).

Nonetheless, Title IX had secured a permanent future, and some important policies and procedures were developed by the 1980s. All colleges and universities receiving federal aid were required to establish clear procedures for charges of sexual harassment. They were prominently posted and, in some cases, worked well. The dominance of women's athletics in discussions of Title IX has overshadowed equally important issues pertaining to access, discrimination, and sexual misconduct. All were important. Other issues received detailed attention from OCR, including gender balance among finalists for faculty positions (Ibid., as well as personal recollection of the author).

Assessing the success of Title IX is difficult. How much progress has been due to Title IX and how much to changing acceptance of women's capacities and rights? If there has been progress, what shall we make of continuing, endemic sexist behavior at the college level—from derogatory attitudes about women at prestigious graduate schools to an apparent epidemic of date rape at the college level? Title IX obviously still has a role to play in curbing these acts of discrimination and violence. Is the glass half full or half empty? Although uniform treatment and full equality of status still eludes us, there has been progress in increasing the proportions of women Ph.D. recipients in fields that were until recently male dominated, as well as rising percentages of women among college faculty and college presidents.[13]

Education of Children with Disabilities

In the nineteenth century, almost no students with disabilities went to public schools. Most remained with their families, segregated from schools of any kind. Among those in institutions that were educational and not merely custodial, the emphasis was on blind and deaf children. In the cases of what were then called "mentally retarded," emotionally disturbed, or hyperactive children, some were committed to asylums where inmates were vaguely defined as "troublesome," "imbecilic," "incorrigible," or "truant." Toward the end of the nineteenth century many of these institutions adopted eugenic explanations of disabilities. Involuntary sterilizations were carried out on a large scale. As numbers swelled in these institutions, overcrowding, physical punishments, sexual assaults by staff, and physical restraints on the inmates occurred. Scandals caused little public concern until the 1970s. During the subsequent 20 years many were exposed and closed down.

A few outstanding institutions for children with disabilities in both the nineteenth and twentieth centuries developed educational methods and did other research in the field. In 1957, Governor Orville Faubus of Arkansas hired an able expert, David Ray, to direct the Arkansas Children's Colony. Ray lectured widely on the need to have such children going to public schools. He later became an adviser to Eunice Shriver, President Kennedy's sister, who lobbied for better government support for children with disabilities. Some states passed legislation requiring schools to admit some such students, but progress was slow. The Massachusetts law of 1972 would become a model for later federal action.

Two court cases helped publicize the issue and supported parents' claims that their children's civil rights were being violated. Members of the Pennsylvania Association for Retarded Citizens (PARC) claimed in 1971 that the state had violated the 14th Amendment's Equal Protection Clause when it allowed schools to reject admission to any child without at least a "mental age of five." Because state officials admitted that the law was wrong, the trial resulted in a consent decree, not a full-blown opinion. The three-judge panel simply said these children's rights had been violated and did not elaborate on the constitutional arguments. Expert witnesses had presented evidence that children with learning disabilities could benefit

---

[13] I am not aware of a comprehensive published history of Title IX, thus McCarthy (1991) is important. Ware (2007) organizes relevant documents. Other relevant works are Fishel and Pottker (1977, Chap. 5), which addresses the development of regulations for Title IX, and Costain (1979, 3–11).

from the services of a free public school system. The Court directed Pennsylvania to expunge from its state code any barriers to the enrollment of these children.[14]

The *PARC* decision addressed children with intellectual disabilities but not those with other disabilities. One year later, suit was brought against the Board of Education of Washington, D.C. The first named plaintiff, 12-year-old Peter Mills, was expelled from fourth grade in a district elementary school as a "behavior problem." The District did not afford him a proper hearing or allow him to enroll in any other public school. The following year. D.C. authorities incarcerated Peter at "Junior Village," and the parents brought suit. Sketches of the other six plaintiffs showed similar histories. U.S. District Judge Joseph Cornelius Waddy ruled that the plaintiffs and all children with disabilities had rights under the Equal Protection Clause and could not be excluded from the public schools. School officials argued that it would be prohibitively expensive; Waddy disagreed. He ordered the District to "provide to each child of school age a free and suitable publicly-supported education regardless of the degree of the child's mental, physical, or emotional disability or impairment."[15]

These cases stood as the legal landmarks of the education rights of children with disabilities. Nonetheless, some advocates were nervous that the upcoming trial in *Rodríguez v. San Antonio* might end with a denial of education as a right under the 14th Amendment. They campaigned instead for an endorsement of these rights under the Civil Rights Act.

This effort succeeded in the form of a one-sentence amendment to the Rehabilitation Act of 1973 known as Section 504. Modeled on the Civil Rights Act, it states: "No otherwise qualified handicapped individual in the United States . . . shall, solely by reason of his handicap, be excluded from the participation in, be denied the benefits of, or be subjected to discrimination under any program or activity receiving Federal financial assistance." Young civil rights staff of Senator Harrison Williams (D-New Jersey) drafted this legislation. Their instincts about *Rodríguez* proved justified. In 1974 the Supreme Court declared, in a 5–4 decision, that the Constitution did not support a right to education. Nonetheless, Section 504 preserved the mantle of civil rights that surrounded special education. Like Title IX for women's education in 1972, Section 504 did not cause great controversy as a simple abstract statement because it was nestled in a bill full of specific requirements and programs (see Scotch 2001, 47–48).

The stage was now set for a comprehensive federal bill supporting special education. *Mills* and *PARC* were being widely cited. Many states were facing lawsuits on their basis. Other states were moving ahead voluntarily on these new responsibilities. In May 1973, the *Washington Post* estimated that there were about 7 million children with disabilities in the country. Of these, approximately 2.8 million were in public schools with special education services, a big rise from the 1960s. One million were excluded from public schools and were not in private schools. A half

---

[14] Pennsylvania Association for Retarded Children v. Commonwealth of Pennsylvania 334 F. Supp. 1257, U.S. Dist. (1971).

[15] Peter Mills v. Board of Education of the District of Columbia, 348 F. Supp. 866 (1972).

million were in private institutions, many receiving no education. Finally, about 2.7 million children with disabilities were in schools where they received no special education. States were already alarmed at the costs, and tensions were arising about the relative share to be provided by the district, state, and federal levels.[16]

Williams' comprehensive Education of All Handicapped Children Act was debated in 1974 and passed in 1975. It had several main provisions. First, each child with a disability would have an individual education plan (IEP). Second, schools were directed to conduct education of the children with disabilities in the "least restrictive" environment, that is, in regular classrooms, to the extent feasible. This provision later became known informally as "mainstreaming." It was founded on the belief that children with disabilities as well as those without disabilities would benefit from daily contact and a normalization of relationships as well as access to the regular curriculum. However, it also brought tensions from teachers who believed that attention to children with disabilities detracted from paying attention to the other students and that some of these children were disruptive. Teachers also argued they were not trained to handle these responsibilities.

To get funds from this law, districts were required to submit a plan for appropriate education of all of their children with disabilities. Even if they declined funds from Williams' act, they were required to accommodate all children with disabilities because discrimination was forbidden by the Rehabilitation Act. The federal government proposed to fund the states for as much as 40 % of the "extra" costs of special education (translating into about 20 % of the total costs of the average special education student). However, federal appropriations were actually much lower than 40 % (see Table 3.2). This shortfall led the hard-pressed states to complain that the law was an "unfunded mandate," but the authority of the federal government held steady: The obligation of the states was based on civil rights, regardless of federal funding.

Table 3.2 Funding of special education costs, percent shares, 1983 through 2010

Date	Federal	State	Local
1983	7	56	37
1988	6	58	36
1994	6	55	39
1999	8	47	45
2010	9	47	44

Sources: Parrish 2001, 4–12, Table 4; 2010 data from Baker et al. 2014
For end-of-the-century information, see New America Foundation (n.d). For a good discussion of these and other figures about relative share and real costs, see Aron and Loprest (2012, 110)

---

[16] Bart Barnes and Andrew Barnes, "Special Education: A New Storm Center," *Washington Post,* May 29, 1973, C1; B. Barnes and A. Barnes, "Handicapped Pupils Face Schooling Crisis," *Washington Post,* May 30, 1974, D1. The Barnes's estimates of numbers of children with disabilities and their schooling categories came from Alan R. Abeson, spokesman for the Council for Exceptional Children.

The regulations for the act were not formulated until nearly the end of President Gerald Ford's term. As with the Title IX regulations, implementation was delayed. The Carter administration took office in January, but the special education regulations went through a further lengthy consideration and appeared in the summer of 1977. By this time, special education had become an expanding item in school budgets, with the states and districts bearing most of the costs and straining under the imperatives of the law. There were also debates about mainstreaming; discipline with children with disabilities; whether severely disabled children should be mainstreamed; the overdiagnosis of disability for children of color; and other issues. Still, special education legislation had (and has) broad bipartisan appeal.

The rising percentage of students with disabilities among the total student population was substantial. The percentage of school students in special education in 1977 was 8.3 %; by 2005 it was 13.8 % (U.S. Department of Education, National Center for Education Statistics 2015a). During that time the federal share of costs remained about level, while the state share decreased and the local share increased (see Table 3.2). It is this expanding percentage of students in special education, not rising costs per pupil, that has made special education the fastest growing budget item in most local districts. It arose over the past 50 years, starting from a situation in which only a tiny minority of children with disabilities were in public schools at all, to today, when it is a permanent and large reality in our schools. This development involved all three levels of the federalist system and all three branches, but it was led by federal courts and its advocates in the Congress, both pressed by interest groups of special education parents and special education professionals. Whatever its flaws, it was a historic shift, and, for the most part, a benefit to children with disabilities.

Another reform initiative addressed the profound discrimination experienced by Native Americans, but space allows only brief mention. These developments in policy governing Native American education, including the Indian Education Act of 1972, contributed to equalization of opportunity by recognizing Native Americans' justified desire for more autonomy in governing their educational institutions and having a genuine voice on commissions and in the newly created Office of Indian Education (for the history of education policy regarding Native Americans, see Szasz 1999; Hale 2002).

The 1978 Reauthorization of ESEA

Advocates and opponents of bilingual education, women's equity in education, and education for children with disabilities continued working through the complicated process of implementation, the approval of regulations and guidelines, and providing the relevant agencies with the needed resources to make a federal program work. In the meantime, the Democrats returned to the White House. President Carter had many problems on his hands, and in education, he was mostly preoccupied with creating a new Department of Education. Meanwhile, veteran staff at the Office of

Education and in Congressional education committees carried on the development of a revised ESEA.

The impetus for a Department of Education arose during the 1976 election campaign, when Carter courted the National Education Association's support; in the process he agreed to support its longtime goal of creating a separate department with Cabinet status. Carter eventually focused on the promised department and gathered various West Wing staff to work on details, especially the issue of which federal programs would be transferred to it from other agencies.

Meanwhile, the reauthorization of ESEA loomed important. Much of the leadership for the reauthorization came from Marshall "Mike" Smith, assistant commissioner of education for policy. Smith was a veteran of ESEA purposes, policies, and problems and a veteran Office of Education official. The commissioner, Ernest Boyer, former chancellor of the State University of New York, advocated in Congress for ESEA along with HEW Secretary Anthony (Joe) Califano. But Boyer was otherwise mostly involved in the disputes about what programs should be in the new Department of Education, while Califano openly opposed losing the Office of Education, which he thought belonged in an organization that combined education with health and welfare matters.

Smith and his colleagues developed the Office of Education's proposed ESEA legislation and conferred with Congressional staff continually. Among the key House staff were Jack Jennings and Chris Cross. Jennings, a Democrat, was majority counsel to the House Subcommittee on Elementary and Secondary Education, and Cross, a Republican, was minority senior staff member. They worked well with each other and with Smith. A lengthy document emerged, went to the President for approval, and then went to the relevant Congressional committees for further negotiations.

Evaluations of Title I in the early 1970s had discovered widespread misuse of funds, questioned whether the funds were properly targeted at kids in high-poverty schools, and saw little evidence that the programs were working to improve academic achievement (McLaughlin 1975; Vinovskis 1999a). In response, Congress in 1974 commissioned a three-year study headed by Paul Hill at the new National Institute of Education (NIE). The legislative report by the House of Representatives' Committee on Education and Labor, when introducing the 1978 bill, stated that the NIE study had convinced them that the funds were now effectively targeted, explaining that while Title I provided only 5 % of the elementary and secondary education budgets nationwide, many poor districts reported levels up to 17 %. As for results, NIE found that Title I students tended not to fall behind their "non-assisted peers." Part of the NIE research was a case study of 12 districts, which showed much better academic gains than in previous evaluations. Carl Perkins, chair of the Education Committee, concluded, "Title I has matured into a viable approach for aiding the disadvantaged."[17]

---

[17] HR. Rep. No. 29-553 at 6-7. (Excerpt of a Report on the Education Amendments of 1978). Available online through HathiTrust at http://www.hathitrust.org/access

The committee's optimistic report would not end criticisms of Title I's efficiency in raising students' scores. In fact, another study was ongoing at the same time. Called the "Sustaining Effects" study, it followed 130,000 students in 300 schools for three years. Study director Launor Carter pointed out the participation problems: Many poor children were in non-Title I schools that did not qualify as having a sufficient concentration of poor families. Conversely, many low-achieving students who were in Title I schools but were not economically disadvantaged were in Title I instructional programs. Furthermore, students with very low achievement levels got little benefit from Title I; those with somewhat higher achievement at the beginning benefited the most. These and other qualms caused Carter to say that Title I was not "a unified or coherent treatment program" and needed a "new program with more intensive and innovative techniques" to bring success to the lowest achieving students (Carter 1984).

The Office of Education staff, in consultation with education experts in Congress, came up with several substantial reforms for the 1978 authorization, working mainly with Congress but giving regular reports to the White House staff and getting their ideas vetted and approved by the Office of Management and Budget. Among these changes were allocating a higher per-pupil expenditure to Title I students in schools with a large concentration of high-poverty families (which Congress set at 55 %); pressing Title I programs to rely less upon "pullout" programs and to integrate Title I students into regular classrooms with special assistance; allowing schools with 75 % or more percentage of children from homes below the poverty line to spend Title I funds on "whole school" programs and improvements; providing matching funds to states that had put money into their own compensatory education programs; providing better professional development for experienced teachers in the field; engaging in better planning and development of bilingual education; encouraging states to equalize resources among districts; deepening parental participation by requiring districts to pay for their transportation to and from meetings; and requiring districts to submit plans about the training of parent council members.

Beyond Title I, the 1978 Amendments had several other titles related to equal opportunity: Title II for basic skills improvement, Title VI for "emergency aid" to desegregating schools, Title VII for bilingual education, Title IX for women's education equity, and Title XI for Indian education.[18] The collaboration and constant communication between Office of Education staff and key Congressional advocates was crucial in producing a reauthorization bill with bipartisan support.

---

[18]Education Amendments of 1978, 92 Stat. 2143 (Washington, D.C.: Public Law 95-561, 95th Cong (1978); interview with Marshall Smith, September 24, 2013; Cross (2014, 70–74); Jennings (2015, 35–42).

Education Policy and Civil Rights in the Reagan Administration

Ronald Reagan was elected in 1980 over Carter on a platform that focused largely on cutting down on "big government." In the field of education, the Education Consolidation and Improvement Act (ECIA) of 1981 moved to decentralize and deregulate the federal role in education while spending less on federal aid. Its major sections were now called "chapters" rather than "titles." Chapter I became the new name for Title I for compensatory education of disadvantaged students in schools with high poverty. Education for children with disabilities also continued in separate legislation. But Chapter II of ECIA was a showcase innovation: a "block" grant. It pulled together 32 small federal programs. The items blocked in Chapter II ranged from the Emergency Schools Assistance Act (ESAA) for desegregation costs, to metric education, environmental education, and other small programs. The states received their share purely on the basis of population and were required to allocate at least 80 % of it directly to districts. Districts were then permitted to allocate the Chapter II funds as they wished among the 32 programs.

This devolution of control came at a time when state and local budgets were tight, and the ECIA bill itself reduced allocations for many programs. There was less money for both Chapter I and Chapter II (in comparison to its 32 constituent programs separately) than had been the case a year before, so the states and districts had to make their decisions about Chapter II allocations in the midst of a funding crisis. Furthermore, Chapter II had a much smaller budget than Chapter I. In many districts, these 32 programs had added up to as little as 1 % of the elementary and secondary school costs, although ranging upward in large city districts that had many more families in poverty and many remaining desegregation activities.

A strong shift of money from urban to suburban and rural, and a shift away from desegregation, resulted from the funding changes. Previously a large share of the funds represented by these 32 separate programs had gone to large urban districts—partly because ESAA was the largest program in the block, and partly because urban school staffs were more likely to apply successfully for grants. But Chapter II funds required no application. The money came just on the basis of school population.

The shift can be seen in these figures: Wilmington, DE, received $3.3 million just from ESAA the year before the block funding; under ECIA, the amount of block funds for all Chapter II purposes the next year was only $1.7 million. St. Louis and Kansas City received $7.0 million between them under ESAA; the next year the entire state of Missouri received $8.7 million for Chapter II overall (Verstegen 1985, 521). Another study showed that 20 urban school districts, including Atlanta, Buffalo, Boston, Chicago, and New York, collectively received $110 million from the ESAA alone in 1980; the next year, they collectively received $38 million for all the programs combined in the block grant (Salomone 1986, 179). Despite the overall reduction in ECIA funds, and perhaps because of the shift from urban districts, school officials in many rural and suburban districts praised ECIA as a modest return to local control, as it was intended to be (Turnbull and Marks 1986, 61, 63).

The Reagan administration proposed large cuts in other education programs. Education advocates in Congress strained against it, settling for budgets larger than the White House proposed but less than many had wished. Within these small annual increases, some of the flagship programs of the 1960s and 1970s were reduced. Rosemary Salomone writes that between 1980 and 1984, federal funding cuts, adjusted for inflation, were as follows: 9.3 % for special education, 19.7 % for compensatory education for disadvantaged students; and 39.8 % for bilingual education (Salomone 1986, 180).

In addition to the shift of priorities in the small block grants—which worked disproportionately against desegregation aid—and targeted cuts in programs for compensatory education, bilingual education, and special education, there was also a slowdown of enforcement in civil rights suits. This was part of the Reagan platform to transfer authority in education to the states and districts. One of the effects of this philosophy was to diminish federal programs that had been intended to increase opportunity.[19] Overall, this was the last period when the federal portion of funding diminished.

The Nation at Risk Report

While federal funding was on the decline, a broad-based push for education reform was on the way. President Reagan's Secretary of Education was Terrel Bell, a veteran education leader from Utah who had served as U.S. Commissioner of Education during the Ford administration. He may have been the most liberal member of the Reagan cabinet, but he was a strong believer in local control. He had advised President Ford to veto the special education legislation in 1975 because he thought it was too costly and intrusive (Bell 1975). Bell had little stature with the President, but he was convinced that America's schools needed reforming, and he asked the White House to appoint a blue-ribbon commission to look into it. When the White House ignored his request, Bell appointed a department commission on his own authority.

The National Commission on Excellence in Education worked with data from researchers at the Education Department, who provided tons of information on the good news and bad news about schools in the U.S. However, two of the scientists on the panel, Gerald Horton, a physicist from Harvard, and Glenn Seaborg, a chemist

---

[19] I do not have data on expenses specifically for Title IX, which bars discrimination against women, as a part of the budget of the Office of Civil Rights in HEW. Salomone (1986, 180) reports that enforcement of Title IX was reduced during the Reagan administration, and that the Reagan administration tried to either block grant or zero budget the Women's Educational Equity Act, which complemented Title IX by providing funds to promote sex equity and eliminate sex-stereotyping in education materials. Women's advocacy groups succeeded in lobbying, and he signed a five-year extension of the program in 1984.

at Berkeley, were not satisfied with the initial staff draft. Horton wanted something more decisive. He and other members crafted a theme of crisis, which framed the research data around alarming trends and gave them a slogan: *A Nation at Risk.* Journalists picked up on this eagerly. There was already much publicity about poor test results and their possible relation to America's competitive position in the world. *Nation at Risk* fanned the fires. The Department of Education counted 700 newspaper articles about the report in the first four months after its publication. Reagan met to congratulate the members. A side effect of this highly publicized report was that it weakened public and Congressional sentiment to abolish the Education Department (Vinovskis 2009).

However, it did not change the determination of the Reagan administration to back away from a federal role in education. In response to a President who said that education was the states' business and a federal report that said there was an urgent crisis, officials in the states took up the slack. It led to a decade of reform activity, resulting in new legislation in most states and capacity building in the state education agencies. The theme was excellence; the goal was to raise average test scores, not necessarily to reduce the gap between some groups and others.

The commission, along with several other reform reports, recommended more homework, higher graduation standards, more academic focus in schools, and better teacher preparation. Many states passed laws incorporating these recommendations. However, within three or four years, journalists and educators were bemoaning the failure of these reforms to increase test scores. The reform movement was fading. Its theory of action, plausible enough, was that if kids worked hard enough, and if teacher-training programs raised their standards, academic achievement would rise. However, that strategy did not work in the short run. By 1985 the National Governors' Association was calling for better testing and task forces to recommend better reforms.

Reagan Faces Reversals: Hawkins-Stafford Bill of 1988

In the waning years of Reagan's second term, Congress reversed some of his policies on education. This effort was led by Augustus "Gus" Hawkins, Democratic Congressman from Los Angeles and chair of the House Committee on Education and Labor, and his co-sponsor, Robert Stafford, a renegade Vermont Republican who believed in a strong federal role in education. Their bill deleted the signature provision of ECIA, the block grants under Chapter II. Hawkins-Stafford increased Chapter I spending staunchly but required the states to make gains on achievement and narrowing gaps. Any state that did not make its target two years in a row was required to review its districts' programs and supervise remediation. Equalization was the goal; tighter monitoring of test scores was the strategy.

The bill also strengthened the role of the National Assessment of Educational Progress (NAEP) by establishing an independent governing body, the National Assessment Governing Board, to set goals for what students should know and be able to do at various grade levels in various subjects. The new ESEA was not a panacea, however. The federal government still yielded to the states the job of setting performance standards, and there was great variability in how ambitious the goals were in different states. Nonetheless, as Jennings emphasizes, the emphasis in the Hawkins-Stafford amendments on accountability was a strong factor in the almost unanimous bipartisan support for the bill; also, the emphasis on standards helped lay the groundwork for the standards movement as the basis for school reform and accountability.[20]

The Era of Standards-Based Reform

George H. W. Bush and the Onset of Reform

As President Reagan's second term ended and George H. W. Bush was elected President, the country was looking for new answers to improve education. President Bush hoped to launch a partnership between the federal government and the states, but a Democratic majority in Congress short-circuited his legislative efforts. Meanwhile, the cadre of "education" governors was growing, and they began to edge toward the use of comparative state test results to spur reform. NAEP had launched an experimental state-by-state administration of the tests, which had the potential to rate states across the nation. Also, independent state-produced tests could be rated relative to the uniform NAEP assessments (Vinovskis 2008, 2009).

After his election Bush suggested a national education summit meeting, to which the governors readily agreed. Held in September 1989, the Charlottesville (Va.) Summit ended with the governors and the President agreeing to improve assessment and accountability. They also called for a set of national goals in education. Prior to the meeting, Governors Bill Clinton of Arkansas (Dem.) and Carroll Campbell of South Carolina (Rep.) co-chaired a meeting in which they noted the disadvantages of students of color and students from low-income families. Equality of opportunity had reentered the picture.

After the summit, the governors and the White House agreed upon six goals, several of which had strong implications for equal opportunity and equalization of results. The goals stated that by the year 2000, all children in America would "start school ready to learn"; 90 % would graduate from high school; all students would demonstrate high competency in English, math, science, history, and geography; the

---

[20] For the provisions of the law, see Augustus F. Hawkins-Robert T. Stafford Elementary and Secondary School Improvement Amendments of 1988, H.R. 5, 100th Cong. (1988). For Hawkins, see "Hawkins, Augustus Freeman (Gus), (1907–2007)." n.d.; for Stafford, see Reagan Walker, "Stafford: Republican Rebel During Reagan's Revolution," *Education Week,* November 2, 1988, http://www.edweek.org/ew/articles/1988/11/02/08450045.h08.html, and essays on "Hawkins-Stafford Amendments," and "Targeting the Achievement Gap" in *Federal Education Policy and the States, 1945–2009* (2009). On the importance of bipartisan support and accountability, see Jennings (2015, 48–49).

U.S. would be first in the world in science and math; all adults would be literate and have the knowledge "to compete in a global economy" and become good citizens; and every school would be free of drugs and violence (Swanson 1991; on the novelty of the aspiration to have all adults gain high-level literacy skills, see Kaestle 1995).

These goals, of course, were optimistic statements. They were attainable only in part, and only if the reform movement could develop better theories about education reform and improved accountability systems. The period 1988 through 1992 was a very "yeasty" time for school reform ideas. NAEP tests at the state level now had the capacity to compare states' performances on basic skills, though hardly anyone thought they should be used as a national "test" for the evaluation of individual students or teacher accountability. The states at the front of the school reform movement were developing state-level standards and curriculum guides. Assessment experts were experimenting with more sophisticated "performance" assessments.

Enter Systemic Education

A key theory was articulated in a 1991 article by Marshall Smith and Jennifer O'Day called "systemic school reform." It crystallized several ideas that had been circulating in school reform circles and became a founding document for the standards-based reform movement. To be "systemic," said Smith and O'Day, the states must create content standards, performance standards, opportunity-to-learn standards (equal access to high-quality education), and student assessments, as well as foster teacher preparation and professional development that focus on the standards. To form a coherent program, all of these elements must be "aligned" (Smith and O'Day 1991).[21]

Historian Maris Vinovskis has analyzed the origins of this idea in the professional experiences of Smith and O'Day. As the director of the Wisconsin Center on Education Research, Smith was immersed in school improvement research, and his participation in the Consortium for Policy Research in Education reinforced his belief that the states should be the actors in developing standards. In 1990, Robert Schwartz, education director at the Pew Charitable Trusts, initiated the Pew Forum on School Reform, which included Smith. The forum began looking at exemplars of content standards from the various states and from abroad. O'Day, an expert policy analyst, was the associate director of the Pew Forum (Vinovskis 1999b, Chap. 7, 175–81).

Smith and O'Day emphasized the problem of underperforming poor and minority students, who were so often in underperforming schools. If reformers did not attend to this problem, not only would those students have unequal opportunity, but

---

[21] Marshall S. Smith and Jennifer A. O'Day 1999, "Systemic School Reform," in *The Politics of Curriculum and Testing* (London, England: Falmer Press, *Politics of Education Yearbook,* 1990): 233–67.

the system itself would not be coherent. The idea of Opportunity to Learn (OTL) standards, which were designed to solve the problem of holding students responsible for meeting challenging standards when they may not have had adequate instruction in those standards, caused great controversy.

There were several problems with OTL standards. Some opponents said it was hard to imagine how one would operationalize indicators for OTL that would go beyond the many existing state policies like teacher certification, curriculum guides, and rules about class size. Some governors opposed them because of the estimated cost of establishing and maintaining OTL systems. Other opponents viewed them as a federal incursion into local control. Others said it would just delay the much-needed standards-based reform movement. In the end, systemic reform without OTL standards became the backbone of the movement, which developed bipartisan support, and, despite great controversies, persisted as the unifying factor in federal and state education policy for 25 years, from the Clinton administration to the present.

Standards-Based Reform Arrives on the Federal Agenda

Governors and chief state school officers had been the prominent leaders in systemic school reform in the 1980s. Yet upon the election of President Clinton in 1992, the federal government reemerged as an education policy maker. Clinton was not shy to renew a strong federal role. He appointed William Riley, popular former education governor of South Carolina, as Secretary of Education and Smith as deputy in charge of drafting and promoting the legislative agenda in education. In addition to its enthusiasm for standards-based reform, the Clinton team focused on the problems of disadvantaged students.

The Education Department developed two bills during the first two years of his administration. The first bill was the reauthorization of ESEA. The Clinton administration renamed it the Improving America's Schools Act (IASA), but many old hands around Washington continued to call it ESEA. Also, the term "chapter" for a section of the law was returned to "title," the pre-Reagan term. IASA proposed to alter the Title I formula to focus resources on districts with the highest poverty concentrations. This lost in a close vote in the House subcommittee. Meanwhile, the Title I threshold for whole-school approaches was lowered from schools with 75 % poverty families to 65 %. IASA introduced the new key provisions requiring districts to test all kids (not just those in Title I) with math and reading assessments that were geared to standards that states would be required to develop and implement. Other equity-related programs besides Title I remained: basic skills (Title II), aid for desegregation (Title VI), bilingual education (Title VII), women's educational rights (Title IX), and Indian education (Title XI).[22]

---

[22] On the legislative history of Title I in 1994, see Jennings (1998, 118–53). For a summary of all the titles, see "Summary of the Improving America's Schools Act," *Education Week*, November 9, 1994, http://www.edweek.org/ew/articles/1994/11/09/10asacht.h14.html

The second bill was called The Goals 2000 Act. It specified how the states and the federal government would collaborate on systemic education, spurring many debates about the proper roles of the federal government. There were also equal opportunity concerns at stake. Smith and O'Day had focused attention on disadvantaged students and underperforming schools. There could be high standards for all children, and that became a mantra of standards-based reform.

The battle lines were typical: liberals vs. conservatives, and centralists vs. localists. But there were wrinkles. Some Democrats wanted national standards, some did not; some also wanted national assessments. Many Republicans supported standards-based reform but wanted the states to be the main actors and not supervised by the federal government. In the compromises that were hammered out, Goals 2000 proposed a system where states were expected to establish content standards, performance standards, opportunity-to-learn standards, and assessments. Each state was required to establish a board to carry out this work. A new national board, called the National Education Standards and Improvement Council (NESIC), would approve state plans, but only on a voluntary basis.

Even though Goals 2000 did not require states to submit their standards to federal authorities, many Republicans reacted negatively to the establishment of NESIC and it remained unfunded by Congress. As for the controversial opportunity-to-learn standards, they remained in the department's description of a proper systemic effort, but researcher Andrew Porter pointed out that there was little incentive for states to develop them, and even less incentive to subject them voluntarily to federal certification (Porter 1995; for the detailed arguments and debates about standards and federal authority in standards-based education, see Ravitch 1995; Jennings 1998; Kaestle and Lodewick 2007).

Republicans made gains in Congress and asserted themselves. They succeeded in abolishing NESIC, squelched the administration's suggestions for a Voluntary National Test, discredited a federally sponsored set of national history/social studies standards, and blocked the reauthorization of ESEA in 2000. The Democrats staved off some Republican assaults with help from some Senate Republicans who were not in tune with the more conservative program.[23] Nonetheless, Goals 2000 established a framework that spread across the country and would remain the central reform instrument from that time to the present. Policy analyst Margaret "Peg" Goertz reported in 2001 that 49 states had content standards in reading and math, 48 of them had assessments to match, and 33 had developed accountability measures that went beyond student test performance. Paul Manna points out that several Republican governors and many business groups supported the standards movement. Furthermore, general public opinion favored the Clinton education agenda. While the administration's retreat from some issues may have looked like a defeat,

---

[23] Maris Vinovskis (2009, 111–20) presents a balanced account of education policy in the Clinton years, with many more details. See the book and sources cited there. See also, among the many books dealing with this period, Cross (2014); DeBray (2006); McGuinn (2006); Manna (2007); Jennings (1998); and Ravitch (1995).

standards-based education was progressing in the states. Ironically, that formula would take on a more authoritarian federal face in the administration of President George W. Bush, a Republican (Manna 2007, 103, 152–54).

Peg Goertz reminded me recently of a metaphor for this significant policy success. Title I of IASA, with its requirement that all districts test all students on assessments that are linked to standards, could be considered the "stick," forcing the standards-reform framework on the districts, while Goals 2000 was the "carrot," the framework to help states and districts create standards-based systems. Conjuring up a different metaphor, Mike Smith said that the ESEA, with its requirements for school-wide testing and system accountability, was the "big engine" pulling all the other cars down the track.[24]

No Child Left Behind: Its Trajectory Under George W. Bush and Barack Obama

Bush Launches New Federal Reforms

President Bush's attraction to standards-based reform was similar to Clinton's. Both had been education governors and enjoyed the reputation of having successfully improved his state's schools. Bush was determined to continue the federal role in school reform, and his advocates fanned out to convince their conservative Republican colleagues that either they were out of step with public opinion or should give the President his preferences in education policy because the rest of his agenda was so attractive to conservative Republicans. But it took more effort than that. Sandy Kress, Bush's main education adviser, circulated the program first as a platform rather than as specific legislation. Bush's allies held meetings with carefully selected members of Congress. The campaign was skillfully done and unconventional. With Kress in charge, the administration and its Congressional allies bypassed the Senate Health Education and Pensions Committee, shunned the participation of education lobby groups, and ignored the staff of the Department of Education. In the wake of the attacks on the World Trade Center on September 11, 2001, many Congress members believed that they should work to pass effective legislation and not appear to be in disarray.

For Democrats, there were some attractive features in Bush's proposed No Child Left Behind Act (NCLB): an emphasis on improving failing schools and narrowing the achievement gap between racial groups, with disaggregated achievement test scores by group for each school available publicly, with some tough incentives and disincentives for schools that did not succeed. Senator Ted Kennedy endorsed the bill later in the process, hoping to get increased Title I money and achievement scores disaggregated by race-ethnic group. He got the scores but not much money.

---

[24] Margaret Goertz and Marshall Smith, personal communications.

His co-sponsorship capped the image of a bipartisan bill (see DeBray 2006). But the goal of reducing achievement gaps was not solely the Democrats' property. Campaigning for the presidency, Bush vowed that his education policy would attack the "soft bigotry of lowered expectations." Speaking at Harvard in the second year of the Bush administration, Secretary of Education Rod Paige, himself African-American, said that the achievement gap "is the civil rights issue of our time," and some leading civil rights lawyers like Christopher Edley of the Harvard Civil Rights Project and Bill Taylor of the Citizens Commission for Civil Rights supported NCLB for its tough approach and for setting an ultimate goal of reducing the gaps.[25]

The Bush team concluded that the Clinton enforcement of Title I had been slack and unproductive. The attempt to ensure that all states would link Title I tests to standards-related tests for the whole student population was still languishing in non-compliance. In response it produced the deepest intrusion into local control since desegregation. Some of its supporters in Congress and out in the states and the schools had second thoughts when they realized how much coercion was to be levied upon local school districts for not very much money. Schools were required to test all students in third through eighth grades annually. States were required to commit themselves to performance standards. Schools that did not come up to their adequate yearly progress (AYP) commitments would eventually be liable for "reconstitution," including sanctions as severe as having new leadership being appointed or being reopened as a charter school. This assumed that the states had the technical capacity to remedy poor performance, which was not always the case.

It began to appear that the rules would generate huge lists of condemned schools, because the end goals were set too high. Elizabeth DeBray (2006) wrote that the unrealistic goals and the concerns about the extent of federal leverage led to a "rocky start" for NCLB. The Bush administration softened some of the demanding features of the law but persisted in the end goal to have all children proficient by 2014. That, some test experts said, was impossible. Robert Linn wrote in 2005, "There is considerable evidence that gains in student performance on the tests tend to be greatest in the first few years after they have been introduced as part of an accountability system and then taper off in later years." Thus, those states that adopted low AYP goals in the early years, expecting to accelerate into higher achievement and smaller gaps later in the process, were working in exactly the wrong way. Said Linn, "It can be anticipated that the AYP goals, which are likely to be hard to meet in the early years, will become increasingly difficult to meet in the out years of the program" (DeBray 2006, 129–43, Rothstein 2004; Linn 2005).

In the latter stages of Congressional consideration, some staff on the Senate Committee on Health, Education, Labor, and Pensions did some research, simulating how many schools would be deemed failing in three of the states known for

---

[25] George W. Bush's speech to the National Association for the Advancement of Colored People, July 16, 2000, is quoted in "Bush Addresses NAACP Convention," ABC News, http://abcnews. go.com/Politics/story?id=123409; Paige is quoted in Cara Feinberg, "Rod Paige Offers High Praise for No Child Left Behind," *Harvard University Gazette,* April 29, 2004, 1; on Edley's support, see DeBray 2006; Taylor's support is documented in Linn (2005) and personal interviews.

reducing the achievement gap: Texas, North Carolina, and Connecticut. Based on the AYPs, almost all the schools in these states would have been rated as "failing." Presented at a meeting within the administration, these data produced a "stunned silence," said a staffer. Another staff member said, "I left just wanting to cry" (Manna 2007, 124–25).

The Bush people and their allies rushed to adjust the AYP formulas, but the results were unsuccessful. Once the bill was passed and in the field, the Bush administration eased off, allowing different kinds of tests to be used and delaying deadlines. Paul Manna argues that the federal NCLB scheme actually relied on "borrowed state capacity" for its implementation, capacity which most states lacked. They realized this and pushed back. Almost all states had a nominal set of content standards by this time, but many were not coherent and not matched by an aligned assessment regime (Manna 2007; DeBray 2006). Standards-based reform had become a consensus position, with bipartisan appeal to centrists in both parties; Democrats on the civil rights left and conservative Republicans agreed with the Kennedy liberals and the Republican leadership in the Congress that there should be no amendments to the law at the end of Bush's first term, just administrative adjustments (Manna 2007; Cross 2014).

Some appraisals of achievement test scores suggest that there was a trough in which the achievement gaps widened during the end of the Clinton second term and for much of the first Bush term. Many factors could be responsible. Most states had not accomplished the reforms of the 1994 reauthorization, and districts were now faced with the Bush administration's new complex reform regime. In the second Bush term, he had an energetic Secretary of Education, Margaret Spellings, and the rules were clarified. Still, there was much criticism of No Child Left Behind (see Goertz 2005).

Enter Obama and Duncan

As President Obama entered the White House, the country was descending into a fiscal crisis and a major recession. State and local budgets were reduced heavily. As part of the American Recovery and Reinvestment Act (ARRA) of February 2009, the President and Congress put a large amount of federal money into high-priority areas to create jobs, relieve local and state budgets, and put money in the pockets of consumers. Secretary Arne Duncan's budget at the Department of Education was nearly doubled with an ARRA allocation of $97.4 billion. The specific program areas receiving stimulus funding were State Fiscal Stabilization ($48.6 billion), college student Pell grants ($16.5 billion), Individuals with Disabilities Education Act funds ($12.2 billion), Title I programs ($10.0 billion), and formula grants and discretionary funds ($10.1 billion). Duncan and his staff had an unusual opportunity to fashion a new version of standards-based reform through these discretionary funds (Executive Office of the President of the United States 2009).

The Duncan team had to decide what to do about No Child Left Behind. It was still the law of the land, but it was widely discredited for its negative incentives and unrealistic achievement goals. States and school districts were in a budget squeeze with predictions that it would get worse in the coming few years. And all of this fell to a new Secretary who had been a successful superintendent of schools in Chicago but had no experience in Washington. Several of his assistant secretaries had not yet been appointed when ARRA was passed. Meanwhile, the department's day-to-day business had to continue amid pressure to articulate a major reform strategy (U.S. Department of Education 2009).

With help from advisers around the country, Duncan and his staff developed a shift away from the NCLB mode of tight monitoring and negative incentives. In addition to Title I and other entitlement programs, the new strategy was to have competitive grants and reward the best state applications with extra funding to implement their plans, a positive incentive. The state plans had to comply with criteria set by the department.

From a critical perspective, there are (at least) two things to be questioned in retrospect: first, Race to the Top rewarded the 19 states deemed to have the best potential for effective reform, that is, the states with the best grant writers and the most broad support for their plan among their stakeholders. The 31 states that did not receive Race to the Top grants either opted out for various reasons or applied and were not chosen. The amounts were not trivial; in the first round, only two awards were announced, $500 million to Tennessee and $100 million to Delaware. Later awards were reduced as the budget dwindled. In any case, the competition left the children of those 31 states who did not receive Race to the Top awards without funds that those states might have used to improve their systems. This was the price for rewarding excellence.[26]

Second, the Education Department under Duncan took a very prescriptive stance. It insisted that every state applying for Race to the Top had to increase the number of charter schools and adopt pay-for-performance as part of salary decisions for teachers. Among the many possible policy options that one might have urged for mandatory implementation, many would have had a better basis in research than simply establishing more charter schools or using student scores in setting teachers' salaries—for example, access to early childhood education or carefully targeted class-size reduction. Research does not support the idea that simply increasing the number of charter schools will improve academic achievement. Charter schools perform about the same as public schools on a national average (C. Lubienski and S. Lubienski 2014). After some criticism from the field on this issue, the department began explaining that it meant to say it wanted more well-monitored, excellent charter schools, but the states got the first message loud and clear.

Similarly, the department created a list of strategies for rescuing failing schools. To get a federal grant for this work, applicants would have to choose one of the four strategies. Some people in the field thought that having to choose from a list of

---

[26] "Delaware and Tennessee Win First Race to the Top Grants," U.S. Department of Education, press release, March 29, 2010, www2.ed.gov/news/pressreleases/2010/03/03292010.html

strategies issued by the federal government foreclosed input from those who knew the particular circumstances, assets, and local constituencies of a given school or district. Jack Jennings studied hundreds of districts that had experience with turnarounds, some with federal grants, some not. He found very mixed results. Three of the federal strategies got low grades; one of them got much higher grades. It seemed to Jennings that the Department of Education was basing its confidence "on a hunch rather than on evidence."[27]

By the beginning of the second Obama term, most of the funds from ARRA were expended. Congress, meanwhile, was gridlocked by partisan conflict, so the No Child Left Behind legislation had not been reauthorized and, at the time of this writing, there seems little prospect of it happening before the end of the second Obama term. In response to this gridlock, the department simply relaxed some of the procedures of NCLB regarding failed deadlines for a district's AYP. This practice was formalized into a state-by-state granting of waivers, giving Duncan a new means of leverage. Each state receiving a waiver had to agree to a long list of the Department of Education's procedures that would substitute for the NCLB approaches. Forty-three states plus the District of Columbia had received waivers by November 2014.[28]

The "era" of standards-based education at the federal level has spanned the administrations of three Presidents: Bill Clinton, George W. Bush, and Barack Obama. Their approaches to school reform shared two features: first, all three put a very strong emphasis on schools with concentrations of economically and educationally disadvantaged children, abiding by the durable Elementary and Secondary Education Act. The central indicator of their success in these efforts was a slight but durable narrowing of gaps in student assessment results. This also took account of rising average scores by group, as well as retention and graduation rates. Second, all three placed the federal government in a strong relationship with the states and schools.

In all three cases, the strategy changes were influenced by reactions to the previous administration. Following Reagan's retreat from a strong federal role in education, Clinton asserted leadership in promoting standards-based reform. In the Bush administration there was widespread opinion that Goals 2000 had not worked well in the 1990s because so many of the states were not complying with Congressional decisions. Thus, it was time to get tough. In the Obama case, it was the opinion, again widely shared, that the Bush version of standards-based reform was too negative in its incentives. A swing toward positive incentives and showcasing success

---

[27] On Jennings' work, see Katherine Gewertz, "Restructuring Schools under NCLB Found to Lag." *Education Week* December 9, 2009; the quotation is from "New Study Questions Turnaround Strategies," *EdNews Blog*, http://blog.ednewscolorado.org/2009/12/09/new-study-questions-turnaround-strategies. For the department's account of the grant program as of 2015, including a map indicating how the four strategies were distributed around the country, see "Turnaround Schools," *Education Week,* June 10, 2015.

[28] Allie Bidwell, "Education Department Drops New NCLB Waiver Guidance: The Waiver Extension Could Lock in Key Obama Administration Education Policies Past 2016," *U.S. News and World Report,* November 13, 2014.

became the rhetoric; in reality, the resources that came with successful competition required states or districts to comply with many specific ideas generated by the Secretary and his top staff.

The Importance of Title I

Background

Title I has a historical importance as the program that led the way in federal efforts to improve educational opportunity. It has generated an ocean of research papers and policy arguments about whether to continue, improve, or abolish the program. Within the research and policy fields there is little consensus on how to interpret test scores such as NAEP in relation to Title I, and little consensus about what would constitute success (eliminating test score gaps across groups, reducing them, or keeping them from getting worse). The program is widely criticized despite increasing scores and slightly declining gaps between race-ethnic groups and decades of solid bipartisan support for the general idea of Title I.

Part of the dominance of Title I in such discussions has to do with the attraction to test scores and Title I's linkage to NAEP. Journalists follow suit, highlighting these test scores, although whether the emphasis on scores is appropriate is an open question. In contrast, consider the field of special education. Although special education's budget exceeds Title I in most districts, and federal support for it now rivals Title I, it does not have a simple annual set of achievement scores to report and receives less notice.

Some critics say that Title I has failed to close the achievement gaps. They also say there is no proof Title I is responsible for the modest narrowing of gaps in the test scores by race-ethnicity because NAEP does not actually identify Title I kids. Therefore, some say, Title I should be discontinued. Thus, Title I is an important topic; it would be an enormous decision to discontinue this durable but plagued symbol of the nation's commitment to improving the education of the children of poverty.

NAEP's Relation to Title I

To satisfy Title I regulations, states had to report academic assessment scores for their districts. As a concession to a long tradition of opposition to national tests, they could devise their own tests, but that meant the scores were not comparable across states. Since 1971, however, NAEP has been taking a representative sample of students across the country and assessing them all on the same material. Those scores were available only for national averages for the first two decades after

NAEP's introduction, due to the same apprehension about a national test and undermining state prerogatives. By the 1990s, however, the states' opposition subsided and state-by-state assessments were developed on a trial basis in 1990. They became routine as of 1996.

NAEP prominently reports two kinds of data on achievement because they map onto the dual goals of Title I and standards-based reform: first, increases in the average scores for all students, and second, the gaps between the scores for students in the different race, ethnic, or income groups. The former is most closely related to the "quality" goal of education reform. (How good is my state doing as a whole compared to other countries or states, and how do my state's scores compare to our own scores for previous years?) The gaps between groups are most closely associated with the "equality" goal. (As the scores rise or fall for various subgroups, are the gaps decreasing or increasing between those groups?)

NAEP has kept comparable national figures since 1971 in reading and since 1973 in mathematics. Some changes were made in content and demands of the assessments during the 1970s and 1980s, but the Department of Education considers the trend lines reliable through to the present (this data series is now called Long-Term NAEP). However, as the changes in the test became more frequent and more fundamental, the NAEP board decided in 1990 to establish a second, more flexible series (Main NAEP) that would keep up with the changes and thus reflect the new work as well. Presently the Department of Education emphasizes the Main NAEP data for the ongoing release of scores and for interpretation of trends since 1990. The department states that the scores on these two series are not comparable to each other, but that *within* each series, the changes made in the test have not caused a break in the trend lines of the scores (U.S. Department of Education, National Center for Education Statistics. 2015b; Beaton and Chromy 2010).

Long-Term NAEP: Trends and Interpretations

For the period before 1990 we have only the Long-Term NAEP, and much analysis has been performed on these data. Nancy Kober, writing in 2001, presented achievement results from the Long-Term NAEP up to 1999. Kober noted that as the NAEP scores for White students in math and reading improved, so did Black scores. But the average scores for Blacks were rising more steeply. Graphs of Black and White scores in mathematics displayed a secular trend, steadily and gradually upward in scores, plus some gradual reduction in gaps by 1999. The reading scores were more bimodal, starting with a large gap of 39 points in 1971, falling to a low gap of 18 points in 1988, and then increasing to a 1999 gap of 29—still 10 points lower than in 1971.

Kober attributed the gaps remaining in 1999 partly to school factors for disadvantaged kids, such as less qualified or less experienced teachers; lower expectations; concentration of low-income students in some schools; school climate less conducive to learning; and disparities in access to preschool. Also, there are community or home factors: the effects of poverty on learning, a legacy of discrimination, and limited learning supports in homes and communities (Kober 2001; Ferguson and Mehta 2004).

Going beyond NAEP, Geoffrey Borman and Jerome D'Agostino performed a meta-analysis of 17 major assessments from 1966 to 1999. They wanted to test the notion that there had basically been no change over time in the effectiveness of Title I in raising achievement scores, which they say is the conventional wisdom. Their findings support the opposite view. The historical record also supports their view. The earliest years of Title I in the late 1960s and into the 1970s were characterized by weak enforcement, widespread abuse of rules by districts, and lack of consensus at all levels about how to improve the education of poor children in underperforming schools. By the 1980s oversight had improved, rules had tightened, and many more districts had accepted the challenge that had been tossed to them 20 years earlier.

Borman and D'Agostino found that Title I students were achieving greater gains in later decades than their similar peers not in Title I programs. To the argument that it still left substantial gaps between them and their non-Title I peers, Borman and D'Agostino argued that the Title I students "would have fallen farther behind" without Title I. To eliminate such gaps altogether would require the elimination of educational disadvantages beyond the school: poor nutrition, health, housing, and low parents' education, all in a negative, symbiotic relationship with poverty (Borman and D'Agostino 1996).

Ronald F. Ferguson reviewed the research on the effectiveness of the following reforms: reducing ability grouping and tracking; eliminating racially biased placements; providing more Black teachers for Black students; decreasing class sizes; and increasing the academic skills of teachers who predominantly taught students of color. For most of these he sees some merit. He summarizes in a clear and sensible conclusion: "Whether the Black-White test score gap would narrow if schools and teachers become more effective is uncertain. I believe it would. However, if the gap were to remain because all children improved, that too would be acceptable." (Ferguson 1998; see also Hedges and Nowell 1998).

The 1980s and 1990s: Studying Actual Title I Students

Despite some upward trend in NAEP scores in the 1980s and 1990s, Title I received much criticism. One interesting study with some positive findings was the "Sustaining Effects Study" headed up by Launor Carter in the early 1980s, relying on three years of data from the mid-1970s. Unlike NAEP data, their data distinguished between students in compensatory education programs (mostly Title I) and those who were not. Their sample included 120,000 students in 300 elementary schools. It could take achievement scores with participation in compensatory education and match them with the poverty status of families and race-ethnicity of the students taking the test. They compared Title I students with students who were described at the beginning as "needing" Title I but not assigned. They found the Title I students' scores higher. Very few datasets had as many variables as the Carter "Sustaining Effects" data, so it is not known in most studies of achievement gaps who had been in Title I; all that is known is students' NAEP scores and their race-ethnicity, sex, and an indicator of family income (free lunch, partial free lunch, no free lunch) (Carter 1984).

By the 1990s there was much debate and publicity about achievement gaps, almost all of it around race-ethnicity. These debates were spurred by episodes of academic racism regarding race and IQ. As a result, the focus in Title I studies switched from family income to students' race-ethnicity.

In 1999, Maris Vinovskis reviewed the history of Title I. Vinovskis is a demographic historian and frequent consultant on both sides of the aisle, focusing on federal program effectiveness. With regard to Title I, Vinovskis judged that "efforts to radically change its approach or focus were ignored or defeated in the early 1980s." A Congressionally managed study called "Prospects" followed three cohorts over six years and concluded that Title I "did not appear to help at-risk students in high-poverty schools to close their academic achievement gaps with students in low-poverty schools." Like the Carter study, the Congressional "Prospects" data included whether students were in Title I or not. The authors reported that (in Vinovskis' words) Title I was "insufficient to close the gap in academic achievement between advantaged and disadvantaged students" (Vinovskis 1999a). I lack the expertise and the space here to evaluate the "Prospects" work. I note, however, that "eliminating" the achievement gap is a high hurdle. If disadvantaged students were not totally closing the gap between their scores and those of advantaged students, they might nonetheless have been keeping it from widening, and Title I might have been a factor. But gaps according to income, though they were not as emphasized, were flat or widening in recent decades, while those between race-ethnic groups were decreasing. (Reardon 2011; also see Jencks and Phillips 1998, Chap. 9).

NAEP Score Gaps after 2000

Analyses of Title I's achievement data after 2000 display similar score trends and the same diversity of judgments as those from the 1970s to the 1990s. Considering the large scope of this essay and the ocean of research literature about the effects of Title I, I shall present the Main NAEP scores for the period from 2000 to 2013 for the gaps by race-ethnicity that have been emphasized most in public discussions (Porter 2005; Clarke 2007; Dee and Jacob 2011; Carnoy and Loeb 2002).

Tables 3.3 and 3.4 display the Main NAEP scores by race-ethnic group in reading and mathematics, for the period from 1992 to 2013, for grades 4, 8, and 12. For example, fourth-grade reading scores for White students begin in 1992 with an average of 224, rising gradually but steadily to an average of 232 in 2013. Average scores of Black students on the same assessments go up and down during the 1990s, and then climb steadily to 206, thus reducing the White/Black achievement gap from 32 to 26. The movements are modest and some changes are not statistically significant, but the trends continue across grade levels, as well as across reading and

Table 3.3 Main NAEP reading scores, 1992–2013: White/Black and White/Hispanic gaps

	1992	1994	1998	2000	2002	2005	2007	2009	2011	2013
Grade 4										
White	224	224	225	225	229	229	231	230	231	232
Black	192	185	193	191	199	200	203	205	205	206
W/B gap	32	39	32	34	30	29	28	25	26	26
Hispanic	197	188	193	197	201	203	205	205	206	207
W/H gap	27	36	32	28	28	26	26	25	25	25
Grade 8										
White	267	267	270	–	272	271	272	273	274	276
Black	237	236	244	–	245	243	245	246	249	250
W/B gap	30	31	26	–	27	28	27	27	25	26
Hispanic	241	243	243	–	247	246	247	249	252	256
W/H gap	26	24	27	–	25	25	25	24	22	20
Grade 12										
White	297	293	297	–	292	293	–	296	–	297
Black	273	265	269	–	267	267	–	269	–	268
W/B gap	24	28	28	–	25	26	–	27	–	29
Hispanic	279	270	275	–	273	272	–	274	–	276
W/H gap	28	23	22	–	19	21	–	22	–	21

Table 3.4 Main NAEP mathematics scores, 1992–2013: White/Black and White/Hispanic gaps

	1990	1992	1996	2000	2003	2005	2007	2009	2011	2013
Grade 4										
White	220	227	231	235	243	246	248	248	249	250
Black	188	193	199	204	216	220	222	222	224	224
W/B gap	32	34	32	31	27	26	26	26	25	26
Hispanic	200	202	205	209	222	226	227	227	229	231
W/H gap	20	27	26	26	21	20	21	21	20	19
Grade 8										
White	270	277	281	285	288	289	291	293	293	294
Black	237	237	242	246	252	255	260	261	262	263
W/B gap	33	40	39	41	36	34	31	32	31	31
Hispanic	246	249	251	253	259	262	265	266	270	272
W/H gap	24	28	30	32	29	27	26	27	22	22
Grade 12										
White	n/a	n/a	n/a	n/a	n/a	157	n/a	161	n/a	162
Black	n/a	n/a	n/a	n/a	n/a	127	n/a	131	n/a	132
W/B gap	n/a	n/a	n/a	n/a	n/a	30		30		30
Hispanic	n/a	n/a	n/a	n/a	n/a	133	n/a	138	n/a	141
W/H gap	n/a	n/a	n/a	n/a	n/a	24	n/a	21	n/a	21

math and across the White/Black gap, suggesting some progress. The scores and gaps follow parallel patterns for eighth graders, and for Hispanic students in 12th grade. The gaps in eighth-grade reading achievement of Black and Hispanic students, as well as for Hispanic students in Grade 12, are narrowed. In general, the upward movement is mostly observed in the assessments from 2002 to 2013, rather than in the period 1992–2000.[29]

In sum, the Main NAEP scores for 1990–2013 move gradually upward, with the three groups mostly parallel but narrowing the gaps slightly. These numbers support an argument made by various researchers: If the Black and Hispanic scores are keeping pace, and if those scores are affected by Title I programs, we should continue and improve Title I. The seriousness of the gap between Whites and students of color has been a central feature of discussions about equality of educational opportunity since at least the 1990s.

But do the NAEP scores by race-ethnicity tell us about Title I? As we have seen, the Title I money goes to individual schools according to the number of parents under the poverty line as defined in the legislation, but the instruction is administered to children selected by their low scores in math and reading, regardless of their race-ethnicity or their families' income. Studies that actually track students in Title I instruction are few, and the ones mentioned above come to rather different conclusions (see Borman and D'Agostino 1996; and Carter 1984). Nonetheless, both recommend that Title I be continued and improved. As a historian interested in the history of educational opportunity, I hold this view. Many other researchers, some mentioned above, have made research-based suggestions for improving Title I programs (Carnoy and Loeb 2002; Dee and Jacob 2011; Ferguson 1998; Jennings 1998).

Some Generalizations

Before moving into the concluding sections of the report, I feel it is worth drawing some key generalizations about the evolution of the federal role in education and developments that laid the foundations for the reforms in play today.

Three Eras in the History of the Federal Role in Education

In the history of the federal role in education, there are "eras" that seem pretty clear. The first is from 1965 (or, if you wish, the National Defense Education Act in 1958) to 1980, when you have several important and controversial additions to the federal repertoire in the direction of equity. From 1980 through 1988, we have the Reagan

---

[29] For mathematics, the fourth-grade scores for Whites move from an average of 220 (in 2000) to an average of 250 (in 2013). Black average scores keep pace, from 188 to 224, reducing the gap from 32 to 24. Hispanic fourth-graders scored an average of 200 in 1990, up to 231 in 2013, leaving the gap essentially level (from 20 to 19). In eighth grade, all three groups' average scores edged up from year to year, virtually parallel.

presidency, the second "era." There is then a transition period under George H. W. Bush, whose inclination was to form a new partnership between states and the federal level but who instead got partisanship as the Democrats voted down his omnibus school reform bill. Thus, he falls between the second and the third era. That third era began in earnest with the presidency of Bill Clinton in 1993. From that time to the present, we have a unifying policy goal: standards-based education reform, spanning a Democratic President, then George W. Bush, a Republican, and Barack Obama, a Democrat.

Conditions for Change

The expansion of the federal role in education that began in 1965 coincided with the escalation of the civil rights movement, a mostly healthy economy, and a Supreme Court that, after a 10-year sleep, was ready to expand the authority of the *Brown* decision by asserting that the 14th Amendment's Equal Protection Clause required the courts to guarantee equal rights in education. During this time, savvy grassroots movements pressed for women's rights and the rights of children with disabilities, and Latino families demanded to see their cultures in their children's schools. This context helped these equity efforts, but still they weren't easy. Still, as James Patterson (1996) argues, the liberal agenda prevailed partly because a majority of people in the United States believed that the country could afford these reforms and that a rising tide would lift all boats.

Congress as the Arena for Advocacy and Compromise

Congress, especially the House of Representatives, was the arena where different interests and different regions began the process of advocacy and compromise. In the case of Title I, Congress spent most of its discussion time debating how the money was going to be divided, not on how the Title I classes might succeed. The resulting compromises ended with too little money spread over too many districts. These compromises were necessary for passage in Congress but impaired the program once in the field.

Lack of Constitutional Authority as a Hindrance

Beyond Congress, Title I advocates had to reckon with the federal role in education having no explicit authority in the Constitution and very little acceptance until the 1950s. That tradition guaranteed that any time there was a federal assertion of authority, it energized those who believed in local and state control. Localism and centralism, the "alter egos" of our Constitutional government, have never been far from educational policy making.

States and Districts Forced to Focus on New Populations

Lorraine McDonnell uses the three-era framework to make some fresh generalizations about the evolution of the federal role. Her depiction of the first era is relevant here. She urges us to think of it as a period of rather urgent interest in monitoring grants and making more specific rules for states and districts. She emphasizes an important point: The federal government was thereby forcing states and districts to focus on particular clients (English language learners, poor students, students of color, and students with disabilities), which was alien to the culture of schools (McDonnell 2005). The states and districts had sometimes distributed their resources in surreptitious, perhaps unconscious ways with deleterious effects: through assignment to ability groups, through tracking, and through the superior resources of some schools in White neighborhoods. Now they were asked to account for distributions, and they were told that money from some grants had to go, not just to some *activity* (like science education), but to certain *students*. This took time and money for school districts as well as an increase in the intrusiveness of state and federal officials; reformers, however, believed that these drawbacks would be outweighed by the fairness and effectiveness of the new categories and programs.

The Numbers Game

This was a time of fast development in budgets, accounting, and in the social sciences in order to judge programs by their output, not their input. Data became king. James Coleman's famous study of the relationship between academic test scores and race, class, school facilities, and other variables became a model for using achievement as a measure of program performance. The Pentagon's new Planning Programing and Budgeting system (PPBS) spread through the cabinet departments and out into other government levels under the influence of Secretary of Defense Robert McNamara. PPBS faded, but it had picked up on the changing standards of accountability. Frank Keppel, new Commissioner of Education for President Kennedy, was appalled that the Office of Education had almost no data on student learning, and he began to develop NAEP behind the scenes, doing it privately (because of the animus against a possible national test) with funds from John Gardner, then-chairman of the Carnegie Corporation in New York. Thus began the era of accountability that focused on actual performance of children in educational programs. It took years before federal and state officials could get legitimate, sufficient, standardized test data from thousands and thousands of school districts, many of them resistant, but in the late 1960s and the 1970s, the seeds were sown (see Dwyer 2005).

The Reality of Delays

Delays in working out regulations and guidelines, pauses for changes in administrations, and other processes can add several years to the gap between the President's signing a bill and the agency in charge sending out notices of a law's activation date. These are the building blocks it takes to initiate a new major policy area from the federal level, as we have seen in our glimpse of the implementation of bilingual education, Title IX, and special education.

Impressive Action Despite the Odds

Given these pitfalls, it is impressive how many equity issues the federal government embraced and how much legislation it produced that affected schools. During the fertile time from the passage of ESEA in 1965 to the end of the 1970s, bilingual education, equal access and treatment for women students, equal access and treatment of children with disabilities, improvements in Native Americans' schools, and other programs took hold.

The Federal Government's Agenda-Setting Role

It is difficult to prove the benefits of these federal education programs, but at the very least, the federal government put them on the agenda with some regulations, expectations, and assistance. In none of these cases is it easy to document educational outcomes. But these items were, with some exceptions, not even on the radar at state and local levels before federal action. In cases where some of the states were ahead, as in special education, bilingual and other areas, federal advocates were able to benefit from this groundwork and use their national scope to generalize the concerns to other states. It's impressive to see that many new equity programs for new target populations developed in such a short time and in such a complicated system as federalism.

The Half-Truth About the Federal Role

The narrative of a relentless, engulfing federal control of education is a half-truth. The trouble with a half-truth is that half of it is true. The half that's true here is that there is a much greater presence of federal programs and rules in America's schools today than there was in 1950.[30] Nonetheless, in 1965 the percent of local budgets provided by the federal government was 7.9 %, while in 2008, it was 8.0 %. From 1965 until 2009, it never went lower than 6.1 % or higher than 8.3 %.

Federal Action Can't Do It Alone

As Jack Jennings reminds us, policy collaboration in a federalist system is not a zero-sum game. An increase in federal activity on school reform may occur at a time of increasing state reform activity. Even the local level may find itself creating more policy rather than less at the time that the role of the federal government and the states increase. Systemic reform, or Common Core, are complicated endeavors and require increased policy activity at all levels.[31]

Not a Straight Evolution

Obviously, given the example of the Reagan reduction of a federal role in education, the evolution is not just linear upward. People may argue about how abrupt and how deep Reagan's attempted reversal was. In this chapter I've emphasized the serious reduction in the budget, the small but symbolically important block grant in ECIA, and the reduction in civil rights enforcement. But Congress, including some Republicans, prevented some of the most severe cuts, saved Title I and other programs from being included in the block grant, and prevented President Reagan from abolishing the new Department of Education.

From Laissez-Faire to Monitoring

Quite apart from the drift toward student achievement scores, the Office of Education had to change its mentality beginning in the 1960s. Far from being avaricious bureaucrats anxious to control state education agencies and their school districts, the Office of Education had, for a century, been a sleepy agency with a strong inclination not to tell anyone what to do. It continually assured people in the field that it had no regulatory ambitions. This caused quite a staff crisis when the new breed came in. Keppel found a staff that was disinclined and untrained to monitor compliance. This applied very much to the desegregation effort, but there was also a

---

[30]This cute but important point is found in my lecture notes from Professor Eric McKitrick's course in mid-nineteenth century America, Columbia University, fall 1966.

[31] In my experience, this important declaration belongs to Jack Jennings, in one private chat, and at a couple of meetings. If it comes initially from Montesquieu, please forgive me.

general disinclination to keep track of education program grants. Quick pressure to get new people and train old veterans shook up the Washington staff. After 1965, the Office of Education gradually became a policy and compliance agency. The vexing question was how much to trust local districts given a history of segregating schools, falsifying conditions, and misappropriating Title I funds. Finding the right balance between trust and compliance remains an ongoing issue, and it requires bureaucratic genius and diplomatic skills to do so.

The Conundrum of the Federal Role in Common Core

The third era, discussed at some length above, ended in an interesting conundrum. The three presidents of the third era, along with their Secretaries of Education and the U.S. Congress, created a federal policy of standards-based education, although the standards themselves were to be forged by each state. Then, after Clinton's forays into possible national standards and national tests were defeated, a group of former governors, educators, and businesspeople began talking about the possibility of a cooperative effort to develop such national standards and tests. This led eventually to the formation of a proposal sponsored by the governors and the chief state school officers to promote a compact called "Common Core." It is quite startling how the states acquiesced in the functions of the big, new collaboration of the National Governors' Association and the Council of Chief State School Officers, which is providing national standards and, through two national contractors, assessments to match. This will have a strong impact on the development of curriculum; indeed, vendors in the private sector have gone into action to offer curriculum materials that will be aligned to the national standards and assessments. The development of standards had until this time been in the hands of the states. In most of the states, reformers persuaded a majority of the public and the school leaders to consent to this new national system. The conundrum is twofold: How did this happen, and where does it leave the role of the federal government? We turn, then, to a brief presentation about the Common Core to understand the complex juncture at which we have arrived.

A National Arena of Education Policy: Common Core

There is an arena of policy formation and dissemination that is properly called "national," in which reforms move across state lines from district to district by informal, nonlegislative means but with some considerable influence. In the early twentieth century, this meant the consolidation of rural districts and the development of a multitrack high school curriculum. In the mid-twentieth century, it involved the articulation of the "comprehensive" American high school, which drew upon ideas from the early twentieth century. In the 1980s, it involved other reform ideas like increased standards and more discipline. Sometimes this "national" dialogue informed state policy makers just as much as federal legislation, depending upon the issue.

Common Core, a recent movement, is a very large and ambitious hybrid of "national" and "federal." The National Governors' Association and the Council of Chief State School Officers proposed nationwide content standards to be shared across states. Common Core advocates argue that it is not a federal but a "national" project. On the other hand, the Department of Education has put its considerable power and resources behind the Common Core. In the first Obama administration, candidates for the Race to the Top were required to join a consortium for multistate assessments, a key ingredient of Common Core. The department funded these two big assessment consortia. More recently the department withdrew NCLB waivers from two states that withdrew from participation in the Common Core. Thus, it seems accurate to say that this is a national project, initiated by the governors and the chiefs but strongly supported by the Department of Education (see Rothman 2011).

Even though the Common Core is mostly the work of the governors and chief state school officers and their staffs, it is nonetheless a strong assertion of authority exercised by a national group over traditional state authority in the area of school curriculum planning and testing. Advocates emphasize that content standards are not the same as curriculum (indeed they are not) and that Common Core provides content standards, not curricula (also true). But planning a school program (including the curriculum) is much influenced by the standards; furthermore, having also agreed to assessments from multistate consortia, the states will experience another strong interstate effect on their curriculum.

Many advocates think that this is an arrangement worth making, usually justified on quality and capacity grounds, which are unevenly distributed across states. Common Core advocates argue that academic performance will be upgraded by adopting these high standards and common assessments. Still, most of what people feared about "national tests" in earlier debates applies here: The consortia have already made compromises about tests of higher-level abilities because assessing these abilities requires more complicated technology and more test time, something that some states want and others do not. We shall see how it plays out.

Equality and Quality With the Common Core

Common Core emphasizes improvement in the quality of the standards. It includes much more analysis and other higher-order skills. This is laudable and exciting but also raises anxieties. Teachers in many states feel the implementation schedule is far too rapid and that they have not had sufficient professional development to teach to the standards well, especially because for many teachers the test scores will count in their performance evaluations. The other source of opposition to the Common

Core is from local-control conservatives who are beginning to make Common Core a major issue in some states.

The possible effects of the Common Core on equity and disparate impact is not receiving as much attention as these other concerns, but it is crucial to the subject of this chapter: How functional for equal opportunity is the coming realignment of authority under the Common Core? Will children from low-income families and children of color be negatively impacted by the new, high demands of the Common Core? Will their teachers be as ready to teach to the Common Core standards as the teachers of more affluent children? Will our underperforming schools be able to teach effectively to these more demanding standards, with less experienced faculty and many children under the stresses of poverty and racial bias? In any case, the kaleidoscope of federalist governance seems to be turning to a new pattern. It will be fascinating to see what kind of a picture we get in five or six years, when the pieces come into clearer focus at the federal, state, and local levels. In particular, we will be interested in how the new alignment of initiative and authority will serve efforts to broaden educational opportunity and reduce gaps in academic achievement.

Federal Funding: A Final Overview

Before engaging in some policy suggestions, it is worth doing a broad review of the federal funding picture of education to provide an overview of the federal portion's size relative to state and local contributions. What appears to be a substantial expansion of the federal role in education occurred during the 50 years following 1965. This period was marked by a generally expansive economy, bipartisan cooperation, the civil rights movement, the augmented role of the United States in a turbulent world, the growing importance of education in the economy, the skills of education reformers in the Congress and the executive agencies, and the strong roles of advocacy groups on education, both traditional and new. But how big an expansion was it?

Table 3.5 displays the changing share of school districts' expenses paid by local, state, and federal government. From these data we can see a prevailing increase in the federal share during this period of strong increase overall in the context of the long-term trends from 1920 to 2012. The downturn in the 1980s was due to policy preferences of the Reagan administration, though resisted with some success by supporters of education in the Congress. The peak, from 2010 to 2012, was due to emergency funds to the Department of Education from Congress in the wake of the 2008 economic crisis. We can assume that those percentages will decrease when the official statistics are posted for 2013 and following.

In the big expansion in the 1960s and 1970s, the federal share of local dollar expenditures grew from 4.4 to 9.8 %, about double. But is that a lot of money? It's worth pointing out that federal dollars are the kind that local administrators want because they are almost all devoted to new kinds of learning, new clients, and

Table 3.5 Federal, state, and local share: public elementary and secondary school budgets

Year	Federal	State	Local
1920	0.3	16.5	83.2
1930	0.4	16.9	82.7
1940	1.8	30.3	68.0
1945	1.4	34.7	63.9
1950	2.9	39.8	57.3
1955	4.6	39.5	55.9
1960	4.4	39.1	56.5
1965	7.9	39.1	53.0
1970	8.0	39.9	52.1
1975	9.0	42.0	49.0
1980	9.8	46.8	43.4
1985	6.6	48.9	44.4
1990	6.1	47.3	46.8
1995	6.8	46.8	46.4
2000	7.3	49.7	43.0
2005	8.3	n.a.	n.a.
2008	8.0	48.0	44.0
2009	9.5	46.7	43.8
2010	13.0	43.0	44.0
2012	12.3	n.a.	n.a.

improvement of instruction; in contrast, much of the remaining approximately 90 % is largely needed for inflexible costs such as building and maintenance, salaries, student transportation, supplies, and similar necessities. So federal money has two rather large impacts: It provides program money and it allows the federal government to influence the agenda of the schools and require some accountability.

Although it is well to remember that the lion's share of the cost of public education falls to the state and local resources, opposition to the growing federal role is not about money as much as it is against new programs that require changes, rules, and accountability that infringe on local control. Whatever the objective of the federal initiatives—desegregation, better science classes, teacher evaluations, improved education of disadvantaged children, or adopting the Common Core—objections to federal assertions can also be justified on philosophical bases that are deeply ingrained in our history and our political preferences about how democracy best works in a very large country.

Some Policy Suggestions

This chapter has taken a broad look at the federal role in education, particularly about issues of equity. It has looked in detail at efforts to raise the achievement of poor children and those of color and ethnicity, as well as improving education for

English language learners, women, and children with disabilities. Now, I offer some policy suggestions for ways to move U.S. education forward.

Reassessing the Federal Role

First, we should de-emphasize the role of the federal Department of Education in K-12 standards-based reform from defining and enforcing the details of school reform to a collegial support role. The states and districts will have an unprecedented challenge to implement the Common Core in addition to their other duties. Common Core has created a host of new policy questions that must be made by states and districts, not by the federal government or the Common Core national administration. These include which assessment system to choose; how to phase in these new assessments and standards into already complex systems of curriculum, testing, and accountability; how to produce or purchase curriculum materials that will serve their needs and comport with Common Core standards; how to provide the requisite teacher education and professional development; and how to guarantee that students in the least effective schools will have equal access to what they need to achieve in the Common Core. Given the importance of these decisions, which will manifest themselves differently in the various states, it may be an opportune time to reconsider the relationship between the federal Department of Education and the states' role in providing high-quality education and increasing educational opportunity.

Aside from challenges of the Common Core, there is a renewed sense among many educators that the states are "where the action is" and that on many matters the states can assess their needs, capacities, and priorities better than the federal government. This is not suggested in the spirit of a "kinder, gentler" face of the department or to "reduce" the federal role but to suggest some changes given the giant workload Common Core will generate for the districts and the states. Furthermore, in this past 23 years of standards-based reform, the states have had ample time to develop reform systems and accountability; most have more capacity than they have ever had.

One example of federal-state cooperation is suggested by a recent article about California having some documented success with a state program of more extensive on-site technical assistance in individual districts (Strunk and McEachin 2014). If such successes continue, the Department of Education could disseminate information about California and subsidize state education agencies so they can create such units or use California's insights to strengthen their present technical assistance programs.

The relationship between Common Core and the Department of Education will continue to exist. It is hard to imagine that there will not be issues where adjustments might have to be made in federal regulations or in Common Core procedures. One important area might be the relation of the Common Core's heightened standards to possible disparate effects on economically disadvantaged students, students of color, or other groups. Perhaps it would be appropriate for the department and the Common Core leaderships to collectively look at how the new, more challenging Common Core standards and activities are affecting the lowest achievers. One of the most important contributions the Department of Education has made during the long era of standards-based school reform has been, with the support of their Presidents, to press the states and districts to put special emphasis on helping low-achieving students coming from low-income families or students of color who so often encounter racial prejudice. I am confident that these and other issues are already under discussion as we move into a more collegial relationship between the department and the states. It will be interesting to see what the next reauthorization of ESEA says about the Common Core, and how the existence of the Common Core will impact on the Department of Education's requirements for receipt of grants such as for Title I.

One of the risks of relying more on the states to carry the ball in school reform is that the states' capacities are uneven, and they differ greatly in the achievement of their students and their progress in reform. The department could ameliorate that by incentivizing state action on various important national priorities. The incentives would be to subsidize the costs of introducing new or improved programs in return for reliable agreements to carry them out. The department could choose to start with two or three areas of reform. For example:

Early Childhood Education Individual states have been the leaders in the reform of early childhood education. (Rose 2010). The results have been quite different in these states that have led in attempting to upgrade early childhood opportunities by improving training and salaries, standards, and facilities. The federal government has endorsed this cause.

School Finance Equity Here again, some states are leaders and are well down the road that ran through many courtrooms. The idea of federal subsidies to help other states was raised in the Department of Education's Commission on School Finance a few years ago and would have the same effect as the early education option: stimulating reform and equalizing education across districts and across states (see Chap. 4).

Technical Assistance As mentioned above, another subsidization idea is to support the state education agencies in providing enhanced technical assistance to districts.

Title I Improvements

Congress and the administration should approve the continuation of Title I, at a higher level of authorization. As we have seen, there is much divided opinion about the effectiveness of Title I in reducing achievement gaps between race-ethnic groups and between students from varying family income groups (free lunch, partial free lunch, and not-free lunch). I am an outsider to this literature, but it seems that the lack of connection between Title I assignment and a student's race or family income level renders most research results inconclusive in judging Title I's effects. The federal government should make a major effort to support research that follows actual Title I students, tracking them through Title I instruction, and probing why children of color are now making better progress on improving scores and narrowing gaps, while children from families with low income are not.

Income inequality, increasing since 1980, has devastating effects on most people in the lowest one-fifth of the population and even above that. With people facing difficulties related to low wages, unemployment, housing, and health care, this would be an illogical time to decrease our support for our main educational program aimed at children from poor families.

Additional Legislation

Major legislation regarding other programs that have attempted to lessen educational disadvantages and bias should be enacted. I do not know as much about current policy controversies in these fields as I do about Title I. I should simply like to say that, as a historian, I believe that the programs included in this essay have achieved historically important breakthroughs yet still need further extension and reform. Because their principal object is to ensure specific group rights and they have been underfunded in the past, I believe that programs regarding these issues— education of children with disabilities; bilingual education and other recognition of the needs of English language learners; women's rights in education and their enforcement, and the improvement of Native American educational resources and governance—should be amply funded to the fullest extent allowed by the resources of the Congress and the nation.

Conclusion

The goal of this chapter was to assess the major efforts by the federal government (with an eye on major advances by the states) to widen educational opportunity. Efforts through the decades have been filled with frustrations, controversies, and imperfections. But in the end, I see progress. Despite their failings, I have come out of the process, on balance, more hopeful about the positive effects these initiatives might still provide.

References

Aron, Lauden, and Pamela Loprest. 2012. Disability and the education system. *The Future of Children* 22(1): 110.

Baker, Bruce D., David G. Sciarra, and Danielle Farrie. 2014. *Is school funding fair? A national report card.* Newark: Education Law Center. http://www.schoolfundingfairness.org

Barley, Numan V. 1997. *The rise of massive resistance: Race and politics in the South during the 1950s*, 2nd ed. Baton Rouge: Louisiana State University Press.

Baugh, Joyce A. 2011. *The Detroit school busing case: Milliken v. Bradley and the controversy over desegregation.* Lawrence: University Press of Kansas.

Beaton, Albert E., and James R. Chromy. 2010. *NAEP trends: Main NAEP vs. long-term trend.* Paper for the NAEP Validity Studies Panel, American Institutes for Research, for National Center for Education Statistics. http://www.air.org/resource/naep-trends-main-naep-vs-long-term-trend

Bell, Theodore, to David Grinstead (White House staff). 1975. Folder 5, Box 801, Office Files of the Commissioner of Education, National Archives and Records Administration, College Park, November 21.

Bestor, Arthur. 1953. *Educational wastelands: The retreat from learning in our schools.* Urbana: University of Illinois Press.

Borman, Geoffrey D., and Jerome D'Agostino. 1996. Title I and student achievement: A meta-analysis of federal evaluation results. *Educational Evaluation and Policy Analysis* 18(4): 309–326.

Bound, John, and Sarah Turner. 2002. Going to war and going to college: Did World War II and the GI Bill increase educational attainment of returning veterans?". *Journal of Labor Economics* 20(4): 784–815.

Carnoy, Martin, and Susanna Loeb. 2002. Does external accountability affect student outcomes? A cross-state analysis. *Educational Evaluation and Policy Analysis* 24 (4: 305f). http://epa.sage-pub.com/content/24/4/305

Carter, Launor F. 1984. The sustaining effects study of compensatory and elementary education. *Educational Researcher* 13(7): 4–13.

Cascio, Elizabeth U., Nora Gordon, and Sarah Reber. 2013. Local responses to federal grants: Evidence from the introduction of Title I in the South. *American Economic Journal: Economic Policy* 5(3): 121–159.

Clarke, Marguerite. 2007. *State responses to the No Child Left Behind Act: The uncertain link between implementation and 'Proficiency for All.'* In Kaestle and Lodewick 2007, 144–76.

Clotfelter, Charles T. 2004. *After Brown: The rise and retreat of school desegregation.* Princeton: Princeton University Press.

Cohen, David K., and Susan L. Moffitt. 2009. *The ordeal of equality: Did federal regulation fix the schools?* Cambridge, MA: Harvard University Press.

Conant, James B. 1959. *The American high school today.* New York: McGraw-Hill.

Costain, Anne. 1979. Eliminating sex discrimination in education: Lobbying for implementation of Title IX. In *Race, sex, and policy problems*, ed. Marian Lief Palley and Michael B. Preston. Lexington: Lexington Books.

Cross, Christopher T. 2014. *Political education: Setting the course for state and federal policy*, 2nd ed. New York: Teachers College Press.

Cubberley, Ellwood P. 1909. *Changing conceptions of education.* Boston: Houghton Mifflin.

Davies, Gareth. 2007. *See government grow: Education politics from Johnson to Reagan.* Lawrence: University Press of Kansas.

DeBray, Elizabeth H. 2006. *Politics, ideology, & education: Federal policy during the Clinton and Bush administrations.* New York: Teachers College Press.

Dee, Thomas S., and Brian Jacob. 2011. The impact of no child left behind on student achievement. *Journal of Policy Analysis and Management* 30(3): 418–446.

Dougherty, Jack. 2004. *More than one struggle: The evolution of Black school reform in Milwaukee.* Chapel Hill: University of North Carolina Press.

Douglas, Davison M. 1995. *Reading, writing, and race: The desegregation of the Charlotte schools*. Chapel Hill: University of North Carolina Press.

Dwyer, Carol Anne (ed.). 2005. *Measurement and research in the accountability era*. Mahwah: Lawrence Erlbaum Associates.

Eidenberg, Eugene, and Roy D. Morey. 1969. *An act of Congress: The legislative process and the making of education policy*. New York: Norton.

Executive Office of the President of the United States. 2009. *Educational impact of the American Recovery and Reinvestment Act*. A report issued by the Domestic Policy Council, October. www.whitehouse.gov/assets/FDPC_Education/Report.pdf

Federal Education Policy and the States, 1945–2009. 2009. *States' impact on federal education policy project*. http://nysa32.nysed.gov/edpolicy/research/es_essay_reagan_achvmnt-gap.shtml

Ferguson, Ronald F. 1998. *Can schools narrow the Black-White test score gap?* In Jencks and Phillips 1998, 318–74.

Ferguson, Ronald F., and Jal Mehta. 2004. An unfinished journey: The legacy of *Brown* and the narrowing of the achievement gap. *Phi Delta Kappan* 85(9): 656–669.

Fishel, Andrew, and Janice Pottker. 1977. *National politics and sex discrimination in education*. Lexington: Lexington Books.

Frum, David. 2000. *How we got here: The 70's*. New York: Basic Books.

Gamson, David. 2007. *From progressivism to federalism: The pursuit of equal educational opportunity, 1915–1965."* In Kaestle and Lodewick 2007.

Goertz, Margaret E. 2005. Implementing the No Child Left Behind act: Challenges for the states. *Peabody Journal of Education* 80(2): 73–89.

Goldin, Claudia, and Lawrence F. Katz. 2008. *The race between education and technology*. Cambridge, MA: Harvard University Press.

Gordon, Nora. 2004. Do federal grants boost school spending? Evidence from Title I. *Journal of Public Economics* 88: 1771–1792.

Graham, Hugh Davis. 1990. *The civil rights era: Origins and development of national policy*. New York: Oxford University Press.

Hale, Lorraine. 2002. *Native American education: A reference handbook*. Santa Barbara: ABC CLIO.

Hawkins, Augustus Freeman (Gus), (1907–2007). n.d. *Biographical directory of the United States Congress*. http://bioguide.congress.gov/scripts/biodisplay.pl?index=h000367

Hedges, Larry V., and Amy Nowell. 1998. *Black-White test score convergence since 1965*. In Jencks and Phillips 1998, 149–181.

Jeffrey, Julie Roy. 1978. *Education for children of the poor: A study of the origins and implementation of the Elementary and Secondary Education Act of 1965*. Columbus: Ohio State University Press.

Jencks, Christopher, and Meredith Phillips (eds.). 1998. *The Black-White test score gap*. Washington, DC: Brookings Institute Press.

Jennings, John F. 1998. *Why national standards and tests: Politics and the quest for better schools*. Thousand Oaks: Sage.

Jennings, Jack. 2015. *Presidents, Congress, and the public schools: The politics of education reform*. Cambridge, MA: Harvard Education Press.

Kaestle, Carl F. 2012 *Testing policy in the United States: A historical perspective*. Paper prepared for the Gordon Commission on the Future of Educational Assessment. http://www.gordoncommission.org/publications_reports/assessment_education.html

Kaestle, Carl F. 1983. *Pillars of the Republic: Common Schools and American Society, 1780–1860*. New York: Hill & Wang.

Kaestle, Carl F. 1990. The public schools and the public mood. *American Heritage* 41: 1.

Kaestle, Carl F. 1995. Literate America: High-level adult literacy as a national goal. In *Learning from the past: What history teaches us about school reform*, ed. Diane Ravitch and Maris Vinovskis, 329–354. Baltimore: Johns Hopkins University Press.

Kaestle, Carl F. Forthcoming. *Uncertain mandate: The formative years of the federal role in education.*

Kaestle, Carl F., and Alyssa E. Lodewick (eds.). 2007. *To educate a nation: Federal and national strategies of school reform.* Lawrence: University Press of Kansas.

Kaestle, Carl F., and Larry Stedman. 1987. Literacy and reading performance in the United States, from 1880 to the present. *Reading Research Quarterly* 22(Winter): 8–46.

Kaestle, Carl F., and Maris A. Vinovskis. 1980. *Education and social change in 19th-century Massachusetts.* Cambridge: Cambridge University Press.

Kober, Nancy. 2001. *It takes more than testing: Closing the achievement gap.* Washington, DC: Center on Education Policy.

Krug, Edward. 1964. *The shaping of the American high school.* New York: Harper & Row.

Linn, Robert. 2005. *Scientific evidence and inference in educational policy and practice: Implications for evaluating adequate yearly progress.* In Dwyer 2005, 24.

Lubienski, Christopher A., and Sarah Theule Lubienski. 2014. *The public school advantage: Why public schools outperform private schools.* Chicago: University of Chicago Press.

Manna, Paul. 2007. *School's in: Federalism and the national education agenda.* Washington, DC: Georgetown University Press.

Martin, Ruby, and Phyllis McClure. 1969. *Title I of ESEA: Is it helping poor children?* Washington, DC: Washington Research Project and the NAACP Legal Defense Fund.

Massey, Douglas S., Jonathan Rothwell, and Thurston Domino. 2009. "The changing base of segregation in the United States." *Annals of the American Academy of Political and Social Science* 626 (74). http://www.ncbi.nlm.nih.gov

McCarthy, Joseph Justin. 1991. *Title IX from 1970 to 1988: A study in educational policy-making* (doctoral dissertation). Cambridge, MA: Harvard Graduate School of Education.

McDonnell, Lorraine M. 2005. No Child Left Behind and the federal role in education: Evolution or revolution? *Peabody Journal of Education* 80(2): 19–38.

McGuinn, Patrick J. 2006. *No Child Left Behind and the transformation of federal education policy, 1965–2008.* Lawrence: University Press of Kansas.

McLaughlin, Milbrey W. 1975. *Evaluation and reform: The Elementary and Secondary Education Act of 1965.* Cambridge: Ballenger Publishing.

Miech, Edward J. n.d. *The necessary gentleman: Francis Keppel's leadership in getting education's act together* (doctoral dissertation). Cambridge, MA: Harvard University, Graduate School of Education.

Miguel, San, and Jr. Guadalupe. 2004. *Contested policy: The rise and fall of federal bilingual education in the United States.* Denton: University of North Texas Press.

Moreno, José F. (ed.). 1999. *The elusive quest for equality: 150 years of Chicano/Chicana Education.* Cambridge, MA: Harvard Educational Review.

New America Foundation. n.d. *Cost of educating children with disabilities.* http://febp.newamerica.net/background-analysis/individuals-disabilities-education-act-funding-distribution

Orfield, Gary. 1969. *Reconstruction of Southern education: The schools and the 1964 Civil Rights Act.* New York: Wiley-Interscience.

Orfield, Gary, and Susan E. Eaton. 1996. *Dismantling desegregation: The quiet reversal of Brown v. Board of Education.* New York: New Press.

Orfield, Gary, Erica Frankenberg, Jongyeon Ee, and John Kuscera. 2014. *Brown at 60: Great progress, a long retreat and an uncertain future.* Los Angeles: University of California at Los Angeles.

Parrish, Thomas B. 2001. Who's paying the rising cost of special education? *Journal of Special Education Leadership* 14(1): 4–12.

Patterson, James T. 1996. *Grand expectations: The United States, 1945–1974.* New York: Oxford University Press.

Patterson, James T. 2001. *Brown v. Board of Education: A civil rights milestone and its troubled legacy.* New York: Oxford University Press.

Peterson, Paul. 1983. Background paper. In *Making the grade: Report of the 20th century fund task force on federal elementary and secondary education policy.* New York: 20th Century Fund.

Porter, Andrew. 1995. The uses and misuses of opportunity-to-learn standards. *Educational Researcher* 24(1): 21–27.

Porter, Andrew. 2005. *Prospects for school reform and closing the achievement gap*. In Dwyer 2005.

Pottinger, Stanley. 1970. *Memo regarding language minority children*, May 25. http://www2.ed.gov/pint/about/offices/list/ocr/docs/lau1970.html

President's Commission on School Finance. 1972. *Schools, people, & money: The need for educational reform*. Washington, DC: U.S. Government Printing Office.

Ravitch, Diane. 1995. *National standards in American education: A citizen's guide*. Washington, DC: Brookings Institution.

Reardon, Sean F. 2011. The widening achievement gap between the rich and the poor: New evidence and possible explanations. In *Whither opportunity: Rising inequality, schools, and children's life chances*, ed. Greg J. Duncan and Richard J. Murnane, 91–116. New York: Russell Sage Foundation/Spencer Foundation.

Reardon, Sean F., Elena Tej Grewal, Demetra Kalogrides, and Erica Greenberg. 2012. Brown fades: The end of court-ordered school desegregation and the resegregation of American public schools. *Journal of Policy Analysis and Management* 31(4): 533–547.

Reese, William J. 1995. *The origins of the American high school*. New Haven: Yale University Press.

Reese, William J. 2013. *Testing wars in the public schools: A forgotten history*. Cambridge, MA: Harvard University Press.

Rose, Elizabeth. 2010. *The promise of preschool: From Head Start to universal pre-kindergarten*. New York: Oxford University Press.

Rothman, Robert. 2011. *Something in common: The Common Core standards and the next chapter in American education*. Cambridge, MA: Harvard Education Press.

Rothstein, Richard. 2004. *Class and schools: Using social, economic and educational reform to close the Black-White achievement gap*. Washington, DC: Economic Policy Institute.

Rury, John L. 2005. *Education and social change: Themes in the history of American schooling*, vol. 2. Mahwah: Lawrence Erlbaum.

Salomone, Rosemary C. 1986. *Equal education under law: Legal rights and federal policy in the post-Brown era*. New York: St. Martin's Press.

San Miguel Jr., Guadalupe. 1987. *'Let all of them take heed' Mexican Americans and the campaign for educational equality in Texas, 1910—1981*. Austin: University of Texas Press.

Schneider, Susan Gilbert. 1976. *Revolution, reaction or reform: The 1974 Bilingual Education Act*. New York: Las Americas Publishing Company.

Scotch, Richard K. 2001. *From good will to civil rights: Transforming federal disability policy*, 2nd ed. Philadelphia: Temple University Press.

Simon, Kenneth A., and W. V. Grant (eds.). 1970. *Digest of educational statistics*. Washington, DC: Office of Education.

Smith, Marshall S., and Jennifer A. O'Day. 1991. Systemic school reform. In *The politics of curriculum and testing, Politics of education association yearbook 1990*, ed. Fuhrman Susan and Malen Betty, 233–267. London: Falmer Press.

Stewner-Manzanares, Gloria. 1988. The bilingual education act: Twenty years later. In *Occasional Papers in Bilingual Education* 6 (Fall). Washington, DC: Office of Bilingual Education and Minority Languages Affairs. http://eric.ed.gov/?id=ED337031

Strum, Phillipa. 2010. *Mendez v. Westminster: School desegregation and Mexican-American rights*. Lawrence: University Press of Kansas.

Strunk, Katharine O., and Andrew McEachin. 2014. More than sanctions: Closing achievement gaps through California's use of intensive technical assistance. *Education Evaluation and Policy Analysis* 36(3): 281–307.

Sundquist, James L. 1968. *Politics and policy: The Eisenhower, Kennedy and Johnson Years*. Washington, DC: Brookings Institution.

Swanson, Beverly B. 1991. An overview of the six national education goals. *ERIC Digest*. www.ericdigests.org/pre-9220/six.htm

Szasz, Margaret Connell. 1999. *Education and the American Indian: The road to self-determination since 1928*, 3rd ed. Albuquerque: University of New Mexico Press.

Turnbull, Brenda J., and Ellen L. Marks. 1986. *The education block grant and intergovernmental relations: Effect at the local level*. Menlo Park: SRI International.

Turner, Susan, and John Bound. 2003. Closing the gap or widening the divide: The effects of the G. I. Bill and World War II on educational outcomes of Black Americans. *Journal of Economic History* 63(1): 145–177.

U.S. Department of Education, 2009. *The American Recovery and Reinvestment Act of 2009: Saving and creating jobs and reforming education*, March 7. www2.ed.gov/policy/gen/leg/recovery/implementation.htm

U.S. Department of Education, National Center for Education Statistics. 2015a. Fast facts: Students with disabilities. (Source: *Digest of Education Statistics, 2012*). https://nces.ed.gov/fastfacts/display.asp?id=64

U.S. Department of Education, National Center for Education Statistics. 2015b. *What are the differences between long-term trend NAEP and main NAEP?* National Assessment of Educational Progress. Accessed January 27, 2015. http://nces.ed.gov/nationsreportcard/about/ltt_main_diff.aspx

U.S. Department of Health, Education, and Welfare, Office of Civil Rights. 1975. *Task-force findings specifying remedies available for eliminating past educational practices rule unlawful under* Lau v. Nichols. Copy in *Bilingual education: A reappraisal of federal policy*, edited by Keith A. Baker and Adriana A. de Kanter. Lexington: Lexington Books, 1983, Appendix B.

Urban, Wayne. 2010. *More than science and Sputnik: The National Defense Education Act of 1958*. Tuscaloosa: University of Alabama Press.

Verstegen, Deborah A. 1985. Redistributing federal aid to education: Chapter 2 of the Education Consolidation and Improvement Act of 1981. *Journal of Education Finance* 10(4).

Vinovskis, Maris A. 1999a. Do federal compensatory education programs really work? A brief historical analysis of Title I and Head Start. *American Journal of Education* 107(3): 187–209.

Vinovskis, Maris A. 1999b. *History & educational policymaking*. New Haven: Yale University Press.

Vinovskis, Maris A. 2008. Gubernatorial leadership and American K-12 educational reform. In *Legacy of innovation: Governors and American public policy*, ed. Ethan Scribnick, 185–203. Philadelphia: University of Pennsylvania Press.

Vinovskis, Maris A. 2009. *From A Nation at Risk to No Child Left Behind: National education goals and the creation of federal education policy*. New York: Teachers College Press.

Ware, Susan (ed.). 2007. *Title IX: A brief history with documents*. Boston: Bedford-St. Martin's.

Webb, Clive (ed.). 2005. *Massive resistance: Southern opposition to the second reconstruction*. New York: Oxford University Press.

Wilkinson III, J. Harvie. 1979. *From Brown to Bakke: The Supreme Court and school integration, 1954–1978*. Oxford: Oxford University Press.

Chapter 4
The Changing Distribution of Educational Opportunities: 1993–2012

Bruce Baker, Danielle Farrie, and David G. Sciarra

Abstract Over the past several decades, many states have pursued substantive changes to their state school finance systems. Some reforms have been stimulated by judicial pressure resulting from state constitutional challenges and others have been initiated by legislatures. But despite gains in school funding equity and adequacy made over the past few decades, in recent years we have witnessed a substantial retreat from equity and adequacy. This chapter builds on the national school funding fairness report annually published by the Education Law Center. We track school funding fairness (the relative targeting of funding to districts serving economically disadvantaged children) for all states from 1993 to 2012. This chapter explores in greater depth the consequences of school funding levels, distributions, and changes in specific classroom resources provided in schools. We find that states and districts applying more effort—spending a greater share of their fiscal capacity on schools—generally spend more on schools, and that these higher spending levels translate into higher staffing levels and lower class sizes as well as more competitive teacher wages.

Keywords School funding • School finance • Funding equity • Funding fairness • Class size • Teacher compensation • School quality • Pay for performance • School poverty

B. Baker (✉)
Graduate School of Education, Rutgers University, New Brunswick, NJ, USA

D. Farrie • D.G. Sciarra
Education Law Center, Newark, NJ, USA

© Educational Testing Service 2016
I. Kirsch, H. Braun (eds.), *The Dynamics of Opportunity in America*,
DOI 10.1007/978-3-319-25991-8_4

Introduction

Over the past several decades, many states have pursued substantive changes to their state school finance systems. Some reforms have been stimulated by judicial pressure resulting from state constitutional challenges and others have been initiated by legislatures. But despite gains in school funding equity and adequacy made over the past few decades, in recent years we have witnessed a substantial retreat from equity and adequacy, and retrenchment among state legislatures, governors, and federal officials across the political aisle, with many contending that the level and distribution of school funding are not primary factors in quality of education.

This chapter builds on the national school funding fairness report annually published by the Education Law Center, in which we apply regression-based methods to national data on all local public school districts to characterize state school finance systems (Baker et al. 2014). Specifically, we evaluate whether those systems lead to consistent targeting of resources to districts serving higher concentrations of children from economically disadvantaged backgrounds.

In this chapter we expand our analysis in two directions. First, our past three national reports have each been based on the most recent three available years of district level data on state and local revenues. In this chapter, we track school funding fairness (the relative targeting of funding to districts serving economically disadvantaged children) for all states from 1993 to 2012. This time period includes substantive changes to state school finance systems in several states, whether as a function of ongoing litigation or proactive legislative change. Further, this period runs through the recent economic downturn, in which several state school finance systems lost significant ground, both in level of overall funding and in fairness of distribution (Baker 2014). Thus we are able to evaluate the extent of backsliding and the partial rebound that has occurred.

Second, this chapter explores in greater depth the consequences of school funding levels, distributions, and changes in specific classroom resources provided in schools. The majority of school spending is dedicated to staffing, with the primary spending tradeoff being the balance between employee salaries and the numbers of employees assigned. Competitive teacher wages and appropriate class sizes are important to the provision of equitable and adequate educational programs and services. The third edition of *Is School Funding Fair* included additional indicators related to (a) pupil-to-teacher ratios across higher and lower poverty districts and (b) the relative competitiveness of teacher wages statewide when compared with nonteachers at similar education level and age. In that report, we provided preliminary evidence that more equitable funding distributions with respect to poverty concentrations did indeed translate to more equitable distributions of pupil-to-teacher ratios. Further, states with higher funding levels tended to have, on average, more competitive teacher wages relative to other professions.

In this chapter, we explore both of these additional measures during a 20-year time period, and we add measures of class size and variation in teacher wages across schools and districts using data from the National Center for Education Statistics

(NCES) Schools and Staffing Survey. Specifically, we explore whether targeting of funding to higher poverty districts translates to reduction of class sizes and the number of students per teacher in higher poverty settings relative to lower poverty ones. We also explore whether targeting of funding to higher poverty settings leads to more competitive wages in those settings. A substantial body of research points to the need not merely for comparable wages, but substantial added compensation to support recruiting and retaining teachers in high-need settings.

Conceptions of Equity, Equal Opportunity, and Adequacy

Reforms across the nation to state school finance systems have been focused on simultaneously achieving equal educational opportunity and adequacy. While achieving and maintaining educational adequacy requires a school finance system that consistently and equitably meets a certain level of educational outcomes, it is important to maintain equal educational opportunity in those cases where funding falls below adequacy thresholds. That is, whatever the level of outcomes attained across a school system, it should be equally attainable regardless of where a child lives or attends school or his or her background.

Conceptions of school finance equity and adequacy have evolved over the years. Presently, the central assumption is that state finance systems should be designed to provide children, regardless of where they live and attend school, with equal opportunity to achieve some constitutionally adequate level of outcomes (Baker and Green 2009a). Much is embedded in this statement and it is helpful to unpack it, one layer at a time.

The main concerns of advocates, policy makers, academics, and state courts from the 1960s through the 1980s were to (a) reduce the overall variation in per-pupil spending across local public school districts; and (b) disrupt the extent to which that spending variation was related to differences in taxable property wealth across districts. That is, the goal was to achieve more equal dollar inputs—or *nominal spending equity*—coupled with *fiscal neutrality*—or reducing the correlation between local school resources and local property wealth. While modern goals of providing equal opportunity and achieving educational adequacy are more complex and loftier than mere spending equity or fiscal neutrality, achieving the more basic goals remains relevant and still elusive in many states.

An alternative to nominal spending equity is to look at the *real resources* provided across children and school districts: the programs and services, staffing, materials, supplies and equipment, and educational facilities provided (Still, the emphasis is on equal provision of these inputs) (Baker and Green (2009b). Providing real resource equity may, in fact, require that per-pupil spending not be perfectly equal if, for example, resources such as similarly qualified teachers come at a higher price (competitive wage) in one region than in another. *Real resource* parity is more meaningful than mere dollar equity. Further, if one knows how the prices of real resources differ, one can better compare the value of the school dollar from one location to the next.

Modern conceptions of equal educational opportunity and educational adequacy shift emphasis away from schooling inputs and onto schooling outcomes—and more specifically equal opportunity—to achieve some level of educational outcomes. References to broad outcome standards in the school finance context often emanate from the seven standards articulated in Rose v. Council for Better Education,[1] a school funding adequacy case in 1989 in Kentucky that scholars consider the turning point in shifting the focus from equity to adequacy in school finance legal theory (Clune 1994). There are two separable but often integrated goals here—equal opportunity and educational adequacy.

The first goal is achieved when all students are provided the real resources to have equal opportunities to achieve some common level of educational outcomes. Because children come to school with varied backgrounds and needs, striving for common goals requires moving beyond mere equitable provision of *real resources.* For example, children with disabilities and children with limited English language proficiency may require specialized resources (personnel), programs, materials, supplies, and equipment. Schools and districts serving larger shares of these children may require substantively more funding to provide these resources. Further, where poverty is highly concentrated, smaller class sizes and other resource-intensive interventions may be required to strive for those outcomes achieved by the state's average child.

Meanwhile, conceptions of educational adequacy require that policy makers determine the desired level of outcome to be achieved. Essentially, adequacy conceptions attach a "level" of outcome expectation to the equal educational opportunity concept. Broad adequacy goals are often framed by judicial interpretation of state constitutions. It may well be that the outcomes achieved by the average child are deemed sufficient. But it may also be that the preferences of policy makers or a specific legal mandate are somewhat higher (or lower) than the outcomes achieved by the average child. The current buzz phrase is that schools should ensure that children are "college ready"[2]

---

[1] As per the court's declaration: "An efficient system of education must have as its goal to provide each and every child with at least the seven following capacities: (i) sufficient oral and written communication skills to enable students to function in a complex and rapidly changing civilization; (ii) sufficient knowledge of economic, social, and political systems to enable the student to make informed choices; (iii) sufficient understanding of governmental processes to enable the student to understand the issues that affect his or her community, state, and nation; (iv) sufficient self-knowledge and knowledge of his or her mental and physical wellness; (v) sufficient grounding in the arts to enable each student to appreciate his or her cultural and historical heritage; (vi) sufficient training or preparation for advanced training in either academic or vocational fields so as to enable each child to choose and pursue life work intelligently; and (vii) sufficient levels of academic or vocational skills to enable public school students to compete favorably with their counterparts in surrounding states, in academics or in the job market. Rose v. Council for Better Education, Inc., 790 S.W.2d 186, 212 (Ky. 1989). https://casetext.com/#!/case/rose-v-council-for-better-educ-inc.

[2] See PARCC website at http://www.parcconline.org.

One final distinction, pertaining to both equal educational opportunity and adequacy goals, is the distinction between striving to achieve equal or adequate outcomes versus providing the resources that yield equal opportunity for children, regardless of their backgrounds or where they live. Achieving equal outcomes is statistically unlikely at best, and of suspect policy relevance, given that perfect equality of outcomes requires leveling down (actual outcomes) as much as leveling up. A goal of school finance policy is to provide the resources to offset pre-existing inequalities that otherwise give one child a greater chance than another of achieving the desired outcome levels.

Money and School Finance Reforms

There is an increasing body of evidence that substantive and sustained state school finance reforms matter for improving both the level and distribution of short-term and long-run student outcomes. A few studies have attempted to tackle school finance reforms broadly, applying multistate analyses over time. Card and Payne (2002) found "evidence that equalization of spending levels leads to a narrowing of test score outcomes across family background groups" (Card and Payne 2002, 49). Most recently, Jackson et al. evaluated long-term outcomes of children exposed to court-ordered school finance reforms, finding that "a 10 % increase in per-pupil spending each year for all 12 years of public school leads to 0.27 more completed years of education, 7.25 % higher wages, and a 3.67 percentage-point reduction in the annual incidence of adult poverty; effects are much more pronounced for children from low-income families" (2015, 1).

Numerous other researchers have explored the effects of specific state school finance reforms over time, applying a variety of statistical methods to evaluate how changes in the level and targeting of funding affect changes in outcomes achieved by students directly affected by those funding changes. Figlio (2004) says that the influence of state school finance reforms on student outcomes is perhaps better measured within states over time, explaining that national studies of the type attempted by Card and Payne confront problems of (a) the enormous diversity in the nature of state aid reform plans, and (b) the paucity of national level student performance data.

Several such studies provide compelling evidence of the potential positive effects of school finance reforms. Studies of Michigan school finance reforms in the 1990s have shown positive effects on student performance in both the previously lowest spending districts[3] and previously lower performing districts.[4] Similarly, a study of Kansas school finance reforms in the 1990s, which also primarily involved a leveling up of low-spending districts, found that a 20 % increase in spending was associated with a 5 % increase in the likelihood of students going on to postsecondary education (Deke 2003).

Three studies of Massachusetts school finance reforms from the 1990s find similar results. The first, by Thomas Downes and colleagues, found that the combination of funding and accountability reforms "has been successful in raising the achievement of students in the previously low-spending districts." (2009, 5) The second found that "increases in per-pupil spending led to significant increases in math, reading, science, and social studies test scores for 4th- and 8th-grade students."[5] The most recent of the three, published in 2014 in the *Journal of Education Finance,* found that "changes in the state education aid following the education reform resulted in significantly higher student performance" (Nguyen-Hoang and Yinger 2014, 297). Such findings have been replicated in other states, including Vermont.[6]

Indeed, the role of money in improving student outcomes is often contested. Baker (2012) explains the evolution of assertions regarding the unimportance of money for improving student outcomes, pointing out that these assertions emanate in part from misrepresentations of the work of Coleman and colleagues in the 1960s, which found that school factors seemed less associated with student outcome differences than did family factors. This was not to suggest, however, that school factors

---

[3] Roy (2011) published an analysis of the effects of Michigan's 1990s school finance reforms that led to a significant leveling up for previously low-spending districts. Roy, whose analyses measure both whether the policy resulted in changes in funding and who was affected, found that the proposal "was quite successful in reducing interdistrict spending disparities. There was also a significant positive effect on student performance in the lowest-spending districts as measured in state tests." (p. 137).

[4] Papke (2005), also evaluating Michigan school finance reforms from the 1990s, found that "increases in spending have nontrivial, statistically significant effects on math test pass rates, and the effects are largest for schools with initially poor performance." (p. 821).

Most recently, Hyman (2013) also found positive effects of Michigan school finance reforms in the 1990s but raised some concerns regarding the distribution of those effects. Hyman found that much of the increase was targeted to schools serving fewer low-income children. But the study did find that students exposed to an additional "12 %, more spending per year during grades four through seven experienced a 3.9 % point increase in the probability of enrolling in college, and a 2.5 % point increase in the probability of earning a degree." (p. 1).

[5] "The magnitudes imply a $1000 increase in per-pupil spending leads to about a third to a half of a standard-deviation increase in average test scores. It is noted that the state aid driving the estimates is targeted to under-funded school districts, which may have atypical returns to additional expenditures." (Guryan 2001, 1).

[6] Downes had conducted earlier studies of Vermont school finance reforms in the late 1990s (Act 60). In a 2004 book chapter, Downes noted, "All of the evidence cited in this paper supports the conclusion that Act 60 has dramatically reduced dispersion in education spending and has done this by weakening the link between spending and property wealth. Further, the regressions presented in this paper offer some evidence that student performance has become more equal in the post-Act 60 period. And no results support the conclusion that Act 60 has contributed to increased dispersion in performance." (2004, 312).

were entirely unimportant, and more recent reanalyses of the Coleman data using more advanced statistical techniques than available at the time clarify the relevance of schooling resources (Konstantopoulos and Borman 2011; Borman and Dowling 2010).

Eric Hanushek ushered in the modern-era "money doesn't matter" argument in a study in which he tallied studies reporting positive and negative correlations between spending measures and student outcome measures, proclaiming as his major finding: "There appears to be no strong or systematic relationship between school expenditures and student performance" (1986, 1162).[7]

Baker (2012) summarized reanalyses of the studies tallied by Hanushek, applying quality standards to determine study inclusion, and finding that more of the higher quality studies yielded positive findings with respect to the relationship between schooling resources and student outcomes (Baker 2012). While Hanushek's above characterization continues to permeate policy discourse over school funding—and is often used as evidence that "money doesn't matter"—it is critically important to understand that this statement is merely one of uncertainty about the direct correlation between spending measures and outcome measures based on studies prior to 1986. Neither this statement, nor the crude tally behind it, ever provided any basis for assuming with certainty that money doesn't matter.

A separate body of literature challenges the assertion of the positive influence of state school finance reforms in general and court-ordered reforms in particular. Baker and Welner (2011) explain that much of this literature relies on anecdotal characterizations of lagging student outcome growth following court-ordered infusions of new funding. Hanushek (2009) provide one example of this anecdote-driven approach in a book chapter that seeks to prove that court-ordered school funding reforms in New Jersey, Wyoming, Kentucky, and Massachusetts resulted in few or no measurable improvements. However, these conclusions are based on little more than a series of descriptive graphs of student achievement on the National Assessment of Educational Progress (NAEP) in 1992 and 2007 and an undocumented assertion that, during that period, each of the four states infused substantial additional funds into public education, focused on low-income and minority students, in response to judicial orders. They assume that, in all other states that serve as a comparison, similar changes did not occur. Yet they validate neither assertion.

Baker and Welner (2011) explain that Hanushek and Lindseth failed to measure whether substantive changes had occurred to the level or distribution of school

---

[7] A few years later, Hanushek paraphrased this conclusion in another widely cited article as "Variations in school expenditures are not systematically related to variations in student performance" (Hanushek 1989). Hanushek describes the collection of studies relating spending and outcomes as follows: "The studies are almost evenly divided between studies of individual student performance and aggregate performance in schools or districts. Ninety-six of the 147 studies measure output by score on some standardized test. Approximately 40 % are based upon variations in performance within single districts while the remainder looks across districts. Three-fifths look at secondary performance (grades 7–12) with the rest concentrating on elementary student performance" (Fig. 25).

funding as well as when and for how long. For example, Kentucky reforms had largely faded by the mid- to late 1990s, yet Hanushek and Lindseth measure postreform effects in 2007. Similarly, in New Jersey, infusions of funding occurred from 1998 to 2003 (or, arguably, 2005). But Hanushek and Lindseth's window includes 6 years on the front end where little change occurred. Further, funding was infused into approximately 30 specific New Jersey districts, but Hanushek and Lindseth (2009) explore overall changes to outcomes among low-income children and minorities using NAEP data, where some of the children tested attended the districts receiving additional support but many did not.[8] Finally, Hanushek and Lindseth concede that Massachusetts did, in fact experience substantive achievement gains, but attribute those gains to changes in accountability policies rather than funding.

In an equally problematic analysis, Neymotin (2010) set out to show that court-ordered infusions of funding in Kansas following *Montoy v. Kansas* led to no substantive improvements in student outcomes. However, Neymotin evaluated changes in school funding from 1997 to 2006 even though the key Supreme Court decision occurred in January 2005 and impacted funding starting in the 2005–2006 school year, the end point of Neymotin's outcome data (Baker and Welner 2011). Finally, Greene and Trivitt (2008) present a study in which they claim to show that court-ordered school finance reforms led to no substantive improvements in student outcomes. However, while those authors offer the conclusion that court-ordered funding increases had no effect, they test only whether the presence of a court order is associated with changes in outcomes; they never once measure whether substantive school finance reforms followed the court order (also see Neymotin 2010).

To summarize, there exists no methodologically competent analyses yielding convincing evidence that significant and sustained funding increases provide no educational benefits, and relatively few do not show decisively positive effects (Baker and Welner 2011). On balance, it is safe to say that a sizable and growing body of rigorous empirical literature validates that state school finance reforms can have substantive, positive effects on student outcomes, including reductions in outcome disparities or increases in overall outcome levels (Baker and Welner 2011).

---

[8] Hanushek (2006) goes so far as to title a concurrently produced volume on the same topic "How School Finance Lawsuits Exploit Judges' Good Intentions and Harm Our Children" [emphasis ours]. The premise that additional funding for schools often leveraged toward class size reduction, additional course offerings or increased teacher salaries, causes harm to children is, on its face, absurd. The book, which implies as much in its title, never once validates that such reforms ever cause observable harm. Rather, the title is little more than a manipulative attempt to instill fear of pending harm in the mind of the uncritical spectator. The book also includes two examples of a type of analysis that occurred with some frequency in the mid-2000s and that also had the intent of showing that school funding doesn't matter. These studies would cherry pick anecdotal information on either or both of the following: (a) poorly funded schools that have high outcomes, and (b) well-funded schools that have low outcomes (see Evers and Clopto 2006; Walberg 2006).

Resources That Matter

The premise that money matters for improving school quality is grounded in the assumption that having more money provides schools and districts the opportunity to improve the qualities and quantities of real resources. The primary resources involved in the production of schooling outcomes are human resources—the quantity and quality of teachers, administrators, support, and other staff in schools. Quantities of school staff are reflected in pupil-to-teacher ratios and average class sizes. Reduction of class sizes or reductions of overall pupil-to-staff ratios require additional staff, and thus additional money, assuming wages and benefits for additional staff remain constant. Quality of school staff depend in part on the compensation available to recruit and retain them—specifically salaries and benefits, in addition to working conditions. Notably, working conditions may be reflected in part through measures of workload, like average class sizes, as well as the composition of the student population.

A substantial body of literature has accumulated to validate the conclusion that both teachers' overall and relative wages affect the quality of those who choose to enter the teaching profession, and whether they stay once they get in. For example, Murnane and Olsen (1989) found that salaries affect the decision to enter teaching and the duration of the teaching career, while Figlio (1997, 2002) and Ferguson (1991) concluded that higher salaries are associated with more qualified teachers. Loeb and Page (2000) tackled the specific issues of relative pay noted above. They showed that:

> Once we adjust for labor market factors, we estimate that raising teacher wages by 10 % reduces high school dropout rates by 3–4 %. Our findings suggest that previous studies have failed to produce robust estimates because they lack adequate controls for non-wage aspects of teaching and market differences in alternative occupational opportunities.

In short, while salaries are not the only factor involved, they do affect the quality of the teaching workforce, which in turn affects student outcomes.

Research on the flip side of this issue—evaluating spending constraints or reductions—reveals the potential harm to teaching quality that flows from leveling down or reducing spending. For example, Figlio and Rueben (2001) note that, "Using data from the National Center for Education Statistics we find that tax limits systematically reduce the average quality of education majors, as well as new public school teachers in states that have passed these limits."

Salaries also play a potentially important role in improving the *equity* of student outcomes. While several studies show that higher salaries relative to labor market norms can draw higher quality candidates into teaching, the evidence also indicates that relative teacher salaries across schools and districts may influence the distribution of teaching quality. For example, Ondrich et al. (2008) "find that teachers in districts with higher salaries relative to non-teaching salaries in the same county are less likely to leave teaching and that a teacher is less likely to change districts when he or she teaches in a district near the top of the teacher salary distribution in that county."

Others have argued that the dominant structure of teacher compensation, which ties salary growth to years of experience and degrees obtained, is problematic because of weak correlations with student achievement gains, creating inefficiencies that negate the relationship between school spending and quality (Hanushek 2011). Existing funds, they argue, instead could be used to compensate teachers according to (measures of) their effectiveness while dismissing high-cost "ineffective" teachers and replacing them with better ones, thus achieving better outcomes with the same or less money (Hanushek 2009).

This argument depends on four large assumptions. First, adopting a pay-for-performance model, rather than a step-and-lane salary model, would dramatically improve performance at the same or less expense. Second, shedding the "bottom 5 % of teachers" according to statistical estimates of their "effectiveness" can lead to dramatic improvements at equal or lower expense. Third, it assumes there are sufficiently accurate measures of teaching effectiveness across settings and children. Finally, this argument ignores the initial sorting of teachers into schools where more marketable teachers head for more desirable settings.

Existing studies of pay-for-performance compensation models fail to provide empirical support for this argument—either that these alternatives can substantially boost outcomes, or that they can do so at equal or lower total salary expense (Springer et al. 2011). Simulations purporting to validate the long-run benefits of deselecting "bad" teachers depend on the average pool of replacements lining up to take those jobs being substantively better than those who were let go (average replacing "bad"). Simulations promoting the benefits of "bad teacher" deselection assume this to be true, without empirical basis, and without consideration for potential labor market consequences of the deselection policy itself (Baker et al. 2013a). Finally, existing measures of teacher "effectiveness" fall well short of these demands (Ibid.).

Most importantly, arguments about the structure of teacher compensation miss the bigger point—the average level of compensation matters with respect to the average quality of the teacher labor force. To whatever degree teacher pay matters in attracting good people into the profession and keeping them around, it's less about how they are paid than how much. Furthermore, the average salaries of the teaching profession, with respect to other labor market opportunities, can substantively affect the quality of entrants to the teaching profession, applicants to preparation programs, and student outcomes. Diminishing resources for schools can constrain salaries and reduce the quality of the labor supply. Further, salary differentials between schools and districts might help to recruit or retain teachers in high-need settings. So, too, does investment in improved working conditions, from infrastructure to smaller class sizes and total student loads. In other words, resources for teacher quality matter.

Ample research indicates that children in smaller classes achieve better outcomes, both academic and otherwise, and that class-size reduction can be an effective strategy for closing racial or socioeconomic achievement gaps (U.S. Department of Education et al. 2003). While it's certainly plausible that other uses of the same money might be equally or even more effective, there is little evidence to support this. For example, while we are quite confident that higher teacher salaries may lead to increases in the quality of applicants to the teaching profession and increases in student outcomes, we do not know whether the same money spent toward salary increases would achieve better or worse outcomes if it were spent toward class size reduction. Some have raised concerns that large-scale class-size reductions can lead to unintended labor market consequences that offset some of the gains attributable to class-size reduction (such as the inability to recruit enough fully qualified teachers). For example, studies of California's statewide class-size reduction initiative suggest that as districts across the socioeconomic spectrum reduced class sizes, fewer high-quality teachers were available in high-poverty settings (Jepsen and Rivkin 2002).[9]

While it would be useful to have more precise cost-benefit analyses regarding the tradeoffs between applying funding to class-size reduction versus increased compensation (Ehrenberg et al. 2001), the preponderance of existing evidence suggests that the additional resources expended on class-size reductions do produce positive effects. Both reductions to class sizes and improvements to competitive wages can yield improved outcomes, but the gains in efficiency of choosing one strategy over the other are unclear, and local public school districts rarely have complete flexibility to make tradeoffs because class-size reduction may be constrained by available classrooms (Baker and Welner 2012). Smaller class sizes and reduced total student loads are a relevant working condition simultaneously influencing teacher recruitment and retention (Loeb et al. 2005; Isenberg 2010). That is, providing smaller classes may partly offset the need for higher wages for recruiting or retaining teachers. High-poverty schools require both strategies rather than an either-or proposition when it comes to smaller classes and competitive wages.

As discussed above, achieving equal educational opportunity requires leveraging additional real resources—lower class sizes and more intensive support services—in high-need settings. Merely achieving equal-quality real resources, including equally qualified teachers, likely requires higher competitive wages, not merely equal pay in a given labor market. As such, higher-need settings may require substantially greater financial inputs than lower-need settings. Lacking sufficient financial inputs to do both, districts must choose one or the other. In some cases, higher need districts may lack sufficient resources to reduce class sizes or provide more intensive support.

---

[9] "The results show that, all else equal, smaller classes raise third-grade mathematics and reading achievement, particularly for lower-income students. However, the expansion of the teaching force required to staff the additional classrooms appears to have led to a deterioration in average teacher quality in schools serving a predominantly Black student body. This deterioration partially or, in some cases, fully offset the benefits of smaller classes, demonstrating the importance of considering all implications of any policy change" (p. 1).

For further discussion of the complexities of evaluating class size reduction in a dynamic policy context, see Sims 2008, 2009; Chingos 2010.

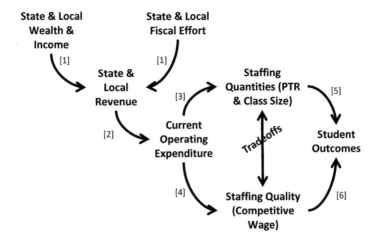

Fig. 4.1 Conceptual map of fiscal inputs & real resources

In this chapter, we explore the relationship between financial inputs and these tradeoffs, both within and across states, and over time. Specifically, we address the following questions:

- What patterns in national and state funding equity and adequacy do we see over the last two decades?
- What patterns do we find in access to important school resources, namely wage competitiveness and staffing ratios, over the same time period?
- What is the relationship between the adequacy and equity of school funding and access to real resources (teacher wages, staffing ratios, and class sizes)?

Measuring Fiscal Input as Well as Real Resource Equity and Adequacy

In this section, we draw on several national data sources to develop indicators of (a) school funding levels and distributions, (b) staffing levels and distributions and (c) relative wage levels and distributions (see Appendix (Table 4A.1) for full list of data sources, years, and measures). Ultimately, our goal is to examine the levels and distributions of fiscal input, staffing, and wages and discern their relationship. Our following analyses use national data sources over time to draw the various connections displayed in Fig. 4.1. First, the amount of effort a state puts forth, in addition to wealth and income, influences the level of resources made available to schools. Revenues available to schools translate to expenditures, and those expenditures may be leveraged to support more competitive wages, hiring and retaining more staff, or both. While we do not in this chapter include measures that connect inputs to student outcomes, we do expect staffing quantities and qualities to substantively influence those outcomes. We also document the relationships between financial resources and the real resources purchased with those financial resources. We explore these linkages in terms of state average levels of resources and within-state distributions of those resources with respect to concentrations of child poverty across districts.

These relationships, while relatively straightforward, have not been systematically documented across all states over time in recent years.[10] Specifically, there is little documentation of the relationship across states between the level of commitment made by states to their public schooling systems and the average competitiveness of teacher wages, and little documentation of the extent to which differences in and changes in spending levels translate to changes in staffing ratios and class sizes.[11]

Evaluating Funding Levels and Fairness

We begin with our model for estimating levels and variation in school districts' state and local revenue. Our objectives are twofold: first, to compare across states the amount a school district would be expected to receive in state and local revenue (and current operating expenditure) if the district was of a given enrollment size (economies of scale) and population density, faced national average labor costs, and served a population with relatively average child poverty levels; second, to evaluate within states the amount that a school district would be expected to receive in state and local revenue (and current operating expenditure) at varied levels of child poverty, holding constant labor costs, district enrollment size, and population density.

The goal here is to make more reasonable comparisons of revenue and expenditure levels across local public school districts from one state and to another. So adjustments are made accordingly in our models. Average spending per pupil might be higher in states with higher labor costs. To compare the purchasing power of that spending, we adjust for those cost differences. Average spending per pupil might also be higher in states where more children attend school in population-sparse, small, rural districts. Thus, we compare spending for districts of otherwise similar size and population density across states—a "what if" analysis assuming a district size of 2000 or more pupils with average population density. Similarly, unified K-12

---

[10] For an earlier analysis that parallel school funding disparities and real resource disparities, see Corcoran et al. 2004.

[11] In the absence of clear documentation of these rather obvious connections between fiscal constraints, wages, and class sizes, a body of literature has emerged that suggests that no such linkage exists, that local public school districts of all types possess more than sufficient resources to achieve competitive, restructured compensation systems, or entirely different service delivery approaches altogether with no consequences resulting from resource reallocation. During the economic downturn, much of that non-peer-reviewed, think-tank-sponsored literature found its way to a special section on the U.S. Department of Education website dedicated to improving educational productivity. Baker and Welner (2012) provide a substantive critique of the reports posted on the website.

districts might have different average spending than K-8 or high school districts; thus we base our comparisons on unified K-12 districts. Finally, we compare revenue and spending predictions for districts of similar child poverty rates, as child poverty influences the costs of achieving common outcome goals (Duncombe and Yinger 2005).

For both objectives, we use a 20-year (1993–2012) set of local public school district data to which we fit the following model:

$$\text{Funding per Pupil} = f\left(\text{Regional Competitive Wages, District Size} \times \right.$$
$$\text{Population Density, Grade Range Served,}$$
$$\left.\text{State} \times \text{Census Child Poverty Rate}\right)$$

To account for variation in labor costs, we use the NCES Education Comparable Wage Index, updated through 2012 by the author of the original index (Extending the NCES CWI 2013). We impute additional years as necessary (see Appendix). We account for district size with a series of dummy variables indicating that a district has (a) under 100 pupils, (b) 101–300 pupils, (c) 301–600 pupils, (d) 601–1200 pupils, (e) 1201–1500 pupils, and (f) 1501–2000 pupils, where the baseline comparison group are districts with over 2000 pupils, a common reference point for scale efficiency. The district size factor is interacted with county-level population density to further correct for cost differences associated with small, sparse, rural districts, separating them from segregated enclaves in population-dense metropolitan areas. Finally, we interact state dummy indicators with district level child poverty rate to estimate the within-state, cross-district distribution of funding with respect to child poverty. The regression model is weighted by district enrollment size.

We then use this model to generate predicted values of the funding measure—total state and local revenues per pupil and current operating spending per pupil—at varied levels of child poverty for each state at national average labor costs, average population density, and efficient size. To compare levels of funding across states, we compare predicted revenue and spending at 10 % census poverty, holding other factors constant. To compare distributions, we construct what we call a "fairness ratio." It is the ratio of the predicted funding level for a high poverty district (30 % census poverty, equivalent to about 60–80 % qualified for the National School Lunch Program), relative to that of a low poverty (0 % census poverty) district. A fairness ratio above 1 indicates that the state provides a greater level of resources to high poverty districts than low poverty districts, while a ratio below 1 indicates that high-poverty districts have fewer resources.

$$\text{Fairness Ratio} = \frac{\text{Predicted Funding at 30\% Poverty}}{\text{Predicted Funding at 0\% Poverty}}$$

Evaluating Resource Levels and Fairness

The next step is to estimate levels of real resources in otherwise comparable settings across states and to estimate variations in real resources with respect to child poverty.

Estimating Staffing Levels and Distributions   Our approach to modeling staffing levels follows the one we used to model funding levels. We use annual data from 1993 to 2012 and apply the same model as above, except putting numbers of teachers per 100 pupils on the left-hand side. Again, the premises are: overall staffing ratios might be higher on average (better) in states with more children in small, low-population-density districts; staffing ratios (given spending levels) might be lower (worse) in states facing higher labor costs; and staffing ratios should vary with respect to children's educational needs, as proxied by district poverty measures.

$$\text{Teachers per 100 Pupils} = f\big(\text{Regional Competitive Wages, District Size} \times$$
$$\text{Population Density, Grade Range Served,}$$
$$\text{State} \times \text{Census Child Poverty Rate}\big)$$

We then use this model to (a) generate predicted values of teachers per 100 pupils at given levels of poverty, within each state and (b) generate a staffing fairness ratio like our funding fairness ratio.

Evaluating the Average Competitiveness of Teacher Wages   As discussed above, one way in which teacher wages matter is that the average relative wage of teachers versus other professions in a given labor market may influence the quality of those entering and staying within the teaching workforce. Here, we use the U.S. Census Bureau's American Community Survey (ACS) annual data from 2000 to 2012 to estimate, for each state, the ratio of the expected income from wages for an elementary or secondary school teacher to the expected income from wages for a non-teacher at the same age and degree level.

Of primary interest here are the differences in competitive wage ratios across states, and ultimately, whether states that allocate more resources to education generally are able to achieve more competitive teacher wages. Here, we compare *annual* wages of teachers to nonteachers, but we also note that variation across states remains similar with a comparison of weekly or monthly wages, although teacher wages do become more comparable to nonteacher wages. Recall that literature on teacher wages and teacher quality suggests that the more competitive the teacher wage (relative to other career options), the higher the expected quality of entrants to the profession.

To generate our competitive wage ratios, we begin with a regression model fit to our 13-year set of ACS data, in which we estimate the relationship between "income from wages" as the dependent variable, a series of state indicators, and an indicator that the individual is a teacher (occupation) in elementary or secondary education (industry). We include an indicator of the teacher's age and education level, and we include measures of hours worked per week and weeks worked per year but do not equate our predicted wages by holding constant these latter two factors in the analyses. We estimate the following model:

$$\text{Income from Wages} = f\left(\text{State Place of Work, k12 Teacher, Age, Education Level,}\right.$$
$$\left.\text{Hours per Week, Weeks per Year}\right)$$

We use this model to generate predicted values for teacher and nonteacher wages at specific age points, for individuals with a bachelor's degree, and then take the ratio of teacher to nonteacher wages. Of particular interest are (a) the differences in the teacher/nonteacher wage ratio across states and (b) the changes over time within states in the teacher/nonteacher wage ratio. That is, are teacher wages more competitive in some states than others? And have teachers generally gained or lost ground? Are these differences in wage competitiveness and gains or losses related back to state funding levels?

Estimating Sensitivity of Resources to Funding Across Districts

For these last two analyses, we link our data on district-level finances with teacher-level data from the NCES Schools and Staffing Survey (SASS), which includes over 40,000 public school teachers, surveyed in waves on approximately 4-year cycles. We use data from the 1993–1994, 1999–2000, 2003–2004, 2007–2008, and 2011–2012 cycles.

Because personnel costs vary across labor markets within states, it is important when evaluating either teacher quantity measures or teacher wages to make direct comparisons only among districts facing similar personnel costs. Further, because livable wages similarly vary across labor markets, but income thresholds for determining whether families are in poverty do not, it also makes sense to compare poverty rates only across local public school districts sharing a labor market (Baker et al. 2013b). A convenient solution is to re-express per-pupil spending measures and child poverty rates for each school district in the nation relative to (as a ratio to) the average per-pupil spending and child poverty rates for all districts sharing that same labor market.

We use a similar strategy for evaluating variations in both class sizes and competitive teacher wages, with the latter comparisons requiring a preliminary step of determining the wage for teachers of comparable qualifications and contractual obligations. This analysis is different from the previous analyses because we are working with samples of teachers and schools where total sample sizes and the distribution of sampled teachers for many states are insufficient for characterizing cross-district equity. As a result, we ask whether nationally, across nonrural labor markets, there exists the expected relationship between the relative funding available to local public school districts, and the class sizes and wages of teachers in those school districts. That is, do schools in districts with better funding tend to have smaller class sizes, more competitive wages, or both?

Class Sizes To estimate the sensitivity of class size variation to spending variation across schools within labor markets, we estimate separate models of departmentalized and self-contained class sizes. We estimate class sizes as a function of (a) relative spending, (b) relative poverty, and (c) grade level taught.

$$\text{Class Size} = f(\text{Relative Spending, Relative Poverty, Grade Level})$$

Teacher Wages While the previous wage indicator compared teacher salaries to nonteachers, this dataset allows us to compare wages among similar teachers within labor markets, but in different school districts. The relative competitiveness of teacher salaries is then examined in the context of the relative poverty and relative funding levels of school districts. This analysis offers further evidence as to whether districts can leverage funding resources to provide more competitive wages to teachers in other, less resourced districts. In other words, does the distribution of funding affect districts' ability to offer competitive wages, and therefore influence the distribution of quality teachers across districts?

We begin by estimating, within each labor market in each state, the relative wage of teachers with a specific set of credentials. We focus on full-time classroom teachers, estimating their salaries (base pay from school year teaching) as a function of (a) experience and (b) degree level within (c) labor market (as defined in the Education Comparable Wage Index, aligned with metropolitan and micropolitan statistical areas). We exclude teachers outside of metropolitan and micropolitan areas because of small sample sizes within rural labor markets. We estimate separate models for each SASS wave.

$$\text{Salary} = f(\text{experience, degree, labor market})$$

Next, we generate the predicted salary for each teacher in each labor market, identifying the average wage for a teacher at given experience and degree level across all schools in each labor market. We then take the ratio of actual salary to predicted salary, which indicates for all teachers in the sample whether their salary is higher or lower than expected. Aggregated to the school or district level, we have a measure of the relative competitiveness of teacher wages in each school or district compared to other schools or districts sharing the same labor market.

The next step is to estimate the sensitivity of these wage variations to spending variations across districts sharing the same labor market. We do this with the teacher-level data, linked to a measure of the relative spending of their school district in its labor market, and the relative poverty rate of the school district in its labor market. We take the district's current operating spending per pupil as a ratio to the average of all other districts in the labor market and do the same with district poverty rate. We estimate together the relationship between relative spending and poverty and the relative competitiveness of teacher's salaries. We include additional dummy variables for grade level taught, again including only nonrural full-time teachers:

$$\text{Salary Competitiveness} = f\left(\text{Relative Spending, Relative Poverty, Grade Level Taught}\right)$$

Findings

We begin by reviewing longitudinal trends in funding levels and funding fairness. We also validate the extent to which state school funding levels are associated with differences in fiscal effort—or the share of gross state product allocated to schools. Next, we summarize changes to the distribution of funding across school districts within states, specifically evaluating the funding fairness profiles of states and how those profiles have changed over the past 20 years. We then proceed to explore average competitive wage levels across states from 2000 to 2012, and pupil-to-teacher ratios across states over the full 20-year period.

We subsequently explore the connections between measures of the level and distribution of financial inputs to schooling, and the level and distribution of staffing quantities and staffing qualities. Specifically, we evaluate whether state spending levels are associated with the state average competitiveness of teacher wages and state average staffing ratios (pupil-to-teacher ratios). Then we explore whether within-state distributions of financial inputs to schooling are associated with within-state distributions of staffing ratios, class sizes, and competitive wages.

Adequacy and Equity of Fiscal Inputs Figure 4.2 presents the national averages of current spending per pupil and state and local revenues per pupil, adjusted for

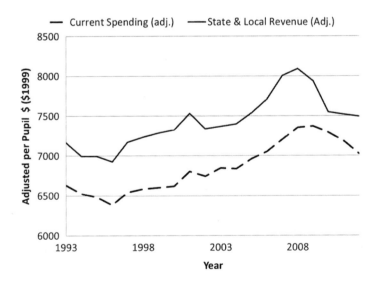

Fig. 4.2 Input price adjusted revenue and spending

changes in labor costs by dividing each district's revenue or spending figure by the comparable wage index for that district. Both revenues and spending are included to illustrate how the two largely move together over time, as one would expect. The Education Comparable Wage Index adjusts for both regional variation in labor costs (input prices) and inflationary change in labor costs. Figure 4.2 shows that on average using district level data weighted by student enrollments, state and local revenues and per pupil spending are up approximately 4.5–5.5 % over the period, reaching a high around 2008 and returning to levels comparable to 2000 by 2012.

Figure 4.3 summarizes the trends in predicted state and local revenue levels for all states, organized by regions. These are combined state and local revenues per pupil, predicted for a district with 10 % child poverty, of 2000 or more pupils at constant labor costs (though not fully corrected for inflation). Of particular interest

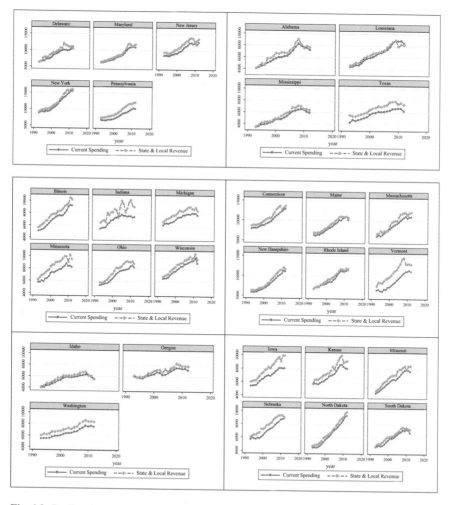

Fig. 4.3 Predicted state and local revenues over time by state

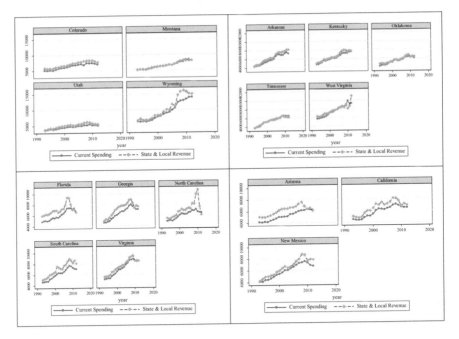

Fig. 4.3 (continued)

are the trends, divergences, and convergences among regionally contiguous states. A notable feature of these figures is the sharp shift in growth trajectories that occurs in most states around 2009 as a function of the recession. New Jersey, for example, experienced a particularly strong downturn. Delaware is the only state in this mix to show no recovery as of yet. Related work has shown that these downturns were largely a function of sharp reductions in state aid, buffered in some cases by increases to local property taxes. But those shifts in responsibility from state funding onto local property tax have potential equity consequences. Average revenue may have rebounded with offsetting property tax increase, but inequity is likely to have increased as a result.

Figure 4.4 illustrates the relationship in 2012 between the percent of gross state product expended on K-12 schools and the average level of state and local revenue. In short, higher effort states do have higher funding levels. Certainly, some relatively low fiscal capacity states like Mississippi apply average effort and still end up with low funding, while high fiscal capacity states like Wyoming or Connecticut are able to apply much lower effort and yield far greater resources. But effort matters above and beyond wealth and income. While some might assume that effort crept upward as fiscal capacity declined during the recession, this assumption is generally wrong. Political proclivity for cutting taxes has led, on average, to reductions in funding effort. Forty-one states reduced effort from 2007 to 2012. Further, 5-year changes in effort are strongly associated with 5-year changes in revenue levels, as

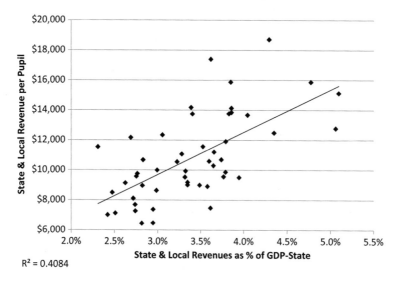

R² = 0.4084

Fig. 4.4 Relationship between effort and revenue (Note: See Appendix (Table 4A.2) for full information by state)

Table 4.1 Numbers of states where funding fairness ratio has improved

		Initial fairness ratio among improved states		
Period	# States that improved fairness	<.95	.95–1.05	>1.05
1993–2012	33	4	9	20
2002–2012	23	3	3	17
2007–2012	21	2	4	15

might be expected (correlation=.7 excluding Alaska). States that reduced effort generally reduced school revenues proportionately.

Current Expenditure "Fairness" (Spending Equity) So what then have been the consequences of the economic downturn for school spending fairness across states? That is, how have higher poverty districts been differentially affected when compared with lower poverty ones? Table 4.1 summarizes numbers of states where funding fairness improved (or not) over specific time periods over the past 20 years. Again, a funding fairness ratio of .95 means that a district with 30 % of children in poverty[12] has only 95 % of the funding of a district with 0 % children in poverty. A fairness ratio of 1.05 indicates that a district with 30 % poverty has 5 % greater funding than a district with 0 % poverty.

From 1993 to 2007 in particular, 40 different states experienced increased funding levels in higher poverty districts relative to lower poverty ones (only 33 sustained the pattern over the entire period from 1993 to 2012). But in the 5 years that

---

[12] Census poverty rate, where a 30 % rate is equivalent to about 80 % free or reduced priced lunch.

followed, 30 states reduced funding fairness, with some of the greatest reductions coming in states that had previously experienced the greatest improvements, including New Jersey.

Table 4.2 summarizes the state-by-state current expenditure fairness ratios and changes over time. As noted in Table 4.1, most states did improve their fairness ratios over the entire period, but many reduced fairness over the past 5 years. Massachusetts improved fairness at the outset of the period, as did New Jersey, but both states taper off in recent years. Other states like Pennsylvania started the period with relatively flat distributions (similar funding in higher and lower poverty districts) and then slid into more regressive distributions over time.

Notably, these findings present a more positive light on funding progressiveness than those in the report *Is School Funding Fair,* because these figures are based on current operating spending per pupil, which includes the expenditure of federal funds. Those federal funds tend to lift (by around 5 %) the levels of funding in the highest poverty districts, thus improving the funding fairness index.

Resource Models

Relative Annual Wage of Teachers Table 4.3 summarizes changes to the state average competitiveness of teacher wages over the past 12 years, and then for the most recent 5 years. Wage competitiveness is expressed as a ratio of teacher wages to nonteacher wages. A ratio less than 1 means teachers earn less than comparable nonteachers. It's important to understand in this case that there are two moving parts—teacher wages and nonteacher wages. Teacher wages can become more competitive if they remain relatively constant but wages of others (at the same age and education level) decline. Teacher wages can become less competitive even if they appear to grow but do so more slowly than wages in other sectors. Put simply, it's all relative, but it is the relative wage that matters. From 2000 to 2012, teacher wages in every state became less competitive, based on our model, a finding that is consistent with similar work by Mishel et al. (2011). It would appear that over the last 5 years, only in Iowa did teacher wages become marginally more competitive. Over the 12-year period, the state average (unweighted) reduction in wage competitiveness was 12 %. Over the period from 2007 to 2012, the state average reduction in wage competitiveness was 8 %.

But, as can be seen in Table 4.4, these estimates tend to jump around, especially in low population states like Alaska. States with persistently noncompetitive teacher wages include Colorado and Arizona. Teacher wages have tended over time to be more competitive in rural states (where nonteacher wages aren't as high), including Montana and Wyoming. Average teacher wages in New York and Rhode Island have also tended to be more competitive, though data are inconsistent across years.

Teachers per 100 Pupils Table 4.5 summarizes changes to the numbers of teachers per 100 pupils over time. Over the entire 20-year period, nearly all states increased

Table 4.2 Spending fairness indices for select years

State	Fairness ratio current operating expenditures per pupil				Change over time			
	1993	2002	2007	2012	1993–2007	20-year change	10-year change	5-year change
Alabama	1.02	1.06	1.04	1.08	0.02	0.06	0.02	0.04
Alaska	2.14	2.44	2.30	1.87	0.17	−0.27	−0.58	−0.44
Arizona	1.20	1.18	1.33	1.05	0.13	−0.15	−0.13	−0.27
Arkansas	1.13	1.11	1.19	1.23	0.06	0.09	0.11	0.03
California	1.17	1.12	1.32	1.20	0.14	0.03	0.08	−0.12
Colorado	1.09	1.05	1.15	1.16	0.06	0.07	0.11	0.01
Connecticut	1.07	1.30	1.21	1.07	0.15	0.00	−0.23	−0.14
Delaware	1.04	1.19	1.64	1.23	0.60	0.19	0.04	−0.41
Dist. of Columbia	1.02	1.06	1.04	1.08	0.02	0.06	0.02	0.04
Florida	1.33	1.28	1.37	1.19	0.04	−0.14	−0.09	−0.18
Georgia	1.22	1.29	1.23	1.20	0.02	−0.01	−0.08	−0.03
Hawaii	1.02	1.06	1.04	1.08	0.02	0.06	0.02	0.04
Idaho	1.25	1.26	1.16	1.18	−0.09	−0.07	−0.08	0.02
Illinois	1.08	0.96	1.07	1.05	−0.01	−0.03	0.08	−0.02
Indiana	1.26	1.53	1.62	1.45	0.36	0.19	−0.08	−0.17
Iowa	1.19	1.33	1.32	1.20	0.13	0.01	−0.13	−0.12
Kansas	1.15	1.33	1.34	1.22	0.19	0.07	−0.11	−0.11
Kentucky	1.17	1.17	1.26	1.22	0.09	0.05	0.05	−0.04
Louisiana	1.03	1.00	1.08	1.33	0.05	0.30	0.32	0.25
Maine	1.12	1.15	1.11	0.99	−0.01	−0.13	−0.16	−0.12
Maryland	0.89	1.17	1.12	1.14	0.23	0.24	−0.04	0.02
Massachusetts	0.95	1.37	1.39	1.25	0.44	0.30	−0.12	−0.14
Michigan	1.04	1.21	1.23	1.20	0.19	0.16	−0.01	−0.02
Minnesota	1.39	1.82	1.71	1.60	0.32	0.21	−0.22	−0.11
Mississippi	1.19	1.26	1.22	1.30	0.03	0.11	0.04	0.08
Missouri	1.25	1.17	1.10	1.05	−0.15	−0.20	−0.11	−0.05
Montana	1.18	1.30	1.54	1.18	0.36	0.00	−0.11	−0.36
Nebraska	1.14	1.09	1.35	1.36	0.21	0.22	0.27	0.01
Nevada	0.61	0.60	0.61	0.57	0.01	−0.03	−0.02	−0.04
New Hampshire	0.80	0.95	0.85	1.07	0.05	0.27	0.12	0.22
New Jersey	1.05	1.42	1.51	1.26	0.46	0.21	−0.16	−0.25
New Mexico	1.11	1.23	1.27	1.29	0.16	0.17	0.06	0.01
New York	0.79	0.91	0.96	0.99	0.17	0.20	0.08	0.02
North Carolina	1.09	1.13	1.26	1.25	0.17	0.17	0.12	0.00
North Dakota	1.34	1.33	1.40	1.43	0.06	0.09	0.10	0.03
Ohio	1.19	1.29	1.25	1.16	0.05	−0.03	−0.12	−0.08
Oklahoma	1.26	1.31	1.30	1.20	0.04	−0.06	−0.11	−0.10
Oregon	1.17	1.35	1.46	1.22	0.29	0.06	−0.13	−0.24
Pennsylvania	1.01	0.90	0.90	0.92	−0.10	−0.08	0.02	0.02

(continued)

Table 4.2 (continued)

State	Fairness ratio current operating expenditures per pupil				Change over time			
	1993	2002	2007	2012	1993–2007	20-year change	10-year change	5-year change
Rhode Island	0.93	1.08	1.11	1.03	0.18	0.10	−0.05	−0.08
South Carolina	1.04	1.28	1.20	1.26	0.16	0.22	−0.01	0.07
South Dakota	1.27	1.50	1.50	1.61	0.23	0.35	0.11	0.12
Tennessee	1.23	1.15	1.21	1.22	−0.02	−0.01	0.07	0.01
Texas	1.13	1.16	1.21	1.19	0.08	0.06	0.03	−0.02
Utah	1.89	1.68	1.78	1.49	−0.11	−0.40	−0.19	−0.29
Vermont	0.90	0.92	1.00	0.86	0.09	−0.04	−0.06	−0.13
Virginia	1.13	1.08	1.07	1.07	−0.06	−0.06	−0.01	0.00
Washington	1.30	1.28	1.29	1.21	−0.01	−0.10	−0.08	−0.09
West Virginia	1.06	1.16	1.14	1.19	0.08	0.13	0.03	0.06
Wisconsin	1.10	1.19	1.21	1.23	0.11	0.13	0.04	0.03
Wyoming	1.37	1.57	1.35	1.04	−0.02	−0.33	−0.52	−0.31

Table 4.3 Summary of changes in wage competitiveness

Period	# States that increased wage competitiveness	State mean change (%)
2000–2012	1	−12
2000–2007	3	−9
2007–2012	1	−8

numbers of staff per 100 pupils. The state average (unweighted) increase was approximately 1 additional teacher per 100 pupils, moving from about 5.5 to about 6.5 total teachers per 100 pupils. Most of those gains occurred prior to 2002. Over the past 10 years, state average staffing increases have been much more modest, and over the past 5 years, nonexistent.

Table 4.6 displays state-by-state ratios of teachers per 100 pupils and changes in those ratios. States including Alabama and Virginia appear to have reduced teachers per 100 pupils by over 1.0 (or around 13–16 %). About half of states continued to increase numbers of teaching staff per 100 pupils. Notably, these figures change over time both as a function of changing numbers of staff and of changing numbers of pupils. States with constant staffing but declining enrollments will show increasing staffing ratios. States with increasing enrollment but no additional staff will show decreasing staffing ratios.

Table 4.4 Teacher/nonteacher wage ratios for select years

State	Wage competitiveness ratio (Teacher/Nonteacher) (%)				Change over time (%)		
	2000	2002	2007	2012	12-year change	10-year change	5-year change
Alabama	83	83	77	71	−12	−12	−6
Alaska	89	104	118	85	−4	−19	−33
Arizona	79	74	70	62	−18	−13	−9
Arkansas	82	84	82	74	−7	−10	−8
California	79	82	82	75	−5	−7	−7
Colorado	81	75	70	68	−13	−6	−2
Connecticut	78	82	76	71	−7	−11	−5
Delaware	82	87	83	75	−7	−13	−9
District of Columbia	74	85	74	68	−7	−18	−6
Florida	85	82	80	73	−11	−8	−6
Georgia	76	76	74	68	−8	−8	−5
Hawaii	95	83	81	77	−17	−6	−4
Idaho	93	92	86	72	−21	−20	−13
Illinois	77	78	79	73	−4	−5	−6
Indiana	87	85	80	70	−17	−15	−10
Iowa	86	87	83	85	−1	−2	3
Kansas	87	80	77	70	−17	−10	−7
Kentucky	84	80	78	71	−13	−9	−7
Louisiana	78	78	79	75	−4	−3	−5
Maine	90	79	90	81	−9	2	−9
Maryland	80	77	78	75	−4	−2	−3
Massachusetts	77	72	77	69	−8	−3	−8
Michigan	93	88	94	78	−15	−10	−16
Minnesota	84	80	75	71	−13	−10	−5
Mississippi	86	81	78	72	−13	−9	−6
Missouri	83	76	78	68	−16	−9	−11
Montana	100	98	93	74	−26	−24	−19
Nebraska	86	82	78	77	−10	−6	−2
Nevada	93	85	84	82	−11	−3	−3
New Hampshire	78	82	75	73	−5	−9	−2
New Jersey	86	81	82	76	−10	−5	−6
New Mexico	77	82	85	78	1	−4	−7
New York	83	80	82	81	−2	1	−1
North Carolina	80	79	75	67	−13	−12	−8
North Dakota	87	86	77	70	−17	−17	−7
Ohio	80	79	82	75	−5	−4	−7
Oklahoma	80	78	76	67	−13	−11	−9
Oregon	93	82	86	75	−17	−7	−11

(continued)

Table 4.4 (continued)

State	Wage competitiveness ratio (Teacher/Nonteacher) (%)				Change over time (%)		
	2000	2002	2007	2012	12-year change	10-year change	5-year change
Pennsylvania	94	92	85	80	−13	−12	−5
Rhode Island	92	87	94	78	−13	−8	−16
South Carolina	86	89	77	73	−13	−16	−4
South Dakota	82	88	78	68	−15	−21	−10
Tennessee	86	74	76	66	−20	−9	−10
Texas	77	78	73	69	−8	−9	−4
Utah	99	93	79	71	−28	−22	−8
Vermont	90	91	95	75	−15	−16	−20
Virginia	76	75	72	63	−14	−12	−10
Washington	79	78	74	69	−11	−9	−5
West Virginia	89	79	79	77	−12	−3	−2
Wisconsin	94	88	84	76	−18	−12	−8
Wyoming	106	91	99	94	−12	3	−5

Table 4.5 Summary of staffing level changes over time

Period	# States that improved staffing ratios	State average change
1993–2012	49	1.06
2002–2012	34	0.21
2007–2012	25	0.03
1993–2007	48	1.03

Relationships Across Adequacy (Level) Measures

Here we explore the relationships among these indicators. Figure 4.5 conveys that states with higher per pupil spending tend to have more teachers per 100 pupils on average. This suggests that, on balance and across states, higher spending on schools is leveraged to increase staffing quantities. The next question is the extent to which these increased overall staffing quantities translate to decreased class sizes, where research literature tends to point to more positive effects on student outcomes.

Figure 4.6 shows that these differences in overall staffing ratios do translate to smaller class sizes, both for self-contained elementary classes and for secondary departmentalized settings. That is, while some may contest the direct relevance of pupil-to-teacher ratios as having influence on schooling quality, the availability of more staff certainly provides the opportunity for, and eventual reality of, smaller classes.

Table 4.6 Predicted staffing ratios for select years

State	Teachers per 100 pupils				Change over time			
	1993	2002	2007	2012	1993–2007	20-year change	10-year change	5-year change
Alabama	5.58	6.41	7.76	6.68	2.18	1.09	0.27	−1.09
Alaska	5.60	5.76	5.77	6.06	0.18	0.46	0.30	0.29
Arizona	4.99	5.26	5.43	5.50	0.44	0.51	0.24	0.07
Arkansas	5.57	6.66	6.55	6.56	0.98	0.99	−0.10	0.01
California	4.03	4.89	4.85	4.40	0.83	0.37	−0.50	−0.46
Colorado	5.12	5.89	5.93	5.67	0.81	0.55	−0.22	−0.26
Connecticut	6.71	7.37	6.92	8.02	0.21	1.31	0.65	1.10
Delaware	5.77	6.54	6.60	6.95	0.83	1.18	0.41	0.35
District of Columbia	5.57	7.78	7.74	8.46	2.17	2.90	0.68	0.72
Florida	5.59	5.49	6.25	7.01	0.66	1.42	1.52	0.77
Georgia	5.30	6.48	7.16	6.79	1.87	1.49	0.31	−0.38
Hawaii	4.90	6.08	6.42	6.57	1.52	1.67	0.49	0.15
Idaho	4.81	5.34	5.39	5.54	0.58	0.73	0.20	0.15
Illinois	5.42	6.14	5.84	6.39	0.43	0.98	0.25	0.55
Indiana	5.33	5.83	5.62	5.85	0.29	0.52	0.02	0.23
Iowa	5.66	6.71	6.92	6.66	1.27	1.00	−0.05	−0.27
Kansas	6.06	6.68	6.89	7.39	0.84	1.33	0.70	0.49
Kentucky	5.45	6.00	6.50	6.17	1.05	0.72	0.17	−0.33
Louisiana	5.81	7.04	7.21	7.10	1.40	1.29	0.06	−0.11
Maine	6.49	7.43	8.04	7.64	1.55	1.15	0.21	−0.40
Maryland	5.90	6.45	7.22	7.13	1.32	1.24	0.68	−0.08
Massachusetts	6.28	8.24	7.61	7.35	1.33	1.07	−0.90	−0.26
Michigan	4.86	5.54	5.56	5.36	0.69	0.50	−0.17	−0.19
Minnesota	5.38	6.20	6.08	6.09	0.70	0.71	−0.12	0.01
Mississippi	5.24	6.10	6.56	6.56	1.32	1.32	0.45	0.00
Missouri	5.44	6.62	6.77	6.84	1.33	1.40	0.23	0.07
Montana	4.91	5.63	5.86	5.98	0.95	1.07	0.35	0.12
Nebraska	5.91	6.65	6.88	6.94	0.97	1.04	0.30	0.07
Nevada	5.47	5.90	5.87	5.81	0.40	0.34	−0.08	−0.05
New Hampshire	5.96	6.84	7.48	7.29	1.52	1.33	0.45	−0.19
New Jersey	7.04	7.78	8.26	8.22	1.22	1.19	0.44	−0.04
New Mexico	5.24	6.66	6.68	6.45	1.44	1.21	−0.22	−0.23
New York	6.52	7.45	7.97	8.10	1.45	1.58	0.65	0.12
North Carolina	5.72	6.56	7.45	6.60	1.73	0.88	0.04	−0.85
North Dakota	5.17	6.26	6.99	7.40	1.82	2.22	1.14	0.41
Ohio	5.41	6.38	5.67	5.76	0.26	0.35	−0.62	0.09
Oklahoma	5.53	6.06	6.05	5.84	0.52	0.31	−0.22	−0.21
Oregon	4.90	4.96	4.18	4.72	−0.71	−0.18	−0.24	0.54
Pennsylvania	5.43	6.25	6.59	7.10	1.16	1.67	0.86	0.51

(continued)

Table 4.6 (continued)

	Teachers per 100 pupils				Change over time			
State	1993	2002	2007	2012	1993–2007	20-year change	10-year change	5-year change
Rhode Island	6.96	7.23	7.70	8.57	0.74	1.62	1.34	0.87
South Carolina	5.56	6.68	7.02	6.50	1.46	0.93	−0.18	−0.53
South Dakota	5.52	6.30	6.52	6.45	1.00	0.93	0.15	−0.07
Tennessee	4.80	6.45	6.47	6.75	1.67	1.96	0.30	0.29
Texas	5.75	6.91	6.95	6.73	1.19	0.98	−0.18	−0.22
Utah	4.17	4.67	4.61	4.38	0.44	0.21	−0.30	−0.23
Vermont	5.48	7.00	7.59	7.49	2.11	2.01	0.50	−0.10
Virginia	6.24	7.45	8.92	7.54	2.68	1.30	0.09	−1.38
Washington	5.56	5.20	5.30	5.13	−0.26	−0.43	−0.07	−0.17
West Virginia	6.19	6.79	5.70	7.08	−0.50	0.89	0.29	1.38
Wisconsin	5.73	6.79	6.70	6.58	0.97	0.85	−0.21	−0.12
Wyoming	6.03	7.51	7.66	7.94	1.63	1.91	0.43	0.28

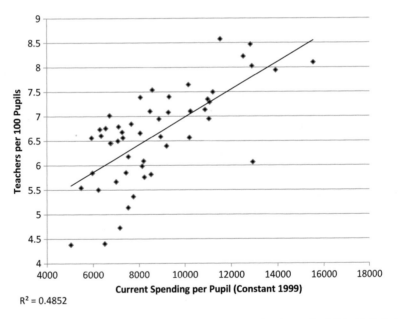

$R^2 = 0.4852$

Fig. 4.5 Spending levels and staffing levels 2011–2012 (Note: See Appendix (Table 4A.2) for full information by state)

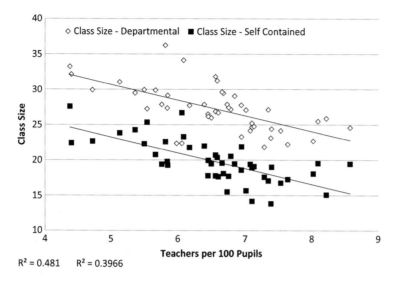

$R^2 = 0.481$ $R^2 = 0.3966$

Fig. 4.6 Relating total staffing and class size (Note: See Appendix (Table 4A.2) for full information by state)

Figure 4.7 shows that variation across states in current spending levels also translates to variation in the competitiveness of teacher wages. We have already seen that states where spending is higher tend to have more teachers per pupil and smaller class sizes, consuming a share of the funds that might also be used for providing more competitive wages.

Figure 4.7 shows that states where school districts spend more also tend to have teacher wages more comparable to nonteachers at the same age and degree level. In other words, combining Figs. 4.5 through 4.7, it would appear that much of the cross-state variation in school spending, which is driven by cross-state variation in fiscal effort, translates into real resource differences likely to matter—more competitive wages, lower pupil-to-teacher ratios, and smaller classes.

Figure 4.8 explores the within-state distribution of resources, asking whether there exists a relationship between current spending fairness across states' school districts and staffing fairness. That is, if current spending per pupil is higher in higher poverty districts within a given state, are staffing concentrations also higher—and vice versa? Do states that provide for fairer distribution of funding yield, on average, fairer distribution of staffing ratios? The answer to that question as seen in Fig. 4.8 is, setting aside outliers (North Dakota and Alaska), yes. See Appendix (Table 4A.2) for full information by state.

Each of the above graphs and related correlations expresses only the relationship across states within the most recent year of data. These graphs do not speak to the question of whether increases or decreases in funding translate to increases or decreases in real resource levels or fairness. Unfortunately, our only real resource measure collected annually from 1993 to 2012 at the district level—thus useful for

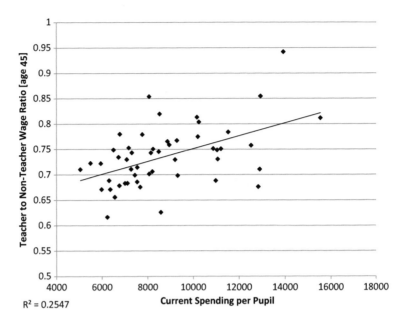

Fig. 4.7 Spending levels and competitive wages (Note: See Appendix (Table 4A.2) for full information by state)

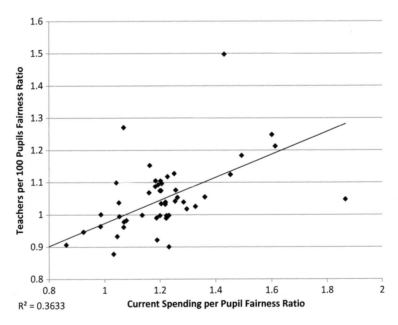

Fig. 4.8 Spending fairness and staffing fairness 2011–2012 (Note: See Appendix (Table 4A.2) for full information by state)

Table 4.7 Fixed effects model of pupil-to-teacher ratio fairness

DV=Teachers per 100 pupils fairness	Fixed effects N=50×20 years			Random effects N=50×20 years		
	Coef.	Std. err.	P>t	Coef.	Std. err.	P>t
Spending measures						
Spending fairness	0.417	0.022	a	0.432	0.020	a
Constant	0.564	0.026	a	0.546	0.026	a
R-Squared						
Within		0.278			0.278	
Between		0.694			0.694	
Overall		0.572			0.572	

[a]p<.01

evaluating both predicted state levels and within-state variation over time—is our pupil-to-teacher ratio measure.

Table 4.7 shows the results of a 20-year fixed effects model (also random effects) of the relationship between annual changes in spending levels and fairness, and pupil-to-teacher ratio fairness. The fixed effects model evaluates year-over-year changes within states. That is, to what extent do within-state changes in spending result in within-state changes in pupil-to-teacher ratio distributions? The random effects model combines evaluation of within-state differences over time with across-state differences. Cross-state differences evaluate the extent that states with fairer (or less fair) distributions of spending have fairer (or less fair) distributions of pupil-to-teacher ratios. R-squared values display the extent of variance that is explained by the models *within* states over time (averaged across states) and *between states* at each point in time (averaged over time). The more substantial variations across states than within any state over time yield more predictable variation (r-squared=.694).

In short, the model shows that when spending fairness improves, so too do staffing ratios in higher poverty districts. Each unit increase in funding fairness (increase in relative spending of higher poverty districts compared to lower poverty districts) translates to an additional 0.4 units of staffing per 100 pupils. Put into more realistic terms, an increase in fairness ratio from 1.0 (flat funding) to 1.25 (modestly progressive funding) leads to an increase in 0.1 of a teacher per 100 pupils in high poverty, relative to low poverty districts.

These differences exist across states but also occur within states over time. The magnitude of the change over time effect is only slightly smaller than the combined change over time and cross sectional effect. In other words, whether across states at all time periods, or within states over time, the responsiveness of pupil-to-teacher ratio fairness to spending fairness is relatively consistent.

To summarize, if we target additional funding to higher poverty settings, that funding translates to increased numbers of teachers and a fairer statewide distribution of staffing ratios in those districts. Of course, the inverse also follows.

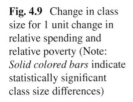

Fig. 4.9 Change in class size for 1 unit change in relative spending and relative poverty (Note: *Solid colored bars* indicate statistically significant class size differences)

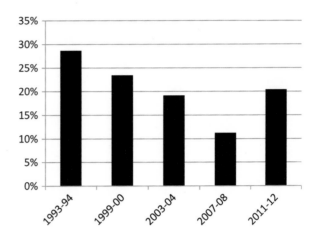

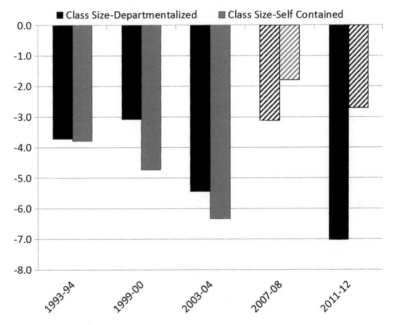

Fig. 4.10 Change in salary competitiveness for 1 unit change in relative spending (Note: *Solid colored bars* indicate statistically significant salary differences)

Figures 4.9 and 4.10 explore within year, over time, relationships between within-state variation in current spending and within-state (within-labor market) variation in (a) class sizes and (b) teacher wages (conditioned on age, experience, teaching assignment, grade level). Both figures are based on within-year (within SASS wave) models. Figure 4.9 shows that within-year (except for 2007–2008) class sizes across districts within metropolitan areas are sensitive to relative spending differences across districts within metropolitan areas. For example, as we move from average to double the average current spending, in 2011–2012, departmental-ized class sizes are reduced by over seven pupils. More realistically, as a district moves from average spending for its labor market to 20 % above average, class sizes are reduced by about 1.4 students (20 % of 7). Such reductions are sufficient to be policy relevant. Recall that these estimates are conditioned on grade level taught and relative district poverty rate and include only nonrural schools.

Figure 4.10 displays the relationship between the competitiveness of teacher salaries to other teachers with similar credentials in similar jobs on the same labor market. Teachers in districts in a given labor market where per-pupil spending is double the labor market average have 20 % higher wages than similar teachers in average spending districts on average in 2011–12. Taken together, Figs. 4.9 and 4.10 support the conclusion that spending variation translates to meaningful real resource variation across children and across districts within the same labor market. These differences are significant, and the resources in question are meaningful.

Conclusions and Implications

The analyses presented validate the conclusion that variations in available revenues and expenditures are associated with variations in children's access to real resources—as measured by the competitiveness of the wages paid to their teachers and by pupil-to-teacher ratios and class sizes. Put simply:

- States that apply more effort—spending a greater share of their fiscal capacity on schools—generally spend more on schools.
- These higher spending levels translate into higher statewide staffing levels—more certified teaching staff per pupil.
- These higher staffing levels translate to smaller statewide class sizes.
- These higher spending levels translate to more competitive statewide teacher wages.
- Districts that have higher spending levels within states tend to provide smaller class sizes than surrounding districts with lower spending levels.
- Districts that have higher spending levels within states tend to provide more competitive teacher salaries than surrounding districts with lower spending levels.

These relationships hold (a) across states, (b) within states over time as resource levels change and (c) across districts within states and labor markets. The connec-tions identified here between school funding and real resource access speak to both equity and adequacy concerns. Equity and adequacy of financial inputs to schooling across states are required if we ever expect to achieve more equitable access to a highly qualified teacher workforce (as dictated in part by the competitiveness of their compensation) and reasonable class sizes.

The loftier goal of equal educational opportunity—or equal opportunity across children to strive for common outcome goals—requires not merely equal real resources, but appropriately differentiated resources, including smaller classes and additional support services with at least equally qualified teachers and other school staff. While the press is on to nationalize those outcome expectations through Common Core Standards and the assessments by which we measure them, our current system for financing schools is in full retreat from the equity and adequacy gains made between 1993 and 2007.

The recent recession yielded an unprecedented decline in public school funding fairness. Thirty-six states had a 3-year average reduction in current spending fairness between 2008–2009 and 2010–2011, and 32 states had a 3-year average reduction in state and local revenue fairness over that same time period. Even after the partial rebound of 2012, 30 states remained less fair in current spending than in 2007. Nearly every state has experienced a long-term (10-year) decline in the competitiveness of teacher wages. Between 2007 and 2012, 33 states saw increases in pupil-to-teacher ratios.

Notably, while equity overall took a hit between 2007 and 2012, the initial state of funding equity varied widely at the outset of the period, with Massachusetts and New Jersey being among the most progressively funded states in 2007. Thus, they arguably had further to fall. Funding equity for many states has barely budged over time and remained persistently regressive, for example, in Illinois, New York, and Pennsylvania. Potential influences on these patterns are also elusive and widely varied. In Missouri, we see the 1990s influence of desegregation orders, which capitalized on the state's matching aid program to generate additional revenue in Kansas City and St. Louis driving spending progressiveness, but when the state adopted a need-weighted foundation aid formula in 2006, spending continued to become more regressive.

We see the more logical influence of school finance reforms in Massachusetts in the early 1990s and in New Jersey in the late 1990s after court orders targeting additional funds to needy districts, yielding an overall pattern of progressiveness. Court orders in New York state (2006) appears to have had little or no influence on equity, and the influence of court orders over time in Kansas have moved the needle only slightly. A better understanding of the role of judicial involvement requires significant additional exploration of these data linked to information on both judicial activity and legislative reforms.

Finally, the coming years will tell us both whether state school finance systems can rebound from the effects of the downturn or whether these effects have become permanent, and they will inform us about the consequences for short- and long-term student outcomes. A significant body of literature has now shown the positive effects of equity and adequacy improvements of the prior 40-plus years of school finance reform. Similar methods applied years from now may reveal the deleterious influences of these dark ages of American public school finance.

Appendix

Table 4A.1 Data sources, years, and measures

Data element	Unit of analysis	Data source	Years available	Years imputed
District level fiscal measures				
Per pupil spending	District	U.S. Census F-33 Public Elementary-Secondary Education Finance Survey (F-33)[a]	1993–2012	
State revenue	District	F-33	1993–2012	
Local revenue	District	F-33	1993–2012	
Federal revenue	District	F-33	1993–2012	
District characteristics				
Enrollment	District	National Center for Education Statistics (NCES), Common Core of Data (CCD)[b]	1993–2012	
Grade ranges	District	CCD	1993–2012	
Pupil/teacher ratios	District	CCD	1993–2012	
Regional cost variation				
Education comparable wage index	District	Taylor's Extended NCES Comparable Wage Index	1997–2012	1993–1996, 2012
Population needs/characteristics				
Child poverty[c]	District	U.S. Census Small Area Income and Poverty Estimates[d]	1995, 1997, 1999, 2000–2012	1993–1994, 1996, 1998
Teacher characteristics				
Teacher/nonteacher wages	Individual worker	IPUMS Census & American Community Survey	2000–2012	
Wages/compensation	Teacher linked to school/district (sample)	NCES Schools and Staffing Survey[e]	1993–1994, 1999–2000, 2003–2004, 2007–2008, 2011–2012	
Class size	School (sample)	NCES Schools and Staffing Survey	1993–1994, 1999–2000, 2003–2004, 2007–2008, 2011–2012	

[a]U.S. Census. Public Elementary–Secondary Education Finance Data
[b]U.S. Department of Education, National Center for Education Statistics. Common Core of Data
[c]See Baker et al. (2013b)
[d]U.S. Census. Small Area Income and Poverty Estimates, School District Data Files
[e]U.S. Department of Education, National Center for Education Statistics. Schools and Staffing Survey

Table 4A.2 Summary data by state

| State | Effort & revenue | | Spending & staffing | | | | | | Fairness | |
	Effort index (%)	State & local revenue ($)	Spending level ($)	Staffing level	Class size – departmental	Class size – Self contained	Wage ratio (%)		Spending Fairness	Staffing Fairness
Alabama	3.3	9013	7263	6.68	29.45	18.09	71.0		1.08	0.98
Alaska	3.4	13,745	12,934	6.06	22.38	26.70	85.4		1.87	1.05
Arizona	2.5	7122	6239	5.50	29.93	22.30	61.6		1.05	0.99
Arkansas	3.8	9554	7296	6.56	31.80	20.69	74.3		1.23	1.12
California	2.7	8104	6503	4.40	32.12	22.41	74.9		1.20	1.00
Colorado	2.8	8959	7000	5.67	29.87	20.77	68.3		1.16	1.07
Connecticut	3.9	15,863	12,901	8.02	22.68	18.07	71.0		1.07	0.96
Delaware	2.7	12,160	11,046	6.95	23.28	21.88	74.8		1.23	1.00
Florida	2.7	7684	6718	7.01	27.08	15.66	73.4		1.19	0.92
Georgia	3.6	8905	7104	6.79	27.16	20.54	68.3		1.20	1.03
Hawaii	3.1	12,339	10,203	6.57			77.5		1.08	0.98
Idaho	2.9	6462	5498	5.54	27.24	25.34	72.2		1.18	1.09
Illinois	3.8	11,911	9202	6.39	27.85	21.98	72.9		1.05	0.93
Indiana	3.6	10,587	7431	5.85	29.14	19.27	69.9		1.45	1.12
Iowa	3.5	11,565	8055	6.66	29.61	19.57	85.4		1.20	1.07
Kansas	3.7	10,693	8065	7.39	23.12	13.83	70.1		1.22	1.00
Kentucky	3.5	8992	7536	6.17	27.72	21.77	71.4		1.22	1.04
Louisiana	2.8	9568	8483	7.10	24.65	14.18	74.5		1.33	1.02
Maine	4.4	12,486	10,162	7.64	22.19	17.26	81.3		0.99	0.96
Maryland	3.8	13,759	10,877	7.13	24.75	19.08	75.1		1.14	1.00
Massachusetts	3.4	14,171	10,993	7.35	27.12	17.07	68.8		1.25	1.13
Michigan	3.8	9862	7756	5.36	29.47	24.26	77.9		1.20	1.10

Minnesota	3.3	11,067	8204	6.09	34.13	23.30	70.6	1.60	1.25
Mississippi	3.6	7471	5951	6.56	26.86	17.77	72.2	1.30	1.02
Missouri	3.3	9932	7666	6.84	29.05	19.44	67.5	1.05	1.04
Montana	3.3	9527	8141	5.98	22.36		74.3	1.18	1.11
Nebraska	3.2	10,550	8870	6.94	27.76	18.58	76.6	1.36	1.05
Nevada	2.8	10,668	8523	5.81	36.23	22.59	81.9	0.57	0.69
New Hampshire	4.0	13,668	11,077	7.29	21.81	17.58	73.0	1.07	1.27
New Jersey	4.8	15,862	12,528	8.22	25.89	15.08	75.8	1.26	1.08
New Mexico	3.3	9185	6775	6.45	26.49	17.78	78.0	1.29	1.04
New York	4.3	18,708	15,540	8.10	25.47	19.53	81.1	0.99	1.00
North Carolina	2.4	7004	6363	6.60	26.69	17.64	67.1	1.25	1.04
North Dakota	2.3	11,538	9316	7.40	24.40	19.01	69.8	1.43	1.50
Ohio	3.7	10,295	8236	5.76	27.86	19.40	75.0	1.16	1.15
Oklahoma	2.9	7371	5987	5.84	27.34	19.78	67.1	1.20	1.07
Oregon	2.6	9133	7159	4.72	29.90	22.66	75.3	1.22	0.99
Pennsylvania	3.9	14,127	10,248	7.10	25.20	18.93	80.3	0.92	0.95
Rhode Island	3.9	13,843	11,532	8.57	24.59	19.44	78.4	1.03	0.88
South Carolina	3.9	9505	7072	6.50	25.98	19.46	73.0	1.26	1.05
South Dakota	2.5	8498	6755	6.45	26.17	19.95	67.8	1.61	1.21
Tennessee	2.7	7263	6559	6.75	27.43	17.71	65.6	1.22	1.03
Texas	3.0	8634	6311	6.73	27.87	15.50	68.8	1.19	0.99
Utah	2.8	6443	5047	4.38	33.23	27.58	71.0	1.49	1.18
Vermont	5.1	15,126	11,214	7.49			75.1	0.86	0.91
Virginia	3.0	9989	8583	7.54	24.14	16.76	62.6	1.07	0.98
Washington	2.8	9752	7529	5.13	31.04	23.82	68.6	1.21	1.10
West Virginia	5.1	12,781	9279	7.08	24.14	19.40	76.7	1.19	1.09
Wisconsin	3.7	11,199	8947	6.58	31.20	20.37	75.9	1.23	0.90
Wyoming	3.6	17,394	13,920	7.94			94.2	1.04	1.10

References

Baker, Bruce D. 2012. *Revisiting the age-old question: Does money matter in education?* Washington, DC: Albert Shanker Institute.

Baker, Bruce D. 2014. Evaluating the recession's impact on state school finance systems. *Education Policy Analysis Archives* 22(91). doi:http://dx.doi.org/10.14507/epaa.v22n91.2014

Baker, Bruce, and Preston Green. 2009a. Conceptions, measurement and application of educational adequacy standards. In *AERA handbook on education policy*, ed. David N. Plank. New York: Routledge.

Baker, Bruce, and Preston Green. 2009b. Does increased state involvement in public schooling necessarily increase equality of educational opportunity? In *The rising state: How state power is transforming our nation's schools*, ed. Bonnie C. Fuscarelli and Bruce S. Cooper, 133. Albany: State University of New York Press.

Baker, Bruce D., and Kevin G. Welner. 2011. School finance and courts: Does reform matter, and how can we tell. *Teachers College Record* 113(11): 2374–14.

Baker, Bruce D., and Kevin G. Welner. 2012. Evidence and rigor scrutinizing the rhetorical embrace of evidence-based decision making. *Educational Researcher* 41(3): 98–101.

Baker, Bruce D., Joseph O. Oluwole, and Preston C. Green III. 2013a. The legal consequences of mandating high stakes decisions based on low quality information: Teacher evaluation in the race-to-the-top era. *Education Policy Analysis Archives* 21(5).

Baker, Bruce D., Lori Taylor, Jesse Levin, Jay Chambers, and Charles Blankenship. 2013b. Adjusted poverty measures and the distribution of title I aid: Does Title I really make the rich states richer? *Education Finance and Policy* 8(3): 394–417.

Baker, Bruce D., David G. Sciarra, and Danielle Farrie. 2014. *Is school funding fair? A national report card.* Newark: Education Law Center. http://www.schoolfundingfairness.org.

Borman, Geoffrey D., and Maritza Dowling. 2010. Schools and inequality: A multilevel analysis of Coleman's equality of educational opportunity data. *Teachers College Record* 112(5): 1201–1246.

Card, David, and A. Abigail Payne. 2002. School finance reform, the distribution of school spending, and the distribution of student test scores. *Journal of Public Economics* 83(1): 49–82.

Chingos, Matthew M. 2010. *The impact of a universal class-size reduction policy: Evidence from Florida's statewide mandate* (Program on Education Policy and Governance Working Paper 10–03). Cambridge, MA: Harvard University.

Clune, William H. 1994. The shift from equity to adequacy in school finance. *Educational Policy* 8(4): 376–394.

Corcoran, Sean, William N. Evans, Jennifer Godwin, Sheila E. Murray, and Robert M. Schwab. 2004. The changing distribution of education finance, 1972 to 1997. In *Social inequality*, ed. Kathryn M. Neckerman. New York: Russell Sage Foundation.

Deke, John. 2003. A study of the impact of public school spending on postsecondary educational attainment using statewide school district refinancing in Kansas. *Economics of Education Review* 22(3): 275–284.

Downes, Tom A. 2004. School finance reform and school quality: Lessons from Vermont. In *Helping children left behind: State aid and the pursuit of educational equity*, ed. John Yinger. Cambridge, MA: MIT Press.

Downes, Tom A., Jeff Zabel, and Dana Ansel. 2009. *Incomplete grade: Massachusetts education reform at 15*. Boston: MassINC. http://www.massinc.org/Research/Incomplete-Grade.aspx.

Duncombe, William, and John Yinger. 2005. How much more does a disadvantaged student cost? *Economics of Education Review* 24(5): 513–532.

Ehrenberg, Ronald G., Dominic J. Brewer, Adam Gamoran, and J. Douglas Willms. 2001. Class size and student achievement. *Psychological Science in the Public Interest* 2(1): 1–30.

Evers, Williamson M., and Paul Clopto. 2006. High-spending, low-performing school districts. In *Courting failure: How school finance lawsuits exploit judges' good intentions and harm our children*, ed. Eric Hanushek, 103–194. Palo Alto: Hoover Institution Press.

Ferguson, Ronald. 1991. Paying for public education: New evidence on how and why money matters. *Harvard Journal on Legislation* 28(2): 465–498.

Figlio, David N. 1997. Teacher salaries and teacher quality. *Economics Letters* 55: 267–271.

Figlio, David N. 2002. Can public schools buy better-qualified teachers? *Industrial and Labor Relations Review* 55: 686–699.

Figlio, David N. 2004. Funding and accountability: Some conceptual and technical issues in state aid reform. In *Helping children left behind: State aid and the pursuit of educational equity*, ed. John Yinger, 87–111. Cambridge, MA: MIT Press.

Figlio, David N., and Kim Rueben. 2001. Tax limits and the qualifications of new teachers. *Journal of Public Economics* (April): 49–71.

Greene, Jay P., and Julie R. Trivitt. 2008. Can judges improve academic achievement? *Peabody Journal of Education* 83(2): 224–237.

Guryan, Jonathan. 2001. *Does money matter? Estimates from education finance reform in Massachusetts* (NBER Working Paper 8269). Cambridge, MA: National Bureau of Economic Research. http://www.nber.org/papers/w8269.

Hanushek, Eric A. 1986. Economics of schooling: Production and efficiency in public schools. *Journal of Economic Literature* 24(3): 1141–1177.

Hanushek, Eric A. 1989. The impact of differential expenditures on school performance. *Educational Researcher* 18(4): 45–62.

Hanushek, Eric A. (ed.). 2006. *Courting failure: How school finance lawsuits exploit judges' good intentions and harm our children*. Palo Alto: Hoover Press.

Hanushek, Eric A. 2011. The economic value of higher teacher quality. *Economics of Education Review* 30(3): 466–479.

Hanushek, Eric A. 2009. Teacher deselection. In *Creating a new teaching profession*, ed. Dan Goldhaber and Jane Hannaway, 168, 172–173. Washington, DC: Urban Institute Press.

Hanushek, Eric A., and Alfred Lindseth. 2009. *Schoolhouses, courthouses and statehouses*. Princeton: Princeton University Press.

Hyman, Joshua. 2013. *Does money matter in the long run? Effects of school spending on educational attainment* (Working Paper). Ann Arbor: University of Michigan. http://www-personal. umich.edu/~jmhyman/Hyman_JMP.pdf.

Isenberg, E. P. 2010. The effect of class size on teacher attrition: Evidence from class size reduction policies in New York State. *US Census Bureau Center for Economic Studies* Paper CES-WP-10-05.

Jackson, C. Kirabo, Rucker Johnson, and Claudia Persico. 2015. *The effects of school spending on educational and economic outcomes: Evidence from school finance reforms* (NBER Working Paper No. 20847). Cambridge, MA: National Bureau of Economic Research. http://www.nber. org/papers/w20847

Jepsen, Christopher, and Steven Rivkin. 2002. *What is the tradeoff between smaller classes and teacher quality?* (NBER Working Paper 9205). Cambridge, MA: National Bureau of Economic Research. http://www.nber.org/papers/w9205.

Konstantopoulos, Spyros, and Geoffrey Borman. 2011. Family background and school effects on student achievement: A multilevel analysis of the Coleman data. *Teachers College Record* 113(1): 97–132.

Loeb, Susanna, and Marianne E. Page. 2000. Examining the link between teacher wages and student outcomes: The importance of alternative labor market opportunities and non-pecuniary variation. *Review of Economics and Statistics* 82(3): 393–408.

Loeb, Susanna, Linda Darling-Hammond, and John Luczak. 2005. How teaching conditions predict teacher turnover in California schools. *Peabody Journal of Education* 80(3): 44–70.

Mishel, Lawrence, Sylvia A. Allegretto, and Sean P. Corcoran. 2011. *The teaching penalty: An update through 2010* (EPI Issue Brief 298). Washington, DC: Economic Policy Institute. http://www.epi.org/publication/the_teaching_penalty_an_update_through_2010/.

Murnane, Richard J., and Randall Olsen. 1989. The effects of salaries and opportunity costs on length of state in teaching. Evidence from Michigan. *Review of Economics and Statistics* 71(2): 347–352.

Neymotin, Florence. 2010. The relationship between school funding and student achievement in Kansas public schools. *Journal of Education Finance* 36(1): 88–108.

Nguyen-Hoang, Phuong, and John Yinger. 2014. Education finance reform, local behavior, and student performance in Massachusetts. *Journal of Education Finance* 39(4): 297–322.

Ondrich, Jan, Emily Pas, and John Yinger. 2008. The determinants of teacher attrition in upstate New York. *Public Finance Review* 36(1): 112–144.

Papke, Leslie E. 2005. The effects of spending on test pass rates: Evidence from Michigan. *Journal of Public Economics* 89(5–6): 821–839.

Roy, Joydeep. 2011. Impact of school finance reform on resource equalization and academic performance: Evidence from Michigan. *Education Finance and Policy* 6(2): 137–167.

Sims, David. 2008. A strategic response to class size reduction: Combination classes and student achievement in California. *Journal of Policy Analysis and Management* 27(3): 457–478.

Sims, David. 2009. Crowding Peter to educate Paul: Lessons from a class size reduction externality. *Economics of Education Review* 28: 465–473.

Springer, Matthew G., Dale Ballou, Laura S. Hamilton, Vi-Nhuan Le, J.R. Lockwood, Daniel F. McCaffrey, Matthew Pepper, and Brian M. Stecher. 2011. *Teacher pay for performance: Experimental evidence from the project on incentives in teaching (POINT)*. Evanston: Society for Research on Educational Effectiveness.

U.S. Census. *Public elementary–Secondary education finance data*. http://www.census.gov/govs/school/

U.S. Department of Education. National Center for Education Statistics. Common Core of Data. http://nces.ed.gov/ccd/ccddata.asp

U.S. Department of Education. National Center for Education Statistics. Schools and Staffing Survey. http://nces.ed.gov/surveys/sass/

U.S. Census. *Small area income and poverty estimates*, School District Data Files. http://www.census.gov/did/www/saipe/data/schools/data/index.html

U.S. Department of Education, Institute of Education Sciences, National Center for Education Evaluation and Regional Assistance. 2003. *Educational practices supported by rigorous evidence: A user friendly guide*. Washington, DC. http://www2.ed.gov/rschstat/research/pubs/rigorousevid/rigorousevid.pdf

Walberg, Herbert J. 2006. *High poverty, high performance schools, districts and states*, 79–102. In Hanushek 2006.

Chapter 5
The Dynamics of Opportunity in America: A Working Framework

Henry Braun

Abstract Since its founding, America has been seen as a land of opportunity, where an individual with skills who was willing to work hard could achieve success and expect his children to do even better. Today we live in turbulent times: A tsunami of change is washing over us, driven by forces operating at multiple levels that have not only led to almost unprecedented inequalities in income and wealth, but also have dramatically restructured the economy and changed the landscape of work. Having sufficient amounts of relevant human and social capital are more critical than ever—and too many Americans are finding they are not equipped to succeed as workers and citizens. Growing inequities in access to opportunities to develop needed capital, strongly linked to socioeconomic status should be cause for grave concern. This chapter presents a framework—gates, gaps, and gradients—that can facilitate understanding of both the dynamics governing the distribution of access to opportunity across the developmental lifespan and the implications of those dynamics for intragenerational and intergenerational mobility. Further, it indicates in broad strokes how this nation can begin to broaden opportunity in order to revitalize the American Dream for the twenty-first century.

Keywords Opportunity • Globalization • Technology • Human capital • Wages • Educational attainment • Skills • Intergenerational mobility • Socioeconomic status (SES) • Unmarried mothers • Unemployment

Introduction

We live in turbulent times—economically, technologically, socially, and politically. A tsunami of change is washing over us, driven by forces operating at all levels: global, national, regional, and local. Some of these forces, such as globalization and technology, are supranational. Some, such as fiscal and trade policy, are decided at

H. Braun (✉)
Lynch School of Education, Boston College, Chestnut Hill, MA 02467, USA

© Educational Testing Service 2016
I. Kirsch, H. Braun (eds.), *The Dynamics of Opportunity in America*,
DOI 10.1007/978-3-319-25991-8_5

137

the national level. Others, such as education and health policies, are the result of a combination of national and state actions. Yet others, such as changes in the demographics of neighborhoods, are influenced by forces at all levels, such as international migration patterns, as well as by local laws and regulations adopted to achieve certain policy objectives or to accommodate the interests of various stakeholders.

Even prior to the Great Recession, stable employment and guaranteed retirement were pledged to fewer and fewer workers. Today, the nation is experiencing not only ongoing "creative destruction" of firms (and of jobs within firms) but also threats to both public and private pensions. Correspondingly, increasing numbers of individuals are either "under water" or confronting that prospect. Although some are able to ride the wave and prosper, they, too, face greater uncertainties. Indeed, for almost everyone, this is the *Age of Anxiety*.

That justifiable anxiety is, in part, a consequence of increasing inequality in both income and wealth driven by trends in labor and capital markets, as well as by differences in opportunities to accumulate relevant human capital. Arguably, today's differences will lead to even greater divergence in opportunities in the future. The implications of such a self-reinforcing, multigenerational cycle—for the economy, for society, and for our democratic polity—are a matter of current debate.[1] I believe that such a prospect is one we cannot afford to ignore. As Nobel Laureate Joseph Stiglitz argues, "An economic and political system that does not deliver for most citizens is one that is not sustainable in the long run. Eventually, faith in democracy and the market economy will erode, and the legitimacy of existing institutions and arrangements will be called into question.[2]

This is certainly not the first time in our country's history that we face great difficulties. In the past, however, there were two beliefs, held by many, that helped to sustain and inspire us to meet the challenges. The first was American exceptionalism—America was unlike (and better than) other countries, truly a light unto the nations. The second was that the U.S. was a land of unprecedented opportunity—no matter their circumstances at birth, individuals could realistically expect to improve themselves through education, hard work, and persistence, and more importantly, their children could aspire to do even better.

These beliefs are harder to maintain today. World events have shaken our belief in American exceptionalism, and reams of statistics—not to mention the experiences of tens of millions of individuals—cast doubt on meaningful opportunity in America being available to all. Indeed, surveys show that many older persons, especially parents, believe that the next generation will not do as well

---

[1] Stiglitz 2012; Cowen 2013.

[2] Joseph Stiglitz, "Climate Change and Poverty Have Not Gone Away," *Guardian*, January 7, 2013, http://www.theguardian.com/business/2013/jan/07/climate-change-poverty-inequality.

as they have—and even fewer adults consider themselves members of the middle class.[3]

Historically, differences in opportunity were associated with race and, indeed, this was the prime motivation for the Great Society legislation pursued by President Lyndon Johnson in the mid-1960s. Although differences by race and ethnicity persist and remain substantial, there is considerable evidence that differences (say, in test scores) by income are now larger than those by race. Moreover, differences by income within a race/ethnicity category are also quite striking (Reardon 2011; Murray 2012). As will be demonstrated in what follows, individual differences in opportunity result in differences in individuals' levels of preparedness to successfully meet the demands of adult life—as workers, citizens and, for most, parents. That level of preparedness is often signified by the term human capital. This chapter focuses on human capital: what it is, how it develops and is accumulated, what is happening to its distribution across the U.S. population, and some possible consequences if current trends continue.

Before diving in, let's look at some data to give us a sense of the state of inequality in America. Following the old adage that a picture is worth a thousand words, we begin with some graphs. Figure 5.1 shows the percentile trajectories for wages and salaries from 1961 to 2000. For about 30 years after World War II, the relationships among the trajectories remained fairly stable, that is, greater prosperity was generally shared. After 1975, and certainly after 1980, the income trajectories began to diverge, quite dramatically. What is especially noteworthy is how the top percentiles

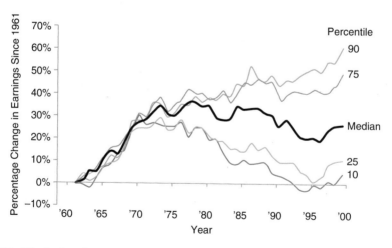

Fig. 5.1 Distribution of real wage and salary earnings for full-year, full-time males workers aged 18–64 as compared to 1961–2000 (Used by permission of The Aspen Institute)

---

[3]Leslie McCall, "Political and Policy Responses to Problems of Inequality: Past, Present and Future" (unpublished presentation, *Opportunity in America* advisory panel meeting, June 2014).

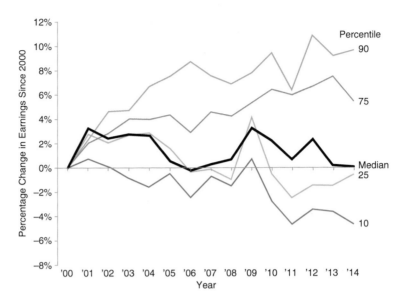

Fig. 5.2 Distribution of real wage and salary earnings for full-year, full-time male workers aged 16 and over, as compared to 2000 (Source: Author's tabulations of the Current Population Survey)

have pulled away from the rest—a striking manifestation of increasing inequality.[4] Figure 5.2 presents an analogous picture but employs 2000 as a new starting point. Clearly the divergence in earnings between the higher and lower percentiles has continued through 2014. Putting the two figures together yields a disturbing picture of increasing inequality.

Figure 5.3, which offers a more focused view of this phenomenon, displays the cumulative change (1979–2010) in real annual wages by income group, defined by percentiles of the income distribution.[5] Evidently, the increases garnered by the top 1 % dwarf those in the 95th—99th and the 90th—95th percent categories. But these are still more than double the 15 % gain of the rest (the "bottom" 90 %) (Thompson 2012). The divergence is even more striking for changes in total annual household income (i.e., including both capital gains and income transfers)—and more striking still if one considers household wealth or shares of the stock market (Piketty 2014; for a quicker look, see Thompson 2012).[6] At the same time, some economists argue

---

[4] Tabulations by Professor David Ellwood, Harvard University.

[5] Economic Policy Institute (State of Working America). It is important to understand that this graph does not follow specific people over time but, rather, is constructed anew each year. Thus, it doesn't tell us anything about the (relative) income mobility or immobility of particular individuals.

[6] Data from the Congressional Budget Office shows that the cumulative growth in average after-tax income (sum of market income and government transfers minus federal tax liabilities) did not vary much across the bottom four quintiles.

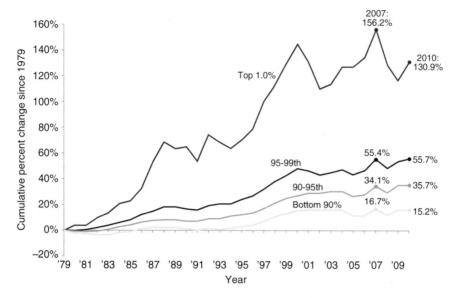

Fig. 5.3 Cumulative change in real annual wages, by wage group, 1979–2010 (Economic Policy Institute, 2012, "Cumulative Change in Real Annual Wages, by Wage Group, 1979–2010", The State of Working America, Washington, DC: Economic Policy Institute, Aug. 22, 2012, www. stateofworkingamerica.org/jobs/figure4H)

that focusing on the trajectory of the "1 %" is misguided, at least with respect to addressing the broader issues of inequality (Mankiw 2013).[7]

Figure 5.4 displays the 50-year trajectories of real wages for different levels of educational attainment, separately for men and women (Autor 2014; see also Acemoglu and Autor 2012, Fig. 3). Although there are some differences between males and females, in general, individuals with higher levels of attainment have done well, while those at the lowest levels have either stagnated (high school diploma) or even lost ground (less than a high school diploma). Who are the individuals in that last category? Table 5.1 offers one answer. It displays the probability of individuals lacking a high school diploma or GED as a function of their family income and their Armed Services Vocational Aptitude Battery (ASVAB) score, a composite measure of developed skills.[8] More than 35 % of individuals coming from poor families with ASVAB scores in the lowest quintile fall in this category of attainment, with the percentages falling with increasing family income and dramatically so with higher ASVAB scores.

---

[7] Tyler Cowen," It's Not the Inequality; It's the Immobility." *New York Times,* April 5, 2015, http://www.nytimes.com/2015/04/05/upshot/its-not-the-inequality-its-the-immobility.html?abt=0002&abg=1.

[8] Data compiled by the Center for Labor Market Studies, Northeastern University. For more information see http://official-asvab.com/index.htm.

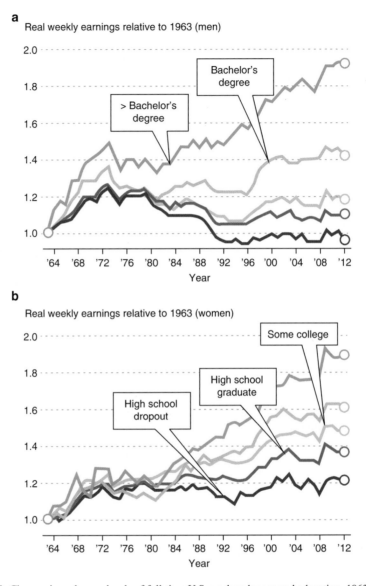

Fig. 5.4 Changes in real wage levels of full-time U.S. workers by sex and education, 1963–2012 (Reproduced from Autor 2014)

The last graph in this series, Fig. 5.5, compares the problem-solving skills of American adults (ages 16–65) to those of other developed countries. Comparisons are displayed for two age classes. This is also very striking: For the oldest age class (55–64), the U.S. is at the top, but for the youngest age class (16–24), the U.S. is at the bottom (OECD 2013, Fig. 3.3).

What do these pictures tell us? Figures 5.1, 5.2 and 5.3 demonstrate that rising income inequality is real. Even when government benefits are taken into account there is still a widening gap between the bottom 50 % and the top 10 %, and even more so if attention focuses on the top 1 % or, especially, the top 0.1 %. Figure 5.4 and Table 5.1 together show that income inequality is strongly related to the amount

Table 5.1 Percent of 24- to 28-year-old adults in the U.S. in 2008 without a high school diploma or GED by ASVAB test score quintile and family's income in their teenaged years in 1997 (Andrew Sum 2014, presentation to *Opportunity in America* panel)

	(A)	(B)	(C)	(D)	(E)	(F)
Family income	Bottom	Second	Middle	Fourth	Top	All
Poor	35.9	15.4	10.6	4.7	0	22.9
1–2* poor	30.0	11.1	6.5	2.3	4.3	15.4
2–3* poor	19.8	8.4	5.2	1.2	0	6.7
3–4* poor	19.0	5.8	7.4	1.2	0	4.0
4 or more * poor	16.3	1.7	.6	0	0	2.1
All	28.3	8.2	3.7	1.5	.5	

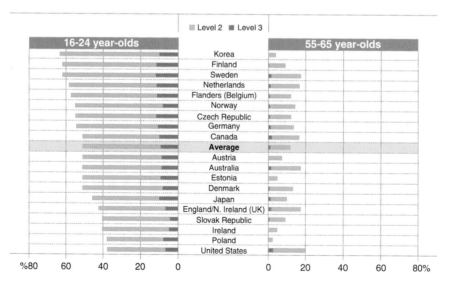

Fig. 5.5 Problem-solving proficiency among younger adults (age 16–24) and older adults (age 55–65) (OECD 2013)
Percentage of adults aged 16–24 and 55–65 scoring at level 2 or 3 in problem solving in technology-rich environments

of education achieved and that those with weak skills and coming from poor families are likely to fall in the lowest category of attainment.[9] It is reasonable to conclude that individuals with low skills are unlikely to earn a good wage while those with high skills have an excellent chance of doing so. In point of fact, there are now millions of individuals with low skills confronting poor job prospects.

Figure 5.5 signals America's relative decline. Today's young adults may not be less literate than their elders (and may well be more proficient with technology), but other countries have charged ahead so that too many of our young adults are not competitive in the global marketplace and, more and more, the global marketplace influences what happens in towns and cities across America. Unfortunately, the problem is not confined to the youngest cohort. As Kevin Carey of the New America Foundation has pointed out, comparisons of literacy skills among 25 to 29-year-olds who are college graduates show that Americans again fall well below the Organisation for Economic Co-operation and Development average.[10] Similar findings hold for numeracy skills (see Fig. 8 of Goodman, Sands, and Coley 2015).

There is a growing consensus that current trends, if left unchecked, pose a serious threat not only to the American Dream, but to the American way of life (Stiglitz 2012; Noah 2013). If that is the case, we must understand these forces and their interactions if we are to have even a possibility of countering their effects. At the same time, given the multiplicity of factors and the range of dynamics among them, it would be naïve to believe that there is a simple fix such as to just "improve education" or "make the income tax more progressive"; rather, it is surely necessary to undertake a broad set of strategies that are systematic, systemic, and sustained. This will be neither simple nor easy.

The chief purpose of this chapter, undertaken under the auspices of the *Opportunity in America* project and funded by Educational Testing Service, is to present a framework that can help us to understand both the dynamics governing the distribution of access to opportunity in America and the implications of those dynamics for intragenerational and intergenerational mobility. It offers some of the relevant evidence and constitutes an initial foray into an exceedingly complex and controversial topic. The ultimate goal of the project is to contribute to a constructive public debate on the implications of increasing inequality and social stratification, however measured, and how we can dramatically expand opportunity in order to revitalize the American Dream for the 21st century.

---

[9] It appears that differences in educational attainment better account for differences in income below the median than they do above the median – especially differences within the top quintile.

[10] Kevin Carey, "Americans Think We Have the World's Best Colleges. We Don't," *New York Times,* June 28, 2014, http://www.nytimes.com/2014/06/29/upshot/americans-think-we-have-the-worlds-best-colleges-we-dont.html.

What Is Opportunity?

Opportunity is defined by Merriam-Webster as *a favorable juncture of circumstances*. For our purposes it can be thought of as the set of paths by which a child's potential develops over time into the broad set of skills, competencies, and dispositions (i.e., the human capital) that will enable him or her to successfully navigate adult life. By inequality of opportunity we mean that the paths for some children present relatively few obstacles to their developmental trajectories; for others, there are many obstacles and, consequently, they are less likely to be able to amass needed human capital.[11]

Not surprisingly, the path a child traverses is strongly related to his or her family's circumstances at birth and the early years that follow. In fact, the data show that those children born with substantial advantages are on track to accumulate a great deal of human capital and, consequently, are very unlikely to fall much below their beginnings, at least with respect to their relative standing on the income ladder.[12] By contrast, those children born into pervasive disadvantage face great difficulties in accumulating human capital and are very unlikely to rise much above their beginnings with respect to their relative standing.[13] As one recent study in Baltimore argues, an impoverished childhood casts a "long shadow" on adult outcomes (Alexander et al. 2014).

Of course there are anecdotes of children "beating the odds" and achieving great success despite an unpromising start.[14] But the data indicate that they are the rare exception and not the rule. And we must ask: Do we want America to be a country where millions of children must be heroes in order to achieve a modicum of security and stability?

---

[11] Although the focus of this chapter is on the distribution of opportunities to develop human capital over the age span of 0–25, there are also differential opportunities in adulthood to productively employ that human capital and continue to amass it through one's lifespan. The former is addressed in a later section on gradients. Relevant factors include general skill-labor market fit, workplace discrimination, and secular economic trends. The latter depends on the nature of employment, the availability and affordability of venues for education and training, and individual choice.

[12] As one reviewer pointed out, the typical child whose father earns $500,000 at age 40 may, when he or she reaches age 40, be earning only $300,000. This would be a manifestation of regression to the mean. The child then may have lost ground on absolute mobility but very little on relative mobility.

[13] See for example, publications based on The Brookings Institution's *Social Genome Project* (Brookings Institution 2013). For a more positive outlook on the impact of sustained and systematic interventions, see Sawhill and Karpilow 2014.

[14] There is some empirical evidence that succeeding against the odds takes a physical and psychological toll that has consequences in later years. See Brody et al. (2013).

The Challenge

Understanding the dynamics underlying current trends and patterns in the distribution of opportunity across income levels and social strata, as well as increasing income inequality and stagnant intergenerational mobility, is critical to formulating meaningful policy responses.[15] This is an exceedingly difficult task, made more challenging because the forces in question have a wide range. They include such factors as global macroeconomic trends, the transmission from parents to children of advantage (or disadvantage) related to family characteristics and resources, and neighborhood environment. Adding to this challenge is that both inequality and intergenerational mobility have been defined in different ways and studied with different populations, sometimes yielding different results (Black and Devereux 2010; Blanden 2013).

We also must take into account personal responsibility—the choices that individuals make along their life path and the consequences of those choices. That is, success in accumulating human capital and, subsequently, in the labor market depends on not only having opportunities but also taking advantage of them (see Chap. 8). Finally, the statistical averages that are often cited, whether of cognitive skills or income, mask enormous variation by geographical location, race/ethnicity, and other factors. This variation must be taken into account not only in understanding inequality but also in formulating policy prescriptions.

In order to sort out and make some sense of the wealth of empirical research that has been carried out, it is helpful to have a framework that can structure a description of how a child's potential and family circumstances at birth, interacting over time with forces large and small, result in a young adult (say, age 25) who is more or less ready to take responsibility for his or her future and lead a life of accomplishment and fulfillment.

The framework we propose is captured by the three-part metaphor of *gates, gaps,* and *gradients*. The next section introduces this framework, which is then used to describe some of the factors that contribute to differences in opportunity and the resulting variation in accumulated human capital. The final section looks forward to some policy actions that could counter current trends.

The Framework: Gates/Gaps/Gradients

The first element of the framework is *Gates*, a metaphor for how opportunity in America is increasingly determined by income, wealth, and socioeconomic status (SES), as well as by race/ethnicity. From birth to, say, age 25, individuals

---

[15] Intergenerational mobility (IGM) is a measure of the probability that a child with parents at one level in society will, as an adult, reside in a different level—higher or lower. The most commonly used scales are income, years of education, and socioeconomic status. Economists sometimes use the term intergenerational elasticity (IGE), which is the opposite of IGM.

accumulate the human capital, broadly conceived, that will play a critical role in their adult outcomes. The dimensions of human capital include a variety of cognitive and noncognitive skills, as well as dispositions, experiences, and flexibility (see Keeley 2007; Pellegrino and Hilton 2012). At each stage of development, the gates represent access or obstacles to opportunities to add human capital, building on whatever potential individuals may have, as well as the human capital they already possess. For individuals born in higher strata (by income, SES, or other) the gates are mostly open, offering access to a multitude of opportunities. For individuals born in lower strata, the gates are mostly closed so that there are fewer opportunities to amass essential high-quality human capital at a developmentally appropriate stage (Fishkin 2014).

The use of the term "gates" is motivated by the gated communities that have sprung up over the last few decades and are perhaps the most visible aspect of the stratification of opportunity. Children born in such privileged communities have multiple opportunities to develop their human capital, while those born outside of them often have fewer.

However, stratification of opportunity goes far beyond these enclaves of privilege. According to some investigators, over the last few decades, residential segregation by income has remained fairly stable and by race/ethnicity has even declined slightly. Others argue that residential segregation by income has increased. All agree, however, that Blacks and Hispanics remain much more segregated than Whites and Asians (Rugh and Massey 2013; Bischoff and Reardon 2013). Neighborhood differences in income are, in turn, strongly associated with differences in private and public investments in children such as parental attention, school quality, the nature and extent of social networks, and so on (Bischoff and Reardon 2013). These and other factors largely determine which gates are open to some children—and closed to others.

Indeed, it is worth noting that as neighborhoods become more homogeneous with respect to income, so do children's peer groups (Ibid.). This homogeneity carries over to school—whether a neighborhood public school or a private school (parochial or nonsectarian). Increasingly, children find themselves in schools segregated by income as well as by race and ethnicity (Coley and Baker 2013).

Stratification by income also leads to neighborhoods that are more homogeneous with respect to percentages of adults in the labor force or facing long-term unemployment, as well as the types of work engaged in by those who are employed. Such patterns are determined in large part by the type and extent of the human capital that adults bring to the labor market, as well as labor market trends in the kinds of occupations with openings, the salaries and benefits offered, and their locations (Levy and Murnane 2013). At the low end of the spectrum, neighborhoods in which a plurality of adult males either are or have been incarcerated are characterized by high unemployment, high levels of crime, and a lack of positive role models.

As noted at the outset, these trends are driven not only by globalization and the rapid advances in technology but also by interactions among market forces, regulatory decisions, and legislation. Inasmuch as how these trends shape parents' or guardians' circumstances, children's opportunities are indirectly—but powerfully—affected by both macroeconomic factors and general societal trends.

Gaps is a metaphor for the differences among individuals in an age cohort at various points in time in the distributions of human capital. The gaps at the start of full adulthood are a consequence of the dynamic interactions between gates and gaps at each stage of the age span (Sawhill and Karpilow 2014). For example, differences at birth related to various gates being open, ajar, or fully closed lead to gaps as early as they can be measured (see Chap. 8). In turn, those gaps interact with the gates at age 5 (strongly correlated with those at birth) to produce additional gaps by age 14. This process evolves through successive transition points to age 25 and beyond. By age 25 there is great variability in the types and magnitudes of human capital that have been accumulated—and much of that variability can be traced back to individuals' family circumstances at birth and in their formative years.

Gates and Gaps Together

It is particularly important to understand how gates and gaps interact over time to produce gates and gaps at the next stage.[16] A good example is provided by individuals applying to college at the end of high school. Students from poorer families with weak grades and low test scores face many closed gates: Not only are top-tier colleges and universities out or reach, but when they enroll at community colleges they find that they must take one or more so-called remedial courses, a path that often leads to dropping out before obtaining a degree or certificate. (Bettinger et al. 2013; National Center for Public Policy and Higher Education Special Report 2010).[17]

Sometimes the gates are less obvious. Students coming from families without college experience are less adept at navigating the admissions and financial aid processes and have fewer resources upon which to draw. In fact, a recent study finds that many able, top-scoring minority students coming from lower SES families don't even apply to top-tier colleges, thinking they don't qualify and couldn't afford them if they were accepted (Hoxby and Avery 2013). This problem stems from the lack of a certain kind of social capital, a lack that is amenable to policy intervention (Hoxby and Turner 2014).

One consequence of this dynamic between gates and gaps is relatively homogeneous college campuses, leading to assortative mating and further divergence in

---

[16] The recognition that such dynamic interactions over, say, ages 0–18 can have powerful effects on the distribution of adult skills is implicit in Brookings Institution, *Social Genome Project,* and explicit in the work of James Heckman and his associates http://heckmanequation.org/content/resource/case-investing-disadvantaged-young-children.

[17] The problem of high school graduates going on to tertiary education but required to take one or more noncredit-bearing courses (sometimes designated as *remedial* or *developmental*) is more pervasive than one that just concerns students from low-income families. While some studies estimate 35–40 % of students entering college need at least one remedial course, other studies place the estimate as high as 60 %.

personal/family trajectories (McClanahan 2014). This divergence is even more pronounced when one looks at the full birth cohort, which includes those who dropped out of high school or completed high school but did not go on for further education or training (see Chap. 7, Fig. 7.13).

Gradients is a metaphor for the strength of the relationships between the dimensions of human capital on the one hand, and various life outcomes on the other. Life outcomes include whether the individual is employed, the nature and remuneration (salary and benefits) of that employment, the possibility of obtaining further education/training, accumulation of wealth, the likelihood of forming stable family units, and having children in the context of those partnerships. The data show that the gradients are typically quite steep; that is, modest differences in human capital can result in substantial differences in outcomes. For example, both the likelihood of full-time employment and the likelihood of having children in the context of a two-parent family are strongly correlated with levels of educational attainment and cognitive skills. Gradients are critical because they account for much of the relative advantage or disadvantage that is passed on to the next generation.

It is worth pointing out that gradients are typically not linear. That is, there are inflection points such that there can be large differences in outcomes for individuals who are close in many facets of human capital. For example, individuals with similar cognitive skills but who differ in whether they obtained a college degree can have very different adult trajectories. On the other hand, differences between inflection points may be less consequential.

In the remainder of the chapter, the gates/gaps/gradients framework will be used to organize some of the voluminous literature concerning the forces and processes driving differences in opportunity, as well as the extent of those differences.

The Dynamics of Inequality

The Birth Lottery

For a newborn, whether the gates to different opportunities are open or closed depends very much on family structure and income. Of course, these are mutually dependent and strongly associated with other relevant factors such as parental education, housing, neighborhood characteristics, and school quality.[18] All these factors have a direct bearing on the investments, private and public, that are made in children.

In general, children born to mothers who are single or in unstable relationships face more closed gates, and the rates of such births vary substantially by mother's race/ethnicity, age, educational attainment, and location. Although nonmarital birth rates are generally declining for all groups, the proportion of all births to unmarried

---

[18] The work of Heckman and his associates is relevant here. For a summary of that work, see Heckman, *Case for Investing.*

mothers is still very high. For example, as of 2012, the proportion of nonmarital births overall was 40.7 %.[19] However, the proportions varied considerably by race/ethnicity: They were 72.6 % for non-Hispanic Blacks, 54 % for Hispanics, and 29 % for non-Hispanic Whites. As one might expect, there is also considerable variation among states in both birth rates and proportions of nonmarital births.[20]

To introduce further nuance to this picture, it appears that less than 20 % of mothers who give birth out of wedlock are truly single; the others are in some form of relationship with the father (Wise 2013). However, these dyads are quite fragile. Follow-up data show that by their fifth birthday, 61 % of these children have experienced the dissolution of the relationship between the parents. By contrast, of children born to married parents, only 18 % have experienced a dissolution by their fifth birthday.[21]

Research supports the criticality of the period from birth to age 5. Not only is brain growth greater than at any other postnatal stage, but also the character of the early learning environment influences patterns of neural growth that in turn are related to the capacity to develop human capital (Fox et al. 2010).[22] By now there is an extensive research base that documents the conditions that strongly predict whether or not a child thrives in this critical period (Barton and Coley 2013). Some of these conditions typically involve monetary investments. They include pre- and postnatal care, good maternal health, adequate shelter and nutrition, living in a nontoxic environment, appropriate medical and dental care, and high quality day care (when needed). Other conditions involve nonmonetary investments. These include establishing a nurturing relationship, parental attention, socioemotional development, as well as cultivation of early language and numeracy skills.

There is an equally extensive research base that demonstrates that the probability that a child experiences something close to the ideal increases with income and stable family structure. Toward the high end of the income ladder, the gates are mostly open and the child is very likely to thrive; that is, grow up healthy and secure—arriving at school ready both cognitively and socioemotionally. Toward the low end of the ladder, many gates are closed and the child is much less likely to

---

[19] Birth rates are usually calculated as the number of births per 1,000 women in a particular category (e.g., unmarried women aged 15–19). Although nonmarital birth rates have been declining, it is still possible for the proportion of nonmarital births overall to be increasing. The explanation is that the proportion is a function of both category-specific birth rates and the distribution of women among the categories.

[20] For example, teen birth rates varied from a low of 13.8 % in New Hampshire to a high of 42.5 % in New Mexico; Centers for Disease Control 2013. For an explanation of the apparent paradox of declining birth rates and high proportions of nonmarital births, see Wise 2013.

[21] Tach's tabulations from the Fragile Families & Child Wellbeing Surveys, Waves 3–4, quoted in Smeeding, *Connecting Inequality and Intergenerational Mobility: Looking Ahead, Not Behind* (unpublished presentation).

[22] There is also evidence of continuing neuroplasticity into adolescence. An experiment in Chicago Public Schools focuses on accelerating the development of the math skills of African-American and Latino ninth and 10th graders who are lagging behind their age peers. See David L. Kirp, "Closing the Math Gap for Boys," Sunday Review, *New York Times,* January 31, 2015.

thrive. Similarly, children who are raised in two-parent families are more likely to find the gates open than are children raised in single-parent families, particularly if the mother is younger and not in a committed relationship (Grannis and Sawhill 2013; Doyle et al. 2009, 1–6; Heckman and Masterov 2007). Whether the gates are mostly open or closed is one manifestation of the constellation of conditions that are typical of higher incomes and/or two-parent families on the one hand, and of lower income and/or single parent families on the other. In both cases, there are powerful implications for future development.

Adequate nutrition can serve as a bellwether indicator of a child's environment. Food insecurity is strongly associated with family structure. Using 2011 survey data, it was found that female-headed households (no spouse) had a 37 % rate of food insecurity, while married couple households had a 14 % rate (Coley and Baker 2013, Fig. 7); both groups saw increases from 2005). Not surprisingly, the relationship between family income and food insecurity is particularly strong. For families with incomes below the poverty level, the rate is 45 %, while for families with incomes at least 1.85 times the poverty level, the rate is only 8 %.

Poverty is also associated with other obstacles to normal development. For example, studies find that lower income mothers report higher rates of maternal depression than do their higher income peers. A depressed individual is less likely to provide the attention and nurturing that are important to an infant thriving. Moreover, in comparison to children born to more affluent families, children growing up in poorer homes are more likely to be exposed to tobacco smoke and have higher blood levels of lead (Aizer and Currie 2014; Coley and Baker 2013, p. 19).

Many toddlers receive care outside of their own home, either in another home (a relative's or other) or in a center (e.g., early learning centers, nursery schools, and preschools). Among children around 4 years old receiving nonparental day care, poor ones were much more likely to receive low-quality care than nonpoor were (Coley and Baker 2013, Table 8). Not surprisingly, family income is strongly associated with the ability to make private expenditures on behalf of children. Data show that, in 2005–2006, parents in the highest income quintile invested nearly $8900 in children's enrichment, while those in the lowest quintile invested slightly more than $1,300, a ratio of 6.8. By comparison, in the years 1972–1973, the ratio was only 4.2 (Duncan and Murnane 2011, Fig. 1.6; see also Kaushal, Magnuson, and Waldfogel 2011).

As noted earlier, the gates to different opportunities tend to be open or closed in tandem. A child born to a young, single mother is more likely to grow up in poverty than one born to parents in a committed, stable relationship. The former is also more likely to live in a stressful environment, less likely to have positive extra-home experiences, such as visits to museums or exhibitions, and to receive beneficial contributions from extended family. It is repeatedly encountering closed gates (or, in other terms, multiple risk factors) that places many children at great disadvantage in their early years and beyond.

Thus, children born to families in different circumstances tend to develop along very different trajectories. Differences in cognitive skills, which are examples of what we here refer to as gaps, appear early on—as early as can be measured (Halle et al. 2009, 87–119; for an international perspective, see Bradbury et al. 2013). By the time children enroll in kindergarten, differences in readiness are striking. These results are consistent with the well-known findings of very large differences in vocabulary among kindergarten children from different SES strata (Hart and Risley 1995).

Clearly, the variation in environmental factors documented above is an important contributor. Direct parental investment in children's cognitive development also plays a role. Survey data reveal large differences by SES quintile. The percentage of kindergarteners whose parents read to them every day ranges from 62 % in the highest quintile to 36 % in the lowest. As one might expect, even within quintiles, there are noteworthy differences by race/ethnicity (Coley and Baker 2013).

Beginning School

The same conditions that are conducive to development from birth to age 5 are important for further development in the elementary grades. To the extent that family circumstances remain reasonably stable, the pattern of gates open or closed at birth is typically replicated at age 5—unless (usually) public interventions are successful in opening those gates that are closed.[23]

Children with more accumulated human capital tend also to have more gates open to new opportunities, such as attending schools that are of higher quality (with respect to such features as teaching staff, safety, and physical plant), more parental involvement in schooling, more extracurricular experiences, and benefiting from good nutrition and adequate medical/dental care. Children with lesser amounts of accumulated human capital are more likely to attend lower quality schools with fewer extracurricular activities. They are also more likely to suffer from health problems (e.g., asthma) and medical/dental problems that result in increased school absences and less engagement when in school.

Children starting behind in K-1 have difficulty catching up. Many are not reading on grade level by the end of grade 3—they are still "learning to read" rather than "reading to learn." Studies show that students who enter kindergarten with little to no text comprehension skills are far behind peers with average or high text comprehension skills, and this gap continues to widen through third grade. A similar trend is found in mathematics—a child entering kindergarten who does poorly in basic numbers skills will only fall further and further behind peers by third grade (Foster and Miller 2007; Bodovski and Farkas 2007).

Of course, an important mission of schools is to close the gaps that are evident on the first day of class. But the schools attended by poor children—many if not most of whom are on the wrong side of the gap—are often ill-equipped to do so. Teachers in these schools are more likely to have fewer years of experience and less likely to have the requisite qualifications than teachers in schools serving more

---

[23] A discussion of such interventions is beyond the scope of this chapter.

affluent students. Moreover, those schools experience greater instability, with respect to both staff and students, so that there are fewer opportunities for students to receive coherent, systematic instruction.

Of course, peer interactions are an important component of schooling. In parallel with increased residential segregation, over the past two decades schools have become more segregated both by income and by race/ethnicity. As commentators have noted, "While the average White student attends a school where poor students account for a quarter to a third of enrollment, the typical Black or Hispanic student attends a school where nearly two-thirds of their peers are low-income" (Orfield et al. 2012, quoted in Coley and Baker 2013, p. 25). They also point out that "38 and 43 % of Black and Hispanic students, respectively, attended schools where 90–100 % of students were minorities."

As poor and minority students make their way through school, they are more likely to experience suspensions, be required to repeat a grade and, eventually, drop out before completing high school. In 2009, students from the lowest family income quintile were about five times more likely to drop out than students from the highest quintile were.[24] Thus, by late adolescence or early adulthood, the gaps in cognitive skills are substantial and likely the result of the interaction of earlier gaps and current school quality. Presumably, this is one of the mechanisms by which later gaps are still strongly associated with family background.

Another kind of gap relates to flexibility and resilience. Those who have had the benefit of open gates—and have taken advantage of the opportunities offered them—find themselves on the right side of the gaps related to flexibility (cognitive skills, maturity, etc.) in adapting to new circumstances or demands. They also have the capacity to recover from setbacks. As an example, poor students who enroll in postsecondary programs are more likely to accumulate college debts that are large in relation to family income and to carry that debt for a long time, particularly if they leave without a degree or a marketable certificate. As a consequence, they will lack the flexibility to respond to job opportunities that require moving and incurring further expenses. On the other hand, students from more advantaged backgrounds are less likely to accumulate substantial debt, more likely to graduate, and are able to call on family resources to take advantage of opportunities, such as unpaid internships, that demand further expenditures.[25]

---

[24] For suspensions, see report of U.S. Department of Education 2014; For dropouts, see SES Indicator, "Poverty and High School Dropouts," blog entry by Russell W. Rumberger, American Psychological Association, May 2013, http://www.apa.org/pi/ses/resources/indicator/2013/05/poverty-dropouts.aspx, and references therein. See also Kearney and Levine (2014).

[25] Suzanne Mettler, "College, the Great Unleveler," *New York Times*, March 1, 2014. For a somewhat different view of college debt, see Chingos 2014.

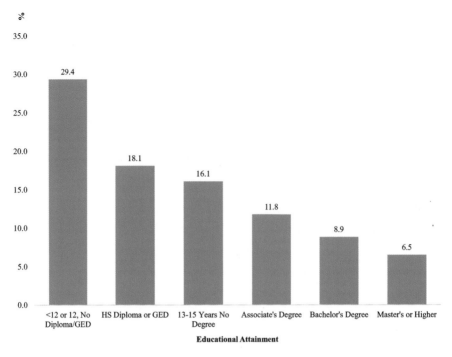

Fig. 5.6 Underutilization rates among U.S. workers (16 and over) by educational attainment, January 2012–August 2013 averages (in %) (see Chap. 7, Fig. 7.12)

Gradients

As noted earlier, the term "gradients" denotes the relationships between accumulated human capital and outcomes in adulthood. One oft-cited example is the relationship between unemployment and educational attainment. During the period from January 2013 to August 2014, the unemployment rate for high school dropouts with no GED stood at 13.9 %, with the rates decreasing with increasing levels of educational attainment; for those with master's degrees or higher, the rate was only 2.9 % (see Chap. 7, Fig. 7.2). Unfortunately, the problem is far worse than first appears. As some labor economists argue, one must also take into account underemployment and hidden unemployment.[26] They define the labor underutilization rate as the sum of the unemployment, underemployment, and hidden unemployment rates. Figure 5.6 shows the labor underutilization rates as a function of educational attainment. The rates range from nearly 30 % for those with no high school diploma and no GED to 6.5 % for those with a master's degree or above (see Khatiwada and Sum, Chap. 7, Fig. 7.12). Even among those with full-time employment, there is a

---

[26] Underemployment refers to individuals who are working fewer hours than they desire. Hidden unemployment refers to individuals who are jobless and not actively seeking work, but indicated that they wanted to work.

Table 5.2 Comparisons of the unemployment rates of U.S. adults 16 and older by educational attainment, 2000 and 2012–2013 (in %) (Sum presentation 2014)

	(A)	(B)	(C)
Educational Attainment	2000	2012–2013	Percentage point change
<12 or 12, no diploma or GED	8.6	14.9	+6.3
H.S. diploma or GED	4.4	9.8	+5.4
13–15 years, no degree	3.5	8.4	+4.9
Associate's degree	2.4	6.2	+3.8
Bachelor's degree	2.0	4.7	+2.7
Master's or higher degree	1.4	3.3	+1.9
All (16+)	4.0	8.0	+4.0

steep gradient in weekly earnings with respect to educational attainment. In 2009, the ratio in weekly earnings for individuals (aged 25 or more) with a bachelor's degree was 1.64 relative to those with a high school diploma and 2.26 relative to high school dropouts. The ratios were quite similar for comparisons both among men and among women.[27]

There are similarly steep gradients on social outcomes, broadly conceived. For example, in 2009, the percentage of mothers who were never married ranged from 20.1 % for those with less than 12 years of education to only 3.3 % for those with 18 or more years of education.[28] Not surprisingly, in 2010, the percentage of births to unmarried women stood at nearly 50 % for those with lower education and at 10 % for those with higher education (Ibid.). These differences by education level have widened substantially over the last three decades.

There is considerable evidence that workplace-related gradients have been getting steeper over time as well. As Table 5.2 shows, from 2000 to 2012–2013, the unemployment rate rose for all levels of educational attainment, but the percentage point increase was greater for those with lower educational attainment.[29] Concomitantly, Table 5.3 shows that for individuals with full-time employment, those with lower educational attainment lost ground absolutely (in inflation-adjusted dollars) from 1979 to 2009; only those with bachelor's degrees or higher gained ground (Chap. 7). Consequently, wage ratios increased substantially over the period. For example, the ratio for those holding a bachelor's degree to those holding a high school diploma went from 1.32 to 1.64, an increase of almost 25 %.

These patterns appear to be the result of a confluence of several forces and trends. Over the last two decades, technology has enabled many jobs to be off-shored, made obsolete, or changed them so dramatically that many fewer workers with different

---

[27] Andrew Sum, personal communication, May 2, 2014.

[28] Timothy Smeeding, "Connecting Inequality and Intergenerational Mobility: Looking Ahead, Not Behind" (unpublished PowerPoint presentation. Madison, WI: Institute for Research on Poverty, 2014).

[29] Current Population Survey monthly household surveys [public use files 2000 and January 2012-August 2013]. Data compiled by the Center for Labor Market Studies, Northeastern University.

Table 5.3 Wages for full-time employment by educational attainment, 1979–2009 (Sum presentation 2014)

Educational attainment	(A) 1979	(B) 2009	(C) Absolute change, 1979–2009	(D) Percent change, 1979–2009
High school dropouts	696	500	−196	−28 %
High school graduates	869	716	−153	−18 %
Some college, including associate degree	942	835	−107	−11 %
Bachelor's degree	1086	1200	+114	+10 %
Master's or higher degree	1170	1535	+365	+31 %
H.S. graduate/H.S. dropout	1.25	1.43	+.18	
Some college/H.S. graduates	1.08	1.17	+.09	
B.A. degrees/H.S. graduates	1.25	1.68	+.43	
Master's or higher/H.S. graduates	1.35	2.14	+.79	

skills are required, as is the case with advanced manufacturing.[30] Some economists argue that technology, in various forms, leads to a "winner take all" economy that produces greater inequality.[31] The combination of technology, globalization, and the broad deregulation of industry that began in the 1980s, with the specter of offshoring in the background, has exerted a downward pressure on wages in the many sectors that are now characterized by both fewer jobs and more job seekers. The decline of private sector unions, along with differences between states in "right to work" laws, has reduced the bargaining power of local workforces. While the decline of the buying power of the minimum wage contributes to the decline of those at the low end of the skill distribution, there is generally an upward pressure on wages for those who possess specialized skills that are scarce and in demand. The driver of this divergence is sometimes referred to as "skill-biased technological change."

More ominously, the "second IT revolution" will feature even faster computers with more powerful forms of artificial intelligence that will automate, partially or fully, many jobs that are now considered to be more skilled (Brynjolfsson and McAfee 2014, 34–37). Even today the new workplace rewards high-level cognitive skills, flexibility, and the capacity to continuously upgrade skills as job requirements change (Levy and Murnane 2013). Moreover, individuals who have found a good place in the new economy are more likely to be offered training and educational opportunities that enable them to keep pace with workplace changes. Those who are in low-wage, low-skill occupations rarely have such opportunities and face many obstacles in trying to obtain new skills on their own (e.g., through enrollment in a community college or vocational training center).

---

[30] Goldin and Katz 2008.

[31] Alan Krueger, "Land of Hope and Dreams: Rock and Roll, Economics, and Rebuilding the Middle Class" (remarks, Rock and Roll Hall of Fame, Cleveland, June 12, 2013).

Why Is Expanding Opportunity Important?

Employing the gates/gaps/gradients framework helps us understand how initial differences in opportunity can be magnified over time, resulting in wide disparities in accumulated human capital and increasing inequality in life outcomes that, in turn, contribute to greater differences in opportunity in the next generation. This cycle leads to what might be termed an *accelerated accumulation of advantage* (or *disadvantage*).[32] An America that offers opportunity to all, we noted at the outset, has been an enduring belief and contributed to the strength of this country—in part by drawing immigrants from all over the world searching for a better life for themselves and for their children. That this was never the case for everyone, and that it may be less true today than many imagine, in no way diminishes its importance and the obligation to promote its resurgence.

That obligation has many facets. It is a moral obligation, particularly to the children born to disadvantage who, nonetheless, deserve a decent chance to realize their potential. Denying them that opportunity is not just a betrayal of America's promise but does a disservice to us all—in greater social costs and lower overall economic growth (Stiglitz 2012).[33] In fact, there is good empirical evidence that greater inequality and the concomitant disparities in opportunity are associated with poorer health and less general satisfaction for everyone, even those on the top rungs of the ladder (Wilkinson and Pickett 2010; Sanger-Katz 2015).

There is some debate about whether increasing inequality portends lower intergenerational mobility (IGM) (Winship and Schneider 2014; Jerrim and Macmillan 2014). Although cross-nationally there is a strong association between greater income inequality and lower IGM, it is less clear whether that pattern holds within a country over time. Recent research suggests that in the U.S., IGM has remained steady, though at rather low levels. IGM appears to be particularly low at the extremes of the income distribution (Chetty et al. 2014a; Corak 2013). However, it will take another 15–20 years for the impact of the recession of 2007–2010 on IGM to fully play itself out.

Irrespective of its consequences for IGM, the increasing separation between rungs of the income ladder has immediate implications for the lives of all. On the one hand, many goods, such as televisions and cell phones, have become both cheaper and better. Indeed, some argue that, from an historical perspective, the percentage of the population that is poor has decreased markedly (Jencks 2015). On the other hand, individuals and families at the low end are spending a greater proportion

---

[32] For a comprehensive review of cumulative advantage, see DiPrete and Eirich 2006.

[33] See interview with Christopher Jencks for a different view. Eduardo Porter, "Income Equality: A Search for Consequences," *New York Times,* March 25, 2014, http://www.nytimes.com/2014/03/26/business/economy/making-sense-of-income-inequality.html. Also see interview with Lane Kenworthy. Eduardo Porter, "Q&A: A Sociologist on Inequality," *New York Times*, March 25, 2014. http://economix.blogs.nytimes.com/2014/03/25/qa-a-sociologist-on-inequality/.

of their disposal income on such necessities as food, rent, utilities, and transportation that relate directly to their ability to invest in themselves and their children.[34]

We appear to be moving from a market economy to a market society, where everything has a price. When this extends beyond goods and services to social practices, it changes social relations and the meanings we attach to those relations (Sandel 2012). More prosaically, but no less importantly, this can be seen in the role of money in political campaigns. With the recent Supreme Court decisions striking down campaign finance restrictions, the influence of wealthy contributors to political campaigns will only grow.

Increasing inequality, in conjunction with other trends and developments, helps to shape civil society and the democratic polity. As we become more segregated by income and education, we typically have less empathy for those with whom we have little contact (Friedman 2005). Such polarization necessarily undermines the notion of a shared future. When and if a large proportion of the population loses faith in the fairness of the social order and the extant political arrangements, then the stability that depends on the "consent of the governed" is threatened. Unfortunately, there is good evidence that differences in opportunity continue to increase over time and that many people have become disengaged from both civil society and the political process (Murray 2012). Looking ahead to the next generation, Putnam (2015) argues that, among high school students and young adults, there is an increasing divergence in this respect between those at the high end of the socioeconomic scale and those at the low end.

Moving Forward

The critical question is whether the dynamics of increasing divergence in opportunities and in life outcomes are self-correcting or self-reinforcing. More simply, was the pattern of shared prosperity seen in the three decades following World War II an anomaly?

Employing a vast trove of historical data, the French economist Thomas Piketty argues that increasing inequality in wealth is the inexorable outcome of a market economy in which, over the long run, the returns to capital outpace the returns to labor and, consequently, result in the increasing concentration of wealth and political power. This trend, he avers, can only be held in check by government action. Such actions should include a global wealth tax as well as greater investments in education and training (Piketty 2014).

---

[34] Planet Money (NPR blog), "How the Poor, the Middle Class and the Rich Spend Their Money," blog entry by Jacob Goldstein, August 1, 2012, http://www.npr.org/blogs/money/2012/08/01/157664524/how-the-poor-the-middle-class-and-the-rich-spend-their-money; Real Time Economics (*Wall Street Journal* blog), "How Rich and Poor Spend (and Earn) Their Money," April 6, 2015, http://blogs.wsj.com/economics/2015/04/06/how-the-rich-and-poor-spend-and-earn-their-money/.

His diagnosis is supported by the economist Alan Krueger, who decries the "erosion of the institutions and practices that supported shared prosperity." He argues that private industry has to take the lead in righting this balance and government's responsibility is to set the conditions for that recommitment to the common good. This seems a bit weak—and he does end with a list of more forceful interventions, including an increase in the minimum wage, financial reform, income tax reform, and greater infrastructure investment.[35]

To be sure, some economists argue that this phenomenon is a natural outgrowth of human variation: Starting with a perfectly equal society, individual differences in talent, energy, and motivation, as well as random shocks, would inexorably lead to an unequal society; moreover, this inequality, however extreme, does not signal unfairness or inefficiency (Mankiw 2013). This view leads to a recommendation of minimal policy interventions. Stiglitz, who is quoted at the outset of this chapter, takes a less benign view: He sees increasing inequality as a signal of market inefficiencies, such as rent-seeking (trying to obtain economic gain without any reciprocal benefit to society), and argues that those with greater resources are in an ever better position to influence laws and regulations to preserve and strengthen these advantages, for their benefit, their families, and associates (Stiglitz 2012).

If one adopts the less sanguine view, then there are certainly formidable barriers to countering the self-reinforcing dynamics of inequality of opportunity. A polarized central government is unlikely to take bold action, especially in light of the unavoidable uncertainties involved in projecting current trends into the future. (This situation is much like the one confronting those who argue for strong action on climate change.) Indeed, budget plans from the House of Representatives prescribe scaling back some of the supports now provided to the poor. Yet at the same time, the Affordable Care Act acts to extend medical insurance to millions of individuals who have done without, although efforts continue to derail or scale it back.

One can certainly hope that some segments of private industry will take the lead. Here there is certainly a mixed picture. On the one hand, the finance industry spends millions on protecting such benefits as the "carried interest" provision in the tax code or on weakening the financial regulations spurred by the Dodd-Frank Act.[36] For the most part, large retailers and fast food chains are resisting an increase in the minimum wage, even though its real purchasing power has plummeted since it was last raised.[37]

On the other hand, there is some evidence that a few corporations are taking a broader view of their responsibilities—not only to their shareholders and customers but also to their employees, the communities in which they are located, and even to

---

[35] Krueger, "Land of Hope."

[36] Paul Krugman, "Obama's Other Success," *New York Times,* August 4, 2014, http://www.nytimes.com/2014/08/04opinion/paul-krugman-dodd-frank-financial-reform-is-working.html/.

[37] On February 19, 2015, Doug McMillon, Walmart President and CEO, announced a program of increases in the minimum wage for current and new associates, as well as for department managers. About a month later, McDonald's followed suit with a wage increase for employees in its corporate-run stores.

society at large. That broader view goes beyond the traditional "bottom line" to consideration of community stability and environmental stewardship (Googins, Mirvis, and Rochlin 2007; Freeland presentation to *Opportunity in America* panel 2014). At present it is hard to determine whether this movement toward *sustainable capitalism* will prove to be long lasting and whether it will have any effect on the dynamics of inequality.

In the search for viable policies and the strategies to build consensus around them, it is necessary to consider some further complications. For example, the family circumstances that play such a critical role in the access to opportunity are not just determined by the impersonal forces we have been discussing. They are also a product of individual choices, sometimes poor ones. To what extent can and should government intervene, at least on behalf of children, to compensate for those choices, for insufficient private investment in the children, or even parental neglect? There can be reasoned disagreement on government's responsibility.

At the same time there is considerable evidence that early interventions, say between birth and age 3, if effective, can yield benefit-to-cost ratios substantially above 1 and considerably greater than those for later interventions can. Moreover, it appears that those early interventions can enhance the effects of later interventions in a virtuous cycle (particularly if they target both cognitive and noncognitive skills) with important implications for later labor market success (Heckman, *Case for Investing*).[38]

Another complication arises because the distribution of opportunity is "lumpy"— it varies substantially by location, as well as by demographic characteristics such as race-ethnicity, immigration status, prison record, and so on. Presumably, the conjunction of these factors can either mitigate or exacerbate access to opportunity. For example, recent data indicate that other things being equal, Blacks are more likely to have lost ground in the distributions of income and wealth during the recession (for a general discussion of race in America, see Orfield 2014).

Over the last decade, certain areas have become hubs of the new economy with a high concentration of well-paying jobs, while others stagnate or decline. For the former, there are spillover effects, so that even those further down the skills ladder derive some benefit from being located in those areas (Acs 2013; Moretti 2013). Although intergenerational mobility may well be stable (or stagnant) overall, it varies very substantially by location. For example, recent work shows that, roughly speaking, for children growing up in below-median income families, upward mobility is highest in the Midwest, lowest in the Southeast, and moderate at the coasts (Chetty 2014b).

Thus, it appears that a viable policy strategy will have to comprise multiple initiatives at various governmental levels, with serious attempts to bring the resources of both the for-profit and nonprofit sectors to bear on the problem. Although the dynamics underlying the current situation are complex, they are not beyond under-

---

[38] As results from the Brookings Institution Social Genome Project make clear, real impact on human capital accumulation results from systematic interventions throughout the a child's development.

standing or mitigation. As one commentator put it: "Rising inequality is a trend, but it is one we have helped create and one we can still change."[39]

References

Acemoglu, Daron, and David Autor. 2012. "What does human capital do?", Review of *The race between education and technology,* by Claudia Goldin and Lawrence F. Katz. *Journal of Economic Literature* 50(2): 426–463.

Acs, Gregory. 2013. *The Moynihan report revisited.* Washington, DC: Urban Institute. http://www.urban.org/UploadedPDF/412839-The-Moynihan-Report-Revisited.pdf.

Aizer, Anna, and Janet Currie. 2014. The intergenerational transmission of inequality: Maternal disadvantage and health at birth. *Science* 344(6186): 856–861.

Alexander, Karl, Doris Entwistle, and Linda Olson. 2014. *The long shadow: Family background, disadvantaged urban youth, and the transition to adulthood.* New York: Russell Sage.

Autor, David. 2014. Skills, education, and the rise of earnings inequality among the 'other 99 percent'. *Science* 344(6186): 843–851.

Barton, Paul, and Richard Coley. 2013. *Parsing the achievement gap, II.* Princeton: Policy Information Center, Educational Testing Service. http://www.ets.org/Media/Research/pdf/PICPARSINGII.pdf

Bettinger, Eric, Angela Boatman, and Bridget Terry Long. 2013. Student supports: Developmental education and other academic programs. *The Future of Children* 23(1): 93–115. http://future-ofchildren.org/publications/journals/article/index.xml?journalid=79&articleid=582.

Bischoff, Kendra, and Sean F. Reardon. 2013. *Residential segregation by income, 1970–2009.* New York: Russell Sage.

Black, Sandra E., and Paul J. Devereux. 2010. *Recent developments in intergenerational mobility* (NBER Working Paper 15889). Cambridge, MA: National Bureau of Economic Research. http://www.nber.org/papers/w15889.

Blanden, Jo. 2013. Cross-country rankings in intergenerational mobility: A comparison of approaches from economics and sociology. *Journal of Economic Surveys* 27(1): 38–73.

Bodovski, Katerina, and George Farkas. 2007. Mathematics growth in elementary school: The roles of beginning knowledge, student engagement, and instruction. *Elementary School Journal* 108(2): 115–130.

Bradbury, Bruce, Corak Miles, Waldfogel Jane, and Washbrook, Elizabeth. 2013. Inequality in early childhood outcomes. In *From parents to children: The intergenerational transmission of disadvantage,* ed. John Ermisch, Markus Jantii, and Timothy Smeeding, 87–119. New York: Russell Sage.

Brody, Gene H., Yu. Tianyi, Chen Edith, E. Miller Gregory, M. Kogan Steven, and R.H. Beach Steven. 2013. Is resilience only skin deep? Rural African-Americans' socioeconomic status-related risk and competence in preadolescence and psychological adjustment and allostatic load at age 19. *Psychological Science* 24(7): 1285–1293.

---

[39] David Leonhardt, "Inequality Has Been Going On Forever … but That Doesn't Mean It's Inevitable," *New York Times magazine,* May 2, 2014, http://www.nytimes.com/2014/05/04/magazine/inequality-has-been-going-on-forever-but-that-doesnt-mean-its-inevitable.html.

Brookings Institution. 2013. *Social genome project: Mapping pathways to the middle class.* Washington, DC: Brookings Institution (April). http://www.brookings.edu/~/media/Centers/ccf/SGP_overview.pdf.

Brynjolfsson, Erik, and Andrew McAfee. 2014. *The second machine age: Work, progress, and prosperity in a time of brilliant technologies.* New York: W.W. Norton.

Centers for Disease Control. 2013. *Births: Final data for 2012,* by Joyce A. Martin, Brady E. Hamilton, Michelle J. K. Osterman, Sally C. Curtin, and T. J. Matthews, 62(9) (National Vital Statistics Reports, December 30). http://www.cdc.gov/nchs/data/nvsr/nvsr62/nvsr62_09.pdf.

Chetty, Raj, Nathaniel Hendren, Patrick Kline, and Emmanuel Saez. 2014a. *Is the United States still a land of opportunity? Recent trends in intergenerational mobility,* NBER working paper 19843. Cambridge, MA: National Bureau of Economic Research.

Chetty, Raj, Nathaniel Hendren, Patrick Kline, and Emmanuel Saez. 2014b. *Where is the land of opportunity? intergenerational mobility in the US, VoxEU.org.* Center for Economic Policy Research. http://www.voxeu.org/article/where-land-opportunity-intergenerational-mobility-us.

Chingos, Matthew M. 2014. *Why student loan rhetoric doesn't match the facts* (Brown Center, Chalkboard 75). Washington, DC: Brookings Institution, July 17. http://www.brookings.edu/research/papers/2014/07/17-student-loan-rhetoric-chingos.

Coley, Richard, and Bruce Baker. 2013. *Poverty and education: Finding the way forward.* Princeton: Policy Information Center, Educational Testing Service. http://www.ets.org/s/research/pdf/poverty_and_education_report.pdf.

Corak, Miles. 2013. Income inequality, equality of opportunity, and intergenerational mobility. *Journal of Economic Perspectives* 27(3): 79–102.

Cowen, Tyler. 2013. *Average is over: Powering America beyond the age of the great stagnation.* New York: Dutton.

Current Population Survey monthly household surveys [public use files, 2000 and January 2012–August 2013]. Data compiled by the Center for Labor Market Studies, Northeastern University.

DiPrete, Thomas A., and Gregory M. Eirich. 2006. Cumulative advantage as a mechanism for inequality: A review of theoretical and empirical developments. *Annual Review of Sociology* 32: 271–297.

Doyle, Orla, Colm P. Harmon, James J. Heckman, and Richard E. Tremblay. 2009. Investing in early human development: Timing and economic efficiency. *Economics and Human Biology,* 7(1) (March). doi: 10.1016/j.ehb.2009.01.002.

Duncan, Greg J., and Richard J. Murnane. 2011. Introduction: The American dream, then and now. In *Whither opportunity: Rising inequality, schools, and children's life chances,* ed. Greg J. Duncan and Richard J. Murnane, 3–23. New York: Russell Sage Foundation/Spencer Foundation.

Fishkin, Joseph. 2014. *Bottlenecks: A new theory of equal opportunity.* New York: Oxford University Press.

Foster, Wayne A., and Merideth Miller. 2007. Development of the literacy achievement gap. *Language, Speech, and Hearing Services in Schools* 38: 173–181. doi:10.1044/0161-1461(2007/018).

Fox, Sharon E., Pat Levitt, and Charles A. Nelson III. 2010. How the timing and quality of early experiences influence the development of brain architecture. *Child Development* 81: 28–40.

Friedman, Benjamin M. 2005. *The moral consequences of economic growth.* New York: Knopf.

Goldin, Claudia, and Lawrence F. Katz. 2008. *The race between education and technology.* Cambridge: Harvard University Press.

Goodman, Madeline J., Anita M. Sands, and Richard J. Coley. 2015. *America's skills challenge: Millennials and the future.* Princeton: ETS Center for Research on Human Capital and Education, Educational Testing Service.

Googins, Bradley K., Philip H. Mirvis, and Steven A. Rochlin. 2007. *Beyond good company: Next generation corporate citizenship.* New York: Palgrave McMillan.

Grannis, Kerry Searle, and Isabel V. Sawhill. 2013. *Improving children's life chances: Estimates from the Social Genome Model.* Social Genome Project Research (49). Washington, DC: Brookings Institution.

Halle, Tamara, Nicole Forry, Elizabeth Hair, Kate Perper, Laura Wandner, Julia Wessel, and Jessica Vick. 2009, June. *Disparities in early learning and development: Lessons from the early childhood longitudinal study—Birth Cohort (ECLS-B).* Washington, DC: Council of Chief State School Officers and Child Trends. http://www.childtrends.org/wp-content/uploads/2013/05/2009-52DisparitiesELExecSumm.pdf.

Hart, Betty, and Todd Risley. 1995. *Meaningful differences in the everyday experiences of young American children.* Baltimore: Brooks Publishing.

Heckman, James J. (n.d.). *The case for investing in disadvantaged young children.* The Heckman Equation. http://heckmanequation.org/content/resource/case-investing-disadvantaged-young-children.

Heckman, James J., and Dimitriy V. Masterov. 2007. The productivity argument for investing in young children. *Applied Economic Perspectives and Policy* 29(3): 446–493. http://aepp.oxford-journals.org/content/29/3/446.extract.

Hoxby, Caroline, and Christopher Avery. 2013. *The missing "One-Offs": The hidden supply of high-achieving, low-income students.* Washington, DC: Brookings Papers on Economic Activity (Spring). http://www.brookings.edu/~/media/projects/bpea/spring%202013/2013a_hoxby.pdf.

Hoxby, Caroline, and Sarah Turner. 2014. *Expanding college opportunities for high-achieving, low income students.* SIEPR Discussion Paper 12–014. Stanford: Stanford Institute for Economic Policy Research.

Jencks, Christopher. 2015. The war on poverty: Was it lost? *New York review of books*, April 2.

Jerrim, John, and Lindsey Macmillan. 2014. *Income inequality, intergenerational mobility and the Great Gatsby curve: Is education the key?* London: Institute of Education, University of London.

Kaushal, Neeraj, Katherine Magnuson, and Jane Waldfogel. 2011. How is family income related to investments in children's learning? In *Whither opportunity: Rising inequality, schools, and children's life chances*, ed. Greg J. Duncan and Richard J. Murnane, 187–206. New York: Russell Sage Foundation/Spencer Foundation.

Kearney, Melissa Schettini, and Phillip B. Levine. 2014. *Income inequality, social mobility, and the decision to drop out of high school*, NBER Working Paper 20195. Cambridge, MA: National Bureau of Economic Research. http://www.nber.org/papers/w20195.

Keeley, Brian. 2007. *Human capital: How what you know shapes your life.* Paris: OECD Publishing. doi:10.1787/9789264029095-en.

Levy, Frank, and Richard Murnane. 2013. *Dancing with robots: Human skills for computerized work.* Washington, DC: Third Way. http://content.thirdway.org/publications/714/Dancing-With-Robots.pdf.

Mankiw, Gregory W. 2013. Defending the 1 %. *Journal of Economic Perspectives* 27(3): 21–34.

McClanahan, Sara. 2014. Diverging destinies: How children are faring under the second demographic transition. *Demography* 41a(4): 607–627. https://muse.jhu.edu/journals/demography/v041/41.4mclanahan.pdf.

Moretti, Enrico. 2013. *The new geography of jobs.* Boston: Mariner Books.

Murray, Charles. 2012. *Coming apart: The state of White America 1960–2010.* New York: Crown Forum.

National Center for Public Policy and Higher Education Special Report. 2010. *Beyond the Rhetoric: Improving college readiness through coherent state policy.* http://www.highereducation.org/reports/college_readiness/index.shtml.

Noah, Timothy. 2013. *The great divergence: America's growing inequality crisis and what we can do about it.* London: Bloomsbury Press.

OECD (Organisation for Economic Co-operation and Development). 2013. *First results from the survey of adult skills*. Paris: OECD Skills Studies, OECD Publishing. doi:10.1787/9789264204256-en.

Orfield, Gary. 2014. A new civil rights agenda for American education. *Educational Researcher* 43(6): 273–292.

Orfield, Gary, John Kucsera, and Genevieve Siegl-Hawley. 2012. *E pluribus … separation: Deepening double segregation for more students*. Los Angeles: The Civil Rights Project, as cited in Coley and Baker, Poverty and Education.

Pellegrino, James W., and Margaret L. Hilton (eds.). 2012. *Education for life and work: Developing transferable knowledge and skills in the 21st century*. Washington, DC: National Academies Press.

Piketty, Thomas. 2014. *Capital in the 21st century*. Cambridge, MA: Harvard University Press.

Putnam, Robert. 2015. *Our kids: The American dream in crisis*. New York: Simon & Schuster.

Reardon, Sean F. 2011. The widening achievement gap between the rich and the poor: New evidence and possible explanations. In *Whither opportunity: Rising inequality, schools, and children's life chances*, ed. Greg J. Duncan and Richard J. Murnane, 91–116. New York: Russell Sage Foundation/Spencer Foundation.

Rugh, Jacob S., and Massey, Douglas S. 2013. Segregation in post-civil rights America: Stalled integration or end of the segregated century? *The DuBois Review: Social Science Research on Race*. doi:10.1017/S1742058X13000180.

Sandel, Michael J. 2012. *What money can't buy: The moral limits of markets*. New York: Farrar, Strauss, and Giroux.

Sanger-Katz, Margot. 2015. How income inequality can be bad for your health. *New York Times*, March 31. http://www.nytimes.com/2015/03/31/upshot/income-inequality-its-also-bad-for-your-health.html?abt=0002&abg=1.

Sawhill, Isabel V., and Quentin Karpilow. 2014. *How much could we improve children's life chances by intervening early and often?*, CCF Brief 54. Washington, DC: Brookings Institution.

Stiglitz, Joseph. 2012. *The price of inequality*. New York: W. W. Norton.

Thompson, Derek. 2012. A giant statistical round-up of the income inequality crisis in 16 charts, *Atlantic*, December 12. http://www.theatlantic.com/business/archive/2012/12/a-giant-statistical-round-up-of-the-income-inequality-crisis-in-16-charts/266074/.

U.S. Department of Education, Office for Civil Rights, Civil Rights Data Collection of 2011–2012, Washington, DC: 2014 (March 21). http://www2.ed.gov/about/offices/list/ocr/whatsnew.html#2014.

Wilkinson, Richard G., and Kate Pickett. 2010. *The spirit level: Why greater equality makes societies stronger*. New York: Bloomsbury Press.

Winship, Scott, and Donald Schneider. 2014. The collapse of the Great Gatsby curve. *e21*, February 3. http://www.economics21.org/research/collapse-great-gatsby-curve.

Wise, Tim. 2013. Explaining conservative deception about out-of-wedlock births in the Black community. *BlackVisions.org*, Aug. 3. http://www.blackvisions.org.

Part II
The Labor Market

Chapter 6
Wages in the United States: Trends, Explanations, and Solutions

Jared Bernstein

Abstract Since the late 1970s, two major developments have occurred regarding wages in the U.S.: the stagnation of real wages for various groups of workers and the increase in wage inequality. This chapter examines these trends in some detail and finds that real wages have performed better for women than men and for the more highly educated relative to those with less educational attainment. However, particularly since 2000, few groups have been spared; even workers with 4-year college degrees have experienced some stagnation in real hourly pay. The chapter examines economic theories of wage determination and finds that while skills often play a critical role in both theory and practice, other important wage determinants, most notably the absence of full employment—the persistently slack labor markets that have prevailed over the stagnation/dispersion period—are often underemphasized. The chapter suggests a number of policy recommendations to offset the problems of wage stagnation and increased wage inequality, including greater skill acquisition as well as policies to promote full employment and strengthen eroding labor standards.

Keywords Wage trends • Wage inequality • Wage policy • Economic theories • Labor markets • Unemployment • Trade deficits • Minimum wage • Unions

Introduction

This chapter provides an in-depth look at historical wage trends in the United States. Though some of the analysis goes as far back as the post-World War II years, most begins in the latter 1970s. This is partly a function of data availability but more of the analysis itself: The two major problems revealed by the analysis—the stagnation of real wages for various groups of workers and the increase in wage inequality—are most evident over the past 35 years or so.

My goal is not simply to show these trends but to explain their movements as well as discuss policy ideas targeted at both wage stagnation and dispersion. Thus,

J. Bernstein (✉)
Center on Budget and Policy Priorities, Washington, DC, USA

© Educational Testing Service 2016
I. Kirsch, H. Braun (eds.), *The Dynamics of Opportunity in America*,
DOI 10.1007/978-3-319-25991-8_6

the first part of the chapter presents empirical trends and the second attempts to explain the factors driving these trends and prescribe policy solutions to improve them.

There are, of course, many determinants of both wage levels and trends, including workers' skills and productivity, their ability to interact productively with technology, institutional factors such as unionization and labor laws (e.g., minimum wages, overtime rules), nonwage costs (e.g., employer-provided health benefits), and macroeconomic factors. While I touch on all the above, I find the latter set of factors—macroeconomic ones—to be both important and often underemphasized in wage analysis. The extent of slack in U.S. labor markets (high levels of unemployment) cannot be overlooked when attempting to explain widespread wage stagnation and dispersion, not to mention recent developments in wage trends that are the subject of considerable debate among both economists and the popular press.[1] Imbalances in trade—persistent U.S. trade deficits—are another seldom broached but germane area of analysis in this space.

Following the empirical section, I review various theories of wage determination common to contemporary economics. Some of these theories, like those that explain the correlation between education levels and wage levels (marginal product theory), have clear linkages to the data (e.g., the ever-present gradient in wage levels by educational attainment). But this theoretical review also finds that most theories assume "equilibrium," or full employment, in the labor market, meaning a tight matchup between the number of jobs and job seekers. In fact, as noted above and stressed throughout, this assumption is highly unrealistic as far as the U.S. labor market over the past few decades—a time of stagnant and diverse wage growth. It is a particularly incorrect assumption in recent years.

The policy recommendation section that follows builds off this conspicuous omission in the theoretical work by incorporating the "slack problem"—the persistent absence of full employment—into the analysis. This means that along with conventional (but still critical) policy interventions like better access to educational opportunities for those facing such barriers, I also suggest such interventions as wage targeting at the Federal Reserve, smarter fiscal policy, direct job creation, improving labor standards, reducing trade deficits, and generally speaking, reducing slack in the job market, which I identify as a key determinant of worker bargaining power, and thus, wage pressures for many in the workforce.

---

[1] See Janet Yellen's speech at the Federal Reserve Bank of Kansas City Economic Symposium, Jackson Hole, WY, August 22, 2014, http://www.federalreserve.gov/newsevents/speech/yellen20140822a.htm, and David Leonhardt, "Trying to Solve the Great Wage Slowdown," *New York Times*, http://www.nytimes.com/2015/01/15/upshot/trying-to-solve-the-great-wage-slowdown.html?abt=0002&abg=1.

Empirical Trends in Wages and Compensation in the U.S.

The seemingly simple question of trends in earnings is, if not complex, then multi-faceted. Are we talking about straight wages or all-in compensation? Medians or averages? Annual, weekly, or hourly earnings? The first concept—annual earnings—invokes questions of labor supply, as in weeks worked per year and hours worked per week. The second—weekly earnings—invokes variation in hours per week. The last concept—hourly earnings—one to which I pay considerable attention to in this section, is a fundamental building block of the living standards of working families.

I also look briefly at recent developments in labor's share of national income, as this key variable has been undergoing tectonic shifts that many economists view as relevant to the important question of growing inequality.

The key findings of this review of many of these trends are as follows:

- Real wages have both become much more dispersed over time, and, for certain groups, also undergone long periods of stagnation.
- Hourly wage trends have been less favorable for men than for women, though hourly pay has undergone long periods of stagnation for middle- and low-wage women as well.
- Real wages across the wage scale received a clear lift during the high-pressure labor market of the full-employment latter 1990s.
- Wages by education reveal a clear and persistent gradient by attainment levels. However, all attainment levels, with the exception of workers with advanced college degrees but including those with four-year degrees, experienced periods of stagnation in the past few decades, with the largest losses among those with the least education.
- Annual earnings by percentile show extreme dispersion at the very top of the pay scale and stagnation among the bottom 90 %.
- To the extent that the data permit it, adding employer-provided benefits to the analysis of compensation does not broadly change these findings.
- In recent years, labor's share of national income has significantly declined.

Hourly Wage Percentiles

As noted, the hourly wage is a fundamental building block of the living standards of working families. When real hourly wages are rising throughout the pay scale, families from all walks of life do not have to work more weeks or hours to get ahead and can thus balance family obligations with less stress. Unfortunately, hourly wage trends in recent decades have not been particularly favorable for most workers, and this in turn has required more family members to work more hours per week and weeks per year to raise family incomes. Mishel et al. (2012) find that 86 % of the increase in annual earnings for middle-income families between 1979 and 2007 was driven by more work, leaving only 14 % attributable to hourly wage growth.

Figure 6.1 shows real hourly wages at the 10th, median (50th), and 95th percentiles from 1979 to 2013, indexed to 100 in 1979 so as to be able to plot them together given their different scales (in 2013, the 10th percentile wage was about $8.40, the median about $16.70, and the 95th was about $52.80).[2]

This one simple figure captures many of the more important trends in real wages over the last 30-plus years. First, the pattern of wage inequality in the 1980s is evident as we see declining low wages, stagnant middle wages, and rising high wages. Next, the very important period of the latter 1990s, when full employment labor markets prevailed for a few years, is evident in the acceleration of all three series. Third, in a point that will become more important in a later section, while middle and low wages diverged in the 1980s, they have since generally converged. Finally, wage growth stagnated again for these lower two groups starting around 2000 and has yet to recover. In fact, real wages for low- and mid-wage workers were dealt another blow in the "Great Recession," although some stabilization can be seen in the most recent data.

Let us pause here and note a truly remarkable development: With the exception of the tight labor markets of the latter 1990s, wage earners in the bottom half of the wage scale have seen little, if any, real hourly wage growth over the past three decades. Given that the workforce has grown older, more highly educated, and more

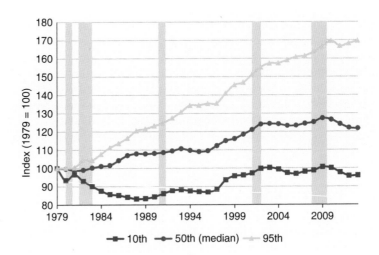

Fig. 6.1 Real hourly wage trends by decile, 1979–2013

---

[2] These data were provided by the Economic Policy Institute and are featured in their State of Working America (I coauthored nine earlier editions of this compendium and thus helped to develop this wage series). The data are constructed from the Current Population Survey and are deflated using the CPI-RS. The sample includes 18- to 64-year-olds.

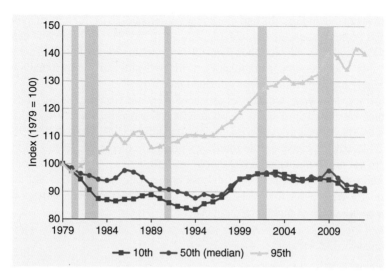

Fig. 6.2 Real hourly wage trends: men

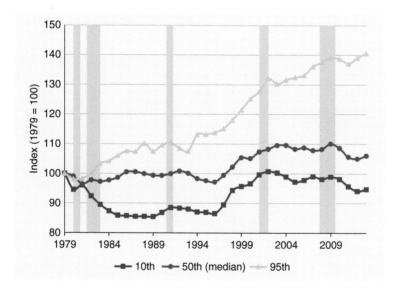

Fig. 6.3 Real hourly wage trends: women

productive over these years only increases the degree to which these trends are both unusual and problematic.

While there are, of course, many subgroups by which to break out wage trends, two of the most important are gender and education. Figures 6.2 and 6.3 are in the same format as Fig. 6.1 but are broken out for men and women. While the inequality pattern is notable in Figs. 6.2 and 6.3, salient differences exist. First, men in the bottom half of the wage scale did worse than women did. This difference is generally associated with the shift in labor demand from production worker jobs to service sector jobs—for example, from manufacturing to health care—a shift that has been particularly tough on non-college-educated men.[3]

However, low-wage workers experienced stagnant (in the case of women) or declining (in the case of men) real hourly wages since the late 1970s. These are trends that have been associated with demand shifts against "less skilled" workers (related to but broader than the industry shifts just noted), the decline in the real value of the minimum wage (a key determinant for women in the 1980s, for example), and slack labor markets. As I discuss in the policy section, that last factor is particularly critical for low-wage workers, as labor market slack hurts them the most and full employment helps the most.

Weekly Earnings by Education

Figure 6.4 shows wage trends—in this case, real weekly earnings, by education level and gender, as plotted by labor economist David Autor in a recent analysis (indexed to "1" in 1964). A few notable developments are apparent.

First, not unlike the decile wage trends, real wages by education level fan out and have generally grown more quickly, or fallen less, for higher-skilled workers compared to lower-skilled ones. This is widely interpreted to reflect skill-biased technological change (SBTC). This is the idea that workers whose skills are complementary to new technologies that are increasingly common in the workplace can command an increasing wage premium. Information technology and computers are the classic example, and economists often invoke SBTC to explain the rising wage of college graduates, for example, compared those a high school graduate.

Though there's surely some validity to the SBTC hypothesis, it actually provides only a limited explanation of the educational wage trends in Fig. 6.4. For example, SBTC predicts a rising college wage premium as employers' unmet skill demands bid up college wages. Yet as the part of the figure for men reveals, the real earnings of men *up to and including a bachelor's degree* generally have been flat since around 2000. Similar trends appear for women, though starting later. For both genders, only those with advanced degrees (about 12 % of the workforce) have experienced steadily rising wages.

It could be that technology-induced skill demands have only been unmet in recent years for the most highly educated workers, but given that only about 12 % of the workforce are in this category, this would introduce a much narrower concept

[3] For example, back in 1990, 16 % of employment was in manufacturing and 7 % in health care. In 2014, the respective shares were 9 % manufacturing and 11 % health care.

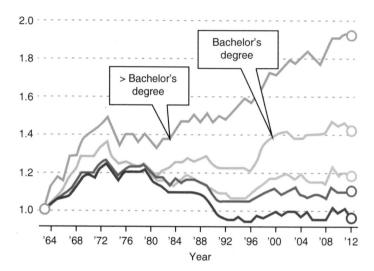

a Real weekly earnings relative to 1963 (men)

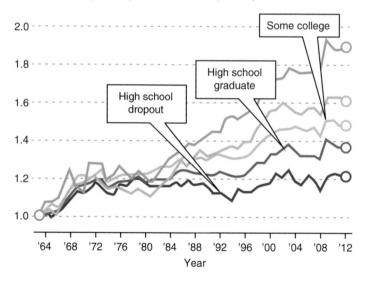

b Real weekly earnings relative to 1963 (women)

Fig. 6.4 Changes in real wage levels of full-time U.S. workers by sex and education, 1963–2012 (Reproduced from Autor 2014)

of SBTC than is generally thought to prevail.[4] Also, economists generally expect a gradient for skill bias, one that would distinguish the wage trends of more highly educated workers from those of less educated workers. But we don't see that very clearly in Fig. 6.4. Instead, other than those with advanced degrees, earnings for workers at all other education levels are pretty flat since around 2000.

In fact, according to these data, college-educated men, who did relatively well compared to other males, experienced earnings growth of less than 1 % per year. For comparably educated women, growth was 1 % per year. The earnings of non-college-educated men stagnated or lost ground since the mid-1970s.

Annual Earnings by Wage Percentile

The wage data I've presented so far show some dimensions of the increase in wage inequality, such as the relative increase for high-wage workers over middle- and low-wage workers by decile, or the increase in relative earnings of more highly educated workers. But to understand the extent of wage dispersion, it is important to examine trends that reach the very top of the earnings distribution. Fortunately, annual earnings data from a high quality source—the administrative wage records from the Social Security Administration—provide such information.[5]

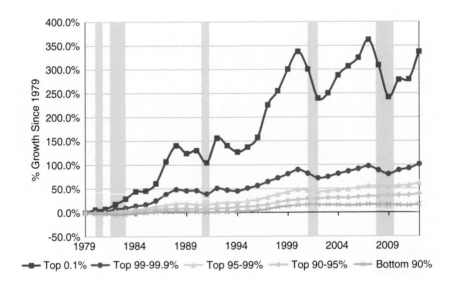

Fig. 6.5 Real annual earnings by wage percentile, 1979–2012

----

[4] The 12 % is the share of workers, 18 and over, in 2013, with at least a master's degree (data are from the Current Population Survey, March Supplement, graciously provided by Danilo Trisi).

[5] These are the earnings reported on employees' W-2 tax forms. They thus exclude self-employment earnings.

Table 6.1 Real annual earnings, 1947–2012 (Source: EPI analysis of Kopczuk et al. 2010 and Social Security Administration wage statistics [http://www.ssa.gov/cgi-bin/netcomp.cgi])

(2012 Dollars)	Top 0.1 %	Top 99 %–99.9 %	Top 95 %–99%	Top 90 %–95%	Bottom 90 %
1947	$316,878	$110,427	$49,737	$35,037	$14,392
1979	$569,521	$220,898	$105,519	$75,191	$27,110
1989	$1,275,327	$322,321	$124,773	$81,316	$27,596
1995	$1,349,802	$333,669	$130,993	$84,333	$27,873
2000	$2,492,254	$418,654	$156,163	$95,332	$31,248
2007	$2,633,800	$435,324	$163,927	$100,801	$31,626
2012	$2,488,525	$444,098	$170,540	$104,641	$31,741
1947–1979	80 %	100 %	112 %	115 %	88 %
1979–1989	124 %	46 %	18 %	8 %	2 %
1989–2000	95 %	30 %	25 %	17 %	13 %
1995–2000	85 %	25 %	19 %	13 %	12 %
2000–2007	6 %	4 %	5 %	6 %	1 %
2007–2012	–6 %	2 %	4 %	4 %	0 %

Figure 6.5 and Table 6.1 show the trends and levels (in 2012 dollars) from this series, with the figure starting in 1979 (and indexed to 0 in that year, thus showing cumulative percent growth) and the table going all the way back to the late 1940s.

The figure shows the dramatic increase in earnings inequality, with especially outsized gains going to the top 0.1 %: Their real earnings grew by more than a factor of 4 over these years. The rest of the top 1 %—the 99th through 99.9th percentile— about doubled, and below that, gains are consecutively diminished. The extreme cyclical movements of the top earnings trends are also notable in the figure. As I've shown in earlier analysis, these movements closely mimic those of equity markets in those years, and the correlation reflects that these high wages include exercised stock options. While many economists think of equity holdings as wealth or, if realized, as income, clearly in this context they are a part of earnings.[6]

To telegraph some of what's coming in my efforts to explain these trends, I note here that it is hard to square this equity-market-driven pattern with theories of wage determination based on, for example, workers' skills or their "marginal product" (their marginal contribution to the firm's output), and such factors could not plausibly gyrate like that (how could workers be highly skilled/productive in one quarter but not the next?). "Occam's razor" would strongly suggest we rely on the simpler explanation: By dint of the increased importance of stock options in their earnings, these workers' labor earnings have become tied to stock market prices, introducing a whole new dimension of wage determinants, including bubbles, busts, corporate governance, and market valuations made in global markets.

After having gained 88 % in the first few postwar decades, the annual earnings of the bottom 90 % grew only 17 % since 1979, from about $27,000 to close to

---

[6]On the Economy; "Rents, Rents, Everywhere, Rents!", blog entry by Jared Bernstein, April 17, 2014, http://jaredbernsteinblog.com/rents-rents-everywhere-rents/.

$32,000, or 0.5 % per year (one-fourth of the 2 % annualized growth rate for this wage class for 1947–79). Moreover, and this is again important to my later interpretation of these trends, most of the gains of the bottom 90 % occurred in a few short years in the latter 1990s, when the job market was unusually tight.

Adding Compensation to Wages

One counterargument to the above observations about the bottom 90 % is that those data cover just the wage part of the pay package. Because workers are known to trade off wages for benefits, to what extent does the addition of employer-provided benefits—largely health and pension coverage—change the story?

Though the data needed to answer that question are somewhat sparse, the answer appears to be "not much at all." New analysis by Bivens et al. (2014) reveals the following:

- Adding a measure of benefits to the hourly pay of production, nonsupervisory workers (blue-collar workers in manufacturing and nonmanagers in services), the trend in hourly compensation is much like that of the bottom 90 % of earnings from the Social Security Administration data: Real compensation doubled from the late 1940s to the late 1970s, and has then grown 8 % since 1979.[7]
- The share of the workforce with employer-provided pension and health coverage declined since 1980: The former was down from about 50 % to 42 %, the latter, down from about 70 % to 52 % (these data cover only private-sector workers; Bivens et al. 2014).
- According to employers' reports of their actual spending on pension and health benefits, their hourly costs for these benefits, inflation adjusted, were up by less than 4 % since 1987, or about 0.1 % per year. And this figure represents the average (as opposed to, say, the median of the 20th percentile worker, whose benefit provision is typically less generous).

In other words, there's no evidence to support the contention that adding benefits to wages changes the trends shown thus far (though it does, of course, raise the levels of pay). The real compensation trend for the occupation classes of workers that saw less wage growth since the late 1970s is much the same as the wage trend. The share of workers with employer-provided health and pension benefits has diminished, and employers' costs for those benefits, on average, have grown only slightly over time.

---

[7] Bivens et al. (2014) assign the average compensation package to the wage of the production, nonsupervisory worker. Generally, the value of benefit packages received by such workers is below the average, so this adjustment may bias compensation levels up to some degree.

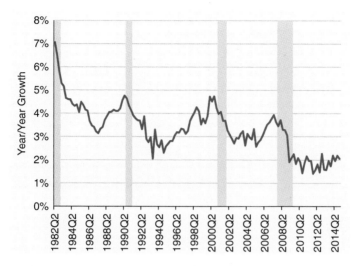

Fig. 6.6 First principal component: Five series, nominal growth

Near-Term Wage Issues

This review of wage and compensation trends would be incomplete without a look at a wage issue that has been generating intense interest in the near-term economy and presents a good example of the role of economic slack in nominal wage trends. Though as of this writing the current economic expansion is over five years old, wage growth, not accounting for inflation, has been flat at around 2 % and unresponsive to what tightening has occurred in the labor market. This persistent lack of responsiveness of wage trends to growth has caught the attention of the Federal Reserve as well as the broader media.[8] Because, until recently, consumer prices have also been growing around 2 %, the media have often framed the issue of stagnant real earnings as the recovery's missing ingredient.

In order to be careful not to "cherry pick" any one wage or compensation series to examine this dynamic, Figure 6.6 plots the first principal component of five different wage and compensation series.[9] This technique is commonly used to summarize numerous data series in a way that pulls out their common signal, in this case, yearly changes in nominal growth since the early 1980s.

The five series are:

• Employment cost index: hourly compensation

---

[8] See Janet Yellen 2014: http://www.federalreserve.gov/newsevents/speech/yellen20140822a.htm and, for a media account, Leonhardt 2015: http://www.nytimes.com/2015/01/18/upshot/driving-the-obama-tax-plan-the-great-wage-slowdown.html?abt=0002&abg=1.

[9] By "cherry picking," I mean that given these "high frequency" quarterly data, analysts can sometimes find one series that makes their particular case as far as whether wage growth is speeding up, slowing down, or neutral. I wanted to avoid that possibility, so I combined these quarterly series.

- Employment cost index: hourly wages
- Productivity series: hourly compensation
- Median weekly earnings, full-time workers
- Average hourly earnings, production, nonsupervisory workers

The series decelerates notably during the "Great Recession" from a peak nominal growth rate of about 4 % and stops falling when it hits about 2 % (about the rate of inflation, implying stagnant earnings), where it has remained. In this regard, the combined series reveals little in the way of wage pressure and thus serves as a useful and potent confirmation of the role of slack in wage formation. Later, I return to the information in this figure in discussing why "wage targeting" would be a useful policy for the Federal Reserve to adopt in its assessment of slack when setting monetary policy.

Labor's Share of National Income

Finally, a more complete understanding of current issues regarding earnings requires a look at a relatively recent phenomenon: the decline in the labor share of national income. One can think of aggregate income as generated by two "factors:" labor and capital. Thus, economists examine factor shares—the shares of national income attributable to each of these factors. Also relevant to this discussion is that most economists assumed factor shares to remain relatively constant over time, an assumption that is difficult to sustain in the face of the recent trend shown below.

As usual, in reality, the division of income is a lot more complicated than these two factors allow. We've already seen that realized stock options show up in earnings data of the top earners. Proprietors' income—self-employed or unincorporated businesses—is also ambiguous and now amounts to 9 % of national income (what part of the income of a physician in private practice is earnings versus profits?). I do not try to finesse these measurement issues here, in part because more careful work that does so comes up with findings similar to those that follow (see, for example, Elsby et al. 2013).

Figure 6.7 plots aggregate compensation as a share of national income since 1959. The pre-2007 average of this series is about 65 % (the straight line in the figure), a value around which the series has apparently wiggled since the late 1960s, giving rise to the widely held assumption noted above of constant factor shares. Since then, however, the series has declined almost 4 percentage points. The equivalent of $555 billion in 2013, about $4000 per worker, has shifted from the labor share to the capital (or profit) share of national income.

Summarizing, we see that real wages have stagnated for many in the workforce in recent years. While the conventional wisdom is that this unfortunate trend has exclusively beset only low-wage or low-skilled (i.e., less educated) workers, the data show otherwise. Other than a brief (but important) boost from the full-employment 1990s, annual earnings for the bottom 90 % of the workforce have

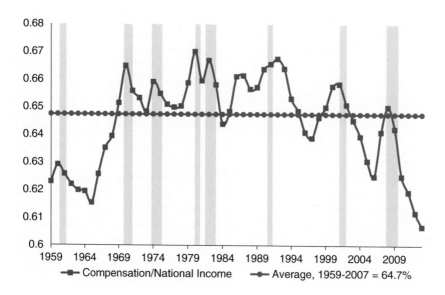

Fig. 6.7 Compensation as share of national income, 1959–2013

been flat since the late 1970s. Even college graduates, specifically men without advanced degrees, have experienced flat real earnings since around 2000. Adding in employer-provided benefits does not change the picture, and aggregating individuals' wages up to national "factor shares" reveals similarly weak outcomes. Most recently, persistent slack in the postrecession job market has led to flat wage growth, stuck at around 2 % in nominal terms, about the rate of inflation, implying flat average compensation in real terms.

In other words, the evidence clearly shows that America has a wage problem. The following sections present ideas as to why and what to do about it.

Theories of Wage Formation

Having documented the relevant trends in the prior section, the rest of the chapter turns to diagnosing what's behind wage, compensation, and labor share trends and prescribing policy solutions that might help to reverse or at least mitigate wage stagnation and inequality. A potentially useful place to start is by briefly reviewing the economic theories of wage determination. Perhaps such theories can point to useful diagnostics as to what's behind the observed trends and prescriptions regarding intervention points. As with all economic theories, the real world is considerably more complex and no single theory adequately explains wage formation.

A notable shortcoming of one group of theories, for example, is that they generally assume full employment: that wages are set at the intersection of supply and demand, either at the level of the firm or the macroeconomy (aggregating up across firms), at full employment. However, as I show below, full employment hasn't been the norm in the U.S. labor market in recent decades. In fact, according to conventional measures, the U.S. labor market has been at full employment only about 30 % of the time since 1980, and this absence of tight labor markets and the bargaining power they deliver to middle- and low-wage workers is an important explanation for the trends documented in part 1. Thus, I divide the discussion of wage-determination theories by whether or not they assume full employment.

Given how wrong that assumption of full employment has been, readers may wonder whether theories that make such an assumption can still add value to our diagnosis and prescriptions. I believe so, as we will see that even theories that ignore the reality of labor market slack offer some useful guidance regarding other aspects of wage determination.

Theories that Assume Full Employment

Perhaps the dominant theory is that in a capitalist economy with "free markets," people are paid their marginal product. The theory dictates that firms hire workers up to the point where their additional contribution to the firm's output fails to cover their cost, that is, up to the point where the marginal product of the last worker hired is zero. To hire beyond that point would be an unnecessary cost to the firm; to hire below that point would leave money on the table as the firm's technology and market share could profitably absorb more production.

While marginal product theory is obviously an abstraction—imagine a business of any magnitude trying to figure out the precise value added by its latest hire—it does have at least one important real world application: One of the most consistent findings in labor economics is that more highly educated workers receive greater pay than those with less education do. According to Bureau of Labor Statistics (BLS) data, the median weekly earnings of full-time workers with a college degree (bachelor's or higher) was $1,194 in 2013. For high school graduates, the comparable figure was $651.

On the other hand, even a passing familiarity with U.S. wage and demographic trends should engender some skepticism regarding the explanatory power of marginal product theory alone, in part because it omits labor market slack and bargaining power (and the negative correlation between the two). For example, Schmitt and Jones (2012) show that low-wage workers are considerably older and more highly educated today than was the case 30 years ago, yet relative to earlier cohorts, they earn less. Of course, it could be the case that the skill requirements of production have changed in ways to lower the marginal product of today's more highly educated low-wage workforce but, there's little evidence for that, and some evidence to the contrary.[10]

In fact, a major finding of this review is that while skill enhancement through better educational opportunities and job training measures are, of course, essential factors in raising individuals' earnings capacities, particularly for the least advantaged, these "supply side" factors are by no means the whole story in wage trends over the past few decades. Even skill acquisition that raises a worker's marginal product may not necessarily boost his or her wage. In sum, there is some evidence for marginal product theory in the differentiation of wage levels by education, though less in terms of trends. Its policy implication is a sound one: better educational opportunities, especially for those facing barriers to access quality schooling. A shortcoming of the theory is its assumption of full employment and lack of any role for bargaining power or broader market failures.

Marginal product is a microeconomic theory in that it refers to the wage formation process at the individual or firm level. In what is perhaps the dominant macroeconomic theory—the neoclassical growth model, which also assumes full employment—aggregate productivity plays a central role in wage growth.

In this theory, average compensation is expected to grow at the rate of productivity, which itself is a function of the interaction of capital (e.g., equipment, structures, hardware, and software) and technology. Things that boost productivity growth, which could be smarter workers (a linkage to marginal product theory) or innovations that speed up output per hour (i.e., productivity), will raise average compensation.

While this theory has some empirical support—there are significant time periods when average compensation grew at the rate of productivity—for our purposes it has numerous shortcomings. First, it is mathematically the case that when compensation grows at the rate of productivity, wages and the labor share of national income will remain constant. However, the previous figure shows that in recent years, this has not been the case, as compensation has declined fairly sharply as a share of income. Second, as the prior section revealed, there is great and increasing dispersion of wages at different levels such that understanding movements in the average wage is obviously insufficient for our purposes.

The neoclassical growth model's focus on productivity, capital investment, and innovation are useful reminders of the importance of these key growth factors. But the fact that neither of these developments—the decline in the wage share of national income and increased wage dispersion—are tractable within the framework (as it assumes constant shares and only includes average wages), not to mention the incorrect full employment assumption, means we will need to look elsewhere for theoretical guidance regarding wage formation.

---

[10] David Autor 2014, in "Polanyi's Paradox," and others argue that technology is neutral toward lower-wage workers.

Theories That Do Not Assume Full Employment

Since periods of full employment have been the exception in recent decades, it is very important to review theories of wage determination that do not assume away this critical fact.

In recent years, economists have been able to tap into larger and more nuanced datasets to build so-called "wage curve" models that explicitly link changes in labor market slack. For example, a particularly timely and useful wage curve model was recently estimated by economists David Blanchflower and Andrew Levin (2013), tracking wage movements across all 50 states for the years 1990–2012, yielding almost 1,200 observations. Their results show strong, inverse correlations between slack and wage growth, implying, for example, "that a doubling of the unemployment rate is associated with a 10 % decline in real wages."

Also relevant to our diagnostic analysis, Blanchflower and Levin find that unemployment is but one measure of slack inversely correlated with wage growth. Their wage-curve model reveals the importance of underemployment (e.g., part-time workers who would rather be full-timers) and "nonparticipation," a measure that captures the extent to which potential workers are out of the labor force, thus contributing to slack but not counted in traditional labor force measures.

"Search models" of wage formation are also instructive. These models start from the observation that unemployment is always far from zero and the matching process of workers seeking jobs is a lot trickier than "frictionless" matches of buyers and sellers on stock exchanges. As Rogerson et al. point out, "there is simply no such thing as a centralized market where buyers and sellers of labor meet and trade at a single price, as assumed in classical equilibrium theory." (2005, 960).

In these models of wage determination, bargaining power plays an important and explicit role. Potential workers and employers bargain over the wage offer, with the parties trying to get the best deal for themselves, that is, the job seekers want to maximize compensation, and the employers want to maximize profits (and thus minimize compensation). How they settle the deal is a function of their "threat points"—essentially, outside options that give them either more or less room to maximize their position in the bargaining process.

For example, a job seeker with considerable savings has the time to drive a harder wage bargain on his or her own behalf relative to someone who needs a paycheck right away. Conversely, an employer who isn't facing much in the way of unmet demand has time to "shop around" for the best worker at the lowest price (wage).

Some of the realities we see in the job market fit into this model. For example, unemployment insurance raises the job seeker's bargaining clout and can facilitate a better match from his or her perspective (more recently, analysts have suggested the new subsidized health insurance options from the Affordable Care Act will play a similar role). High unemployment strengthens employers' hands in this bargain, as workers have fewer options and thus less bargaining clout. In fact, one of the key findings of my own work in this area is that the bargaining power provided to workers from full employment conditions—or missing in periods of slack—is an important wage determinant in contemporary U.S. labor markets.

A related theory is "efficiency wage theory," under which for a variety of reasons, employers will adjust a certain worker's wages above that worker's outside options, given their skill level and experience. The reason for the above-market wage might be to increase the worker's effort or their allegiance to the firm, or, to reduce turnover and thus avoid losing sunk costs associated with hiring and training.

The idea that paying workers more might increase their productivity (very different from the neoclassical assumption that productivity determines the wage) and lower turnover costs to the firm has been offered as an explanation why increases in the minimum wage fail to trigger the predicted job losses engendered by equilibrium wage theory (the idea that any employer who paid a worker above the market wage would go out of business). In other words, higher labor costs engendered by the wage increase are absorbed by improved productivity. On the other hand (barring a wage floor), if demand is weak, workers are plentiful, and skill demands are low—or skilled workers are amply supplied—firms may be more willing to invoke turnover or "shirking risk" rather than pay a higher "efficiency" wage.

Before closing this brief tour, it is useful to make a final stop at "institutionalist" theories of wage formation. The idea here—and parts of this were sprinkled through all of the above—is that entrenched societal institutions, laws, and norms play a key role in how earnings are distributed. Moreover, these institutionally determined outcomes have less to do with marginal product than any of the theories above would dictate. Unions, political power, the ideology of policy makers from Congress to the Federal Reserve, the setting and enforcement of labor standards (minimum wages, overtime rules, workplace safety), immigration practices—all of these are large and determinant forces outside the narrow scope of marginal product.

There's some evidence to support these more nuanced models—wage curve, efficiency wages, search models, and institutionalist approaches—some of which I show in the next section. For example, an institutionalist framework would predict that international trading regimes can pit blue-collar workers in high-wage countries against those in low-wage countries, leading to wage gains in the latter at the expense of some classes of workers in the former.[11] Below, I show evidence from my own work (with Dean Baker) on wage curve analysis. And unlike many of the other models, the role of labor market slack in these more nuanced models leads to some of the policy ideas I recommend.

A memorable quip in economic modeling is that while all models are wrong, some models are useful. While many of the theories have shortcomings in the real world, especially the assumption of full employment, there are useful ideas in all of them, ideas that I pull out and suggest in the next section on policy ideas to address the wage challenge.

---

[11] Actually, standard trade theory ("Stolper/Samuelson") makes this same prediction.

Diagnosis and Prescription: What's behind Wage Stagnation and Earnings Inequality and What Can Be Done to Reverse It?

The causes of the trends documented in the previous section are typically attributed to these factors:

Globalization: Increased international trade, or globalization, is frequently raised in this context because increased trade has placed American workers in the tradable goods sector in competition with their counterparts from lower-wage countries, essentially increasing the implicit supply of labor. Of course, workers displaced from the tradable sector then compete with others in the nontradable sector. This creates the potential for greater labor market slack, particularly if, as has been the case in the U.S., net exports are negative (we run trade deficits).

Technology and the Need for Greater Skills in the Workforce: Those who favor this explanation maintain that as technology has pervaded the workplace, employers' skill demands have increased to the disadvantage of those lacking such skills. This was discussed above under the rubric of SBTC. This explanation relates to marginal product theory.

Eroded Institutions: Reaching back to institutionalist theories of wage formation, others claim that the erosion of the real value of the minimum wage, union density, and labor standards has hurt many in the labor force who heretofore benefited from the protection of these institutional forces.

Absence of Full Employment: As stressed throughout, labor market slack is one of the most important problems facing middle- and low-wage workers. The full-employment 1990s, for example, were the only period since the latter 1970s when real low and median wages rose at the rate of productivity growth. In recently completed research shown below by Baker and me, we find solid evidence that lower unemployment disproportionately raises the pay of the lowest paid workers and has virtually no impact on those at the top of pay scale. In other words, full employment's impact on the patterns of wage growth is inequality reducing (Bernstein and Baker 2013).

Figure 6.8 tells an important part of this historical story. Using the Congressional Budget Office's estimates of the lowest unemployment rate consistent with stable inflation, it shows the percent of quarters when unemployment has been "too high" in the sense of being above the full employment unemployment rate. Over the period when real wages grew across the wage scale (see Table 6.1 above, specifically the trend from 1947 to 1979), unemployment was "too high" only 30 % of the time, meaning the job market was at full employment 70 % of the time. Since then, this share has flipped: unemployment has been too high 70 % of the time. And, of course, these are the years when wage growth was both stagnant for many and widely dispersed.

Of course, full employment wasn't the only difference between these two periods—I've already stressed other relevant differences, including globalization. But it

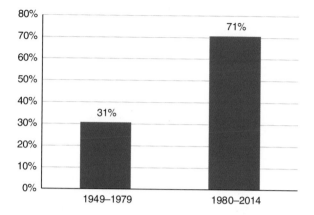

Fig. 6.8 Percent of time unemployment has been "Too High" (Source: Congressional Budget Office, Bureau of Labor Statistics)

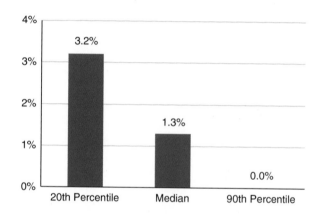

Fig. 6.9 Change in real wages by wage level given 30 % decline in unemployment rate (Bernstein and Baker 2013)

is one important factor. Figure 6.8 also poses a stark challenge to those wage determination theories that assume away the problem of labor market slack.

How important a factor is the absence of full employment? Results from Bernstein and Baker (2013) are presented in Fig. 6.9, which come from panel regressions of all states using annual data from 1979 to 2014, shows the impact on wages at different percentiles from a 30 % decline in the unemployment rate (not a 30 percentage point decline; an example of a 30 % decline would be from 7 % to 4.9 %).

These results show that such a decline raises real wages the most at the bottom of the pay scale, less than half that much at the middle of the pay scale, and not at all at the top. Moreover, other results from our work show a similar pattern for hours worked, implying that full employment boosts both hourly wages and hours worked, and does so progressively (more so at the low end of the pay scale than at the high end).

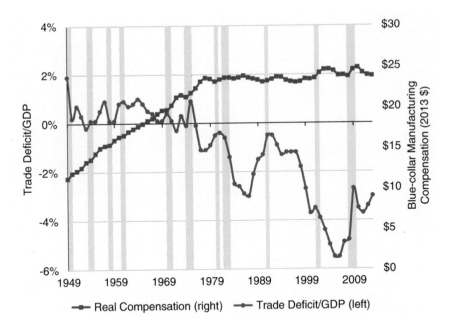

Fig. 6.10 Trade deficit/GDP and manufacturing compensation, 1949–2013

In considering policy interventions to address the impact of these various forces on wage stagnation and inequality, begin with globalization and consider the manufacturing wage. In real terms, the real hourly compensation of production workers (i.e., workers in blue-collar occupations) more than doubled from about $10 to $25 between the late 1940s and the late 1970s (see blue line with squares in Fig. 6.10). Since then, despite productivity gains in the sector, real compensation has hardly changed at all (in 2013 dollars, it was about $23.50 in 1979 and $23.80 in 2013).[12]

Economists often ascribe trade penetration to these figures—the fact that workers in the tradable goods sector were exposed to much more global competition in the latter period when pay stagnated. But I think a more nuanced story is necessary, one that points toward a policy solution: It's not more trade that has hurt blue-collar workers in manufacturing, it's trade *deficits* (the red line in Fig. 6.10 with circles). Over the period when production worker wages doubled, the trade surplus averaged 0.5 % of GDP (1947–79); since then, the trade deficit has been negative in every year, ranging from minus 0.4 % to minus 5.5 % of GDP, and averaging minus 2.6 %.

As economist Josh Bivens has shown, when we run trade deficits of these magnitudes for that long, we are exporting large numbers of manufacturing jobs and

---

[12] I use the same technique as Bivens et al. (2014) to convert public manufacturing wage data for production workers into compensation data, i.e., I multiply the hourly wage by the ratio of National Income and Product Accounts aggregate manufacturing compensation to wages.

significantly damaging the ability of the sector to effectively grow and provide remunerative, high-value–added jobs for production workers. Bivens finds that our persistent trade deficits have reduced labor demand for non-college-educated workers in tradable sectors, leading to an annual earnings loss of 5.5 %, or $1,800 for full-time, full-year workers.[13] Of course, if diminished labor demand in one sector was fully offset in another sector, our persistent trade deficits might not be a problem. But an inherent point in Bivens' analysis, one that ties into a theme in this review, is that displaced workers from one sector add to labor market slack (unemployment and underemployment) in other sectors, exerting downward pressure on earnings for broad swaths of affected workers.

In other words, *globalization* is a major factor in the negative wage trends shown above, and the pursuit of more balanced trade is one important way to help reverse those trends. As Bernstein and Baker argue in a *New York Times* piece,[14] exchange rate policy is key to pursuing that balance, especially given the widely accepted fact that some of our trading partners, including but not solely the Chinese, place our manufacturers at a competitive disadvantage by suppressing the value of their currencies relative to the dollar, thus making their imports cheaper in dollar terms and exports more expensive in foreign currency terms. We offer various policy ideas to push back at such currency management, from legislation treating currency management as a violation of international trading rules that leads to offsetting tariffs to explicit reciprocity arrangements. If a country wants to buy our Treasuries, we must be able to buy theirs (which is not always the case now).

Turning to *higher educational attainment*, there is, of course, no question that more highly educated workers have, on average, higher wages and lower unemployment. At the same time, Figure 6.4 shows that real trends over time have not been particularly favorable, even for those with 4-year college degrees, especially men.

This latter point poses a challenge to skills-based explanations of wage inequality, a point that has been acknowledged even by economists closely associated with those explanations. David Autor, for example, argued that education-only explanations for rising inequality "can suck all the air out of the conversation," adding that "… all economists should be pushing back against this simplistic view."

David Card, a prominent economist who has often been a skeptic of SBTC explanations, as well as someone who has consistently documented the educational wage premium, explains the rationale behind Autor's caveat: "I don't think the college-to-noncollege wage premium gives you any insight into why such a large share of the economic gains has accrued to such a tiny share of the population."[15] The phenom-

---

[13] Josh Bivens 2013. "Using Standard Models to Benchmark the Costs of Globalization for American Workers Without a College Degree," http://s3.epi.org/files/2013/standard-models-benchmark-costs-globalization.pdf

[14] Jared Bernstein and Dean Baker, "Taking Aim at the Wrong Deficit," *New York Times*, November 6, 2013, http://www.nytimes.com/2013/11/07/opinion/taking-aim-at-the-wrong-deficit.html.

[15] Both the Card and Autor quotes are referenced here: Jared Bernstein, "Inequality's Roots: Beyond Technology," Economix, *New York Times*, November 18, 2013, http://economix.blogs.nytimes.com/2013/11/18/inequalitys-roots-beyond-technology/?_php=true&_type=blogs&_r=1.

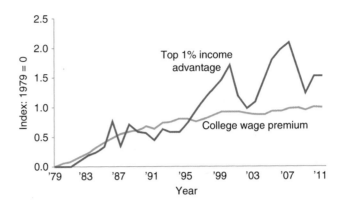

Fig. 6.11 Growth of the top 1 % income advantage and the college wage premium, 1979–2011 (Source: Mishel's analysis of Piketty and Saez [Jan 2013 update, Table A-6] and Current Population Survey Outgoing Rotation Group microdata) (Note: College wage premium reflects regression-adjusted wage advantage of those with a college degree or more)

enon Card is describing here can be gleaned from Fig. 6.5, showing the extent to which the top 0.1 % of wage earners have pulled away from the pack, including the rest of the top 1 % (i.e., the 99.0–99.9th percentiles). Surely, the vast majority of both groups are college educated, yet the differential in their wage growth rates are striking. Card is also referring to the deceleration of the (4-year) college wage premium (relative to the high school wage) observed in Fig. 6.4 (note how both high school and college weekly earnings broadly track each other since 2000).

These wage dynamics are most evident in Fig. 6.11, made by labor economist Larry Mishel.[16] The light blue line shows the flattening college premium, regression-adjusted, against the trend in income of the top 1 % relative to that of the bottom 90 %. The latter moves in the familiar pattern seen in Fig. 6.5, including cyclical gyrations that are clearly related to stock market returns, as opposed to any skill differentials. In fact, it is implausible to view these varied series of the very top fractile incomes or earnings as related to employers' skill demands. There's no conceivable model that would explain such cyclical movements within that framework.

The key insight from the perspective of this chapter is the following: Providing workers with more education or training will often translate into higher earnings. Encouraging and allowing such persons to achieve their intellectual, productive, and earnings potential must be a central goal of public policy. Moreover, higher educational attainment is increasingly important, because even if the education wage premium is not rising much, it remains highly elevated. Also, as Reeves has pointed out (see Chap. 13), educational attainment is a key mobility determinant for children from disadvantaged backgrounds.

---

[16] Working Economics (Economic Policy Institute blog), "Greg Mankiw Forgets to Offer Data for his Biggest Claim," blog entry by Lawrence Mishel, June 25, 2013, http://www.epi.org/blog/greg-mankiw-forgets-offer-data-biggest-claim/.

But we should also be aware that while, on average, such interventions will raise someone's earnings—assuming adequate labor demand, a key issue I explore below—it will not render him or her immune from trends that have flattened the trajectory of real wages for most education categories.

Furthermore, the stabilization of the college wage premium and the decline in the ratio of middle- to low-wage workers challenge the SBTC theory, as its prediction that technology's dissemination generates increasingly unmet skill demands predicts increased wage divergence by decile or skill level. The fact that the top 0.1 % have pulled so far from the pack while the wages of the bottom 90 % generally have stagnated is similarly inconsistent with both SBTC and simple marginal product stories.[17] In this regard, the education solution for rising inequality—versus basic wage stagnation faced by an individual—may be more limited than most advocates recognize.

In effect, the education/wage debate needs clarification. On the one hand, there clearly exists a positive wage gradient by education level. On the other, the SBTC story is incomplete in that more education alone won't solve the wage problem. It is not hard, however, to square these observations. On average, an individual is better off with more education or training, much as marginal product theory would predict. But (a) that doesn't inoculate him or her from stagnant trends within educational classes, and (b) it doesn't speak to the wage needs of those who are not likely or able to move up the education ladder. A comprehensive wage policy agenda must be mindful of all of these nuances.

Finally, it is essential to note that increasing the earnings capacity of individual workers does not simply mean "finish college," though that's a laudable goal for many. It should also include work-based learning such as apprenticeship programs and on-the-job training, as articulated in a recent paper by Holzer and Lerman (2014). These authors find that such policies can provide much needed upward earnings mobility for many who may be less likely to benefit from a 4-year college degree.

Reinstating the power of eroded labor market institutions is also necessary. The federal minimum wage remains over 20 % below its peak in the late 1960s, and while many states have acted independently to raise the wage floor, others, particularly in the South, have not. The most recently introduced proposal by White House and Congressional Democrats is to increase the federal minimum from its current level of $7.25 to $10.10 in three annual increments, and then index it to inflation. According to recent analysis by the Congressional Budget Office, which employs standard assumptions from the minimum wage literature about the impacts of the policy, the increase would raise the pay of 24.5 million low-wage workers, though

---

[17]Economists developed a "hollowing out" hypothesis to explain some of these patterns in ways intended to support an altered version of SBTC, but their evidence was particular to certain time periods and inconsistent with others. See Mishel 2013.

the CBO also predicts that 500,000 jobs would be lost due the mandated increase in labor costs.[18]

Policy analyst Ross Eisenbrey (2014) provides a very useful review of a broad set of other important labor standards that need attention in the interest of raising pay for workers with limited bargaining power. His recommendations include:

- Updating/increasing the salary threshold below which salaried workers are eligible for overtime pay: This threshold—the so-called "salary test"—is not indexed to inflation, meaning that unless policy makers act, nominal earnings growth will increasingly exempt salaried workers from time-and-a-half pay, even when their occupational duties mean they should be nonexempt (there is a "duties test" but it is less reliably applied in practice than the salary threshold). Simply adjusting the current threshold for inflation based on its nominal value back in the mid-1970s would more than double it from $455 to about $980.
- Improving the enforcement of "wage and hour" rules: Incidence of "wage theft" (not paying workers what they are contractually owed), misclassification (classifying regular employees as self-employed who are thus ineligible for minimum wages, overtime, and other established protections), and nonpayment of overtime has led to significant wage losses for many lower-paid workers.
- Leveling the playing field for union organizing: Eisenbrey presents extensive evidence of both legal and structural changes that have tilted the balance against those interested in boosting the number and ability of workers to engage in collective bargaining, thus blocking an essential rebalancing of bargaining power. Reversing this tilt requires allowing unions to organize subcontracted workers, crackdowns (versus "wrist slaps") on employers who illegally block organizing drives, reducing waiting periods between drives and elections, and providing union advocates the same access to potential members that employers currently enjoy.

In addition, one of economics' most unfortunate and unrealistic assumptions is that the job market is typically at full employment, barring occasional cyclical downturns, an assumption clearly belied by the second bar in Fig. 6.8. Instead, in the interest of generating balanced and lasting real wage growth, policy makers must pursue full employment. This goal is particularly germane for less advantaged and minority communities, as even when the overall job market is at full employment, their portion of the market can still be too slack to enforce a more equitable distribution of wages.

Getting back to full employment requires fiscal and monetary stimulus, particularly in periods like the recent past, where such actions are necessary to offset the residual weakness in the private sector stemming from the bursting of the housing bubble and the financial crisis. Interestingly, the monetary authorities—the Federal

---

[18] CBO, "The Effects of a Minimum-Wage Increase on Employment and Family Income," February 18, 2014. The budget office finds that 16.5 million workers benefit directly from the increase and projects that another 8.5 million indirectly benefit from "spillovers"—the tendency of employers to raise wages of those just above the new minimum.

Reserve—have in recent years quite explicitly stressed persistent labor market slack as a rationale for their fairly aggressive monetary stimulus. Clearly, they have been in the mode of weighting the full employment side of their dual mandate.

That said, an important idea has surfaced recently that exists right at the intersection of wage policy and monetary policy: wage targeting by the Federal Reserve. The central bank, particularly under Chair Janet Yellen, is known to use a "dashboard" of indicators to determine slack in the economy and thus to guide its macro-management role of balancing growth and price pressures.[19] For a variety of reasons—including the difficulty assessing slack using more traditional measures such as unemployment (due to declines in the labor force), the "flattening of the Phillips curve" (i.e., price inflation has become less sensitive to unemployment), and the general stability of the Fed's most prominent price inflation gauge[20]—some analysts have suggested that tracking nominal wage trends (as summarized in Fig. 6.6 above) would improve the Fed's ability to more accurately determine when economic pressures are building in the labor market.

Researchers at Goldman Sachs, for example, in an analysis that carefully tracks the impact on inflation and unemployment of the various types of indicators or rules the Fed uses to guide interest rate policy, conclude "…that the benefits of focusing on wage inflation are substantial when slack is difficult to measure and wage growth acts as a reliable cross check for the true amount of spare capacity" (Stehn 2014, 1). Importantly, they argue that upweighting wage targeting could reduce the likelihood of a premature tightening of monetary policy that would throw the economy off the path to full employment too soon. In the interest of both stronger recoveries and more broadly shared wage growth, I judge wage targeting to be an important idea worthy of more research.

Unlike monetary policy, fiscal policy has been highly problematic, as Congress has pursued "austerity measures"—reducing budget deficits even as output gaps persist. For example, various analysts found that fiscal drag reduced real GDP growth in 2013 by 1.5 percentage points. Conventional rules of thumb imply that the unemployment rate was 0.75 of a percentage point higher than it otherwise would have been. That amounts to over 1 million jobs, and coincidentally, about 10 % of the actual 2013 unemployment rate, invoking real wage elasticities of the magnitudes in Fig. 6.9.

Especially given the slack labor markets in disadvantaged communities even in good times, another essential policy for achieving full employment is direct job creation. While the idea of direct job creation may invoke images from the 1930s of men in camps undertaking large public infrastructure projects, contemporary versions are quite different. Donna Pavetti reviews a program that was effectively implemented as part of the Recovery Act, the Temporary Assistance for Needy

---

[19] "Janet Yellen's Dashboard," 2014, Brookings Institution, http://www.brookings.edu/research/interactives/2014/janet-yellens-dashboard.

[20] That is, the core personal consumption deflator, which, as I show in my blog entry at On the Economy, "Price Inflation and Wage Inflation," http://jaredbernsteinblog.com/price-inflation-and-wage-inflation/, has basically moved between 1 and 2 % for over 10 years.

Families Emergency Fund, wherein the federal government significantly subsidized the pay of targeted workers who found jobs in any sector (public, private, nonprofit, etc.) (Pavetti 2014).

Not only did this program provide jobs for about 250,000 workers, it did so at a cost below that of other Recovery Act job creation measures.[21] Moreover, some follow-up evidence suggests that subsidized workers kept their jobs even after the subsidy ended. To be sure, program rules must forbid displacement (the substitution by employers of a subsidized worker for a nonsubsidized one) and be vigilantly enforced. But Pavetti (2014) convincingly argues that a scaled-up, national version of this direct job creation program would be a strong antidote for persistent labor market slack, especially for the hard to employ.

Conclusion

For much of the last 3½ decades, trends in real wages for various different groups in the workforce have been stagnant or worse. As shown above, this is true for middle- or low-wage deciles, most education levels, the bottom 90 % of annual earners, and even the national share of labor-based income. Adding compensation does not change this picture, though it does raise the level of earnings at any point in time.

However, those at the very top of the wage scale— at the top 1 % or even more so, at the top 0.1 %—and those with advanced degrees have consistently posted strong gains, even accounting for temporary losses associated with the business cycle (and the loss of equity-based earnings). Thus, two key observations that surface from the empirical analysis are real wage stagnation and increased wage inequality.

Theories of wage formation highlight the role of education and skills in promoting higher earnings, the role of macroeconomic variables—specifically labor market slack vs. tautness—the role of labor market standards and institutions, and the critical role of worker bargaining power. All of these factors are important if policy makers are to undertake measures to address the wage problems identified throughout. Research on educational premiums shows that more schooling is clearly associated with higher earnings, a fact that is already widely reflected in policy debates.

On the other hand, a problem that is both more immediate and longer lasting, as shown in Fig. 6.8, is the persistence of slack labor markets and its strong corollary, diminished bargaining power for low- and middle-wage workers. Moreover, this problem is generally missing from both many theories of wage determination, which assume full employment, as well as the broader analysis of wage trends. Remarkably, many policy discussions of what to do about wages assume full employment, which naturally elevates supply-side (versus demand-side) solutions like education and training. I've stressed throughout that these are, of course, essen-

---

[21] Compare, for example, cost per job values in Pavetti's Appendix Table 1 with cost per job figures discussed in this analysis. See Council of Economic Advisers 2009, Table 4.

tial weapons in the fight against wage stagnation and inequality, but they are insufficient.

Full employment and robust labor standards are equally important, perhaps even more so in the sense that absent ample job quantity, even skilled workers risk being underemployed. In that regard, I hope this review will remind policy makers that the most holistic approach to pushing back on stagnant and unequal wage trends is the best. Our interventions in this space must, of course, recognize and attack skills deficits. But they must also attack trade deficits, the absence of full employment, and the erosion of labor standards. Yes, this constitutes a highly comprehensive and challenging agenda, but that is what it will take to address the wage difficulties that have been faced by most workers in the U.S. labor force for far too long.

Finally, there are numerous aspects of wage analysis that I left out of this analysis not because they are unimportant in my judgment but because, though others may disagree, I view them as less central. Some labor market analysts believe that the pace at which technology is replacing workers has accelerated in recent years, with profound effects on jobs and incomes for many in the workforce. I've examined these arguments and found them lacking in convincing evidence, at least for now. But it is an issue very much worth tracking.[22]

Though I mentioned the role of immigration in various places, I did not give this explanation—the increased supply of low-skilled immigration as a factor depressing wages—much weight in the above analysis. There is a large literature on this question and the general consensus is that such supply effects have hurt the wages of those who are substitutes for low-wage immigrant labor while having little impact, or even a positive impact, on those who are complements. In the U.S. labor market, the latter—complements—vastly outnumber the former, though the negative impact of supply effects on the wages of, say, high-school dropouts or disadvantaged minorities, should not be overlooked.

While I focused quite closely on wage trends of various income classes, I did not examine issues around wage mobility (tracking cohorts of workers across time). Such analysis is useful but data are scarce relative to the type of information upon which I focused, and what evidence there is suggests little change in the pace of mobility over time. If that is the case, then the problems of more stagnation and more inequality cannot be said to be offset by greater mobility.

Finally, it may fairly be argued that given how "gridlocked" federal politics are today, few policy makers would be interested in tackling these issues. I acknowledge the limits of our current political system to deal with the wage problem documented throughout, but an analysis of these political constraints is beyond the scope of this chapter. However, these wage challenges are not going away anytime soon,

---

[22] Jared Bernstein, "Before Blaming the Robots, Let's Get the Policy Right," Economix, *New York Times,* February 17, 2014, http://economix.blogs.nytimes.com/2014/02/17/before-blaming-the-robots-lets-get-the-policy-right/?_php=true&_type=blogs&_r=0; On the Economy; "Where's the Automation in the Productivity Accounts," blog entry by Jared Bernstein, http://jaredbernstein-blog.com/wheres-the-automation-in-the-productivity-accounts/

and perhaps, in more cooperative times, future policy makers may find the analysis and policy recommendations to be useful.

Acknowledgments The chapter acknowledges the input of Jesse Rothstein, Ben Spielberg, the Economic Policy Institute (for much of the data on hourly wage percentiles), and the members of the ETS project of which this is a part. Any mistakes are my own.

References

Autor, David. 2014. *Polanyi's paradox and the shape of employment growth*. Draft of paper presented at the Federal Reserve Bank of Kansas City's economic policy symposium, Jackson Hole, WY (August 21–23). https://www.kansascityfed.org/publicat/sympos/2014/GD2.pdf.

Bernstein, Jared, and Dean Baker. 2013. *Getting back to full employment: A better bargain for working people*. Washington, DC: Center for Economic Policy and Research. http://cepr.net/documents/Getting-Back-to-Full-Employment_20131118.pdf.

Bivens, John, Elise Gould, Lawrence Mishel, and Heidi Shierholz. 2014. *Raising America's pay: Why it's our central economic policy challenge*. Washington, DC: Economic Policy Institute. http://www.epi.org/publication/raising-americas-pay/.

Blanchflower, David G., and Andrew T. Levin. 2013. *Labor market slack and monetary policy, full employment*. Washington, DC: Center on Budget and Policy Priorities.

Council of Economic Advisers. 2009. *Estimates of job creation from the American Recovery and Reinvestment Act of 2009*. Washington, DC (May). https://www.whitehouse.gov/assets/documents/Job-Years_Revised5-8.pdf.

Eisenbrey, Ross. 2014. Improving the quality of jobs through better labor standards. In *Center on Budget and Policy Priorities, full employment*. http://www.pathtofullemployment.org/wp-content/uploads/2014/04/eisenbrey.pdf.

Elsby, Michael W. L., Bart Hobijn, and Ayşegül Şahin. 2013, *The decline of the U.S. labor share*. Washington, DC: Brookings Institution (Fall). http://www.brookings.edu/~/media/Projects/BPEA/Fall%202013/2013b_elsby_labor_share.pdf.

Holzer, Harry J., and Robert I. Lerman. 2014. Work-based learning to expand jobs and occupational qualifications for youth. In *Center on Budget and Policy Priorities, full employment*. http://www.pathtofullemployment.org/wp-content/uploads/2014/04/holzerlerman.pdf.

Kopczuk, Wojciech, Emmanuel Saez, and Jae Song. 2010. Earnings inequality and mobility in the United States: Evidence from social security data since 1937. *Quarterly Journal of Economics*, http://elsa.berkeley.edu/~saez/kopczuk-saez-songQJE10mobility.pdf.

Mishel, Lawrence, Josh Bivens, Elise Gould, and Heidi Shierholz. 2012. *The state of working America*, 12th ed. Ithaca: Cornell University Press.

Mishel, Lawrence, John Schmitt, and Heidi Shierholz. 2013. *Assessing the job polarization explanation of growing wage inequality*. Washington, DC: Economic Policy Institute, (January 11). http://www.epi.org/publication/wp295-assessing-job-polarization-explanation-wage-inequality/.

Pavetti, LaDonna. 2014. Subsidized jobs: Providing paid employment opportunities when the labor market fails. In *Center on Budget and Policy Priorities, full employment*. http://www.pathtofullemployment.org/wp-content/uploads/2014/04/pavetti.pdf.

Piketty, Thomas, and Emmanuel Saez. 2013 (update). *Income inequality in the United States, 1913–1998*. NBER Working Paper 8467. Cambridge, MA: National Bureau of Economic Research.

Rogerson, Richard, Robert Shimer, and Randall Wright. 2005. Search-theoretic models of the labor market: A survey. *Journal of Economic Literature* 43 (December). http://home.uchicago.edu/shimer/wp/search-survey.pdf.

Schmitt, John, and Janelle Jones. 2012. *Low-wage workers are older and better educated than ever*. Washington, DC: Center for Economic and Policy Research. http://www.cepr.net/documents/publications/min-wage3-2012-04.pdf.

Stehn, Jari. 2014. *The case for a wage Taylor rule*. New York: Goldman Sachs Research, June 4.

Chapter 7
The Widening Socioeconomic Divergence in the U.S. Labor Market

Ishwar Khatiwada and Andrew M. Sum

Abstract The first 10 years of the 2000s were the worst decade of job-creating performance experienced by the United States in the entire post-World War II era. The unemployment rate skyrocketed as high as 9.6 %, tied with 1982 and 1983 as the highest unemployment rates since the end of the Second World War. Yet the unemployment rate only provides part of the story of the United States' weak labor market. This chapter goes well beyond the official unemployment statistics to look at the total pool of underutilized labor, including those who are working part time but cannot obtain full-time work (the underemployed) and those who have stopped looking for a job but want to be in the full-time work force (the hidden unemployed). It also rigorously examines the full array of labor market problems among U.S. workers in various education and income groups in 2013–2014 as well as providing relevant comparisons dating back to 1999–2000. We find that widening labor market outcome gaps have contributed to the growth of earnings and income disparities over the decade and a half since 1999–2000. Groups at the top end of the educational and income scales have come to experience virtually full employment and high earnings, while those at the bottom are dealing with unemployment and poverty that have sunk to levels last seen during the Great Depression.

Keywords Unemployment • Underemployment • Hidden unemployment • Underutilized labor • Labor market • Educational attainment • Household income • Inequality

I. Khatiwada (✉)
Center for Labor Markets and Policy, Drexel University, Philadelphia, PA, USA

A.M. Sum
Northeastern University, Boston, MA, USA

© Educational Testing Service 2016
I. Kirsch, H. Braun (eds.), *The Dynamics of Opportunity in America*,
DOI 10.1007/978-3-319-25991-8_7

197

Introduction

Even with an unemployment rate that stood only a little above 5 % in early 2015, in reality, the labor markets of the nation began performing poorly starting with the arrival of the 2000s and have yet to fully recover. The first 10 years of the 2000s decade hit the nation's workers particularly hard, with some economists and other social science analysts referring to 2000–2010 as the "Lost Decade." (Chinn and Frieden 2011). After achieving full employment in its labor markets in 2000, the nation experienced a recession in early 2001 that lasted 8 months. It was followed by a largely jobless recovery marked by rising unemployment and other labor market problems that lasted close to 2 years (NBER 2015). Four years of job growth were then followed by the Great Recession of 2007–2009 and a slow jobs recovery that sharply increased the national unemployment rate and other labor underutilization problems through 2010.

It was the worst decade of job-creating performance experienced by the United States in the entire post-World War II era. The aggregate number of payroll wage and salary jobs over the decade fell by approximately 1.9 million, a stark contrast to the gains of 22.4 million jobs in the 1990s and nearly 19 million in the 1980s. After beginning the 2000s with an unemployment rate of only 4.0 % in 2000, the lowest since 1969, it skyrocketed to 9.6 %, which was tied with 1982 and 1983 as the highest unemployment rates since the end of the Second World War.[1] Yet the reason we say that the recovery has been weak is that the unemployment rate only provides part of the story. A serious understanding requires going well beyond the official unemployment statistics to look at the total pool of underutilized labor, including those who are working part time but cannot obtain full-time work (the underemployed) and those who have stopped looking for a job but want to be in the full-time work force (the hidden unemployed).[2] It also requires going beyond just the averages to include a careful examination of labor market problems as distributed by educational attainment and household income.[3]

This report is devoted to performing such an analysis, rigorously examining the full array of labor market problems among U.S. workers in various education and income groups in 2013–2014 as well as providing relevant comparisons dating back to 1999–2000. The findings will examine the extent to which the combined underutilization problems among the nation's workers have increased in recent years and the distribution of such labor market problems across key socioeconomic classifications of workers as represented by their educational attainment and household income groups.

---

[1] For an overview of national unemployment rates from 1947 to 2000, see U.S. Council of Economic Advisers 2002.

[2] For a recent review of the labor market problems of young college graduates in obtaining jobs related to a college degree, see Katherine Peralta, "College Grads. Taking Many Low Wage Jobs," *Boston Globe*, March 10, 2014.

[3] See Sum and Khatiwada 2012 for a more careful explanation of these labor underutilization measures.

This report also studies how many Americans fared in the labor market, including those with incomes below the official poverty threshold, as well as taking a broader look at those struggling economically—examining statistics on income inadequacy for the "near poor" (those between 100 and 125 % of the poverty line) and those considered low income (those earning a maximum of double the official poverty line).

These widening labor market outcome gaps have contributed to the growth of earnings and income disparities over the decade and a half since 1999–2000. Groups at the top end of the educational and income scales have come to experience virtually full employment and high earnings, while those at the bottom are dealing with unemployment and poverty that have sunk to levels not seen since the Great Depression.

Defining Labor Underutilization

First, let us define the labor underutilization categories that we will examine regarding U.S. workers. Our estimates of these labor underutilization problems among workers in recent years (2013–2014) are based on findings of the Current Population Survey (CPS) of American households (Fig. 7.1). The CPS is sponsored jointly by the U.S. Census Bureau and the U.S. Bureau of Labor Statistics (BLS) and is the primary source of national labor force statistics.

The unemployed are those who did not work for pay or profit in the reference week of the survey but had actively looked for a job in the past 4 weeks and could

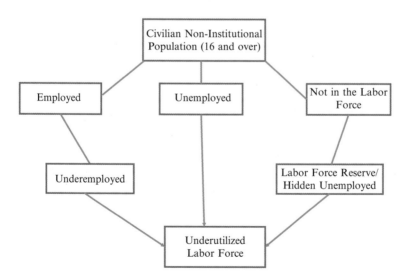

Fig. 7.1 Measuring the unemployed, underemployed, the hidden unemployed, and the underutilized labor force

have taken one if offered. Those persons who were not classified as employed or unemployed are placed into the "not in labor force" category.

The estimates of the numbers of the employed and unemployed are combined to form an estimate of the civilian labor force (Fig. 7.1). By dividing the number of unemployed persons by the civilian labor force, an estimate of the unemployment rate can be obtained. The unemployment rate is the most widely cited measure of labor underutilization in the national and local media, but it covers only a fraction of the labor market problems encountered by workers, especially less educated and low-income workers.

A second labor market problem is that of underemployment. An underemployed person is one who worked part time (under 35 h in the reference week) but desired and was available for full-time work.[4] Nationally, the numbers of underemployed increased sharply during the Great Recession and remained high (7–8 million persons per month) in the early years of the recovery. On average, the underemployed typically work only 21–22 h per week, barely half the mean number of weekly hours worked by the full-time employed. They receive less per hour in wages and thus less than half the mean weekly earnings of the full-time employed. There is a more than a short-time cost to being underemployed. Recent national research evidence has shown that working part time has no statistically significant effect on increasing one's hourly earnings over the long term, which means being underemployed not only leads to earnings losses in the short run but perpetuates them for years to come.[5]

A third measure of labor underutilization is the so-called "hidden unemployed," or the labor force reserve. This is a fairly sizable group of individuals within the "not in labor force" population. Individuals in this group have not actively looked for a job in the past 4 weeks but expressed a desire for immediate employment at the time of the CPS. Their absence from the labor force reduces their current earnings and future incomes from work.

A subset of this group of the hidden unemployed is referred to by the Bureau of Labor Statistics as the marginally attached. These individuals must have looked for a job at some time in the past 52 weeks and been available to take a job in the reference week. Their numbers are typically only 40 % as high as the total number of the hidden unemployed. But we are focused on measuring the entire pool of hidden unemployed, not just the marginally attached.[6]

Finally, in this chapter, we develop a count of the total pool of underutilized workers in the nation (for a review of the BLS alternative measures of labor underutilization, see U.S. Bureau of Labor Statistics 2008). The underutilized represents the sum of the official unemployed, the underemployed, and the hidden unem-

---

[4] For an overview and assessment of the rising incidence of underemployment problems during the Great Recession, see Sum and Khatiwada 2010, pp. 3–13.

[5] For evidence on the limited effectiveness of part-time jobs in raising the future wages of U.S. workers, see Tienda et al. 2010; Blau and Kahn 2013.

[6] The labor force reserve or hidden unemployed is typically more than twice as large as the marginally attached labor force. For example, in July 2013, the number of persons in the labor force reserve was 6.86 million, while the marginally attached labor force was only 2.53 million.

ployed. We also estimate a labor underutilization rate. This underutilization rate is calculated by dividing the number of underutilized workers by the adjusted civilian labor force. The adjusted civilian labor force represents the sum of the civilian labor force and the numbers of hidden unemployed.

In this report, we will provide estimates of four labor underutilization measures (unemployment rate, underemployment rate, hidden unemployment rate, and labor underutilization rate) for all workers 16 and over.

Defining the Educational Attainment and Household Income Groups

The report is organized primarily around presenting these numbers in relation to the following:

- Educational attainment groups: Workers are assigned to one of six educational attainment groups, ranging from those with no high school diploma or GED to those with a master's or higher degree, including a professional degree (law, medicine, etc.)

  - No high school diploma or GED certificate
  - High school diploma or GED, no college
  - 13–15 years of schooling, no college degree (some college)
  - Associate's degree
  - Bachelor's degree
  - Master's or higher degree

- Household income groups: Workers are categorized into six household income groups, ranging from a low of $20,000 in annual income to a high above $150,000

  - Under $20,000
  - $20,000 to $40,000
  - $40,000 to $75,000
  - $75,000 to $100,000
  - $100,000 to $150,000
  - $150,000 and over

- Combinations of educational attainment/household income group

Disparities in the incidence of each of the four labor market problems across these groups will be presented and highlighted. The size of these disparities in labor market outcomes in 2013–2014 across socioeconomic groups will be shown to be far higher than those prevailing in 1999–2000, at the end of the labor market boom years of the 1990s. First, we will look at the unemployment rate.

Identifying Labor Underutilization Problems across Education and Household Income Groups in the U.S.

Unemployment Problems Among Workers Across Education and Income Groups in 2013–2014

The average unemployment rate of U.S. workers between January 2013 and December 2014 was 6.8 %.[7] But there is much more to the story. Around that average rate of unemployment stands a significant degree of inequality. Findings in Figs. 7.2, 7.3, and 7.4 show these socioeconomic disparities in unemployment rates in 2013–2014.

By Educational Attainment Group When looking at educational attainment groups, unemployment rates varied quite widely. The unemployment rate was highest by far for those workers who did not have a high school diploma or GED, decreasing steadily with increased years in school (see Fig. 7.2). Workers that were high school dropouts or without a GED fared the worst with an unemployment rate of 13.9 %. The rate fell to 8.4 % for those that were high school graduates or held a GED,

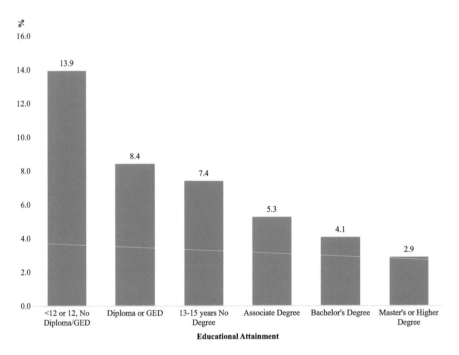

Fig. 7.2 Unemployment rates among workers (16 and over) by educational attainment, 2013–2014 averages (in %)

---

[7] In 2009 and 2010, the unemployment rate of U.S. workers was 9.5 %.

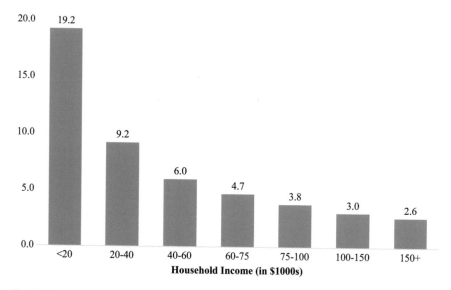

Fig. 7.3 Unemployment rates among workers (16 and over) by household income, 2013–2014 averages (in %)

continuing downward to 4.1 % for those with a bachelor's degree and a low of 2.9 % for those with a master's degree or higher. The least educated workers were almost five times more likely to be unemployed than those with the highest levels of formal educational attainment.

To illustrate the degree to which workers in different educational groups were affected by the rise in unemployment rates, we compared their unemployment rates in 2013–2014 with those in 1999–2000 (see Table 7.1). Unemployment rates rose for members of each of the six educational groups; however, the absolute size of these increases was higher the less education one had completed. High school drop-outs and graduates with no college experienced unemployment rate increase of about 4 percentage points, while workers with a bachelor's or higher degree saw unemployment rates rise by 2 percentage points or less. The unemployment rate gap between high school graduates and bachelor's degree holders widened from only 2.3 percentage points in 1999–2000 to 4.3 percentage points in 2013–2014.

By Household Income Group Unemployment rates of workers also varied quite considerably across household income groups.[8] Unemployment rates were highest

[8] These statistics come from monthly Current Population Surveys, where respondents are asked to report total combined income received by the household members during the past 12 months. The

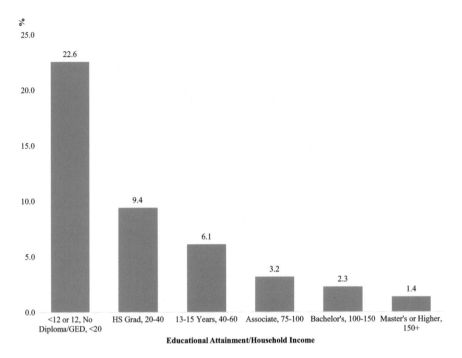

Fig. 7.4 Unemployment rates among workers (16 and over) by educational attainment and household income, 2013–2014 averages (in %)

among lower-income workers and fell steadily and steeply as household income increased (see Fig. 7.3). Workers in the lowest household income group (under $20,000) had an unemployment rate of 19.2 %, with the rate falling to under 9.2 % for those with household incomes of $20,000–40,000. Workers in households with low-middle to middle incomes ($40,000–75,000) had unemployment rates of 5–6 %, with the rate under 3 % for workers in the most affluent households (those with annual incomes of $150,000 or more). Workers in the lowest income group were seven times more likely to be unemployed than those in the most affluent households in 2013–2014.

By Separate Educational Attainment/Household Income Groups To identify the link between unemployment rates, educational attainment and household income, workers were combined into 36 separate educational attainment and household income groups, with unemployment rates calculated for each. The groups ranged from high school dropouts in households with low incomes ($20,000 per year) to workers with a master's or higher degree that were in the most affluent households

incomes are reported in categorical form. The income includes wage and salary income, farm/nonfarm, self-employment incomes, Social Security/Supplemental Security Incomes, pensions/interests/dividends incomes, net rental income, cash public assistance income, unemployment or workers' compensation incomes, pension or retirement incomes, and all other incomes.

Table 7.1 Comparisons of the unemployment rates of adults 16 and older by educational attainment, 1999–2000 and 2013–2014 (in %)

Educational attainment	(A) 1999–2000	(B) 2013–2014	(C) Percentage point change
<12 or 12, no diploma or GED	9.7	13.9	+4.2
H.S. diploma or GED	4.4	8.4	+4.0
13–15 years, no degree	3.6	7.4	+3.9
Associate's degree	2.6	5.3	+2.7
Bachelor's degree	2.1	4.1	+2.0
Master's or higher degree	1.5	2.9	+1.4
All (16 and over)	4.1	6.8	+2.7

Source: Monthly CPS household surveys, public use files, 1999–2000 and 2013–2014, tabulations by authors

($150,000 or more per year). The range in unemployment rate proved extraordinarily broad. The unemployment rates for these workers ranged from a high of 22.6 % for workers from low-income households and no high school diploma, to 9.4 % for high school graduates with below average incomes ($20,000–$40,000,) to a low of only 1.4 % for workers in the most affluent households ($150,000 and over) that held a master's or higher degree. Workers from the lowest income households who did not have a high school diploma were 16 times more likely to be unemployed than the best educated workers from the most affluent households (see Fig. 7.4). Well-educated Americans from high-income families lived in a super full employment labor market, while less educated, low-income workers were facing Depression-level unemployment rates.

Underemployment Problems Among U.S. Workers

Underemployment problems of U.S. workers rose substantially during the Great Recession of 2007–2009 and its early aftermath, setting new record highs (Sum and Khatiwada 2010, pp. 3–10). In 1999–2000, there was an average of only 3.3 million persons per month who worked part time but desired full-time work. By 2013–2014, this number had risen by more than 130 % to 7.6 million.[9]

By Educational Attainment Group Underemployment rates of workers were strongly associated with individuals' educational attainment; with the rates being the highest for the least educated workers and falling progressively for those with more education (see Fig. 7.5). The underemployment rate for workers without a high school diploma or GED was 9.9 %, falling to 6.8 % for those with a diploma or GED. Rates dropped to 3.1 % for those with a bachelor's degree and only 2.0 %

---

[9] In 2009–2010, on average, 8.9 million persons per month were working part time but desired full-time work.

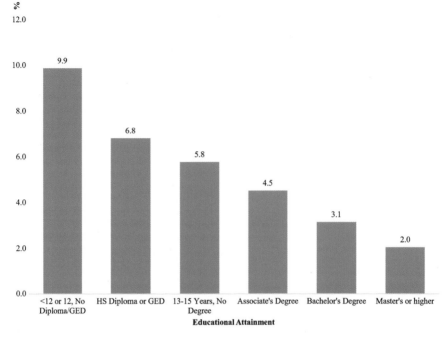

Fig. 7.5 Underemployment rates among employed workers (16 and over) in 2013–2014 by educational attainment, annual averages (in %)

for those with a master's or higher degree. The least educated workers were five times more likely to experience underemployment problems than the best educated workers during 2013–2014.

By Household Income Group The incidence of underemployment among workers also varied considerably by the level of household income. Underemployment rates were highest for workers in the least affluent households, with rates decreasing steeply as annual household income grew (see Fig. 7.6). Workers in the least affluent households (earning less than $20,000 per year) had an underemployment rate of 14.2 %, with the rate falling sharply to 7.7 % and 3.9 % for low-middle and middle-income workers and dropping to 2.6 % for workers in families earning $100,000–$150,000 per year. The most affluent workers (income above $150,000) had an underemployment rate of just 2 %. Low-income workers were seven times more likely to be underemployed than the most affluent workers.

By Separate Educational Attainment/Household Income Groups The underemployment rates of workers in 2013–2014 varied sharply and systematically across the various educational attainment/household income groups (see Fig. 7.7). The lowest income workers who had not completed high school had an underemployment rate of 17.7 %. The underemployment rate fell sharply to 7.8 % for low-income workers who were high school graduates and reached a low of only 1 % for

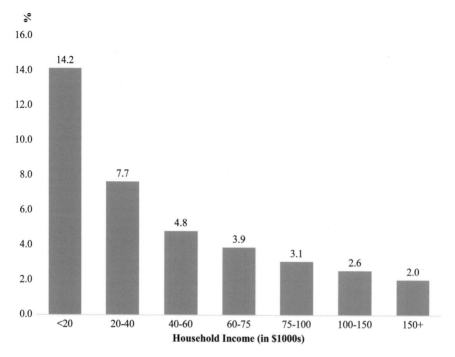

Fig. 7.6 Underemployment rates among employed workers (16 and over) in 2013–2014 by household income, annual averages (in %)

the highest income workers with a master's or higher degree. The least educated and lowest income workers were 17 times more like to be underemployed than the most affluent workers who held graduate and professional degrees.

The overall level and incidence of underemployment problems increased substantially between 1999–2000 and 2013–2014 (see Table 7.2). In 1999–2000, the underemployment rate was only 2.4 % but rose sharply to 5.2 % in 2013–2014. In both time periods, underemployment problems were strongly linked to combinations of unemployment and household income. In each of these groups, the underemployment rate rose over this time period; however, the size of these percentage-point increases varied quite widely across those groups. At the bottom, the underemployment rates of low income without a high school diploma/GED increased by nearly 9 percentage points from 8.8 to 17.7 % between 1999–2000 and 2013–2014; among low-income-high school graduates, the underemployment rate doubled from 4.3 to 9.9 % over the same time period. At the top of the education ladder (bachelor's degree and above) with incomes over $75,000, the underemployment rates rose by only 1.4 percentage points or less. The size of the percentage point increase in underemployment among low-income high school dropouts and graduates was 4–12 times as high as that at the top. Underemployment rates have become massively more unequal over time. The steep weekly wage losses from

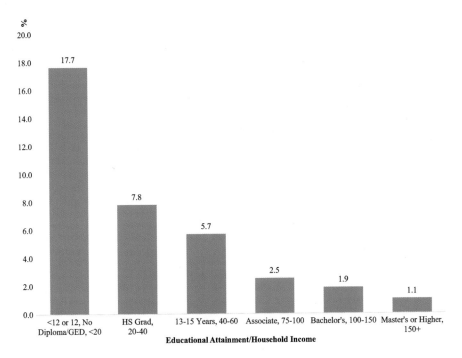

Fig. 7.7 Underemployment rates among workers (16 and over) by educational attainment and household income, 2013–2014 annual averages (in %)

Table 7.2 Comparisons of the underemployment rates of employed adults by household income and educational attainment in 1999–2000 and 2013–2014 (in %)

Educational attainment/household income	(A) 1999–2000	(B) 2013–2014	(C) Percentage point change
No diploma or GED, under $20,000	8.8	17.7	+8.9
H.S. diploma or GED, under $20,000	4.3	9.9	+5.6
H.S. diploma or GED, $20,000–40,000	3.1	7.8	+4.7
13–15 years, $40,000–60,000	1.6	4.7	+3.1
Associate's degree, $60,000–75,000	1.0	3.4	+2.4
Bachelor's degree $75,000 and over	0.6	2.0	+1.4
Master's or higher, $75,000 and over	0.6	1.3	+0.7
All	2.4	5.2	+2.8

Source: Monthly CPS household surveys, public use files, 1999–2000 and 2013–2014, tabulations by authors

being underemployed took a severe toll at the bottom of the wage distribution, creating more wage inequality over time.

The Problems of Hidden Unemployment Among Workers in 2013–2014

A third set of labor market problems facing workers is that of the hidden unemployed, or members of the so-called labor force reserve (for a discussion of this concept, see Ginzberg 1978). The number of persons in the labor force reserve and the marginally attached tend to rise sharply during recessions and jobless recoveries.[10] Although they do not count toward official unemployed figures, their joblessness contributes to personal wage losses and output losses just as if they were unemployed. Their more limited work experience resulting from these periods of hidden unemployment will also have negative effects on future employability and earnings.

Hidden Unemployment Rates Among Workers

By Educational Attainment Group Hidden unemployment rates were strongly associated with the educational attainment of workers in 2013–2014 (see Fig. 7.8). The incidence of hidden unemployment was highest for workers with no high school diploma or GED, with the likelihood of being part of the hidden unemployed decreasing as the level of educational attainment increased (see Fig. 7.8). Workers who were the least educated (those with no high school diploma or GED) had a hidden unemployment rate of just under 9 %, with rates dropping to 4 % for those who had graduated from high school or completed some college but were without a degree.[11] Those workers with a bachelor's or higher degree had a 2 % or lower rate of incidence of hidden unemployment. Workers with the lowest educational attainment were four and five times more likely to suffer hidden unemployment problems than the best educated.

By Household Income Group The likelihood of being a member of the hidden unemployed in 2013–2014 also was strongly linked to the household incomes of potential workers. As with the unemployed and underemployed, the lowest income individuals in the adjusted labor force were the most likely to be members of the hidden labor force. Nearly one in every ten individuals with household incomes below $20,000 was in the ranks of the hidden unemployed (see Fig. 7.9). The probability of hidden unemployment continued to decline as household income grew, dropping to 3 % for middle-income workers and under 2 % for those with household incomes over $100,000. Workers in the lowest income groups were between five

---

[10] The members of the marginally attached and discouraged workers tend to rise during recessions and jobless recoveries. See Cohany (2009).

[11] High school students not reported separately also had a very high hidden rate of unemployment. Close to 22 % of these individuals in the labor force were hidden unemployed in 2013–2014.

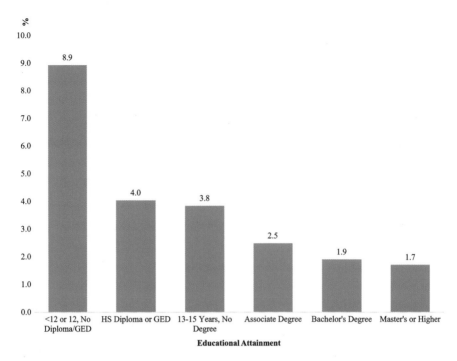

Fig. 7.8 Hidden unemployment rates among workers (16 and over) in 2013–2014 by educational attainment, annual averages (in %)

and six times more likely to suffer a hidden unemployment problem than the nation's most affluent workers in the 2013–2014 time period.

By Separate Educational Attainment/Household Income Groups The rates of hidden unemployment among workers in 2013–2014 varied considerably across the 36 different educational attainment/household income groups. Hidden unemployment problems were most prevalent among high school dropouts in the lowest income group, who had a hidden unemployment rate just under 13 %, which dropped to 4.4 % for lower-middle income high school graduates (see Fig. 7.10). The most affluent, best educated workers had a hidden unemployment rate under 1 %. Workers with the lowest educational attainment living in the lowest income households were 15 times more likely to suffer a hidden unemployment problem than the most affluent and most highly educated workers in 2013–2014. Hidden unemployment was virtually an unknown phenomenon among the most affluent and educated.

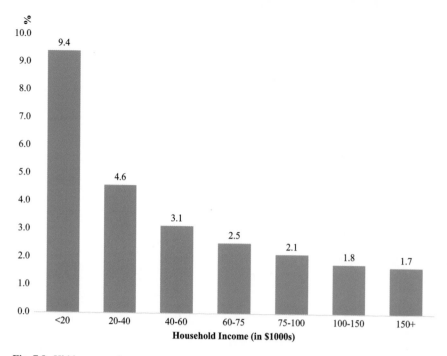

Fig. 7.9 Hidden unemployment rates among the adjusted labor force (16 and over) by household income, 2013–2014 annual averages (in %)

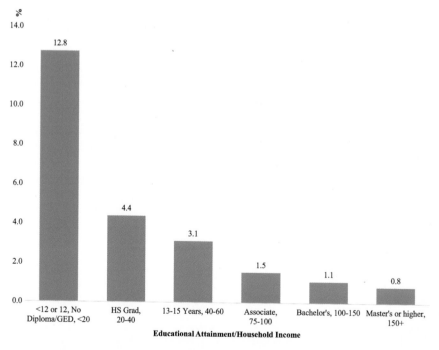

Fig. 7.10 Hidden unemployment rates among workers (16 and over) by educational attainment and household income, 2013–2014, annual averages (in %)

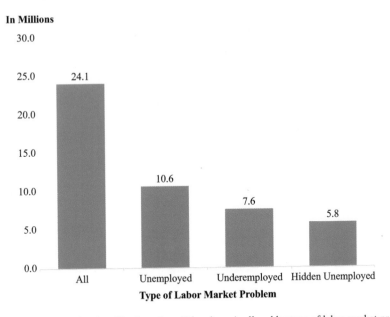

Fig. 7.11 Numbers of underutilized workers (16 and over), all and by type of labor market problem, 2013–2014 averages (in millions)

Labor Underutilization Problems in the U.S. in 2013–2014

The three labor market problems of unemployment, underemployment, and hidden unemployment can now be combined to form a pool of "underutilized labor."[12] The estimated average monthly number of unemployed in 2013–2014 was 10.6 million (see Fig. 7.11). That number, however, was exceeded by the combined total of underemployed and hidden unemployed (7.6 million underemployed and 5.8 million hidden unemployed, or 13.4 million altogether). The joint pool of underutilized labor was equal to 24.1 million, or 14.9 % of the adjusted resident labor force of the nation in 2013–2014.[13] Thus, approximately one of every six members of the resident labor force experienced some type of labor underutilization problem.

---

[12] The U.S. Bureau of Labor Statistics U-1 through U-6 framework for estimating labor problems includes a measure (U-6) that is somewhat similar to ours. It counts in the numerator the sum of the unemployed, the underemployed, and the marginally attached, which are a subset of the hidden unemployed. See U.S. Bureau of Labor Statistics 2008, 2014.

[13] In 2009–2010, representing the labor market trough of the Great Recession, 29.1 million persons were members of the labor force underutilized pool (14.7 million unemployed, 8.9 million underemployed, and 5.5 million hidden unemployed).

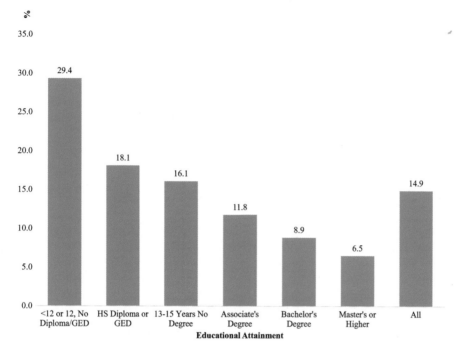

Fig. 7.12 Labor force underutilization rates among workers (16 and over) by educational attainment, 2013–2014 annual averages (in %)

Labor Underutilization Rates Among Workers

By Educational Attainment Group The rates of labor force underutilization among workers in 2013–2014 varied widely by educational attainment. Given our previous findings on each individual labor market problem, it should come as no surprise to discover that the highest rate of underutilization was found among the least educated workers and declined as educational attainment increased (see Fig. 7.12). Those workers who did not possess either a high school diploma or GED had an underutilization rate of 29.4 %, which dropped to 18.1 % for those with a high school diploma. Four-year college graduates had an underutilization rate of just under 9 %, while those workers holding a master's or higher degree had only a rate of 6.5 %. The least educated workers were between three and four times more likely to be part of the underutilized labor force than the best educated workers in the 2013–2014 time period.

Comparisons of the labor underutilization rates of workers by educational attainment in 1999–2000 with those for 2013–2014 are presented in Table 7.3. These underutilization rates increased over time in every educational group, but the percentage point sizes of these increases were substantially greater at the bottom of the education distribution than at the top. The size of these increases was highest among

Table 7.3 Labor force underutilization rates of workers 16 and older by educational attainment, 1999–2000 and 2013–2014 (in %)

Educational attainment	(A) 1999–2000	(B) 2013–2014	(C) Percentage point change
<12 or 12, no diploma or GED	20.4	29.4	+9.0
H.S. diploma or GED	9.7	18.1	+8.4
13–15 years, no degree	7.9	16.1	+8.2
Associate's degree	5.8	11.8	+6.0
Bachelor's degree	4.5	8.9	+4.4
Master's degree	3.5	6.5	+3.0
All (16 and over)	9.1	14.9	+5.8

Source: Monthly CPS household surveys, public use files, 1999–2000 and 2013–2014, tabulations by authors

those lacking a high school diploma/GED (9 %), stayed at 8 % for high school graduates and those with some college but no degree, and rose by only 4.4 and three percentage points for bachelor's degree holders and those with a master's or higher degree, respectively. In 1999–2000, there was only a five-point gap between the underutilization rates of high school graduates and those workers with a bachelor's degree. By 2013–2014, this gap had widened to nine points.

By Household Income Group Labor force underutilization problems among workers during the 2013–2014 time period also were strongly associated with household income. The rate of labor force underutilization was greatest for low-income workers (under $20,000), with rates falling sharply and steadily as household income grew (see Fig. 7.13). The labor underutilization rate for workers in households with an annual income below $20,000 was 37 %, with the rate falling to 20 % and 13 % for low-middle and middle-income workers and finally dropping to 6 % for members of the highest income households ($150,000 or more per year). Workers in low-income households were roughly six times more likely than the most affluent to experience a labor underutilization problem in 2013–2014. Their labor market problems are clearly massively different from one another, with a gap of 31 percentage points.

By Separate Educational Attainment/Household Income Groups

Labor underutilization rates also were calculated for 36 educational attainment/household income groups. There was tremendous variability in these rates across these 36 separate groups of workers. Underutilization problems were most severe by far for the lowest income and least educated workers, easing as both household income and educational attainment increased (see Fig. 7.14). Workers without a high school diploma or a GED and from families with incomes under $20,000 had an underutilization rate of nearly 44 %. This rate fell to 20 % for low-middle-income, high school graduates and to 13 % for those with some college and in a middle-income household, dropping to only 3 % for workers that held a master's or higher degree in a household with annual earnings of $150,000 or more. The least

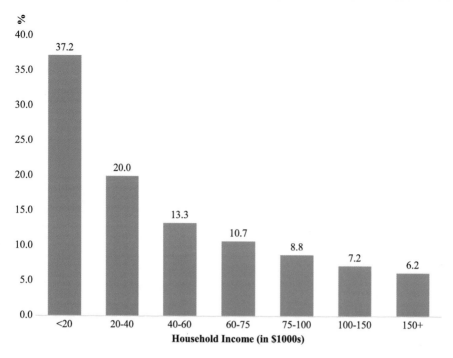

Fig. 7.13 Labor force underutilization rates among workers (16 and over) by household income, 2013–2014 annual averages (in %)

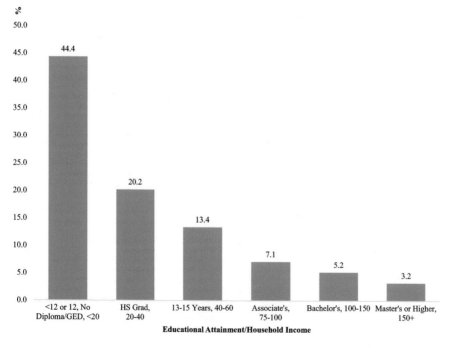

Fig. 7.14 Labor underutilization rates among workers (16 and over) by educational attainment and household income, 2013–2014 annual averages (in %)

Table 7.4 Comparisons of the labor underutilization rates of adults 16 and older by educational attainment and household income groups, by gender and race-ethnic group, 2013–2014 annual averages (in %)

Group	(A) Men	(B) Women	(C) Black	(D) Hispanic	(E) White, not Hispanic
No diploma or GED, under $20,000	41.3	48.3	59.7	36.8	47.0
H.S. diploma under $20,000	38.1	38.0	45.5	34.3	35.6
H.S. diploma or GED, $20,000–$40,000	20.0	20.4	24.1	20.9	18.8
13–15 years, $40,000–$60,000	13.0	13.7	16.4	14.5	12.0
Associate's degree, $60,000–$75,000	8.0	8.7	10.5	9.2	7.8
Bachelor's degree, $100,000–$150,000	4.6	5.8	6.8	5.7	5.0
Master's or higher $150,000 and over	2.4	4.2	4.1	3.6	3.2
All	14.3	15.5	23.3	19.3	12.2

Source: Monthly CPS household surveys, public use files, 2013 and 2014, tabulations by authors

educated and lowest income workers were nearly 14 times more likely to suffer labor underutilization problems than the most affluent and best educated workers were in 2013–2014.

We also identified the degree to which these patterns of labor force underutilization across educational attainment and household income groups may have varied across gender and race-ethnic group, estimating such rates for both men and women and for Blacks, Hispanics, and White non-Hispanics separately (see Table 7.4). The overall underutilization rates of men and women followed similar patterns to the overall numbers.

But across the three major race-ethnic groups, the overall labor underutilization rates varied widely from a low of under 12 % for White non-Hispanics to 19 % for Hispanics to 23 % for Blacks. The patterns of these findings across educational attainment and household income groups are quite similar. All three groups experienced substantial drops in labor underutilization rates as their household income and educational attainment improved. In Fig. 7.15, we present findings for two groups at both extreme portions of the distribution for each race-ethnic group. Hispanic and Black low-income high school dropouts faced underutilization rates of 37 % and nearly 60 %, respectively.[14] In contrast, those with a master's or higher

---

[14] The labor force underutilization rate among native-born Hispanics without a high school diploma or a GED was much higher than their foreign-born peers. In 2013–2014, the underutilization rate among native-born Hispanics was 36 % compared to 22 % among their foreign-born peers.

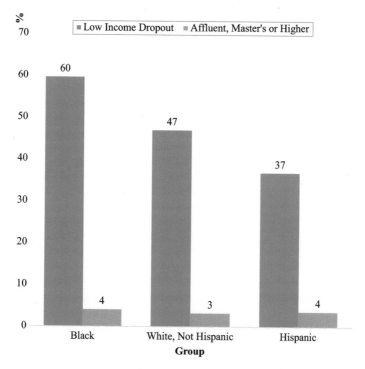

Fig. 7.15 Comparisons of the labor underutilization rates of low-income, high school dropouts and affluent adults with a master's degree or higher by race-ethnic group, 2013–2014 annual averages (in %)

degree in the highest income group had underutilization rates of only 3–4 % for each race-ethnic group. The large disparities in labor underutilization rates across socioeconomic groups are, thus, common to both men and women as well as across Blacks, Hispanics, and Whites, with Blacks facing the highest underutilization rates overall. (Appendix 7A contains a number of tables regarding labor underutilization rates by gender and race-ethnic groups, illustrating the depth of family income inadequacy problems. For detail about associations between educational attainment/household income groups by gender and race-ethnicity, see Appendix 7B).

The Findings of Logistic Probability Models to Predict Labor Underutilization among Workers in 2013–2014

The above findings on the labor market problems of adults have primarily focused on variations in these problems across educational attainment and family income groups with a few separate breakouts of key findings for gender and race-ethnic groups. To illustrate the independent effects of other demographic variables on the

Table 7.5 Predicated probabilities for selected individuals 16 and older of being an underutilized member of the nation's labor force in 2013–2014 (in %)

	Characteristics of individual	Probability (%)
(1)	16- to 24-year-old, Black, male, native born, high school dropout, family income under $20,000	66.7
(2)	16- to 24-year-old, White, male, native born, high school graduate, family income under $20,000	45.5
(3)	25- to 34-year-old, White, male, native born, high school graduate, family income $20,000-$40,000	14.1
(4)	35- to 44-year-old, White, male, native born, some college, family income $40,000-$75,000	8.2
(5)	45- to 54-year-old, White, male, native born, associate's degree, family income $75,000-$100,000	5.5
(6)	55- to 64-year-old, White, male, native born, bachelor's or higher degree, family income $150,000 and over	4.5
	RELATIVE DIFFERENCE FROM TOP TO BOTTOM	15

underutilization rates of workers in 2013–2014, we have estimated a set of logistic probability models of their underutilization status over this 2-year period (for a description of this process and full detail about the logistic probability regression model, see Appendix 7C, including Table 7C.2).

The findings of the logistic probability regression model of the underutilized status of workers in 2013–2014 can be used to predict the probability of a given labor force participant with specific demographic and socioeconomic traits being underutilized at the time of the CPS household surveys in 2013–2014. The predicted probabilities of being underutilized in the labor market of six male individuals with very different demographic and socioeconomic backgrounds are presented in Table 7.5 (the specific formula used to generate these probability estimates is explained in Appendix 7D).[15]

The first individual was a young (16- to 24-year-old) Black, native born male who was a high school dropout and lived in a low-income household (annual income under $20,000). His predicted probability of being underutilized in the labor market was an extraordinarily high 66.7 %. If this individual had been White and had a high school diploma and lived in a low-income family, his predicted probability of being underutilized was also quite high at 45.5 %. As the age of the respondent and family income increased, the predicted probability of being underutilized declined. A 25- to 34-year-old White, male high school graduate from a low-middle-income family ($20,000–$40,000) had a 14 % probability of being underutilized.

If the respondent's age rose to 35–44, his education increased to 13–15 years with no formal degree, and his family income increased to the $40,000–75,000 range, then his probability of being underutilized declined to 8.2 %. A native born

---

[15]The estimated impact of gender on the probability of being underutilized was quite small (<1 percentage point), thus, we have limited our analysis to males only though the results for women would be quite similar.

55- to 64-year-old male with a bachelor's or higher degree who lived in an affluent family ($150,000 or higher) had only a 4.5 % probability of being underutilized.

The findings of the above analyses are quite clear. Young, poorly educated adults from low-income families faced underutilization rates of historic proportions. They encountered Depression-era unemployment and other labor market problems in 2013–2014. Even young high school graduates from low-middle-income families faced high rates of labor underutilization. In contrast, older males (45–64) with a bachelor's or higher degree and above average incomes experienced very low labor underutilization rates that would have to be considered the equivalent of super full employment in the labor market. America's labor markets have become extremely stratified by age, education, and family income since 2000. Gaps in labor underutilization rates between the top and bottom of the distribution exceeded 60 percentage points, representing more than 15 times difference in relative terms.

The Labor Underutilization Problems of the Nation's Young Adults (16–29) in 2013–2014

Since the end of the nation's labor market boom years of the 1990s, national labor markets have been characterized by a "great age twist" in the structure of employment rates.[16] While the nation's older adults (57 and older) had higher employment rates in 2010–2011 than they did in 1999–2000, all younger adults had lower employment rates. These declines were sharpest with the youngest age groups. As was the case in many other OECD (Organisation for Economic Co-operation and Development) countries, U.S. teens fared the worst in the labor market by far, followed by 20–24 year olds, and 25–29 year olds (Sum et al. 2014a).

The annual average employment rates of the nation's teens (16–19 years old) fell from 45 % in 1999–2000 to only 28 % in 2013–2014 (see Fig. 7.16).[17] Steep declines in employment rates were experienced by the nation's teens in every age, gender, race-ethnicity, and family income group, but employment rates remained lowest among the youngest teens (16–17), Blacks and Hispanics, high school students and dropouts, and low-income youth.

The employment/population ratio (E/P) of the nation's young adults (20–24) fell by 10 percentage points over the same time period, creating a new historical low for young U.S. adult men, while the ratio for 25–29 year olds dropped from 81 to 74 %, a seven percentage point decline. The deteriorating employment prospects for teens have had negative impacts on their employability as young adults here and in most other OECD nations. They have seen reduced ability to form independent households, leading more to remain living at home with one or both parents (for estimates

---

[16]For a detailed review and assessment of the changing labor market experiences of teens and young adults (20–24) in the U.S., see Sum et al. 2014b.

[17]See Josh Sanbum, "Fewest Young Adults (18–24) in 60 Years Have Jobs," *Business.com,* February 9, 2012.

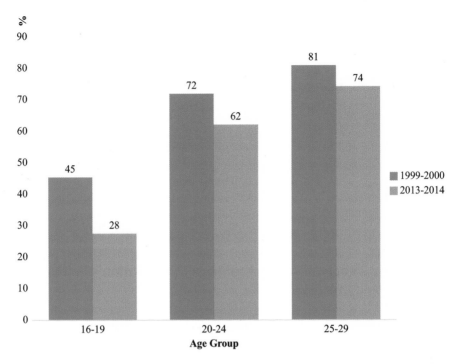

Fig. 7.16 Trends in the employment/population ratios of teens and young adults (20–24, 25–29) in 1999–2000 and 2013–2014 (in %)

of earnings losses among young unemployed workers, see Ayres 2013). These same factors also have led to a reduction in marriage rates among the young, which has helped raise the share of new births taking place out of wedlock to all-time highs.[18] With that said, part of the decline in employment for young people can be attributed to more young people being enrolled in colleges/schools. But the largest decline occurred among teens who were not enrolled (Table 7.6).

These income and family formation developments have contributed in an important way to declining real incomes of young families with children and to higher rates of poverty among them. Young families' incomes (a family head under 30 years of age) have been subject to widening inequality over the past few decades, with the top decile (one-tenth) of families' gains equaling close to half of all young family incomes (McLaughlin et al. 2010). Wealth gaps among young households have increased to an even greater degree, with the top 10 % capturing 86 % of the net worth of young households in 2007 (Sum and Khatiwada 2009).

Given the high and rising degrees of labor underutilization among the nation's teens and young adults, we also estimated a logistic probability model of labor

---

[18] Over 50 % of all births to women under 30 in 2011 were out of wedlock, the first time ever that a majority of such births took place outside of marriage.

Table 7.6 Employment-population ratio of 16- to 24-year-old by school enrollment status, 1999–2000 and 2013–2014 averages

Enrollment status	Age group	1999–2000	2013–2014	Absolute change
Not enrolled	16–19	61	46	−15
	20–24	78	70	−8
	Total	73	64	−8
Enrolled	16–19	38	21	−17
	20–24	58	48	−10
	Total	45	31	−13
Total	16–19	45	28	−18
	20–24	72	62	−10
	Total	60	47	−12

Source: Monthly CPS household surveys, public use files, 1999–2000 and 2013–2014, tabulations by authors

underutilization among those labor force participants under age 30 in 2013–2014. For full detail, see Appendix 7E.

We have picked five young males (from ages 16–19 to 25–29) with different race-ethnicity, educational attainment, and family income backgrounds and used the logistic probability model to estimate their predicted probability of being underutilized in 2013–2014 (see Table 7.7).

Our first individual is a teenaged Black male, who was a high school dropout and lived in a low-income family. His predicted probability of being underutilized was an astonishingly high 73 %. If we made this young man a White male and raised his age to 20–24 but kept his education and family income status unchanged, his estimated probability of being underutilized still remained at 47 %. If this same young man's educational attainment was raised to that of a high school graduate and his family income raised to $20,000–$40,000, then his probability of being underutilized fell to 26.8 %.

If his educational attainment was increased to that of an associate's degree and his family income increased to a middle-income level, his probability of being underutilized dropped to 14.2 %. Our final individual is a 25- to 29-year-old White non-Hispanic male who was native born, had a bachelor's or higher degree, and lived in an upper middle-income family ($75,000–100,000). His predicted probability of being underutilized was only 6.8 %, *or* basically only one-eleventh as high as that of our first individual (the Black, male, teen dropout from a low-income family). The distribution of labor underutilization rates among our nation's young adults in 2013–2014 was extraordinarily varied, with potentially severe adverse consequences for future family formation, income and earnings inequality, and the economic and social well-being of children in these families.

Table 7.7 Predicted probabilities of selected young adult labor force participants being underutilized in 2013–2014 (in %)

	Traits of individual	Probability of being underutilized (%)
(1)	16- to 19-year-old, Black, male, native born, high school dropout, low income	73.0
(2)	20- to 24-year-old, White, male, native born, high school dropout, low income	47.1
(3)	20- to 24-year-old, White, male, native born, high school graduate, $20,000–$40,000 income	26.8
(4)	20- to 24-year-old, White, male, native born, associate's degree, $40,000–$75,000 income	14.2
(5)	25- to 29-year-old, White, male, native born, bachelor's or higher degree, $75,000–$100,000 income	6.8
	RELATIVE DIFFERENCE FROM TOP TO BOTTOM	11

Trends in Labor Underutilization Rates Among Adults (16 and Over) by Educational Attainment and Household Income, 1999–2000 to 2013–2014

In our prior analyses of the labor underutilization rates of the nation's working-age population, we tracked variations in these rates across educational attainment and household income groups in 2013–2014. In this section of our chapter, we compare key findings from the 2013–2014 surveys with those for 1999–2000, when the national economy was operating under full employment conditions in its labor markets (see Table 7.8).

In 1999–2000, the overall labor underutilization rate was 9.1 %, varying from a high of about 30 % among low-income dropouts to only under 3 % for bachelor's and higher degree holders with household incomes above $75,000.

By 2013–2014, the aggregate labor underutilization rate had increased to 14.9 %. Each demographic, educational attainment, and household income group of labor force participants encountered an increase in its labor underutilization rates, but the percentage point sizes of these increases varied quite widely across these groups (see Fig. 7.17). Low-income workers with a high school diploma or less in formal schooling saw their labor underutilization rates rise by 14–16 percentage points. At the lower end of the distribution of underutilization rates were bachelor's or higher degree recipients from upper-income families. Their underutilization rates rose by only to two to three percentage points over this 14-year period. Adults with a master's or higher degree and a family income greater than $75,000 faced a labor underutilization rate of only 4 % in 2013–2014, two percentage points higher than in 1999–2000.

America's adults clearly faced a deep set of widening gaps in their labor underutilization rates since 1999–2000. At the top of the distribution are low-income adults with only a high school diploma or less education with underutilization rates of 38–44 %—a Depression-era labor market environment. High school graduates

Table 7.8   Labor force underutilization rates of U.S. workers (16 and older) in selected educational attainment and household income groups in 1999–2000 and 2013–2014 (in %)

Educational attainment/household income	(A) 1999–2000	(B) 2013–2014	(C) Percentage point change
No diploma or GED, under $20,000	30.5	44.4	+13.9
H.S. diploma or GED, under $20,000	22.4	38.1	+15.7
H.S. diploma or GED, $20,000–$40,000	9.8	20.2	+10.4
13–15 Years, $40,000–$60,000	5.9	13.4	+7.5
Associate's degree, $60,000–$75,000	3.3	8.4	+5.0
Bachelor's degree, $75,000 and over	2.7	5.5	+2.8
Master's and higher degree, $75,000 and over	2.1	4.1	+2.0
All	9.1	14.9	+5.8

Source: Monthly CPS household surveys, public use files, 1999–2000 and 2013–2014, tabulations by authors

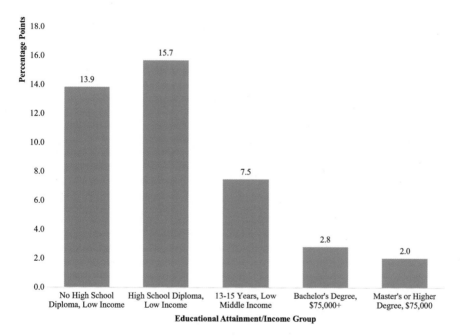

Fig. 7.17   Percentage point increases in labor underutilization rates among selected educational and household income groups of workers, 1999–2000 to 2013–2014

from low-middle-income families faced a 20 % labor underutilization rate, equivalent to several points above the worst during the Great Recession of 2007–2009. At the bottom of the distribution are college graduates (bachelor's and above) with affluent family incomes who live in a world characterized by super full employment. These are radically different labor market worlds.

Income Problems of Underutilized Workers, 2012–2013

The previous sections of this chapter have been focused on the labor underutilization problems of workers in an array of educational attainment and household income groups, also looking at gender, age, and race-ethnic groups. This section of the chapter now assesses another set of issues related to the impact on income of underutilized workers.

A labor underutilization problem by itself does not have to automatically lead to poverty or low-income status. For example, an unemployed worker may experience only a short duration of unemployment (2–4 weeks) that does not have a major impact on annual income. The unemployed worker may be a young household member who does not contribute to household income in a substantive way, or the unemployed or underemployed persons may be a secondary earner whose temporary loss of income does not reduce the household's income below the poverty line or low-income standard.

But labor underutilization problems following the 2007–2009 recession were accompanied by steep increases in the mean durations of unemployment, with long-term unemployment problems (26 weeks or more) increasing in share to over 37 % in 2014.[19] These long-term unemployment spells create higher mean annual earnings losses despite the existence of unemployment benefits. The steep rise in underemployment with its high weekly wage losses also sharply reduces the earnings of this group, placing individuals at risk of income inadequacy.

We will begin our analysis of the links between labor underutilization problems and income inadequacy problems with a brief overview of the three measures of income inadequacy and their values for selected families and individuals in 2012–2013. This will be followed by an examination of the links between labor underutilization and incidence of income inadequacy problems both overall and for workers in each major educational attainment subgroup (for a review of the official poverty measures of the federal government and alternative measures of poverty, see U.S. Census Bureau 2010). We will also provide separate breakouts of these income inadequacy problems by combinations of educational attainment and labor underutilization status, showing the degree to which U.S. labor markets today are affected.

The Three Income Inadequacy Measures

Three separate measures of income inadequacy are used in this report, which are the poverty income thresholds of the federal government: those who are poor, near poor, or low income. These are defined as follows:

---

[19] In 2010–2011, more than 47 % of the nation's unemployed had been out of work for 26 weeks or longer.

- Poor: Annual money income, pretax, below the official poverty line for persons or families by family size and age composition.
- Poor or near poor: Annual money income below 125 % of the official poverty line.
- Low income: Annual money income below 200 % of the official poverty line.[20]

For 2013, the values of the income thresholds defining each of these measures for a single individual and three types of families are displayed in Table 7.9. The poverty income thresholds ranged from $12,119 for a single nonelderly individual to $23,624 for a four-person family with two children under 18. By definition, the values of the low-income thresholds were twice the value of the poverty line, ranging from $24,238 to $47,248 in our examples.

The Poverty Rates of Workers by Underutilization Status and Educational Attainment

The poverty rates of workers (including the hidden unemployed) by labor force underutilization status in March 2013–2014 are displayed in Table 7.10.[21] Findings are presented for all workers and for men and women separately by educational attainment for our six educational groups.

Overall, slightly over 9 % of all workers were members of poor families in March 2013–2014. The underutilized, however, were nearly 4.7 times as likely to be poor as their counterparts who were not underutilized (27.1 % vs. less than 5.8 %) (see Fig. 7.18). Clearly, being underutilized substantially increases the probability of poverty among workers. Among the underutilized, the likelihood of being poor also was associated with educational attainment Slightly more than 38 % of the under-

Table 7.9 The annual money incomes equivalent to the poverty line, the poverty/near poverty line, and the low-income threshold for selected individuals and families, 2013

Person or family	(A) Poverty line	(B) Poverty/near poverty line	(C) Low-income threshold
Single individual under 65	$12,119	$15,149	$24,238
Two-person family, no own children	15,142	18,928	30,284
Three-person family, one own child under 18	18,751	23,439	37,502
Four-person family, two children under 18	23,624	29,530	47,248

[20] A number of poverty researchers and income analysts began using this definition of low income in the late 1990s. See Acs et al. (2000).

[21] Poverty status is based on the annual income received by the respondent's family in the prior calendar year; i.e., 2012 or 2013.

Table 7.10 Poverty rates of persons 16 and older[a] in 2012–2013 by labor force underutilization status in March 2013–March 2014, total and by gender and educational attainment level (2-year averages)

Gender	Educational attainment	Poverty rate (%)			
		(A) Underutilized	(B) Not Underutilized	(C) Total	(D) Difference (A−B)
Male	<12 or 12, No H.S. diploma	34.1	15.9	21.2	+18.2
	H.S. diploma/GED	25.8	6.3	10.1	+19.5
	Some college	21.1	5.0	7.7	+16.1
	Associate's degree	16.3	3.5	4.9	+12.8
	Bachelor or higher degree	13.7	2.2	3.3	+11.5
	M.A. or higher degree	12.9	1.5	2.1	+11.4
	Total	24.2	5.3	8.3	+18.9
Female	<12 or 12, No H.S. diploma	43.9	17.6	26.6	+26.3
	H.S. diploma/GED	33.6	8.9	13.7	+24.7
	Some college	28.0	8.3	11.7	+19.7
	Associate's degree	24.3	5.4	7.8	+18.9
	Bachelor or higher degree	18.6	2.7	4.3	+15.9
	M.A. or higher degree	15.1	1.6	2.5	+13.5
	Total	30.4	6.5	10.2	+23.9
Total	<12 or 12, No H.S. diploma	38.4	16.5	23.4	+21.8
	H.S. diploma/GED	29.2	7.4	11.7	+21.7
	Some college	24.5	6.6	9.7	+17.9
	Associate's degree	20.9	4.5	6.5	+16.4
	Bachelor or higher degree	16.2	2.5	3.8	+13.8
	M.A. or higher degree	14.1	1.5	2.3	+12.6
	Total	27.1	5.8	9.2	+21.3

Source: 2013 and 2014 March CPS Supplements, public use files, U.S. Census Bureau, tabulations by authors
[a]Restricted to members of labor force and labor force reserve

utilized without a high school diploma or GED were poor (Fig. 7.19). The poverty rate fell to 29 % for those with a high school diploma, and to only approximately 15 % for those with a bachelor's or higher degree.

Data on the underutilization status of workers was combined with findings on their educational attainment to produce estimates of these joint factors on the probability of being poor (see Fig. 7.20). Of those underutilized workers with no high school diploma, 38 % were poor. This poverty rate declined to 29 % for those underutilized workers with a high school diploma. Of those workers not underutilized,

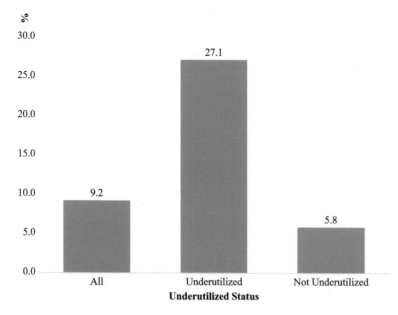

Fig. 7.18 Poverty rates of persons 16 and older in 2012–2013 by labor underutilization status in March 2013–March 2014

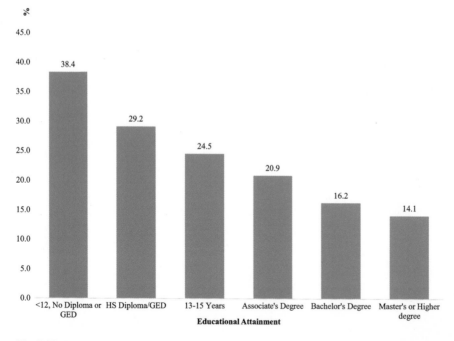

Fig. 7.19 Poverty rates of underutilized U.S. workers (16 and over) by educational attainment, March 2013–March 2014 (in %)

the poverty rate fell to only 2.5 % for those with a bachelor's degree and to only 1.5 % for those with a master's or higher degree. America's best educated workers who were not underutilized faced close to a zero rate of poverty, while the less educated, underutilized individuals faced extremely high rates of poverty in the 30–40 % range.

Poverty/Near Poverty Problems of the Underutilized

Our second measure of income inadequacy focuses on those persons with annual family incomes below 125 % of the poverty line: the poor and near poor. Overall, from March 2013 to March 2014, approximately one of every eight workers (12.5 %) was a member of a poor or near-poor family (see Table 7.11 and Fig. 7.21). Among the underutilized, however, one-third were poor or near poor versus only 8.6 % of the not underutilized, a relative difference of nearly four times.

Among the underutilized, the poverty/near poverty rates of workers varied across educational attainment groups, being highest for those with the least education and falling with the level of educational attainment (see Fig. 7.22). Those underutilized workers lacking a high school diploma or GED faced a poverty/near poverty rate of

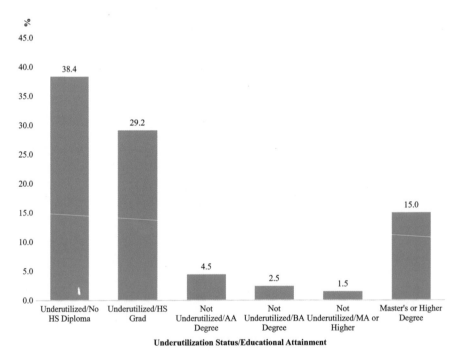

Fig. 7.20 Poverty rates of workers (16 and over) by underutilized status and educational attainment, March 2013 and March 2014 (in %)

Table 7.11 Poverty/near poverty rates of 16 and older persons[a] in 2012–2013 by labor force underutilization status in March 2013 and March 2014, total and by gender and educational attainment level

| Gender | Educational attainment | Poverty/near poverty rate (%) | | | |
		(A) Underutilized	(B) Not Underutilized	(C) Total	(D) Difference (A − B)
Male	<12 or 12, No H.S. diploma	44.1	23.4	29.4	+20.8
	H.S. Diploma/GED	32.6	9.7	14.1	+22.9
	Some college	26.4	7.4	10.6	+19.0
	Associate's degree	21.5	5.2	7.1	+16.2
	Bachelor or higher degree	17.8	3.2	4.5	+14.6
	M.A. or higher degree	16.1	1.9	2.7	+14.2
	Total	30.9	7.8	11.5	+23.1
Female	<12 or 12, No H.S. diploma	51.4	24.7	33.8	+26.7
	H.S. Diploma/GED	40.5	13.3	18.6	+27.2
	Some college	34.4	12.1	15.9	+22.3
	Associate's degree	29.8	8.1	10.9	+21.7
	Bachelor or higher degree	22.9	3.8	5.7	+19.1
	M.A. or higher degree	16.7	2.1	3.1	+14.6
	Total	36.5	9.4	13.7	+27.1
Total	<12 or 12, No H.S. diploma	47.3	23.8	31.2	+23.4
	H.S. Diploma/GED	36.1	11.3	16.1	+24.8
	Some college	30.4	9.7	13.2	+20.7
	Associate's degree	26.3	6.8	9.2	+19.5
	Bachelor or higher degree	20.5	3.5	5.1	+17.0
	M.A. or higher degree	16.5	2.0	2.9	+14.5
	Total	33.6	8.6	12.5	+25.0

Source: 2013 and 2014 March CPS Supplements, public use files, U.S. Census Bureau, tabulations by authors
[a]Restricted to members of labor force and labor force reserve

47 %. This rate declined to 30 % for those with 1–3 years of college, and to a low of 16 % for those with a master's or higher degree. The least well educated underutilized workers were about 2.3 times as likely to be poor or near poor as their counterparts with a four-year or higher college degree.

The findings on the underutilization status of workers were combined with their educational attainment to estimate poverty/near poverty rates for various subgroups

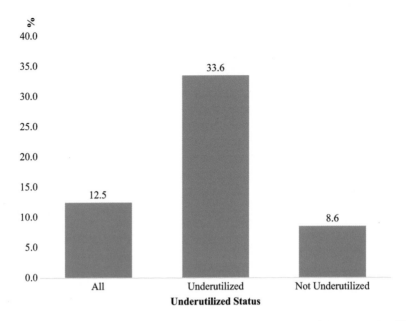

Fig. 7.21 Poverty/near poverty rates of workers (16 and over) in 2012–2013 by labor underutiliza-tion status, March 2013–March 2014

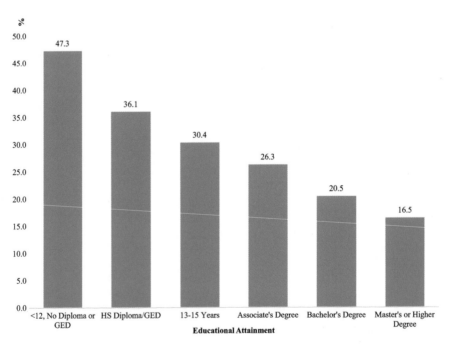

Fig. 7.22 Poverty/near poverty rates of underutilized U.S. workers (16 and over) by educational attainment, March 2013–March 2014 (in %)

of such workers. The poverty/near poverty rates of these workers ranged quite widely across these various subgroups (see Fig. 7.23). Close to 50 % of underutilized, high school dropouts were poor/near poor versus slightly more than one-third of high school graduates. Among those workers who were not underutilized, just 11 % of high school graduates were members of poor/near poor families and under 3 % of those with a bachelor's or higher degree. Poverty/near poverty rates of underutilized high school dropouts were 17 times greater than those of the college educated who were not underutilized.

Low-Income Problems of Workers by Labor Underutilization and Educational Attainment

Our final measure of the income inadequacy problems of workers is that of their low-income status; that is, a family income that is twice the poverty line or less. Approximately one in four workers was living in low-income families in March

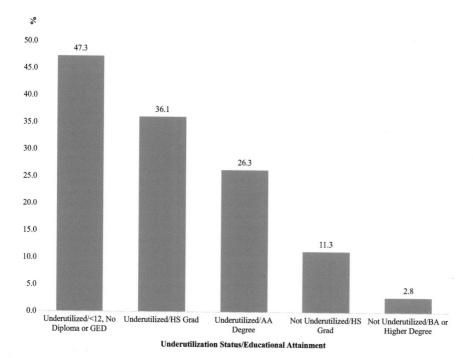

Fig. 7.23 Poverty/near-poverty rates of selected groups of workers (16 and over) by underutilized status and educational attainment, March 2013–March 2014 (in %)

2013–2014 (see Fig. 7.24). Among those with an underutilization problem, one-half

(51 %) had household income below our low-income threshold. In comparison, among those who were not underutilized, the incidence of such low-income problems was only 19 %, or less than two-fifths that of the underutilized.

Again, the incidence of income inadequacy problems among underutilized workers varied across educational groups, being highest for the less educated and falling with additional levels of educational attainment. Two-thirds of the underutilized who lacked a high school diploma or GED were low income versus 55.6 % of high school graduates and 33 % of those with a bachelor's degree (see Fig. 7.25). Clearly, even among the well educated, labor underutilization creates severe low-income problems, though they fare far better than their less educated peers.

In the final set of analysis, we generated estimates of low-income problems among various groups of workers categorized by their educational attainment and labor underutilization status. Both factors together have a massive impact on the likelihood of being low income in 2013–2014. At the upper end of the distribution of low-income rates are high school dropouts who were underutilized in the labor market. Two-thirds of these individuals were low income. Even among high school graduates, a majority (55.6 %) of the underutilized had household income below the low-income threshold (see Fig. 7.26).

Among those who were not underutilized, the incidence of low-income problems was only 8.8 % for those with a bachelor's degree and only 4.7 % for those with a master's or higher degree (see Table 7.12). The least well-educated members of the underutilized were 14 times as likely to be low income as the best educated mem-

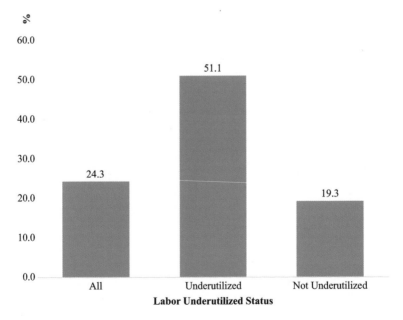

Fig. 7.24 Low-income rates of workers (16 and over) in 2012–2013 by labor underutilization status, March 2013–March 2014

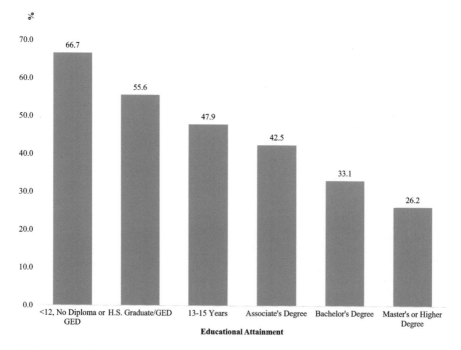

Fig. 7.25 Low-income rates of underutilized workers (16 and over) by educational attainment, March 2013–March 2014 (in %)

bers of those workers who were not underutilized in the labor market. Clearly, the division of American workers into a low-income/not-low-income status is substantially influenced by formal schooling and labor underutilization status. Being underutilized by itself was also found to be significantly influenced by educational attainment.

Conclusion

From 2000 to 2014, the labor market problems of U.S. workers were characterized by a massive degree of inequality across socioeconomic strata. The nation's labor market problems were very unevenly distributed across workers based on differences in household incomes and educational attainment. In comparison to college-educated and affluent workers, younger, race-ethnic minority, less educated, lower-income workers faced extraordinarily high rates of labor underutilization in the form of unemployment, underemployment, and hidden unemployment. We found that on every labor market outcome measure, the gap between affluent, college-educated and low-income, less-educated groups have widened. Both during the Great Recession of 2007–2009 as well as the subsequent weak GDP and jobs

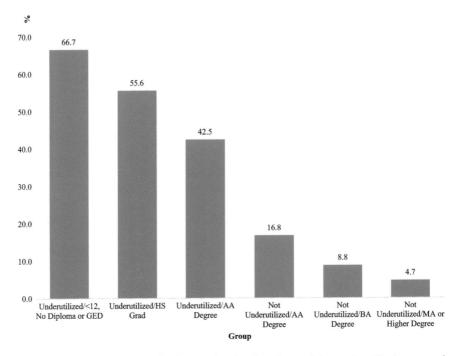

Fig. 7.26 Low-income rates of selected educational attainment/labor underutilized groups of workers (16 and over), March 2013–March 2014 (in %)

recovery through 2014, workers at the lower end of the socioeconomic ladder have faced labor market problems similar to that of the Great Depression era, while those at the higher end of the socioeconomic ladder experienced near full employment labor market conditions. Unsurprisingly, we found that the income inadequacy status of U.S. workers was heavily influenced by their formal schooling and labor force underutilization status.

These findings make it abundantly clear that labor market problems across educational groups interact substantially with household income. Being less educated and low income places one at a sharply higher risk of labor market underutilization, while for America's best educated and affluent workers, the problem isn't nonexistent, but nearly so. These findings make it quite clear that it is difficult to talk about the "average" unemployment rate or the "average" labor underutilization rate in such labor markets. As economic analysts often agree, "the average is over" (Cohen 2013).

Limitations of the U.S. labor market in recent years have taken a tangible toll on the nation's less educated and low-income workers; contributing to growing earnings and wage inequality and family income inequality, and to poverty and other problems associated with low incomes. A full employment economy similar to that of the 1994–2000 period helped raise weekly wages, annual earnings, and family incomes, bringing rising family income inequality at least temporarily to a halt, and

Table 7.12 Low-income rates of 16 and older persons[a] in 2012–2013 by labor force underutilization status in March 2013 and March 2014, total and by gender and educational attainment level

| Gender | Educational attainment | Low-income rate (%) | | | |
		(A) Underutilized	(B) Not Underutilized	(C) Total	(D) Difference (A − B)
Male	<12 or 12, No H.S. diploma	64.4	46.9	52.0	+17.5
	H.S. Diploma/GED	52.8	23.5	29.1	+29.3
	Some college	44.0	17.9	22.3	+26.1
	Associate's degree	37.7	14.0	16.7	+23.7
	Bachelor or higher degree	29.7	7.9	9.8	+21.9
	M.A. or higher degree	26.7	4.5	5.7	+22.2
	Total	49.0	18.1	23.0	+30.9
Female	<12 or 12, No H.S. diploma	69.6	47.6	55.2	+22.0
	H.S. diploma/GED	59.3	29.5	35.4	+29.8
	Some college	51.8	25.4	30.0	+26.4
	Associate's degree	46.0	19.1	22.6	+26.9
	Bachelor or higher degree	36.2	9.7	12.3	+26.5
	M.A. or higher degree	25.7	4.9	6.3	+20.8
	Total	53.4	20.6	25.8	+32.8
Total	<12 or 12, No H.S. diploma	66.7	47.2	53.3	+19.5
	H.S. diploma/GED	55.6	26.1	31.8	+29.6
	Some college	47.9	21.6	26.1	+26.3
	Associate's degree	42.5	16.8	19.9	+25.7
	Bachelor or higher degree	33.1	8.8	11.1	+24.3
	M.A. or higher degree	26.2	4.7	6.0	+21.5
	Total	51.1	19.3	24.3	+31.8

Source: 2012 and 2013 March CPS Supplements, public use files, U.S. Census Bureau, tabulations by authors
[a]Restricted to members of labor force and labor force reserve

reduced poverty problems, including among children. Restoring economic opportunity in the United States cannot take place without a much more favorable labor market environment.

Appendices

Appendix 7A: Labor Underutilization Rates by Gender and Race-Ethnic Groups

In the main part of the chapter, we analyzed variations in an array of labor market problems (unemployment, underemployment, hidden unemployment, and labor underutilization) across workers in various educational and household income groups in labor markets in 2013 and 2014. For gender and race-ethnic groups, we also presented selected findings for combinations of educational attainment and household income.

This appendix provides more detailed findings on the labor underutilization rates of workers in each gender and five race-ethnic groups (Asian, Black, Hispanic, Other, White, not Hispanic). For each of these seven groups as well as all workers, we provide estimates of labor underutilization rates in 2013–2014 for six educational attainment groups cross-tabulated by household income in seven income categories ranging from a low of under $20,000 (which we refer to as low income) to a high of $150,000 or more, which we refer to as the most affluent group of workers in the U.S.

Table 7A.1 provides the estimates of these labor underutilization rates for all workers (16 and over), including the hidden unemployed. As revealed in the main report, the labor underutilization rates of workers varied widely across educational attainment groups, ranging from a high of 29 % among those lacking a high school diploma, to 18 % for high school graduates with no college, to a low of just 6.5 % for those workers holding a master's or higher degree (see Table 7A.1).

For each gender and race-ethnic group, we have compared the estimates of labor underutilization rates from those workers lacking a high school diploma and those with a master's or higher degree (see Table 7A.2) and taken the ratio of these two

Table 7A.1 Labor force underutilization rates of persons 16 and older by household income level, educational attainment: 2013–2014 averages (in %)

Educational attainment	Household income level (in 1000 s)							
	<20	20–39	40–59	60–74	75–99	100–149	150+	Total
<12 or 12, No H.S. Diploma	44.4	26.5	22.1	21.0	21.5	21.1	21.3	29.4
H.S. Diploma/GED	38.1	20.2	14.2	11.7	10.0	9.6	9.6	18.1
Some college	34.7	19.3	13.4	11.9	10.2	9.4	10.4	16.1
Associate's degree	33.0	16.2	10.6	8.4	7.1	5.9	6.5	11.8
Bachelor or higher degree	28.0	16.0	10.1	8.1	6.4	5.2	5.1	8.9
M.A. or higher degree	27.5	16.7	9.9	7.3	5.8	4.3	3.2	6.5
Total	37.2	20.0	13.3	10.7	8.8	7.2	6.2	14.9

Source: Monthly CPS, public use files, 2013 and 2014, U.S. Census Bureau, tabulations by authors

Table 7A.2 Comparisons of the labor underutilization rates of workers lacking a high school diploma with those holding a master's or higher degree, all and by gender and race-ethnic group, 2013–2014 averages (in %)

Group	(A) Lacking a high school diploma	(B) Master's or higher degree	(C) Col. A/Col. B
All	29.4	6.5	4.5*
Men	26.6	5.7	4.7*
Women	33.6	7.3	4.6*
Asian	21.4	6.7	3.2*
Black	46.1	9.3	5.0*
Hispanic	25.4	8.6	3.0*
Other races	44.0	7.7	5.7*
White, not Hispanic	28.6	6.0	4.8*

Source: Monthly CPS, public use files, U.S. Census Bureau, tabulations by authors

estimates (see Column C). The labor underutilization rate of high school dropouts was 29 % versus slightly below 6 % for those with a master's or higher degree. The relative difference in underutilization rates for these two groups of workers was between four and five times.

Very similar ratios prevailed among both men and women. Across the five race-ethnic groups, these relative differences in labor underutilization rates ranged from lows of 3.0–3.2 among Asian and Hispanic workers to highs of 5–6 among Black and other races, including Native American and those of mixed races. With the exception of Asians, where high school dropouts faced a labor underutilization rate of 21 %, dropouts in both gender and other four race-ethnic groups often experienced underutilization rates in the 25–46 % range. Such high underutilization rates sharply reduce their expected annual earnings, and when combined with low incomes of other family members, they often place such individuals at high risk of poverty and other income inadequacy problems.

The underutilization rates of workers in seven household income groups were calculated separately, both overall and for gender and race-ethnic groups. In Table 7A.3, we compare these labor underutilization rates for workers in low-income (under $20,000) and affluent households ($150,000 and over). Overall, 37.2 % of the workers from low-income households were underutilized versus only 6.2 % in affluent households, a relative difference of six times.

These large absolute and relative gaps in labor underutilization rates between affluent and low-income workers prevailed among both gender groups and each race-ethnic group in 2013–2014. Thirty-seven percent of both low-income male and female workers faced labor underutilization problems, five to six times as high as those encountered by affluent workers of both genders. Among the five race-ethnic groups, low-income workers faced underutilization rates of 32–46 % in four of these race-ethnic groups (the rate for Asians was 32 %), with relative differences typically in the four to six times range. Across the board, low-income workers in every demographic group clearly experienced labor underutilization rates well above those of

Table 7A.3 Comparisons of the labor underutilization rates of workers from low-income families (under $20,000) with those from the most affluent ($150,000 and over), all and by gender and race-ethnic group, 2013–2014 (in %)

Group	(A) Low-income	(B) Affluent households	(C) Low-income/affluent
All	37.2	6.2	6.0*
Men	36.9	5.8	6.4*
Women	37.5	6.7	5.6*
Asian	31.9	5.2	6.2*
Black	46.1	9.3	5.0*
Hispanic	35.1	8.1	4.3*
Other races	46.4	11.0	4.2*
White, not Hispanic	34.0	5.8	5.8*

Source: Monthly CPS, public use files, U.S. Census Bureau, tabulations by authors

the nation's most affluent workers, contributing to rising earnings and family income inequality and to widening gaps in family income inadequacy problems.

The incidence of problems of labor underutilization across educational groups was strongly, positively correlated with household income differences in labor underutilization rates. As a consequence, there are very large differences in labor underutilization rates across combinations of educational attainment/household income groups among workers, both overall and within each gender and race-ethnic group (see Table 7A.4).

Forty-four percent of low-income workers who lacked a high school diploma were underutilized in 2013–2014 (Table 7A.4). As educational attainment rose, even low-income workers were less likely to experience such labor market problems. Among the nation's most affluent workers with a master's or higher degree, only 3.2 % were underutilized in 2013–2014. The absolute percentage point gap between these two radically different groups of workers was 41 percentage points, or 14 times in relative terms. For each gender and race-ethnic group, the relative difference in labor underutilization rates between these two groups of workers was in the double digits range and came close to or exceeded 15 times for men, Black, White, non-Hispanic workers, and other races, including Native American and those of mixed races. Tables 7A.5, 7A.6, 7A.7, 7A.8, 7A.9, 7A.10, and 7A.11 break down the labor underutilization rates of gender and race-ethnicity separately by household income level and education. Tables 7A.12, 7A.13, and 7A.14 display labor force underutilization rates of Black, Hispanic, and non-Hispanic White workers broken out by poverty, poverty/near poverty, and low-income status in six educational groups.

Table 7A.4 Comparisons of the labor underutilization rates of workers from low-income families lacking a high school diploma to workers from the most affluent families with a master's or higher degree, all and by gender and race-ethnic group, 2013–2014 (in %)

Group	(A) Low-income, lacks diploma	(B) Affluent, master's or higher	(C) Low-income/ affluent
All	44.4	3.2	14*
Men	41.3	2.4	17*
Women	48.3	4.2	11*
Asian	35.9	2.8	13*
Black	59.7	4.1	15*
Hispanic	36.8	3.6	10*
Other races	60.3	3.0	20*
White, not Hispanic	47.0	3.2	15*

Source: Monthly CPS, public use files, U.S. Census Bureau, tabulations by authors

Table 7A.5 Labor force underutilization rates of men 16 and older by household income level, educational attainment, 2013–2014 averages (in %)

Educational attainment	Household income level (in 1000 s)							
	<20	20–39	40–59	60–74	75–99	100–149	150+	Total
<12 or 12, No H.S. diploma	41.3	23.8	19.7	19.1	20.5	20.7	21.5	26.6
H.S. Diploma/GED	38.1	20.0	13.8	11.5	9.9	9.2	9.2	17.5
Some college	34.9	20.0	13.0	11.7	9.4	9.2	10.8	15.4
Associate's degree	32.9	15.9	10.4	8.0	6.4	4.8	5.6	10.8
Bachelor or higher degree	28.9	15.8	9.4	7.7	5.7	4.6	4.6	8.1
M.A. or higher degree	26.5	16.9	10.0	7.0	4.9	3.6	2.4	5.7
Total	36.9	19.9	13.1	10.6	8.4	6.9	5.8	14.3

Source: Monthly CPS, public use files, U.S. Census Bureau, tabulations by authors

Table 7A.6 Labor force underutilization rates of women 16 and older by household income level, educational attainment, 2013–2014 averages (in %)

Educational attainment	Household income level (in 1000 s)							
	<20	20–39	40–59	60–74	75–99	100–149	150+	Total
<12 or 12, No H.S. diploma	48.3	31.0	26.6	23.9	23.2	21.8	20.9	33.6
H.S. Diploma/GED	38.0	20.4	14.7	12.1	10.1	10.1	10.1	19.0
Some college	34.5	18.8	13.7	12.2	11.1	9.7	9.8	16.8
Associate's degree	33.1	16.4	10.9	8.7	7.7	7.0	7.5	12.7
Bachelor or higher degree	27.3	16.3	10.7	8.4	7.2	5.8	5.7	9.6
M.A. or higher degree	28.5	16.5	9.8	7.5	6.5	4.9	4.2	7.3
Total	37.5	20.2	13.6	10.9	9.2	7.6	6.7	15.5

Source: Monthly CPS, public use files, U.S. Census Bureau, tabulations by authors

Table 7A.7 Labor force underutilization rates of 16 and older by family income level, educational attainment level for Asian adults, 2013–2014 averages

Educational attainment	Household income level (in 1000 s)							
	<20	20–39	40–59	60–74	75–99	100–149	150+	Total
<12 or 12, No H.S. diploma	35.9	18.4	18.7	14.6	15.5	19.1	13.2	21.4
H.S. Diploma/GED	32.0	15.0	12.8	15.8	11.5	8.1	7.1	15.4
Some college	36.4	21.1	17.1	13.4	12.9	9.9	13.2	18.0
Associate's degree	27.1	15.2	11.9	9.0	7.3	6.5	8.5	11.3
Bachelor or higher degree	30.6	20.4	11.9	10.2	8.5	5.2	5.7	10.5
M.A. or higher degree	22.4	13.6	9.9	9.3	8.2	5.3	2.8	6.7
Total	31.9	17.6	13.1	11.7	9.6	6.3	5.2	12.2

Source: Monthly CPS, public use files, U.S. Census Bureau, tabulations by authors

Table 7A.8 Labor force underutilization rates of 16 and older by family income level, educational attainment level for Black adults, 2013–2014 averages

Educational attainment	Household income level (in 1000 s)							
	<20	20–39	40–59	60–74	75–99	100–149	150+	Total
<12 or 12, No H.S. diploma	59.7	38.8	34.2	33.2	34.8	26.4	33.8	46.1
H.S. Diploma/GED	45.5	24.1	19.0	16.7	13.2	13.2	13.6	27.2
Some college	41.2	21.6	16.4	16.1	13.7	11.3	14.7	22.5
Associate's degree	39.1	16.7	13.2	10.5	10.1	8.9	12.1	17.2
Bachelor or higher degree	35.4	17.6	11.1	9.0	7.2	6.8	6.8	12.4
M.A. or higher degree	34.3	19.0	11.7	7.7	9.0	3.3	4.1	9.3
Total	46.1	23.6	17.0	14.1	11.8	9.2	9.3	23.3

Source: Monthly CPS, public use files, U.S. Census Bureau, tabulations by authors

Table 7A.9 Labor force underutilization rates of 16 and older by family income level, educational attainment level for Hispanic adults, 2013–2014 averages

Educational attainment	Household income level (in 1000 s)							
	<20	20–39	40–59	60–74	75–99	100–149	150+	Total
<12 or 12, No H.S. diploma	36.8	22.8	18.9	16.1	18.6	17.8	17.7	25.4
H.S. diploma/GED	34.3	20.9	15.7	14.0	13.2	11.5	13.2	20.4
Some college	34.7	19.7	14.5	14.0	10.9	10.3	8.5	17.8
Associate's degree	33.8	16.9	12.3	9.2	8.3	6.1	7.0	14.0
Bachelor or higher degree	28.8	16.9	9.9	9.1	7.1	5.7	6.3	11.1
M.A. or higher degree	29.6	14.4	13.0	7.9	6.6	5.7	3.6	8.6
Total	35.1	20.8	15.2	12.9	11.3	9.3	8.1	19.3

Source: Monthly CPS, public use files, U.S. Census Bureau, tabulations by authors

Table 7A.10 Labor force underutilization rates of 16 and older by family income level, educational attainment level for Native American/other adults, 2013–2014 averages

	Household income level (in 1000 s)							
Educational attainment	<20	20–39	40–59	60–74	75–99	100–149	150+	Total
<12 or 12, No H.S. diploma	60.3	39.0	38.9	42.8	23.2	34.2	41.4	44.0
H.S. diploma/GED	46.8	26.6	20.1	22.2	15.2	14.5	12.0	26.4
Some college	43.1	21.5	18.7	14.1	15.0	14.1	18.8	21.9
Associate's degree	41.8	21.6	15.3	14.0	10.4	8.4	1.6	17.2
Bachelor or higher degree	28.8	13.8	12.2	5.9	9.4	7.2	9.0	10.8
M.A. or higher degree	31.5	19.2	8.1	13.1	4.0	5.3	3.0	7.7
Total	46.4	24.5	18.9	16.6	12.4	11.5	11.0	21.9

Source: Monthly CPS, public use files, U.S. Census Bureau, tabulations by authors

Table 7A.11 Labor force underutilization rates of 16 and older by family income level, educational attainment level for White adults, 2013–2014 averages

	Household income level (in 1000 s)							
Educational attainment	<20	20–39	40–59	60–74	75–99	100–149	150+	Total
<12 or 12, No H.S. diploma	47.0	28.5	22.4	22.2	22.2	21.4	20.9	28.6
H.S. diploma/GED	35.6	18.8	12.8	10.0	8.8	8.8	8.7	15.3
Some college	30.9	18.1	12.0	10.6	9.3	8.8	9.6	13.9
Associate's degree	30.5	15.7	9.7	7.8	6.5	5.6	6.0	10.4
Bachelor or higher degree	25.7	15.1	9.7	7.7	6.0	5.0	4.8	8.0
M.A. or higher degree	26.6	17.0	9.4	6.7	5.1	4.1	3.2	6.0
Total	34.0	18.6	11.9	9.5	7.8	6.7	5.8	12.2

Source: Monthly CPS, public use files, U.S. Census Bureau, tabulations by authors

Table 7A.12 Poverty rates of 16 and older persons[a] in 2012–2013 by labor force underutilization status in March 2013 and March 2014 by selected race and educational attainment level

		Poverty rate (%)			
Race	Educational attainment	(A) Underutilized	(B) Not Underutilized	(C) Total	Difference (A–B)
Black	<12 or 12, No H.S. diploma	51.0	24.3	37.2	+26.7
	H.S. diploma/GED	44.0	13.0	22.1	+31.0
	Some college	32.7	10.6	15.9	+22.1
	Associate's degree	25.5	7.7	10.8	+17.7
	Bachelor or higher degree	21.9	3.7	5.9	+18.3
	M.A. or higher degree	19.8	1.8	3.4	+18.0
	Total	39.2	9.9	17.1	+29.2

(continued)

Table 7A.12 (continued)

		Poverty rate (%)			
Race	Educational attainment	(A) Underutilized	(B) Not Underutilized	(C) Total	Difference (A−B)
Hispanic	<12 or 12, No H.S. diploma	41.8	20.5	26.1	+21.3
	H.S. diploma/GED	32.4	11.5	15.9	+20.9
	Some college	25.1	8.4	11.6	+16.7
	Associate's degree	32.0	6.5	9.8	+25.5
	Bachelor or higher degree	22.5	4.6	6.8	+18.0
	M.A. or higher degree	17.3	2.3	3.5	+15.0
	Total	33.8	11.6	16.1	+22.2
White	<12 or 12, No H.S. diploma	29.6	10.2	16.3	+19.3
	H.S. diploma/GED	22.3	5.2	8.1	+17.0
	Some college	21.7	5.5	7.9	+16.2
	Associate's degree	18.4	3.6	5.2	+14.9
	Bachelor or higher degree	13.8	2.0	3.0	+11.7
	M.A. or higher degree	11.1	1.3	1.8	+9.8
	Total	20.9	3.9	6.2	+16.9

Source: 2013 and 2014 March CPS Supplements, public use files, U.S. Census Bureau, tabulations by authors
[a]Restricted to members of labor force and labor force reserve

Table 7A.13 Poverty/near poverty rates of 16 and older persons[a] in 2012–2013 by labor force underutilization status in March 2013 and March 2014 by selected race and educational attainment level

		Poverty/near poverty rate (%)			
Race	Educational attainment	(A) Underutilized	(B) Not Underutilized	(C) Total	Difference (A−B)
Black	<12 or 12, No H.S. diploma	60.3	32.7	46.0	+27.6
	H.S. diploma/GED	51.8	19.4	28.9	+32.4
	Some college	38.3	15.1	20.7	+23.2
	Associate's degree	32.2	11.2	14.8	+21.0
	Bachelor or higher degree	26.2	5.2	7.8	+21.0
	M.A. or higher degree	23.7	2.7	4.5	+21.0
	Total	46.3	14.3	22.2	+32.0

(continued)

Table 7A.13 (continued)

Race	Educational attainment	Poverty/near poverty rate (%)			
		(A) Underutilized	(B) Not Underutilized	(C) Total	Difference (A − B)
Hispanic	<12 or 12, No H.S. diploma	53.7	29.9	36.2	+23.8
	H.S. diploma/GED	41.8	17.1	22.3	+24.6
	Some college	31.9	12.5	16.1	+19.4
	Associate's degree	35.9	10.3	13.7	+25.6
	Bachelor or higher degree	27.8	6.5	9.1	+21.3
	M.A. or higher degree	19.4	3.6	4.8	+15.8
	Total	43.1	17.2	22.4	+25.9
White	<12 or 12, No H.S. diploma	34.9	14.8	21.1	+20.1
	H.S. diploma/GED	27.8	8.0	11.3	+19.7
	Some college	27.0	8.1	10.8	+18.9
	Associate's degree	23.9	5.5	7.5	+18.4
	Bachelor or higher degree	17.7	2.9	4.2	+14.8
	M.A. or higher degree	13.2	1.6	2.3	+11.5
	Total	25.9	5.8	8.5	+20.0

Source: 2013 and 2014 March CPS Supplements, public use files, U.S. Census Bureau, tabulations by authors
[a]Restricted to members of labor force and labor force reserve

Table 7A.14 Low-income rates of 16 and older persons[a] in 2012–2013 by labor force underutilization status in March 2013 and March 2014 by selected race and educational attainment level

Gender	Educational attainment	Low income rate			
		(A) Underutilized	(B) Not Underutilized	(C) Total	Difference (A − B)
Black	<12 or 12, No H.S. diploma	75.8	53.9	64.5	+21.9
	H.S. Diploma/GED	72.7	38.0	48.2	+34.7
	Some college	57.4	31.2	37.6	+26.3
	Associate's degree	49.7	24.1	28.5	+25.6
	Bachelor or higher degree	41.2	13.3	16.8	+27.9
	M.A. or higher degree	36.0	6.7	9.3	+29.3
	Total	64.7	28.6	37.5	+36.1

(continued)

Table 7A.14 (continued)

Gender	Educational attainment	Low income rate			
		(A) Underutilized	(B) Not Underutilized	(C) Total	Difference (A−B)
Hispanic	<12 or 12, No H.S. diploma	75.3	58.0	62.5	+17.3
	H.S. diploma/GED	64.7	39.7	45.0	+25.0
	Some college	53.7	30.3	34.8	+23.3
	Associate's degree	52.4	26.2	29.6	+26.2
	Bachelor or higher degree	43.5	14.3	17.8	+29.2
	M.A. or higher degree	31.8	8.2	10.0	+23.6
	Total	64.4	37.2	42.7	+27.2
White	<12 or 12, No H.S. diploma	53.6	32.8	39.3	+20.8
	H.S. diploma/GED	45.6	19.7	24.0	+26.0
	Some college	42.6	17.6	21.3	+25.0
	Associate's degree	39.1	13.9	16.7	+25.2
	Bachelor or higher degree	28.7	7.6	9.4	+21.1
	M.A. or higher degree	22.6	3.9	5.0	+18.7
	Total	41.6	13.9	17.5	+27.7

Source: 2013 and 2014 March CPS Supplements, public use files, U.S. Census Bureau, tabulations by authors
[a]Restricted to members of labor force and labor force reserve

Appendix 7B: Associations Between Educational Attainment/ Household Income by Gender and Race-Ethnic Groups

Findings on the unemployment rates of workers have focused on the links between educational attainment/household income and unemployment status for all workers combined. We also looked at the associations between educational attainment/ household income and unemployment status to see whether they prevailed among both gender groups and across major race-ethnic groups. We estimated unemployment rates of workers in seven selected educational attainment/household income groups by gender and for Black, Hispanic, and White non-Hispanic workers. Key findings are displayed in Table 7B.1.

For men and women, the unemployment rate patterns were very similar. Both male and female workers with limited formal schooling and low incomes faced extremely high unemployment rates ranging from 21 to 24 %, while those with a high school diploma and below average incomes ($20,000–40,000) encountered unemployment rates between 8 and 10 %, and those with a bachelor's or higher degree and incomes above $100,000 experienced unemployment rates of 2 %.

Table 7B.1 Unemployment rates of workers by gender and race-ethnic group in selected educational attainment and family income groups, 2013–2014 (in %)

Educational/income group	(A) Men	(B) Women	(C) Black	(D) Hispanic	(E) White not Hispanic
H.S. Dropout, <$20,000	21.2	24.5	38.2	15.7	25.8
H.S. graduate, <$20,000	21.5	18.4	26.9	16.2	18.2
H.S. graduate, $20,000–$40,000	10.4	8.3	12.8	9.1	8.5
13–15 Years, $40,000–$60,000	6.3	5.9	8.2	6.2	5.5
Associate degree, $60,000–$75,000	3.7	3.4	4.9	3.9	3.2
Bachelor's degree, $100,000–$150,000	2.3	2.3	3.5	1.3	2.1
Master's or higher degree, $150,000 plus	1.2	1.7	2.1	1.3	1.4
All	7.0	6.6	12.3	8.3	5.5

Source: Monthly CPS household surveys, public use files, 2013 and 2014, tabulations by authors

In the aggregate, unemployment rates across these three major race-ethnic groups varied from a low of 5.5 % among White non-Hispanics to a high of 12.3 % among Black non-Hispanics. In each race-ethnic group, however, the unemployment rates of workers were strongly linked to their educational attainment and household incomes. Among low-income high school dropouts and high school graduates with no college, unemployment rates varied from 16 to 38 %. They fell steadily and steeply with additional education and income for each race-ethnic group, falling to 6–8 % for those with some college and low-middle incomes to lows of 1–2 % for affluent workers with a master's or higher degree. These gaps in unemployment rates across workers by schooling/household income were substantial for each race-ethnic group.

Appendix 7C: Logistic Probability Models Showing Effects of Demographics on Underutilization Rate of Workers

We have estimated a set of logistic probability models to illustrate the independent effects of various demographic variables on the underutilization rates of workers in 2013–2014.

The dependent variable in this logistic probability model is *UNDERUTIL*, a dichotomous variable that takes on the value of 1 if the respondent was underutilized at the time of the CPS and the value of zero if he or she was an active member of the labor force but was not underutilized.[22] The right-hand side predictor variables include the gender, age, race-ethnic origin, nativity status, disability status, educational

---

[22] With the exception of members of the labor force reserve, all other nonparticipants in the civilian labor force are excluded from the analysis.

attainment, and the annual family income category of the household. The base group of labor force participants for this analysis consists of White non-Hispanic, native born males, who were 55–64 years old, faced no physical or mental disability limiting their work ability, held a bachelor's or higher degree, and lived in a family with an income above $150,000. Members of the base group faced an expected probability of being underutilized of 4 %. Definitions of each of these predictor variables are displayed in Table 7C.1.

The findings of the logistic probability regression displayed in Table 7C.2 reveal that the probability of a labor force participant being underutilized in 2013–2014 was significantly associated with age, race-ethnicity, disability status, educational attainment, and family income background (see Table 7C.2).[23] The youngest members of the labor force (those under 25 years of age) were significantly and substantially more likely than the older members of the base group (55–64) to be underutilized. Those participants 25–44 years of age (key members of the so-called prime aged work force) faced a labor underutilization probability less than three percentage points above the base group. Older adults (65 and over) faced a 1.8 percentage point greater probability of being underutilized relative to the base group of 55–64 year olds.

The gender of respondents had only a modest independent impact on the likelihood of being underutilized. Women with traits similar to those of men were about one percentage point more likely to be underutilized than males. Members of each minority race-ethnic group were more likely to be underutilized than comparable, White non-Hispanic peers; however, the impact was substantially higher for Black non-Hispanics than for Asians or Hispanics. Holding all other background traits constant, Black labor force participants were nearly 8.4 percentage points more likely than White non-Hispanics to be underutilized in the labor market.

The educational attainment of these labor force respondents had strong independent impacts on their probability of being underutilized. Relative to members of the base group who held a bachelor's or higher degree, persons in each other educational group were more likely to be underutilized, with the size of the impacts being considerably higher for the less educated. High school students were nearly 20 percentage points more likely to be underutilized than four-year or higher college graduates. High school dropouts were between 14 and 15 percentage points more likely to be underutilized than those with bachelor's or higher degrees. The likelihood of being underutilized fell to seven percentage points for high school graduates and to only two percentage points for those holding an associate's degree.

The annual family income of the respondent had significant impacts on their probability of being underutilized in the labor market. Relative to the affluent members of the base group (those living in families with incomes above $150,000), members of each other income group were significantly more likely to be underutilized, with the size of these impacts declining with family income. Those labor

---

[23] The logistic coefficients on the independent variables were converted into estimated marginal probability effects. A standard practice in the literature is to calculate these marginal probability effects at the means of all right hand side variables. We can convert the logit regression coefficients (Bs) into a set of marginal effects by multiplying the value of each logistic coefficient (B) by (P) and (1-P), where P is the percent of workers in the sample who were underutilized in 2013–2014.

Table 7C.1 Definitions of the variables appearing in the logistic probability model of being an underutilized labor force participant

Variable	Definition
UNDERUTIL	=1 if underutilized
	=0
Female	=1 if female
	=0 if other
Asian	=1 if Asian
	=0 if other race
Black	=1 if Black
	=0 if other race
Hispanic	=1 if Hispanic origin
	=0 if not Hispanic
Native American	=1 if Native American
	=0 if else
Native	=1 if native born
	=0 if else
Disabled	=1 if faces a physical/mental disability
	=0 if else
Age 16–24	=1 if age 16–24
	=0 if else
Age 25–34	=1 if age 25–34
	=0 if else
Age 35–44	=1 if age 35–44
	=0 if else
Age 45–54	=1 if age 65–74
	=0 if else
Age 65–74	=1 if age 55–64
	=0 if else
HSDROP	=1 if a high school dropout
	=0 if else
HSGRAD	=1 if a high school graduate
	=0 if else
SOMECOLL	=1 if 13–15 years, no degree
	=0 if else
AA DEGREE	= if person holds an associate's degree
	=0 if else
INCOME<20	=1 if household income under $20,000
	=0 if else
INCOME 20–40	=1 if household income between $20,000 and $40,000
	=0 if else
INCOME 40–75	=1 if household income between $40,000 and $75,000
	=0 if else
INCOME 75–100	=1 if household income between $75,000 and $100,000
	=0 if else
INCOME100–150	=1 if household income between $100,000 and $150,000
	=0 if else

Table 7C.2 Findings of the logistic probability model of the underutilized status of individual members of the labor force in 2013–2014

Variable	(A) Logit coefficient	(B) Sig. of coefficient	(C) Marginal probability at the mean
Constant	−3.081	0.01	
Female	0.067	0.01	0.012
Asian	0.114	0.01	0.021
Black	0.465	0.01	0.084
Hispanic	0.121	0.01	0.022
Native American/other	0.416	0.01	0.075
Native Born	0.027	0.01	0.005
Disabled	0.596	0.01	0.108
Age 16–24	0.707	0.01	0.128
Age 25–34	−0.040	0.01	−0.007
Age 35–44	−0.168	0.01	−0.030
Age 45–54	−0.178	0.01	−0.032
Age 65 and over	0.099	0.01	0.018
High school student	1.099	0.01	0.198
High school dropout	0.815	0.01	0.147
High school graduate	0.406	0.01	0.073
13–15 Years, no degree	0.262	0.01	0.047
Associate's degree	0.129	0.01	0.023
FAMINC <$20,000	1.760	0.01	0.318
FAMINC $20,000–$39,000	1.008	0.01	0.182
FAMINC $40,000–75,000	0.547	0.01	0.099
FAMINC $75,000–$99,000	0.259	0.01	0.047
FAMINC $100,000–$149,000	0.113	0.01	0.020

−2 Log likelihood = 1187291, Nagelkerke R Square = .150, Chi Square = 142955, Sig. = .01, DF = 22, N = 1,644,646

force participants living in the lowest income households (an annual income under $20,000) were 32 percentage points more likely to be underutilized than the most affluent group. This impact fell to 18 percentage points for those in families with incomes between $20,000 to $40,000, to 10 percentage points for those with incomes between $40,000 and $75,000, and to only 2–5 percentage points or less for those with family incomes between $75,000 and $150,000.

Appendix 7D: Estimating the Probability of a Person with Given Background Traits Being Underutilized in 2013–2014

The logistic regression coefficients can be used to estimate the probability of a person with given characteristics being underutilized in 2013–2014. The procedure for estimating the probability of a person being underutilized with given traits is relatively straightforward. The probability that a given person being underutilized is equal to the following:

$$P_i = \frac{e^{\alpha+\beta x}}{1+e^{\alpha+\beta x}}$$

To calculate the values of P_i, we begin by calculating the value of $\alpha+\beta x$ for an individual with given traits, X_i (e.g., gender, race-ethnic origin, age, education, nativity, disability, family income level). The values of the α and β's are those generated by the logistic regression model. We then calculate the value of $e^{\alpha+\beta xi}$. The value of the denominator is simply equal to $1+e^{\alpha+\beta xi}$. The ratio of these two values would then yield the estimated probability of college attendance for this individual.

Appendix 7E: Logistic Probability Model of Labor Underutilization for Labor Force Participants Under 30

The following are details regarding estimates of a logistic probability model of labor underutilization among labor force participants under 30 in 2013–2014 (see Table 7E.1). The base group for this analysis is a 25- to 29-year old White non-Hispanic male who was not disabled, held a bachelor's or higher degree and lived in a family with an income over $150,000.[24]

Similar to our findings for all working-age adults (16 and over), gender had only a very modest impact on the labor underutilization rate of teens and young adults. Holding all other demographic and socioeconomic traits constant, young women were slightly under one percentage point less likely than males to be underutilized.[25] Teens and young adults (20–24 years old) faced much higher rates of labor underutilization than their older peers (25–29 years old). A teen labor force participant (or a member of the labor force reserve) was nearly 11 percentage points more likely than his or her peers 25–29 years old to be underutilized, while a 20–24 year old was about six percentage points more likely to be underutilized than his older peers.

Members of each race-ethnic group were significantly more likely than White non-Hispanics to be underutilized. The estimated sizes of these independent impacts of race-ethnic group varied from lows of two to three percentage points among Asians and Hispanics to a high of nine percentage points among Black non-Hispanic youth. The educational attainment of these youth also had frequently strong impacts on the probability of being underutilized at the time of the 2013–2014 surveys. Relative to their base group peers with a bachelor's or higher degree, those young adults who lacked a high school diploma or GED were nearly 14 percentage points more likely to be underutilized. High school graduates were 10 percentage points

---

[24] The expected probability of labor underutilization among the base group was only 5.9 percentage points.

[25] Male teens and those 20–24 were heavily hit by changing employment developments over the 2000–2014 time period, including the high loss of blue-collar jobs that impacted young men more than young women.

Table 7E.1 Findings of the logistic probability model of the underutilized status of individual members of the young adult labor force under age 30 in 2013–2014

Variable	(A) Logit coefficient	(B) Sig. of coefficient	(C) Marginal probability at the mean
Constant	−2.777	0.01	
Female	−0.038	0.01	−0.005
Asian	0.206	0.01	0.026
Black	0.713	0.01	0.090
Hispanic	0.197	0.01	0.025
Native American/Other	0.443	0.01	0.056
Native Born	0.162	0.01	0.021
Disabled	0.798	0.01	0.101
Age 16–19	0.859	0.01	0.109
Age 20–24	0.457	0.01	0.058
High school student	0.947	0.01	0.120
High school dropout	1.117	0.01	0.141
High school graduate	0.790	0.01	0.100
13–15 Years, no degree	0.381	0.01	0.048
Associate's degree	0.233	0.01	0.029
FAMINC < $20,000	0.923	0.01	0.117
FAMINC $20,000–$39,000	0.365	0.01	0.046
FAMINC $40,000–75,000	0.130	0.01	0.016
FAMINC $75,000–$99,000	−0.002	–	0.000
FAMINC $100,000–$149,000	−0.045	0.05	−0.006

Note: Implies not statistically significant
−2 Log likelihood =364601, Nagelkerke R Square = .142, Chi Square = 36761, Sig. = .01, DF =19, N =377,096

more likely to be underutilized than bachelor's degree holders. The impact drops to only 5 percentage points for those with 13–15 years of schooling but no degree and to under three percentage points for those with an associate's degree.

Family income of respondents also affects an independent impact on the probability of young adults being underutilized in the labor market, but the negative impacts are primarily concentrated among low-income and low-middle-income youth. Those young adults with household incomes under $20,000 had a probability that was 12 percentage points higher of being underutilized than their affluent peers, and those young adults with incomes between $20,000 and $40,000 had a five to six percentage point higher probability of experiencing an underutilization problem. There were no significant differences between upper-middle-income youth and the most affluent families.

The above findings illustrate quite dramatically that among the young as well as among all workers, age, race-ethnic origin, educational attainment, and family income status played jointly large roles in shaping the incidence of underutilization problems in 2013–2014.

References

Acs, Gregory, Katherin R. Phillips, and Daniel McKenzie. 2000. *Playing the rules but losing the game: America's working poor*. Washington, DC: Urban Institute.

Ayres, Sara. 2013. *The high cost of youth unemployment*. Washington, DC: Center for American Progress.

Blau, Francine, and Lawrence M. Kahn. 2013. The feasibility and importance of adding measures of actual experience to cross-section data collection. *Journal of Labor Economics* 31(April): S17–S58.

Census Bureau, U.S. 2010. *Income, poverty, and health insurance coverage in the United States: 2009*. Washington, DC: U.S. Government Printing Office.

Chinn, Menzie D., and Jeffrey Frieden. 2011. *Lost decades*. New York: W.W. Norton and Co.

Cohany, Sharon. 2009. Ranks of discouraged workers and other marginally attached to the labor force rise during recession, *Issues in labor statistics*. Washington, DC: U.S. Bureau of Labor Statistics, April.

Cohen, Tyler. 2013. *Average is over: Powering America beyond the age of the great stagnation*. New York: Penguin Group.

Ginzberg, Eli. 1978. *Good jobs, bad jobs, and no jobs*. Cambridge, MA: Harvard University Press.

McLaughlin, Joseph, Andrew Sum, Ishwar Khatiwada, and Sheila Palma. 2010. *Trends in the levels and distribution of young family incomes, 1979–2009*. Washington, DC: Children's Defense Fund.

NBER (National Bureau of Economic Research). 2015. *U.S. business cycle expansions and contractions*. www.nber.org/cycles.

Sum, Andrew, and Ishwar Khatiwada. 2009. The wealth of the nation's young. *Challenge* (November/December): 96–100.

Sum, Andrew, and Ishwar Khatiwada. 2010. The nation's underemployed in the great recession of 2007–2009. *Monthly Labor Review* (November): 3–13.

Sum, Andrew, and Ishwar Khatiwada. 2012. Endnotes: Going beyond the unemployment statistics: The case for multiple measures of labor underutilization. *Mass Benchmarks* 14(2): 19–24.

Sum, Andrew, Ishwar Khatiwada, and Walter McHugh. 2014a. Deteriorating labor market fortunes of teens: Consequences for future young adult employment in our nation, *Challenge* (May/June).

Sum, Andrew, Martha Ross, Ishwar Khatiwada, and Mykhaylo Trubskyy. 2014b. *The changing labor market fortunes of teens (16–19) and young adults (20–24) years old in the nation's 100 largest metropolitan areas during the lost decade*. Washington, DC: Brookings Institution, March.

Tienda, Marta, V. Joseph Hotz, Avner Ahituv, and Michelle Bellessa. 2010. Employment and wage prospects of Black, White, and Hispanic women. In *Economics and public policy*, ed. Human Resource, 129–160. Kalamazoo: W.E. Upjohn Institute for Employment Research.

U.S. Bureau of Labor Statistics. 2008. *The unemployment rate and beyond: Alternative measures of labor underutilization*. Washington, DC, June.

U.S. Bureau of Labor Statistics. 2014. *The employment situation: February 2014*. Released March 8. Washington, DC.

U.S. Council of Economic Advisers. 2002. Economic report of the president, February. Washington, DC: U.S. Government Printing Office.

Part III
Education and Opportunity

Chapter 8
Gates, Gaps, and Intergenerational Mobility: The Importance of an Even Start

Timothy M. (Tim) Smeeding

Abstract This chapter focuses on how intergenerational mobility is affected by children's earliest life experiences from conception through preschool. These experiences are important because of their effects on outcomes later in life. One consequence is that intervening early is the most cost-effective way to put a child on course to pass through the gates that determine adult success and thereby reduce differences in mobility among children born in different circumstances. Using a life-cycle model, we examine the evidence on trends in factors that affect child development. The evidence we assess leads to the conclusion that opportunity and mobility are declining for lower and even middle class children as changes in family life, parenting practices, economic inequality, unresponsive social institutions, and increasingly economically homogeneous neighborhoods all point to a serious decline in the factors that are associated with greater mobility. We conclude that the decline in opportunity and mobility for current generations of American children is likely the biggest negative effect of the continuing U.S. inequality boom in income, wealth, and consumption. The paper ends by outlining a series of policies that would help restore opportunity in America by intervening early in the life course.

Keywords Intergenerational mobility (IGM) • Dynamic complementarity • Economic opportunity • Childhood outcomes • Human capital • Life-cycle model • Early childhood education • Childcare • Maternal health • Health care • Health insurance • Socioeconomic status (SES) • Unmarried mothers

The author thanks Educational Testing Service for its support in completing this paper. I also thank Henry Braun, Irwin Kirsch, and Andy Sum for their comments on an earlier draft. I also appreciate the comments of two referees, Steve Barnett and Bhash Mazumder, as well as the editorial help of Henry Braun, Larry Hanover, Deborah Johnson, and David Chancellor in completing this chapter. All errors of commission and omission are the responsibility of the author alone.

T.M.(T.) Smeeding (✉)
University of Wisconsin-Madison, Madison, WI 53706, USA

© Educational Testing Service 2016
I. Kirsch, H. Braun (eds.), *The Dynamics of Opportunity in America*,
DOI 10.1007/978-3-319-25991-8_8

Introduction: How Can We Make the Start More Even?

Efforts to address economic opportunity are not enough as we seek to improve American society. That's because addressing economic opportunity does not deal with another problem: a lack of intergenerational mobility (IGM). Without more widespread opportunities to improve childhood outcomes and do a better job of building human capital for all children, we are not likely to see a systematic increase in relative social and economic intergenerational mobility—movement up (or down) in socioeconomic class within a family from one generation to the next (see, for instance, Jencks and Tach 2006; Smeeding 2015).

Policy makers concerned about IGM need to think about how to overcome barriers in order to create more opportunity for those left behind and how to make greater opportunity translate into more mobility. In the parlance of the *Opportunity in America* project, we need to open more gates to opportunity for more children. And we need to reduce the gaps in successful outcomes between the children of the haves and have-nots, with the latter passing through key transition points with positive momentum instead of confronting closed gates at each point, falling further and further behind.

To guide our analysis, we need a framework to map out progress in reducing barriers that inhibit equalizing opportunity and IGM. The traditional literature on IGM does not help us much in this task. Most scholarly discussions of IGM focus on the question of income mobility for children once they have reached adulthood. Some of these studies tell us overall mobility has not declined in recent decades, which is unsurprising for an economy where income gains were widespread and living standards rose across the distribution up until the early 1980s (compare Mazumder 2015 and Smeeding 2015 with Chetty et al. 2014). We also know from national and cross-national research that there is substantial "stickiness" at both the top and bottom of the U.S. IGM matrix of parental and child incomes, with about 35–40 % of children that start in families at the top or the bottom of the heap ending up there as adults (Jäntti et al. 2006). Finally, we know that the resource levels separating the poor from the rich have grown in magnitude since the inequality generation was born in the 1980s, meaning that even with constant mobility, the consequences of ending up at one end or the other of the adult outcome distribution are much greater now because the dispersion in outcomes is much wider due to growing inequality in income and wealth.

If we are to advocate for policies to enhance opportunity and improve IGM for the next generation, we need to look at the factors affecting today's and tomorrow's children's chances at upward mobility, both in a relative and an absolute sense. A life-cycle approach begins to do this by setting up markers of success along the road to greater IGM from conception onward. By viewing IGM from this perspective, we are able to observe factors that increase or decrease equality of opportunity and mobility, and therefore, those that affect gates and gaps. These include both policies and institutions that open or close gates, and actions and choices made by individuals that either help to reduce opportunity gaps for themselves and their children or have the opposite effect—to widen them.

In this chapter, I focus on just a few steps along this continuum but the ones that I believe are the most important—those earliest in life. Increasingly, scientific evidence on child development and success focuses on the very earliest developmental periods (Aizer and Currie 2014; Mazumder et al. 2010). Thus we argue that worrying about a child's chances of success in life by starting with preschool is not starting too early but rather at least two or three steps too late. Indeed preschool is the final step along the life cycle that we address in this chapter.

We begin by asking what makes a difference early in life. We consider just a sample of the evidence on child differences by social and economic origin that is accumulating in all social and behavioral science fields, as well as the brain sciences. We then review recent changes in the five most important factors that propel or hinder progress at early (and later) life stages: family structure and stability; parenting practices; economic inequality; social institutions; and neighborhoods and the role of place. These factors interact with one another and together strongly influence both opportunity and mobility. We also discuss how these dynamics will be playing out in a very different world, one in which there is no racial or ethnic majority but ever-larger numbers of children of color.[1]

The goal is to produce a healthy, active, curious, happy, and engaged child for the first day of elementary school. With this in mind we examine how children are affected by these forces in three early life stages: prenatal and family birth status; early home life, health, and childcare during ages 6 months to 3 or 4 years; and family life, neighborhood, and preschool during ages 4–6. Evidently, there are large gaps in outcomes related to school readiness that are systematically linked to the contextual factors listed above. In particular, we need to determine if the gap between the top and bottom of the child well-being distribution has narrowed or widened along this path. Finally, we will conclude with some suggestions on policy levers that can increase the chances of success for children born to disadvantage.

Throughout the chapter, we must ask what the "proper" roles of government are and society is in this process. How might we target public investment in children's (and in some cases their parents') development—in their education, health, safety, and so on—to compensate for lower private investment and less capable parenting? Resources can play a significant role at strategic transition points in the life cycle (i.e., places where more investment on the part of parents or institutions can make a big difference in children's outcomes). Some come early and are addressed here, such as parent-child interactions and the development of cognitive skills and character (grit, social competency, perseverance, and good habits), while others come later in life. The latter include schooling choices, paying for college, providing funding to enable acceptance of an unpaid internship, direct job provision in family firms (nepotism), or helping a first entrance into the housing market. But in all cases, disparities in child outcomes appear at the earliest stages of life. And there is

---

[1] See, for instance, Frey 2014 and the section entitled "The 5 Big Factors That Determine Early Development."

ever mounting evidence that the early childhood period, when the brain is most malleable, is the time where interventions for at-risk children might be most cost-effective (Heckman and Mosso 2014).

The scope of this investigation includes not only the poor but also the lower middle class. Stagnant earnings and flat or falling incomes, such as those that most workers are now experiencing, suggest that the barriers we identify are a worry for strapped middle classes, not just poor families with children (Shapiro 2015). There is a need for wages and incomes to rise in real terms for those now in the middle class. There is a difference between making a life on a poverty budget that provides just enough to barely shelter, feed, and clothe one's children, and one that is based on a budget sufficient to support a "well raised" child. In this regard, the important issue of the split in these costs between parents/families and the public sector and even the private sector arises.[2] Hence mobility is an issue for middle class families, not just the poor.

The present study is not simply an academic one: Opportunity and social mobility are growing popular and political issues. The belief in the opportunity to reach the American Dream is being seriously questioned today.[3] It once was a strongly and widely held view that if you worked hard and played by the rules, you could get ahead in America. But that has changed. Today, only 42 % of Americans agree that if you work hard, you'll get ahead, while just less than half (48 %) believe that was once but no longer true. Also notably, less than one-third of Black Americans believe that hard work gets you ahead, while one-seventh never believed this was true. Indeed, flat incomes indicate hard work and recovery from the Great Recession have not yet paid off for the middle classes.

More to the point for IGM analysis, most Americans (55 %) believe that one of the biggest problems in the country is that not everyone is given an equal chance to succeed in life. And according to Galston (2014), other recent surveys have shown the same result— parents' confidence in their children being better off than they are is at or near the lowest point ever recorded:

> (W)hen the August 2014 NBC/WSJ poll asked "Do you feel confident or not confident that life for our children's generation will be better than it has been for us?", only 21 percent expressed confidence, down from 30 % in 2012. During the same month, the CBS poll asked, "Do you think the future of the next generation of your family will be better, worse, or about the same as your life today?", only 23 % responded "better" compared to fully 50 % who said "worse."
>
> In June, CNN/ORC found that only 34 % of respondents believed that most children would grow up to be better off than their parents, while 63 % expected the children to be worse off. And the Heldrich Center at Rutgers' Bloustein School found in August that only 16 % of Americans expect job, career, and employment opportunities to be better for the

---

[2] Kirkegaard (2015) suggests that public finance support for U.S. children is amassed mainly in the tax code and therefore supports rich children much more than poor ones. Absent changes in federal funding to favored new investment in children, new methods to pay must be found. The new institution of Social Impact Bonds (SIBs), where the public sector pays back private investments in outcomes that reduce future public costs, might help in such instances. For more, see Liebman (2011) and Costa (2014).

[3] Data collected in July and August 2014; Jones et al. 2014.

next generation than for the current generation, compared with 40 % in November of 2009, just months after the official end of the Great Recession (Galston 2014).

And families are not just imagining retrenchment, they are living it. A recent Brookings Institution report (Shapiro 2015) notes that in 2000, 16 % of households were headed by people without high school diplomas, and an additional 51 % were headed by people without college degrees. From 2002 to 2012, the median income of the group without high school diplomas declined at an average annual rate of 2.4 % across age cohorts year after year; the median income of the group without college degrees fell at an average annual rate of 1 % across age cohorts year after year. That tells us that two-thirds of American households have suffered persistent income losses from 2002 to 2012, a period that included eight years of economic "expansion" and two years of serious recession.

Overall then, it appears that most Americans express significant concerns about the economic future of their children and themselves. But they also are questioning their beliefs in America being an equal opportunity society, a principle widely thought by many to be our highest social value.[4] Restoring opportunity in America has to become an important and continuing national priority.

What Makes a Difference Early in Life?

In this section, we introduce the life-cycle model. We then provide a brief review of what we know about early influences on health, behavior, and learning, establishing the following:

- Child development starts at conception, influenced by prenatal health and intra-uterine environment, and these factors have important longer-term effects, according to evidence from test of the fetal origins hypothesis.
- Brain development differs between rich and poor children from conception onward.
- Health status, health care access, and parenting are the keys to successful early child development (after birth but before formal preschool).
- Poor health and bad birth outcomes make it harder for such children to catch up with others as life progresses according to the "dynamic complementarity" hypothesis.
- Difficulties persist in providing high-quality preschool experiences for poor children.

---

[4] "[Only] in America is equality of opportunity a virtual national religion, reconciling individual liberty—the freedom to get ahead and 'make something of yourself'—with societal equality. It is a philosophy of egalitarian individualism. The measure of American equality is not the income gap between the poor and the rich, but the chance to trade places" Reeves (2014).

Gates and Gaps and the Life-Cycle Model

In a recent pair of cross-national research volumes, the authors and editors took the life-cycle approach to studying the relationship of parental education and income to child outcomes from birth to age 30 (Smeeding et al. 2011a; Ermisch et al. 2012). Figure 8.1 summarizes their model of the process from birth to adulthood for one generation, moving across six life stages from origin (parental socioeconomic status, or SES) to destination (children's adulthood SES). Parental investments and social institutions affect each step, where intermediate gains or losses are measured in multiple domains.

This structure allowed us to combine evidence from different cohorts at different times, with every outcome in every country being ranked by adult educational differences. Taken as a whole, these studies suggest a powerful effect of parental SES on child outcomes in health, cognitive testing, sociobehavioral outcomes, school achievement, and adult social and economic outcomes. Examination of standardized outcomes across 11 countries found a definite and universal pattern: the higher

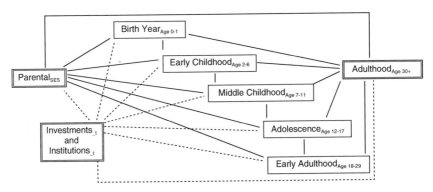

Table A. Variable Definitions and Examples of Proposed Measures at Different Points in the Life Course

Parental SocioEconomic Variables (Parental$_{SES}$)   *Measures:* Education, Income, Earnings, SES, Occupation, Wealth, Employment
Childhood/Early Adulthood Life Stages Birth Year (age 0-1), Early Childhood (age 2-6), Middle Childhood (age 7-11), Adolescence (age 12-17), Early Adulthood (age 18-29)   *Measures:* Educational attainment, cognitive measures, socio-emotional behavior, employment/labor market, health/physical
Investments $_t$ and Institutions $_t$ Are assumed to be different public and private investments and institutions contributing to children's development that vary by country.
Adulthood (Age 30+)   *Measures:* Child SES, Income, Education, Employment, Labor Market Attachment

Fig. 8.1 A model of intergenerational transmission of advantage by life stage (Ermisch et al. 2012)

the adult SES as measured by educational attainment, the larger the positive effect on children's outcomes as they crossed each transition point.

The gaps among children ranked by parental education were observed from birth onward and did not diminish as they got older. Although in some cases the gaps widened, this was not always the case. Notably, the slopes of the relationships between parental SES and child outcomes were most steep in the United States.[5]

The same structure facilitates the assessment of how various cohorts of United States children will be affected by growing gaps in parental SES (education, earnings, wealth, and income). In this chapter we concentrate only on the first two stages in Fig. 8.1: conception and birth through early childhood.[6]

What We Know about Early Influences on Health, Behavior, and Learning: A Very Brief Review

Child development starts at conception. The fetal origins hypothesis first suggested by Barker (1995) hypothesizes that pre-birth experiences have long-term effects on health. Ever mounting evidence suggests that maternal impoverishment during the prenatal period has a substantial causal impact on infant health and long-term outcomes (Aizer and Currie 2014). Behaviors (smoking, drinking, substance abuse—each holding other factors constant) and exposure to toxins all exert a negative influence on in-utero child health, full-term birth, birth weight, and early child well-being (Lien and Evans 2005). Exposure to harmful environmental factors such as pollution, violence, and stress also take their toll on mothers and children alike (Currie et al. 2009; Currie and Walker 2011). Nutritional and health effects in-utero are also important to long-term outcomes for children—the findings of multiple studies suggest the growing importance of such effects (Mazumder et al. 2010, 2015; Almond and Mazumder 2011; Almond et al. 2012; Almond and Currie 2011).

Mothers born in a high-disease environment were also more likely than other women to have low-birth-weight offspring and to be suffering from diabetes when they gave birth, suggesting a strong intergenerational environmental component to poor health (Almond et al. 2011; Aizer and Cunha 2012; Smeeding 2015). Disadvantaged women also have greater exposure to, and are more susceptible to, contagions such as seasonal influenza. Hence, they may be disproportionately affected by pandemics which, in turn, can negatively affect fetal development. There are a number of factors that can potentially explain disadvantaged women's greater susceptibility. These include that disadvantaged women are more likely to

---

[5] But not all the steps were filled in for any one country, save Sweden, where the paper by Mood et al. (2012) covers all the steps in the life course. In the larger study, most outcomes were measured for only one cohort. For more, see Ermisch et al. (2012), especially Chap. 2.

[6] In this review we draw heavily on recent reviews of the child development literature by Aizer and Currie 2014; Magnuson and Duncan 2014; Heckman and Mosso 2014; Duncan and Magnuson 2013.

live in crowded homes, are more reliant on public transportation, are less able to stay home from work when ill, are less likely to be immunized, and are less likely to believe the influenza vaccine to be effective (Wooten et al. 2012; Sanders 2012; Quinn et al. 2011). Finally, women who are poor, minority, or both are also more likely to be the victims of domestic violence (Vest et al. 2002). The literature on maternal health, exposure to toxins and the like, and poverty strongly suggest that from conception through birth, children from lower-income families are at a disadvantage in comparison to those born to higher-income families.

Moreover, there is evidence that poor birth outcomes and low birth weight have effects that are liable to persist through childhood and even into adulthood. In a recent paper, Figlio and colleagues (2014) find that the effects of poor neonatal health on adult outcomes are largely determined early in life and continue for all births to rich and poor families alike and to families at all levels of educational attainment (Figlio et al. 2014). However, children with poor neonatal health born to highly educated families perform much better in the longer run than do those with good neonatal health born to poorly educated families, suggesting that patterns of nurture and early child development can at least partially overcome poor health at birth. Their findings are very much in keeping with the literature on the positive relationship between household income and health status in childhood and adulthood (Hoynes et al. 2012; Dahl and Lochner 2012) and are consistent with the notion that parental inputs and neonatal health are complements rather than substitutes, a "dynamic complementarity" that we return to below.

Recent research has focused on understanding how environmental experiences, including stress and poverty, affect the underlying neurocognitive, biological, and physiological processes of development. This phenomenon is often referred to as the way that "poverty gets under the skin." About five years ago, early research identified abnormal levels of, and fluctuations in, cortisol (the "stress" hormone) as the primary underlying mechanism (McEwen and Gianaros 2010; Champagne and Mashoodh 2009; Seeman et al. 2010). More recently, given that stress-related, elevated levels of cortisol in the mother can affect the placenta, researchers have focused on the potential negative effects of maternal stress on fetal outcomes. Comparisons of siblings suggest that those who were apparently exposed to higher-than-average levels of cortisol in utero have lower IQ levels at age 7 and complete one less year of schooling (Aizer et al. 2012). In some recent studies, environmental experiences are linked to individual differences in developmental outcomes through stable and permanent changes in genetic expressions (Essex et al. 2013).

Although genetic endowments are largely invariant during development, there is considerable change in the epigenome—the biochemical system that regulates gene expression. Moreover, the epigenome has been found to be particularly responsive to environmental conditions, including poverty directly (Hanson et al. 2013; Essex et al. 2013; Boyce 2012; Sameroff 2010). Research has also found that early maternal stressors are related to epigenetic changes in their children during adolescence, with implications for their mental health (Hanson et al. 2014; Knudsen et al. 2006; Shonkoff et al. 2012). Finally in a recent study of great importance, Noble et al. (2015) provide the strongest evidence to date that socioeconomic disparities, particularly in income, are associated with large differences in cognitive development. Investigating patterns in brain structure across social and economic status, they found that children from lower-income families had relatively large differences in brain surface area in comparison to children from higher-income families, likely predictive of future differences in cognitive development.

Postpartum health and development (but prior to pre-preschool) is also important for child outcomes (Beller 2009). Several studies have documented the relationship between the amount and type of speech directed at a child by caregivers during the course of a typical day and the child's later expressive language and vocabulary (Weisleder and Fernald 2013; Rowe 2012). Studies of parenting and children's self-regulation also point to associations between parents' early support of their children's autonomy with later assessments of children's executive function (Landry et al. 2006; Bernier et al. 2010). Because higher-income parents are typically better educated and also have more money to invest, their children tend to have better outcomes than children of lower-income parents (Guryan et al. 2008; Yeung et al. 2002; Kaushal et al. 2011). Further, child-parent interactions, such as those outlined above, may be more productive for children born healthier. In other words, prenatal and postpartum investments may be complementary in producing better child outcomes (Bono et al. 2012; Hsin 2012).

In fact, research on the malleability of cognitive and language abilities shows these skills to be highly responsive to both positive *and* negative influences (Fox et al. 2010; Shonkoff 2010). In effect this suggests that newborn health and postnatal investments are complementary. This hypothesis, termed "dynamic complementarity," implies that the impacts of general parental investments, as well as early childhood education on child outcomes, will be greater for children who enter the preschool period with higher levels of cognitive and socioemotional skills (Aizer and Cunha 2012). In particular, preschool settings that are designed to expose children to sensitive caregiving environments should increase children's socioemotional skills much more among children with more sensitive caregivers in their home environments (Duncan 2014). This process of dynamic complementarity is still just a hypothesis, and one whose negative effects can be overcome by consistent, strong investments in children from the beginning of their lives, even for the most disadvantaged children (Cunha and Heckman 2007, 2008; Camilli et al. 2010; Heckman and Mosso 2014).

Thus, despite some uncertainty, the available evidence suggests that the consequences of initial health disadvantages associated with being born to a poor mother are likely to be exacerbated over time without intensive policy and practice interventions. Unfortunately, children with poorer initial health endowments typically receive fewer postnatal investments, and the investments they do receive may be less effective due to dynamic complementarity. This mechanism can explain not only the considerable persistence of in-utero conditions in later-life outcomes, but also why the long-term impact of low birth weight is greater when children are born into poverty and other unsatisfactory circumstances (Figlio et al. 2014). In terms of the framework of this project, early gaps can easily become larger and increasingly more difficult to reduce. However, continuous investments before the preschool period can still make an important difference in outcomes.

Preschool Investments

The life-cycle model leads us to the topic of preschool and its effectiveness. Although about 70 % of children overall have attended a preschool-like program, the rate is much higher among the top two quintiles of the income distribution (nearly 90 %) than among the three bottom-income quintiles (65 %) (Duncan and Magnuson 2013; Magnuson et al. 2012). Currently, about 25 % of children do not attend preschool at all before they enter kindergarten, while some unknown fraction of children are privately reared in strong developmental childcare and early education systems from ages 1 or 2. Because lower-income children are least likely to be enrolled compared to higher-income children, and because income gaps in early development forecast lower levels of human capital accumulation, improving enrollment and attendance for low-income children should be a first priority for policy.[7] But in this area, the United States pales in comparison to other nations. According to the Organisation for Economic Co-operation and Development (OECD 2015, chart PF3.1.A) public expenditure on childcare and early education services was less than 0.5 % of GDP in 2011, placing the U.S. last among rich OECD countries in such efforts. Surprisingly, African-American children are, if anything, more likely than comparable White children to be enrolled in school- or center-based care at age 5, though often of lesser quality (Magnuson et al. 2006; Magnuson and Waldfogel 2005).

Any discussion about preschool for disadvantaged children must begin with the much maligned, but currently irreplaceable, Head Start program, the oldest and largest federally funded preschool program in the United States. Head Start not only provides early childhood education, care, and services for children but also tries to promote parental success. Although recent critical federal evaluations suggest that the effects of Head Start on learning and cognitive outcomes begin to fade in the second grade and later disappear, others defend the program as having positive longer-term outcomes for children and parents (Duncan and Magnuson 2011).

For instance, employing a quasi-experimental design, Sabol and Chase-Lansdale (2015) examined whether children's participation in Head Start promoted parents' educational advancement and employment. They found that parents of 3-year-old Head Start children had steep increases in their own educational attainment by the time the child was 6, with strong effects particularly for African-American parents.

---

[7] We also note that there are other demographic groups that have comparatively low levels of preschool enrollment—Hispanic children and children of immigrants. No doubt, part, but not all, of the lower rates of enrollment can be attributed to their families having lower incomes. But both language barriers and cultural factors are also likely influences that play a role in the lower levels of enrollment among Hispanic children and children of immigrants (Takanishi 2004).

Further, Head Start centers offering full-day service boost cognitive skills more than other centers, while Head Start centers offering frequent home visits are especially effective at raising noncognitive skills in children and adults (Cunha and Heckman 2008; Cunha et al. 2010; Walters 2014). Carneiro and Ginja (2014) provide new estimates of long-term impacts of Head Start on health and behavioral problems, suggesting that participation in the program reduces the incidence of behavioral problems, health problems, and obesity of male children as teens, lowers depression and obesity among adolescents, and reduces engagement in criminal activities and idleness for young adults.

What skill development strategies will likely have the greatest payoff in preschools? Heckman and colleagues[8] have continued to establish that we need to better understand the mechanisms through which successful early childhood programs work. And their evidence suggests those that appear to work best affect the so-called "soft skills," social and behavioral outcomes such as character building, self-control, and conscientiousness, in comparison to cognitive skills which often fade out early in elementary school (Heckman 2012; Kautz et al. 2014). For instance, those young children and their parents who practice small acts of self-control find it easier to perform big acts in times of crisis. Quality preschools and parenting coaches have produced lasting effects by encouraging young parents and students to observe basic etiquette and practice small but regular acts of self-restraint (Roberts et al. 2014).

Simple things like showing up also matter. Research from the Consortium on Chicago School Research at the University of Chicago suggests almost half of 3-year-olds and more than a third of 4-year-olds enrolled in pre-K are "chronically absent"—defined as missing more than 10 % of days—from Chicago's pre-K program and, further, these absences are strongly correlated with negative outcomes in elementary school learning (Ehrlich et al. 2013). Such findings reinforce the connection between health and learning and, in particular, the dynamic complementarity of bad health and poor early childhood education outcomes as the child transfers from preschool to elementary school.

The most encouraging news is that there are successful models of preschool on which to build. One example of a public preschool program that has developed exemplary curricula by integrating proven literacy, math, and social skills interventions and then implemented them, is the Boston Pre-Kindergarten Program (Duncan and Murnane 2013). Rigorous evaluation reveals large impacts on vocabulary, math, and reading but smaller impacts on executive function (Duncan and Murnane 2013; Weiland and Yoshikawa 2013). Another is Chicago's Child Parent Center education program. This program engages not only with the children but also with their parents to foster better learning at home and to help families address the myriad challenges they face. The program comprises a dedicated parent resource teacher and a school community representative who engage parents both inside and outside the program. Students who participate in the program are better prepared for kindergarten, perform better on standardized tests, are less likely to need special education

---

[8] Heckman et al. 2013; Heckman and Mosso 2014; Heckman and Kautz 2014; Kautz et al. 2014.

services, and are more likely to graduate from high school and be successful in life (Chetty et al. 2011). The program is now funded in the Chicago area by a series of Social Impact Bonds, where the public sector pays back private investments in outcomes that reduce future public costs (Costa 2014).

In summary, we are finally coming to understand the importance of maternal and child health, as well as maternal behaviors related to poverty, substance abuse, bad neighborhoods, stress, pollution, and domestic violence. Together these toxic ingredients make a powerful negative cocktail of dynamic complementarity that is hard to overcome without strong and continuous interventions as a child moves from birth through preschool. Further study and examination of evidence on child outcomes are beginning to tell us not only what conditions matter, but also what treatments appear to offer effective counterweights. To reduce disparities in opportunity, we must take advantage of these findings.

The Five Factors That Determine Early Development

Here we briefly review five separate, but often highly intercorrelated, factors or forces that influence child development and, ultimately, IGM by determining whether the gates to opportunities are open, slightly ajar, or closed for the child. Unless we are able to counter the distributions of advantage and disadvantage that are influenced by each of these factors, we will not be able to meaningfully increase opportunity or mobility for those children born to disadvantage. We begin with the two most closely related factors: family structure early in life and parenting. These are followed by economic factors (money), social institutions, and neighborhoods.

Family Structure

Family formation and parenting practice are treated together, as they are often highly intertwined and because they matter a great deal from a child's earliest days through adolescence and beyond. Many analysts believe that family composition and stability may matter even more than income for equality of opportunity and IGM. As McLanahan and coauthors (McLanahan 2014; McLanahan and Jacobsen 2013) and Cherlin (2014) have established, we are seeing a growing parental class divide in America—in income, education, neighborhood, and especially family formation.

Children born into continuously married families have much higher economic mobility than those in single-parent families, especially those headed by unmarried mothers. In this regard, we must recognize the long, steady decline of marriage. In 1960, only 12 % of adults aged 25–34 had never married; by the time they were 45 to 54, the never-married share had dropped to 5 %. But by 2010, 47 % of Americans 25–34 had never married, and based on present trends, their share will be about

25 % in 2030 when they're 45–54 (Wang and Parker 2014). This is a stunning decline that befuddles demographers and social policy wonks alike. The growth in the number of single unmarried mothers in the United States has both been massive and concentrated among the least educated (no high school degree), as well as those, especially in their 20s, who have graduated high school and even may have some postsecondary education. These women are typically more educated than the men who fathered their children and do not want to marry men who do not have an education or regular jobs. Some scholars believe that changes in the labor market have been particularly important in reducing the marriageability of undereducated men (Wilson 1996). Others argue that incarceration and street violence have drastically reduced the numbers of Black men who are eligible for marriage.[9]

Because family differences begin at birth, it is often useful to characterize the middle ground of an issue by looking at the extremes. If we examine both what is considered to be the best and the worst ways to become a parent, we can better understand the genesis of "diverging destinies" (McLanahan 2014; McLanahan and Jacobsen 2013). The "best" way to become a parent is through living the American Dream. The process is the same for men and women alike: Finish school, find a decent job, find a partner you can rely on, make plans for a future together including marriage as a commitment device (see Lundberg and Pollak 2013), and then have a baby. Following this path will likely mean that parents are age 25 or older, more educated, and more likely to have a stable marriage. They have better parenting skills and smaller families, along with more income, auxiliary benefits, and assets to support their children. For their children, these characteristics translate into open gates for opportunity.

At the other extreme, the step "have a baby" (between the ages of 16 and 22) moves to the top of the list, preceding all the other steps. These parents typically have not finished school, do not have a steady or well-paying job, do not have a stable marriage or steady partnership, and likely never had a plan. They have less education (high school or less), are younger and less skilled, and have lower wages and fewer benefits and more multipartner fertility. The result of this personal choice is less social and economic stability, as well as fewer resources and opportunities for their children (Smeeding et al. 2011b; Carlson and Meyer 2014; Smeeding 2015). For single women under 30, almost 70 % of pregnancies are also unintended (Sawhill 2014). And there is now strong evidence that unintended pregnancies produce poorer outcomes in children (Ibid.).

Changes in fertility/marriage, cohabitation/divorce, maternal employment, and maternal education are therefore reinforcing differences in income inequality (see below) and further reducing IGM among children. Perhaps the relationship between children and their mothers is the most important mechanism of how families affect development. Better educated women are more likely to obtain jobs with higher earnings and family leave benefits, allowing these mothers to invest more time and

---

[9] Justin Wolfers, David Leonhardt, and Kevin Quealy. "1.5 Million Missing Black Men," *New York Times*, April 20, 2015, http://www.nytimes.com/interactive/2015/04/20/upshot/missing-black-men.html?abt=0002&abg=0

money in their children. They are also more likely to have fewer children, and children born later in life. Mother's age at childbirth matters because it is a strong indicator of the child's future economic mobility.

Parenting

The quality of parenting is also highly unequal because of differences in parental endowments with respect to skills (type and amount) and economic resources (income and wealth). Hours spent reading to a young child or talking with a young child make a big difference in later outcomes. Soft skills such as conflict resolution or how to respond to setbacks are also usually better taught by those who have those skills—typically those with more education. And, of course, parental educational attainment is highly correlated with childhood education; high-skill parents not only realize the value of education but also make every effort to make sure their children succeed in reaching a high level of educational attainment.

Top-quintile spending on children's' enrichment (special classes, music, camps, and other experiences) is now almost $8900 per year, three times that of low-income quintile parents, who spend about $1320 on the same goods and services (Kaushal et al. 2011). These differences, confirmed in multiple studies, suggest that long before preschool, children born to highly educated and stable families acquire strong foundations in both cognitive and behavioral skills.[10] Using a composite measure of parenting quality,[11] researchers have established that the children of parents in the lowest quartile (lowest one-fourth) do worse on multiple outcomes at every stage of the life cycle in comparison to those born to the highest-quartile parents, with differences in success rates on the order of 30–45 % at *each* stage.

Economic Inequality: Money Matters—A Lot

There is a range of opinions about general trends in IGM, the trends in top-decile and bottom-decile income mobility, and the complicated relationship between income/wealth inequality and IGM. Nonetheless, almost all researchers agree that because differences in parental incomes between the top and bottom quintiles have grown substantially, the stakes for remaining at the bottom or the top of the distribution are now much larger, even with constant mobility parameters, because the rungs of the income ladder are much further apart. Figure 8.2 uses the Congressional Budget Office (2011) estimates of after-tax and transfer incomes for families with

---

[10] Readers should consult Kalil et al. 2012; Philips 2011.

[11] The Reeves and Howard (2013) parenting scale is based on Children of the National Longitudinal Survey of Youth "HOME" assessments at various life stages, which includes pictures, observation, interviews, etc., as well as information about literacy activities.

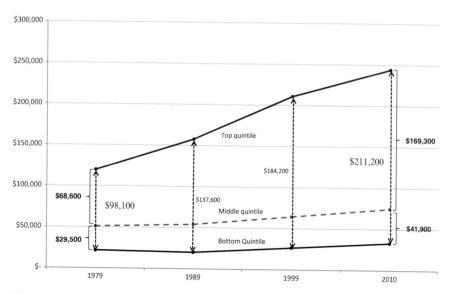

Fig. 8.2 After-tax and transfer disposable income for households with children: mean income in bottom, middle, and top quintiles, 1979–2010 (Source: Congressional Budget Office, http://www.cbo.gov/sites/default/files/cbofiles/attachments/44604-AverageTaxRates_Supplemental.xlsx)

children to show that the family income gap rose by almost $113,000, or 115 %, from 1979–2010.[12] This is a huge change across a fairly short time span.

This figure raises an important question: Should we be more concerned about relative or absolute mobility? The former refers to how children rank in terms of an outcome variable such as income relative to their parents' rank; the latter refers to the level of income that a child achieves and whether it is higher or lower than their parents' incomes (see Chap. 13). For example, do we care about absolute class gap or relative class gaps in child outcomes? In Fig. 8.2, both the top- and bottom-quintile children are better off in income terms in 2010 than in 1979, but the gap between them has widened. However, fully half of the gain in real incomes in the bottom 20th percentile is because of the increase in the cost of insured health care, which is assigned to the poor as income. Of course, the cost of health care insurance rises for the other quintiles, too, but is a much smaller fraction of their incomes and income gains (CBO 2011), hence overstating the income gains to the poor.

---

[12] Because of the growth in the very top income shares, how much is it driven by the top 1 % in any given year? If we use the mean of other percentiles to gauge the change at the top, then how much smaller or bigger are the differences between top and bottom? The gap between the bottom and the top, where the top is the 81st–90th, grows $48,900, or 49.9 %, over this period; the gap using the 91st–95th percentile as the top grows $68,800, or 70.1 %. And if the top is the 96th–99th percentile, the gap grows $115,000, or 117.2 %.

Further, Fig. 8.2 shows that middle class children[13] are losing more ground relative to top-end children than are those at the bottom relative to the middle. The top-to-middle gap has expanded from $68,600 to $169,300, or by over $100,000, from 1979–2010, while the middle-to-bottom gap rose from $29,500 to $41,900, or by about $12,400, over this same period.[14] It therefore appears that the top-end children are leaving the middle (and everyone else!) behind and helps explain why most "middle class" Americans worry about their children's future socioeconomic status, and why we see consistent calls for inclusive prosperity and shared growth (Summers and Balls 2015).

In a world where wages for most education groups are flat, as David Autor's (2014; Fig. 8.2) recent review of full-time workers makes clear, one finds that incomes and wages are stagnant or worse for undereducated men, not to mention relatively flat wages over the past decade even for men who are college graduates. This phenomenon also emerges for women since 2007 (Fig. 8.3). Even if women's wages at the bachelor's degree level have flattened since the Great Recession, women's rising wages over the longer term are in contrast to men's, except for the most educated men with post-bachelor's degrees. Beyond the diverging patterns of individual wages, the increase in assortative mating—whereby members of the same social and economic class are more likely to marry each other—substantially compounds income differences across families.[15] Evidently, these "mated" high-skill parents are at a substantial advantage in comparison to lower-income men or women who fail to marry or partner and have only a single income to support their families.

If anything, the Great Recession likely has made differences in wages and incomes much worse, as we see increasingly widespread differences in employment and wages by education and age, with income gains mainly above the bachelor's degree level, where the IGM correlation of parents and kids' education is highest (Fig. 8.3; Torche 2011). Cross-national research suggests that the premiums in pay for the highest educated are the largest in the U.S., meaning that the minority who attain a bachelor's degree and beyond do most well in the U.S. labor market compared to their lesser educated counterparts (Autor 2014; Blanden et al. 2014; Ermisch et al. 2012). Much of this difference comes from the lack of progress in educational attainment in the United States compared to other rich nations (OECD 2014).

---

[13] Middle class children are those in households with the mean income of middle-quintile families with children.

[14] Again, the reader must be careful as most of the gains in the lowest income class over this period—just about half—can be attributed to including the value of Medicaid and the State Children's Health Insurance Program in the incomes of households with children, where the value of Medicaid is far above the willingness of these households to pay for it.

[15] One can perform this operation by combining the incomes of men and women at each education level in Figure 8.3, producing a perfectly assortatively mated outcome by educational attainment that looks much like Figure 8.2. McCall and Burke (2014) show that the combined earnings rankings of husbands and wives at the upper end is actually a total sum of 160–170 (where husbands and wives are ranked by earnings quintiles from 10 to 100).

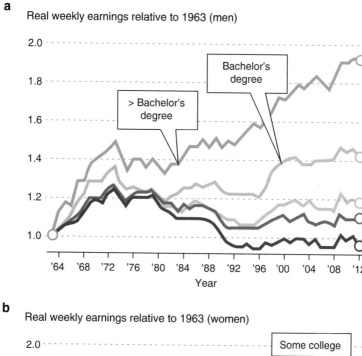

a

Real weekly earnings relative to 1963 (men)

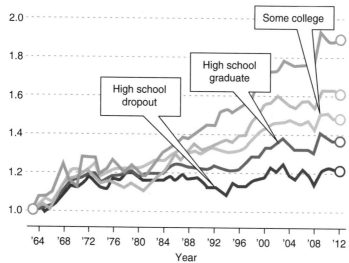

b

Real weekly earnings relative to 1963 (women)

Fig. 8.3 Changes in real wage levels of full-time U.S. workers by sex and education, 1963–2012 (Reproduced from Autor 2014)

Of course, both earned incomes matter for all two-parent families. For families with children under 14, the United States has by far the largest number of two-parent full-time workers among the rich OECD countries. Nearly 60 % of children under 14 living in coupled households have both parents working full time in the

U.S., far more than in most other nations. For instance, German and Dutch couples with dual full-time earners represent less than 20 % of all two-parent working households.[16] But because of the Great Recession and the high rates of long-term unemployment that are still present, along with the disappearance of middle-wage jobs, maintaining steady full-time work is often difficult (Kenworthy and Smeeding 2014). Also, changes in housing markets and plant closings have led to a situation where, if one parent loses his or her job, the family is not able to move to another location due to the risk of selling their home at a loss or giving up the one remaining job that they have. In fact, the growth of low-wage service jobs since the Great Recession fits well with the U.S. having by far the largest number of workers who work weekends and evenings (Hamermesh and Stancanelli 2014). There is also evidence that median incomes rose from 1979, and especially from 2000 to 2007, in the United States due almost exclusively to added hours of work and not higher wages (Mishel 2013). These work patterns pose both economic and time costs on all parents who are also raising children, especially on single parents.

Although money matters, as we have established above, it is not just about income. Consumption and wealth also matter (Fisher et al. 2015). When one looks at the placement of children across the consumption and wealth distributions, we find that they are located in very different parts of the distribution compared to the positions of elders and childless adults. Children are overrepresented in the bottom half of all of these distributions, leading to concerns about their upward mobility, certainly in comparison to the minority of advantaged children who are located at the top of the wealth and consumption scales.

None of the current analyses of inequality or IGM have captured the full effect of net worth (assets, debt, and wealth) on consumption or income by considering all three measures of well-being simultaneously for the same households—although we know that each gives a different and important perspective on the distribution of economic well-being, and, most likely, a different outcome when considering the effects of inequality on IGM (Pfeffer 2011). For instance, recent work by Pfeffer and Hällsten (2012) and the Federal Reserve's Survey of Consumer Finances (SCF) (Yellen 2014) show that since 2001 (with wealth measured in early 2013), wealth inequality had increased and income inequality with it, especially at the top. And overall financial wealth has increased by 20 % since the time of both surveys, mainly to the benefit of those with the highest wealth levels. In particular, Pfeffer and Hällsten (2012) establish that the impact of parental wealth on children partly operates through its insurance-like effects for children (i.e., a "private family safety net"). Higher wealth creates the ability to purchase higher-quality childcare (e.g., a nanny), to afford higher-priced homes for better quality local preschools, or to pay

---

[16] OECD Family Policy Database 2014. Chart LMF1.1.A "Children in couple households by parental employment status, 2011," http://www.oecd.org/els/family/LMF_1_1_Children_in_fami-lies_by_employment_status_Jul2014.pdf

for tuition for private preschools.[17] Reeves (2013) and Smeeding (2014) refer to this as the "glass floor" effect, and it makes a difference from childbirth onward.

Social Institutions

In the United States, as in other rich nations, we are aware of a set of social institutions and social policies that are intended to ameliorate some of the differences in opportunity that come from differences in private incomes and wealth. The two most important are health care and public education (in the present case, high-quality preschools).[18] The major social institution that almost all children experience from conception through preschool is the health care system, especially the pediatricians and other health professionals who are a part of that system. The U.S. health care system does not yet provide high-quality care to all of its poor and middle class children. The availability of such care is especially important for children who are born with chronic exposure to toxins (e.g., lead), as well as parental smoking, alcohol, and substance abuse. Hence the children who would most benefit from high-quality, chronic-illness-oriented health care are the ones least likely to be receiving it. The passage and start of the Affordable Care Act may in time make a difference in patterns and continuity of care, but much can be done to improve it.

The second institution is the school system, including both subsidized and publicly provided early childhood education. The interaction between parental and child education has been studied at least back through Becker and Tomes (1979, 1986). Tests of their model by others (e.g., Solon 2014) have established that intergenerational correlations in socioeconomic status (or IGM) in later life can arise from the greater knowledge and financial ability of better-off parents to invest in their children's human capital, from children's genetic or cultural inheritance, or a combination of all.[19] Hence, in the opinions of many analysts, the schooling system, including preschool, often serves to reinforce existing patterns in IGM that are the consequence of differences in parenting, family stability, and parental education, as well as economic differences (Reardon 2011).[20]

---

[17] These differences also work well later in life to finance 529 college savings plans and pre-fund college with tax-free interest and capital gains, as well as the greater ability to do more for well-timed inter-vivos transfers, especially for the following generations. See Kirkegaard 2015; Fisher et al. 2015.

[18] For poor children, one might add the legal and child protective service system, the child support system, and the childhood disability systems, but they are beyond the scope of this chapter.

[19] Because these different sources of intergenerational status transmission produce similar empirical results, distinguishing the processes from one another is therefore a difficult task. But new research by Seshadri et al. (2014) presents a model of human capital accumulation that isolates the direct effect of parents' human capital on children's human capital and finds substantial evidence of strong parental spillover effect on children's educational attainment.

[20] Also Sean F. Reardon, "No Rich Child Left Behind," The Great Divide, New York Times, April 27, 2013, http://opinionator.blogs.nytimes.com/2013/04/27/no-rich-child-left-behind/

Finally, the methods by which health care and schooling are supported by public policy in the United States differ substantially from those in other developed nations. Instead of direct and universal open access to health care and preschool, we regressively subsidize these and other goods such as housing in good neighborhoods and college expenses using income tax subsidies that benefit the rich far more than the poor (Kirkegaard 2015).

Neighborhoods and the Role of Place

Neighborhoods and residential contexts clearly affect prospects for IGM. Previous research by Sharkey (2013) and others suggests that economic segregation can at least in part explain IGM patterns. School quality, exposure to community violence, elements in the physical environment (air pollution, noise, lead), and long-term exposure to neighborhood disadvantage can and do affect academic trajectories, child cognitive development, and later economic outcomes as seen above (Aizer and Currie 2014). For those living in a high-poverty neighborhood, the odds of falling down the income ladder as adults—being worse off than their parents—are 50 % on average, even for those children who have not grown up in a poor family. In other words, neighborhoods matter in terms of schooling and other attributes; structural clustering of disadvantages contributes to these factors reinforcing each other to produce bad outcomes, above and beyond the contributions of individual families' characteristics. In fact, a recent study by Chetty and Hendren (2015) concludes that "neighborhood effects are substantial, especially for children in low-income families. The county in which a child grows up explains nearly half as much of the variation in his/her earnings as his/her parents' incomes."

Declining manufacturing sector employment in inner cities, accompanied by the outmigration of Whites and the rising Black middle class in the 1990s and 2000s, left behind pockets of concentrated disadvantage (Wilson 1987, 1996; see also Chap. 2). From 1980 to 2010, economic segregation by neighborhood grew, while racial segregation per se changed by little. These poor and still racially segregated neighborhoods are characterized not just by high rates of poverty and crime, but also by high rates of unemployment, single parenthood, and multiple-partner fertility (Kneebone 2014). And while these neighborhoods were heavily populated by Blacks in the '80s and '90s, Murray (2012) shows similar patterns in formerly White middle class neighborhoods as well. Of course there are good urban neighborhoods, with clean parks and play spaces, new schools and childcare centers, readily available high-quality health care, and little crime. But these are largely occupied by well-to-do parents who pay housing and property tax prices to segregate themselves and their families (Brodmann and Massey 2014; Kirkegaard 2015).

The Changing Race and Ethnicity of American Children

There are stark differences in mobility rates for different racial groups, especially between Whites and African-Americans. Half the Black children growing up in families in the lowest income quintile remain stuck there as adults (51 %), compared to just one in four Whites (23 %) (Smeeding 2015). Mobility is also lower for Hispanic children than White children. Research on differences in mobility between Blacks and Whites reveal stark differences: On average, Blacks experience less upward mobility and Whites experience less downward mobility. In fact, Whites are on average 20–30 percentage points more likely to experience upward mobility than are Blacks. Mazumder (2014) finds that Black men raised in middle class families are 17 percentage points more likely to be downwardly mobile than are White men raised in the middle (38 % of Black men fall out, compared with 21 % of White men). A range of personal and background characteristics—such as parental occupational status, individual educational attainment, family wealth, and marital status—all help explain this gap.

We know far less about the mobility of ethnic minorities, especially immigrants, because they are not part of older panel datasets. For instance, the Panel Study of Income Dynamics and various National Longitudinal Surveys help assess IGM but are constrained by study and sample designs that began with the original adult samples in the 1960s or 1970s and followed their children, hence excluding all immigrant groups who have not "married into" the dataset, especially the large recent immigrant cohorts that are not captured at all (Duncan and Trejo 2015). What we know about Hispanic IGM, for instance, is sparse and, again, includes only those who emigrated before the recent immigration boom (see Duncan and Trejo 2015; Acs 2011). For instance, there is limited data about economic mobility among Hispanic families, who tend to have lower incomes compared to non-Hispanic Blacks and Whites but more stable family structures than do Blacks.[21]

Most importantly, perhaps, the racial and ethnic makeup of today's children is changing rapidly (Frey 2014). In 2011, for the first time, less than half of the children born in America were to two White Anglo-American partners. Soon most children will be minority children, including White Anglo children. By 2050, Anglo-Americans will be less than half of the population (compared to aging baby boomers, the vast majority of whom are White Anglo-American). Hispanics, Asians, and multiracial populations are expected to double in size over the next 40 years as the result of immigration, higher birth rates among minority populations already here, and more interracial marriages. While these changes will challenge the nation's legal, political, and economic systems, they are already beginning to affect the youngest of the emerging majority who are just now entering our school systems. Indeed one should not forget that the children whose mobility we are trying to improve early on are not likely to be White and Anglo-Saxon by heritage

---

[21] One more promising approach is for future studies to begin with the current population and trace back to find their parental heritage instead of the other way around (Grusky et al. 2015).

(Frey 2014). In succeeding decades, the combination of this explosion with the diminishing numbers of the White Anglo baby boomers will produce intergenerational competition over governmental resources (see Brownstein and Taylor 2014).

Using the Gates-Gaps Metaphor to Examine Opportunity and Mobility Early in Life

Having reviewed some of the evidence on the major economic, demographic, and social forces and factors that impede upward mobility for our youngest, most vulnerable children, we briefly return to the three life-cycle gates. Our goal is to examine the evidence regarding trends in the distributions of opportunity and of outcomes; that is, in comparison to earlier cohorts, have the distributions for very young children growing up in the twenty-first century become more dispersed (i.e., greater inequality) or more concentrated (i.e., lesser inequality)?

Remember that gates represent access (open gates) or obstacles (closed gates) to the opportunities to accumulate human capital and to have the possibility of upward mobility. We have divided the early life-cycle age span into three segments, with endpoints chosen to match critical transition points. Now we look at the gaps at each point to see if they are increasing, which would signal the cumulative widening of differences across children as they age. We pay attention here both to the gaps we find at each transition point and, where possible, the trends that may affect patterns in gaps for future generations.

Transition 1: Prenatal and Family Birth Status

The first step involves being born at a normal birth weight to a nonpoor, mature (partnered or, better, married) mother who has at least a high school diploma. While we know a little about trends in life quality at birth (Aizer and Currie 2014), we know from the diverging destinies literature mentioned above that 41 % of U.S. births are out of wedlock (vs. 11 % in 1970) and half of all births to women under 30 are out of wedlock (Hamilton et al. 2013). A majority of these births are unplanned as young adults "drift" into parenthood because of failed contraception or ambivalence about school and life goals (Sawhill 2014).

And for these parents, family complexity, defined here as having one or more children with someone who is not the birth parent of his or her earlier child, is greatest. Multiple-partner fertility leads to very unstable lives for children and adults, replete with communication and coordination issues across parents, complicated living arrangements, and much less available time for rearing of children (Carlson and Meyer 2014; Amato et al. 2014).

The facts are that marriage rates have fallen for all types of parents in their 20s, especially for White parents who, in earlier cohorts, were much more likely to marry by age 30 (Murray 2012; Cherlin 2014). But, somewhat surprisingly, the marriage rates for college graduates have held almost constant, along with relatively low divorce rates, over the past 40 years. This bifurcation in family formation patterns is a large component of the "diverging destinies" that young children face today.

Although never-married motherhood is rising among all women, we see in Fig. 8.4 that the fraction of never-married mothers with children under 18 is more than 20 % for those who did not graduate secondary school and 15 % for high school graduates, as compared to 3 % for those with a bachelor's degree or more. And these differences have been almost continually expanding over the past 40 years. Not only is out-of-wedlock childbearing highest among the least educated, but these births occur mainly to younger mothers, most of whom are poor or near poor, and most of whom have unstable living conditions in terms of both partners and living conditions (Edin et al. 2012; Tach 2015). Over their lifetimes, these mothers have more children per woman on average than the typical mother (Smeeding et al. 2011b). In contrast, well-educated parents have fewer children later (in marriage) under much better economic circumstances (McLanahan 2014; Sawhill 2014).

Looking at unmarried mothers by education group in Fig. 8.5, we can get at the differences in being raised by an unmarried parent. These figures suggest that out-of-wedlock childrearing almost has not changed at all since 1980 for college-educated

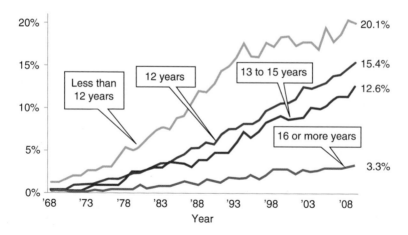

Fig. 8.4 Never-married mothers by education attainment (Source: Brookings tabulations of the Current Population Survey, Annual Social and Economic Supplement. Sawhill [2010], Fig. 10, 26; The *Economics of Inequality, Poverty, and Discrimination in the 21st century* by Robert S. Rycroft. Reproduced with permission of Praeger in the format Republish in a book via Copyright Clearance Center. Notes: The sample includes noninstitutionalized, civilian women ages 16–64 with a child under age 18 living in their house. Never-married mothers are those who have never been married)

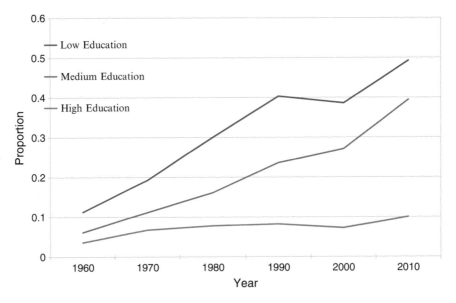

Fig. 8.5 Unmarried mothers by mothers' education (Source: IPUMS Census/ACS; Tach 2015)

(High Education) women, despite large increases among high school educated (Medium Education) and less educated (Low Education) women. These trends suggest widening differences and are not at all reassuring.[22] To be sure, the choice to have an unplanned child early in life handicaps both the parent(s) and the child, reducing absolute and relative mobility for both (Smeeding 2015).

Transition 2: Life at Early Ages, Post-Birth but before Preschool (6 Months to 3–4 Years)

In the face of low levels of education, instability, and meager income, most young single parents, including cohabiting mothers, live stressful lives that are neither good for themselves nor for their children (Aizer and Currie 2014). Various studies document that time spent with young children in reading and personal interaction is much more developmentally oriented in older and more educated married-couple families than in younger single-unmarried-mother families. These differences are then mirrored by large differences in early language development (Kalil et al. 2012; Phillips 2011).

---

[22] Of course one way to reduce this problem is reducing young unwanted pregnancy, which we turn to in the next section of the chapter.

What is the evidence on the ways that developmental differences open up early in life? One important set of tests comparing children at 9 and 24 months of age was conducted by Halle et al. (2009) and nicely summarizes child development issues over this period. Halle et al. examined disparities in child outcomes at 9 and 24 months in 2008 using the Early Childhood Longitudinal Birth Cohort. They found that gaps in outcomes by race, ethnicity, parental income, and education were evident at 9 months and grew larger by 24 months. These gaps were evident across cognitive, social, behavioral, and health outcomes. Infants and toddlers from low-income families scored lower on a cognitive assessment than infants and toddlers from higher-income families, were less likely to be in excellent or very good health at both 9 and 24 months, and were less likely to receive positive behavior ratings at 9 and 24 months.

Nearly half of all infants and toddlers—approximately 1.5 million children—in families with incomes below 200 % of poverty at 9 and 24 months of age had multiple risk factors. The most prevalent risk factors were low family income and low maternal education at both 9 and 24 months (see Appendix). Equally important, given the demographic changes underway in the U.S., infants and toddlers from more at-risk backgrounds (i.e., children from racial/ethnic minority groups whose home language was not English, and/or who had mothers with low maternal education) scored lower on cognitive and positive behavior ratings (Fig. 8.6). In each of these minority groups, scores were below those for non-Hispanic White children and, in each case, differences were larger at 24 months than at 9 months.

When a child is getting ready to enter preschool, his or her first educational institution, several factors are important for whole child development, including the

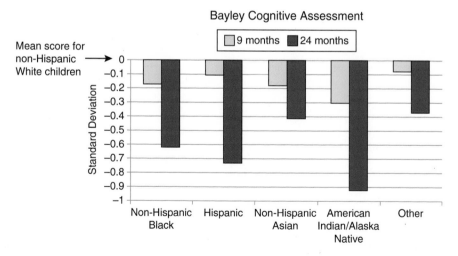

Fig. 8.6 Racial and ethnic cognitive disparities at ages 9 and 24 months (Source: Disparities in Early Learning and Development: Lessons from the Early Childhood Longitudinal Study – Birth Cohort (ECLS-B) – Executive Summary by Halle, Tamara, and Nicole Forry. Reproduced with permission of Child Trends Inc. in the format Republish in a book via Copyright Clearance Center)

home environment, parental skills, and behaviors as reviewed above. With respect to health issues, parental mental health is liable to be a major barrier to well-child development, along with other barriers such as poor nutrition, vision problems, hearing deficits, undertreated asthma, anemia, and dental pain. These are all more common in low-income families, and are critical to readiness before the onset of formal care or schooling.

Transition 3: Preschool and Early Childhood Education (Ages 4–6)

The goal is to have children with pre-reading and foundational math skills and school-appropriate behavior by first grade. More specifically, the goals for all early childhood education programs, with parental inputs and reinforcement, are to create a "mobility mentality" consisting of a growth mindset (the belief that success is learned, not preordained), instilling confidence in children to succeed, and raising their aspirations, as well as those of their parents. They also need the grit and character development to see setbacks as hurdles to overcome, not impenetrable walls, and the persistence, if they confront a closed gate, to find ways to open it or discover other paths. Fostering these characteristics in children from disadvantaged backgrounds, along with instilling in parents the ability to take these lessons home with them and apply them, are crucial elements.

But the challenge is great. Only 38 % of American 3-year-olds are enrolled in early childhood education programs (as compared to an average of 70 % among the 34 richest OECD nations; OECD 2015). Moreover, U.S. children tend to enter early childhood education at age 4. Even then, only 66 % of 4-year-olds were enrolled in 2012 (the OECD average was 84 %), a slight decrease from 68 % in 2005, when the OECD average was 79 %.[23]

It is well documented that there are large gaps in early childhood education and school readiness by parental education and income, which were most pronounced in the U.S. compared to other Anglo nations and which only recently have begun to stabilize (Bradbury et al. 2012). These gaps are larger now than in the past, in part because parents at the top spend vastly more in time and money on developmentally oriented goods and activities than those at the bottom (Kaushal et al. 2011; Kalil et al. 2012). We know that high-quality early childhood education programs are critical for development. Quality programs include productive teacher-child interactions, encouragement from teachers, and opportunities to engage with varied materials. Teacher quality and retention are also key ingredients for producing better outcomes for disadvantaged children. But these conditions are hard to establish or maintain in low-income areas (Duncan 2014).

---

[23] See OECD (2014) and figures in the section entitled "What Makes a Difference Early in Life?".

President Obama's national drive to improve early childhood education for these children is central to the effort to overcome these gaps but is hampered by differential state take-up rates in expanding preschool to all children (Duncan and Magnuson 2011). Cross-national research in Denmark and France, where universal early childhood education is the norm, shows that effective high-quality preschools do reduce the slope of the relationship of achievement to family education background. But even so, the remaining differences in both cognitive and behavioral outcomes are still significant when outcomes are ranked by parental education (Bingley and Westergaard-Nielsen 2012; Dumas and Le Franc 2012). This suggests that while early childhood education can improve opportunity and mobility from the bottom, it is not by itself the "magic bullet" for achieving desirable levels of IGM.

Cumulative Gaps?

In many ways, the U.S. system of supports and institutions performs well enough to maintain but not reduce SES-related outcome gaps once school begins (Ermisch et al. 2012; Duncan and Magnuson 2013). Hence, the gap at the beginning of elementary school is key—assuming smaller gaps upon the start of grade school would in fact be maintained and not exacerbated. We do know from longitudinal studies that there are large gaps at 9 months that widen by 24 months. This is worrisome because cross-sectional studies reveal wide gaps based on pre-K assessments at ages 4–5 (see Bradbury et al. 2012).[24] Thus, we need effective, scalable, and replicable interventions before preschool, as well as through the preschool period, if we are to make progress in improving mobility for children coming from disadvantaged backgrounds.

Summary

Essentially all the factors key to healthy child development are very much affected by parental circumstances at a point in time, and almost all the trends in differences in child development (or gaps) by parental incomes, education, and SES are on the upswing at early ages. Conditions at birth, family background, parenting, neighborhoods, social institutions, and economic circumstances all make it more difficult for low-income children, especially minority children, to successfully cross each transition point on their way to elementary school.

The social policy challenges are many, and are not just situated in the health and learning domains; the greater challenge is that medical and educational professionals

---

[24] Whereas the data we have on young children follows the same children from ages 9–24 months, we do not have follow-up data on the same children as they exit preschool or enter elementary school.

must interact with social services and deal with fractured patterns of family life, in addition to the children themselves. Effective action requires the integration of policies across the health, education, and family assistance silos if we are to become more successful in boosting mobility from below.

Policy Levers to Open Gates, Reduce Gaps, and Moderate Cumulative Gaps Early On

America is finally beginning to awaken to the reality that the next generation *is* at risk.[25] But we need to pay more than lip service to make a difference in children's chances for upward mobility. Moreover these challenges confront federal, state, and local authorities, as well as faith-based organizations, nongovernmental organizations, and even some organizations in the for-profit sector. In this final section we focus on some emerging green shoots of hope that need to be nurtured if we are to make progress in opening more opportunity gates and closing the gaps that emerge along the developmental trajectory. We begin with the prevention of unwanted pregnancies and children who begin life with a parent who is not yet prepared. We then move onto other policies that can make a difference in the lives of young children.

Unwanted Pregnancy at Young Ages: An Agency Problem

Despite the somewhat gloomy data cited above, the U.S. is making some progress in improving children's life chances through the reduction in the numbers of early unplanned pregnancies. For example, U.S. fertility is at an all-time low, reaching a rate of only 1.86 children per woman of childbearing age in 2013. More importantly, fertility has reached this record low because of falling birthrates among teens and women in their early 20s, bringing the U.S. teen pregnancy rate closer to that in other rich countries (Hamilton et al. 2013; Curtin et al. 2014). Much of this success is due to the dissemination of long-acting reversible contraceptives, which are much more effective than conventional birth control (Secura et al. 2014; Sawhill 2014).

Money Makes a Difference in Parenting

An important point established above is that money makes a difference, and especially so for young low-income children. An ever-growing number of studies have shown that refundable tax credits improve child outcomes in health, including birth

---

[25] This is more than 30 years after the then-Secretary of Education, Ted Bell, sounded the alarm in 1983 with the publication of *A Nation at Risk*.

outcomes for mothers, and the learning of young children.[26] Receiving aid from the Supplemental Nutrition Assistance Program (SNAP), a program for needy families with young children, has been shown to improve childhood health and learning outcomes as well significantly reduce the incidence of "metabolic syndrome" (obesity, high blood pressure, and diabetes). For women, SNAP serves to increase economic self-sufficiency (Almond et al. 2011; Hoynes et al. 2012). More generally, supplementing incomes for low-income families with children has a large number of positive effects, as summarized by Duncan et al. (2011), Duncan (2014), and Cooper and Stewart (2013). Specifically, cash transfers from the child tax credit and earned income tax credit (EITC) and SNAP of perhaps $1500 to $2000 per child per year lead to better outcomes for children and parents, especially longer-term important positive developmental effects on very young children.

Building on these findings, one policy strategy is to push for a stronger EITC (including one for single adults), larger refundable child allowances, and a higher minimum wage (Sawhill and Karpilow 2014; Heinrich and Smeeding 2014a, b). Although such a package would help mitigate poverty, there is also a critical need for a labor market solution that leads to more, accessible, better-paying jobs targeted at the poor and nonpoor (see Chaps. 6 and 11).

Many low-income parents are stretched thin working in one or more low-paying jobs at odd hours, making childcare almost impossible to schedule (Reeves and Rodrigues 2014). The effects of inflexible work schedules and the lack of paid days off on a parent's ability to provide emotional and physical care for young children, as well as the detrimental effects of parental stress on children's cognitive development, are all too apparent in such situations. And so another foundational element in parental assistance would be the enforcement of the Fair Labor Standards Act so that work schedules consistent with good parenting at younger ages are planned and maintained.[27]

Prenatal and Early Parenting Programs

Because good parenting is so important for child outcomes, one should try to make better parents, too. But in the new policy realm of parental improvement, ideas and efforts so far outstrip evidence of success, with a few exceptions (King et al. 2013). The starting point is prenatal health, where young about-to-become-parents must learn the importance of in-utero health and the costs of some of their own habits for child outcomes (Aizer and Currie 2014). The Nurse Home Visiting Program has been shown to be highly effective when properly deployed and when follow-up to emergent home-based problems is coordinated with local social service agencies

---

[26] For a nice summary see Duncan et al. 2014; also see Evans and Garthwaite 2014; Hoynes et al. 2012; Dahl and Lochner 2012; Milligan and Stabile 2009.

[27] Lest we forget, the U.S. is the only rich nation without some form of national paid family leave post childbirth.

(Annie E. Casey Foundation 2014; Haskins et al. 2009; Mosle et al. 2014). Still, substantial systematic differences exist in children's home learning experiences, and the few existing parenting programs that have shown promise often are not widely accessible, either due to the demands they place on parents' time and effort or cost. The widespread use, low cost, and ease of scalability of text messaging make it an attractive approach to support parenting practices (York and Loeb 2014). One exemplar program that seems to clearly make a difference in mobility and parenting just about the time of preschool is the Home Instruction for Parents of Preschool Youngsters (HIPPY) program for lower-income families with children ages 3–5. The program seeks to effectively train parents to be their child's first teacher while at the same time reducing child hyperactivity. Rigorous evaluations in New York found that the program significantly improved child reading scores (Sawhill and Karpilow 2014).

The Role of the Pediatrician

A second major type of parental-child intervention is centered on pediatricians and their role in early childhood development. The pediatrician and the parent are the bedrock of early child health and development. It is therefore essential that the physician treat the child and the parent as a single entity. Uncovering basic health issues, from allergies and asthma to hearing loss or diabetes, each require not only early detection but also successful chronic-care interventions. The burden of the habitual behaviors needed to overcome childhood asthma, for instance, requires competent parenting and regular application of medicine, cleanliness, and a host of other tasks. But that care management cannot be effectively delivered if a parent suffers from depression or high levels of stress. Health care targeting two generations at once holds the promise to improve both child outcomes and parent responsiveness to disease management programs, especially when that care is linked to social support services delivered by programs like the Nurse Home Visiting Program (Glied and Oellerich 2014). Pediatricians are often well positioned to assess children's well-being but usually do not ask about parental risk factors to children's health, such as smoking. One example is the SEEK Project, which trains health professionals to screen for parental risk factors and then refer the family to appropriate resources to address the problems.

Preschool: The Importance of Quality

In addition to cognitive training, there is overlap in skills training for the labor market and family formation among children and parents alike. Soft skills such as conflict resolution or how to respond to setbacks should be emphasized more in preschools *and* in parenting classes (Cunha and Heckman 2007, 2008). Because we do not yet have a good substitute for Head Start, we need to improve the model (Barnett 2011). One way to expand childcare may be to make such care more affordable through new, targeted subsidies for early childhood care (Ziliak 2014). A closer look at the programs that seem to work best in Boston and Chicago is a good starting point.

Conclusion

Americans have always been more tolerant of income inequality than their European forbearers; perhaps this was because the average standard of living was increasing across the board and because the "rising tide was lifting all boats." Americans also believed that inequality was acceptable because there was lots of movement up and down the income ladder. If one worked hard and followed the rules, he or she had a good chance of rising to the top (the "Horatio Alger" ideal). But the U.S. now faces a fourfold threat: stagnant growth in standards of living for all below the top rungs of the income ladder; a growing gap between the rich and the rest; high rates of early unplanned children by parents who are not prepared to raise them, and low rates of upward mobility that threaten belief in equality of opportunity.

Nowhere is this more apparent than in the recent patterns of uneven child development at early ages. To paraphrase Robert Putnam (2015), "our kids" are not doing well and need help to succeed. Larger majorities do not believe their children's generation will be as well off as they were. If we are to restore opportunity and improve upward mobility in the United States, we need to start very young and we need to begin right now.

Appendix

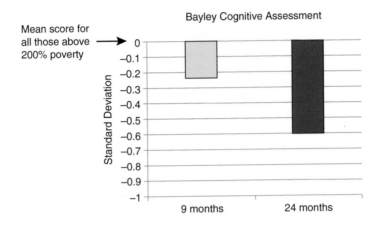

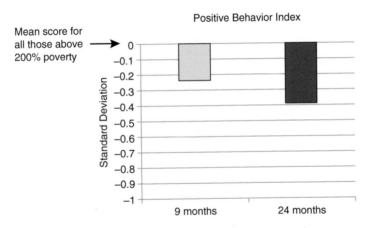

Fig. 8A.1 Disparities in cognitive and socio-behavioral outcomes by income level at 9 and 24 months (Source: Disparities in Early Learning and Development: Lessons from the Early Childhood Longitudinal Study – Birth Cohort (ECLS-B) – Executive Summary by Halle, Tamara, and Nicole Forry. Reproduced with permission of Child Trends Inc. in the format Republish in a book via Copyright Clearance Center)

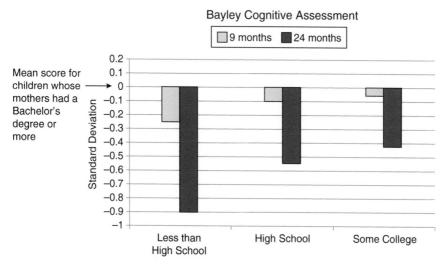

Fig. 8A.2 Disparities in cognitive and socio-behavioral outcomes by education of mother (Source: Disparities in Early Learning and Development: Lessons from the Early Childhood Longitudinal Study – Birth Cohort (ECLS-B) – Executive Summary by Halle, Tamara, and Nicole Forry. Reproduced with permission of Child Trends Inc. in the format Republish in a book via Copyright Clearance Center)

References

Acs, Gregory. 2011. *Downward mobility from the middle class: Waking up from the American dream*, Pew Charitable Trusts, Economic Mobility Project, September.

Aizer, Anna, and Flávio Cunha. 2012. *The production of human capital: Endowments, investments and fertility*, NBER Working Paper 18429. Cambridge, MA: National Bureau of Economic Research.

Aizer, Anna, and Janet V. Currie. 2014. The intergenerational transmission of inequality: Maternal disadvantage and health at birth. *Science* 344(May): 856.

Aizer, Anna, Laura Stroud, and Stephen Bubka. 2012. *Maternal stress and child outcomes: Evidence from siblings*, NBER Working Paper 18422. Cambridge, MA: National Bureau of Economic Research.

Almond, Douglas, and Janet Currie. 2011. Killing me softly: The fetal origins hypothesis. *Journal of Economic Perspectives* 25(3): 153–172. doi:10.1257/jep.25.3.153.

Almond, Douglas, and Bhashkar Mazumder. 2011. Health capital and the prenatal environment: The effects of Ramadan observance during pregnancy. *American Economic Journal: Applied Economics* 3(4): 56–85.

Almond, Douglas, Hilary W. Hoynes, and Diane W. Schanzenbach. 2011. Inside the war on poverty: The impact of food stamps on birth outcomes. *The Review of Economics and Statistics* 93(2): 387–403.

Almond, Douglas, Janet Currie, and Mariesa Herrmann. 2012. From infant to mother: Early disease environment and future maternal health. *Labour Economics* 19(4): 475–483.

Amato, Paul, Alan Booth, Susan McHale, and Jennifer Van Hook. 2014. *Families in an era of increasing inequality: Diverging destinies* Springer International Publishing, Vol. 5 of National Symposium on Family Issues, October 23.

Annie E. Casey Foundation. 2014. *Creating opportunity for families: A two-generation approach.* KIDS COUNT Policy Reports. Baltimore: Annie E. Casey Foundation (November 12). http://www.aecf.org/resources/creating-opportunity-for-families/?utm_source=datacenter&utm_medium=web&utm_campaign=two%20gen%20report&utm_content=publications.

Autor, David H. 2014. Skills, education, and the rise of earnings inequality among the 'other 99 percent'. *Science* 344(6186): 843–851.

Barker, David. 1995. Fetal origins of coronary heart disease. *British Medical Journal* 311: 171. doi: http://dx.doi.org/10.1136/bmj.311.6998.171.

Barnett, W. Steven. 2011. Effectiveness of early educational intervention. *Science* 333(6045): 975–978.

Becker, Gary S., and Nigel Tomes. 1979. An equilibrium theory of the distribution of income and intergenerational mobility. *Journal of Political Economy* 87(December): 1153–1189.

Becker, Gary S., and Nigel Tomes. 1986. Human capital and the rise and fall of families. *Journal of Labor Economics* 4(July): S1–S39.

Beller, Emily. 2009. Bringing intergenerational social mobility research into the twenty-first century: Why mothers matter. *American Sociological Review* 74: 507–528.

Bernier, Annie, Stephanie M. Carlson, and Natasha Whipple. 2010. From external regulation to self-regulation: Early parenting precursors of young children's executive functioning. *Child Development* 81(1): 326–339.

Bingley, Paul, and Niels Westergaard-Nielsen. 2012. Intergenerational transmission and day care. In Ermisch et al. 2012, 190–204.

Blanden, Jo., Robert Haveman, Timothy Smeeding, and Kathryn Wilson. 2014. Intergenerational mobility in the United States and Great Britain: A comparative study of parent-child pathways. *Review of Income and Wealth* 60(3): 425–449.

Bono, Del, John Ermisch Emilia, and Marco Francesconi. 2012. Intrafamily resource allocations: A dynamic structural model of birth weight. *Journal of Labor Economics* 30: 657–706.

Boyce, Thomas W. 2012. *A biology of misfortune: How social stratification, sensitivity, and stress diminish early health and development.* Institute for Research on Poverty New Perspectives Lecture, University of Wisconsin-Madison, February 8. http://www.irp.wisc.edu/publications/focus/pdfs/foc291.pdf.

Bradbury, Bruce, Miles Corak, Jane Waldfogel, and E. V. Washbrook. 2012. *Inequality in early childhood outcomes.* In Ermisch et al. 2012.

Brodmann, Stephanie, and Douglas Massey. 2014. *Spheres of influence: The social ecology of racial and class inequality.* New York: Russell Sage.

Brownstein, Ronald, and Paul Taylor. 2014. *The next America: Boomers, millennials, and the looming generational showdown.* Philadelphia: Perseus Books.

Camilli, Gregory, Sadako Vargas, Sharon Ryan, and W. Steven Barnett. 2010. Meta-analysis of the effects of early education interventions on cognitive and social development. *Teachers College Record* 112(3): 579–620.

Carlson, Marcia, and Daniel R. Meyer (eds.). 2014. Family complexity. *The Annals of the American Academy of Political and Social Science*, July.

Carneiro, Pedro, and Rita Ginja. 2014. Long-term impacts of compensatory preschool on health and behavior: Evidence from Head Start. *American Economic Journal: Economic Policy* 6(4): 135–173.

CBO (Congressional Budget Office). 2011. *The distribution of income and federal taxes.* Washington, DC: http://www.cbo.gov/sites/default/files/cbofiles/attachments/49440-Distribution-of-Income-and-Taxes.pdf.

Champagne, Frances A., and Rahia Mashoodh. 2009. Genes in context gene-environment interplay and the origins of individual differences in behavior. *Current Directions in Psychological Science* 18(3): 127–131.

Cherlin, Andrew J. 2014. *Labor's love lost: The rise and fall of the working-class family in America*. New York: Russell Sage.

Chetty, Raj, John Friedman, Nathaniel Hilger, Emmanuel Saez, Diane Schanzenbach, and Danny Yagan. 2011. How does your kindergarten classroom affect your earnings? Evidence from Project STAR. *Quarterly Journal of Economics* 126(4): 1593–1660.

Chetty, Raj, and Nathaniel Hendren. 2015. *The impacts of neighborhoods on intergenerational mobility: Childhood exposure effects and county-level estimates*. Cambridge, MA: Harvard University and National Bureau of Economic Research. http://scholar.harvard.edu/files/hendren/files/nbhds_paper.pdf.

Chetty, Raj, Nathaniel Hendren, Patrick Kline, and Emmanuel Saez. 2014. Where is the land of opportunity? The geography of intergenerational mobility in the United States. *Quarterly Journal of Economics* 129(4): 1553–1623.

Cooper, Kerris, and Kitty Stewart. 2013. *Does money affect children's outcomes? A systematic review*. York: Joseph Rowntree Foundation, October. http://sticerd.lse.ac.uk/dps/case/cr/casereport80.pdf.

Costa, Kristina. 2014. *Fact sheet: Social impact bonds in the United States*. Washington, DC: Center for American Progress, February 12. https://www.americanprogress.org/issues/economy/report/2014/02/12/84003/fact-sheet-social-impact-bonds-in-the-united-states/.

Cunha, Flavio, and James J. Heckman. 2007. The technology of skill formation. *American Economic Review* 97(May): 31–47.

Cunha, Flavio, and James J. Heckman. 2008. Formulating, identifying and estimating the technology of cognitive and noncognitive skill formation. *Journal of Human Resources* 43: 738–782.

Cunha, Flavio, James J. Heckman, and Susanne M. Schennach. 2010. Estimating the technology of cognitive and noncognitive skill formation. *Econometrica* 78(3): 883–931.

Currie, Janet, Matthew J. Neidell, and Johannes F. Schmieder. 2009. Air pollution and infant health: Lessons from New Jersey. *Journal of Health Economics* 28(3): 688–703.

Currie, Janet, and Reed Walker. 2011. Traffic congestion and infant health: Evidence from E-ZPass. *American Economic Journals-Applied Microeconomics* 3(January): 65–90.

Curtin, Sally C., Stephanie J. Ventura, and Gladys M. Martinez. 2014. *Recent declines in nonmarital childbearing in the United States,* NCHS Data Brief No. 162. U.S. Centers for Disease Control, National Center for Health Statistics, August. http://www.cdc.gov/nchs/data/databriefs/db162.pdf.

Dahl, Gordon B., and Lance Lochner. 2012. The impact of family income on child achievement: Evidence from the earned income tax credit. *American Economic Review* 102: 1927–1956.

Dumas, Christtelle, and Arnaud Lefranc. 2012. *Early schooling and later outcomes*. In Ermisch et al. 2012.

Duncan, Brian, and Stephen J. Trejo. 2015. *Assessing the socioeconomic mobility and integration of U.S. immigrants and their descendants*. In Grusky, Smeeding, and Snipp 2015, 108–134.

Duncan, Greg. 2014. *Optimal preschool policies for low-income children*. Presented to the University of Wisconsin-Madison, Institute for Research on Poverty seminar series, September 18.

Duncan, Greg J., and Katherine Magnuson. 2011. The nature and impact of early achievement skills, attention and behavior problems. In Duncan and Murnane 2011, 47–69.

Duncan, Greg J., and Katherine Magnuson. 2013. Investing in preschool programs. *Journal of Economic Perspectives* 27(2): 109–131.

Duncan, Greg J., Katherine Magnuson, and Elizabeth Votruba-Drzal. 2014. Boosting family income to promote child development. *Future of Children* 24(1): 99–120.

Duncan, Greg J., Pamela Morris, and Chris Rodrigues. 2011. Does money really matter? Estimating impacts of family income on young children's achievement with data from random-assignment experiments. *Developmental Psychology* 47: 1263–1279. doi:10.1037/a0023875.

Duncan, Greg J., and Richard J. Murnane. 2011. *Whither opportunity? Rising inequality, schools, and children's life chances*. New York: Russell Sage Foundation/Spencer Foundation.

Duncan, Greg J., and Richard J. Murnane. 2013. *Restoring opportunity: The crisis of inequality and the challenge for American education*. Cambridge, MA: Harvard Education.

Edin, Kathryn, Stefanie DeLuca, and Ann Owens. 2012. Constrained compliance: Solving the mystery of MTO lease-up rates and why mobility matters. *Cityscape* 14(2): 181–194.

Ehrlich, Stacy B., Julia A. Gwynne, Amber Stitziel Pareja, and Elaine M. Allensworth. 2013. *Preschool attendance in Chicago public schools: Relationships with learning outcomes and reasons for absences: Research summary.* Chicago: University of Chicago, September. https://ccsr.uchicago.edu/publications/preschool-attendance-chicago-public-schools-relationships-learning-outcomes-and-reasons.

Ermisch, John M., Markus Jäntti, and Timothy M. Smeeding. 2012. *From parents to children: The intergenerational transmission of advantage.* New York: Russell Sage.

Essex, Marilyn J., W. Thomas Boyce, Clyde Hertzman, Lucia L. Lam, Jeffrey M. Armstrong, Sarah M.A. Neumann, and Michael S. Kobor. 2013. Epigenetic vestiges of early developmental adversity: Childhood stress exposure and DNA Methylation in adolescence. *Child Development* 84(1): 58–75.

Evans, William N., and Craig L. Garthwaite. 2014. Giving mom a break: The impact of higher EITC payments on maternal health. *American Economic Journal: Economic Policy* 6(2): 258–290.

Figlio, David, Jonathan Guryan, Krzysztof Karbownik, and Jeffrey Roth. 2014. The effects of poor neonatal health on children's cognitive development. *American Economic Review* 104(December): 3921–3955.

Fisher, Jonathan, David Johnson, Timothy Smeeding, and Jeffrey Thompson. 2015. *The demography of inequality: Income, wealth and consumption, 1989–2010.* Working paper. Presented to the Population Association of America, April.

Fox, Nathan A., Pat Levitt, and Charles A. Nelson. 2010. How the timing and quality of early experiences influence the development of brain architecture. *Child Development* 81(1): 28–40.

Frey, William H. 2014. *Diversity explosion: How new racial demographics are remaking America.* Washington, DC: Brookings Institution Press.

Galston, William A. 2014. *Declining optimism among the Obama coalition.* 2014. Washington, DC: Brookings Institution, September 23. http://www.brookings.edu/blogs/fixgov/posts/2014/09/23-american-values-survey-american-dream-galston?.

Glied, Sherry, and Don Oellerich. 2014. Two-generation programs and health. *Future of Children* 24(1): 79–97.

Grusky, David, Timothy Smeeding, and C. Matthew Snipp. 2015. Monitoring social mobility in the 21st century. *Annals of the American Academy of Political and Social Science* 657 (January).

Guryan, Jonathan, Erik Hurst, and Melissa S. Kearney. 2008. Parental education and parental time with children. *Journal of Economic Perspectives* 22(3): 23–46.

Halle, Tamara, Nicole Forry, Elizabeth Hair, Kate Perper, Laura Wandner, Julia Wessel, and Jessica Vick. 2009. *Disparities in early learning and development: Lessons from the Early Childhood Longitudinal Study—Birth Cohort (ECLS-B).* Washington, DC: Child Trends.

Hamermesh, Daniel, and Elizabeth Stancanelli. 2014. *Long workweeks and strange hours.* IZA DP No. 8423, August. Bonn: Institute for the Study of Labor. http://ftp.iza.org/dp8423.pdf.

Hamilton, Brady, Joyce A. Martin, Michelle J. K. Osterman, and Sally C. Curtin. 2013. *Births: Preliminary data for 2013 National vital statistics reports 63, No 2. May 29.* U.S. Centers for Disease Control, National Center for Health Statistics http://www.cdc.gov/nchs/data/nvsr/nvsr63/nvsr63_02.pdf.

Hanson, Jamie L., Nicole Hair, Dinggang Shen, Feng Shi, John H. Gilmore, Barbara L. Wolfe, and Seth D. Pollak. 2013. Family poverty affects the rate of human infant brain growth. *PLOS One* 8 (December 11): doi:10.1371/journal.pone.0080954.

Hanson Jamie L., Brendon M. Nacewicz, Matthew J. Sutterer, Amelia A. Cayo, Stacey M. Schaefer, Karen D. Rudolph, Elizabeth A. Shirtcliff, Seth D. Pollak, and Richard J. Davidson. 2014. Behavior problems after early life stress: Contributions of the hippocampus and amygdala. *Biological Psychiatry.* doi:10.1016/j.biopsych.2014.04.020.

Haskins, Ron, Christina Paxson, and Jeanne Brooks-Gunn. 2009. *Social science rising: A tale of evidence shaping public policy*, Future of Children, Policy Brief. Princeton: Princeton University. http://futureofchildren.org/futureofchildren/publications/docs/19_02_PolicyBrief.pdf.

Heckman, James J. 2012. *Hard evidence on soft skills*, Lampman Lecture, University of Wisconsin-Madison, Institute for Research on Poverty, May. http://www.irp.wisc.edu/newsevents/other/lampman/2012Lampman-Heckman.pdf.

Heckman, James J., and Tim Kautz. 2014. Fostering and measuring skills: Interventions that improve character and cognition. In *The myth of achievement tests: The GED and the role of character in American life*, ed. J.J. Heckman, J.E. Humphries, and Tim Kautz, 293–317. Chicago: University of Chicago Press.

Heckman, James J., and Stefano Mosso. 2014. The economics of human development and social mobility. *Annual Review of Economics* 6: 689–733.

Heckman, James, Rodrigo Pinto, and Peter Savelyev. 2013. Understanding the mechanisms through which an influential early childhood program boosted adult outcomes. *American Economic Review* 103(6): 2052–2086. http://dx.doi.org/10.1257/aer.103.6.2052.

Heinrich, Carolyn, and Timothy Smeeding. 2014a. *Building human capital and economic potential*, Fast Focus No. 21–2014, Institute for Research on Poverty, University of Wisconsin-Madison, September. http://www.irp.wisc.edu/publications/fastfocus/pdfs/FF21-2014.pdf.

Heinrich, Carolyn, and Timothy Smeeding. 2014b. *Building economic self-sufficiency*, Focus on Policy No. 2, Institute for Research on Poverty, University of Wisconsin-Madison, September. http://www.irp.wisc.edu/publications/policybriefs/pdfs/PB2-SelfSufficiency.pdf.

Hoynes, Hilary, Diane Whitmore Schanzenbach, and Douglas Almond. 2012. *Long run impacts of childhood access to the safety net*, NBER Working Paper 18535. Cambridge, MA: National Bureau of Economic Research, November. http://www.nber.org/papers/w18535.

Hsin, Amy. 2012. Is biology destiny? Birth weight and differential parental treatment. *Demography* 49(4): 1385–1405.

Jäntti, Markus, Brent Bratsberg, Knut Reed, Oddbjørn Raaum, Robin Naylor, Eva Österbacka, Anders Björklund, and Tor Eriksson. 2006. *American exceptionalism in a new light: A comparison of intergenerational earnings mobility in the Nordic countries, the United Kingdom and the United States*, IZA Discussion Papers 1938, Institute for the Study of Labor.

Jencks, Christopher, and Laura Tach. 2006. Would equal opportunity mean more mobility? In *Mobility and inequality: Frontiers of research from sociology and economics*, ed. Stephen B. Morgan, David L. Grusky, and Gary S. Fields. Stanford: Stanford University Press.

Jones, Robert P., Daniel Cox, and Juhem Navarro-Rivera. 2014. *Economic insecurity, rising inequality, and doubts about the future: Findings from the 2014 American values survey*. Washington, DC: Public Religion Research Institute, September 23. http://publicreligion.org/site/wp-content/uploads/2014/09/AVS-web.pdf.

Kalil, Ariel, Rebecca Ryan, and Michael Corey. 2012. Diverging destinies: Maternal education and the developmental gradient in time with children. *Demography* 49: 1361–1383.

Kaushal, Neeraj, Katherine Magnuson, and Jane Waldfogel. 2011. How is family income related to investments in children's learning? In Duncan and Murnane 2011, 187–206.

Kautz, Tim, James Heckman, Ron Diris, Baster Weel, and Lex Borghans. 2014. *Fostering and measuring skills: Improving cognitive and non-cognitive skills to promote lifetime success*. Paris: OECD. http://www.oecd.org/edu/ceri/Fostering-and-Measuring-Skills-Improving--Cognitive-and-Non-Cognitive-Skills-to-Promote-Lifetime-Success.pdf.

Kenworthy, Lane, and Timothy Smeeding. 2014. The United States: High and rapidly-rising inequality. In *Inequality and its impacts*, vol. 2, ed. Brian Nolan, Wiemer Salverda, Daniele Checchi, Ive Marx, Abigail McKnight, István György Tóth, and Herman G. van de Werfhorst, 695–717. Oxford: Oxford University Press.

King, Christopher T., Rheagan Coffey, and Tara C. Smith. 2013. *Promoting two-generation strategies: A getting started guide for state and local policy makers*. Austin: University of Texas at Austin LBJ School of Public Affairs. http://fcd-us.org/resources/promoting-two-generation-strategies-getting-started-guide-state-and-local-policy-makers.

Kirkegaard, Jacob F. 2015. *The true levels of government and social expenditures in advanced economies*, Peterson Institute, Policy Brief 15–4, Washington DC, March. http://www.piie.com/publications/pb/pb15-4.pdf.

Kneebone, Elizabeth. 2014. *The growth and spread of concentrated poverty, 2000 to 2008–2012*, Brookings Metropolitan Studies Research Brief. Washington, DC: Brookings Institution, July 31. http://www.brookings.edu/research/interactives/2014/concentrated-poverty#/M10420.

Knudsen, Eric I., James J. Heckman, Judy L. Cameron, and Jack P. Shonkoff. 2006. Economic, neurobiological, and behavioral perspectives on building America's future workforce. *Proceedings of the National Academy of Sciences*.

Landry, Susan, Karen Smith, and Paul Swank. 2006. Responsive parenting: Establishing early foundations for social, communication, and independent problem-solving skills. *Developmental Psychology* 42(4): 627–642.

Liebman, Jeffrey. *Social impact bonds*. 2011. Washington, DC: Center for American Progress, February 9. https://www.americanprogress.org/wp-content/uploads/issues/2011/02/pdf/social_impact_bonds.pdf.

Lien, Diana Stech, and William N. Evans. 2005. Estimating the impact of large cigarette tax hikes: The case of maternal smoking and low birth weight. *Journal of Human Resources* 40(2): 373–392.

Lundberg, Shelly, and Robert Pollak. 2013. *Cohabitation and the uneven retreat from marriage in the United States: 1950–2010*, NBER Working Paper 19413, Cambridge, MA: National Bureau of Economic Research. http://www.nber.org/papers/w19413.

Magnuson, Katherine, and Greg J. Duncan. 2014. *Can early childhood interventions decrease inequality of economic opportunity?* Presented to the Federal Reserve Bank of Boston Conference, Inequality of Economic Opportunity in the United States, October 17–18.

Magnuson, Katherine, and Jane Waldfogel. 2005. Early childhood care and education: Effects on ethnic and racial gaps in school readiness. *Future of Children* 15(1): 169–196.

Magnuson, Katherine, Claudia Lahaie, and Jane Waldfogel. 2006. Preschool and school readiness of children of immigrants. *Social Science Quarterly* 87: 1241–1262.

Magnuson, Katherine, Jane Waldfogel, and E.V. Washbrook. 2012. *The development of SES gradients in skills during the school years: Evidence from the U.S. and U.K.* In Ermisch et al. 2012.

Mazumder, Bhashkar. 2014. Black-White differences in intergenerational economic mobility in the United States. *Economic Perspectives* 38(1): 1–18.

Mazumder, Bhashkar. 2015. *Estimating the intergenerational elasticity and rank association in the US: Overcoming the current limitations of tax data*. Chicago: Federal Reserve Bank of Chicago, April. http://www.iza.org/conference_files/inequality_2015/mazumder_b3665.pdf.

Mazumder, Bhashkar, Douglas Almond, Kathleen Parka, Eileen M. Crimmins, and Caleb E. Finch. 2010. Lingering prenatal effects of the 1918 Influenza Pandemic on Cardiovascular disease. *Journal of Developmental Origins of Health and Disease* 1(February): 26–34.

Mazumder, Bhashkar, Douglas Almond, and Reyn Van Ewijk. 2015. Fasting during pregnancy and children's academic performance. *Economic Journal*.

McCall, Leslie, and Derek Burk. 2014. *Beyond the work-income debate: Gender and class inequalities in resource pooling*. Presented to the Plenary Panel of the Complex Inequalities and Global Dimensions of Gender Conference, University of Stockholm, June.

McEwen, Bruce S., and Peter J. Gianaros. 2010. Central role of the brain in stress and adaptation: Links to socioeconomic status, health, and disease. *Annals of the New York Academy of Sciences* 1186: 190–222.

McLanahan, Sara. 2014. *Family and mobility*. Presentation to the U.S. Administration for Children and Families seminar on Intergenerational Socials and Economic Mobility, Washington, DC, May 16.

McLanahan, Sara, and Wade Jacobsen. 2013. *Diverging destinies revisited*. Draft presentation for Penn State University conference, August 16.

Milligan, Kevin, and Mark Stabile. 2009. Child benefits, maternal employment, and children's health: Evidence from Canadian child benefit expansions. *American Economic Review* 99(2): 128–132.

Mishel, Lawrence. 2013. *Trends in U.S. work hours and wages over 1979–2007*, Issue Brief 348, January 30. Washington, DC: Economic Policy Institute. http://www.epi.org/publication/ib348-trends-us-work-hours-wages-1979-2007/.

Mood, Carina, Jan O. Jonsson, and Erik Bihagen. 2012. *Socioeconomic persistence across genera-tions: Cognitive and noncognitive processes.* In Ermisch et al. 2012, 53–84.

Mosle, Anne, Nisha Patel, and Jennifer Stedron. 2014. The top ten for 2gen, *Ascend.* Washington, DC: Aspen Institute, October. http://b.3cdn.net/ascend/1b324c19707d1e43c6_p4m6i2zji.pdf.

Murray, Charles. 2012. *Coming apart: The state of White America, 1960–2010.* New York: Crown Publishing.

Noble, Kimberly G., Suzanne M. Houston, Natalie H. Brito, Bartsch Hauke, Kan Eric, Joshua M. Kuperman, Akshoomon Natacha, David G. Amaral, Cinnamon S. Bloss, Libiger Ondrej, Nicholas J. Schork, Sarah S. Murray, B.J. Casey, Chang Linda, Thomas M. Ernst, Jean A. Frazier, Jeffrey R. Gruen, David N. Kennedy, Peter Van Zijl, Mostofsky Stewart, Walter E. Kaufmann, Kenet Tal, Anders M. Dale, Terry L. Jerniga, and Elizabeth R. Sowell. 2015. Family income, parental education and brain structure in children and adolescents. *Nature Neuroscience* 18: 773–778. doi:10.1038/nn.3983.

OECD (Organisation for Economic Co-operation and Development). 2014. *Education at a glance—U.S. Country note.* Paris: Author. http://www.oecd.org/edu/United%20States-EAG2014-Country-Note.pdf.

OECD. 2015. *Public spending on childcare and early education.* OECD Family Database- Social Policy Division – Directorate of Employment, Labour and Social Affairs, PF3.1. http://www.oecd.org/els/soc/PF3_1_Public_spending_on_childcare_and_early_education.pdf.

Pfeffer, Fabian. 2011. Status attainment and wealth in the United States and Germany. In *Persistence, privilege, and parenting: The comparative study of intergenerational mobility,* ed. Timothy Smeeding, Robert Erikson, and Markus Jäntti. New York: Russell Sage.

Pfeffer, Fabian T., and Martin Hällsten. 2012. *Mobility regimes and parental wealth: The United States, Germany, and Sweden in comparison,* Population Studies Center Research Report 12–766. http://www.psc.isr.umich.edu/pubs/abs/7676.

Phillips, Meredith. 2011. Parenting, time use, and disparities in academic outcomes. In Duncan and Murnane 2011.

Putnam, Robert. 2015. *Our kids: The American dream in crisis.* New York: Simon and Schuster.

Quinn, Sandra Crouse, Supriya Kumar, Vicki S. Freimuth, Donald Musa, Nestor Casteneda-Angarita, and Kelley Kidwell. 2011. Racial disparities in exposure, susceptibility, and access to health care in the U.S. H1N1 Influenza Pandemic. *American Journal of Public Health* 101(2): 285–293.

Reardon, Sean. F. 2011. The widening academic achievement gap between the rich and the poor: New evidence and possible explanations. In Duncan and Murnane 2011.

Reeves, Richard. 2013. *The glass floor.* Washington, DC: Brookings Institution, November. http://www.brookings.edu.

Reeves, Richard. 2014. Equality, opportunity, and the American dream. *National Journal* (August 14). http://www.nationaljournal.com/economy/equality-opportunity-and-the-american-dream-20140820.

Reeves, Richard, and Kimberly Howard. 2013. *The parenting gap.* Washington, DC: Brookings Institution. http://www.brookings.edu.

Reeves, Richard, and Edward Rodrigue. 2014. *Do unpredictable hours undermine upward mobil-ity?* Washington, DC: Brookings Institution, December 11. http://www.brookings.edu.

Roberts, Brian W., Carl Lejuez, Robert F. Krueger, Jessica M. Richards, and Patrick L. Hill. 2014. What is conscientiousness and how can it be assessed? *Developmental Psychology* 50(5): 1315–1330.

Rowe, Meredith L. 2012. A longitudinal investigation of the role of quantity and quality of child-directed speech in vocabulary development. *Child Development* 83: 1762–1774.

Sabol, Terri J., and P. Lindsay Chase-Lansdale. 2015. The influence of low-income children's par-ticipation in Head Start on their parents' education and employment. *Journal of Policy Analysis and Management* 34(Winter): 136–161.

Sameroff, Arnold. 2010. A unified theory of development: A dialectic integration of nature and nurture. *Child Development* 81(1): 6–22.

Sanders, Nicholas J. 2012. What doesn't kill you makes you weaker: Prenatal pollution exposure and educational outcomes. *Journal of Human Resources* 47: 826–850.

Sawhill, Isabel. 2010. *Do we face a permanently divided society?* Presented at Tobin Project Conference on Democracy and Markets: Understanding the Effects of America's Economic Stratification, April 30–May 2, 2010. http://www.tobinproject.org/sites/tobinproject.org/files/assets/Sawhill%20%20Do%20we%20face%20a%20permanently%20divided%20society.pdf.

Sawhill, Isabel. 2014. *Generation unbound: Drifting into sex and parenthood without marriage.* Washington, DC: Brookings Institution Press, September.

Sawhill, Isabel, and Quentin Karpilow. 2014. *Raising the minimum wage and redesigning the EITC.* Washington, DC: Brookings Institution, January 30, http://www.brookings.edu/research/papers/2014/01/30-raising-minimum-wage-redesigning-eitc-sawhill.

Secura, Gina M., Tessa Madden, Colleen McNicholas, Jennifer Mullersman, Christina M. Buckel, Qiuhong Zhao, and Jeffrey F. Peipert. 2014. Provision of no-cost, long-acting contraception and teenage pregnancy. *New England Journal of Medicine* 371(October 2): 1316–1323. doi:10.1056/NEJMoa1400506.

Seeman, Teresa, Elissa Epel, Tara Gruenewald, Arun Karlamangla, and Bruce S. McEwen. 2010. Socio-economic differentials in peripheral biology: Cumulative allostatic load. *Annals of the New York Academy of Sciences* 1186(February): 223–239. doi:10.1111/j.1749-6632.2009.05341.x.

Seshadri, Ananth, Sang Yoon (Tim) Lee, and Nicolas Roys. 2014. *The causal effect of parental human capital on children's human capital,* working paper, University of Wisconsin-Madison, Economics Department, October.

Shapiro, Robert. 2015. *Income growth and decline under recent U.S. Presidents and the new challenge to restore broad economic prosperity.* Washington, DC: Brookings Institution, March 5. http://www.brookings.edu/research/papers/2015/03/05-income-growth-decline-economic-prosperity-shapiro.

Sharkey, Patrick. 2013. *Stuck in place: Urban neighborhoods and the end of progress toward racial equality.* Chicago: University of Chicago Press.

Shonkoff, Jack P. 2010. Building a new biodevelopmental framework to guide the future of early childhood policy. *Child Development* 81(1): 357–367.

Shonkoff, Jack P., Andrew S. Garner, The Committee on Psychosocial Aspects of Child and Family Health, Committee on Early Childhood, Adoption, and Dependent Care, and Section on Developmental and Behavioral Pediatrics. 2012. Lifelong effects of early childhood adversity and toxic stress. *Pediatrics* 129: e232–e246.

Smeeding, Timothy. 2014. *Social mobility: Three reasons to worry about the future,* Social Mobility Summit Series. Washington, DC: Brookings Institution, February 26. http://www.brookings.edu/blogs/social-mobility-memos/posts/2014/02/26-3-reasons-to-worry-about-the-future.

Smeeding, Timothy. 2015. *Multiple barriers to economic opportunity in the United States.* Presented to the Federal Reserve Bank of Boston Conference, Inequality of Economic Opportunity in the United States, October 17–18, 2014 (Revised).

Smeeding, Timothy M., Robert Erikson, and Markus Jäntti (eds.). 2011a. *Persistence, privilege and parenting: The comparative study of intergenerational mobility.* New York: Russell Sage.

Smeeding, Timothy M., Irwin Garfinkel, and Ronald Mincy (eds.). 2011b. Young disadvantaged men: Fathers, families, poverty, and policy. *Annals of the American Academy of Political and Social Science* 635.

Solon, Gary. 2014. Theoretical models of inequality transmission across multiple generations. *Research in Social Stratification and Mobility* 35(March): 13–18.

Summers, Lawrence, and Ed Balls. 2015. *Report of the commission on inclusive prosperity.* Center for American Prosperity, Washington, DC, January. https://cdn.americanprogress.org/wp-content/uploads/2015/01/IPC-PDF-full.pdf.

Tach, Laura. 2015. Social mobility in an era of family instability and complexity. In Grusky, Smeeding, and Snipp 2015, 83–96.

Takanishi, Ruby. 2004. Leveling the playing field: Supporting immigrant children from birth to eight. *Future of Children* 14(2): 61–79.

Torche, Florencia. 2011. Is a college degree still the great equalizer? Intergenerational mobility across levels of schooling in the U.S. *American Journal of Sociology* 117(3): 763–807.

Vest, Joshua R., Tegan K. Catlin, John J. Chen, and Ross C. Brownson. 2002. Multistate analysis of factors associated with intimate partner violence. *American Journal of Preventative Medicine* 22: 156–164.

Walters, Christopher. 2014. *Inputs in the production of early childhood human capital: Evidence from Head Start*, NBER Working Paper 20639. Cambridge, MA: National Bureau of Economic Research. http://www.nber.org/papers/w20639.

Wang, Wendy, and Kim Parker. 2014. *Record share of Americans have never married, as values, economics and gender patterns change*, Pew Research Report. Washington, DC: Pew Research, September 24. http://www.pewsocialtrends.org/2014/09/24/record-share-of-americans-have-never-married/.

Weiland, Christina, and Hirokazu Yoshikawa. 2013. Impacts of a prekindergarten program on children's mathematics, language, literacy, executive function, and emotional skills. *Child Development* 84(6): 2112–2130.

Weisleder, Adriana, and Anne Fernald. 2013. Talking to children matters: Early language experience strengthens processing and builds vocabulary. *Psychological Science* 24(11): 2143–2152.

Wilson, William Julius. 1987. *The truly disadvantaged*. Cambridge, MA: Harvard University Press.

Wilson, William Julius. 1996. *When work disappears*. New York: Knopf.

Wooten, Karen G., Pascale M. Wortley, James A. Singleton, and Gary L. Euler. 2012. Perceptions matter: Beliefs about influenza vaccine and vaccination behavior among elderly White, Black and Hispanic Americans. *Vaccine* 30(November 6): 6927–6934. doi:10.1016/j.vaccine.2012.08.036. Epub 2012 Aug 30.

Yellen, Janet L. 2014. *Perspectives on inequality and opportunity from the survey of consumer finances*. Presentation to the Conference on Economic Opportunity and Inequality, Federal Reserve Bank of Boston, October 17. http://federalreserve.gov/newsevents/speech/yellen20141017a.htm.

Yeung, W. Jean, Miriam R. Linver, and Jeanne Brooks-Gunn. 2002. How money matters for young children's development: Parental investment and family processes. *Child Development* 73(November–December): 1861–1879.

York, Benjamin, and Susanna Loeb. 2014. *One step at a time: The effects of an early literacy text messaging program for parents of preschoolers*, NBER Working Paper 20659. Cambridge, MA: National Bureau of Economic Research. http://papers.nber.org/papers/W20659.

Ziliak, James. 2014. *Making child care more affordable for working families*, Hamilton Project Report. Washington, DC: Brookings Institution, July 11. http://www.hamiltonproject.org/blog/making_child_care_more_affordable_for_working_families/.

Chapter 9
Quality and Equality in American Education: Systemic Problems, Systemic Solutions

Jennifer A. O'Day and Marshall S. Smith

Abstract After briefly reviewing the unequal opportunities outside schools that contribute to the disparities in educational achievement, attainment, and various indicators of adult success, this chapter zeroes in on addressing inequities within K-12 education. We argue that disparities within the educational system are the product of institutional structures and cultures that both disenfranchise certain groups of students and depress quality overall. Systemic causes require systemic solutions, and we envision a three-pronged systemic remedy: a continuous improvement approach for addressing the quality of educational opportunities for underserved students as well as of the system as a whole; targeted high-leverage interventions consistent with the overall approach but focused on key transition points and needs; and stronger connections between schools and other institutions and systems affecting the development and well-being of children and youth. We then outline a change strategy that incorporates both pressure and support for improvement from three distinct but interacting sources: government and administrative policy (federal, state, and local); professional accountability and networking; and collective engagement of parental, community, and advocacy organizations. We end the chapter with a consideration of recent developments in California and the degree to which they lay the groundwork for moving an equity agenda in the state.

Keywords Opportunity • Achievement gap • Accountability • Human capital • Standards-based reform • Continuous improvement approach • Interventions • High-poverty schools • Preschool • Parental education • Segregation • Title I • No Child Left Behind • Common Core

We thank David K. Cohen, Richard J. Murnane, Henry Braun, Bill Honig, and Susan Fuhrman for their instructive and insightful comments on an earlier draft of the chapter. We also thank the Spencer Foundation, the American Institutes for Research, the Carnegie Foundation for the Advancement of Teaching, and Educational Testing Service for the resources, time, and intellectual support to complete this work. All errors of fact and inference are the responsibility of the authors.

J.A. O'Day (✉)
American Institutes for Research, San Mateo, CA, USA

M.S. Smith
Carnegie Foundation for the Advancement of Teaching, Stanford, CA, USA

I. Kirsch, H. Braun (eds.), *The Dynamics of Opportunity in America*,
DOI 10.1007/978-3-319-25991-8_9

An Unequal Present

Education is the great equalizer—or so goes the promise. Yet the chapters in this book and decades of data belie that promise. It is not that educational achievement and attainment are unimportant to mobility and future success—the data confirm that they are. It is that—despite reform attempt after reform attempt—educational achievement and attainment continue to reflect student background: parent education, access to preschool, childhood nutrition and health, individual and neighborhood poverty and segregation. This chapter is about that persistent pattern and what it might take to substantially change it.

Let's Start with the Children

Born with virtually limitless potential and genetically predisposed to language, learning, and social enterprise, our children represent at once the promise of our society's future and the vestiges of its past and present failures. Much of this book is about those failures—or more specifically about a certain kind of societal break-down: the systematic denial of opportunity across generations of Americans based on their class, race, geographic location, gender, or national origin. For the children of these Americans, the chance to grow into their full potential is sharply con-strained and sometimes squelched altogether by social structures, endemic beliefs, and policies beyond their control or that of their families.

Who are these children? Primarily they are our young people growing up in pov-erty. Over 16 million children in the U.S. are officially classified as living in pov-erty; this is 20 % of all children and 25 % of those under the age of 5. Moreover, 40 % of poor children live in "extreme poverty"—that is, in families with annual incomes less than half of the poverty level for a family of four ($11,746). These figures are significantly confounded by race, as children of color are more than twice as likely to be poorer than White children, and a full one-third of all children of color live and grow up in poor households (Children's Defense Fund 2014).[1]

The external conditions in which these young people live and learn have impor-tant implications for their preparedness for and participation in school.[2] Consider the most basic needs: food and shelter. In this the most prosperous nation in the

---

[1] Recent data from the National Center for Educational Statistics (NCES) find that 51 % of U.S. schoolchildren are eligible for the free and reduced price meal program, which some observers have as a majority of U.S. students being in poverty (http://www.washingtonpost.com/local/educa-tion/majority-of-us-public-school-students-are-in-poverty/2015/01/15/df7171d0-9ce9-11e4-a7ee-526210d665b4_story.html). A more accurate label of "low income" for the figure in this article is used by the original report from the Southern Education Foundation http://www.southerneduca-tion.org/Our-Strategies/Research-and-Publications/New-Majority-Diverse-Majority-Report-Series/A-New-Majority-2015-Update-Low-Income-Students-Now).

[2] See Duncan and Murnane's (2014) excellent treatment of these topics.

world, one in nine children lacks adequate access to food and basic nutrition, which negatively impacts development and school performance (Jyoti et al. 2005). Black and Latino children are twice as likely to be food insecure as their White counterparts. Inadequate nutrition is both a result of insufficient family income and the deterioration of the neighborhoods in which these children live. There are whole census tracts in some U.S. urban centers that are veritable "food deserts," areas that lack grocery stores where residents can buy fresh meat and produce, forcing them to rely instead on prepackaged nutrition-depleted processed foods.[3] Poor nutrition plus inadequate health care combine to contribute to higher rates of serious medical conditions like asthma, diabetes, and obesity as well as developmental, behavioral, or social delays. And children in poor families are twice as likely not to receive preventive dental and medical care than their more advantaged counterparts and significantly less likely to have health insurance (Children's Defense Fund 2014).

With respect to opportunities for learning and social development, children from poor families are similarly disenfranchised, as low-income parents have few resources to devote to enrichment activities. Indeed, Duncan and Murnane (2014) report that in 2005–2006, the gap between what lower-income and higher-income families spent on enrichment activities was $8000 annually, a figure that had tripled since 1972 as inflation-adjusted income disparities grew. Moreover, many children in low-income families live in situations where their parent(s) have little support in parenting and must rely on the TV to babysit.[4] When of an age for preschool, the majority of low-income students do not attend because there are none available or because their families cannot bear the cost.[5] A large body of evidence indicates that too many of these children enter school with a working vocabulary and number skills of far less than more advantaged children and without socialization experiences that prepare them for making the most of kindergarten (Yoshikawa et al. 2013). Moreover, children who do not attend a preschool such as Head Start are less likely to graduate from high school and go to college and more likely to get pregnant in teenage years or be imprisoned (Deming 2009).

As they get older, many of these young people have little access to community affordances that middle-income children take for granted—parks, playing fields, sports teams, safe havens. Segregation is a major culprit here. Though residential segregation by race has declined slightly in recent decades, segregation by income

---

[3] The language in the 2008 Farm Bill defined a food desert as an "area in the United States with limited access to affordable and nutritious food, particularly such an area composed of predominantly lower income neighborhoods and communities" (Title VI, Sec. 7527). See U.S. Department of Agriculture (2009). The entire area of West Oakland in California's prosperous San Francisco Bay Area is a case in point. See McClintock (2008).

[4] This problem is exacerbated for children of single parents, who are four times more likely to be poor than children of married couple families (Children's Defense Fund 2014).

[5] The Children's Defense Fund (2014) reports that the average cost of center-based care for infants is greater than the annual in-state tuition for public colleges in 35 states and Washington, D.C. For 4-year-olds the average cost is more than college tuition in 25 states and D.C. Only 16 % of 3- to 4-year-olds attend state-run preschools, and fewer than 40 % nationally were enrolled in any kind of preschool during the period from 2009 to 2011.

has increased: in 2010, 28 % of lower-income households were located in majority low-income neighborhoods, up from 23 % in 1982 (Reardon and Bischoff 2011; Fry and Taylor 2012). And high poverty generally means low services; many of these neighborhoods lack everything from banks to grocery schools to good schools. What they don't lack are sources of stress and trauma. Too many poor children live in neighborhoods that are not safe of drugs, crime, and sometimes physical as well as emotional harm. Often they live in such conditions throughout school and beyond—it becomes one of the few constant features of their young life. And these conditions make academic learning, both inside and outside school, difficult.

While some children in these circumstances—whether through family and community supports, their own personal resilience, or intervention of a successful program or school—are able to overcome the predicted pattern of intergenerational poverty, many others are not. The widening income gaps and erosion of the middle class exacerbate and extend the problem, and the lack of a coherent support infrastructure means that few children and their families have access to avenues out of poverty.[6]

---

[6] Segregation and public and private divestment in high-poverty neighborhoods, particularly those of color, is not the product of residential choice but rather of decades of discriminatory practices and policies (Massey and Denton 1993; Rothstein 2013). Moreover, current approaches to providing safety nets and advancement for the residents of these neighborhoods are woefully lacking. In the U.S., unlike many other nations, the responsibility for health, social services, and income support is spread between the federal government, states, and communities. Though the federal government finances a large portion of these services the funds are distributed according to different rules of multiple programs that have sprung up over the years. Many state governments and communities also provide lists of services for the poor, sometimes in the same sectors as the federal government. While the various levels of government may attempt to act rationally, the forces of politics and ideologies work to create a mix of services that differ in quality and scope from state to state and community to community and often fail miserably to meet the needs of the community. In addition, in many communities and settings, churches and other nongovernmental organizations provide services, some funded by governments and other by philanthropy. All of this creates a bewildering and incoherent patchwork of organizations that, in many settings where there are concentrations of the poor, are often opaque and inadequate to meet daily needs, much less provide the sense of security necessary for the recipients of the services to figure out how to improve their own lives.

The product of distributed federalism in the U.S. that is exemplified by the often-incoherent provision and delivery of support for children from low-income families is unlike the governments of the countries such as Finland, Singapore, and South Korea. The Finnish central government, for example, supports well-organized and coherent systems for delivering health, family support, preschool, and other benefits for all of its population. The importance of predictable and high quality social services for children growing up in poor families is detailed in other chapters of this report. The effects of the incoherence on the probability for success in schools are large and pervasive.

Where Do the Schools Fit In?

Residential segregation, poverty, low levels of parental education, and limited access to social supports and preschool learning all influence students' educational achievement and attainment, which in turn are strong predictors of adult earnings and civic participation. In this equation, education is a key intervening variable.

We led this chapter with a litany of the environment's challenges for children from low-income families and the importance of social services and enrichment opportunities to support their readiness for school at age 5 and their learning in school as children, youth, adolescents, and young adults. The average number of hours per year that a student is in public school is roughly 1000. The average number of waking hours for the same student during a year is roughly 5500. During the 4500 h a middle-income student is awake and out of school, the student has a myriad of opportunities for learning experiences that children in low-income families are not offered.

Yet inequalities outside schools do not let schools off the hook. Schools are our society's central institution serving students from all backgrounds and—in theory—supplying them with the knowledge and skills they need to have a fair shot at success in adulthood. That schools *can* make a difference in children's life trajectories is evident from the isolated but powerful examples of highly effective high-poverty schools that produce success for students who would otherwise be unlikely to progress at pace, graduate, or attend college (see, for example, Cunningham 2006; Kannapel and Clements 2005; Reeves 2003; and Carter 1999). There are even examples of whole districts that have significantly and substantially narrowed gaps in achievement and attainment among groups of students over time.[7] We discuss several of these in greater detail later on.

Unfortunately, such places are the exception rather than the rule. Indeed, as the Equity and Excellence Commission (2013) notes, "The current American system exacerbates the problem [of unequal opportunities outside school] by giving these children less of everything that makes a difference in education." (U.S. Department of Education 2013, 14). What is this "everything" of which the Equity Commission writes?

Unequal Resources

One way to approach this question is to consider the most basic learning situation for students in school: the instructional unit. Cohen et al. (2003) define the instructional unit as teachers and students interacting in the presence of content. In this conceptualization, all three of these elements—students, teachers, and content—could be considered resources that provide opportunities for student learning.

---

[7] These examples include such districts as Long Beach and Garden Grove in California; Union City, NJ; and Montgomery County, MD.

Let's start with students, as the makeup of a school's student body influences access both to high-quality teachers and to challenging content. Poor children are increasingly concentrated in schools and classrooms with other poor children, reflecting both residential segregation and student placement policies within schools. In 2011–2012, 19 % of public school students[8] attended high-poverty schools (greater than 75 % poverty) and 44 % attended schools with at least 50 % poverty; these figures were up from 12 to 28 %, respectively, in 1999–2000.[9] With respect to race, Black and Latino students attend schools with nearly twice as many students who are poor as White students do. Pervasive in cities, school segregation is also pronounced even in predominantly White suburbs, where 40 % of Black and Latino students attend intensely segregated schools that are at least 90 % Black and Latino (Orfield 2009, 2013).

Studies carried out over several decades find a consistent independent effect of school-level poverty (in addition to the effect of individual poverty) and racial composition on student achievement (see, for example, Perry and McConney 2010; Rumberger and Palardy 2005; and Caldas and Bankston 1997). Concentration of poor students and students of color in certain schools affects the learning environment in multiple ways. Students in these schools are more likely to be in classrooms with schoolmates who have behavior problems and low skills. Student mobility rates in such schools are also higher, which increases disruption in learning for both mobile and nonmobile students (Raudenbush et al. 2011). But most importantly, the concentration of poor students is correlated with the levels of other resources— teachers and other adults, curriculum and instructional materials, facilities, and so on.

In this array of school-based resources, teachers are the most critically important for supporting learning, and study after study indicates that children of color and children in poverty are less likely to be taught by qualified, experienced, and effective teachers (Clotfelter et al. 2010; Isenberg et al. 2013). Summarizing research across varying measures of quality, Adamson and Darling-Hammond (2011) report that students of color in low-income schools are three to 10 times more likely to have unqualified teachers than students in predominantly White schools. Neighborhood environment and low salaries are among the obstacles to recruiting qualified staff in these schools, but poor working conditions—including inadequate support from school administration, disruptions, and limited faculty input in decision making—contribute to a 20 % average annual departure rate among teachers in high-poverty schools (Simon and Johnson 2013; Ingersoll 2004). The constant faculty churn makes it difficult for teachers in these schools to develop a strong sense of professional community, adds to the instability that children in these

---

[8] Educational statistics use eligibility for free and reduced price lunch as a proxy for poverty. Students are eligible for free lunch if their family income is below 130 % of the poverty level; eligibility for reduced-price lunch extends from 130 to 185 % of the poverty level.

[9] For the most NCES recent data, see Snyder (2014, Tables 102.50, 216.30, and 216.60), retrieved from http://nces.ed.gov/programs/coe/indicator_clb.asp on April 12, 2015. Also see Owens et al. (2014).

schools face in other parts of their lives, and exacerbates staff recruitment challenges. Moreover, departing teachers are disproportionately replaced with novices, who on average are less effective than their more experienced peers (see Henry et al. 2012; Kane et al. 2006; Papay and Kraft Forthcoming). Once these teachers obtain a little experience and skill, they also often depart (to be replaced with a new round of novices), creating a pattern of reshuffling of teachers from poor to not-poor schools, high-minority to low-minority schools, and urban to suburban schools (Ingersoll et al. 2014).

Next to teachers in importance is the content to which students are exposed, but again poor students and students of color get less than their more advantaged peers (Schmidt and McKnight 2012). For example, high schools serving Black and Latino students are less likely to offer advanced mathematics, Advanced Placement (AP), and gifted and talented courses than schools serving mostly White students. And in schools that do offer such courses and programs, students of color are less likely to be enrolled in them (Theokas and Saaris 2013).

Underlying many of these differences are disparities in fiscal resources available to schools. Variations in both state and local wealth and commitment to education mean that children in districts in one state may have substantially greater resources than those in another state, and children in one community may have the benefits of substantially different resources than those in another district in the same state. At the state level, the highest spending state (New York) spends three times more per pupil than does the lowest spending state (Utah) (Dixon 2014). Not surprisingly, there is considerable overlap between lower spending states and those with the highest levels of poverty among school-age children. Within states, the same pattern is evident, though there is considerable variation across states in the spending disparities among local districts within their borders. For example, in 2009 states in the Northeast had the highest funding inequities across districts (averaging about $2000 per student, or 14 % of the total) while states in the West were among the most equitable with an average disparity of approximately $1100 (New America Foundation 2012).

The bottom line is that while poor students need more resources to even hope to reach the level of opportunity of more advantaged students, they actually receive less.

Organizational Dysfunction and Unequal Practices

Differences in resource amounts are only part of the story. Often neglected by their districts, high-poverty schools are more likely than those of more advantaged students to be dysfunctional organizations with low levels of trust among the adults, ineffective leadership, and incoherent educational programs. Buildings are often poorly maintained and environments are unfriendly (and sometimes unsafe) for staff and students alike. Morale and commitment are often low, making it difficult to motivate and sustain improvements, especially in the face of high faculty turnover.

Even more damaging are the attitudes toward the students. Low expectations in these schools (and of these schools by their district leadership) have been well documented (see, for example, Boser et al. 2014). Placement policies systematically track poor students and students of color away from higher-level courses, even when they have demonstrated the requisite skills. Discriminatory application of discipline and special education policies results in disproportionate numbers of Black and Latino students (particularly males) being removed from their classes through suspension, expulsion, and placement into restricted environments for "emotionally disturbed" children.[10] Often these practices are implemented with the best of intentions and with a belief that the policies are fair to all students. The resulting pattern is nonetheless discriminatory, whatever the intentions.

The disparities in opportunities outside school are thus compounded by disparities within our educational systems. It is therefore hardly surprising that the National Assessment of Educational Progress (NAEP) records achievement gaps in mathematics of two or more years between Black or Latino eighth-grade students and Whites as well as between students from low and high-income families. The gaps for reading are slightly smaller. Nor given these patterns is it surprising to find that White students graduate at a rate 13 and 17 points higher than Black and Latino students, respectively (Stetser and Stillwell 2014).

Though these patterns are pervasive and persistent, they are not immutable. Over the past six decades, we have learned a great deal about the learning process, the contributors to unequal outcomes for students, and what it takes to change complex systems. We have also achieved a beginning level of success.

Signs of Progress

One sign of progress is the positive trend for American students on several aggregate measures of achievement compared both to their counterparts in other developed nations and to the historical data on outcomes here in the U.S.[11] For example, in 2011, the average scale score in mathematics for all U.S. eighth graders on the Third International Mathematics and Science Study (TIMSS) was 509, nine points above the international average of 500 and 16 points above the U.S. score of 493 in 1995. This represented the sixth largest gain among the 31 countries that took the assessment in both years. (We focus on eighth grade throughout these analyses because they provide a better estimate of overall schooling than those in the earlier grades and represent the whole population of a cohort better than 12th-grade scores,

---

[10] These practices have been well documented in the October 1, 2014, "Dear Colleague" letter from Catherine E. Lhamon, Assistant Secretary for Civil Rights, U.S. Department of Education (Lhamon 2014).

[11] The numbers in this section are based on analyses of NCES data using the NCES Data Explorer (nces.ed.gov/nationsreportcard/NAEPdata/) and International Data Explorer (nces.ed.gov/surveys/international/ide/).

which do not include dropouts.) In science, U.S. eighth-graders scored ninth at 525, a 12-point gain from 1995 even though science had not been a specific focal point of the U.S. education reform efforts. It is important to note that all of the nations that scored better than the U.S. had substantially lower rates of poverty.[12] Finland, for instance—with which the U.S. is often (negatively) compared—has a poverty rate of only 5 %. By way of comparison, Massachusetts, whose TIMSS scores are the highest of the U.S. state participants in the assessment, has a poverty rate somewhere around 13–15 % and scores that are substantially greater than those of Finland. Indeed, Massachusetts' science results would place it second in the world if it were a country.[13]

Achievement and attainment trends on U.S. measures reflect an even clearer pattern of growth. Eighth-grade mathematics scores on the Main NAEP increased 15 points between 1996 and 2013, a gain of roughly 1.3 grade levels. In NAEP reading, average eighth-grade scores went from 257 in 1994 to 266 in 2013, an increase of nine points, or a little less than one grade level.

With respect to achievement gaps between groups of students, the picture is more mixed. The good news is that there was some narrowing of the gaps between Whites and Blacks and between Whites and Hispanics in mathematics, with a smaller narrowing in reading. In general the growth was consistent over the past two decades for all of the groups, with Whites gaining less than Blacks and Hispanics.

By contrast, there was virtually no overall reduction in the gaps between poor (defined as eligible for free and reduced price lunch) and nonpoor students. In eighth-grade mathematics, for example, both groups increased their performance by 18 points between 1996 and 2013, and the gap remained 27 points or about 2.5 grade levels. Duncan and Murnane (2014) and Reardon (2011) find the same pattern of a reduction in the gaps between White students and Black and Hispanic students while income gaps stay the same or increase.

A second sign of progress is the recent increase in high school graduation rates. The U.S. Department of Education recently released a report showing an overall average freshman graduation rate of 81 % for the nation in 2012–2013. Murnane (2013) in a comprehensive paper points out that the rate was stagnant from 1970 to 2000 and since then shows a substantial overall increase, with especially large

---

[12] Most international organizations measure the poverty rate somewhat differently. They use the metric of 50 % of the disposable median income in the country as the measure of poverty. Using this metric, the Organisation for Economic Co-operation and Development (OECD) number of roughly 22 % of U.S. children in families under the poverty level is very similar to the U.S. number. It places the U.S. 29th of 34 OECD countries—the four countries with higher rates than the U.S. are Chile, Mexico, Bulgaria, and Israel. (See OECD Family Database, CO2.2: Child poverty, http://www.oecd.org/els/soc/CO2_2_ChildPoverty_Jan2014.pdf. See also Max Fisher, "Map: How 35 Countries Compare on Child Poverty (The U.S. Is Ranked 34th)", *Washington Post,* http://www.washingtonpost.com/blogs/worldviews/wp/2013/04/15/map-how-35-countries-compare-on-child-poverty-the-u-s-is-ranked-34th/).

[13] In eighth-grade TIMSS math in 2011, Massachusetts scored 560, Finland 514, the U.S. average was 510, and the international average was 500. In eighth-grade science, Massachusetts scored 567, behind only Singapore; Finland scored 552, the U.S. 525, and Ontario 521.

increases for Hispanic and African-American students. Using a different metric (adjusted status completion rates for 20–24 years), which he convincingly argues has greater validity than "average freshman graduation rate", Murnane finds an overall 6 % increase in completion rates from 2000 to 2010 to 83.7 %. During this time period, Whites gained 4.5 points to 86.3 %, while Blacks gained 10.2 points and Hispanic students jumped 13.9 points, both to roughly 78 %.[14]

We suggest two main takeaways from these data. First, the predominant force driving the gaps—and overall achievement levels—is family income and the concomitant conditions associated with it (see previous section).[15] While race differentials controlled for income have not disappeared, they have declined. This suggests that the independent effect of race/ethnicity is decreasing and that a good portion of the overall racial gap might be explained by the disproportionate percentages of African-American and Latino youth living in poverty. This is not to say that race should be ignored. Quite the contrary. The related effects of discrimination and language and the very high levels of poverty and especially intergeneration poverty among Blacks and Hispanics make it imperative that these issues be treated together.

A second takeaway is that there is both some momentum to build on and much more to be done. The achievement gaps both by race/ethnicity and by income remain unconscionably large, with significant impact on the quality of life and work for far too many of our nation's children. In addition, the positive momentum in achievement appears to apply primarily to tests of more procedural knowledge and of the curriculum of the 1990s and early 2000s NAEP and TIMSS. We do not see the same pattern of improvement, for example, on the Programme for International Student Assessment (PISA), which assesses the ability of students to *apply* their knowledge and skills in mathematics, science or reading to analyze novel situations and solve complex problems—the very type of performance needed for success in the twenty-first century. On PISA, the U.S. performance has remained fairly stable since the assessment was initiated in 2003, hovering around the international average in science and reading and substantially below the international average in math. This suggests the need to extend and deepen our improvement efforts in education.

The Common Core State Standards for Mathematics and English Language Learning and Next Generation Science Standards (or similar college and career readiness standards) may be a good step in this direction as they are reflective of the types of knowledge and skills that PISA assesses and that students will need in adulthood. To successfully move in this direction, however, requires that we learn from previous reform efforts, a subject to which we now turn.

---

[14] See U.S. Department of Education, "U.S. High School Graduation Rate Hits New Record High", http://www.ed.gov/news/press-releases/us-high-school-graduation-rate-hits-new-record-high; see also Murnane (2013).

[15] It is likely that accumulated family wealth is also a key factor—perhaps even more so than income, but we have no way of validly linking wealth to the NAEP trends.

Observations from 60 Years of Equity Reforms: There Are No Silver Bullets

Americans have a penchant for quick fixes and easy solutions. We like to do things quickly and if we don't see results right away, we move on to the next new and improved approach. In no arena is this American predilection toward the fast and easy more evident than in education. We have been through numerous reform efforts in the past 60 years, many of them focused specifically on reducing the gaps in opportunities enjoyed by more and less advantaged groups in our society and our schools. We have targeted money at the problem through supplemental funding streams, like the federal Elementary and Secondary Education Act (ESEA) and state categorical programs, and through a myriad of state fiscal equity suits and policies. We have tracked and detracked students, tried homogenous grouping by ability and heterogeneous cooperative learning in the classroom. We have tried pullout and push-in instructional approaches to give extra support to students who need it. We have focused exclusively on academics only to turn around and chide ourselves for ignoring the whole child. We have thought teacher testing and formal qualifications on the front end were the answer to low educator quality, moving more recently to test-driven teacher evaluation as the new required solution. And the list goes on.

While often these solutions have a faddish quality to them—that is, they are popular for a time and then die out when the next new thing or new leader comes along—they are not necessarily without merit or void of at least a promising research base. Indeed, in the past 15 years there has been considerable interest in and policy support for adoption and use of what has come to be referred to as "evidence-based practices." The idea is straightforward: figure out "what works"—usually these are very targeted interventions with a reasonable effect size found in one or more rigorous research studies; adopt and implement the practice at scale; and finally, realize the expected improvements in overall outcomes and gap closings. A corollary to this theme is often the idea that if we adopt multiple evidence-based practices, benefits will cumulate to an overall larger effect.[16]

In the main, we believe that the focus on evidence and effectiveness has been a positive development and has contributed to some portion of the gap closings cited above. But almost invariably, when individual interventions are implemented at scale in schools and districts, the results are far less than anticipated and sometimes disappear altogether. While there are many contributing factors, we see two main interrelated explanations for the diminished effects. First, implementation challenges across multiple and varying contexts lead to uneven and sometimes unforeseen results. Second, individual interventions, usually focused on a specific targeted disparity, often leave untouched the systemic contributors that underlie and

---

[16] For example, see Grannis and Sawhill (2013) for a thoughtful discussion of implications of the Social Genome Project and an estimate of the cumulative benefits of a set of research-based strategies.

perpetuate that disparity. We review each of these problems below and draw out several lessons for moving forward.

Lesson One: Implementation Dominates Impact

It has been said that implementation is 90 % of impact. The very same intervention applied in one school, locale, or state may yield quite different results than when employed in another. Problems of inadequate resources, weak commitment, or poor fit are often cited to explain disappointing outcomes. This situation is not unique to education; in fact, the field of implementation science, which grew out of concerns about the limited uptake of evidence-based practices in medicine, seeks to apply research on implementation patterns and strategies to improve their application and use across a wide range of social domains. "Implementation varied" is probably the most commonly reported finding across decades of policy and program evaluations. Yet implementation considerations generally get short shrift when policy makers and administrators are considering options and calculating expected impact. Decades of implementation research have yielded a panoply of implementation lessons that could be applied to considerations for equity-oriented policies. Here we focus on three that are integral to our vision of how a more equitable education system would need to operate.

Context Matters

Research on organizational learning and change holds that all change is history dependent. Schools, districts, and even states differ in their educational histories, including the past performance trajectories, their experience with particular strategies and interventions previously tried, and the expectations that derive from these experiences. They also differ in the makeup of both the adult and the student populations in their systems and the histories that each of these groups has had with schooling, inequality, and change. Varying cultures, conditions, and structures across organizational units and systems can influence the ways in which local actors interpret and act on any given reform or intervention (O'Day 2002, 2008; Spillane et al. 2006). Weatherly and Lipsky's (1977) seminal piece on "street-level bureaucrats," which examined variation across three districts in their implementation of special education in Massachusetts, spawned a host of increasingly sophisticated analyses of the causes and manifestations of contextual variation in implementation.

Attempts to constrain such variation through emphases on fidelity, scripted instructional programs, and one-size-fits-all policies do not solve the problem, as they often inhibit professional judgment and responsiveness to individual student and local system needs. Indeed, such approaches may be counterproductive.[17]

Capacity Is a Key Determinant of Implementation Quality and Results

At the heart of many of the differences in implementation across contexts is their variation in local capacity. Scholars have taken differing approaches to delineating the elements of capacity that matter for improving student outcomes. (Beaver and Weinbaum 2012). All would agree that *human capital*—the knowledge and skills of individual actors and of the collective body of actors—in a system or site has broad implications for how a given intervention, program, or policy is understood, whether the actors are able to carry out the required or suggested actions, the degree to which the system can adapt to changing conditions and threats to implementation, and so on. Many research-based efforts, from bilingual education to new math or literacy curricula to teacher evaluation rubrics, fail because those who would implement them lack the requisite knowledge and skills. Most observers would also include the amount and appropriateness of available *material resources*—such as money, instructional materials, and facilities—in notions of organizational or system capacity. Sometimes these resources are the target of particular reform efforts; often they can determine the success or failure of any given strategy.[18]

While people and resources are critical, they are not enough, however. Another aspect of organizational capacity is what several researchers have termed *program coherence*. Coherence in education implies shared goals and frameworks and the presence of working conditions, structures, and routines that support those goals and allow the actors in the system to focus on their attainment (Newmann et al. 2001; Beaver and Weinbaum 2012).[19] Like human and material capital, program

---

[17] For example, during the era of Reading First grants, in systems focused on preventing such variation, observers would often encounter references to the "literacy police," administrators whose job it was to ensure that all teachers were following the program on a daily basis as scripted. The intent was to ensure that all students has access to research-based literacy instruction, but teachers argued that the program was often ill-suited to their particular population, including English language learners, special education students, or others who needed specialized attention. Similarly, professional development programs that are designed for *all* teachers often fail to meet the differentiated needs of most and may not align with the particular issues at a given school or grade level.

[18] One clear example is the implementation of class size reduction in California. While districts received state funds to reduce class sizes in K-3 to 20 or fewer students, many districts, particularly urban systems with already overcrowded and understaffed schools, lacked the classroom space and a pool of qualified teachers to make these reductions effectively. This led to a reliance on portable classrooms and the hiring of large numbers of under-credentialed and novice teachers, who were disproportionately assigned to work in schools serving poor students and students of color. As a result, this massive reform effort, intended to benefit low-income students and schools, actually exacerbated disparities in access to qualified and experienced teachers and adequate facilities (Bohrnstedt and Stecher 2002).

[19] Conversely, program coherence implies an absence of factors that detract from or inhibit implementation.

coherence is not equitably distributed across schools and districts. We have already noted the organizational dysfunction that characterizes many high-poverty schools, caused by years of neglect, environmental stresses, and high rates of staff turnover. A similar observation could be made of many low-capacity districts. One manifestation of this incoherence is either a flitting from one reform effort to another in search of the panacea or the accumulation of multiple interventions and programs—some well-intended and researched but all vying for attention and resources. Lack of coherence in high-poverty schools and districts makes it difficult for teachers and administrators to select and adapt strategies that build on one another and enhance their ability to systematically address the learning needs of their students.

Implementation Is a Social Process

The past few decades have brought increasing attention to the importance of social capital and trust for diffusing effective practices and for enhancing learning and improvement in the conduct of one's daily work. Social capital resides in the relationships between and among people, groups, and organizations (Coleman 1988). For effective implementation to occur, these relationships must be activated, not just once but through multiple interactions on an ongoing basis.[20] Unfortunately the isolation of schools and teachers that is common in American education systems generally is exacerbated in high-poverty contexts where turnover and lack of trust impede the development of strong relationships that can mobilize implementation of evidence-based practices. Thus, even those interventions that are specifically designed to benefit such systems and the children and adults in them often never find their way where they are most needed. Attempts to ensure spread and implementation through administrative mandates do little to solve this problem and often lead to superficial compliance without deep understanding or committed action. When the pressure subsides, so does reform.

Lesson Two: Piecemeal Reforms Leave Systemic Contributors Untouched

Underlying many of these implementation challenges is the fact the isolated and piecemeal reforms often fail to address underlying systemic contributors to the very situation or inequity that they are attempting to address. Take the example of incentive programs that are designed to attract more qualified and effective teachers to work in high-poverty schools but leave untouched the dismal working conditions that cause turnover in the first place (Ingersoll 2004; Simon and Johnson 2013). Or

---

[20] See Rogers et al. (2009) for a discussion of the importance of social relationships in implementation, and Gawande 2013 for how this plays out in healthcare. For a discussion of the role of social learning in the conduct of one's daily, see Bransford et al. (2015) and Bryk et al. (2010).

consider school accountability policies that penalize schools for low performance but let districts off the hook, leaving unaddressed the policies and practices that concentrate low-performing students and inexperienced teachers in those schools and pay insufficient attention to building the capacity for long-term improvement.

In each of the implementation challenges discussed above, the success of individual reforms is constrained or thwarted by conditions endemic to the system itself. What's more, incoherence and instability in the policy environment make it difficult to identify and change these conditions. Superintendents, school boards, and legislators come and go, but disparities in resources and practices go on, bolstered by institutionalized structures and beliefs. Edicts from the federal government and states are often contradictory and ill suited to the specific and varied conditions across contexts. Fragmented governance, politics, top-down compliance, inadequate data systems, bureaucratic human resource policies, and isolation of schools from other systems and organizations affecting children's welfare combine to reinforce existing disparities in resources and processes. On the ground, schools in high-poverty neighborhoods lack the information, trust, and capacity they need to examine their practices and results over time and are pulled in multiple and conflicting directions by the mixed messages they receive. High-stakes testing and accountability measures can compound these issues and have the effect of drawing attention to avoiding consequences for adults rather than ensuring progress for students.[21]

Seeing the limitations in the current system as insurmountable barriers, some politicians and reformers have turned to charter schools and school choice as answers, a way to remove regular public schools—particularly those serving poor students and students of color—from a system that has repeatedly failed these children. Though promising in many ways, however, charters are no more a panacea than any other intervention. They free schools from many constraints and allow more innovation and experimentation, but much of the research suggests that most charter schools are quite similar to public schools in both their organization and results (Raymond et al. 2013). Charters could serve as a learning ground for the larger system and the field as a whole, and some districts have made use of their charters in this way. In most cases, however, mechanisms for feeding information back into the larger system, in ways that it can be effectively used, are either limited or absent altogether. As a result, charters as a whole do little to address the situation for the vast majority of underserved students in American schools.[22]

---

[21] For discussions of the effects of current high stakes testing policies on schools, see Schoen and Fusarelli (2008); Berliner (2011); and Cawelti (2006).

[22] Schools associated with a few of the charter management organizations (CMOs)—deliberately formed groups of charter schools that are similar in vision and strategy—do show signs of significant success. They include Aspire, KIPP, Achievement First, and High Tech High among others. One way of thinking about these CMOs is that they are public systems freed from many of the regulatory constraints of regular public districts and schools. Another way to think about them is that they could be compared to effective districts as they serve many of the same functions and demonstrate similar characteristics.

Vision of a More Equitable Education System

What are the implications of our discussion of educational inequalities and lessons from equity-based reforms? What might a more equitable education system look like? And how might we more effectively move in that direction, not only for a few schools and districts but across whole systems and states? In the next section, we draw on our previous discussion and on 20 years of systemic standards-based reform to sketch out a vision of how a more equitable education might operate in the U.S. We argue that to address the deep and pervasive inequities we've described requires a system-wide focus on quality improvement within a standards-based framework, combined with targeted interventions to address particular and pervasive disparities within schools, and coordinated efforts between schools and other agencies and organizations serving children and their families. In the final two sections of the chapter we turn to the problem of motivating and supporting change toward such a vision and provide an example of a state working to move in this direction.

Three assumptions frame the focus and limit scope of the vision we present. First, we recognize that the ecosystem in low-resourced and often dysfunctional environments in cities and rural areas affects both the social system outside of the schools and the schools themselves. We thus assume that changes in both the out-of-school opportunities and the within-school opportunities are necessary if we wish to dramatically reduce student achievement and attainment gaps. However, we also assume—with considerable evidence to back this up—that schools can make a major difference. Though we believe it is necessary to figure out promising ways to ensure that all children have a real opportunity to be ready for school, that they and their families live in supportive environments, and that they have opportunities for employment beyond their schooling, we leave this task to other authors in other chapters of this volume. We focus here on the schools.

Second, we assume the American educational system will not change in its general form in the next decade or two. We do not propose to "blow up the system," however appealing that might be to some. While we expect that technology will influence to some considerable extent how students learn and teachers teach—especially as older teachers retire and new teachers come in having been raised in the Internet era—we anticipate that for the foreseeable future we will continue to have schools where most students come together to learn, that this learning will take place over 13 grade levels (K-12), and in classes of 15–30 students. We also expect that districts and district school boards will continue to exist and set the rules at the local level and bargain with the local unions. We expect charter schools to remain as an alternative for some small portion of students.

Finally, we recognize that the conditions we outlined in the beginning of this chapter do not simply diminish opportunities for traditionally underserved students. They also depress the quality of schooling for all—or at least the vast majority of—students in U.S. schools. International comparisons demonstrate the limitations of American educational opportunity. These data and our earlier discussion suggest quality and equality are interactive concepts. Any approach to improving equality of opportunity must pay attention first and foremost to the quality of the schools and school systems and their ability to improve conditions for students over time. At the same time, any attempt to improve the quality and outcomes of our educational systems overall will be successful only to the extent that it also reduces disparities and fosters success for those who have traditionally been least successful in school.

The Foundation: A Quality School System

Our analysis of the recent era of educational reform in the U.S. as well as of more successful systems both here and abroad leads us to posit two core elements of a high quality system: a standards-based and supportive policy framework and a continuous improvement approach at all levels of the system.

Coherent Standards-Based Policy Framework

The odds of success for a school with a population that has lacked important opportunities are substantially increased if it operates in a supportive environment where its internal (school) and external (district, state, and federal) leadership are all pulling in the same direction. This is the central tenet of standards-based reform, a systemic improvement strategy first articulated in the late 1980s and subsequently spread through federal and state policy across the nation. In its original conception, standards-based reform encompassed three key components: *challenging standards* stating what students should know and be able to do for graduation and at different points in their schooling, a coherent system of *mutually reinforcing policies* designed to build capacity and focus to ensure that all students had access to opportunities to achieve those standards, and a *redesigned governance system* in which top-down direction was combined with bottom-up discretion, knowledge, and professional energy of school people and their communities (Smith and O'Day 1991). This early conception grew out of efforts of professional associations to professionalize teaching and define standards in the disciplines, research evidence on the limitations of top-down mandates that only intensified current practice, and an analysis of the ways in which a fragmented policy and governance structure hindered the spread of effective school-based innovations and overall improvement efforts. Equity goals have been at the heart of standards-based strategies since their inception, reflecting the belief that all students should have access to high-quality curriculum and instruction and that a coherent set of policies guiding instructional content, professional development, resource allocation, assessment, and accountability could stimulate and support change in that direction (O'Day and Smith 1993, 272).

Over the past two decades, stimulated in part by federal action in ESEA and Goals 2000 legislation, all states have adopted standards and have instituted at least some degree of policy alignment to those standards. Most are currently in the process of shifting to a new generation of college and career-ready standards that better reflect the depth of knowledge and skills needed in the fast-paced and complex world of the twenty-first century. Indeed, the notion that states should articulate and use content standards to guide their education systems—unheard of in the U.S. before the 1980s—has now become conventional wisdom. The pervasiveness of some form of standards-based reform at the state level not only makes it difficult to envision a system in the near future without such standards; it also provides a plausible explanation for at least some of the achievement gains and gap closings observed in the NAEP and TIMSS results cited earlier.

Yet standards and aligned policies are not enough. While systemic in nature, standards-based approaches have fallen prey to many of the same implementation challenges we discussed above for more piecemeal efforts. Early emphasis on support for capacity building, for example, never fully materialized or was not sustained in most jurisdictions. And the notion of an altered governance structure that would allow for context-embedded solutions and responsiveness gave way to an almost singular focus on accountability and top-down mandates (many of them federal) during the No Child Left Behind (NCLB) era. The Obama administration's use of the waiver process to allow for greater state flexibility does not adequately address this problem, for while changing some of the parameters of the NCLB requirements, the Department of Education has maintained the strong focus on accountability as a central lever for change. It has even extended the accountability emphasis to single out test-based teacher evaluation as the favored approach for improving teacher quality (see Jennings 2015 for a fuller discussion).

We continue to believe that a state-level systemic approach based on thoughtful and challenging content standards can provide a scaffolding and structure for the academic activities of schools and classrooms. Multiple states provide existence proofs for this assertion. In addition, within this general approach, we see the Common Core and Next Generation Science Standards as significant and positive steps forward, both because of the content of the standards themselves and because of the potential for collaboration and mutual learning across states.[23] In particular, the increased emphasis on using language orally and in written form and the focus on depth and understanding rather than on algorithms can provide a stronger base for students to successfully enter the environment beyond schooling than is presently offered in most schools.

Yet the promise of the standards to improve overall system quality and reduce disparities for poor students and students of color cannot be realized without focused and persistent attention to implementation and the processes of change and system improvement.

---

[23] Even with the political pushback against the Common Core State Standards per se, we see a trend toward greater depth and commonality in the standards across states. We expect for a large majority of states this trend will hold.

A Continuous Improvement Approach

The second core element of a high-quality system is the simple but demanding concept of continuous improvement, which is a logical extension of our earlier observations about the importance of contextual conditions and systemic contributors to the success of any effort to improve outcomes for traditionally underserved students. An outgrowth of W. E. Deming's work in Japan, continuous (quality) improvement has been a focus for research and organizational change efforts in both public service and private industry for decades. A recent comprehensive review of this work identified five core features of quality improvement across a variety of approaches:

1. It is focused on system outcomes for a defined population of beneficiaries—*and* on the processes that lead to those results;
2. It uses variation in performance (including "failure") as opportunities for learning and improvement;
3. It takes a system perspective, with the understanding that systems are designed to get the results they produce, so if you want to change the results, you have to change the system;
4. It is evidence-based, including measurement of not only outcomes but processes (and resources), and this measurement is embedded in the day-to-day work of the system and its participants: and
5. It involves a specific and coherent methodology and processes. Some of the more familiar methods include PDSA (Plan-Do-Study-Act) cycles, "Six Sigma," and "LEAN."[24]

While specific methodologies differ, continuous improvement processes generally start with identification and analysis of a problem of practice in the given system, followed by repeated cycles of inquiry in which a plan for addressing that problem is developed, tested, revised based on data, and then implemented more broadly (or retested anew), followed by new data and more refinement. Most authors discuss quality improvement as a necessarily ongoing activity, often involving multiple cycles over periods of 7–10 or even more years to address major performance problems. For Tony Bryk and his colleagues at the Carnegie Foundation for the Advancement of Teaching, a critical feature of an improvement approach is not simply the repetition of the cycles of planning, action, and feedback but also the integration of continuous improvement processes into the *daily* work of individuals *throughout* the system.[25] Collaboration and active involvement of system participants allows for more effective individual and organizational learning, diffusion of promising practices, and adaptation to changing conditions (both internal and external)—all aspects of the implementation challenges discussed earlier. Such collaboration has repeatedly been identified as a central feature of more effective schools

---

[24] See Park et al. (2012) for a review and synthesis of the continuous improvement literature. For a more detailed treatment, see Langley et al. (2009).

[25] See Park et al. (2012) and Bryk et al. (2011) for more detail on the conceptual underpinnings of the promising work of the Carnegie Foundation for the Advancement of Teaching.

and districts (see, for example, Purkey and Smith 1983; Sykes et al. 2009). When expanded across systems in what the Carnegie Foundation calls "networked improvement communities," such collaboration allows for collective examination of both common and context-specific patterns of change and adaptation (Bryk et al. 2011).

Continuous improvement approaches have been put to productive use in many sectors and have had a particularly profound impact on improvement of health care organizations, both in the U.S. and internationally.[26] One longer-term example in education is that of the Long Beach School Unified School District in Southern California, which has been consistently applying these concepts over the period of two decades with a focus on increasing outcomes for traditionally underserved students, who make up over 70 % of the student population.[27] That work has been documented in three case study reports published by the Harvard Business School since 2006.[28] Winner of the prestigious Broad Prize in 2003 and a finalist in 2007 and 2009, Long Beach has also recently been named as one of the top three school systems in the country by McKinsey & Company in terms of sustained and significant improvements. The impact of those improvements can be seen not only in overall gains in student achievement and graduation but in narrowing of gaps over time: gains for the district's African-American, Latino, and poor students on the state's Academic Performance Index between 2002 and 2012 were approximately 50 % higher than those for Whites.

---

[26] See, for example, the work of the Institute for Healthcare Improvement (IHI) at http://www.ihi.org/Pages/default.aspx

[27] One small example of how this process works in Long Beach is the development of the district's K-8 mathematics program over an eight-year period. The approach began in 2003 when a single teacher (Si Swun) applied the principles of Singapore Math to his own fifth-grade classroom, with remarkably positive results. Singapore Math combines the development of students' conceptual understanding of mathematics with the automaticity of basic math facts and procedures. Within a year, other teachers in his school were adjusting their math instruction in similar ways, also to good effect. The district decided to test out the approach in other contexts, first in fifth-grade classrooms in five high-need schools. Based on positive results in these schools, the pilot program (entitled MAP²D) was spread to 15 schools, with expansion in several of these to second and third grades. The testing and expansion to new schools and grades continued over the next several years until the district had enough data to warrant full implementation across all elementary schools. In addition to teachers and schools following the progress of their own students, the district research office conducted a quasi-experimental evaluation of the implementation and effects of the program. The first evaluation report, based on 2005–2006 data, found that the students in the MAP²D classrooms were scoring significantly and substantially higher than comparison students and almost as well as students of higher socioeconomic status in other schools. Subsequent evaluations bolstered these findings. In 2009, Long Beach partnered with Fresno Unified School District to expand the approach beyond the elementary grades into middle school, assessing the results across the two systems and revising the process. For an evaluation of MAP²D in Long Beach, see Anderson and Gulek (2008); for details on the partnership in mathematics with Fresno, see Duffy et al. (2011).

[28] See the three case studies of varying aspects of Long Beach's work during this extended period—produced by the Public Education Leadership Project of Austin Harvard University's graduate schools of education and business: Austin et al. 2004, 2006; Honan et al. 2004.

Next door to Long Beach is Garden Grove. In a variation of the strategy, over a 14-year period, Garden Grove has focused on improving its human capital in all areas of the district to similarly positive results (Knudson 2013). Other documented district examples include Union City, NJ; Montgomery County, MD; and Hillsborough and Orange Counties, FL (see, for example, Kirp 2013). The Sanger School District in California's impoverished central valley demonstrates these principles for a smaller, mostly rural district (David and Talbert 2013).

These are only a few of the U.S. examples. At the state level, Massachusetts and Texas fit the pattern of a sustained effort based on evidence to improve all parts of the system. And internationally, much has been written about the improvement processes of Finland, Singapore, and the province of Ontario in Canada. Two key questions emerge that are particularly relevant for our discussion of equity.

Continuous Improvement (CI) and Outcome Accountability

The most obvious question is how a continuous improvement approach differs from typical school and district accountability models instantiated in NCLB and other common policies (Hargreaves and Braun 2013). After all, outcome accountability also focuses on the application of data to identify where things are not working—and particularly where they are not working for traditionally underserved students. For example, the reporting of student outcomes disaggregated by historically significant subgroups has been a main contribution of Title I legislation since 1994. However, we see at least four fundamental differences that distinguish an accountability-based approach and a continuous improvement approach.

First, accountability-based models usually focus exclusively on collecting and analyzing data on student outcomes. But without systematic information about the antecedent processes, teachers, schools, and districts will have difficulty connecting those outcomes with their likely causes; nor will they be able to meaningfully assess the impact of actions they take to alter those outcomes.[29] By contrast, the focus in CI is on the improvement of practice, and so detailed information about particular practices is part and parcel of the analytic method. Moreover, the analytical methods employed are specifically designed to facilitate meaningful connections between processes and outcomes.

A second difference between the two approaches is the perspective on failure. In CI, mistakes and failures are expected; they are both the basis for identifying the focal problem of practice and are opportunities for collective learning about how to make things better. In addition, frequent, rapid cycle tests of possible solutions also help to minimize harmful mistakes when the knowledge base for any particular problem or remedy is weak. By contrast, failure and mistakes in typical accountability systems are more frequently opportunities for blame and negative consequences than for assistance and learning. As a result, participants often try to hide problems rather than address them openly and may even "cook the books" to avoid

---

[29] See O'Day (2008) for a more complete discussion of this issue.

recriminations and penalties. The test cheating scandals in which teachers and administrators change student answers to "improve" their scores are reflective of this problem.[30]

The approach to context is a third difference. Accountability models typically mandate not only the targets and measures but also the solutions to unsatisfactory outcomes, irrespective of their appropriateness for a given context—and often irrespective of the strength of the evidence behind them. In continuous improvement, all solutions are contextualized, and trials across multiple contexts provide information about which solutions are likely to work for whom and under what conditions.

Finally, the two approaches differ with respect to the primary source of accountability. In most education systems today, accountability is something that comes from outside the school or district. Local actors have not been involved in setting their goals or often even in determining their strategies. In continuous improvement, while there may be some externally determined targets, the primary source of accountability is internal among members of the organization and its clients and focused on the practices and feedback loops they have put in place. Case studies of low-performing schools conducted by Consortium for Policy Research in Education researchers found that this internal accountability distinguished those schools that were able to improve their performance over time from those that did not (Abelmann et al. 1999).

Continuous Improvement and Equity

A second question particularly relevant to the topic of this chapter is whether a continuous improvement approach will actually lead to reductions in opportunity and outcome gaps among students. While we believe that such an approach will foster the *conditions* under which strategies for reducing disparities can be most successful, we would argue that addressing these inequalities must be an *explicit* goal of the system for this to happen in a systematic way. The case of Montgomery County, MD, provides an example of how this process works in practice.

When Jerry Weast became superintendent of the Montgomery County district in 1999, he instituted a continuous improvement approach to address the large and nationally comparable gaps between White students and their African-American and Hispanic counterparts. GIS mapping of regions in the county that were high poverty, high minority, and low achieving provided a graphic catalyst for community-wide dialogue about educational disparities and race. Discussions across the district helped to identify structural contributors (like course placement policies in high school that tended to keep Hispanic and African-American students from higher-level courses because they lacked the prerequisites) as well as adult norms and attitudes that prevented full access for some students. Multiple sources of data—including frequent "walk through" observations using formal protocols in individual

---

[30] See, for example, Fair Test's 2011 fact sheet on these issues: *Tests, Cheating and Educational Corruption,* http://fairtest.org/sites/default/files/Cheating_Fact_Sheet_8-17-11.pdf

school sites—helped district leaders to identify particular manifestations of unequal opportunity and to design interventions such as full-day kindergarten, small classes, and rigorous curriculum models, which they targeted to high-poverty schools. They monitored for success of these actions over time while creating a system-wide culture of collaboration focused on both excellence and equity. By the end of Weast's 12-year tenure, Montgomery County had significantly reduced gaps among racial groups across multiple performance indicators: achievement on state tests in elementary school, completion of algebra in eighth grade, SAT and Advanced Placement (AP) results, and high school graduation. Indeed, the county posted higher AP participation and success rates for African-American students than the nation did for students as a whole (Weast 2014).

Similar examples of a focus on equity and access within a process of continuous improvement can be found in most of the districts previously mentioned. In Fresno, for instance, a six-year partnership with the University of California has produced sophisticated data systems to uncover disparities in course-taking patterns and other opportunities for underserved students, which the district and its partners have systematically addressed with substantial success through ongoing work with school counselors, principals, and district administrators. Less than 200 miles away, the Oakland Unified School District has been working with local funders and nongovernmental organizations (NGOs) to monitor and address disparities for African-American youth in seven areas through the African-American Male Achievement Initiative. Based on data collected and analyzed by the district and the Urban Strategies Council, the initiative focuses attention to students' developing identity, social emotional health, and academic learning to reduce achievement and graduation gaps, increase attendance, and eliminate disparities in disciplinary actions and incarceration. In these and similar cases, continuously improving districts explicitly and systematically interrogate their data to ferret out disparities that might not be immediately apparent, collaborate to tease out potential root causes and devise strategies, and test and evaluate those strategies over time.

Targeted Strategies to Reduce Inequalities: Four High-Leverage Approaches

As these examples demonstrate, a great strength of embedding continuous improvement into the fabric of a school system is that the system can more readily identify gaps in outcomes and opportunities among students and efficiently target action in those areas. These include ongoing monitoring of access to such resources as qualified teachers and teacher time, advanced courses, and appropriate and high-quality instructional materials as well as elimination of disparities in disciplinary actions and extracurricular opportunities. In this section, we highlight four high-leverage arenas in which such targeted attention and action for students can help to level the playing field and substantially reduce within-system inequalities. They are

development of a physically and emotional safe school environment; a strong emphasis on cultivating robust language capacities in all students; a methodology (tiered instruction) for systematically thinking about the nature and intensity of interventions; and attention to key transition points that may be particularly difficult for disadvantaged youngsters to traverse and require special interventions.

Ensuring Safe and Supportive School Environments

Safety is one of the first things that parents think about when their child goes off to school. Schools in high-poverty neighborhoods are much more likely to be unsafe. Minorities and "different" children often face emotional and physical safety problems in all schools.[31] At a basic level, physical safety and protection from outside influences capture the public discourse, and districts and schools across the country use a variety of approaches to ensure that safety. We address here the issue of physical and emotional safety in terms of conditions and actions inside the school.

The idea of supportive school culture and climate has been an important element in the school reform discourse for years. Such an environment supports not only a positive place to work but also a more effective organization.

Recent research has broadened this concept to focus on a broad span of social–emotional skills and dispositions of students and adults that support productive interaction and respect for everyone in the school. These skills and dispositions are captured in the research on Social-Emotional Learning (SEL)[32] and undergird the development of a school with a physically and emotionally safe environment. SEL is the label for a growing movement throughout the U.S. for schools and districts to move beyond a narrow focus on academic content and skills.[33] It emphasizes five interrelated sets of cognitive, affective, and behavioral competencies: self-awareness, self-management (often called self-regulation), social awareness (including the capacity for empathy), ability to establish and maintain healthy and rewarding relationships, and responsible decision-making. The competencies provide a framework for specific and detailed interventions such as the "Second Step" and the "Steps to Respect" programs.[34]

---

[31] See, for example, Lippman et al. 1996; Erica Weiler 2003, "Making School Safe for Sexual Minority Students," *Principal Leadership,* June, http://www.nasponline.org/resources/principals/GLBQT%20Safety%20NASSP%20December%202003.pdf

[32] For a deeper discussion of SEL, see the website of the Collaborative for Social and Emotional Learning (CASEL) at http://www.casel.org/social-and-emotional-learning/outcomes/. See also the website for PromotePrevent, http://sshs.promoteprevent.org/publications/prevention-briefs/social-and-emotional-learning

[33] States are taking account of SEL. For example, Massachusetts has a set of guidelines for implementing SEL. See http://www.doe.mass.edu/bullying/SELguide.pdf

[34] For a review of the research on social-emotional learning and Second Step, see the Committee for Children website at http://www.cfchildren.org/Portals/0/SS_K5/K-5_DOC/K-5_Review_Research_SS.pdf

Schools that pursue these goals do so explicitly: Students and parents are regularly engaged, and teachers work to ensure that classroom behavior and opportunities meet the goals of SEL. This kind of focus takes time and energy to implement well but it seems to be worth the effort. A rich literature of studies provides clear and positive evidence on many of the SEL dimensions. For example a recent meta-analysis of SEL's effect on achievement found an average gain of 10 percentile points while other studies have found clear positive effects of SEL interventions on areas such as bullying.[35] The implementation of SEL in a school can do more than change the ways that students behave in classrooms and the halls. It also creates an environment where students can be different from the norms established by advertisements and video. It can change the way people think about each other.

The components of SEL are exemplified in the use of "restorative justice," or "restorative practices," a set of principles and practices focused on promoting respect, taking responsibility, and strengthening relationships.[36] The idea of restorative justice has a long history in areas other than schooling and in a variety of cultures. It changes the focus from punishment to repairing harm. In many schools, instances of bullying, fighting, and threatening have led to disproportionate numbers of students of color and males being subjected to punitive discipline—suspensions and expulsions—that remove them from instructional settings. Restorative justice deals directly with this issue. Oakland and San Francisco have made restorative practices key components of their equity and improvement agendas.

Developing Language Skills

The limits of my language means the limits of my world.
—Wittgenstein

Language development is affected by everything that happens to a child—from the mother's prenatal nutrition and habits (smoking, drinking, drugs) to language use in the home, including whether the child is read to or expected to ask and answer questions and engage in extended dialogue. The well-known Hart and Risley study (1995), comparing children in poor, low-income, and middle-income families, found huge differences in the amount and quality of expressed and understood language, favoring the children in the more advantaged families.[37] The literature on preschool and language development is clear. Young children living in poverty who have not attended preschool are very likely to be behind in their language develop-

---

[35] For a meta-analysis of the multiple effects of social-emotional learning interventions, see Durlak et al. 2011.

[36] For a review of the effects of restorative justice programs, see Latimer and Kleinknecht 2000. For additional description of restorative justice and its relation to SEL, see the report of the Restorative Practices Working Group at http://www.otlcampaign.org/sites/default/files/restorative-practices-guide.pdf

[37] See Hart and Risley (1995). See also http://www.naeyc.org/blogs/gclarke/2013/10/new-research-early-disparities-focus-vocabulary-and-language-processing

ment when they enter kindergarten. Students in this situation should be carefully monitored as they learn to read, with special attention to broadening their vocabulary and increasing their facility and comfort with the academic language of the schools. If the interventions come early and with sufficient intensity, the odds are good that students will gain the necessary skills and breadth of language that they need to succeed educationally. The new evidence of robust and positive long-term effects of Head Start is particularly promising in this regard.[38]

Once in school, students continue to learn conversational and academic oral English through the first years of schooling as they are also learning how to read and comprehend text. Without a strong language base, reading comprehension in the higher grades is a great challenge. By middle school, the teachers in the content areas assume that a student can understand the language in the classroom, integrate knowledge with past experience, and understand complex literary and nonfiction texts. Secondary teachers often have too little time and too many students to systematically identify and help students who are struggling to keep up.[39]

The need (and opportunity) for strong language development has been intensified by the college and career-ready standards recently adopted by most states. These standards emphasize learning to use oral language to explain answers to problems, make a logical argument based on evidence, interpret text, and retell stories. Academic language is part of word problems in mathematics and in science explanations. History, as told in books, movies, or video, is a matter of understanding a complex story; without strong language skills a student struggles. The assessments for the Common Core mathematics standards contain problems with large "stems"—two or three paragraphs of setting out the problem before the questions are posed. Even in math, the capacity to understand the language of the problem is critical to knowing how to set up and execute its solution (see Bransford et al. 2015; Snow et al. 1998).

For students who come to school speaking a language other than English at home, language development takes a particular form and challenge. On the one hand, the research is pretty clear on the cognitive benefits of bilingualism for all students.[40] In addition, in an increasingly global economy, students with native fluency in other languages and cultures can be a wonderful national resource. On the other hand, English language learners (ELLs) in schools face the double challenge of learning increasingly sophisticated and demanding content and learning a new language at the same time. Combining instruction in their native language with instruction in English can be an effective way to increase acquisition of English, ensure higher levels of content learning, and enable maintenance and development

---

[38] For a general discussion of the effects of Head Start and other early childhood programs, see Heckman 2011. For long-term effects, see Deming (2009) (http://www.people.fas.harvard. edu/~deming/papers/Deming_HeadStart.pdf) and Gibbs et al. (2011) (http://www.nber.org/papers/w17452.pdf).

[39] For a delineation of these issues, see Johnson et al. n.d.; Vaughn et al. 2008.

[40] For reviews of the research on the cognitive benefits of bilingualism, see Goldenberg (2008) and Bialystok (2011).

of ELLs' native languages. Bilingual education—particularly dual immersion programs—can also spread the benefits of bilingualism to native English speaking students.[41] Making it possible for students in low-income areas to be in bilingual classes whenever they enter the U.S., but especially in the early years, would be challenging to accomplish but well worth the effort.

Implementing a Tiered Approach to Intervention

Response to Intervention (RTI) is a three-tiered methodology that provides a structure for teachers to select and implement an appropriate intervention for a student or students who require special attention.[42] Without some well-organized and defined strategy, students will slip through cracks. One major goal of RTI is to address problems very early to reduce the odds of students experiencing failure.

The first tier of RTI is a well-organized and effectively implemented curriculum and inclusive instructional approach: All students are involved and expected to be mastering the content, and instruction is specifically designed to address the wide range of learner needs, strengths, and backgrounds.[43] Regular monitoring of student learning is a critical aspect of first-tier instruction, with the goal of addressing problems or barriers to learning before they become serious. Interim assessments can play a role in this monitoring but are often not timely or fine grained enough to enable the teacher to respond effectively to individual student needs. More critical is the teacher's capacity to observe how well students are learning the material on a minute-by-minute and day-by-day basis through the use of formative assessment and observation along the lines described by Black and Wiliam (2009). Black and Wiliam see this process as continuous, with the focus on preventing students from long-term confusion or withdrawing their attention from learning. With a strong core instructional program that is inclusive and incorporates formative assessment practices, 75–80 % of students can be sufficiently served.

The second tier of RTI is for students for whom the core program is insufficient; that is, for those who regularly do not seem to be keeping up or who consistently lose attention. This could be due to not having the background to understand the material, to something going on in their lives outside of the classroom, or even to losing confidence in their capacity to learn the content. When a teacher observes a student struggling in class, his or her response will depend on that teacher's own capacity and on the resources available in the school. If initial adjustments to the

---

[41] For effects of two-way bilingual education, see for example, Marian et al. (2013).

[42] For a definition and description of RTI, see the RTI Action Network website, http://www.rtinetwork.org/learn/what/whatisrti

[43] One approach to developing a truly inclusive first-tier instructional approach is to follow the principles of Universal Design for Learning (UDL). According to its creators, UDL "drew upon neuroscience and education research, and leveraged the flexibility of digital technology to design learning environments that from the outset offered options for diverse learner needs." For a detailed discussion of the variability of learners and the UDL approach, see Meyer et al. (2014).

core instructional program (Tier 1) don't have an effect, more intensive intervention may be necessary. For example, a possible second-tier approach for students having trouble learning to read may be remediation by a tutor such as a Reading Recovery specialist.[44] The degree of intensity is an important decision, as is the nature of the intervention. For students who have lost (or never had) confidence in their capacity, one of the strategies suggested by Carol Dweck (2006) in her Mindset research might be appropriate.[45] Nationally, approximately 10–15 % of students may require the second-tier interventions to supplement the regular instructional program. These numbers may well be higher in high-poverty schools.

The third tier of intervention is more intensive and responds to a continuing problem that could not be effectively addressed through other interventions within the regular classroom. It could entail a meeting to consider providing the student with special services under a federal 504 plan or even an individualized educational plan (IEP).[46] Prior to that, however, there should be a set of second-tier services and appropriate support and analysis of the student's problems.

Attending to Transition Points

RTI provides a framework for intervention at all levels of schooling. Without careful and well-implemented interventions, too many students, especially those from low-income families, will fall through the cracks, lose confidence about how they are doing in school, and try to avoid notice until they are old enough to leave school. The problems can come at any time during a student's educational career.

Yet there are predictable times during a student's voyage through school when problems are both more likely and particularly consequential for future success.[47] Often these critical points occur during major transitions in a student's schooling and are especially problematic for traditionally underserved students. For many of these transition points, there may not be an individual teacher or other adult in a position to be aware of problems; targeted support systems to help clear students' paths during these times are thus critical.

---

[44] For general information on Reading Recovery, see the Reading Recovery Council website http://readingrecovery.org/reading-recovery/teaching-children/basic-facts. For evaluation findings, see Consortium for Policy Research in Education (2013).

[45] The studies and interventions used by Carol Dweck seek to change students' mindset from believing that their intelligence is fixed and determines their school performance to one where they believe that if they work harder, study more, and pay greater attention in school their grades would increase. For a description, see Dweck (2012).

[46] For detailed description and delineation of differences between 504 plans and an IEP, see Understood Team, *The Difference between IEPs and 504 Plans,* http://www.ncld.org/students-disabilities/iep-504-plan

[47] See Kieffer et al. (2011). For a consideration of transition from middle school to high school, see Kathy Christie and Kyle Zinth, "Ensuring Successful Student Transitions from the Middle Grades to High School," http://www.adlit.org/article/32116/. Also see Neild (2009).

The first major transition occurs in kindergarten. A child who comes into kindergarten having had rich language experiences, having developed self-regulatory behaviors, liking to count, and able to share will do well in school. Note that SEL skills are particularly important. Alternatively, if the child missed the opportunities to build these competencies—for example, if he or she never had preschool experience or opportunity to develop these skills in the home—the child may struggle. A child lacking these experiences and skills may not show clear indications for a while, but signs of insecurity, frustration, difficult classroom behavior, and data from diagnostic instruments should alert teachers. Students from low-income homes are disproportionately likely to enter school with some of these challenges as more than half do not attend preschool. In some schools a teacher may be overwhelmed and unable to adequately treat every student, but a school that uses an SEL model and systematically practices a form of RTI is likely to be ready for this. In effective kindergartens in high-poverty schools, students take diagnostic assessments of their language and other skills very early, and there is a regular and systematic approach to working with the students and possibly their parents to catch up. In many chaotic elementary schools with new or poorly trained kindergarten teachers, however, few such supports exist.[48]

A second major transition point occurs toward the end of third grade. The expectation in American schools is that by this time students will be comfortable reading appropriate texts, gaining information from them, and demonstrating their comprehension of the material they have read. The shorthand for this expectation is that prior to fourth grade students learn to read; from fourth grade on, students read to learn. What this means instructionally is that in many schools the intense focus on learning to read subsides in fourth grade, and students who have not mastered comprehension skills and strategies will likely struggle to keep up. We see two implications of this pattern. First, it is critical that all students receive high-quality reading instruction and rich language experiences prior to fourth grade. Second, for those who haven't, a well-designed RTI second-tier intervention must be available to remedy the gaps.

The moves from elementary to middle and middle to high schools are other major transition points in a student's educational career, as is going from secondary school to a community college, four-year college, or to work. In each of the transitions, the rules and expectations for students change. For example, in the move from elementary to middle school, students must suddenly negotiate the rules and personalities of a half dozen teachers rather than one, the stakes are higher, and the academic demands—including homework—are much greater. Moreover students at this age change physically, and the impact of their social world intensifies, now

---

[48] Large numbers of students with these issues might signal the need for more interventions at home. Nongovernmental organizations such as Home Instruction for Parents of Preschool Youngsters (HIPPY), provide information about alternative interventions or strategies that might be used to provide support to parents and, through them, to students. Organizations such as "Too Small to Fail" provide advice and guidance. See the HIPPY USA website at www.hippyusa.org/ and the Next Generation website at http://thenextgeneration.org/tags/too-small-to-fail

aggravated by social media. These changes may be especially challenging for students who lack support at home and may lead some to decide that school is not worth the effort or not relevant to their lives. In addition, pressures and dangerous alternatives outside school can capture students' attention and provide less constructive kinds of social and emotional support. Having a trusted adult at school or in the community, with whom a student may honestly and openly discuss problems and plans, can help individual students navigate both the demands of school and the potholes of adolescent development. Unfortunately, such role models and trusting relationships with adults are too often lacking in schools, especially for low-income students of color. Small schools and learning communities, where students and teachers can get to know one another; advisory classes; and special initiatives like the Manhood Development Program in Oakland, CA, are examples of strategies that districts and schools have employed to help build the needed connections between students and caring adults.

There are also consequential decisions about courses that students and their teachers need to make in seventh, eighth and ninth grades to prepare for high school. If a student misses taking Algebra 1 by ninth grade, for example, the consequences are often considerable. Because of master-schedule problems in secondary schools, this can result in students being left out of the math sequence and out of the academic track. Some studies indicate that low-income and immigrant students without counselors or trusted advisors do not realize the importance of this sort of planning.

Ninth grade appears to be a particularly important year for academic intervention (Allensworth and Easton 2007). For this reason, some districts and states are implementing "early warning indicator" systems to identify ninth-graders who are at risk for dropping out. Based on research by the Consortium on Chicago School Research, for example, Chicago Public Schools adopted a "freshman year on-track indicator" and began providing schools with real time data about which ninth-graders were and were not on track for graduation as well as guidance on how to help students get back on track. A new report on this initiative indicates that Chicago's on-track rate rose 25 percentage points from 2007 to 2013, and that this increase occurred across all racial/ethnic groups, genders, and incoming achievement levels. What is more, the improvements were largely sustained in later grades, contributing to higher grades and increased graduation rates down the road (Roderick et al. 2014).

Another increasingly popular approach to improving graduation rates and better preparing students for transition to adulthood is to provide multiple pathways to graduation. All pathways are intended to prepare students for postsecondary opportunities, but they are designed to tap into varying student interests and real world realities (Symonds et al. 2011). More and more districts and schools are thus beginning to offer sequences of courses focused on occupational domains or issues in today's society. A student in one pathway might focus on health care; his or her math, science, and literature courses would reflect this theme. Another student might follow a pathway focused on the environment or the building trades. These pathways provide relevance and might also include opportunities for students to apprentice in their areas of interest (see Chap. 10). In many settings, the high schools are connected to community colleges, which provide additional courses with the same pathway focus once the students have graduated from high school. Early-college high school programs make such connections even before graduation and have demonstrated success in rigorous studies of their effects for low-income students (Berger et al. 2010).

Finally on the transition theme, many students who graduate from secondary school and go on to college (including community colleges) find out they need remedial courses before they can take courses for credit. Nationally, the figure for such students is approximately 60 % of the incoming cohort (Southern Regional Education Board 2010). Many are low income or ELL. Most fail to pass the required exams and drop out before even passing one credit-bearing course. This pattern is costly and devastating for many low-income students and for local regions and whole states as well. Exemplars of successful approaches include that of El Paso, Texas, where the local districts, community colleges, and local university have worked together for years to ensure equitable access and success. Another approach is to focus on improving student success in gatekeeper courses within the community colleges. Recent work of the Carnegie Foundation for the Advancement of Teaching, for example, has produced a powerful technology-supported intervention for students in developmental mathematics courses in community colleges. Given these alternatives, the task may now be less a conceptual challenge than the political problem of making serious changes in the colleges (Yamada 2014).

Taken together these leverage points provide a crude template for schools and districts committed to not allowing any student to fail.

Beyond School: Connecting Schools with Services and Institutions in the Community

As we noted earlier, the entire environment in which students live influences their development and success in school. We have emphasized the importance of good medical care, healthy food, a supportive and language-rich environment, and at least a year of preschool as important preparation for academic learning. These conditions and other opportunities outside of school continue to be important determinants of students' success and resilience in school. While we have described the negative side of some of the poorest communities and neighborhoods, there are often NGOs, churches, and government agencies available and capable of providing support and services for the students during those 4500 waking hours outside of school.

Connecting schools with other systems is not a new idea in the U.S. In the early 1900s, John Dewey, Jane Addams, and others argued for schools in the cities to be the center of a neighborhood's life by being the center and provider for social life and services. Later on, the Mott family, working through their foundation in Michigan, supported schools that served multiple services, a model and philosophy that spread through many parts of the country. In 1974, amendments to ESEA included the creation of a small grants program for Community Schools that enabled funds to support model community schools directly as well as state activities in support of community education. This program was ended in the consolidation of programs in 1982, but the federal government came back in 1997 to support twenty-first century After Schools programs and, more recently, twenty-first century Learning Centers.

In 2014, the Coalition for Community Schools held a national forum with 1400 participants. The coalition's concept is broad and includes making full use of the school (open all of the time) for the community, health services, and social services. This concept is often called the full-service community school program, and it has schools all across the nation. Using the school as a hub, a community school organization coordinates education and social service organizations all through the neighborhood, including businesses, colleges, adult education, family support activities, and other NGOs.

Another strong organization in this area is Integrated Student Supports (ISS), which is a school-based approach to promoting students' academic success by providing academic and nonacademic support services including tutoring, mentoring, linking students to health care and families to counseling, education, food banks, and employment. Integration around individual student needs is the key factor.

Perhaps the best-known example of the systemic community-based approach— and surely one of the most expensive—has been the Harlem Children's Zone (HCZ), which takes up a 100-block area in Harlem's largely African-American area of New York City. HCZ connects students and their families with the entire panoply of social and educational services; where services have not existed, the organization has raised the resources to create them. HCZ has even created its own small network of schools that admit interested students through a lottery process.[49] Recently the federal government launched a program of competitive grants called Promise Neighborhoods that is modeled after the Harlem Children's Zone; in the last four years, over 40 districts in the nation have received Promise Neighborhood grants.[50]

Other settings—such as Long Beach and El Paso—have focused on developing strong collaborations between their school systems and the local community colleges and public universities, particularly those engaged in teacher preparation and development. In Oakland, the schools host farmers' markets in neighborhoods with no grocery stores. And in Silicon Valley, the John Gardner Center at Stanford works with a number of communities to link data from local social service agencies and community-based organizations to identify patterns and gaps and to ensure that students needing service have access to what they need.

---

[49] See Wikipedia (http://en.wikipedia.org/wiki/Harlem_Children's_Zone) for a description and citations on the Harlem Children's Zone. Also, for a recent analysis that suggests that the schools in the Children's Zone are responsible for observed academic gains, see Dobbie and Fryer (2011).

[50] For information about the Promise Neighborhood awards, see the U.S. Department of Education website at http://www2.ed.gov/programs/promiseneighborhoods/awards.html

Studies of these and similar efforts generally find small positive or insignificant effects on school achievement. But the afterschool activities are often not well coordinated with the instruction that students receive during the regular school day. Some interventions—such as those that connect children with food and medical service, young adolescents with counseling, and schools with teacher training institutions—have a high degree of face validity, even if they do not have evidence of a direct impact on student achievement. An integration of the Gardner Center's data strategy with health, nutrition, and some basic academic and social support services would provide a neighborhood or community with what seems to be the critical core interventions of all of these general programs and a mechanism to make sure the system is working with the students who most need assistance.

The bottom line is that there is a lot of energy around these issues across the nation. The systemic nature of the interventions and the urgency of the need for the populations they serve make a compelling case for their existence in every high-poverty neighborhood. It appears to us to be very unlikely that the achievement gaps can be closed substantially without interventions that mobilize neighborhoods that lack resources for their children around a set of strategies that engage the community-based organizations, the local governments, and the private sector.

Getting From Here to There: The Problem of Change at Scale

This vision of a more equitable system addresses the key shortcomings of past and current efforts to reduce achievement and opportunity gaps. It provides a framework to promote and extend system coherence, embeds improvement efforts in specific systemic contexts, balances whole system change with targeted interventions for underserved and struggling students, and recognizes the importance of connecting schools with other organizations and agencies affecting children and their families.

But envisioning what might be a more effective system is one thing; moving in this direction and doing it at scale is something else. For this discussion we incorporate an observation from decades of implementation research: Effecting change requires a context-appropriate balance of pressure and support—pressure to engender action and support to increase its effectiveness (McLaughlin 1987). This observation about organizational and system-level change is consistent with theory and research on individual performance, which is generally defined as an interactive function of individual motivation, ability, and situation (Rowan 1996).

We see three potential sources of pressure and support to move educational systems in the direction we have suggested: governmental and administrative policy at the federal, state, and local levels; professional networks and norms; and community and stakeholder constituencies.

Designing Governmental Policy to Motivate and Support Improvement and Equity

Governmental and administrative policy at the federal, state, and local levels has been the predominant source of external pressure and support for educational change in the U.S.—particularly with regard to equalizing opportunities for poor students, students of color, and English learners. Over the past six decades, this source has generally become more centralized, with states providing an increased portion of school funding (and demanding greater accountability for how those funds are spent) and the federal government taking more of a role in not only enforcing equality but also influencing the core direction of schooling. With respect to the balance between pressure and support, the scales at these two levels have recently tipped toward pressure and compliance, though requirements are often tied to categorical funding streams that wear the guise of inducements and fiscal support rather than blanket mandates.

We have noted earlier how this emphasis on compliance can actually thwart improvement and lead to unintended negative consequences for underserved students, even when they are the intended beneficiaries. In addition, because policy is made at all levels of the system, schools are frequently confronted with a panoply of conflicting rules, overlapping programs, and fragmented directions that divert attention and prevent real change.

To move toward a system that facilitates continuous improvement where it matters most—in the schools—will require a reconceptualization of the roles of the three levels of government and a rebalancing of emphasis between pressure and support, with greater attention going to providing long-term support for improvement than has been the case in recent years. At the core of this reconceptualization are the twin principles of (a) common commitment at all levels to the goals of equal opportunity, achievement, and attainment, and (b) governmental restraint and focus to achieve these goals. By restraint we mean that each level of government must fully consider the likely tradeoffs and potential unintended consequences before it creates new rules, strong incentives, and/or legislation based on ideology, politics, or even some evidence of effectiveness. The question must be, will the proposed action actually motivate and support greater equity and higher quality, or will it disrupt ongoing improvement processes and stress the schools and the teachers?[51]

A first step for all levels of government on the road to help schools and districts to achieve the improvement and equal opportunity vision is to model the ideas of continuous improvement within their own operations and to reach out to create

---

[51] For example, when Congress passed the No Child Left Behind Act in 2001, it put in place a set of accountability provisions that no state could feasibly achieve (primarily that 100 % of all students would be proficient on the state standards-aligned assessments by 2014). The Obama administration has provided waivers from many of these provisions, thus giving states an alternative to designating all of their schools as failing. But the department predicated these waivers on state actions—such as using student test scores to evaluate teachers—that were not relevant to the substance and purpose of the waiver.

more collaborative environments with other levels of government and with other sectors that influence the quality and equality of educational opportunity. This will not be an easy task for bureaucracies that have been stove-piped and focused on regulating their clients rather than supporting them in their improvement efforts, but there are examples of some states that have been moving in this direction. At the federal level, the task will be even harder, given the current level of political polarization.

Assuming that reorienting the federal and state systems toward improvement is possible, we suggest below that each level of government has a distinct and important role to play in motivating and supporting movement toward both high-quality systems and equal opportunity.

Federal Role and Policy

As the 10th Amendment to the Constitution implies, the basic responsibilities and practices of delivering education are left to the states and districts. And, as the 14th Amendment provides, the federal government has a responsibility to protect and support when needed those who require assistance to receive equal opportunity.

Following from these constitutional provisions, a simple test for suggesting what the federal government should—and should *not*—do in K-12 education is to apply two criteria:

- Does the activity protect or directly support the U.S. constitutional and legislated rights of schoolchildren to receive equal opportunity to a high quality education?
- Does the activity apply to the entire nation and is it more efficiently and effectively delivered by the federal government than it would be by states and districts?

Implementing these criteria would reduce the current portfolio of the U.S. Department of Education and clarify its role around a more highly focused set of responsibilities. The reasons for such a reduction include the great diversity of U.S. students and school environments; the complexity of effective teaching and school management; and the all too real danger of ideology, politics, and regulatory zeal overriding useful evidence within administrations and the Congress. We suggest instead a federal role that works to ensure equity and provides resources but eschews the one-size-fits-all prescription of education practice to states, districts, and schools. This view of the federal role calls for increasing the resources and capacities for support of the programs and policies that directly influence equal educational opportunity.

The activities of our proposed new role may be organized into four groups: protecting and supporting the rights of all students to equal educational opportunity; ensuring equal opportunity for specific groups of students protected under federal law; providing financial resources to equalize educational opportunity for all students; and supporting research, innovation, data about the health of the system and resources for improvement.

Protecting and Supporting the Rights of All Students to Equal Opportunity

The U.S. Office of Civil Rights (OCR) in the Department of Education has the critical function of enforcing civil rights laws affecting educational opportunity—such as the Civil Rights Act of 1964, the various desegregation decisions starting with *Brown v. Board*, Title IX, and Section 504 of the Disabilities Act. To achieve its mission, OCR balances the roles of enforcer/regulator with providing support to districts and schools to promote greater equity. Both approaches—reflecting the "pressure and support" functions mentioned above—are now part of the office's repertoire. As the climate of education reform changes to improvement rather than adherence to regulations, we suggest greater emphasis be placed on the support approach. This change in direction might require more resources.[52]

Ensuring Equal Opportunity for Students Protected Under Federal Law

Federal programs to support specifically protected groups of students include the Education for all Handicapped Act (EHA); Title III of ESEA, which supports the efforts to improve the teaching and learning of students whose native language is not English[53]; and the two programs for Native Americans, one in the Department of Education and the other in the Department of the Interior.[54] These programs differ dramatically in size, delivery strategy, and level of financial appropriation. Unfortunately, because legislative and regulatory environments tend to change slowly and protect vested interests, the programs do not necessarily reflect our new understanding of student learning and the opportunities that have appeared because of new emphases on innovation and strategies for improvement. An important step for each might be to have outside groups of experts and stakeholders carry out thorough and sustained (five-year) studies on how well these programs are working and to recommend changes.

---

[52] See OCR website at http://www2.ed.gov/about/offices/list/ocr/index.html.

[53] Title III of ESEA, intended to support ELLs, should be substantially modified and retained as a symbol and a vehicle for capacity building and innovation. The past decade has provided a great deal of new research on approaches to teaching ELL students. We have now considerable knowledge about dual immersion and other approaches to bilingual education that suggest that students derive added benefits from learning two languages without losing effectiveness in either. The current instantiation of Title III limits the opportunities for states, districts, and schools to apply this new information in a systematic way and should be changed.

[54] Title XI Education Amendments of 1972 contains an anti-discrimination provision that protects women. There is no specific education program—the Office of Civil Rights in the Department of Education administers the provision.

Eliminating Resource Inequities—Title I and New Strategies

Title I of ESEA provides funds to high-poverty schools beyond the base of resources provided by state and local funding. The highest poverty schools receive funds to improve the entire school ("school-wide" schools). Less-high-poverty schools receive funds on the basis of number of students on free and reduced price lunch and then use these funds to help low-achieving students (targeted assistance schools). Title I is the best known and largest of the programs that serve the goal of equal opportunity. It has been the object of much political attention, partly because it provides a large amount of money targeted to poor and low-scoring students and partly because the Title I law carries requirements that all states must have academic standards and assessments and administer a federal accountability system to meet the requirements for receiving Title I funds. We propose to curtail the federal accountability provisions in the current version of Title I (NCLB) to include only two elements: reporting of disaggregated results by subgroups, which would continue to be a gauge of equality of opportunity, and a requirement that each state develop a system of accountability appropriate to its context that includes measures to motivate and support improvement and a reduction of achievement, attainment, and opportunity gaps.

The core and historical purpose of Title I would remain. The funds for Title I should be increased and more highly targeted toward high-poverty schools than they are now (over half the schools and almost all of the districts in the nation receive Title I funds), and many of the legislative and regulatory requirements on the specific uses of the funds should be eliminated. The comparability and supplement-not-supplant provisions should be maintained. In fact, in high-poverty schools, Title I should be able to operate as an accelerator of school reform that supports continuous improvement and interventions targeted to ameliorate specific student challenges as they journey through the school.

Even though Title I is a large program, however, it does not come even close to closing the finance equality gap. Any independent observer of educational opportunity in the U.S. would see three glaring and generally ignored sources of gross disparities of resources that favor the well-to-do in our nation. In the initial section of this chapter we pointed out the great differences in wealth and in the resources available to students among the states, among districts within states, and among schools within districts; as a nation, we tend to turn a blind eye toward these disparities. The only entity available to help reduce state differences in resources for public education is the federal government. Great variation of resources among districts within states would logically be a problem to be solved by states; again logically, the within-district, among-schools disparities would be remedied by the districts. However, in this section of the paper we opt to address all three levels of resource inequality. Our reason is that the federal government could play a substantial role in accomplishing progress toward equality in all three of the areas: among states, within states, and within districts. This focus would call for new activities and resources from the Department of Education.

A serious move toward equalizing resources among states, controlling for effort and wealth, would accelerate equal opportunity across the nation for many low-income students of all races. A goal might be to bring all states to at least the 50th percentile of the current average per-pupil expenditure among states by 2020. This would require new resources from the federal government, which should be partially matched by states. Particularly in the South, many states lack the financial resources and infrastructure to provide the money to support high quality and effective K-12 schools for all of their schoolchildren.[55]

Meeting the within-state (among district) variation in resource allocation is a somewhat different problem. Attaining equalization among districts should be part of the states' commitment to equal opportunity. Here the federal government might figure out how to motivate state efforts to adopt something like a weighted pupil formula.

The third leg of this fiscal equity stool would be to address within-district inequalities among schools. Here the federal government might take an immediate and powerful step. This approach would require a subtle but significant change to the comparability provision in Title I of the ESEA, a provision that requires the resources available to the Title I schools within a district to be comparable *on average* with the resources available to non-Title I schools. In the current provision, the resources are defined as "services," such as number of teachers. Because schools with large populations of students from low-income families often have younger and less experienced teachers (due to teachers moving to other schools and to teacher turnover), the total amount paid to teachers, and thus the total expenditures in these schools, are often less than in schools with more affluent populations. We suggest that the comparability provision should be changed to require districts to equalize *actual* expenditures per pupil instead of "services." A study by the Department of Education found that such a change in regulation could "bring a substantial increase in funding for low-spending, high-need schools" (Stullich 2011, 1). These extra funds would be used to improve the quality of the school, for example, by lowering class size or having reading specialists or counselors.

We are not naïve about the possibilities of enacting any of these three finance proposals. In a Congress where tax cuts are dominant, the idea of investing in the education of students in states other than the congressman's own state does not seem likely to find many advocates. And, even the third proposal, to alter the comparability provision in Title I, has been proposed many times and rejected, with some major education groups leading the opposition. Yet, these three actions, by themselves, would alter the calculus of inequality in the country. They would create huge new opportunities for millions of children and could even engender trust in the public that the rhetoric of equal opportunity is real.

---

[55] See Houck and DeBray (Forthcoming) for a thoughtful discussion of how the federal government might stimulate these equalization reforms.

Supporting Research, Innovation, and Data for Improvement

The Department of Education should also continue to carry out research and data collection and analysis, focused on improving teaching and learning and on innovation in areas such as technology. As a goal, the department's research efforts should move more toward theoretically driven efforts that carefully aggregate knowledge to increase our understanding of key issues in developing an effective education system for all students. The research results and data from government-funded research should all be as openly available as possible through a Creative Commons license to allow all researchers access to the new knowledge and for those interested to be able to use the data to replicate and possibly illuminate the original results.[56] Explorations into innovative ways of using new knowledge and opportunities made possible with technology should be a significant second focus of the research. A third area of activity involves the collection and analysis of data on the status of the system, which has been a function of the department since its original instantiation in 1867. Such data collection requires constant attention and improvement to provide the best possible information and data for researchers, policy makers, and the public to use.

This discussion of a more limited and focused role of the federal government implies a need to eliminate or consolidate a substantial number of current federal programs while refocusing others. We believe that such a consolidation should focus on two purposes. The first would be to support overall continuous improvement strategies in districts and schools; the second would be to kick-start within-district and among-district equalization strategies.

Role of State Governments to Ensure Quality and Opportunity

The basic roles of the states, granted to them under the 10th Amendment and built into their state constitutions and legislation, include responsibilities for all aspects of the education system from governance to finance to curriculum to supporting, enhancing, and monitoring quality education for all public school students in the state.[57]

---

[56] Preservation of anonymity and protection of human subjects can be more complex with qualitative data than with large-scale survey or assessment data, and demands for transparency and replication must be tempered by the feasibility of making these data available without jeopardizing the anonymity of particular individuals. See www.CreativeCommons.org for information about the Creative Commons licenses.

[57] States differ substantially in their political and administrative structures with respect to education. In some states, the state department of education exercises the primary leadership, policy, and administrative functions; in other states, the governor and state board of education have the primary leadership and policy roles. We refer to the state as a whole in this chapter, irrespective of which particular agency or branch of state government carries out a given function. Of course, similar variation in governance structure occurs at the local level; in some districts, the mayor has

In general, states delegate many of their responsibilities to local districts through legislation and their constitutions. They maintain full control of the responsibilities to actively build and monitor a legislative and regulatory framework that guides the districts as they implement much of the remainder of the responsibilities. States are responsible for decisions about common statewide content and performance standards, assessments, accountability, data collection requirements, and regulations about certifying and training teachers. They also manage and provide oversight for federal and state categorical programs. The financing of public education is generally shared, but state legislation or constitutions determine the framework for the finance system. Local districts manage the fundamental tasks of teaching and exercising the day-to-day responsibilities for educating the youth.

An unfortunate fact is that states and local governments and schools have implicitly or explicitly discriminated against low-income individuals and those of color in schools for well over a century. We have documented gaps between rich and poor schools and districts in finance, in prepared teachers, and in other materials in schools that provide clear evidence of these practices.

In order to move resolutely toward the goal of equal opportunity for all, states must develop, maintain and improve well-functioning education systems that support continuous improvement and high quality teaching and learning for all schools and students throughout the state. If the system is dysfunctional, the least advantaged among us will suffer the greatest.

We suggest three broad roles for the state in motivating and supporting educational quality and opportunity for all students:

- Establish a vision and set of priorities for educational improvement in the state—that is, to set the direction
- Provide resources and infrastructure to support continuous improvement toward this vision
- Establish a fair accountability system that stimulates action and tracks progress—particularly progress towards equity

Setting the Direction: State Standards and Priorities

We have already noted that robust and challenging standards for what students should know and be able to do can serve to define equity goals and guide continuous improvement toward those goals. Adoption and support for district implementation of new generation standards and assessments and establishing aligned policies to help guide curriculum development, educator training and accountability is an important role for states. As states transition to new standards and assessments and work to make the necessary changes in other parts of the system, it is especially crucial for them to pay attention to low-income districts, schools, and regions of the

---

substantial authority while in most others the superintendent and the local board are in charge. Again, we focus on the level of the system in general rather than on the roles of specific actors.

state that have fewer resources than others to carry out implementation. Analysis of statewide data can help states set priorities for moving forward to ensure that all students have access to the standards.

But standards and priorities are only one step toward setting direction for the state. Equally important is ensuring consistency in the signals to local districts and schools through consistent leadership and sustained commitment to improvement. This has been and continues to be a major challenge in the majority of states. All too often, state leaders do not have a deep understanding of the nature of the problems; state bureaucracies are locked into patterns that are directive and punitive rather than supportive; and lobby groups work to maintain current practices, often by guiding the votes of legislators and the behavior of the administrators. These practices will not change quickly, but they can be ameliorated over time. Though not yet fully successful, leaders in states such as Massachusetts, Connecticut, Minnesota, Texas, and now California have made substantial progress. The key is sustaining the work over time. One- or two-term leadership is not enough; change of the sort we describe here takes a decade or more to embed itself into the fabric of the system. The task is not easy—the commitment to sustain a policy direction that is based on continuous improvement and equal opportunity is difficult to keep up without succumbing to the siren call of "magic bullets." But it is necessary. And we suspect that strategic mobilization within the profession and among community stakeholders will be necessary to reach a common vision and ensure that state governments actually stay the course (see below).

Providing Resources and Infrastructure to Support Continuous Improvement and Equity

Standards and commitments will, of course, be meaningless without action to back them up. One of the most important roles for states to play is to provide the resources and build the infrastructure necessary to support local capacity for improvement and equity. We highlight three arenas in which state resources and infrastructure are most important: human capital, finance, and data.

A Strong Professional Workforce

Many states face serious human capital issues that hold back improvement and perpetuate inequity. These include teacher shortages, inadequate pre-service training, limited capacity of current teachers for teaching the new content or teaching all students, and a limited supply of well-trained principals. Moreover, the challenge of creating and maintaining a continuous improvement environment and implementing a thoughtful intervention system requires changes in the responsibilities of educators throughout the system. Education systems cannot provide high-quality schooling for all students without high-quality education professionals. The costs of building professional capacity may seem high, but the cost for not doing so is far higher.

States are in a critical position to ensure all students have access to high quality and effective school personnel. A first step is to support the recruitment of talented and interested people to enter the profession. Currently many young people do not see teaching as a desirable option because of a political atmosphere that seems to target teachers, relatively low pay, perceived job insecurity due to uncertain budgets and high-stakes accountability, and the poor reputation of teacher training programs.[58] State political leaders can join with university presidents and others to use the bully pulpit and incentives to upgrade the quality of pre-service training and increase the attractiveness of teaching.

A second step is to create the conditions for teachers and principals to grow in their jobs. High-quality mentoring in the first two years shows solid effects, and we have learned much in the past two decades about designing effective ongoing professional learning. A substantial new body of evidence, for example, indicates that both human and social capital are critical to the development of high-quality teachers and schools (Hargreaves and Fullan 2012). States can provide support to build a strong statewide infrastructure for professional development, including the creation of networks among teachers, schools, and districts. This is particularly important for low capacity and isolated regions of the state to ensure equity.

Finally, a critical role for the state is to ensure equitable access for all children to high-quality teachers. Specific tenure and seniority provisions in some state laws may exacerbate the low quality and ongoing churn of educators in schools and districts serving high needs students. The recent *Vergara* lawsuit in California was predicated on the idea that there is a set of laws and practices that systematically ensure that poor children, on average, have the least qualified and experienced teachers.[59] Whatever one's position is on the lawsuit per se, that the state has a role in ensuring equitable distribution of high-quality teachers should be undeniable. A first step would be to review potential disparate impact of policies currently in place and to improve working conditions in high-poverty schools.

The implications of not meeting these challenges will fall most heavily on the students most in need. The well-to-do communities of the nation will not suffer from the failures to meet these human capital challenges; they will get the first choices in a tight teacher market. It is the children in the central cities, the small, poor rural communities, and in other places where there are large populations of the low-income families that will suffer.

---

[58] See, for example, Jill Tucker, "Bay Area Schools Scramble for Qualified Teachers amid Shortage, *SFGate,* October 12, 2014, http://www.sfgate.com/education/article/Bay-Area-schools-scramble-for-qualified-teachers-5818410.php

[59] See the *Vergara v. California* entry in Wikipedia for background information on the suit, the specific state statutes involved, and additional citations. http://en.wikipedia.org/wiki/Vergara_v._California

Adequate and Fair Funding

We have already suggested something concrete the state governments might do to ensure finance equality across the districts state—legislate and implement a weighted pupil formula or an equivalent approach.[60] This action can be taken in the current environment, as demonstrated by California. It will require new revenue and time, but as we suggested earlier, the change could be spread over time and partially supported by the federal government. States should also seek ways to stimulate within-district equalization. Each of these actions would very positively alter the current unequal resource allocation problems in many states.

A fair and equitable finance system also must face the challenges of providing extra support for the groups of high-risk students that do not fit into the categories of the protected because of race or poverty. Special treatment is necessary for four additional groups of at-risk students that together may constitute up to 4–6 % of all of the nation's children in school: foster children (400,000 in the U.S.), children with incarcerated parents (2.7 million), homeless children (500,000 in any given year), and children/youth who suffer from a serious mental disorder (estimated four million nationally, many of whom are not served by special education).[61]

Effective Data Infrastructure

We have already considered the importance of data to continuous improvement; we believe the state is in the best position to ensure that the data infrastructure is sufficiently robust and adaptable. Beyond this the state must be able to point to examples of effective use of data as integral to continuous improvement and as offering a methodology for use throughout all of their districts and schools. This is particularly

---

[60] We recognize the difficulty of creating weighted pupil formulas in states where high percentages of school funding comes from local sources.

[61] Embedded in the federal education code are programs directed at some of these students, but even where there is a targeted program, the federal contribution to the support of the students is de minimis. For the federal homeless program, for example, the average support to a school for a homeless child is roughly $40 per year. Many states have similarly small programs for different groups of students. Others are unserved. Their in-school and out-of-school lives are chaotic and depressing, and each of these groups has a very high dropout rate. When they enter their teenage years, far too many suffer from drug or alcohol addiction and many of the males are eventually incarcerated. Even considering the overlaps among categories, the sum of students in these groups in any given year is likely between 2 and 3 million, or roughly 4–6 % of the public school children in the nation. For details on specific groups of these children, see the following sites: http://www.endhomelessness.org/ and http://www.mercurynews.com/breaking-news/ci_24294107/fears-another-lost-generation-youth-homeless-numbers-rising (homeless youth); http://www.osborneny.org/images/uploads/printMedia/Initiative%20CIP%20Stats_Fact%20Sheet.pdf; http://www.acf.hhs.gov/programs/cb/faq/foster-care4; and http://www.childtrends.org/?indicators=foster-care (foster youth); and http://www2.nami.org/Template.cfm?Section=federal_and_state_policy_legislation&template=/ContentManagement/ContentDisplay.cfm&ContentID=43804 (youth with mental disabilities).

important in low-capacity regions and districts that cannot do all the needed data work on their own.

Establishing an Accountability System that Supports Improvement

We expect that in the next few years, the locus of education accountability will largely shift from the federal to the state governments. Although they have shared the responsibility in law, the federal government has dominated since NCLB was passed in 2002. Over the past 25 years, the concept of accountability has driven a lot of positive and negative activity in schools and districts. For much of this time, accountability has been a one-way street. Schools and teachers have been held accountable for performance goals set by the federal government and states have been required to meet these goals to avoid being penalized. Only in extreme situations did districts face consequences for failing to meet performance goals, and never for failing to provide sufficient resources or assistance to their low-performing schools. The idea of reciprocity was not part of the mix.

In reciprocal accountability, the entities that hold schools and teachers accountable and control the provision of resources should share in the responsibility for the quality of the practices and student outcomes. Few would argue this premise. Yet while we acknowledge and document that many schools that are predominantly poor and African-American or Hispanic do not receive even the same level of resources as schools of the well-to-do (much less the level of resources they need), we still hold them to the same standards as the largely well-to-do schools.

For a high-stakes assessment to be fair, all students should have equitable opportunities and resources (Messick 1989). Clear and understandable reviews of the resource quality of a school and district should be conducted regularly. States should review their internal frameworks for assessing quality to make reasoned judgments about the opportunities available in districts and schools. Performance and quality measures for schools and districts should be transparent and reported.

The discussions about accountability are almost all focused on the details: How many years of testing should there be? Should the goals be set for 3, 5, or 10 years? Should we require penalties? As the states take over the responsibility to design and manage their accountability system, state leaders should first step back and decide what they want to accomplish. If they want a valid and effective system, they first need to address the glaring issues of inequality. They might also establish goals as well as monitor and provide support to districts and schools that have trouble maintaining progress. Reasonable long-term state goals might be high-quality education for all and equal outcomes for all subgroups of students. An overall short-term goal would be steady progress on the quality and outcome indicators by schools, districts and the state.

District Responsibilities

Of all the levels of governance, local districts have the most direct influence on what happens in schools. They are responsible for recruiting, assigning and supporting teachers; setting instructional policy; ensuring appropriate and efficient management of schools; allocating resources; and establishing an infrastructure to support system learning and ensure equity. The approaches that districts take to accomplishing these tasks will vary depending on the students they serve and the conditions in which they operate. There are 13,500 public school districts and 95,000 schools in the United States. Almost two-thirds of districts have fewer than 1500 students.

Among this diverse population of local systems are varying capacities and challenges. Most small districts, for example, rely on regional or county offices of education to provide expertise about technology, teacher recruitment, special education, and other federal and state programs and policies. Traditionally the quality of reform implementation will depend on the capacity of the state and regional entities to reach out and provide support. Right now the support role of these organizations often conflicts with their regulatory responsibilities, which often take precedence. We suggest that the balance needs to shift more toward improvement and support at all levels, particularly the local level, where it is likely to make the most difference. If the responsibilities of the federal government and states shifted more toward improvement in the ways we have suggested, the local and regional organizations could focus more effectively on improvement as well. This would be beneficial both to smaller, lower-capacity districts and to larger systems with greater capacity that have often been thwarted in efforts to more effectively serve the students by fragmented, compliance-oriented state laws and agencies.

We see four main arenas in which district action can motivate and support both quality and equality. The first concerns districts' role in establishing a culture of continuous improvement focused on the success of all students. We have already described several systems that have demonstrated some success in this regard. These are systems that have established common goals and metrics to measure progress toward attaining those goals. Particularly important is that the metrics include information that allows system and school leaders to identify specific gaps and areas for improvement. Dashboards reflecting these multiple measures can allow district leaders to allocate attention and resources (including human, material, and intellectual resources) to address identified problems of practice. Providing support for cross-school and cross-functional collaboration and learning, in addition to establishing a culture of trust where failure is understood and used as an opportunity for growth, are also part and parcel of such a system.

A second arena in which districts can foster positive change is through the establishment of a systemic approach to equitable resource allocation based on student and school needs. There are various models for more effective within-district allocation, all of which rely on clear alignment between system goals and budgeting processes. Whatever budgeting system a district uses, monitoring the effectiveness of programs and strategies is crucial to ensure that resources flow to more effective strategies and less effective ones are pruned away or revised.

Of course, the district's most valuable resources are its people, particularly its teachers and administrators. Thus, establishing an effective human capital system that ensures quality and supports continuous learning is perhaps the district's most critical function. Although educator quality is a goal at all levels of the system, districts have particular roles to play at key junctures: recruitment, tenure decisions, and evaluation cycles. Because the pools from which districts and schools recruit staff are primarily local, some districts have even established relationships with local pre-service programs or established their own teacher residency and adminis-trator training programs to ensure that those pools are filled with candidates likely to meet their needs. And once hiring decisions have been made, districts can do a great deal to provide structure, time, and support for coordinated learning within and across schools and to engage teachers and administrators as professionals in their own learning processes. In all these functions, as well as in negotiating con-tracts, building a strong and productive relationship with the unions is critical and generally beyond the capacity of individual schools.

A final role is to engage the broader public, manage the inevitable politics of American education at the local level, and connect schools and students with other child-related agencies and organizations that can help address students' broader needs. For many larger districts, these reforms would be carried out in intensely political environments. School boards are often steppingstones to higher elected office. Campaigns cost money that needs to be raised from donors. Local boards generally accept state law and regulation—but may greatly influence the implemen-tation of the reforms. Unfortunately school boards in these cities routinely roll over their superintendents every three to five years and seem to be always on the outlook for "magic bullets" that will assuredly and easily raise student achievement. Stability, focus, adaptation, and a continuous strategy and commitment to meeting the needs of all students are a recipe that is only attractive when your constituency is seen to be benefiting.

Increasing Professional Accountability and Support

Governmental and administrative policy, no matter how well designed, is insuffi-cient to achieve the goals we have described. We see the education profession itself as a needed second source of both pressure and support for improvement. Decades of policy implementation research have demonstrated that teaching is too complex to be effectively governed by bureaucratically defined rules and routines. Teachers not only require specialized knowledge, as do all professionals, but must be able to apply their knowledge and skills in specific contexts (students, content, school set-ting, etc.) to the benefit of their clients (students). In mature professions, the requi-site knowledge is articulated in professionally determined standards of practice, and members of the profession assume responsibility for defining and enforcing those standards. This is professional accountability.

In earlier work, O'Day (2002, 2008) argued that professional accountability offered a promising complement to policy actions in support of improvement by focusing attention on the core process of instruction, the need for ongoing learning of the adults in the system, and the norms of professional interchange. By professional interchange, we mean placing the needs of the client at the center of professional work, collaborating with other professionals to address those needs, and committing to the improvement of practice as part and parcel of professional responsibility.

Professional accountability is thus closely tied with the more recent concept of professional capital put forward by Andy Hargreaves and Michael Fullan (2012). Defining professional capital as comprising human capital (knowledge and skills), social capital (relationships among professionals and between professionals and other stakeholders), and decisional capital (the ability to make discretionary decisions), these authors use the experience of Ontario and other school systems to argue that professional capital sits at the heart of effective efforts to improve outcomes for students.

Professional accountability/professional capital can motivate and support continuous improvement and equity in education in several ways (O'Day 2008). First, the focus on both instructionally relevant processes and student outcomes sets the stage for improvement cycles in which actions are systematically related to results in an ongoing progression of individual and organizational learning. Second, the emphasis on professional knowledge makes it more likely that educators will be able to posit reasonable hypotheses within those cycles and interpret and act on the information they receive. Third, inculcating norms of professional collaboration will increasingly put educators into situations in which they can benefit from the knowledge and skills of peer; when this collaboration reaches across contexts, it will provide opportunities for educators to challenge their own and each others' existing assumptions about the capabilities of students and effective practices. Fourth, professional accountability expands the incentives for improvement, with particular emphasis on the intrinsic motivators that bring teachers into teaching in the first place—a commitment to students and identity as an educator (O'Day 1996; Finnigan and Gross 2007; McLaughlin and Talbert 2001). Finally, to the extent that the profession's focus on the needs of clients encompasses a commitment to reducing opportunity and outcome disparities, professional accountability can help sustain an equity agenda over time.

We see the emergence of professional learning communities (PLCs) within and across school sites in recent years as a manifestation of the potential power of professional capital and professional accountability. Where they work well—as in Sanger Unified School District in California—PLCs operate as communities of practice (Wenger 2000) in which participants work together to address a shared problem of practice, developing common norms and tools to facilitate the process over time. They follow protocols similar to the Plan-Do-Study-Act cycles in which they identify a problem, plan how to address it, do what they set out to do, study the results—often through examination of assessment data or student work—and then act upon this information to refine the next cycle of inquiry and improvement. In Sanger, this process is structured around four key questions:

1. What do we want our students to learn?
2. How will we know when they have learned it?
3. How will we respond when learning has not occurred?
4. How will we respond when learning has already occurred?

Participation in the PLCs is seen as part of what it means to be a teacher in the school or district, and the patterns of professional responsibility and inquiry among teachers are mirrored in communities of principals and of administrators within the central office. In Sanger, PLCs have been the cornerstone of the improvement process since 2004 and have moved this high-poverty, high-English-learner district from being one of the lowest performing in the state to one that has been nationally recognized as a model of exceptional turnaround (David and Talbert 2013). Similar, if somewhat less pronounced, examples of a PLC-based strategy have occurred in districts across the U.S.

Professional associations and networks are also avenues for the development and diffusion of professional norms and practices and can be vehicles for taking the principles of PLCs and continuous improvement to scale across districts and even across states. Organizations like the National Council of Teachers of Mathematics or the California Subject Matter Projects have been significant forces for changing teaching practices and norms and for maintaining relationships among discipline-based professionals over time. Recently, efforts to implement the Common Core State Standards have become a focal point for the work of many such networks and professional associations, with the commonality of the standards providing the basis for collaboration across contexts. Networks of schools or districts are playing a similar role at the organizational level, providing opportunities for mutual learning and improvement.

The ten CORE districts in California, for example, have developed common metrics and are engaged in mutual learning activities to implement the Common Core State Standards, increase achievement and attainment, and reduce disparities for the over one million students they collectively serve.[62] Their efforts have become models for others in the state and have helped to inspire similar partnerships among groups of smaller districts focused on shared problems, such as improving instruction and outcomes for California's substantial population of English language learners. It is important to note that while these are formal partnerships across school systems, it is the professional learning and relationships within them that drive the work. It is also important to note, in the context of this volume, that the focus in these efforts is on improving both quality and equality within the educational systems involved.

---

[62] The district partners in CORE include Los Angeles, Long Beach, Garden Grove, Santa Ana, Fresno, Sanger, Clovis, Sacramento City, San Francisco, and Oakland Unified School Districts.

Mobilizing an Engaged Citizenry

Professional accountability is not enough, however. There have been many examples in recent years of equity-focused reform efforts—even some with fair support among educators—that fell to partisan politics and pushback from a public that didn't understand or agree with the rationale for the changes. Often, public and political support for the status quo is based on deep-seated beliefs about meritocracy, the scarcity of educational goods, and the inability of some children to take advantage of opportunities when offered (Oakes and Lipton 2006). Behind these beliefs sits a power structure that preserves advantages for wealthier and more privileged communities at the expense not only of less privileged communities but also the nation as a whole (Stiglitz 2012). To create and sustain meaningful policies and practices to equalize opportunities for low-income students and students of color requires more than technical solutions and more than an engaged profession. It also requires public constituency and mobilization.

We see this mobilization as necessarily occurring on two levels. One is the coordination of efforts at the "grass tops"—that is through building coalitions among the leaders of the many education stakeholder groups—everyone from higher education institutions to employer groups, parent organizations, advocacy and civil rights groups, and health care and community-based organizations that work with children in other capacities. Political figures and public agency representatives may be a part of these coalitions, but they focus primarily on gathering support and involvement of organized constituencies outside the more formal education system and political structure.

In the past few years, the social sector has seen increased interest in and use of collective impact strategies that employ such coalition efforts to address particularly intractable and complex social problems. The concept of collective impact seems to have emerged from the Strive Together initiative in Cincinnati, which brought together local leaders to tackle the student achievement crisis in greater Cincinnati and northern Kentucky. Defining system change as community-wide transformation in which various partners (a) productively use data to improve their decision making and (b) constantly weigh the impact of their decisions on both their own institutions and the broader ecosystem that work to improve the lives of children, the leaders of Strive Together posited a four-pillar theory of action for collective impact: establishing a shared community vision, instituting evidence-based decision-making and shared accountability among the partners to improve selected outcomes, using continuous improvement approaches to identify and spread promising practices to improve community-level outcomes, and aligning financial and other resources to support and sustain improvement (Edmondson and Hecht 2014, 6–7).

Though Strive Together may have coined the phrase, others have instituted similar collective efforts, sometimes over decades (e.g., El Paso). All are based on the theme that cross-sector, cross-organization coordination is more likely to contribute to large-scale, sustained social change than are the isolated actions of individual organizations and agencies. Within this coordinated approach, the goal of eliminating disparities is a core principle. While such partnerships are not without their challenges, they not only lead to greater short-term success but can also build an infrastructure for identifying shared interests and maintaining a focus on addressing inequities across changes in superintendents and political environments.

In addition to grass-tops approaches like collective impact strategies, grass roots organizations and social movements can create pressure for maintaining focus on equal opportunities within and beyond education. One goal of community-organizing efforts in education is to ensure the accountability of policy makers and local education leaders to students, parents, and the community for providing full opportunities to students in high-poverty communities and communities of color (Renee and McAlister 2011). The power of community organizing comes from the base of community members, rather than an elite set of leaders.

While much of community organizing is adversarial in nature, intended to keep up the pressure for addressing the needs of underserved students, organizing can also provide important support to local school districts. Working in conjunction with researchers and educators, local community members can help to identify problems requiring attention, gather data not available to most educators, and maintain consistency of focus across changes in leadership and conditions (Oakes and Lipton 2006). Such has been the case, for example, in efforts in Oakland and Los Angeles as these districts have confronted and eliminated discriminatory discipline and suspension policies that systematically denied children of color, particularly boys and young men, access to classroom instruction.[63] Community organizing has contributed to documented success in increasing and more equitably distributing educational resources, ensuring access to college preparatory curricula, and establishing more effective recruitment and retention strategies in hard-to-staff schools.

Conclusion

We began this chapter with a brief review of how curtailed opportunities outside school exacerbate, and are exacerbated by, those inside the educational system to virtually disenfranchise large numbers of low-income students and students of color and perpetuate conditions of poverty across generations. We have offered a set of lessons from decades of education reform efforts and have applied those to

---

[63] For example, the Urban Strategies Council in Oakland was instrumental in analyzing data that led to an agreement between the district and the OCR to address egregious disparities in suspension and expulsions of African-American and Latino boys. In Los Angeles, community demonstrations supported efforts of the district administration to push for school board policies that ended use of the ambiguous and racially discriminatory "willful defiance" justification for suspension and that decriminalized all but the most dangerous infractions of school policy. Over a five-year period from 2007–2008 to 2012–2013, the suspension rate declined from 8.1 to 1.5 %, moving from almost 75,000 days lost to a little over 12,000. (See *LA School Report*, October 14, 2013. Retrieved at http://laschoolreport.com/la-unified-suspension-rate-accelerating-down-to-1-5-percent/) Keeping students in classrooms is a critical aspect of ensuring equity and access.

sketching out how a more equitable system might operate. And we have suggested a three-pronged strategy of governmental action, professional networking and accountability, and public engagement and constituency building to provide the pressure and support for moving in this direction. But is such an approach possible at scale? Examples like Montgomery County, MD, and Long Beach, CA, provide some evidence of feasibility at the local level. But what about whole states—and, in particular, what about those that are currently failing so many of the nation's poor students and those of color?

Recent developments in California provide some basis for optimism and help demonstrate how the sources of pressure and support can possibly work together to turn a diverse and complex state in the direction of equity and long-term improvement.[64] Let's be clear: We neither offer California as an exemplar of a mature continuously improving system, nor as one that has demonstrated extraordinary achievement for its traditionally underserved students. Rather, we suggest that the state has taken an important step forward, building a foundation for equity and improvement that was almost unimaginable even five short years ago.

Let's begin with a little context. California educates over 6.2 million students, or about one in every eight public school children in the U.S. California's students are among the most diverse and disadvantaged in the nation, with approximately 59 % coming from low-income families, compared with 48 % nationally.[65] Seventy-five percent are students of color, including 53 % Hispanics, 9 % Asian-Americans, and 6 % African-Americans, among others. Over 1.4 million, or 23 %, of the state's students are officially classified as English language learners, compared to 9.1 % nationally (Snyder 2014). California's ELLs represent by far the largest number and percent of such students among all U.S. states—indeed, almost one-third of English learners in the U.S. attend school in the Golden State.

The state has not done well by this increasingly diverse population of students. In 2013, California students who were eligible for free and reduced-price lunches ranked from 49th (grade 4 math) to 42nd (grade 8 reading) among similarly low-income students in other states on NAEP. And achievement gaps (between Whites and African-Americans or Hispanic students and between those eligible and not eligible for the school lunch program) were similar to the corresponding gaps nationally, ranging from 25 to 33 points—or about 2.3 to three grade levels across both subjects and grades.

A major reason for this poor performance in the past few decades has been California's dysfunctional system of education—found "fundamentally flawed" by a massive independent investigation of the state's school finance and governance

---

[64] For a more detailed discussion of the current policy environment in California and the approach and actions that led to the changes, see O'Day 2015.

[65] These figures use eligibility for free and reduced price lunches as a proxy for low income. Data for California come from the California Department of Education Data Quest figures for 2013–14. The national figure is taken from the Southern Education Foundation (2013) and pertains to 2011 enrollment.

systems in 2007 (Loeb et al. 2008, 8). Among the themes of the 23 independent reports of this "Getting Down to Facts" (GDTF) investigation were the following:

- Overregulation and proliferation of categorical funding streams had led to fragmentation, contradictory policies, and an emphasis on compliance over effective teaching and learning;
- Funding for education was sorely inadequate (lagging well behind national averages and difficult to increase due to Proposition 13's constitutional cap on property taxes), unnecessarily complex, and "inequitable by any measures";
- The state lacked a coherent system for recruiting, developing, and retaining high-quality teachers; and
- Administrators had neither the data systems nor analytic capacity to enable system learning and improvement.

Mistrust and lack of leadership at the state level delayed action on the synthesis report's recommendations, and less than a year after it was released, California was plunged into a severe fiscal crisis. Already inadequate district budgets were slashed. Teachers and administrators were laid off, class sizes soared, and most legislators and education leaders were too busy treading water to see a way forward.

That was six years ago. Today the policy landscape and prospects for the future have taken a decided turn for the better. Passage of Proposition 30 in November 2012 brought $6 billion per year in new revenues into state coffers, directed primarily at K-12 and higher education (Fensterwald 2014). The Local Control Funding Formula (LCFF) passed in June 2013 has simplified the school finance system, ensured greater equity for targeted student populations across (and hopefully within) school districts, and provided flexibility so that local educators can develop coherent strategies for serving their students and communities. Moreover, stakeholder groups across the state—including the California Teachers Association, state legislators and administrators, higher education and business leaders, advocacy groups, and local educators—have united in support of the Common Core State Standards, and the state legislature allocated an additional $1.25 billion explicitly for implementation in 2013. Perhaps most surprising, the prevalent attitude appears to be on digging in for the long haul, and talk of "capacity building" and "continuous improvement" have become more common, even among politicians in Sacramento.

Many factors have combined to create this new window of opportunity in California education. We highlight a few of these, using the framework of the three sources of pressure and support outlined in the previous section.

Restraining the Role of Government: Focusing on the Long Term

California is an excellent example of how restraining and focusing the role of government can lay the groundwork for greater equity and improvement. With the election of Jerry Brown in 2010, the state's leadership team set out a methodical plan to accomplish two goals: right the broken funding and governance system, and provide coherent support for deep transition to the Common Core at the school and classroom levels. A first step was restoring funding for education as the state began its economic recovery; without this move, the other steps would have been difficult, if not impossible, both politically and fiscally. But at the heart of the fiscal transformation has been passage and implementation of the LCFF, which has two major components: (a) a more equitable allocation formula to districts, based on the numbers of students, with additional weights for counts and concentrations of students in poverty, English learners, and foster youth; and (b) the removal of categorical funding streams, and with them, the myriad of conflicting, burdensome, and top-down regulations that made it difficult for local districts to develop coherent, context-specific improvement strategies.

The second focus has been to support effective implementation of the Common Core. The governor, State Board of Education, Department of Education, and state legislature have all united around this goal, and the legislature's allocation of an additional $1.25 billion for capacity building for Common Core standards implementation had both symbolic and material benefits toward its realization. In addition, policies for curriculum and instructional guidance (recommendations of texts and development of instructional frameworks), teacher licensure, admissions criteria for the state's public universities, and accountability systems have been or are being aligned to support Common Core implementation. Each of these areas reflects the same state restraint as in LCFF, with the state playing a supportive and advisory role and placing much greater discretion with districts to respond to their local contexts.

Perhaps one of the boldest and most illustrative moves of the state was the decision to end use of the existing California Standards Tests in spring 2014, before the new Common Core standards-aligned assessments were ready for full implementation. Believing that continued administration of the old tests would send mixed signals to teachers and schools—and recognizing that students and adults could benefit from a run-through with the new assessment formats and technology—state leaders pushed back against accountability demands from the federal government and instead expanded the Smarter Balanced Assessment Consortium (SBAC) field test to include all students in the relevant grades across the state. This move was accompanied by a systematic collection and analysis of data on the implementation of the field test to inform state and local leaders about their readiness for the official SBAC administration set for spring 2015.

State leaders have also maintained focus by eschewing "reforms" that they believed were not in the best interests of the state or would detract from the fiscal and Common Core foci. Most notably, they declined to apply for an NCLB waiver because it would have required creation of a state test-based teacher evaluation system, which they felt would both violate state law and jeopardize the emerging coalition in support of Common Core implementation.

Building Public and Stakeholder Constituency for Improvement

None of the changes above would have been possible without the ongoing mobilization both of the leaders ("grass tops") of education stakeholder groups in the state and grassroots organizing among parents and voters in the communities. Community organizers along with statewide advocacy groups and professional associations rallied support for passage of Proposition 30 in 2012, which brought new dollars into the system through institution of a tax on the wealthiest 3 % of Californians. These same organizations remained active in the massive effort to press the state legislature to pass LCFF and have been involved in providing input into its refinement over the past two years. Indeed, local community and parent input is a core requirement in the development of the Local Control Accountability Plan, in which each district outlines its locally determined goals and allocations for addressing the general state priorities in education.

The momentum and sense of accomplishment from the successful LCFF campaign has also carried over to a sense of optimism and common purpose around Common Core implementation. Informal stakeholder meetings in 2013 led to the formation of a statewide Consortium for Implementation of the Common Core, with involvement from state agencies, local districts, county offices of education, charter management organizations, business, higher education, advocacy groups, teachers unions, and professional associations. The purpose of this consortium is to enable coordination of effort, fill in gaps where needed and feasible, and maintain an active broad-based constituency of support for continuous improvement and standards implementation.

Leveraging and Strengthening Professional Networks

Of course, the heart of educational improvement relies on building professional engagement, commitment, and capacity—including the needed social capital to spread more effective practices. In California this has taken the form of involving professional associations and the teachers unions in Common Core coalitions, as well as mobilizing professional networks like the California Subject Matter Projects to focus teacher attention and learning on the knowledge and practices needed for effective Common Core-aligned instruction. Leading districts in the state have provided exemplars of continuous improvement strategies, and networks and partnerships of local districts have generated opportunities for focused learning across contexts and across levels of the systems involved.

A combination of pressure and support from each of these arenas has been instrumental in laying the foundation for a more equitable state education system and one that enables rather than precludes a continuous, standards-based approach to improvement. Yet California's progress in this direction is still precarious, and several key challenges face state policy makers and local educators over the next few years.

First, it is unclear what will happen when the expectedly low results of the new SBAC assessments are released in summer 2015: Will the public and its politicians have the patience for the long-term improvement process needed? Second, it is also unclear whether the local planning processes put in place for LCFF will generate the kinds of strategic coherence and consistency needed to ensure deep and equitable implementation of the new standards. Trust between equity advocates and local educators is still inchoate, and LCFF remains an experiment in the eyes of many. If results for traditionally underserved students are insufficiently transparent or compelling, the pullback to categorical funding streams and requirements will be strong—and demoralizing. A third challenge is the as-yet-undefined nature of the new accountability system and the lack of a unified vision for accountability that can actually support continuous improvement. Finally, the greatest challenge is the most obvious: How will the state build the individual and organizational capacity at the local level to enable the instructional shifts in classrooms across the state? California has almost 300,000 teachers, and they carry the burden for success of the Common Core and of the education enterprise more generally. Establishing the infrastructure to support them in this transition is an unprecedented challenge that the state has yet to fully address.

We have ended with an extended description of the situation in California because we believe that it provides reasons for hope as well as lessons for other states and jurisdictions. If we can move education in the most complex and challenging state system in the country, then other less troubled and more successful systems should also be able to make progress. California's example suggests the importance of both leadership and stakeholder engagement, of flexibility combined with coherence and focus, and of adequacy and equity of resources.

It also suggests the magnitude of the challenge to take such a vision to all of the other 49 states. Yet, there is hope and some evidence that change is possible. There are scattered examples of states such as Massachusetts and Texas that have proposed reforms and stayed with them over at least a decade. A substantial number of districts across the country have moved toward continuous improvement models as the core of their reforms, based on a growing recognition that accountability without investment in improvement does not work. Networks of superintendents and teachers exist in many states. Almost everyone in education understands we need standards and curricula that prepare students for intellectually rigorous work and that teachers need substantial support to implement the new curricula. Many of the ingredients for serious reform exist—this story is not over.

References

Abelmann, Charles, Richard Elmore, Johanna Even, Susan Kenyon, and Joanne Marshall. 1999. *When accountability knocks, will anyone answer?* CPRE Research Report RR-42. Philadelphia: University of Pennsylvania, Consortium for Policy Research in Education.

Adamson, Frank, and Linda Darling-Hammond. 2011. *Speaking of salaries: What it will take to get qualified, effective teachers in all communities.* Washington, DC: Center for American Progress.

Allensworth, Elaine M., and John Q. Easton. 2007. *What matters for staying on track and graduating in Chicago public high schools.* Chicago, IL: Consortium on Chicago School Research. Accessed 17 Dec 2014.

Anderson, Eric M., and James C. Gulek. 2008. *Evaluation of MAP2D elementary math program.* Long Beach Unified School District, Office of Research, Planning and Evaluation.

Austin, James E., Jennifer M. Suesse, and Robert B. Schwartz. 2004. *Long Beach Unified School District (A): Change that leads to improvement (1992–2002).* Cambridge, MA: Harvard University, Public Education Leadership Project.

Austin, James E., Allen Grossman, Robert B. Schwartz, and Jennifer M. Suesse. 2006. *Managing at Scale in the Long Beach Unified School District.* Cambridge, MA: Harvard University, Public Education Leadership Project.

Beaver, Jessica K., and Elliot H. Weinbaum. 2012. *Measuring school capacity, maximizing school improvement,* CPRE Policy Brief RB-53. Philadelphia: University of Pennsylvania, Consortium for Policy Research in Education.

Berger, Andrea, Nancy Adelman, and Susan Cole. 2010. The early college high school initiative: An overview of five evaluation years. *Peabody Journal of Education* 85(3): 333–347.

Berliner, David. 2011. Rational responses to high stakes testing: The case of curriculum narrowing and the harm that follows. *Cambridge Journal of Education* 41(3): 287–302.

Bialystok, Ellen. 2011. Reshaping the mind: The benefits of bilingualism. *Revue Canadienne de Psychologie Expérimentale* (Canadian Journal of Experimental Psychology) 65(4): 229–235.

Black, Paul, and Dylan Wiliam. 2009. *Developing the theory of formative assessment. education assessment evaluation and accountability* 21: 5–31. http://teacherscollegesj.edu/docs/47-developingthetheoryofformativeassessment_12262012101200.pdf.

Bohrnstedt, George W., and Brian M. Stecher (eds.). 2002. *What we have learned about class size reduction in California.* Sacramento: California Department of Education.

Boser, Ulrich, Megan Wilhelm, and Robert Hanna. 2014. *Power of the Pygmalion effect: Teachers' expectations strongly predict college completion.* Washington, DC: Center for American Progress.

Bransford, John D., Ann L. Brown, and Rodney R. Cocking. 2015. *How people learn: Brain, mind, experience, and school,* Expanded ed. Washington, DC: National Academies Press.

Bryk, Anthony S., Penny Bender Sebring, Elaine Allensworth, John Q. Easton, and Stuart Luppescu. 2010. *Organizing schools for improvement: Lessons from Chicago.* Chicago: University of Chicago Press.

Bryk, Anthony, M. Louis, and Grunow Alicia. 2011. Getting ideas into action: Building networked improvement communities in education. In *Frontiers in sociology of education,* ed. Maureen T. Hallinan. New York: Springer.

Caldas, Stephen J., and Carl Bankston. 1997. Effect of school population socioeconomic status on individual academic achievement. *Journal of Educational Research* 90(5): 269–277.

Carter, Samuel Casey. 1999. *No excuses: Lessons from 21 high-performing high-poverty schools.* Washington, DC: The Heritage Foundation.

Cawelti, Gordon. 2006. The side effects of NCLB. *Educational Leadership* 64(3): 64–68.

Children's Defense Fund. 2014. *The State of America's children: 2014.* Washington, DC: Author.

Clotfelter, Charles T., Helen F. Ladd, and Jacob L. Vigdor. 2010. Teacher credentials and student achievement in high school a cross-subject analysis with student fixed effects. *Journal of Human Resources* 45(3): 655–681.

Cohen, David K., Stephen W. Raudenbush, and Deborah Loewenberg Ball. 2003. Resources, instruction, and research. *Educational Evaluation and Policy Analysis* 25(2): 119–142.

Coleman, James S. 1988. Social capital in the creation of human capital. *American Journal of Sociology* 94(4): S95–S120.

Consortium for Policy Research in Education. 2013. *Evaluation of the i3 scale-up of reading recovery: Year one report, 2011–2012*, CPRE Research Report-76. Philadelphia: University of Pennsylvania, Consortium for Policy Research in Education.

Cunningham, Patricia M. 2006. High-poverty schools that beat the odds. *The Reading Teacher* 60(4): 382–385.

David, Jane L., and Joan E. Talbert. 2013. *Turning around a high-poverty district: Learning from Sanger*. San Francisco: Cowell Foundation.

Deming, David. 2009. Early childhood intervention and life-cycle skill development: Evidence from Head Start. *American Economic Journal: Applied Economics* 3(3): 111–34.

Dixon, Mark. 2014. *Public education finances: 2012: 2012 Census of governments*. Washington, DC: U.S. Census Bureau. http://www.census.gov/content/dam/Census/library/publications/2014/econ/g12-cg-aspef.pdf.

Dobbie, Will, and Roland G. Fryer Jr. 2011. Are high-quality schools enough to increase achievement among the poor? Evidence from the Harlem children's zone. *American Economic Journal: Applied Economics* 3(3): 158–87.

Duffy, Helen, Jim Brown, Stephanie Hannan, and Jennifer O'Day. 2011. *Separate paths, common goals: Cross-district collaboration on mathematics and english learner instruction*. San Mateo: California Collaborative on District Reform.

Duncan, Greg J., and Richard J. Murnane. 2014. *Restoring opportunity: The crisis of inequality and the challenge for American education*. Cambridge, MA: Harvard Education Press.

Durlak, Joseph A., Roger P. Weissberg, Allison B. Dymnicki, Rebecca D. Taylor, and Kriston B. Schellinger. 2011. The impact of enhancing students' social and emotional leaning: A meta-analysis of school-based universal interventions. *Child Development* 82(1): 405–432.

Dweck, Carol S. 2006. *Mindset: The new psychology of success*. New York: Random House.

Dweck, Carol. 2012. *Boosting achievement with messages that motivate*, Canadian Education Association. http://www.lib.usf.edu/tutoring/files/2012/02/Boosting_Achievement_Spring07-Dweck.pdf.

Edmondson, Jeff, and Ben Hecht. 2014. Defining quality collective impact. *Stanford Social Innovation Review* 8 (Fall), 6–7.

Equity and Excellence Commission. 2013. *For each and every child: A strategy for education equity and excellence*. Washington, DC: Author. http://www2.ed.gov/about/bdscomm/list/eec/equity-excellence-commission-report.pdf.

Fensterwald, John. 2014. "Latest—but outdated—Ed Week survey ranks California 50th in per pupil spending." *EdSource Today*, January 14, 2014.

Finnigan, Kara S., and Betheny Gross. 2007. Do accountability policy sanctions influence teacher motivation? Lessons from Chicago's low-performing schools. *American Educational Research Journal* 44(3): 594–630.

Fry, Richard, and Paul Taylor. 2012. *The rise of residential segregation by income*. Washington, DC: Pew Research Center.

Gawande, Atul. 2013. Slow ideas: Some innovations spread fast. How do you speed the ones that don't? *New Yorker*, July 29, 2013.

Gibbs, Chloe, Jens Ludwig, and Douglas L. Miller. 2011. *Does Head Start do any lasting good?* Working Paper 17452. Cambridge, MA: National Bureau of Economic Research.

Goldenberg, Claude. 2008. Teaching english language learners what the research does—and does not—say. *American Educator* 32(2): 8–44.

Grannis, Kerry S., and Isabel V. Sawhill. 2013. *Improving children's life chances: Estimates from the Social Genome Model*. Washington, DC: Brookings Institution.

Hargreaves, Andy, and Henry Braun. 2013. *Data-driven improvement and accountability*. Boulder: National Education Policy Center.

Hargreaves, Andy, and Michael Fullan. 2012. *Professional capital: Transforming teaching in every school*. New York: Teachers College Press.

Hart, Betty, and Todd L. Risley. 1995. *Meaningful differences in the everyday experience of young American children*. Baltimore: Brookes Publishing.

Heckman, James. 2011. The economics of inequality: The value of early childhood education. *American Educator* 2011, 34–47. https://www.aft.org//sites/default/files/periodicals/Heckman. pdf.

Henry, Gary T., C. Kevin Fortner, and Kevin C. Bastian. 2012. The effects of experience and attrition for novice high-school science and mathematics teachers. *Science* 335(6072): 1118–1121.

Honan, James P., Jennifer M. Suesse, and Robert B. Schwartz. 2004. *Long beach unified school district (B): Working to sustain improvement (2002–2004)*. Cambridge, MA: Public Education Leadership Project, Harvard University.

Houck, Eric A., and Elizabeth DeBray. Forthcoming. *The shift from adequacy to equity in federal education policymaking: A proposal: How ESEA could reshape the state role in education finance*. New York: Russell Sage Foundation.

Ingersoll, Richard M. 2004. *Why do high-poverty schools have difficulty staffing their classrooms with qualified teachers?* Washington, DC: Center for American Progress and Institute for America's Future.

Ingersoll, Richard, Lisa Merrill, and Daniel Stuckey. 2014. *Seven trends: The transformation of the teaching force, updated April 2014*, CPRE Report RR-80. Philadelphia: University of Pennsylvania, Consortium for Policy Research in Education.

Isenberg, Eric, Jeffrey Max, Phillip Gleason, Liz Potamites, Robert Santillano, Heinrich Hock, and Michael Hansen. 2013. *Access to effective teaching for disadvantaged students*. Washington, DC: Institute for Educational Sciences.

Jennings, Jack. 2015. *Presidents, Congress, and the public schools: The politics of education reform*. Cambridge, MA: Harvard Education Press.

Johnson, Evelyn S., Juli Pool, and Deborah R. Carter. n.d. *Screening for reading problems in grades 4 through 12*. New York: RTI Action Network, http://www.rtinetwork.org/essential/ assessment/screening/screening-for-reading-problems-in-grades-4-through-12.

Jyoti, Diana F., Edward A. Frongillo, and Sonya J. Jones. 2005. Food insecurity affects school children's academic performance, weight gain, and social skills. *Journal of Nutrition* 135(12): 2831–2839.

Kane, Thomas, J., Jonah E. Rockoff, and Douglas O. Steiger. 2006. *What does certification tell us about teacher effectiveness? Evidence from New York city*, NBER Working Paper 12155. Cambridge, MA: National Bureau of Economic Research. http://www.nber.org/papers/ w12155.pdf.

Kannapel, Patricia. J., and Stephen K. Clements, with Diana Taylor and Terry Hibpshman. 2005. *Inside the black box of high-performing high-poverty schools*. Lexington: Prichard Committee for Academic Excellence.

Kieffer, Michael J., William H. Marinell, and Nicky Stephenson. 2011. *The middle grade student transitions study: Navigating the middle grades and preparing students for high school graduation*. New York: New York University, Research Alliance for New York City Schools. http:// steinhardt.nyu.edu/scmsAdmin/media/users/jnw216/RANYCS/WebDocs/MiddleGradesTransitions-WorkingBrief-Final.pdf.

Kirp, David L. 2013. *Improbable scholars: The rebirth of a great American school system and a strategy for America's schools*. Oxford: Oxford University Press.

Knudson, Joel. 2013. *You'll never be better than your teachers: The Garden Grove approach to human capital development*. San Mateo: California Collaborative on District Reform. http:// cacollaborative.org/publication/youll-never-be-better-your-teachers-garden-grove-approach-human-capital-development.

Langley, Gerald J., Moen Ronald, Kevin M. Nolan, Thomas W. Nolan, Clifford L. Norman, and Lloyd P. Provost. 2009. *The improvement guide: A practical approach to enhancing organizational performance*. San Francisco: Jossey-Bass.

Latimer, Jeff, and Steven Kleinknecht. 2000. *The effects of restorative justice program: A review of the empirical*. Ottawa: Department of Justice Ottawa, Canada.

Lhamon, Catherine E. 2014. *Dear colleague letter: Resource comparability*. Washington, DC: Office of Civil Rights, U.S. Department of Education, October 1. http://www2.ed.gov/about/offices/list/ocr/letters/colleague-resourcecomp-201410.pdf.

Lippman, Laura, Shelley Burns, and Edith McArthur, Statistics. 1996. *Urban schools: The challenge of location and poverty,* Washington, DC: U.S. Department of Education, National Center for Education Statistics. http://nces.ed.gov/pubs/96184all.pdf.

Loeb, Susanna, Anthony Bryk, and Eric Hanushek. 2008. Getting down to facts: School finance and governance in California. *Education Finance and Policy* 3(1): 1–19.

Marian, Viorica, Anthony Shook, and Scott R. Schroeder. 2013. Bilingual two-way immersion programs benefit academic achievement. *Bilingual Research Journal* 36: 167–186.

Massey, Douglas S., and Nancy A. Denton. 1993. *American apartheid: Segregation and the making of the underclass*. Cambridge, MA: Harvard University Press.

McClintock, Nathan. 2008. *From industrial garden to food desert: Unearthing the root structure of urban agriculture in Oakland CA*, ISIS Fellows Working Paper 2007-08.32. Berkeley: University of California-Berkeley, Institute for the Study of Societal Issues. http://escholarship.org/uc/item/1wh3v1sj.

McLaughlin, Milbrey Wallin. 1987. Learning from experience: Lessons from policy implementation. *Educational Evaluation and Policy Analysis* 9(2): 171–178.

McLaughlin, Milbrey, and Joan Talbert. 2001. *Professional communities and the work of high school teaching*. Chicago: The University of Chicago Press.

Messick, Samuel. 1989. Validity. In *Educational measurement*, 3rd ed, ed. R.L. Linn, 13–103. New York: American Council of Education.

Meyer, Anne, David H. Rose, and David Gordon. 2014. *Universal design for learning: Theory and practice*, Wakefield: CAST. http://www.cast.org/our-work/publications/2014/universal-design-learning-theory-practice-udl-meyer.html#.VTa1cGbxpek.

Murnane, Richard J. 2013. U.S. high school graduation rates: Patterns and explanations. *Journal of Economic Literature* 51(June): 370–422.

Neild, Ruth C. 2009. Falling off track during the transition to high school: What we know and what could be done. *The Future of Children* 19 (1). http://futureofchildren.org/publications/journals/article/index.xml?journalid=30andarticleid=38andsectionid=84.

New America Foundation. 2012. *School finance inequity*. Federal Education Budget Project. http://febp.newamerica.net/k12/rankings/schofiineq/print.

Newmann, Fred M., Bets Ann Smith, Elaine Allensworth, and Anthony S. Bryk. 2001. Instructional program coherence: What it is and why it should guide school improvement policy. *Educational Evaluation and Policy Analysis* 23(4): 297–321.

Oakes, Jeannie, and Martin Lipton. 2006. *Teaching to change the world*, 3rd ed. New York: McGraw-Hill Higher Education.

O'Day, Jennifer A. 1996. Introduction: Incentives and improvement. In *Rewards and reform: Creating educational incentives that work*, ed. Susan H. Fuhrman and Jennifer A. O'Day, 1–16. San Francisco: Jossey-Bass.

O'Day, Jennifer A. 2002. Complexity, accountability, and school improvement. *Harvard Educational Review* 72(3): 293–329.

O'Day, Jennifer A. 2008. NCLB and the complexity of school improvement. In *No Child Left Behind and the reduction of the achievement gap: Sociological perspectives on federal educational policy*, ed. Alan R. Sadovnik, Jennifer A. O'Day, George W. Bohrnstedt, and Kathryn M. Borman. London: Routledge.

O'Day, Jennifer A. 2015. A window of opportunity: The politics and policies of Common Core implementation in California. In *Challenging standards: Navigating conflict and building capacity in the era of the Common Core*, ed. Jonathan A. Supovitz and Spillane James. Lanham: Rowman & Littlefield Publishers.

O'Day, Jennifer A., and Marshall Smith. 1993. Systemic reform and educational opportunity. In *Designing coherent education policy: Improving the system*, ed. Susan Fuhrman, 250–312. San Francisco: Jossey-Bass.

Orfield, Gary. 2009. *Reviving the goal of an integrated society: A 21st century challenge*. Los Angeles: Civil Rights Project/Proyecto Derechos Civiles. January.

Orfield, Gary. 2013. Housing segregation produces unequal schools: Causes and solutions. In *Closing the achievement and opportunity gap: What America must do to give every child an even chance*, ed. Prudence L. Carter and Kevin G. Welner, 40–60. New York: Oxford University Press.

Owens, Ann, Sean F. Reardon, and Christopher Jencks. 2014. *Trends in school economic segregation, 1970 to 2010*. http://cepa.stanford.edu/content/trends-school-economic-segregation-1970-2010.

Papay, John, P., and Matthew A. Kraft. Forthcoming. Productivity returns to experience in the teacher labor market: Methodological challenges and new evidence on long-term career improvement. *Journal of Economics*.

Park, Sandra, Stephanie Hironaka, Penny Carver, and Nordstrum Lee. 2012. *Continuous improvement in education*. Stanford: Carnegie Foundation.

Perry, Laura, and Andrew McConney. 2010. Does the SES of the school matter? An examination of socioeconomic status and student achievement using PISA 2003. *Teachers College Record* 112(4): 7–8.

Purkey, Stewart C., and Marshall S. Smith. 1983. Effective schools: A review. *Elementary School Journal* 83(4): 427–452.

Raudenbush, Stephen W., Marshall Jean, and Emily Art. 2011. Year-by-year cumulative impacts of attending a high-mobility elementary school on children's mathematics achievement in Chicago, 1995–2005. In *Whither opportunity: Rising inequality, schools, and children's life chances*, ed. Greg J. Duncan and Richard J. Murnane. New York: Russell Sage.

Raymond, Margaret E., Edward Cremata, Devora Davis, Kathleen Dickey, Kristina Lawyer, Yohannes Negassi, Margaret E. Raymond, and James L. Woodworth. 2013. *National charter school study*. Stanford: Center for Research on Educational Outcomes, Stanford University.

Reardon, Sean F. 2011. The widening academic achievement gap between the rich and the poor: New evidence and possible explanations. In *Whither opportunity: Rising inequality, schools, and children's life chances*, ed. Greg J. Duncan and Richard J. Murnane. New York: Russell Sage.

Reardon, Sean F., and Kendra Bischoff. 2011. Income inequality and income segregation. *American Journal of Sociology* 116(4): 1092–1153.

Reeves, Douglas B. 2003. *High performance in high poverty schools: 90/90/90 and beyond*. Englewood: Center for Performance Assessment.

Renee, Michelle, and Sara McAlister. 2011. *The strengths and challenges of community organizing as a reform strategy: What the research says*. Providence: Brown University, Annenberg Institute for Reform.

Roderick, Melissa, Thomas Kelley-Kemple, David W. Johnson, and Nicole O. Beechum. 2014. *Preventable failure: Improvements in long-term outcomes when high schools focused on the ninth grade year*. Chicago: Consortium on Chicago School Research.

Rogers, Everett, Arvind Singhal, and Margaret Quinlan. 2009. Diffusion of innovations. In *An integrated approach to communication theory and research*, ed. Don W. Stacks and Michael B. Salwen. London: Routledge.

Rothstein, Richard. 2013. *For public schools, segregation then, segregation since: Education and the unfinished march*. Washington, DC: Economic Policy Institute. http://s2.epi.org/files/2013/Unfinished-March-School-Segregation.pdf.

Rowan, Brian. 1996. Standards as incentives for instructional reform. In *Rewards and reform: Creating educational incentives that work*, ed. Susan H. Fuhrman and Jennifer A. O'Day. San Francisco: Jossey-Bass.

Rumberger, Russell W., and Gregory J. Palardy. 2005. Does segregation still matter? The impact of student composition on academic achievement in high school. *Teachers College Record* 107(9): 1999–2045.

Schmidt, William H., and Curtis C. McKnight. 2012. *Inequality for all: The challenge of unequal opportunity in American schools*. New York: Teachers College Press.

Schoen, La. Tefy, and Lance D. Fusarelli. 2008. Innovation, NCLB, and the fear factor: The challenge of leading 21st-century schools in an era of accountability. *Educational Policy* 22(1): 181–203.

Simon, Nicole S., and Susan Moore Johnson. 2013. *Teacher turnover in high-poverty schools: What we know and can do*. Working Paper, Project on the next generation of teachers. Cambridge, MA: Harvard Graduate School of Education. http://isites.harvard.edu/fs/docs/icb.topic1231814.files/Teacher%20Turnover%20in%20High-Poverty%20Schools.pdf.

Smith, Marshall S., and Jennifer A. O'Day. 1991. Systemic school reform. In *The Politics of curriculum and testing, Politics of Education Association yearbook 1990*, ed. Susan Fuhrman and Betty Malen, 233–267. London: Falmer Press.

Snow, Catherine, Susan M. Burns, and Peg Griffin. 1998. *Preventing reading difficulties in young children*. Washington, DC: National Academy Press.

Snyder, Thomas D. 2014. *Mobile digest of education statistics, 2013 (NCES 2014-085)*. Washington, DC: U.S. Department of Education, National Center for Education Statistics, Institute of Educational Sciences.

Southern Education Foundation. 2015. A new majority: Low income students now a majority in the nation's public schools. *Research Bulletin* (January). http://www.southerneducation.org/getattachment/4ac62e27-5260-47a5-9d02-14896ec3a531/A-New-Majority-2015-Update-Low-Income-Students-Now.aspx

Southern Regional Education Board (SREB). 2010. *Beyond the rhetoric: Improving college readiness through coherent state policy,* June. http://www.highereducation.org/reports/college_readiness/.

Spillane, James P., Brian J. Reiser, and Louis M. Gomez. 2006. Policy implementation and cognition: The role of human, social, and distributed cognition in framing policy implementation. In *New directions in education policy implementation*, ed. Meredith I. Honig, 47–64. Albany: SUNY Press.

Stetser, Marie, and Robert Stillwell. 2014. *Public high school four-year on-time graduation rates and event dropout rates: School years 2010–11 and 2011–12: First look, NCES 2014-391*. Washington, DC: U.S. Department of Education. National Center for Education Statistics.

Stiglitz, Joseph E. 2012. *The price of inequality*. New York: W.W. Norton.

Stullich, Stephanie. 2011. *The potential impact of revising the Title I comparability requirement to focus on school-level expenditures*. Washington, DC: U.S. Department of Education. https://www2.ed.gov/rschstat/eval/title-i/comparability-requirement/comparability-policy-brief.pdf.

Sykes, Gary, Jennifer O'Day, and Timothy Ford. 2009. The district role in instructional improvement. In *Handbook on education policy research*, ed. Gary Sykes, Barbara Schneider, and David N. Plank. New York: Routledge.

Symonds, William C., Robert Schwartz, and Ronald F. Ferguson. 2011. *Pathways to prosperity: Meeting the challenge of preparing young Americans for the 21st century*. Cambridge, MA: Harvard University Graduate School of Education, Pathways to Prosperity Project. http://dash.harvard.edu/bitstream/handle/1/4740480/Pathways_to_Prosperity_Feb2011-1.pdf?sequence=1.

Theokas, Christina, and Reid Saaris. 2013. *Finding America's missing AP and IB students*. Washington, DC: The Education Trust, June. http://1k9gl1yevnfp2lpq1dhrqe17.wpengine.netdna-cdn.com/wp-content/uploads/2013/10/Missing_Students.pdf.

U.S. Department of Agriculture. 2009. *Access to affordable and nutritious food: Measuring and understanding food deserts and their consequences—report to Congress*. Washington, DC: Author.

U.S. Department of Education. 2013. *For each and every child—a strategy for education equity and excellence*. Washington, DC: Author.

Vaughn, Sharon, Jack M. Fletcher, David J. Francis, Carolyn A. Denton, Jeanne Wanzek, Jade Wexler, Paul T. Cirino, Amy E. Barth, and Melissa A. Romain. 2008. Response to intervention with older students with reading difficulties. *Learning and Individual Differences* 18(3): 338–345. doi:10.1016/j.lindif.2008.05.001.

Weast, Jerry D. 2014. Confronting the achievement gap: A district-level perspective. In *Improving the odds for America's children: Future directions in policy and practice*, ed. Kathleen McCartney, Hirokazu Yoshikawa, and Laurie B. Forcier. Cambridge, MA: Harvard Education Press.

Weatherley, Richard, and Michael Lipsky. 1977. Street-level bureaucrats and institutional innovation: Implementing special-education reform. *Harvard Educational Review* 47(2): 171–197.

Weiler, Erica. 2003. Making school safe for sexual minority students. *Principal Leadership* 4(4): 10–13. http://www.nassp.org/portals/0/content/48927.pdf.

Wenger, Etienne. 2000. Communities of practice and social learning systems. *Organization* 7(2): 225–246.

Yamada, Hiroyuik. 2014. *Communities colleges pathways' program success: Assessing the first two years' of effectiveness of statway*. Washington, DC: Carnegie Foundation for the Advancement of Teaching, November.

Yoshikawa, Hirokazu, Christina Weiland, Jeanne Brooks-Gunn, Margaret R. Burchinal, Linda M. Espinosa, William T. Gormley, Jens Ludwig, Katherine A. Magnuson, Deborah Phillips, and Martha J. Zaslow. 2013. *Investing in our future: The evidence base on preschool education*. New York: Society for the Research on Child Development.

Chapter 10
Restoring Opportunity by Expanding Apprenticeship

Robert I. Lerman

Abstract Restoring opportunity requires jobs that can generate middle class incomes. Notwithstanding concerns about the declining share of middle-wage jobs, this chapter argues that building a robust apprenticeship system in the U.S. can sharply increase earnings and the share of American workers entering rewarding careers. By emphasizing "learning by doing" as a paid employee, apprenticeships are especially effective in preparing workers to gain a valued occupational qualification. They enhance youth development by providing a more engaging experience than schooling does and by linking young people to mentors. They encourage employers to upgrade jobs and develop job ladders. Apprenticeships currently represent a much smaller share of the workforce in the U.S. than in most other advanced countries. This chapter contends that expanding apprenticeship is feasible and a highly cost-effective strategy for restoring opportunity.

Keywords Apprenticeship • Labor market • High-skill jobs • Middle-skill jobs • Low-skill jobs • Job training • Unemployment • Wages • Occupations • Community colleges • Career academies • Career and technical education (CTE) • Licensing • Certification

Introduction

Central to concerns about opportunity in America is the erosion of middle class jobs. Economist David Autor (2010) highlights the polarization in the U.S. labor market, with computerization eliminating middle-skill jobs while shifting low-skill workers into poorly paid and difficult-to-automate service professions.

R.I. Lerman (✉)
Urban Institute, Washington, DC, USA

American University, Washington, DC, USA

IZA, Bonn, Germany

© Educational Testing Service 2016
I. Kirsch, H. Braun (eds.), *The Dynamics of Opportunity in America*,
DOI 10.1007/978-3-319-25991-8_10

A *Financial Times* report[1] on the United Kingdom found that, "Jobs are being created at the top and bottom of the skills scale, while those in the middle tier—including office administrators and blue-collar process operators—are losing out. The trend is intensifying the 'hour glass economy,' where new technologies increase low-skilled jobs but eliminate many in the middle that require intermediate skills." High youth unemployment rates in the U.S. and especially in Europe exacerbate these trends by keeping many workers from gaining initial work experience. According to *The Economist*, rapid technological change is lowering the costs of replacing workers with robots and wages are stagnating even as economic growth has resumed.[2]

Opportunity is becoming increasingly difficult to sustain in the context of widening educational divides that increase the supply of workers without a college education who need jobs. Although rates of high school graduation have increased in general, including for less advantaged groups, the majority of all workers and the vast majority of young minority male workers leave school without any qualification beyond high school. Low proficiency in literacy and numeracy is the norm for high school graduates (with no college), according to data from the Organisation for Economic Co-operation and Development's (OECD) Programme for the Assessment of Adult Competencies (PIAAC) (Holzer and Lerman 2015). The vast majority of high school graduates attend college, but as of 2014, only about 46 % of 25- to 34-year-old Americans had achieved an associate's (A.A.) or bachelor's (B.A.) degree. Young men, especially minority men, are particularly at risk, with only a modest share graduating either a two- or four-year college. Among 25- to 34-year-olds, 29 % of African-American and 19 % of Hispanic men had attained an A.A. or B.A. degree as of March 2014.[3]

The lack of work experience among youth is another major concern. Only one in three Black 18- to 22-year-old men held a job in March 2014; more than half had no work experience at all in 2013. Because work experience contributes substantially to career success, the high rates of joblessness of young people can weaken their long-term opportunities.

Are these trends inevitable and impervious to policy? Or can wise skill development approaches help engage young people and expand their job opportunities, partly by preserving middle class jobs? This chapter considers the potential of robust apprenticeship systems for increasing opportunity by raising skills, productivity, and wages, thereby increasing the chances for young people to find and hold jobs providing middle class incomes.

---

[1] Weitzman, Hal, and Robin Harding. "Skills Gap Hobbles US Employers," *Financial Times,* December 13, 2011.

[2] "The Economics of Low Wages: When What Goes Down Doesn't Go Up." *Economist*, May 2, 2015.

[3] These figures come from the author's tabulations of the March 2014 Current Population Survey (CPS). The estimates may overstate the share of Black men with high levels of education as the data exclude men in jail or prison. In addition, the CPS is likely to undercount Black men just as the decennial census does, and these men probably have lower levels of education than men counted in the CPS.

The chapter begins by defining apprenticeship and describing why apprenticeship should be a central component of the nation's approach to preparing people for careers. Next, we consider whether apprenticeships, or any training, can restore opportunity in the context of a hollowing out of the middle of the distribution of jobs. Specifically, we describe skill requirements and alternative approaches to preparing and upgrading the skills of individuals for these occupations. Programs of academic education and apprenticeship programs emphasizing work-based learning have often competed for the same space, but the full picture reveals they can complement each other significantly. Then, we show how apprenticeship can affect the demand side of the market, encouraging firms to transform jobs into high-skill career positions. We consider the evidence on the costs and effectiveness of apprenticeship training in several countries. Of particular interest is the evidence on the impacts of apprenticeship on firms and new findings on whether apprenticeship training locks workers into specific occupations and limits their occupational mobility. The analysis examines the costs and benefits of apprenticeship versus school-based alternatives aimed at preparing young people for careers. We go on to discuss recent policy developments in the United States and the implications for the feasibility of expanding apprenticeship. The concluding section answers the question on the role of apprenticeship systems in rebuilding middle class jobs.

Defining Apprenticeship and Explaining Its Advantages

Apprenticeship training is a highly developed system for raising the skills and productivity of workers in a wide range of occupations, with demonstrated success abroad and scattered examples of success domestically. Apprentices are employees who have formal agreements with employers to carry out a recognized program of work-based and classroom learning as well as a wage schedule that includes increases over the apprenticeship period. Apprenticeship prepares workers to master occupational skills and achieve career success. Under apprenticeship programs, individuals undertake productive work for their employer; earn a salary; receive training primarily through supervised, work-based learning; and take academic instruction that is related to the apprenticeship occupation. The programs generally last from 2 to 4 years. Apprenticeship helps workers to master not only relevant occupational skills but also other work-related skills, including communication, problem solving, allocating resources, and dealing with supervisors and a diverse set of co-workers. The course work is generally equivalent to at least 1 year of community college.

In Austria, Germany, and Switzerland, extensive apprenticeships offer a way of upgrading the quality of jobs, especially in manufacturing, commercial, and managerial positions.[4] In these countries, apprenticeships begin mostly in the late high

---

[4]For a list of occupations using apprenticeships in several countries, see the occupational standards section of the American Institute for Innovative Apprenticeship website at www.innovativeapprenticeship.org

school years, absorbing 50–70 % of young people on their way to valued occupational qualifications (Hoffman 2011). OECD reports (2009, 2010) highlight the role of a robust apprenticeship system in limiting youth unemployment.

Apprenticeships within the U.S. and elsewhere show how construction occupations can reach high wages and high productivity. The question is whether the model can be extended and attract firms to upgrade other occupations. Apprenticeship expansion holds the possibility of substantially improving skills and careers of a broad segment of the U.S. workforce. Completing apprenticeship training yields a recognized and valued credential attesting to mastery of skill required in the relevant occupation.

Apprenticeships are a useful tool for enhancing youth development. Unlike the normal part-time jobs of high school and college students, apprenticeships integrate what young people learn on the job and in the classroom. Young people work with natural adult mentors who offer guidance but allow youth to make their own mistakes (Halpern 2009). Youth see themselves judged by the established standards of a discipline, including deadlines and the genuine constraints and unexpected difficulties that arise in the profession. Mentors and other supervisors not only teach young people occupational and employability skills but also offer encouragement and guidance, provide immediate feedback on performance, and impose discipline. In most apprenticeships, poor grades in related academic courses can force the apprentice to withdraw from the program. Unlike community colleges or high schools, where one counselor must guide hundreds of students, each mentor deals with only a few apprentices.

Apprenticeships are distinctive in enhancing both the worker supply side and the employer demand side of the labor market. On the supply side, the financial gains to apprenticeships are strikingly high. U.S. studies indicate that apprentices do not have to sacrifice earnings during their education and training and that their long-term earnings benefits exceed the gains they would have accumulated after graduating from community college (Hollenbeck 2008). The latest reports from the state of Washington show that the gains in earnings from various education and training programs far surpassed the gains to all other alternatives (Washington State Workforce Training and Education Coordinating Board 2014). A broad study of apprenticeship in 10 U.S. states also documents large and statistically significant earnings gains from participating in apprenticeship (Reed et al. 2012).

These results are consistent with many studies of apprenticeship training in Europe, showing high rates of return to workers. One recent study managed to overcome the obstacle that such studies tend to face where unmeasured attributes explain both who is selected for an apprenticeship and how well apprentices do in the labor market (Fersterer et al. 2008); the authors did so by examining how an event unrelated to the apprenticeship (the firm staying in or going out of business) caused some apprentices to have full apprenticeships while others found their apprenticeships cut short. The estimates indicated that apprenticeship training raises wages by about 4 % per year of apprenticeship training. For a three- to four-year apprenticeship, post-apprenticeship wages ended up 12–16 % higher than they otherwise would be. Because the worker's costs of participating in an apprenticeship are often minimal, the Austrian study indicated high overall benefits relative to modest costs.

On the demand side, employers can feel comfortable upgrading their jobs, knowing that their apprenticeship programs will ensure an adequate supply of well-trained workers. Firms reap several advantages from their apprenticeship investments. They save significant sums in recruitment and training costs, reduced errors in placing employees, avoiding excessive costs when the demand for skilled workers cannot be quickly filled, and knowing that all employees are well versed with company procedures. Because employers achieve positive returns to their investments in apprenticeship, the worker and the government can save significantly relative to conventional education and training. After reviewing several empirical studies, Muehlmann and Wolter (2014) conclude that "...in a well-functioning apprenticeship training system, a large share of training firms can recoup their training investments by the end of the training period. As training firms often succeed in retaining the most suitable apprentices, offering apprenticeships is an attractive strategy to recruit their future skilled work force..."

One benefit to firms rarely captured in studies is the positive impact of apprenticeships on innovation. Well-trained workers are more likely to understand the complexities of a firm's production processes and therefore identify and implement technological improvements, especially incremental innovations to improve existing products and processes. A study of German establishments documented this connection and found a clear relationship between the extent of in-company training and subsequent innovation (Bauernschuster et al. 2009). Noneconomic outcomes are difficult to quantify, but evidence from Europe suggests that vocational education and training in general is linked to higher confidence and self-esteem, improved health, higher citizen participation, and higher job satisfaction (Cedefop 2011). These relationships hold even after controlling for income.

In the United States, evidence from surveys of more than 900 employers indicates that the overwhelming majority believe their programs are valuable and involve net gains (Lerman et al. 2009). Nearly all sponsors reported that the apprenticeship program helps them meet their skill demands—87 % reported they would strongly recommend registered apprenticeships; an additional 11 % recommended apprenticeships with some reservations. Other benefits of apprenticeships include reliably documenting appropriate skills, raising worker productivity, increasing worker morale, and reducing safety problems.

While apprenticeships offer a productivity-enhancing approach to reducing inequality and expanding opportunity, the numbers in the U.S. have declined in recent years to about one-tenth the levels in Australia, Canada, and Great Britain. Some believe the problems are inadequate information about and familiarity with apprenticeship, an inadequate infrastructure, and expectations that sufficient skills will emerge from community college programs. Others see the main problem as an unwillingness of U.S. companies to invest no matter how favorable government subsidy and marketing policies are. In considering these explanations, we should remember that even in countries with robust apprenticeship systems, only a minority of firms actually hires apprentices. Because applicants already far exceed the number of apprenticeship slots, the main problem today is to increase the number of apprenticeship openings that employers offer. Counseling young people about potential apprenticeships is a sensible complementary strategy to working with the companies, but encouraging interest in apprenticeship could be counterproductive without a major increase in apprenticeship slots.

The high levels of apprenticeship activity in Australia, Great Britain, and Canada demonstrate that even companies in labor markets with few restrictions on hiring, firing, and wages are willing to invest in apprenticeship training. While no rigorous evidence is available about the apprenticeship's costs and benefits to U.S. employers, research in other countries indicates that employers gain financially from their apprenticeship investments (Lerman 2014).

Although apprenticeship training can prepare workers for a wide range of occupations, including medicine and engineering, apprenticeships are perhaps most appropriate for skilled positions that do not require a B.A. degree. A key question is whether these are the very jobs the country is losing and, if so, whether sufficient jobs amenable to apprenticeship will remain.

Patterns and Trends of Middle-Level Occupations

What are the mid-level or skilled sub-B.A. occupations that are most amenable to apprenticeship and significantly affected by the "hollowing out" of the middle class? Classifying mid-level occupations by a single distribution (say, by educational attainment or a score on a cognitive test) fails to capture the wide variety of skills required to master and be productive at specific jobs or occupations. One approach is to use wage as a proxy for skill in the particular job or occupation. Wages may be viewed as incorporating the skill levels along various dimensions together with the market valuation of those skills. However, wages reflect not only skill but also the riskiness, job satisfaction, responsibility, status, and flexibility of jobs and occupations. A second issue is that skill requirements and expertise required in an occupation might not change, but the wage return to the occupation might. Third, wages sometimes are a reward for tenure on the job; seniority often matters. Fourth, wage differences can come about from differences in bargaining power of workers in various fields. For example, the pay of longshoremen can depend on the ability of their representatives to gain strong returns because of the high costs of strikes relative to wage increases. Fifth, wages for the same occupation often differ widely across geographic areas, partly because of area differentials in the price of housing. Sixth, classifying occupations by mean wages can miss the wage variability within occupations.

A major proponent of the hollowing-out thesis ranks detailed occupations by their average wages in a base period (Autor 2010). Middle-skill jobs are in occupations in the middle segment of the average wage distribution in that period. Using his approach, Autor finds that middle-skill occupations are declining rapidly relative to high- and low-skill positions. One of the main reasons is the increased power of computers to automate routine tasks that many middle-skill positions have long undertaken. Similar trends are apparently occurring in other countries. A paper by Goos et al. (2009) finds that middle-wage occupations declined as a share of employment in 16 countries.

The Autor approach provides a useful perspective but is subject to several limitations. One is the failure to capture the often wide distribution of wages within detailed occupations. Many sub-B.A. occupations can generate high wages at the top levels of quality and productivity. For example, the differences in wage levels, skill, and status are substantial between the occupations "cook at a restaurant" and "chefs and head cooks." Cooks are low paid, but chefs command a median wage that is about 25 % higher than the overall national median. Despite their limited formal education (only 13 % have a B.A. or higher), the top 25 % of chefs earn as much as or more than the median wage of four out of 10 college occupations (50 % or more with B.A. degrees). Were cooks and lower-level chefs upgraded to a status of high quality and productivity, earnings for a noncollege occupation could compete with earnings of many college occupations.

Occupations with above-average earnings and with a majority of workers without a B.A. cover a wide range of fields. Among them are construction managers, buyers and purchasing agents, lodging managers, appraisers, court reporters, various types of technicians, aircraft mechanics, police officers, police supervisors, and operators of gas plants.

In another approach to examining occupational trends, Holzer and Lerman (2009) use U.S. Bureau of Labor Statistics (BLS) estimates of education and training requirements to classify broad occupational categories. High-skill occupations are those in the professional/technical and managerial categories, while low-skill occupations are those in the service and agricultural categories. Middle-skill occupations are all the others, including clerical, sales, construction, installation/repair, production, and transportation/material moving. With this classification, middle-skill jobs show a decline but still make up roughly half of all employment today. In a 2013 article, Autor and Dorn predict middle-skill jobs will survive when they embody such human skills as interpersonal interaction, adaptability, and problem solving. Among other jobs, they cite medical paraprofessionals; plumbers; builders; electricians; heating, ventilation, and air-conditioning installers; automotive technicians; customer-service representatives; and even clerical workers who are required to do more than type and file.

A key question raised by Autor and others is how to characterize jobs that require "… situational adaptability, visual and language recognition, and in-person interaction." On one hand, preparing meals and driving a truck through city traffic are difficult to automate. Because these jobs need only modest training and attributes common across the population (dexterity, good eyesight, and language recognition), Autor sees them as commanding only low wages. But even these jobs could in principle involve pathways to reach "artisan" status.

Several occupations requiring a middle level of skills and good wages have increased a good deal since 1986, including medical therapists (such as respiratory, recreational, and radiation therapists) by 30 %, carpenters (20 %), heavy vehicle maintenance specialists (25 %), and heating and air conditioning positions (21 %).

Taking Education, Training, and Labor Market Interactions into Account

The idea that education and training institutions should prepare people for current and future jobs raises several questions: Do jobs simply materialize from a single technology or family of technologies that effective employers eventually implement? Or, do employers confront a range of technologies, all of which can allow the company or public employer to remain competitive? Moreover, how does the choice of technology interact with the system of preparing or retraining workers?

An older literature (Piore and Doeringer 1971), now rarely cited, looked closely at segmented labor markets, where some employers choose to train, hire from within, and keep workers for long periods, while others operate mostly on the spot market, hiring and firing frequently and providing little training. Subsequently, many authors have highlighted that businesses have the choice to become "high road" vs. "low road" employers. For example, Osterman and Shulman (2011) insist that "firms have choices about how to organize work." They find examples of firms producing the same good or service using technologies that generate more or fewer skilled jobs paying good wages. In a landmark article providing a theoretical rationale for employer occupational training, Acemoglu and Pischke (1999) demonstrated how firms might optimize their hiring and training strategies in several ways, depending on the structure of the labor market and the potential permanence of the jobs.

Actual jobs and compensation vary widely within occupations, suggesting that the nature of work may depend on institutional settings that can lead different firms to choose different technologies to produce the same good or service. Given that production may be undertaken using a variety of skill distributions, the key policy questions become: 1) what are the skills within occupations that raise long-term wages and productivity, and, 2) what are the best approaches to educating and training workers to reach high levels of productivity and wages?

Skill Requirements for Workers to Reach Middle Class

The skills required for middle-level occupations are far from obvious. One issue is the appropriate level of generic academic skills. Another is the appropriate level of specificity in occupational skills. A third is the role of generic, nonacademic skills, such as communication, motivation, and responsibility. Some of all three types of skills are required for nearly all jobs, but the levels vary across occupations.

In the case of general academic requirements, U.S. education reformers have boldly claimed that "… *all* students — those attending a four-year college, those planning to earn a two-year degree or get some postsecondary training, and those seeking to enter the job market right away—need to have comparable preparation in high school" (Achieve 2005). Despite strong evidence against this proposition (Lerman 2008), this idea is taken seriously and has led to the creation of the Common Core standards at the high school level. The curriculum is in the process of implementation and is likely to crowd out occupation-based programs.

The evidence strongly suggests that occupational and nonacademic skills are far more significant from the employer perspective than are exposure to high-level academic courses. For example, data from a survey asking a representative sample of U.S. workers what skills they use on the job (Handel 2007) indicate that only 19 % use the skills developed in Algebra I, only 9 % use the skills for Algebra II, and less than 15 % of workers ever write anything five pages or more. On the other hand, upper blue-collar and even lower blue-collar workers need to know how to read and create visuals, such as maps, diagrams, floor plans, graphs, or blueprints—skills typically learned in occupation-specific courses. Moreover, certain nonacademic skills are clearly critical. Workers report the importance of problem-solving and communication skills, teaching and training other workers, dealing with people in tense situations, supervising other workers, and working well with customers.

One useful categorization of these skills comes from the 1992 Secretary's Commission on Achieving Necessary Skills (SCANS) report in the U.S. After researching the literature, consulting with experts, and conducting detailed interviews with workers and/or supervisors in 50 occupations, SCANS identified five groups of workplace competencies: the ability to allocate resources (time, money, facilities); interpersonal skills (such as teamwork, teaching others, leadership); the ability to acquire and use information; understanding systems; and working well with technology. The key personal qualities highlighted by SCANS and many surveys of employers include responsibility, self-esteem, sociability, self-management, and integrity and honesty. Hanover Research (2011) provides an updated analysis of lists of various twenty-first century generic skills.

In a survey of 3,200 employers that focused on four large metropolitan areas in the U.S., the responses indicated that such personal qualities as responsibility, integrity, and self-management are as important as basic skills or more so (Holzer 1997). In another large survey undertaken in the mid-1990s of 3,300 businesses (the National Employer Survey), employers ranked attitude, communication skills, previous work experience, employer recommendations, and industry-based credentials above years of schooling, grades, and test scores (Zemsky 1997). In a 2007 survey of employers in Washington state, about 60 % of employers reported difficulty in hiring (Washington State Workforce Training and Education Coordinating Board 2008). They experienced less difficulty finding workers with adequate reading, writing, and math skills than with appropriate occupational, problem solving, teamwork, communication, and adaptability skills as well as positive work habits and a willingness to accept supervision. Punctuality, reliability, and avoidance of drug and alcohol abuse are also critical. In a 2002 survey of 27,000 employers in the United

Kingdom, 23 % of employers reported a significant number of their staff were less than fully proficient in their jobs. Skill shortfalls were most common in communication, teamwork, other technical and practical skills, customer handling, and problem solving and least common in numeracy and literacy (Hillage et al. 2002).

Evidence confirming the importance of noncognitive/nonacademic skills has been accumulating in academic literature as well. Heckman et al. (2006) find that except in the case of college graduates, noncognitive skills (as measured by indices of locus of control and self-esteem) exert at least as high an impact—and probably a higher one—on job market outcomes than do cognitive skills (word knowledge, paragraph comprehension, arithmetic reasoning, mathematical knowledge, and coding speed as measured by the Armed Forces Vocational Aptitude Battery).

In a recent study, Lindqvist and Vestman (2011) document the differential impacts of cognitive and what they term as noncognitive skills on the earnings of Swedish men. They used special data on a representative sample of the Swedish male population matched with education, earnings, and information on cognitive and noncognitive skills obtained in the military enlistment process through interviews with psychologists. Persistence, social skills, and emotional stability were the key noncognitive skills measured and scored from the interview. Lindqvist and Vestman found that cognitive and noncognitive skills are both positively related to employment and earnings. In the low to mid ranges of skills, noncognitive skills exert a higher impact on wages than do cognitive skills.

The sociocultural approach provides some revealing examples of how skills are used in context and how nonacademic skills are often developed and used as part of a "community of practice" (Stasz 2001). Nelsen (1997) points out that workplaces not only require formal knowledge—facts, principles, theories, math, and writing skills—but also informal knowledge—embodied in heuristics, work styles, and contextualized understanding of tools and techniques (Nelsen 1997). In her revealing case study of auto repair workers, Nelsen argues that social skills of new workers are very important for learning the informal knowledge of experienced workers, such as captured in stories, advice, and guided practice. Unfortunately, according to Nelsen, the social skills learned at school are not necessarily the same as the ones most useful at work.

What about occupational skills? Often, firms, labor representatives, and government reach agreement on what is required for a qualification that will allow employers to have confidence in the capabilities of their young workers. In several countries, skill requirements for occupations develop through the operation of apprenticeship programs and other training programs. Sometimes, the occupational qualifications fit within a broad framework of national vocational qualifications running from basic to intermediate to advanced levels (for a review of national qualification frameworks in Europe, see Cedefop 2012).

Taking a Look at Other Nations

In the United Kingdom, the National Vocational Qualification (NVQ) system speci-
fies requirements for proficiency that vary widely across types of occupations and
over levels within occupations.[5] It is a modular system that recognizes workplace
learning and competence based on evidence of performance at the workplace. The
NVQ system takes skill gradations in each defined field into account and allows
workers to gain documentation for each level, whether attained with one employer
or many. The ultimate goal is that employers place a value on attaining a qualification level, giving workers an incentive to learn on the job. Although this system has
not worked as effectively as planned (Eraut 2001), the NVQ approach offers one
example of how certifying the attainment of skills can provide the basis for measuring the heterogeneity of skills.

One effort to develop occupational or industry standards in the U.S.—the
National Skill Standards Board (NSSB)—failed to develop relevant, rigorous, portable, and well-recognized skill standards to guide training and provide reliable
signals to worker and employers. However, occupation-specific skills standards
exist in the U.S. through state-level licensing and certification. These forms of occupation qualifications are expanding. Today, about one in five workers requires a
state license to practice his or her occupation, up from less than 5 % in the early
1950s (Kleiner 2006). Much of this increase has resulted from rapid growth in traditionally licensed occupations such as physicians, dentists, and attorneys. But the
number of licensing laws has been increasing as well. In the U.S., licensing rules
vary widely across states, with many states regulating occupations as varied as
alarm contractor, auctioneer, manicurist, and massage therapists. Although licenses
ostensibly offer some quality assurance to consumers among all providers, Kleiner
finds evidence of licensure playing more of a role in raising prices than assuring
quality.

School-based and dual work-based/school-based systems try to ensure that occupational qualifications are widely accepted by employers. In primarily school-based
programs, decisions about what is necessary to prepare young people for particular
careers are often made by the faculty of postsecondary institutions. Often, training
colleges—such as U.S. community colleges and for-profit schools—decide themselves (sometimes in consultation with potential employers) what constitutes qualifications in quite detailed occupations, such as domestic air conditioner and furnace
installer, medical receptionist, and medical coder.[6] Other standards directly involve
employers and government entities.

Occupational standards are prerequisites for the functioning of apprenticeship
programs, which involve work- and school-based learning leading to a credential

---

[5] For an overview on NVQ and other qualification systems in the United Kingdom, see material
provided by the Qualifications and Learning Authority at http://www.qca.org.uk

[6] Curricula for certificates in these occupations appear in the catalog for the Kentucky technical
college system. See http://kctcs.edu/en/students/programs_and_catalog.aspx

documenting the individual's occupational qualifications. This issue has been tackled abroad in a variety of ways. Australia has developed the national Training Package (collections of competency standards gathered into qualifications) for all industry areas, while previously qualifications were only available in a limited range of occupations and industries (Smith 2012). The development of Training Packages is one activity of the nation's ten national Industry Skills Councils. In Canada, the Interprovincial Standards Red Seal Program helps develop occupational standards that allow for effective harmonization of apprenticeship training and assessment in each province and territory (Miller 2012). The Red Seal program's standards incorporate essential skills (reading, document use, writing, numeracy, oral communication, thinking, digital technology, and lifelong learning), common occupational skills (that apply to a small range of occupations), and specific occupational skills.[7]

In England, the Sector Skills Councils and their employers design the content of each apprenticeship using the design principles of a national Apprenticeship Blueprint (Miller 2012). The secretary of state appoints and Sector Skills Councils commission an Issuing Authority to promulgate standards for specific apprenticeships. As of 2012, there were 200 operating apprenticeship frameworks and an additional 118 under development. At the same time, employers have considerable flexibility in implementing their apprenticeship programs. France uses Apprenticeship Training Centers to help design and deliver the classroom-based components of apprenticeship, with skill standards often developed by Professional Consultative Committees (Dif 2012). They operate under frameworks established by the National Commission for Vocational Qualifications.

In Switzerland, the Federal Office for Professional Education and Technology, together with cantons, employers, trade associations, and unions, participate in framing the occupational standards for about 250 occupations (Hoeckel et al. 2009). The canton vocational education programs implement and supervise the vocational schools, career guidance, and inspection of participating companies and industry training centers. Professional organizations develop qualifications and exams and help develop apprenticeship places. Occupational standards in Germany are determined primarily by the "social partners," including government, employer, and employee representatives (Hoeckel and Schwartz 2009). The chambers of commerce advise participating companies, register apprenticeship contracts, examine the suitability of training firms and trainers, and set up and grade final exams.

The content of skill requirements in apprenticeships includes academic courses and structured work-based training. In each field, the requirements are to complete the coursework in a satisfactory manner and demonstrate the apprentice's ability to master a range of tasks. In some systems, there are a set of general tasks that apply to a family of occupations (say, metalworking) and tasks that apply to a specific occupation (say, tool mechanics or metal construction and shipbuilding). While the tasks vary widely across occupations, all involve the application of concepts and academic competencies.

---

[7] See the documents linked at http://www.red-seal.ca/tr.1d.2@-eng.jsp?tid=51 for examples.

The coverage of occupational standards for apprenticeship extends well beyond the traditional construction crafts. In the U.K., for example, specific apprenticeships are available within such broad categories as business, administration and law; arts, media, and publishing; health and public services; retail and commercial enterprise; and information technology and communication. Common apprenticeships in Switzerland include information technology specialists, commercial employees, pharmacy assistants, and doctor's assistants. German standards cover over 300 occupations, including lawyer's assistants, bank staff workers, industrial mechanics, industrial managers, retail workers, commercial sales, and computer networking. While much of the training is specific to the occupation, nearly all fields learn skills in closely related occupations. For example, apprentices in industrial management learn accounting, procurement, production planning, staffing, and logistics.

The ability to raise the quality of jobs and workers across occupations appears to help achieve relatively low levels of wage inequality. The enhanced occupational skills and productivity result in increased wages for workers who in other societies have low or average wages. As of the mid-1990s, the evidence showed wage inequality was especially low in countries that used apprenticeships extensively, including Austria, Germany, and Switzerland (Martins and Pereira 2004).

The Timing and Flexibility of Apprenticeship Training

Countries have developed a variety of approaches for training workers to become effective in intermediate level occupations—those that require considerable skill but not a B.A. degree. Systems vary with respect to the level and duration of general education, the timing of occupation-specific education and training, and the split between classroom- and work-based learning. Waiting too long to incorporate occupation-focused education and training runs the risk of high levels of disengaged students and forcing a highly academic approach on many students who would do better in a more concrete setting that emphasizes applications. This argument is especially strong to the extent that school requirements are poorly matched to the job market opportunities facing most young people.

On the other hand, beginning an occupation-focused program too early might trap youth in unrewarding fields and limit their adaptability and upward mobility. Work-based learning is appealing, but critics worry that the training will be too specific and firms will fail to offer sufficient positions. Still, several countries train skilled craftsmen through apprenticeships. However, for many other occupations, some systems rely entirely on school-based systems and some on work-based apprenticeship models that incorporate some classroom instruction.

Although discussions of skill preparation systems generally focus on the work- vs. school-based distinction, the quality, depth, and portability of what students or apprentices learn are at least as important. The skills learned in school-based programs are not necessarily of greater general applicability than those learned in apprenticeship programs. It depends on the specifics of what is being taught and the likelihood that the worker will stay with the training occupation or an adjacent occupation. Depending on the program's content, workers may or may not be able to sustain the gains from training when moving to another firm with the same occupation or in other occupations.

The portability of the skills learned in occupation-specific programs is a common concern about apprenticeships or any occupation-specific training. Several questions are relevant. How likely is the worker to stay in the occupation and/or with the firm? Will the worker be able to sustain the gains from training when moving to another firm but staying in the same occupation? How transferable are the skills learned to other occupations? How do the earnings gains of workers trained in occupation-specific programs compare with those of workers receiving only general postsecondary education?

How skill portability varies with the mode of learning and the curricula is unclear, a priori. As Geel and Gelner (2009) point out, learning even a highly specific skill can yield benefits outside the narrow occupation.

For example, an adolescent who wants to become a clockmaker should not necessarily be considered poorly equipped for future labor market requirements, even though his industry is small and shrinking. Rather, he is well equipped because his skill combination is very similar to skill combinations of other occupations in a large and growing skill cluster, which includes, for example, medical technicians or tool makers. Despite a seemingly very narrow and inflexible skill combination in his original occupation, he is nonetheless very flexible and well prepared for future labor market changes due to the sustainability of his acquired skills and his current skill cluster.

To operationalize the concept of skill specificity, Geel and Gelner (2009) and Geel et al. (2011) begin with an insight borrowed from Lazear (2009) that all skills are general in some sense, and occupation-specific skills are composed of various mixes of skills. The authors compile the key skills and their importance for nearly 80 occupations. They then use cluster analysis to estimate how skills are grouped within narrow occupations. This approach recognizes that skills ostensibly developed for one occupation can be useful in other occupations. It identifies occupational clusters that possess similar skill combinations within a given cluster and different skill combinations between clusters. Next, indices for each narrow occupation measure the extent to which the occupation is relatively portable between occupations within the same cluster and/or relatively portable between the initial occupation and all other occupations. The authors use these indices to determine how portability affects mobility, the wage gains and losses in moving between occupations, and the likelihood that employers will invest in training.

The authors test their hypotheses on the basis of empirical analyses of German apprentices. One finding is that while only 42 % of apprentices stay in their initial occupation, nearly two-thirds remain with either the occupation they learned as an apprentice or another occupation in the cluster using a similar mix of skills. Second, those trained in occupations with more specific skill sets are most likely to remain in their initial occupation or move to occupations within the same cluster. Third, apprentices actually increase their wages when moving to another occupation within the same cluster but lose somewhat when moving to another cluster. Fourth, as Geel et al. (2011) show, employers are especially likely to invest in apprenticeships with the most specific skill sets.

Other strong evidence of the high returns and transferability of German apprenticeship training comes from Clark and Fahr (2001). They examine the returns to apprenticeship for those who remain in the original apprentice occupation as well as losses that do or would occur from transferring to another occupation. The overall rates of return to each year of apprenticeship range from 8 to 12 % for training in firms of 50 workers or more and from about 5.5 to 6.5 % for firms of two to 49 workers. Transferring to another occupation can offset these gains, but the reduction is zero for those who quit and only 1.7 % for those who are displaced from their job and shift to another occupation.

As found by Geel and Gellner (2009), the wage penalty varies with the distance from the original occupation. There is no penalty at all from displacement into a somewhat related occupation. Göggel and Zwick (2012) show the net gains or losses from switching employers and occupations differ by the original training occupation, with apprentices in industrial occupations actually experiencing wage advantages, while those in commerce, trading, and construction see modest losses. Finally, Clark and Fahr (2001) present workers' own views on their use of skills learned in apprenticeship training on their current jobs. Not surprisingly, 85 % of workers remaining within their training occupation use many or very many of the skills they learned through apprenticeship. This group constitutes 55 % of the sample. But, even among the remaining 45 %, about two of five workers reported using many or very many of the skills from their apprenticeship and one in five used some of the skills. Overall, only 18 % of all former apprentices stated they used few or no skills learned in their apprenticeships.

The findings show that the skills taught in German apprenticeship training are often general. Even when bundled for a specific occupation, the skills are portable across a cluster of occupations. Moreover, apprentices are quite likely to remain in occupations that use the skills they learned in their initial occupation. Apprenticeship skills do vary in terms of specificity and portability. But when the skills are less portable, firms are more likely to make the necessary investments and workers are less likely to change occupations significantly.

The general component of training is presumably stronger in school-based programs, because they are financed by government and/or individuals themselves. For this reason, some favor school-based systems, arguing that firm-based apprenticeship training limits mobility and adaptability (Hanushek et al. 2011). Yet, it is far from clear that these programs, especially the purely academic tracks in U.S. secondary schools and U.S. community colleges, offer more mobility. A high percentage of students drop out of both academic secondary and community college programs. Also, many of the community college programs are at least as specific as apprenticeship programs. Certificate programs within community colleges are almost entirely devoted to learning a narrow occupational skill, such as courses to become a phlebotomist, childcare assistant, or plastics-processing worker. Many U.S. school-based programs take place in for-profit colleges offering narrow programs, such as truck driving, medical assistant, and medical insurance billing and coding. Furthermore, skills often erode when they go unused. To the extent students learn general skills but rarely apply them and wind up forgetting them, their training is unlikely to offer upward mobility.

While community college and private for-profit students often take highly specific occupational courses, apprentices all take some general classroom courses. Thus, apprentice electricians learn the principles of science, especially those related to electricity. In most countries, collaboration takes place between public vocational schools and apprenticeship programs. In the U.S., apprentices often take their required "related instruction" in classes at community colleges or for-profit colleges (Lerman 2010). From this perspective, apprenticeship programs should be viewed as "dual" programs that combine work- and school-based learning, albeit with an emphasis on work-based learning.

In the case of other OECD countries, the mix of school- vs. employer-based programs used to prepare young people for careers varies widely (OECD 2009, 2010). Secondary school students in Belgium and Sweden participate at high rates in vocational education but have very low rates of participation in work-based programs. In contrast, most of the vocational education in Germany, Switzerland, and Denmark revolves around work-based learning, including apprenticeships.

Apprenticeship training is attractive in limiting the gaps between what is learned at school and how to apply these and other skills at the workplace. An extensive body of research documents the high economic returns to workers resulting from employer-led training (Bishop 1997). Transmitting skills to the workplace works well with supervisory support, interactive training, coaching, opportunities to perform what was learned in training, and keeping the training relevant to jobs (Pellegrino and Hilton 2012). These are common characteristics of apprenticeships. Employer-based training like apprenticeship often bears fruit in the form of higher levels of innovation (Bauernschuster et al. 2009), net gains to firms that train during and soon after the training, and externalities, such as benefits for other employers and the public when workers are well trained to avoid the consequences of natural or manmade disasters. Generally, apprenticeships and other forms of employer-based training are far less costly to the government. Moreover, the government generally gains by paying little for the training while reaping tax benefits from the increased earnings of workers.

What Policies Can Encourage Firms to Adopt Apprenticeship in the U.S.?

Today, apprenticeships make up only 0.2 % of the U.S. labor force, far less than the 2.2 % in Canada, 2.7 % in Britain, and 3.7 % in Australia and Germany. In addition, government spending on apprenticeships is tiny compared with spending by other countries as well as compared with what it costs to pay for less effective career and community college systems that provide education and training for specific occupations. While total government funding for apprenticeship in the U.S. is only about $100 to $400 per apprentice annually, federal, state, and local government spending annually per participant in two-year public colleges is approximately $11,400 (Cellini 2009). Not only are government outlays sharply higher, but the cost differentials are even greater after accounting for the higher earnings (and associated taxes) of apprentices compared to college students. Given these data, we can attribute at least some of the low apprenticeship penetration to a lack of public effort in promoting and supporting apprenticeship and to heavy subsidies for alternatives to apprenticeship.

However, the historical reasons for apprenticeship's low penetration in the U.S. are less important than the potential for future expansion.[8] Recent experience in Britain and in selected areas in the U.S. suggests grounds for optimism, but the barriers to expansion are significant.

One is limited information about apprenticeship. Because few employers offer apprenticeships, most employers are unlikely to hear about apprenticeships from other employers or from workers in other firms. Compounding the problem is both the difficulty of finding information about the content of existing programs and the fact that developing apprenticeships is complicated for most employers, often requiring technical assistance that is minimal in most of the country. Experiences in England and South Carolina demonstrate that effective marketing is critically important for expanding the number of firms offering apprenticeships.

Another barrier is employer misperceptions that apprenticeship will bring in unions. There is no evidence that adopting an apprenticeship program will increase the likelihood of unionization, but reports about such close links persist. An additional barrier is the asymmetric treatment of government postsecondary funding, with courses in colleges receiving support and courses related to apprenticeship receiving little financial support. Policies to reduce the government spending differentials between college subsidies and apprenticeship subsidies can help overcome this barrier.

Another significant complication to developing more apprenticeships is that U.S. apprenticeships are categorized in three different ways: registered apprenticeships with the Department of Labor's Office of Apprenticeship (OA), unregistered apprenticeships, and youth apprenticeships. Official data generally fail to track unregistered apprenticeships; evidence suggests their numbers exceed registered apprenticeships.[9] Small youth apprenticeship programs operate in a few states. Tiny budgets and an excessive focus on construction have hampered expansion of the registered apprenticeship system. The federal government spends less than $30 million annually to supervise, market, regulate, and publicize the system. Many states

---

[8] For a detailed look at the barriers to expanding apprenticeship in the U.S., see Lerman (2013).

[9] Data from the combined 2001 and 2005 National Household Education Surveys indicate that 1.5 % of adults were in an apprenticeship program in the prior year (NCES 2008). If these data were accurate, the number of unregistered apprentices would far exceed registered apprenticeship.

have only one employee working under their OA. In sharp contrast, Britain spends about one billion pounds (or about $1.67 billion) annually on apprenticeship, which would amount to nearly $8.5 billion in the U.S., after adjusting for population.

Unlike programs in Austria, Germany, and Switzerland, the U.S. apprenticeship system is almost entirely divorced from high schools and serves very few workers under 25. Only a few states, notably Georgia and Wisconsin, now operate youth apprenticeship programs that provide opportunities to 16- to 19-year-olds. State funding pays for coordinators in local school systems and sometimes for required courses not offered in high schools. In Georgia, 143 of 195 school systems currently participate in the apprenticeship program and serve a total of 6,776 students. These apprentices engage in at least 2,000 h of work-based learning as well as 144 h of related classroom instruction. The Wisconsin program includes one- to two-year options for nearly 2,000 high school juniors or seniors, requiring from 450 to 900 h in work-based learning and two to four related occupational courses. The program draws on industry skill standards and awards completers with a certificate of occupational proficiency in the relevant field. Some students also receive technical college academic credit. In Georgia, the industry sectors offering apprenticeships range from business, marketing, and information management to health and human services and technology and engineering. The Wisconsin youth apprenticeships are in food and natural resources, architecture and construction, finance, health sciences, tourism, information technology, distribution and logistics, and manufacturing.

Bipartisan Initiatives and New Proposals

Both the administration and some members of Congress have proposed expanded funding for apprenticeship. President Obama included $500 million per year for 4 years in his fiscal year 2015 budget. Senators Tim Scott (Republican from South Carolina) and Cory Booker (Democrat from New Jersey) have proposed providing tax credits to employers hiring apprentices.

In December 2014, the Obama administration issued a competitive grant announcement that will allocate about $100 million to expand apprenticeship.[10] The administration used its discretion to apply funds from the user fees paid by employers to hire foreign workers as part of the H-1B temporary immigration program. As a result, the grants are oriented toward expanding apprenticeships in occupations that often use H-1B workers from abroad. The industry areas include advanced manufacturing, business services, and health care. Competitors for the grant will have access to funding of $2.5 million to $5 million over 5 years. The key goal is to increase apprenticeship options for workers, but other goals include reaching out to underrepresented groups.

---

[10] See U.S. Department of Labor, Employment and Training Administration, Notice of Availability of Funds and Funding Opportunity Announcement for the American Apprenticeship Initiative, 2015 at http://www.dol.gov/dol/grants/FOA-ETA-15-02.pdf

Whether to emphasize apprenticeships beginning in late high school or after high school involves tradeoffs. High school programs improve the likelihood of government funding for academic courses related to apprenticeships. Given the consensus that the government should fund students through secondary school, paying for the related instruction of high school apprentices becomes a nondiscretionary part of budgets. When apprentices are beyond high school, government funding for related instruction must come out of discretionary expenses. International experience demonstrates the feasibility of youth apprenticeships; youth are able to attain serious occupational competencies while completing secondary education.

Apprenticeships in the late teenage years improve the nonacademic skills of youth at a critical time. In countries with little or no youth apprenticeship, structured work experience is less common, limiting the ability of youth to develop critical employability skills such as teamwork, communication, problem solving, and responsibility. Early apprenticeships can help engage youth and build their identity (Halpern 2009; Brown et al. 2007). Apprentices work in disciplines that are interesting and new; they develop independence and self-confidence through their ability to perform difficult tasks. Youth try out new identities in an occupational arena and experience learning in the context of production and making things.

From an economic perspective, apprenticeships for youth can be less costly for employers. Wages can be lower partly because youth have fewer medium- and high-wage alternatives and partly because youth have fewer family responsibilities, allowing them to sacrifice current for future income more easily. While Swiss firms invest large amounts of dollars in their apprenticeship programs, they pay their young apprentices very low wages during the apprenticeship period. Another economic advantage is that starting earlier in one's career allows for a longer period of economic returns to training.

For the U.S., scaling apprenticeship in the last years of high school is difficult. The aversion to tracking students too early into an occupational sequence is a common objection to youth apprenticeship. Importantly, high school officials are generally averse to adding youth apprenticeship to their already extensive agenda, including implementing Common Core standards and school and teacher accountability standards as well as dealing with charter schools and vouchers. In the early 1990s, opposition to youth apprenticeship in the U.S. came from unions and others who worried about eroding the apprenticeship brand with less intensive training programs.

To build a robust apprenticeship system in the U.S., even with new resources, the strategies will require branding at the state and/or federal levels and marketing at both the general and the firm level. I suggest five strategies: two could be accomplished at the state level, and three would be the responsibility of the federal government.

The State Role

Develop High Level and Firm-Based Marketing Initiatives

Britain's success in expanding apprenticeships from about 150,000 in 2007 to over 850,000 in 2013 offers one example for how to create successful national and decentralized marketing initiatives. Alongside various national efforts, including the National Apprenticeship Service and industry skill sector councils, the British government provided incentives to local training organizations to persuade employers to create apprenticeships. A similar model could be developed in the U.S. state governments could build a state marketing campaign together with incentives and technical support to community colleges and other training organizations to market apprenticeships at the individual firm level. However, simply marketing to firms through existing federal and state agencies may not work if the staff lacks the marketing dynamism, sales talent, and passion for expanding apprenticeship. Pay for performance is recommended: Technical education and training organizations would earn revenue only for additional apprenticeships that each college or organization managed to develop with employers.

Every apprenticeship slot stimulated by the college/training organization increases the work-based component of the individual's education and training and reduces the classroom-based component. Assume the work-based component amounts to 75 % of the apprentice's learning program and the school-based courses are only 25 % of the normal load for students without an apprenticeship. By allowing training providers to keep more than 25 % of a standard full-time-equivalent cost provided by federal, state, and local governments in return for providing the classroom component of apprenticeship, the community colleges and other training organizations would have a strong incentive to develop units to stimulate apprenticeships. State and local governments could provide matching grants to fund units within technical training organizations to serve as marketing arms for apprenticeships. The marketing effort should encourage government employers as well as private employers to offer more apprenticeships.

South Carolina's successful example involved collaboration between the technical college system, a special unit devoted to marketing apprenticeship, and a federal representative from the Office of Apprenticeship. With a state budget for Apprenticeship Carolina of $1 million per year as well as tax credits to employers of $1000 per year per apprentice, the program managed to stimulate more than a sixfold increase in registered apprenticeship programs and a fivefold increase in apprentices. Especially striking is that these successes—including 4000 added apprenticeships— took place as the economy entered a deep recession and lost millions of jobs. The costs per apprentice totaled only about $1250 per apprentice calendar year, including the costs of the tax credit.

Build on Youth Apprenticeship Programs

State government spending on youth apprenticeship programs amounts to about $3 million in Georgia and $2 million in Wisconsin. Although these programs reach only a modest share of young people, the U.S. could make a good start on building apprenticeship if the numbers in Georgia could be replicated throughout the country. The focus would be on students who perform better in work- than purely school-based settings and are less likely than the average student to attend college or complete a B.A. degree. To create about 250,000 quality jobs and learning opportunities, the gross costs of such an initiative would be only about $105 million, or about $450 per calendar year, or about 4 % of current school outlays per student-year. Moreover, some of these costs would be offset by reductions in teaching expenses, with more students spending greater amounts of time in work-based learning and less time in high school courses. Having fewer students have to repeat grades will save costs as well. In all likelihood, the modest investment would pay off handsomely in the form of increased earnings and associated tax revenues as well as reduced spending on educational and other expenditures.

Good places to start are career academies—schools within high schools that have an industry or occupational focus—and regional career and technical education (CTE) centers. Over 7,000 career academies operate in the U.S. in fields ranging from health and finance to travel and construction (Kemple and Willner 2008). Career academies and CTE schools already include classroom-related instruction and sometimes work with employers to develop internships. Because a serious apprenticeship involves learning skills at the workplace at the employer's expense, these school-based programs would be able to reduce the costs of teachers relative to a full-time student. If, for example, a student spent two days per week in a paid apprenticeship or 40 % of time otherwise spent in school, the school should be able to save perhaps 15–30 % of the costs. Applying these funds to marketing, counseling, and oversight for youth apprenticeship should allow the academy or other school to stimulate employers to provide apprenticeship slots. Success in reaching employers will require talented, business-friendly staff who are well trained in business issues and apprenticeship.

To implement this component, state governments should fund marketing and technical support to career academies to set up cooperative apprenticeships with employers, either using money from state budgets or federal dollars. The first step should be planning grants for interested and capable career academies to determine who can best market to and provide technical assistance to the academies. Next, state governments should sponsor performance-based funding to units in academies so they receive funds for each additional apprenticeship. Private foundations should offer resources for demonstration and experimentation in creating apprenticeships within high school programs, especially career academies.

The Federal Role

Extend Use of Current Postsecondary and Training Subsidies to Apprenticeship

In nearly all other countries, the government is responsible for the classroom-based component of apprenticeship. One approach to making this jump in the U.S. is to use existing postsecondary programs to finance or at least subsidize the classroom portion of apprenticeships. Already, localities can use training vouchers from the Workforce Investment Act for apprenticeship. To encourage greater use of vouchers for apprenticeship, the federal government could provide one to two more vouchers to Workforce Investment Boards for each training voucher used in an apprenticeship program. Another step is to encourage the use of Trade Adjustment Act (TAA) training subsidies to companies sponsoring apprenticeships just as training providers receive subsidies for TAA-eligible workers enrolled in full-time training. In addition, policies could allow partial payment of TAA's extended unemployment insurance to continue for employed individuals in registered apprenticeship programs.

Allowing the use of Pell grants to pay at least for the classroom portion of a registered apprenticeship program makes perfect sense as well. Currently, a large chunk of Pell grants pays for occupationally oriented programs at community colleges and for-profit career colleges. The returns on such investments are far lower than the returns to apprenticeship. The Department of Education already can authorize experiments under the federal student aid programs (Olinsky and Ayres 2013), allowing Pell grants for some students learning high-demand jobs as part of a certificate program. Extending the initiative to support related instruction (normally formal courses) in an apprenticeship could increase apprenticeship slots and reduce the amount the federal government would have to spend to support these individuals in full-time schooling.

The GI Bill already provides housing benefits and subsidizes wages for veterans in apprenticeships. However, funding for colleges and university expenses is far higher than for apprenticeship. Offering half the GI Bill college benefits to employers hiring veterans into an apprenticeship program could be accomplished by amending the law. However, unless the liberalized uses of Pell grants and GI Bill benefits are linked with an extensive marketing campaign, the take-up by employers is likely to be limited.

Designate Best Practice Occupational Standards for Apprenticeships

To simplify the development of apprenticeships for potential employers, a joint Office of Apprenticeship-Department of Commerce team should designate one or two examples of good practice with regard to specific areas of expertise learned at work sites and subjects learned through classroom components. The OA-Commerce team should select occupational standards in consultation with selected employers who hire workers in the occupation. Once selected, the standards should be published and made readily accessible. Employers who comply with these established standards should have a quick and easy path to registration of the program. In addition, workforce professionals trying to market apprenticeships will have a model they can sell and that employers can adopt and/or use with modest adjustments. Occupational standards used in other countries can serve as starting points to the Labor-Commerce team and to industry groups involved in setting standards and in illustrating curricula.

Develop a Solid Infrastructure of Information, Peer Support, and Research

The federal government should sponsor the development of an information clearinghouse, a peer support network, and a research program on apprenticeship. The information clearinghouse should document the occupations that currently use apprenticeships not only in the U.S. but also in other countries along with the list of occupation skills that the apprentices master. It should include the curricula for classroom instruction as well as the skills that apprentices should learn and master at the workplace. Included in the clearinghouse should be up-to-date information on available apprenticeships and applicants looking for apprenticeships. The development of the information hub should involve agencies within the Department of Commerce as well as the OA.

The research program should cover topics especially relevant to employers, such as the return to apprenticeship from the employer perspective and the net cost of sponsoring an apprentice after taking account of the apprentice's contribution to production. Other research should examine best practices for marketing apprenticeship, incorporating classroom and work-based learning by sector, and counseling potential apprentices.

Conclusions

Expanding apprenticeship is a potential game-changer for improving the lives of millions of Americans and for preventing further erosion of the middle class. Apprenticeships widen routes to rewarding careers by upgrading skills, including occupational skills but also math, reading, and employability skills. Taking math, reading, and writing in the context of using these competencies in the workforce will increase the motivation of many workers and the efficacy of the delivery process. Given the ability of workers to learn more, remain well motivated, and notice how to make innovations at the workplace, firms will have an increased incentive to adopt "high road" strategies and make them work. Such an approach may be one of the only ways the firm can attract and sustain workers.

Apprenticeships can also increase the efficiency of government dollars spent on developing the workforce. Instead of spending over $11,000 per year on students in community college career programs, why not shift resources toward far more cost-effective apprenticeship programs? Apprenticeship programs yield far higher and more immediate impacts on earnings than community or career college programs yet cost the student and government far less. Community college graduation rates, especially for low-income students, are dismally low. Even after graduating, individuals often have trouble finding a relevant job. For students in postsecondary education, foregone earnings are one of the highest costs. In contrast, participants in apprenticeships rarely lose earnings and often earn more than if they did not enter an apprenticeship. Further, apprentices are already connected with an employer and can demonstrate the relevant credentials and work experience demanded by other employers. Another advantage is the net gains flowing to employers from apprenticeship programs.

The key question is not whether the shift in emphasis from community and/or career colleges toward apprenticeships is desirable but whether it is feasible. Although some argue that the free U.S. labor market and the weak apprenticeship tradition pose insurmountable barriers to scaling apprenticeship, the dramatic increases in apprenticeship in Britain offer strong evidence that building a robust apprenticeship program in the U.S. is possible.

We are well along with the task of persuading policy makers about the desirability and feasibility of apprenticeship. With the Obama administration's grants for the American Apprenticeship Initiative, as of this writing, we were expecting a mix of approaches beginning in the summer of 2015 aimed at expanding apprenticeship. In addition, employers would learn about the returns to apprenticeship as a result of their own experience and expected evaluations. Still, structural barriers remain that limit the development of a robust apprenticeship system in the U.S.

It is past time for federal and state governments to make a genuine effort to build an extensive and high value apprenticeship system. Without such an effort, we will never know whether U.S. employers will follow the patterns of other countries, create a significant number of apprenticeship slots, and recognize the gains to firms from such investments if we do not try. Institutional change of this magnitude is difficult and will take time but will be worthwhile in increasing earnings of workers in middle-skill jobs, widening access to rewarding careers, enhancing occupational identity, increasing job satisfaction, and expanding the middle class.

References

Acemoglu, Daron, and Jörn-Steffen Pischke. 1999. Beyond Becker: Training in imperfect labour markets. *Economic Journal* 109(4): F112–F142.

Achieve, Inc. 2005. *Rising to the challenge: Are high school graduates prepared for college and work?* Washington, DC: Achieve, Inc. http://www.achieve.org/files/pollreport_0.pdf.

Autor, David. 2010. *The polarization of job opportunities in the U.S. labor market: Implications for employment and earnings.* Washington, DC: Center for American Progress and the Hamilton Project. http://economics.mit.edu/files/5554.

Autor, David, and David Dorn. 2013. The growth of low-skill service jobs and the polarization of the US labor market. *American Economic Review* 103(5): 1553–1597.

Bauernschuster, Stefan, Oliver Falck, and Stephan Heblich. 2009. Training and innovation. *Journal of Human Capital* 3(4): 323–353.

Bishop, John. 1997. What we know about employer-provided training: A review of the literature. In *Research in labor economics*, vol. 16, ed. Soloman Polachek, 19–87. Greenwich/London: JAI Press.

Brown, Alan, Simone Kirpal, and Felix Rauner (eds.). 2007. *Identities at work*. Dordrecht: Springer.

Cedefop. 2011. *Vocational education and training is good for you: The social benefits of VET for individuals,* Research Paper 17. Luxembourg: Publications Office of the European Union.

Cedefop. 2012. *Expenditure on public and private educational institutions per student, at secondary and post-secondary non-tertiary levels of education* (image). http://www.cedefop.europa.eu/EN/Files/3899-img1-1-graph_11-2008.jpg.

Cellini, Stephanie. 2009. Crowded colleges and college crowd-out: The impact of public subsidies on the two-year college market. *American Economic Journal: Economic Policy* 1(August): 1–30.

Clark, Damon, and René Fahr. 2001. *The promise of workplace training for non-college-bound youth: Theory and evidence from German apprenticeship,* IZA Discussion Paper 378. Bonn: IZA. http://www.iza.org/en/webcontent/publications/papers/viewAbstract?dp_id=378.

Dif, M'hamed. 2012. France. *'Possible futures for the Indian apprenticeships system' project.* Interim Report to the World Bank, ed. Erika Smith and Ros Brennan Kemmis. Victoria: University of Ballarat.

Eraut, Michael. 2001. The role and use of vocational qualifications. *National Institute Economic Review* 178(October): 88–98.

Fersterer, Josef, Jorn-Steffen Pischke, and Rudolf Winter-Ebmer. 2008. Returns to apprenticeship training in Austria: Evidence from failed firms. *Scandinavian Journal of Economics* 110(4): 733–753.

Geel, Regula, and Uschi Backes-Gellner. 2009. *Occupational mobility within and between skill clusters: An empirical analysis based on the skill-weights approach,* Working Paper No. 47. Swiss Leading House on Economics of Education, Firm Behavior and Training Policies. Zurich: Swiss Federal Office for Professional Education and Technology. http://ideas.repec.org/p/iso/educat/0047.html.

Geel, Regula, Johannes Mure, and Uschi Backes-Gellner. 2011. Specificity of occupational training and occupational mobility: An empirical study based on Lazear's skill-weights approach. *Education Economics* 19(5): 519–535.

Göggel, Kathrin, and Thomas Zwick. 2012. Heterogeneous wage effects of apprenticeship training. *Scandinavian Journal of Economics* 114(3): 756–779.

Goos, Maarten, Alan Manning, and Anna Salomons. 2009. Job polarization in Europe. *American Economic Review* 99(2): 58–63.

Halpern, Robert. 2009. *The means to grow up. Reinventing apprenticeship as a developmental support in adolescence.* New York: Routledge.

Handel, Michael. 2007. *A new survey of workplace skills, technology, and management practices (STAMP): Background and descriptive statistics.* Presented at National Research Council workshop on future skills. Washington, DC. May 23.

Hanover Research. 2011. *A crosswalk of 21st century skills*. Washington, DC: Author. http://www.
    hanoverresearch.com/wp-content/uploads/2011/12/A-Crosswalk-of-21st-Century-Skills-
    Membership.pdf.
Hanushek, Eric, Ludger Woessman, and Lei Zhang. 2011. *General education, vocational educa-
    tion and labor-market outcomes over the life-cycle*, NBER Working Paper 17504. Cambridge,
    MA: National Bureau of Economic Research.
Heckman, James, Jora Stixrud, and Sergio Urzoa. 2006. The effect of cognitive and noncognitive
    abilities on labor market outcomes and social behavior. *Journal of Labor Economics* 3(24):
    411–482.
Hillage, Jim, Jo. Regan, Jenny Dickson, and Kirsten McLoughlin. 2002. *Employers skill survey:
    2002*, Research Report RR372. London: Department for Education and Skills.
Hoeckel, Kathrin, and Robert Schwartz. 2009. *A learning for jobs review of Germany*. Paris:
    OECD.
Hoeckel, Kathrin, Simon Field, and W. Norton Grubb. 2009. *A learning for jobs review of
    Switzerland*. Paris: OECD.
Hoffman, Nancy. 2011. *Schooling in the workplace: How six of the World's best vocational educa-
    tion systems prepare young people for jobs and life*. Cambridge, MA: Harvard Education Press.
Hollenbeck, Kevin. 2008. *State use of workforce system net impact estimates and rates of return*.
    Presented at the Association for Public Policy Analysis and Management (APPAM) confer-
    ence, Los Angeles. http://research.upjohn.org/confpapers/1.
Holzer, Harry. 1997. *What employers want: Job prospects for less-educated workers*. New York:
    Russell Sage.
Holzer, Harry, and Robert Lerman. 2009. *The future of middle skills jobs*, Center on Children and
    Families, CCF Brief 47. Washington, DC: Brookings Institution.
Holzer, Harry, and Robert Lerman. 2015. *Cognitive skills in the U.S. labor market: For whom do
    they matter?* Washington, DC: U.S. Program for the assessment of adult competencies. http://
    static1.squarespace.com/static/51bb74b8e4b0139570ddf020/t/54da7582e4b0cb4c49fc0d9d/
    1423603074704/Holzer_Lerman_PIAAC.pdf
Kemple, James, with Cynthia J. Willner. 2008. *Career academies: Long-term impacts on labor
    market outcomes, educational attainment, and transitions to adulthood*. New York: MDRC.
Kleiner, Morris. 2006. *Licensing competition: Ensuring quality or stifling competition*. Kalamazoo:
    W. E. Upjohn Institute for Employment Research.
Lazear, Edward. 2009. Firm-specific human capital: A skill-weights approach. *Journal of Political
    Economy* 117: 914–940.
Lerman, Robert. 2008. *Widening the scope of standards through work-based learning*. 30th
    research conference of the Association for Public Policy and Management. Los Angeles
    (November).
Lerman, Robert. 2010. Apprenticeship in the united states: Patterns of governance and recent
    developments. In *Rediscovering apprenticeship. Research findings of the International Network
    on Innovative Apprenticeship (INAP)*, ed. Erica Smith and Felix Rauner. London/New York:
    Springer.
Lerman, Robert. 2013. Expanding apprenticeship in the United States: Barriers and opportunities.
    In *Contemporary apprenticeship: International perspectives on an evolving model of learning*,
    ed. Alison Fuller and Lorna Unwin. London/New York: Routledge.
Lerman, Robert. 2014. Do firms benefit from apprenticeship investments? *IZA World of Labor.*
    http://wol.iza.org/articles/do-firms-benefit-from-apprenticeship-investments-1.pdf
Lerman, Robert, Lauren Eyster, and Kate Chambers. 2009. The benefits and challenges of regis-
    tered apprenticeship: The sponsors' perspective. Washington, DC: U.S. Department of Labor,
    Employment and Training Administration. http://www.urban.org/UploadedPDF/411907_reg-
    istered_apprenticeship.pdf
Lindqvist, Erik, and Roine Vestman. 2011. The labor market returns to cognitive and noncognitive
    ability: Evidence from the Swedish enlistment. *American Economic Journal: Applied
    Economics* 3(1): 101–128.

Martins, Pedro, and Pedro Pereira. 2004. Does education reduce wage inequality? Quantile regression evidence from 16 countries? *Labour Economics* 11: 355–371.

Miller, Linda. 2012. "Canada" and "England". In *'Possible futures for the Indian apprenticeships System' project*, Interim report to the World Bank, ed. Erika Smith and Ros Brennan Kemmis. Victoria: University of Ballarat.

Muehlemann, Samuel, and Stefan C. Wolter. 2014. Return on investment of apprenticeship systems for enterprises: Evidence from cost-benefit analyses. *IZA Journal of Labor Policy*. http://www.izajolp.com/content/3/1/25.

NCES (National Center for Education Statistics). 2008. *Recent participation in formal learning among working-age adults with different levels of education.* Washington, DC: U.S. Department of Education. http://nces.ed.gov/pubs2008/2008041.pdf.

Nelsen, Bonalyn. 1997. Should social skills be in the vocational curriculum? evidence from the automotive repair field. In *Transitions in work and learning: Implications for assessment*, ed. Alan Lesgold, Michael Feuer, and Allison Black. Washington, DC: National Academy Press.

OECD (Organisation for Economic Development and Co-operation). 2009. *Learning for jobs.* Paris: OECD.

OECD. 2010. *Off to a good start: Jobs for youth.* Paris: OECD.

Olinsky, Ben, and Sarah Ayers. 2013. *Training for success: A policy to expand apprenticeships in the United States.* Washington, DC: Center for American Progress. https://www.americanprogress.org/issues/labor/report/2013/12/02/79991/training-for-success-a-policy-to-expand-apprenticeships-in-the-united-states/.

Osterman, Paul, and Beth Shulman. 2011. *Good jobs America.* New York: Russell Sage.

Pellegrino James W., and Margaret L. Hilton, (eds.). 2012. *Education for life and work: Developing transferable knowledge and skills in the 21st century.* Committee on Defining Deeper Learning and 21st Century Skills. Division on Behavioral and Social Sciences and Education. National Research Council. Washington, DC: National Research Council.

Piore, Michael, and Peter Doeringer. 1971. *Internal labor markets and manpower policy.* Lexington: D.C. Heath and Company.

Reed, Deborah, Albert Yung-Hsu Liu, Rebecca Kleinman, Annalisa Mastri, Davin Reed, Samina Sattar, and Jessica Ziegler. 2012. *An effectiveness assessment and cost-benefit analysis of registered apprenticeship in 10 states.* Washington, DC: U.S. Department of Labor, Office of Apprenticeship. http://wdr.doleta.gov/research/FullText_Documents/ETAOP_2012_10.pdf.

Secretary's Commission on Achieving Necessary Skills. 1992. *Learning a living: A blueprint for high performance. A SCANS report for America 2000.* Washington, DC: U.S. Department of Labor.

Smith, Erika. 2012. Australia. In *'Possible futures for the Indian apprenticeships system' project.* Interim Report to the World Bank, ed. Erika Smith and Ros Brennan Kemmis. Victoria: University of Ballarat.

Stasz, Catherine. 2001. Assessing skills for work: Two perspectives. *Oxford Economic Papers* 3: 385–405.

Washington State Workforce Training and Education Coordinating Board. 2008. *Workforce training results report: Apprenticeship.* Olympia, WA. http://www.wtb.wa.gov/Documents/WTR_Apprenticeship.pdf, http://wtb.wa.gov/WorkforceTrainingResults.asp.

Washington State Workforce Training and Education Coordinating Board. 2014. *2014 workforce training results by program.* Olympia, WA. http://wtb.wa.gov/WorkforceTrainingResults.asp.

Zemsky, Robert. 1997. Skills and the economy: An employer context for understanding the school-to-work transition. In *Transitions in work and learning: Implications for assessment*, ed. Alan Lesgold, Michael Feuer, and Allison Black. Washington, DC: National Academy Press.

Chapter 11
Improving Opportunity Through Better Human Capital Investments for the Labor Market

Harry J. Holzer

Abstract While education levels in the U.S. have risen in recent years, students from disadvantaged backgrounds have fallen behind other Americans in college attainment amid increasing college dropout rates. The causes of this growing gap include weaker academic preparation in their K-12 years (and earlier); lower wealth and liquidity that make it harder to pay tuition and other costs; worse information about and lower familiarity with higher education; and pressure to work full-time while being enrolled to help support their families. In addition, disadvantaged college students are heavily concentrated in weaker and under-resourced institutions such as community colleges, which generate fewer graduates. Even when students gain credentials like associate degrees, the degrees often do not have strong labor market value because of students' poor labor market information and the weak incentives of public institutions to respond to the labor market by creating more classes in high-demand fields. And high-quality career and technical education opportunities in the U.S., such as "sectoral" training and work-based learning, have not been developed to the extent possible to provide students a wider range of pathways to careers from which to choose. Efforts to improve these outcomes must therefore focus on three goals: (1) improving completion rates at our public colleges by strengthening student supports; (2) expanding postsecondary options, at the bachelor's level or below, that have labor market value; and (3) developing additional pathways to good-paying jobs through work-based learning and high-quality career and technical education, beginning in secondary schools.

This chapter was initially prepared as a paper for the conference on *Opportunity in America*, sponsored by the Educational and Testing Service (ETS) in Princeton, NJ, on December 9–10, 2014. The author thanks Greg Duncan, Richard Murnane, and David Neumark for very helpful comments.

H.J. Holzer (✉)
McCourt School of Public Policy, Georgetown University, Washington, DC, USA

American Institutes for Research, Washington, DC, USA

I. Kirsch, H. Braun (eds.), *The Dynamics of Opportunity in America*,
DOI 10.1007/978-3-319-25991-8_11

Keywords Human capital • Labor market • Economic opportunity • Educational opportunity • Educational attainment • Career and technical education (CTE) • Apprenticeship • Career academies • Career pathways • Sectoral training • Worker skills • Dropout prevention • Two-year colleges • Four-year colleges

Introduction

Since about 1980, labor market inequality has increased quite dramatically in the United States. Gaps in earnings between highly educated workers—such as those with college diplomas or graduate degrees—and those without them have roughly doubled in magnitude. The high labor market "return" to education creates strong incentives for workers to invest in various kinds of "human capital," such as higher education degrees. Indeed, attaining some type of college credential is perhaps the strongest predictor of upward mobility for young people from low-income families, both across generations or within them, so the incentives for the poor to invest in higher education should be as strong as, or even stronger, than for anyone else.

It is therefore somewhat surprising that, during much of the past 35 years, the growth of higher education credentials among young Americans has been quite modest, especially among those from lower- and middle-income families, while gaps in higher educational attainment between children from poor and nonpoor families have actually grown wider during this period. Though there has been a surge in postsecondary educational attainment among young Americans since 2000, and especially since the Great Recession began in 2007, poor children continue to lag behind in such attainment, and earnings gaps between college graduates and others remain very high.

In this chapter I review the factors that limit postsecondary skills attainment among low-income students. I argue that, although the incentives are very strong for poor students to obtain these degrees, a range of personal and institutional barriers as well as market failures often prevent them from doing so.

To improve economic opportunity in the job market, we must therefore enhance the ability of low-income students to obtain college degrees and other credentials that reflect skills that are valued in the labor market. I will argue for a range of policies and practices that should improve the odds that poor young people attain some type of college credential—such as a bachelor's (B.A.) degree and higher, an associate (A.A.) degree, or an occupational certificate. I will also argue that improving a range of other skill-building pathways for poor students—including high-quality career and technical education; various models of work-based learning, such as apprenticeship; and other approaches, such as career pathways and training in particular employment sectors (sectoral training) —would improve their opportunities in the labor market as well.

Investing in Human Capital: Why Does Postsecondary Educational Attainment Lag behind for the Poor?

Theory and Evidence

The theory of human capital investment, as developed by Gary Becker (1996), Jacob Mincer (1974) and others, posits that (all else equal) a rise in labor market returns to any particular skill, or an educational credential that signals the attainment of that skill, should generate higher investments in that skill or credential. So if demand for those with higher education rises in the labor market, and the earnings premium for having a college diploma (relative to high school) increases, more students will enroll in college and obtain that degree. This increase in the supply of college graduates should, in turn, reach a point that it offsets the higher demand and causes the earnings premium to fall to its earlier level.

Of course, this scenario assumes no other complications in the adjustment process, including market failures of any kind, and no other limits on the potential supply of skilled labor. If, for example, there are lags in the time needed for such skill development, then the adjustment process might take many years to complete, and in the presence of imperfect information and foresight among students, the supply of skilled workers over time could potentially overshoot the new equilibrium, causing wages of skilled workers to oscillate, as they have in some markets for highly educated workers (Freeman 1971).

On the other hand, the ability of students to make these additional investments at all might be limited—if, for example, the marginal students in these markets have lower scholastic ability, their information about market returns is incomplete, or they face higher costs of investing in the skills. Indeed, among low-income students, it is quite possible that all of these complications could limit their investment decisions over time.[1]

If the theoretical responses of investments in skills to market increases in pay premia for those skills are therefore somewhat ambiguous, what does the empirical evidence show? The important and well-known book by Claudia Goldin and Lawrence Katz, *The Race between Education and Technology* (2008), offers us perhaps the clearest long-term evidence on this issue. They show that, due to technological developments in a variety of industries, the labor market return to *high school* diplomas rose sharply in the early part of the twentieth century, and in response, the supply of high school graduate labor rose over the first several decades of the century, just as predicted by the human capital model.

Indeed, the process continued until the higher wage premium associated with high school graduation had disappeared by mid-century. Goldin and Katz note that the rise in high school enrollments and graduation reflected not only private

---

[1] This discussion assumes that the market return to a completed degree is at least as high for the disadvantaged as for other students, which appears to be the case (Backes, Holzer, and Velez 2014).

investment decisions but also a major public policy response to increase the teaching capacities of public high schools and encourage (or require) more such enrollments.[2]

In the last few decades of the twentieth century, a similar process occurred in which technological change (plus globalization and other institutional forces) likely increased the demand for *college* graduates and caused their relative wages to rise as well.[3] But, unlike the earlier episode, there was relatively little rise in the supply of highly skilled workers until the end of the century. Though Autor (2014) notes that higher enrollments in college finally increased the supply of highly educated labor after the year 2000, and especially after the onset of the Great Recession in 2007, this increase was sufficient only to stabilize the premium associated with college rather than reduce it.[4]

Furthermore, Bailey and Dynarski (2011) have shown that the response of college enrollments and attainments to the higher college wage premiums of the 1980s and 1990s varied strongly by family income, with higher responses among high-income students than lower-income ones. Accordingly, the gap in B.A. attainments that already existed by family income grew larger over time. Other evidence (e.g., Holzer and Dunlop 2013) also showed rising enrollments in A.A. programs among poorer students and minorities after 2000, while Whites/nonpoor students showed greater increases in B.A. enrollments and attainments, thus contributing to widening earnings gaps as well.

Explaining the Rising Attainment Gaps among Disadvantaged Students

What accounts for the rising gap in educational attainment between disadvantaged and other students in the past 30 years?

Importantly, we must distinguish *enrollment* rates in higher education from *completion* rates among those who enroll. The data show quite large increases in enrollments over time among the poor and minorities as well as nonpoor and/or White

---

[2] Mandatory high school enrollment up to a certain age (usually 16) in most states was a mechanism by which higher high school enrollment was required.

[3] College enrollments and supply actually rose substantially in the late 1960s and early 1970s in response to the Vietnam War because college students were deferred from being drafted; this caused the college wage premium to decline substantially in the 1970s (Freeman 1976). But enrollments declined after the war ended, and the positive shift in labor demand for college graduates appears to have begun around 1980. The associated rise in the college premium was not sufficient to dramatically raise the supply of such graduates for the next few decades. Labor economists have long debated the extent to which the rising college premiums of this period mostly reflect labor demand and supply factors (Goldin and Katz 2008); (Autor et al. 2008) or other institutional forces like weaker unions and lower statutory minimum wages (Card and Dinardo 2007).

[4] By most accounts, real wages did not rise for college or high school graduates after 2000, only rising for those with graduate degrees beyond the B.A. (e.g., Mishel et al. 2012–2013).

students. Indeed, some evidence suggests that enrollment rates have come close to converging across these groups, conditional on graduating from high school. And, since high school graduation rates have improved markedly for the poor in the past few decades (Murnane 2013), and certain high school reforms show great success in improving the access of the poor and minorities to college enrollment (Bloom and Unterman 2014), college enrollment rates among minorities and the poor should continue to grow over time. Even among the dwindling numbers of high school dropouts, college enrollment options might also grow among those who obtain a GED as the preparation and tests that determine receipt of this degree grow more rigorous over time.[5]

But college completion rates among enrollees have worsened over time (Bound et al. 2009), with large gaps evident by race and family income, especially at four-year colleges and universities (Holzer and Dunlop 2013). For instance, Holzer and Dunlop show that completion rates at four-year colleges and universities (within approximately 8 years of graduating from high school) average over 60 % for the entire population but just over 30 % for disadvantaged students.[6] At A.A. programs in two-year colleges, completion rates are more comparable across these groups (at about 35 %) but are generally low for all students, and the concentration of disadvantaged or minority young people is much higher at these schools than for middle-class students or Whites.[7]

What accounts for these gaps? The research by Bound, Lovenheim, and Turner and others shows that a number of factors contribute to lower college completion rates among the disadvantaged. These include:

- weaker academic preparation in the K-12 years;
- lower wealth and associated liquidity constraints limiting ability to pay tuition and other college expenses;
- worse information about and lower familiarity with higher education; and
- pressure to support a family by working full-time during enrollment.

If anything, the gaps in earlier academic achievement, and therefore preparation for college, across family income groups have also grown over time (though they have fallen somewhat by race—Magnuson and Waldfogel 2008; Reardon 2011), thus contributing to differences in their educational outcomes. But, even within

---

[5] The effects of the more traditional GED on college attainment or earnings appeared to be modest at best (Murnane and Tyler 2000; Heckman et al. 2010). Those who pass the newer, more rigorous one will likely show greater impacts on these outcomes, though we do not yet know if pass rates will decline.

[6] Disadvantaged students in this study refer to those from the bottom quarter of the socioeconomic status distribution, which presumably measures longer-term family income better than annual income. The data on completion are derived from the 2000 panel of the National Educational Longitudinal Survey (NELS).

[7] Completion rates are somewhat higher if measured for those in certificate as well as A.A. programs at two-year colleges, though the average wages they generate are lower. On the other hand, completion rates calculated for community college enrollment populations that include adults and not just a cohort of youth out of high school are usually much lower than 35 %.

groups of students with fairly uniform achievement levels, large gaps in completion rates between poor and other students are observed (Backes et al. 2014).

What role is played by the rising costs of higher education in America (College Board 2013b)? If capital markets operated fully efficiently, academically able students from low-income families would be able to fully borrow for whatever human capital investments they were capable of making. But evidence has shown that accumulated family wealth (especially through the housing market) and access to financial aid have some impact on student enrollment and attainment (Lovenheim 2011; Brown et al. 2009), thus suggesting that capital markets are highly imperfect in overcoming wealth differences across families and lack of access to liquid wealth (often known as "liquidity constraints") among the disadvantaged.[8] And, as the financial costs of two- and four-year public institutions continue to rise, because of reductions in state financial assistance to these institutions (College Board 2013b), these constraints may grow more serious over time.

It is also clear that information about the world of higher education is highly imperfect, especially among first-generation college enrollees from disadvantaged families. Indeed, when applying to college, low-income students are much more likely to attend the two- or four-year colleges located closest to where they live, which (for poorer and minority students) are likely lower-tier public colleges; as a result, there is often some significant undermatching between high-achieving students from low-income families and the colleges they attend (Bowen et al. 2005, 2009). Such undermatching appears to at least partly reflect differences in information about school quality available to the disadvantaged compared to other students, as well as in the likelihood of being accepted to higher-quality schools.[9] Accordingly, fairly small increments in information on higher education can have sizable effects not only on whether such students enroll but also where (Goodman 2013; Hoxby and Turner 2014), while assistance with filling out financial aid forms can have a significant impact as well (Bettinger et al. 2012).

Also, full-time work, and therefore part-time enrollment, is strongly associated with lower completion rates (College Board 2013a); this pressure to work is no doubt especially strong among single parents of small children. And a greater lack of social capital and supports among such students likely impedes their ability to successfully complete classes and accumulate credits as well.

---

[8] In perfect capital markets, high-ability students should have no difficulty borrowing the funds needed to cover the costs of investing in college, as such investments should be regarded by the markets as relatively safe and generating a strong return. But very imperfect information about student ability or other factors reduces the funding available for investments in higher education; this, in turn, forces students to rely more heavily on their own family income or wealth, which causes many from lower-income or lower-wealth families to be "liquidity constrained." It is also likely that disadvantaged students choose to rely less heavily on loans, the repayment and debt servicing of which might be more burdensome to, and impose more risk on, those with lower incomes (unless repayment were fully income-contingent).

[9] Undermatching could, of course, also reflect personal preferences if disadvantaged students might feel more out of place at more elite schools socially or worry about the higher costs of attending.

On top of these *personal* factors, the *institutions* they attend matter as well (Bound et al. 2009). Even controlling for K-12 achievement, students who attend four-year colleges have much higher completion rates than those at two-year colleges, as we noted above, and within the former group, completion rates rise with college quality. In other words, given groups of students are more likely to graduate when they attend elite private colleges and universities, as well as the flagship state universities, than when they attend less selective public colleges. And it is in the less selective colleges and universities that much of the recent increases in college enrollments have occurred. Thus, raising the access of lower-income youth to four- instead of two-year colleges, and to more selective ones within the former, might actually raise their graduation rates.[10]

Why do completion rates vary by institution? For one thing, the elite colleges have much more resources per student and can provide a range of academic and personal supports that cannot be matched at less selective schools. They also provide other benefits to students struggling to finish their degree programs. For instance, the more affluent schools can afford more sections of courses, thus enabling more students to fit them into their schedules; at the less selective schools, more rigid scheduling makes it harder for students to complete their chosen programs—especially if the students are working full time. The higher quality of the student peer groups at the more selective schools likely also contributes to these effects (Sacerdote 2001).

Even within institutions, finishing a program depends on what supports are available to students and also to their chosen fields of study. The data tell us that, all else equal, those majoring in science, technology, engineering or math (STEM) have somewhat lower completion rates, as the level and difficulty of work required in STEM classes is higher and requires greater levels of earlier math preparation (Backes et al. 2014).

But, perhaps more surprisingly, the harder fields of study are not always the ones with the lowest completion rates. Using administrative data from the state of Florida, Backes, Holzer, and Velez find the lowest completion rates in both two- and four-year colleges among those majoring in fairly nondescript humanities fields like "general studies" or "liberal studies." And large subsets of students end up in these fields, especially in A.A. degree programs and among disadvantaged students.[11] Rates of completion are also higher in more technical certificate programs than in A.A. programs, perhaps partly because the former are completed much more quickly.

---

[10] This argument, of course, runs counter to the one frequently made that affirmative action actually hurts the educational attainment of minorities by enabling them to attend school where they are too disadvantaged academically to succeed. The evidence in support of this claim does not appear persuasive (Holzer and Neumark 2006).

[11] In the Florida data, 55 % of students in A.A. programs overall major in the humanities, usually reflecting "general studies" or "liberal studies," while for disadvantaged students (defined here as those eligible for free or reduced-price lunch) the comparable fraction is 60 %.

Another type of institution is the for-profit colleges, which have recently grown in size and now consume quite large fractions of federal student aid.[12] Recent analysis (Cellini 2012; Deming et al. 2013) shows lower completion rates in the for-profit schools, somewhat lower earnings among those who complete them, and higher debt burdens among those who do not complete them.

What About Earnings?

Ultimately, the institution of higher education that one attends, the field of study one chooses, and the degree that one does or does not complete all have important effects on one's future earnings.

As is widely known, the average labor market returns to the B.A. degree (relative to a high school diploma) have roughly doubled since 1980, and now those with B.A.'s earn nearly 80 % more than high school graduates (Autor 2014). For those who have continued beyond the B.A. and completed some type of graduate degree, returns have grown even more substantially; this has occurred even in the past decade or so, when the returns to the B.A. have flattened (as enrollments and attainment of the B.A. have risen).

Returns to the A.A. degree have also risen over time, especially for females, though not by as much as those for B.A. degrees and higher (Kane and Rouse 1995; Acemoglu and Autor 2010; Bailey and Belfield 2013).[13] But vocational certificates can generate important earnings gains for low-income students as well and take much less time to complete than A.A. or B.A. degrees. In fact, those with certificates in high-demand or technical fields—such as health care or advanced manufacturing—frequently earn more than those with A.A.'s (and even some with B.A.'s) in humanities or "liberal studies," though less than those with more technical A.A. degrees (Backes et al. 2014).[14] More generally, the field of study one chooses has very large effects on earnings, implying that the average return to a particular academic credential can be somewhat misleading about any particular individual's true prospects.

---

[12] For instance, over a quarter of Pell financial aid now goes to students at for-profit schools (College Board 2013b).

[13] To infer changing returns over time, the estimated returns to community college in Bailey and Belfield can be compared to those estimated earlier in Kane and Rouse, though the data and samples used differ somewhat between the two studies. Acemoglu and Autor (2010) use consistent data and sampling methods over time, but they only list years of schooling completed rather than the A.A. degree. One can roughly infer the changing returns to the A.A. degree over time in their work by looking at returns for those with 14 years of schooling.

[14] Carnevale et al. (2011) and Owen and Sawhill (2013) also emphasize the high variance in returns across fields and the fact that the earnings of some certificate or A.A. degree holders can exceed those of B.A. holders at the lower end of the B.A. distribution.

For those who do not complete their degree programs, there is still some return in the form of higher earnings to credits attained. But those who drop out of two- and four-year college programs often do so before they have attained many credits, in addition to losing the "sheepskin effect" of completing and attaining the degree. This is especially true for those with poor academic preparation in the K-12 years, who often need remediation when they attend community colleges and cannot take many courses for credit until they have successfully completed these remedial programs (Bettinger et al. 2013; Long 2014).

All of this implies that many college-going students from disadvantaged families will ultimately enjoy much less economic success than the average earnings of college graduates imply. Too many of them will go to A.A. programs or less selective four-year colleges where completion rates in general are low; once there, some will likely be trapped in non-credit-bearing remediation classes from which they cannot emerge. Others will choose fields of study at these institutions with even lower-than-average completion rates and low labor market compensation. And many will drop out before having accumulated enough credits to gain much compensation, even in fields that the labor market does value.

Besides the weak academic preparation that many of these students bring to college, and the generally low resources of the institutions they attend, are there other problems which lead to the discouraging outcomes we've described? I believe there are problems of too little *information* and too weak *incentives* at the community colleges and other public four-year colleges and universities.

Most students get virtually no career (or even academic) counseling before or during college; most never obtain any workforce services of the type routinely provided in a jobs (or "one-stop") center financed by the U.S. Department of Labor. Indeed, the student experience at most two-year colleges has been described by one prominent researcher as a "shapeless river" in which students float along but receive little structure or guidance, and little assistance even while navigating across programs (Scott-Clayton 2011; Jenkins and Cho 2012). This stands in sharp contrast to some traditional proprietary vocational colleges (Rosenbaum 2002), where course-taking and curricula are very structured and job placement assistance is strong. Though some studies (Wiswall and Zafar 2013; Long et al. 2014) show that new information on the labor market has just limited influence on student choices, it seems likely that these effects would be greater among the disadvantaged (whose choices right now seem to reflect so little attention to market returns).[15]

But, even if student choices were better informed and therefore more optimal, they would be constrained by limited teaching capacity in high-demand fields and other institutional features that are common at two-year colleges and the less prestigious four-year programs where resources are very limited. Because instructors

---

[15] Altonji et al. (2012) reviews the literature on choices of student major and emphasizes how early choices about studying certain fields (like math and science), often made under great uncertainty about the future, constrain later choices of major in response to labor market developments.

and equipment are frequently more expensive in the high-demand fields, and because subsidies from most states are still based primarily on student "seat time," regardless of academic or subsequent labor market success; college administrators have little incentive to expand instructional capacity in these high-cost fields (Holzer 2014).[16]

Are There Other Pathways to Labor Market Success Besides College?

One of the reasons that returns to college have grown so much in the U.S. is that those for a high school diploma have diminished, especially for young men. Indeed, most American employers have little reason to believe that the average high school graduate brings occupational or technical skills to the workplace that they will value, or strong communication or analytical skills, or even strong basic cognitive ones. Indeed, on a recent test of skills among workers in 24 Organisation for Economic Co-operation and Development (OECD) countries, Americans scored quite low on literacy or problem-solving proficiency and especially on numeracy; this was especially true among those without postsecondary education. And the skills of non-college-going high school graduates have diminished in recent years as college enrollment rates have risen, so the pool of non-college-going high school graduates looks relatively worse over time.[17]

Yet in other European countries like Germany, employers are willing to pay high school graduates more, at least partly because they know these young people will bring some analytical and technical skills to jobs that they value. The same seems much less true in the U.S. today.

For students who might not be bound for college or universities right away, especially right after high school, a range of other approaches to enhance their labor market skills are being developed and implemented in a number of states and localities. These include high-quality career and technical education programs in high school, work-based learning models like apprenticeships, and innovative approaches to adult training like sectoral models. We consider each of these approaches below.

---

[16]While Rosenbaum's (2001) study argues that proprietary occupational colleges more successfully link their students to the labor market than do community colleges, the recent evidence on the broader category of proprietary (or for-profit) colleges has been less positive (Deming et al. 2013).

[17]See OECD (2013) for results from a new cross-national evaluation of adult literacy known as PIAAC (Programme for the International Assessment of Adult Competencies), which largely confirm earlier findings from the PISA (Programme for International Student Assessment) tests given at earlier ages.

Career and Technical Education

Traditionally, non-college-bound students, especially those from minority or disadvantaged backgrounds, have enrolled in vocational education in the U.S. or been "tracked" there against their will. These programs prepared students mostly for low-wage jobs, often in declining sectors. Beginning in the 1960s, resentment from minority families and communities over tracking led to declining enrollments in these programs, though they were not reformed for decades. Even when the school-to-work programs of the 1990s briefly received federal funding (Neumark 2007), traditional vocational programs went largely untouched. And, though their quality has improved somewhat in recent years, career and technical education (CTE) programs have not become a large-scale alternative to academic programs that prepare students for "college only."[18]

But a number of newer CTE models have been emerging that no longer force students to choose between college and "career" and instead try to prepare them for both (Holzer et al. 2013). Best known of these programs are the career academies, which are programs within more general high schools that prepare students for careers in a particular sector, such as health care, information technology, or finance. Students take courses within the academy as well as outside of it and often find part-time or summer work within the sector. Evaluation evidence shows strong and lasting impacts on the earnings of enrollees, especially disadvantaged young men, whose earnings remain nearly 20 % higher than those in the control group 8 years after enrollment, at least partly because of the greater labor market exposure that academy students receive (Page 2012). There is also no evidence of lasting effects (positive or negative) on high school completion or college enrollment (Kemple 2008). More recent versions of career academies put more emphasis on maintaining strong college preparatory curricula while still maintaining the emphasis on specific sectors and careers.

Other models, perhaps less well known or less rigorously evaluated, also try to prepare students for both college and careers. These include the High Schools that Work in many Southern states; Linked Learning in California; and high-tech high schools (Holzer et al. 2013). High school programs that provide strong career-based instruction and a seamless entry into college (especially the kinds of "early college high schools" reviewed in Schwartz and Hoffman 2014) look particularly promising. Virtually all students at these schools get some career exposure and exploration. Wherever possible, high-quality academic material is incorporated into work- or project-based learning to contextualize the material and make it more relevant to students. Links to employers in targeted industries, and professional development

---

[18] Some recent changes have been driven by the latest reauthorization of the Carl T. Perkins Act in 2007, which provides $1 billion for state and local CTE programs. The current version of Perkins requires states to identify growing or high-wage "career clusters" and to generate "paths of study" to move students into these sectors. There is also evidence that the extent to which CTE students take math and science courses in high school has risen in recent years. See Holzer et al. 2013.

for staff, is emphasized as well. A network of "pathway states" aims to expand the best models and increase student and school participation in them.[19]

Work-Based Learning

Work-based learning models, sometimes called "learning while earning," have enjoyed a recent surge of interest, even outside of school CTE programs. These models include internships, co-op programs at colleges, apprenticeships, and "career pathways."

Many such programs provide students with paid work experience as well as a postsecondary credential of value in the labor market (Holzer and Lerman 2014b). At a time when young people are experiencing low employment rates (due to the Great Recession and weak labor market recovery afterward), combining work experience with postsecondary attainment is an appealing option. The paid work experience might better motivate low-income students to complete their training and also contextualizes the learning.

Apprenticeships, in particular, give students strong paid-work experience while they gain an occupational credential. Early on, the wages they receive might be somewhat below market levels so employers don't have to fully bear the cost of such training.[20] But this means that public sector costs are quite low, while employers also seem to like the program. German companies, in particular, have introduced such programs in the U.S., though not necessarily in identical form to the well-known apprenticeship model widely used in Germany.[21]

In the U.S., certain states—like South Carolina, Wisconsin, and Georgia—are encouraging employers to expand apprenticeships through marketing campaigns and modest financial incentives to help offset costs (Lerman 2014). Indeed, while employers often find them appealing, few would develop them completely on their own due to a variety of market failures.[22]

Incumbent worker training is another model of work-based learning. A range of states have provided subsidies for such training, at least before the Great Recession began (Hollenbeck 2008). The training was mostly limited to nonprofessional and

---

[19] Much of this work has been based on an influential report entitled *Pathways to Prosperity* (Symonds et al. 2011). See also Hoffman (2011).

[20] As Becker has pointed out, the more general the training, the less employers will be willing to pay for it, because workers could leave at any time before employers recoup the costs of their investments.

[21] Nelson Schwartz, "Where Factory Apprenticeship is Latest Model from Germany." *New York Times*, November 27, 2013.

[22] Economists, in particular, often wonder why certain activities that benefit both workers and employers are not undertaken more frequently on their own. A range of market failures, such as high fixed costs for organizing such programs, limited information about their benefits, and wage rigidities (such as the minimum wage) that limit firms' abilities to share training costs with workers, could impede these undertakings.

nonmanagerial starting employees, and the training was usually designed to help them advance within the companies (or to prevent them from being laid off). To prevent the training from being too narrowly focused (or too "customized," in more modern lingo) on the needs of the specific employer, especially when public funds for the training are being provided, the states attempt to ensure that skills are at least somewhat general and "portable" to other employers and sectors. Evidence suggests positive impacts both on workers and on their performance in the workplace (Holzer et al. 1993; Ahlstrand et al. 2003; Hollenbeck 2008.)

Sectoral Training/Career Pathway Programs

Training outside of the workplace that nonetheless targets jobs in a particular growing or high-wage sector, with the active involvement of particular employers, is known as "sectoral training." Workforce intermediaries bring together employers in that sector, training providers (either community colleges or others) and workers. The intermediaries help provide the workers with access to needed supports and services, including transportation and childcare. The intermediaries also work with providers and employers to make sure that the training fits the employers' needs. If successful, employers come to trust the intermediaries over time to screen workers and refer only those with strong skills and work habits.

Rigorous evaluations (Maguire et al. 2010; Roder and Elliott 2011) have shown that sectoral programs can generate large impacts on the earnings of adults and youth—of 30% or more—within 2 years of the onset of training. But the training generally works only for disadvantaged workers with quite strong basic skills and job readiness rather than the "hard to employ." Questions also remain about the extent to which impacts survive over time, particularly after workers leave their current jobs and maybe even that sector of employment.

Many states have begun efforts to scale up "sectoral" models by creating partnerships between community colleges and employers or industry associations (National Governors Association 2014). Efforts in many cities and substate regions of the country have been undertaken as well (National Fund for Workforce Solutions 2014).[23] The Obama administration has also embraced "demand driven" or "job driven" training as ways to meet the needs of the long-term unemployed and other disadvantaged workers.[24]

But little data exists to date measuring the outcomes achieved, in terms of numbers of workers trained or employed in these broader efforts, much less what the

---

[23] The National Fund is an effort funded by several philanthropic foundations to expand and scale sectoral training models at the city or regional level. It currently operates at over 30 sites around the country.

[24] See the White House (2014) for a very recent report by the Office of the Vice President on how to encourage more state and local workforce boards to engage in demand-driven (or "job driven") training.

impacts are on worker earnings. Tensions can sometimes exist between the time it takes to build local or state "partnerships" between employers, intermediaries, and service providers, on the one hand, and the often-changing skill needs of employers and workers in a dynamic labor market on the other. Making sure that these models are not just windfalls for employers who would otherwise provide the training themselves, or that the training serves at least somewhat disadvantaged workers— whom employers might be reluctant to hire—requires some vigilance on the part of intermediaries or state officials.

Finally, a number of states are trying to develop "career pathways" that combine classroom work in a certificate or A.A. program with various amounts of work experience as they move up an occupational ladder of some type. For instance, students might first become a certified nursing assistant and then a licensed practical nurse, with some ultimately becoming registered nurses. A network of states are receiving technical assistance and support for developing a range of these programs (CLASP 2014) within broader career pathway "systems." But little evidence exists to date on the impacts of these efforts (Fein et al. 2013).

Policy Implications

Based on the preceding discussion, a policy agenda to expand opportunities of disadvantaged Americans to build more labor market skills would include the following goals:

- improve completion rates at two- and four-year colleges;
- expand postsecondary options that have labor market value; and
- develop additional and alternative pathways to skill-building and work experience through expanding high-quality CTE and work-based learning

Improving College Completion Rates

Perhaps the best thing we could do to improve college completion rates for disadvantaged students would be to improve their academic preparation in the K-12 years. An enormous research and policy literature already exists on this topic, to which I can add relatively little. But it is clear that any such policies need to emphasize both equity and accountability, with more resources going to poor students and communities and strong performance incentives guiding their use. This can be accomplished with stronger curricula (which could be encouraged through widespread implementation of the Common Core and its Next Generation Science Standards), teacher professional development, and incentives based on teacher performance in salary determination, along with higher compensation for strong teachers in math and science and in segregated or high-poverty areas.[25] High school reforms that are modeled on successes like the Small Schools of Choice in New York, along with other dropout prevention efforts (Balfanz 2010), would help as well.

Given their K-12 performance, increasing the access of disadvantaged students to better colleges and universities would clearly improve their education and employment outcomes. One way to do so would be to provide better information on college choice to high school students as they prepare to apply for college. The evidence to date indicates that even small and low-cost improvements in disseminating information among such students can improve the quality of the colleges to which they apply (Hoxby and Turner 2014). Merely requiring all students to take the ACT exam can generate more information about college quality for these students, which ultimately increases enrollments at better colleges (Goodman 2013; Hyman 2013). Changes in recruitment practices, with flagship and elite colleges reaching out to more disadvantaged students and/or those in poorer neighborhoods, would help as well.

Once disadvantaged students apply more frequently to better colleges, they might also be given better chances of being accepted in the admissions process—through some adjustment of the relative weights applied to traditional academic performance measures (like grades and especially standardized test scores) versus disadvantaged backgrounds and other measures of merit and character (Bowen et al. 2005, 2009). To some extent, this is happening already, as the flagship public universities feel pressure to adjust their affirmative action admissions policies; though the Supreme Court has not yet fully struck-down race-based admissions policies, it has clearly indicated it regards them as its least preferred method of increasing diversity on campuses.[26] Using family- or place-based measures of disadvantaged in place of race in admissions decisions will likely generate student bodies with somewhat lower representation of Blacks and Hispanics but higher representation of low-income and disadvantaged students of all races (Long 2004).

Of course, another way of improving the access of disadvantaged students to better-resourced colleges and universities would be to redistribute public resources more equitably between flagship and nonflagship schools. The evidence suggests that state higher education subsidies may be regressive, given the greater generosity most state legislatures show to their flagship schools (though the exact evidence depends on the range of public resources that are included in the calculations).[27] Of course, these legislatures tend to believe that the flagships contribute more to state

---

[25] See, for instance, the report by the Equity and Excellence Commission (U.S. Department of Education 2012b; Duncan and Murnane 2014; Chetty et al. 2011.

[26] In its most recent ruling on affirmative action in higher education admissions, in Fisher v. University of Texas, the Supreme Court affirmed that race could be used as one of many factors to generate a diverse student body, but only if it had exhausted all other potential remedies and found them to fail in generating such diversity.

[27] See Hansen and Weisbrod (1969) for the beginning of a longstanding argument on the regressive nature of state subsidies to higher education, and Johnson (2005) for evidence that these subsidies are more income-neutral when we also consider the progressive nature of the state taxes that finance them.

economic development, and their alumni tend to be well represented among (or influential with) state legislators, making any such redistribution very hard to achieve.

Still, we spend nearly $200 billion of public funds each year on higher education in America, and perhaps those funds could be spent more efficiently and generate a stronger set of academic outcomes. For one thing, a range of supports provided to improve academic outcomes are in need of some reform. These include financial aid, developmental (or remedial) education, tutoring/coaching, and the formation of learning communities.

Individual financial aid can come from the federal government in the form of Pell grants, loans, and/or work study; the institutions themselves also provide such aid. The research evidence suggests that simplicity and transparency increase student access to aid, while conditioning continuation of the aid (at least to some extent) on satisfactory academic outcomes (for example, through merit scholarships) improves performance incentives and outcomes (Dynarski and Scott-Clayton 2007; Patel et al. 2013).[28] A set of Pell grant reforms have been suggested recently based on these principles (College Board 2013a; Baum and Scott-Clayton 2013). Student loans, which have recently become more burdensome to students who drop out of college or have some difficulty finding well-paying jobs after graduating, could also be made less burdensome by moving repayments to an income-contingent basis, among other reforms (Akers and Chingos 2014).[29] And even providing assistance to low-income parents as they fill out financial aid forms seems to help (Bettinger et al. 2012).

The methods by which two-year and four-year colleges choose students for remediation, and then deliver it, are greatly in need of reform (Long 2014). Students are often required, for instance, to pass Algebra I, though this math is not necessary for the occupational degree in question, or they are required to pass other exams that are often shown to be unrelated to subsequent student performance in for-credit classes (Scott-Clayton 2012).[30] In its current form, the provision of remediation generally has little positive effect on academic outcomes of students or even negative effects (Clotfelter et al. 2013).[31]

---

[28] On the other hand, Cohodes and Goodman (2014) show evidence that generous merit scholarships to in-state public university students can actually reduce the quality of the institution they attend, thus reducing college completion rates as well.

[29] Susan Dynarski, "What We Mean When We Say Student Debt Is Bad." *New York Times*, August 8, 2014.

[30] While math proficiency generally and skill in algebra specifically (Holzer and Lerman 2014a) seem to contribute to one's earnings, there is much less evidence that proficiency in algebra contributes to success in completing community college or to the earnings of these students. Long (2014) argues that literacy might be more foundational for these students in terms of their ability to complete college classes.

[31] Negative effects might occur, for instance, if students have only limited time or financing for higher education and such time is consumed in non-credit-generating remediation rather than credit-accumulation in real courses.

Accordingly, reforms that would accelerate remediation and integrate it into teaching or training classes would likely be successful (Bettinger et al. 2013). One such model, the Integrated Basic Education and Skills Training (I-BEST) program in the state of Washington, has generated strong outcomes and is regarded as a promising (though expensive) alternative to standalone remediation (Zeidenberg et al. 2010). Delivery of remediation could also be made more effective by accelerating it and better integrating it into labor market training or information.

The provision of a range of other supports—such as childcare or other income supports—can be made more accessible by programs like "Single Stop," which applies the one-stop concept of service delivery at college (often two-year) campuses. Mandatory participation of students in counseling or support classes has shown some benefits, as has "coaching" more in general (Bettinger et al. 2012). Requiring students to attend class full time while giving a generous package of income and other supports (as done in Accelerated Study in Associate Programs, or ASAP, at the City University of New York), can improve program completion rates as well (Scrivener and Weiss 2013).

Expanding Postsecondary Options with Labor Market Value

As indicated above, it is not enough just to increase college completion rates for disadvantaged students; we also need to improve the labor market value of the credentials they seek and attain.

States and regions are setting up many partnerships between community colleges and employer groups, with the hope of expanding sectoral training and career pathway programs that better connect disadvantaged workers to high-demand sectors and good-paying jobs (National Governors Association 2014). But before these efforts can replicate the best programs and achieve some real scale, some other reforms must be undertaken to address the problems of limited student information and institutional incentives described above.

On providing information, we need to undertake a major effort to improve the availability and quality of career counseling that students get. Ideally, this would begin in high school for every student. But as students approach either two- or four-year colleges, especially in the public sector, they should obtain counseling on career pathways and job availability in their state and region as well as nationally. This counseling could be delivered through the nation's job centers (formerly called One-Stops), though now most students never set foot in them. The job centers could perhaps be expanded with satellite offices on public campuses, especially community colleges, with appropriate efforts to ensure the quality of counseling will be maintained or improved. Online data sources (such as College Measures) that provide detailed information on earnings among graduates of specific colleges could also help in this regard.

Importantly, the data needed for such up-to-date counseling efforts are becoming more available. With federal support and encouragement, states are linking their college and labor market administrative data at the micro level and making them more accessible to researchers and policy makers (Zinn and Van Kluenen 2014). Such data could be summarized on an annual basis and presented in a manner that counselors could use to better inform student decisions, especially for those seeking an occupational credential.[32]

A variety of approaches could be used to improve the incentives of colleges and employers to increase job-relevant training capacity. Some of these have been incorporated in the recently reauthorized Workforce Innovation and Opportunity Act, though its capacity and budget remains quite small (National Skills Coalition 2014); and the Office of the Vice President has recently published a report on a variety of other ways of encouraging more "job driven" training (White House 2014).

In addition, I think it is important to impose some accountability through performance-driven subsidies for public colleges at the two- and even four-year level (Holzer 2014). A number of states are, in fact, beginning to do so (National Conference of State Legislatures 2014) by tying their subsidies for specific colleges to a range of student academic outcomes in a variety of ways. I would expand this approach to include postcollege employment as well as academic outcomes among the ones that determine the levels of subsidies, and with heavy weight on both sets of outcomes for disadvantaged or minority students. The federal government could also use a variety of competitive grants programs to encourage the states in this endeavor.

The administrative data described above are uniquely suited to the purpose of implementing this strategy. And there are other pitfalls that would need to be avoided—e.g., colleges would now have an incentive to "cream" or "skim" by admitting higher-quality students than before. But careful implementation of these standards, perhaps using some type of value-added measures for labor market performance among a college's enrollees and graduates (or "risk adjustment" based on their initial characteristics), could help avoid these pitfalls while we learn what really works or doesn't in this area (Bailey and Xu 2012).[33]

---

[32] See Jacobson (2013) for a vision of how individual students might ultimately use such data to calculate average completion rates and subsequent earnings for students like themselves at particular colleges or universities and with particular majors at each of them. At least potentially, students might be able to make much better-informed choices about colleges to attend and majors to pick using such data.

[33] The "Gainful Employment" regulations recently implemented by the U.S. Department of Education, on for-profit colleges and certificate programs at public ones, are another attempt to impose accountability, by focusing on debt incurred relative to incomes earned by students after college.

Expanding High-Quality CTE and Work-Based Learning

High-quality career and technical education, beginning in high school and then continuing in college (through career pathway programs), could provide disadvantaged young people with a wider range of options leading to ultimate economic success. Apprenticeships and other work-based learning models could also play an important role.

The expansion of these programs, through the replicating and scaling of apparently successful models, would once again need to occur mostly at the state and local levels. A variety of states are already moving in this direction, working with major employers to increase education and training options for work in their industries.[34]

The federal government could, once again, play a more useful role in this process. By distributing roughly $1 billion in funding to states and localities through the Perkins Act, the federal agencies already have a vehicle through which they can encourage the adoption of higher-quality CTE models with more universal appeal. Recently proposed reforms to Perkins (U.S. Department of Education 2012a) would help such an effort, though there is always resistance from the CTE community to implementing them.[35] The Labor Department's Youth Career Connect grants could also encourage this process. And the Obama administration's recent announcement of a grants program to encourage apprenticeship (Wilson 2014) could also be the first of a number of steps to expand them as well.

Conclusion

Above I have listed a set of factors that render higher education in the U.S. less effective at helping disadvantaged students gain skills and labor market success than it otherwise might be. These factors include the weak academic preparation of poor students, the financial constraints they face, and their poor information about college options; they also include the relatively lower quality of the institutions (both two- and four-year, both for- and not-for-profit) that they attend, and the weak information about the labor markets that limit their choices, as well as the weak incentives for colleges to respond to that labor market. I then outline a set of policies and programs at the federal and state levels to improve college completion rates, labor market success for college graduates (at both the two- and four-year levels), and access to high-quality career and technical education as well as work-based learning among those students.

But a number of factors, both economic and political, could limit the effectiveness of these approaches. For one thing, a full 7 years after the beginning of the

---

[34] See Jobs for the Future (2014).

[35] See, for instance, Association of Career and Technical Education (2012).

Great Recession, our nation's job market remains relatively weak, and young workers continue to show greatly reduced employment and earnings as a result (Altonji et al. 2014).[36] Because education and training are designed to prepare a more skilled supply of labor to meet employer demands, any such ongoing weakness might make these approaches less successful—especially if we train lots of individuals for jobs that they cannot get afterward. We hope that the nation's slow but steady recovery from this downturn will proceed and that its overall sluggishness will not continue to weaken the job market outcomes of young people indefinitely.[37]

Even if the labor market strengthens in the aggregate, labor demand now seems very dynamic and fluid across sectors of the economy. This means skills that are in high demand today might not be tomorrow as labor demand shifts (because of new technologies and globalization) often occur in unpredictable ways. Accordingly, workers trained for specific careers and sectors must also have a broad range of "portable" skills, some general and some specific, that will enable them to move between firms and sectors over time. Ongoing availability of assistance in retraining (or what some observers call "lifelong learning") as well as finding new sectors of employment should also be part of any such plan.

An ample supply of well-educated workers would hopefully also encourage employers to demand more of their labor rather than more fully automating their workplaces or sending such jobs overseas. The recent arrival of several hundred German manufacturers in the U.S. in the last few years and their expansion of production facilities here (while domestic companies continue to cut back in this area) indicates the potential for labor demand expansion if we were to generate a well-trained labor force over time[38]

Regardless of what policies we implement in this area, large numbers of American workers will have weak education and skills as well as low earnings over

---

[36] As of late 2014, the national unemployment rate hovers around 6 %. But no doubt this figure understates the degree of slack in the labor market, because many job-seekers have either dropped out of the labor force (Jared Bernstein and Harry J. Holzer. "A Win-Win Approach to Increase the Future Labor Force," PostEverything, *Washington Post*, September 11, 2014) and/or taken part-time jobs when they prefer full-time ones.

[37] Some commentators (e.g., Lawrence Summers, "On Secular Stagnation," *Reuters*, December 6, 2013) have suggested that the U.S. might be experiencing "secular stagnation," in which we cannot generate sufficient aggregate demand to move us back toward full employment. But Summers ("Supply Issues Could Hamper US Economy," *Washington Post*, September 7, 2014) and others have also worried about declines in labor force participation, perhaps partly in response to poor labor market opportunities, that occur even among those well below retirement age and which could limit potential economic growth over time. See Bernstein and Holzer (2014) for suggestions on how job training and work-based learning programs could be used to expand the earnings potential and labor force participation among these groups.

[38] For instance, the Siemens Corporation built a gas turbine engine manufacturing plant in North Carolina in 2012–2013, but only after it had made arrangements with local community and 4-year colleges to generate a steady stream of technicians and engineers for employment there. On the other hand, the German companies seem to come primarily because of proximity to the U.S. consumer market, low energy prices, and low regulations. We do not want to assume that any increase in the supply of skilled labor will automatically generate its own demand.

time. Accordingly, increases in a range of other work supports will be necessary—including expansions of the earned income tax credit (EITC) for those who currently benefit very little, like childless adults and noncustodial parents; and paid parental leave.[39] Moderate increases in the federal and state minimum wages could supplement these reforms (Sawhill and Karpilow 2014),[40] while efforts to address a specific set of barriers in the labor market—for instance, for those with criminal records—would be helpful as well (Council of State Governments 2013).

In addition, the nation's political and fiscal situations remain fairly bleak, especially at the federal level. Political polarization and paralysis limit federal action on almost any issue, and the combination of low taxes and very high spending on retirement programs will limit our ability to act for years (or likely decades) to come.

Yet, if we can devise policies to make our ongoing public expenditures (of nearly $200 billion) more effective without requiring much in the way of new resources, such actions could still draw some bipartisan support. And, if federal action fails to materialize, perhaps a more practical set of executives and legislators at the state level could move ahead on this agenda.

References

Acemoglu, Daron, and David Autor. 2010. Skills, tasks and technologies: Implications for employment and earnings. In *Handbook of labor economics*, vol. 4b, ed. Orley Ashenfelter and David E. Card. North Holland: Amsterdam.

Ahlstrand, Amanda, Laurie J. Bassie, and Daniel P. McMurrer. 2003. *Workplace education for low-wage workers*. Kalamazoo: W.E. Upjohn Institute for Employment Research.

Akers, Beth, and Matthew Chingos. 2014. *Is a student loan crisis on the horizon?* Policy brief. Washington, DC: Brookings Institution.

Altonji, Joseph, Erica Blom, and Costas Meghir. 2012. *Heterogeneity in human capital investments: High school curriculum, College majors and careers*, NBER Working Paper 17985. Cambridge, MA: National Bureau of Economic Research. http://www.nber.org/papers/w17985.

---

[39] See MDRC (2014) for a description of this promising pilot study that increases the EITC available to childless adults in New York City. Also see Waldfogel (2007) for policy suggestions on how to expand paid leave availability for (low-income) parents.; Nelson Schwartz, "Where Factory Apprenticeship is Latest Model from Germany." *New York Times*, November 27, 2013.

[40] Economists typically fear that higher minimum wages could reduce employer demand for low-wage workers. The research evidence suggests that such effects are likely modest (or even zero), as long as they are moderate in magnitude—which means kept at 50 % or below the median worker's wages (Neumark and Wascher 2009; Dube 2014). Indexing the legal minimum to either inflation or the median wage would keep it from eroding over time, though if it is indexed at a relatively high level this could also generate larger disemployment effects (Harry Holzer, "Pitfalls of Pay Increases," *Washington Post*, December 10, 2013).

Altonji, Joseph, Lisa B. Kahn, and Jamin D. Speer. 2014. *Cashier or consultant? Entry labor market conditions, field of study, and career success,* NBER Working Paper 20531. Cambridge, MA: National Bureau of Economic Research. http://www.nber.org/papers/w20531.

Association for Career and Technical Education. 2012. *ACTE and NASDCTEc respond to Department of Education Perkins Blueprint.* Washington, DC: Association for Career and Technical Education.

Autor, David. 2014. Skills, education, and the rise of earnings inequality among the 'other 99 Percent'. *Science* 344(6186): 843–851.

Autor, David, Lawrence Katz, and Melissa Kearney. 2008. Trends in US wage inequality: Revising the revisionists. *Review of Economics and Statistics* 90(2): 300–323.

Backes, Benjamin, Harry J. Holzer, and Erin Dunlop Velez. 2014. *Is it worth it? Postsecondary education and labor market outcomes for the disadvantaged,* CALDER Working Paper. Washington, DC: National Center for Analysis of Longitudinal Data in Education Research, American Institutes for Research. http://www.air.org/sites/default/files/downloads/report/Postsecondary%20Education%20and%20Labor%20Market%20Outcomes%20for%20the%20Disadvantaged_9.15.14.pdf.

Bailey, Thomas, and Clive Belfield. 2013. Community college occupation degrees: Are they worth it. In *Preparing today's students for tomorrow's jobs in Metropolitan America,* ed. Laura W. Perna. Philadelphia: University of Pennsylvania Press.

Bailey, Martha, and Susan Dynarski. 2011. Inequality in postsecondary education. In *Whither opportunity? Rising inequality, schools, and children's life chances,* ed. Greg J. Duncan and Richard Murnane. New York: Russell Sage Foundation/Spencer Foundation.

Bailey, Thomas, and Di Xu. 2012. *Input-adjusted graduation rates and college accountability: What is known from twenty years of research?* New York: Community College Research Center, Columbia University.

Balfanz, Robert. 2010. *Building a grad nation: Progress and challenge in reducing the high school dropout epidemic.* Baltimore: Johns Hopkins University.

Baum, Sandy, and Judith Scott-Clayton. 2013. *Redesigning the Pell grant program for the 21st century,* Policy brief. Washington, DC: The Hamilton Project, Brookings Institution.

Becker, Gary. 1996. *Human capital,* 2nd ed. Chicago: University of Chicago Press.

Bettinger, Eric, Bridget Terry Long, Phil Oreopoulos, and Lisa Sanbonmatsu. 2012. The role of application assistance and information in college decisions: Results from the H&R block FAFSA experiment. *Quarterly Journal of Economics* 127(4): 1205–1242.

Bettinger, Eric, Angela Boatman, and Bridget Terry Long. 2013. Student supports: Developmental education and other academic programs. *The Future of Children* 23(1): 93–126. http://futureofchildren.org/publications/journals/article/index.xml?journalid=79andarticleid=582.

Bloom, Howard, and Rebecca Unterman. 2014. Can small schools of choice improve educational prospects for disadvantaged students? *Journal of Policy Analysis and Management* 33(2): 290–319.

Bound, John, Michael Lovenheim, and Sarah Turner. 2009. *Why have college completion rates declined? An analysis of changing student preparation and collegiate resources,* NBER Working Paper 15566. Cambridge, MA: National Bureau of Economic Research. http://www.nber.org/papers/w15566.

Bowen, William, Martin Kurzweil, and Eugene Tobin. 2005. *Equity and excellence in American higher education.* Charlottesville: University of Virginia Press.

Bowen, William, Matthew Chingos, and Michael McPherson. 2009. *Crossing the finish line: Completion at America's public colleges.* Princeton: Princeton University Press.

Brown, Meta, John Karl Scholz, and Ananth Seshadri. 2009. *A new test of borrowing constraints in education,* NBER Working Paper 14879. Cambridge, MA: National Bureau of Economic Research. http://www.nber.org/papers/w14879.

Card, David, and Jonathan Dinardo. 2007. The impact of technological change on low-wage workers: A review. In *Working and poor,* ed. Rebecca M. Blank, Sheldon Danziger, and Robert F. Schoeni. New York: Russell Sage.

Carnevale, Anthony, Nicole Smith, and Jeff Strohl. 2011. *Help wanted: Projections of jobs and education requirements through 2018.* Washington, DC: Center for Education and the Workforce, Georgetown University.

Cellini, Stephanie. 2012. For-profit higher education: An assessment of costs and benefits. *National Tax Journal* 65(1): 153–180.

Chetty, Raj, John N. Friedman, and Jonah E. Rockoff. 2011. *The long-term impacts of teachers: Teacher value-added and student incomes in adulthood,* NBER Working Paper 17699. Cambridge, MA: National Bureau of Economic Research. http://www.nber.org/papers/w17699.pdf.

CLASP (Center for Law and Social Policy). 2014. *Shared vision, strong systems: The alliance for quality career pathways framework version 1.0.* Washington, DC: CLASP. http://www.clasp.org/issues/postsecondary/pages/aqcp-framework-version-1-0.

Clotfelter, Charles, Helen F. Ladd, Clara Muschkin, and Jacob L. Vigdor. 2013. *Developmental education in North Carolina community colleges,* CALDER Working Paper. Washington, DC: National Center for Analysis of Longitudinal Data in Education Research, American Institutes for Research, American Institutes for Research.

Cohodes, Sarah, and Joshua Goodman. 2014. Merit aid, college quality, and college completion: Massachusetts' Adams scholarship as an in-kind subsidy. *American Economic Journal: Applied Economics* 6(4): 251–285.

College Board. 2013a. *Rethinking Pell grants.* Washington, DC: College Board.

College Board. 2013b. *Trends in student aid.* Washington, DC: College Board.

College Measures. www.collegemeasures.org. Accessed 20 Sept 2014.

Council of State Governments Justice Center. 2013. *Integrated reentry and employment strategies: Reducing recidivism and promoting job readiness.* Washington, DC: Council of State Governments Justice Center. https://www.bja.gov/Publications/CSG-Reentry-and-Employment.pdf.

Deming, David, Claudia Goldin, and Lawrence Katz. 2013. For-profit colleges. *The Future of Children* 23(1): 137–163.

Dube, Arin. 2014. *Designing thoughtful minimum wage policies at the state and local levels.* In Kearney, Harris, and Anderson 2014.

Duncan, Greg, and Richard Murnane. 2014. *Restoring opportunity.* New York: Russell Sage.

Dynarski, Susan, and Judith Scott-Clayton. 2007. *College grants on a postcard: A proposal for simple and predictable federal student aid.* Washington, DC: Hamilton Project, Brookings Institution.

Fein, David, Howard Rolston, David Judkins, and Karen N. Gardiner. 2013. *Learning what works in career pathways: The ISIS evaluation.* Paper presented at the Association of Public Policy and Management Annual Research Conference, Washington, DC.

Freeman, Richard. 1971. *The market for college-trained manpower.* Cambridge, MA: Harvard University Press.

Freeman, Richard. 1976. *The over-educated American.* Cambridge, MA: Harvard University Press.

Goldin, Claudia, and Lawrence F. Katz. 2008. *The race between education and technology.* Cambridge, MA: Harvard University Press.

Goodman, Sarena. 2013. *Learning from the test: Raising selective college enrollment by providing information.* Washington, DC: Board of Governors, Federal Reserve Bank.

Hansen, W. Lee, and Burton Weisbrod. 1969. The distribution of costs and direct benefits of public higher education: The case of California. *The Journal of Human Resources* 4(2): 176–191.

Heckman, James, John Humphries, and Nicholas Mader. 2010. *The GED,* NBER Working Paper 16064. Cambridge, MA: National Bureau of Economic Research Working Paper.

Hoffman, Nancy. 2011. *Schooling in the workplace.* Cambridge, MA: Harvard Education Press.

Hollenbeck, Kevin. 2008. *Is there a role for public support of incumbent workers on-the-job training?* Working Paper 08–138. Kalamazoo: W. E. Upjohn Institute for Employment Research.

Holzer, Harry. 2014. *Improving education and employment outcomes for disadvantaged students.* In Kearney, Harris, and Anderson 2014.

Holzer, Harry, and Erin Dunlop. 2013. *Just the facts Ma'am: Postsecondary education and labor market outcomes in the US*, CALDER Working Paper. Washington, DC: National Center for Analysis of Longitudinal Data in Education Research, American Institutes for Research.

Holzer, Harry, and Robert Lerman. 2014a. *Cognitive skills in the US labor market: For whom do they matter?* Prepared for conference on PIAAC. Washington, DC: American Institutes for Research.

Holzer, Harry, and Robert Lerman 2014b. Work-based learning for youth. *Challenge* (July–August).

Holzer, Harry, and David Neumark. 2006. Affirmative action: What do we know? *Journal of Policy Analysis and Management* 25 (2).

Holzer, Harry, Richard N. Block, Marcus Cheatham, and Jack H. Knott. 1993. Are training subsidies for firms effective? The Michigan experience. *Industrial and Labor Relations Review* 46(4): 625–636.

Holzer, Harry, Dane Linn, and Wanda Monthey. 2013. *The promise of high-quality career and technical education*. Washington, DC: The College Board.

Hoxby, Caroline, and Sarah Turner. 2014. *Expanding college opportunities for high-Achieving, low income students,* SIEPR Discussion Paper 12–014. Stanford: Stanford Institute for Economic Policy Research.

Hyman, Joshua. 2013. *ACT for all: The effect of mandatory college entrance exams on postsecondary attainment and choice,* Working Paper. Ann Arbor: University of Michigan.

Jacobson, Louis. 2013. *Using data to improve the performance of workforce training.* Washington, DC: The Hamilton Project, Brookings Institution.

Jenkins, Davis, and Sung-Woo Cho. 2012. *Get with the program: Accelerating community college students entry into and completion of programs of study,* Working paper. New York: Community College Research Center, Columbia University.

Jobs for the Future. 2014. *Pathways to prosperity network: State progress report.* Boston: Jobs for the Future.

Johnson, William. 2005. *Are public subsidies to higher education regressive?* Unpublished paper, University of Virginia.

Kane, Thomas, and Cecelia Rouse. 1995. Labor market returns to two-year and four-year colleges. *American Economic Review* 85(3).

Kearney, Melissa S., Benjamin H. Harris, and Karen L. Anderson (eds.). 2014. *Policies to address poverty in America* (June). Washington, DC: Hamilton, Project, Brookings Institution.

Kemple, James. 2008. *Career academies: Long-term impacts on work, education and transitions to adulthood.* New York: MDRC.

Lerman, Robert. 2014. Expanding apprenticeship opportunities in America. In Kearney, Harris, and Anderson 2014.

Long, Mark. 2004. Race and college admissions: An alternative to affirmative action? *Review of Economics and Statistics* 86(4): 1020–1037.

Long, Bridget Terry. 2014. Addressing the academic barriers to success in higher education. In Kearney, Harris, and Anderson 2014.

Long, Mark C., Dan Goldhaber, and Nick Huntington-Klein. 2014. *Do student college major choices respond to changes in wages?* Paper presented at National Center for Analysis of Longitudinal Data in Education Research (CALDER) Research Conference, American Institutes of Research, Washington, DC (February).

Lovenheim, Michael. 2011. The effect of liquid housing wealth on college enrollment. *Journal of Labor Economics* 29(4): 370–422.

Magnuson, Katherine, and Jane Waldfogel (eds.). 2008. *Steady gains and stalled progress: Inequality and the Black-White test score Gap.* New York: Russell Sage.

Maguire, Sheila, Joshua Freely, Carol Clymer, Maureen Conway, and Deena Schwartz. 2010. *Tuning into local labor markets.* Philadelphia: PPV.

MDRC. 2014. *Paycheck plus: Making work pay for Low-income single adults,* Policy brief. New York: MDRC.

Mincer, Jacob. 1974. *Education, experience and earnings.* Chicago: University of Chicago Press.

Mishel, Lawrence, Josh Bivens, Elise Gould, and Heidi Shierholz. 2012–2013. *The state of working America,* 12th Ed. Ithaca: Cornell University Press.

Murnane, Richard. 2013. US high school graduation rates: Patterns and explanations. *Journal of Economic Literature* 51(2): 370–422.

Murnane, Richard, and John Tyler. 2000. Who benefits from obtaining a GED? Evidence from high school and beyond. *Review of Economics and Statistics* 82(1): 23–37.

National Conference of State Legislatures. 2014. *Performance-based funding for higher education.* http://www.ncsl.org/research/education/performance-funding.aspx.

National Fund for Workforce Solutions. www.nfwsolutions.org. Accessed 17 Sept 2014.

National Governors Association Center for Best Practices. 2014. *State sector strategies coming of age: Implications for state workforce policymakers.* Washington, DC: NGA Center for Best Practices.

National Skills Coalition. Federal policy: Workforce innovation and opportunity Act. http://www.nationalskillscoalition.org/federal-policy/workforce-investment-act. Accessed 17 Sept 2014.

Neumark, David. 2007. *Improving school-to-work transitions.* New York: Russell Sage.

Neumark, David, and William Wascher. 2009. *Minimum wages.* Cambridge, MA: MIT Press.

OECD (Organisation for Economic Co-operation and Development). 2013. *OECD Skills Outlook 2013.* Paris: OECD Publishing. http://skills.oecd.org/skillsoutlook.html.

Owen, Stephanie, and Isabel Sawhill. 2013. *Should everyone go to college?* Policy brief. Washington, DC: Brookings Institution.

Page, Lindsay. 2012. Understanding the impact of career academy attendance: An application of the principal stratification framework for causal effects accounting for partial compliance. *Evaluation Review* 36(2): 99–132.

Patel, Reshma, Lashawn Richburg-Hayes, Elijah de la Campa, and Timothy Rudd. 2013. *Performance-based scholarships: What have we learned?* New York: MDRC.

Reardon, Sean F. 2011. The widening achievement gap between the rich and the poor: New evidence and possible explanations. In *Whither opportunity: Rising inequality, schools, and children's life chances*, ed. Greg J. Duncan and Richard J. Murnane, 91–116. New York: Russell Sage Foundation/Spencer Foundation.

Roder, Anne, and Mark Elliott. 2011. *A promising start: Initial impacts of year up on low-income students careers.* New York: Economic Mobility Corporation.

Rosenbaum, James. 2001. *Beyond college for all: Career paths for the forgotten half.* New York: Russell Sage.

Rosenbaum, James. 2002. *Beyond college for all.* New York: Russell Sage.

Sacerdote, Bruce. 2001. Peer effects with random assignment: Results for Dartmouth roommates. *Quarterly Journal of Economics* 116(2): 684–704.

Sawhill, Isabel, and Quentin Karpilow. 2014. *A no-cost proposal to reduce poverty and inequality,* Center for Children and Families policy brief. Washington, DC: Brookings Institution.

Schwartz, Robert, and Nancy Hoffman. 2014. *Career pathways: A route to upward mobility.* Paper presented at the Conference on Education for Improving Mobility, Thomas B. Fordham Institute, New York.

Scott-Clayton, Judith. 2011. *The shapeless river: Does a lack of structure inhibit student progress at community colleges?* Working paper. New York: Community College Research Center, Columbia University.

Scott-Clayton, Judith. 2012. *Do high-stakes placement exams predict college success?* Working paper. New York: Community College Research Center, Columbia University.

Scrivener, Susan, and Michael Weiss. 2013. *More graduates: Two-year results from an evaluation of accelerated study in associates programs (ASAP) for developmental education students.* New York: MDRC.

Symonds, William, Robert Schwartz, and Ronald Ferguson. 2011. *Pathways to prosperity: Meeting the challenge of preparing young Americans for the 21st century.* Cambridge, MA: Graduate School of Education, Harvard University.

U.S. Department of Education. 2012a. *Investing in America's future: A blueprint for transforming career and technical education*. Washington, DC. http://www.ed.gov/news/speeches/investing-americas-future-blueprint-transforming-career-and-technical-education.

U.S. Department of Education. 2012b. *For each and every child: A strategy for achieving equity and excellence in education*. Report by the Commission on Equity and Excellence. Washington, DC.

Waldfogel, Jane. 2007. Work-family policies. In *Reshaping the American workforce in a changing economy*, ed. Harry Holzer and Demetra S. Nightingale. Washington, DC: Urban Institute Press.

White House. 2014. *Ready to work: Job-driven training and American opportunity*. Washington, DC.

Wilson, Scott. 2014. Obama announces $600M in grants programs to prepare workers for jobs. *Washington Post,* April 16.

Wiswall, Matthew, and Basit Zafar. 2013. *How do college students respond to public information about earnings?* Staff Reports 516. New York: Federal Reserve Bank.

Zeidenberg, Matthew, Sung-Woo Cho, and Davis Jenkins. 2010. *Washington State's integrated basic education and skills training (I-BEST) program: New evidence of effectiveness*, Working Paper. New York: Community College Research Center, Columbia University. http://ccrc.tc.columbia.edu/publications/i-best-new-evidence.html.

Zinn, Rachel, and Andy Van Kluenen. 2014. *Making workforce data work*. Washington, DC: Workforce Data Quality Campaign.

Part IV
Politics and the Road Ahead

Chapter 12
Political and Policy Responses to Problems of Inequality and Opportunity: Past, Present, and Future

Leslie McCall

Abstract There is surprisingly little research on American norms of economic inequality and opportunity, particularly in the era of rising inequality since the 1980s. In this chapter, I describe three political and policy responses to problems of inequality and opportunity and examine how they square with public opinion. Each approach is characterized by a particular mix of views concerning inequality (of outcomes) on the one hand and opportunity on the other. The "equalizing opportunity" approach places greater emphasis on equalizing opportunities than on equalizing outcomes, and even goes so far as opposing the equalization of outcomes in principle. This approach tends to be more identified today with conservatives than with liberals, but it has had broad-based appeal for much of American history. The "equalizing outcomes" approach places greater emphasis on equalizing outcomes than on equalizing opportunity, but it embraces both. It typically sees the goal of equalizing opportunities as being met implicitly through government tax and transfer policies that reduce disparities in disposable income. This approach is identified strongly with liberals. The "equalizing outcomes to equalize opportunity" approach is the one introduced in this chapter as the most consistent with public norms today. It occupies the middle of the political spectrum and fuses concerns about both opportunity and inequality. The way forward is to eschew a one-sided focus on either equal outcomes or equal opportunities so that Americans' views are better reflected in both political discourse and public policy.

Keywords Equalizing opportunity • Equalizing outcomes • Equalizing outcomes to equalize opportunity • Economic inequality • Economic opportunity • Income

I am very grateful for feedback on this chapter from three reviewers, Katherine Cramer, Martin Gilens, and Larry Hanover, and from participants in seminars at the University of Wisconsin's Department of Political Science, the University of Chicago School for Social Administration, and the Aalborg University Department of Political Science. Funding for some of the research reported here was gratefully provided by the Russell Sage Foundation and the National Science Foundation.

L. McCall (✉)
Department of Sociology, Institute for Policy Research, Northwestern University, Evanston, IL, USA

© Educational Testing Service 2016   415
I. Kirsch, H. Braun (eds.), *The Dynamics of Opportunity in America*,
DOI 10.1007/978-3-319-25991-8_12

inequality • Racial inequality • Gender inequality • Public opinion • Media coverage • Political campaigns • Income redistribution • Human capital

Introduction

Those of us who have grown up in the United States tend to have a pretty good handle on American culture. But for one particular aspect of American culture—norms of economic inequality and opportunity—there may be more than first meets the eye. Indeed, relatively little research exists on this subject, particularly in the era of rising inequality since the 1980s. Without such research, we naturally fall back on our social antennae, which are not likely to be reliable given the necessarily limited scope of our experiences and networks. Add to this that many commentators inhabit relatively elite positions in society (e.g., professors, journalists, pollsters, and politicians), and the result is often a chasm between elite and public understandings of the issue. This is *not* a chasm that characterizes only one side of the political aisle, however.

In this chapter, I describe three political and policy responses to problems of inequality and opportunity and examine how they square with public opinion about the topic. Each approach is characterized by a particular mix of views concerning the two related issues of opportunity and inequality (of outcomes).

- "Equalizing opportunity": This approach not only places greater emphasis on equalizing opportunities than on equalizing outcomes, it pits one against the other and actively opposes equalizing outcomes as a policy objective. This approach tends to be more identified today with conservatives than with liberals, but it has had broad-based appeal over the long course of American history and is considered by many to be the dominant ideology of the nation.
- "Equalizing outcomes": This approach, at the other end of the spectrum, places greater emphasis on equalizing outcomes than on equalizing opportunity but embraces both. It typically sees the goal of equalizing opportunities as being met implicitly through government tax and transfer policies that reduce disparities in disposable income. This approach is identified strongly with liberals.
- "Equalizing outcomes to equalize opportunity": This approach occupies the middle of the spectrum, *fusing* notions of opportunity and inequality. A central argument of this chapter is that it has emerged as an alternative to the previous two approaches, which have been the dominant forces historically but have important limitations in our present era. This middle approach also has illuminating roots in history, where equalizing outcomes had become the strategy of last resort in the battle to equalize opportunities across race and gender. In this approach, the job market and educational institutions are the focus of a joint strategy to equalize outcomes and opportunities, in contrast to the "equalizing outcomes" approach that emphasizes government tax and transfer policies. Among elites, this approach is more identified with liberals than with conservatives, but I argue

that it potentially has broader popular support among the general public, as well as among elites, with new possibilities that have yet to fully crystalize.

These approaches have not developed in a strictly chronological fashion over time; nor do they overlap precisely onto partisan orientations. Nevertheless, as I hope will become clear, there are good reasons to organize the discussion along the lines of the past, present, and future, and to roughly categorize these approaches along a continuum of partisan and political ideology, as indicated above. However, it is crucial to keep in mind that partisan boundaries are undergoing shifts and are not necessarily identical for elites and the general public.

The Legacy of the Past

> But America is more than just a place … it's an idea. It's the only country founded on an idea. Our rights come from nature and God, not government. We promise *equal opportunity, not equal outcomes*.
> – Paul Ryan's speech upon becoming Mitt Romney's running mate (Norfolk, VA, August 11, 2012, emphasis added)

It has long been an article of faith that what Americans stand for is equality of opportunity and not equality of outcomes. Relative to their European counterparts, Americans are considered "exceptional" in this regard: Europeans place greater emphasis on equality of outcomes, achieved through government policies that redistribute income, provide access to health care and retirement security, and protect the right to bargain for higher wages and other workplace benefits. By contrast, Americans emphasize the importance of individual responsibility and freedom from government intervention. They seek to level the playing field so anyone can succeed no matter their economic or social background (Lipset 1996). In terms of government policy, this has translated into a commitment to expand access to education. The U.S. was a pioneer of compulsory schooling, general and college preparatory curricula for all students, and the expansion of higher education, first through the "high school for all movement" and second through the strategy of providing "college for all" (Goldin and Katz 2008; Rosenbaum 2001).

Although often not associated with government policy per se, another central vehicle in the achievement of equality of opportunity in the United States has been robust economic growth. It would hardly suffice to educate a population for ever-higher-skilled jobs if such jobs were few in number; thus, educational and employment opportunity go hand in hand. The contrast between the U.S. and Europe in this respect was especially stark during the postwar period in which economic growth was both swift and equitably distributed in the U.S. (Levy 1987). Europe, by comparison, was recovering and rebuilding in the aftermath of war and relied on direct government aid and the expansion of the welfare state to do so, often with pressure from labor parties. Although many of the welfare state functions that were instituted in Europe were simultaneously deployed in the U.S., they were implemented through the back door here, so to speak, with government subsidies given to employers who then furnished health-care and retirement benefits to their employees. The hidden nature of these subsidies meant that government was rarely associated with, or given credit for, the ensuing benefits (Strasser et al. 1998; Howard 1997). This only reinforced the image of the United States as the land of unfettered economic opportunity, an image that dates back at least to Alexis de Tocqueville's *Democracy in America*.

This approach, then, is what I will call the "equal opportunity" approach, along the lines of Paul Ryan's quotation at the top of this section. It rests politically on a combination of government policies and an economic environment that together created educational and employment opportunities for a broad swath of the American population. Direct government redistribution is notably and often explicitly absent from this picture.

Nonetheless, there would always be those for whom the land of opportunity was beyond reach. For these individuals, a set of safety net programs has been in place since the New Deal. These programs have a contested history, but by and large they were expanded throughout the postwar decades. Their two-tiered structure—one means-tested serving low-income populations (e.g., "welfare" and food stamps) and one universal (e.g., Social Security)—remains in place. However, the means-tested programs, and particularly income support, became increasingly conditional on the requirement to work, circling back to the notion that opportunities for gainful employment are ultimately a better remedy for economic hardship than transfers of income are.

As important in the struggle for inclusion, especially by those who had been explicitly and legally denied a piece of the American pie, were policies that regulated equal access to educational institutions and the labor market. Here, too, the U.S. was a pioneer in developing strategies that expanded economic and educational opportunities, this time to those groups that had been discriminated against by virtue of their race/ethnicity, gender, or both. In the face of resistance to integration by employers and White workers, however, the anti-discrimination approach proved insufficient on its own. Affirmative action policies were then enacted to ensure a fair representation of women and minorities in universities and the workplace (MacLean 2006). This ignited a debate—perhaps more explicit than ever before—between the "equal opportunities" (i.e., anti-discrimination) and "equal outcomes" (i.e., affirmative action) strategies. Arguably, this opposition spilled over into discussions of the terms of government-provided income support to the poor, given the racial identification of the poor as African-American by the majority White population. Assistance that was directed toward creating employment opportunities was therefore considered more acceptable—and enjoyed greater popular support—than cash support.

The debate between these two opposing strategies continues to this day, as reflected in Ryan's first vice presidential campaign speech. It is critical, however, to recognize the broader resonance of the "equal opportunities" approach; it should not be seen as a dictum of only one of the two parties. As I will show in the next section, when President Obama began placing greater emphasis on the issue of income inequality in late 2011, Independent and Democratic leaning commentators worried that the message would appeal only to a narrow base of party activists and alienate the majority of Americans who, they argued, cared more about opportunity than inequality. And the establishment of a genuinely open opportunity society would require many of the policies that Democrats endorse in both the "equal outcomes" and "equalize outcomes to equalize opportunities" approaches, as also will become clear in subsequent sections.

But before turning to the present, and to what we know about how Americans think about such issues, I want to underline three features of past debates that have important implications for how we think about current and future debates.

First, the original struggle for inclusion by African-Americans, other racial minorities, and women was premised on fundamental rights of equality, but it was also premised on the vitality of the economy, the ongoing expansion of a high-quality educational system, and the equitable nature of both. Living standards rose in absolute terms across the income distribution, *and* relative differences among income groups declined. However, once the foundation of shared prosperity began to crack in the era of stagflation (1970s and 1980s), a more overtly zero-sum politics gained ascendancy, amplifying the tension between opportunities and outcomes and reinforcing popular opposition to outcomes-based measures such as affirmative action and welfare.

Second, and related, is that the "equal opportunities" approach arose, paradoxically, during a period in which outcomes were actually becoming more equal. This prompts the question of whether equitable outcomes were (and are) an implicit part of the definition or perception of an equal opportunity society. One example that suggests that they are is affirmative action, which equalized (occupational and educational) outcomes *as a way to enforce* equal opportunity policies. Indeed, affirmative action is considered an equal opportunity policy. More generally, racial and gender gaps in test scores, graduation rates, and occupational employment—that is, measures of inequality of outcomes—are frequently employed to symbolize the lack of equal educational and employment opportunities. When this happens, unequal outcomes function as indicators of unequal opportunities, and equal outcomes function as gateways to equal opportunities (Young 1958; Bell 1973; Roemer 1998). In the next section, I will refer to this approach as the middle-ground "equalize outcomes to equalize opportunities" approach.

Finally, the "equal opportunities" approach was put in place at a time when the goal was to rectify racial and gender inequalities and to ameliorate the conditions of the poor. It was not put in place to address the kind of economic inequality that we are encountering today, nor the targeting of the top "1 percenters" that this has entailed. Thus, part of the opposition to an "equal outcomes" approach may have been the result of opposition to the "undeserving" poor, racial and/or gender equality, or heightened economic anxieties that exacerbated intergroup competition, rather than to an "equal outcomes" approach *per se*. In other words, an "equal outcomes" approach—untethered from past associations in a postwelfare reform era—may be more palatable today or in the future.

All of this is to say that the "equal opportunities" approach is more nuanced, and even more internally contradictory, than commonly thought.[1] In practice, the achievement of equal opportunities is intertwined in important respects with the achievement of more equitable outcomes, particularly in the postwar period when contemporary norms of equality were given shape. And the slogan of "equal opportunities" may prove malleable in the face of new configurations of inequality as we go forward.

The Present Era of Rising Inequality

The growing income gap has become the central issue in American politics.
– "Income Gap is Issue No. 1, Debaters Agree," *Washington Post*, December 7, 1995

[C]orporate profits are setting records… [b]ut the real average hourly wage is five percent lower than it was a decade ago.
– Robert Dole, eventual Republican nominee, *New York Times*, February 14, 1996

If Americans care about "equal opportunities" and not "equal outcomes," how did we arrive at a point in the mid-1990s when Republican candidates—including Robert Dole, quoted above, as well as Patrick Buchanan—were stumping openly about the growing divide in economic fortunes (Ladd and Bowman 1998; Jacoby 1997)? And what happened to the preoccupation with opportunity? In this section, I bring public opinion to bear on these questions. Even though Americans may be more sensitized to issues of inequality now than in the past, both public opinion data and media coverage reveal that they were attuned to it in the 1990s as well. As I describe below, a majority of Americans have in fact expressed a desire for less inequality since at least the late 1980s. The preference for a more equitable distribution of income cannot, therefore, be attributed only to recent media and political attention to the topic, as is often assumed.

Proceeding from this baseline, my goal in this section is twofold. In an effort to better understand exactly *how* the public thinks about inequalities of both outcomes and opportunities, I first provide a brief overview of the best available survey data on attitudes about income inequality, perceptions of executive and worker pay and pay gaps, and beliefs about the role of individual responsibility and structural factors in shaping opportunities to "get ahead" (as the survey questions put it). I also describe the ways in which views about income inequality are interconnected with—rather than counterposed to—views about economic opportunity, as well as the consequences this has for policy preferences. Second, I discuss how, beginning as early as the late 1980s and culminating in the 2012 presidential election, inequality and opportunity became more explicitly interconnected in elite discourses as well, first among journalists and then among politicians. Recalling the second approach

---

[1] And in this respect parallels the contradictory nature of "American Dream" ideology (Hochschild 1995).

introduced above, this has led to a new set of narratives about problems of inequality and opportunity, as well as to a corresponding set of new policy proposals to address such problems.

Before discussing the content of public opinion, however, it is worth saying a few words about the primary source of public opinion data that informs my analyses. The best available information comes from the General Social Survey. The GSS was devised in the early 1970s to chronicle everything from religious beliefs to family formation practices to priorities for government spending. However, coverage of attitudes concerning inequality and opportunity was thin, and what did exist focused on subjects that were topical at that time, namely poverty and gender and racial inequality (as discussed in the previous section). As a result, the time series of public opinion data reported in this section begins in 1987, when the international counterpart to the GSS, the International Social Survey Program, introduced its first Social Inequality Module, which was incorporated into all of the participating country-level surveys. The module was then replicated in 1992, 1996, 2000, 2008, 2010, and 2012. (In 1996, 2008, and 2012, the modules were only partially replicated and only in the U.S.)

It should be underscored that none of the longest running and most respected surveys in the United States or elsewhere have ever contained a detailed battery of relevant questions on a routine basis. This is indicative, I would suggest, of the extent to which these topics constitute a new domain of inquiry, and one that was perhaps so taken for granted that it failed to inspire rigorous investigation until only recently.[2] In the past decade, however, a number of relevant survey questions have been fielded and I will draw on these in my discussion as well. In particular, wherever possible, I will compare public views to those of economic elites taking part in a representative pilot survey of the top wealth holders in the Chicago area conducted by Benjamin Page and colleagues (the Survey of Economically Successful Americans, or SESA).[3] This survey replicated many of the questions on inequality and opportunity found in the GSS.

Public Beliefs About Inequality and Opportunity

To begin with attitudes toward income inequality, Fig. 12.1 plots trends over time in responses to the only three questions about income inequality that have been replicated in each of the survey years mentioned above. The most straightforward of the three questions asks respondents' feelings as to whether "income differences in America are too large." This question solicits agreement or strong agreement by a substantial majority of Americans today—roughly two-thirds. Desires for less inequality are also consistently high over time, a trend that supports the claim that I

---

[2] In the pre-rising-inequality era, see, e.g., Hochschild (1981), Kluegel and Smith (1986), and Vanneman and Cannon (1987) for in-depth studies of beliefs about inequality.

[3] Page et al. 2013. Analyses of the SESA data are taken from McCall and Chin (2013).

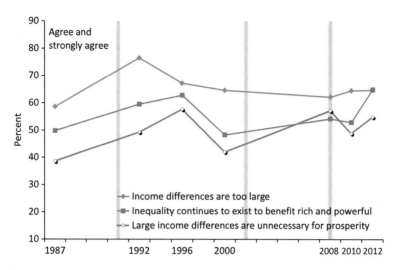

Fig. 12.1 American concerns about inequality, 1987–2012 (Source: Author's analysis of the General Social Survey. Notes: Response categories also include "neither agree nor disagree," "disagree," and "strongly disagree." Shaded lines indicate years of economic recession)

made earlier about the timing and cause of opposition to inequality. American opposition to inequality is not primarily a fleeting consequence of social movement activism or political leadership, as it predates episodes such as the Occupy Wall Street movement and President Obama's seizing upon the issue in his 2012 reelection campaign.

Nonetheless, attitudes do shift over time in revealing ways. According to the bottom two lines in Fig. 12.1, a majority of Americans agree or strongly agree with two specific statements about the ill effects of the income gap. In 2012, between 55 and 65 % of Americans believed that the benefits of inequality are neither widely shared (in response to a question whether "inequality continues to exist because it benefits the rich and powerful") nor strictly required to create the kinds of incentives that fuel economic growth and prosperity (in response to a question whether "large differences in income are not necessary for prosperity"). These skeptical attitudes toward inequality exhibit a clear peak in the mid-1990s and again in the most recent survey year of 2012, relative to the base year of 1987 and also relative to a dip in concerns in 2000.[4] This pattern will help in deciphering how Americans connect perceptions of economic opportunity to perceptions of income inequality, a subject to which I will return at the end of my review of the public opinion data.

Turning to the topic of disparities in pay (rather than income), public opinion polls since at least the 1970s reflect widespread opposition to CEO pay, with well

---

[4] Moreover, the peaks are strongly significant after controlling for a large number of compositional and political shifts, such as polarization in partisan views, which I discuss further below and in McCall (2013, Chap. 3).

over two-thirds of Americans saying CEOs are overpaid.[5] Based on data that are of higher quality than polls but more infrequent, Americans are also generally aware of (1) the rise in executive pay, (2) the stagnation of worker pay, and (3) the widening of pay disparities. For instance, the ratio between the median estimate of executive pay and worker pay more than doubles from 13:1 in 2000 to 32:1 in 2010, as shown in Fig. 12.2. Although these ratios significantly understate the dramatic increase in earnings inequality, the median desired ratio is still remarkably low—4:1 in 2000 and 7:1 in 2010—and also dwarfed by the median desired ratio among the top 1 %, which is 50:1. It is therefore unlikely that preferences for less inequality would be substantially altered by a more accurate appraisal of the scale of executive pay, because they are already so low (see McCall and Chin 2013, Table 3, for a more in-depth analysis of this point). Among the general public, knowledge of growing pay inequality is also driven by dramatically higher estimates of executive pay rather than by significantly lower estimates of worker pay. In fact, it is evident to most Americans that worker pay has been largely stagnant for the past couple of decades.

Despite knowledge of rising inequality and desires for a more equitable distribution of both income and earnings, do Americans nevertheless maintain their faith—perhaps blindingly so—in the land of opportunity? On the one hand, as Fig. 12.3 shows, over 90 % of Americans, including the top 1 %, do indeed believe that hard

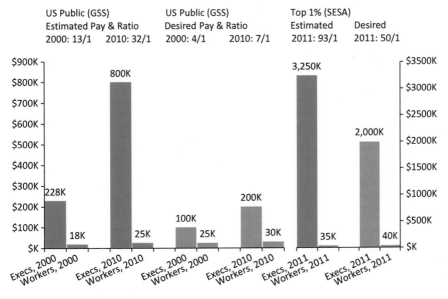

Fig. 12.2 American perceptions of occupational pay and pay inequality (Source: Author's analysis of the General Social Survey, the International Social Survey Program, and the Survey of Economically Successful Americans. Note: Data are in current (non-inflation-adjusted) dollars. Median estimates are presented (e.g., median estimated pay and median desired pay) and ratios of these estimates are taken)

---

[5] Assorted public opinion polls dating back to the 1970s (McCall 2013, 211).

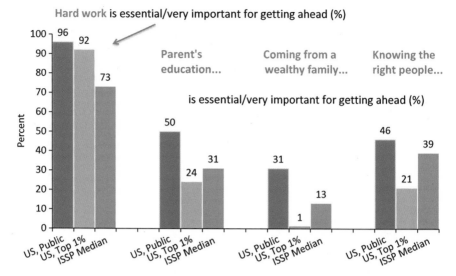

Fig. 12.3 American and international perceptions of economic opportunity (Source: Author's analysis of the General Social Survey [2010; U.S. Public], the International Social Survey Program [2010, ISSP Median], and the Survey of Economically Successful Americans [2011, US Top 1 %]. Notes: Other response categories for GSS and ISSP are "somewhat important," "not very important," and "not at all important." Response categories for SESA include "very important," "somewhat important," and "not very important at all," and therefore only "very important" is shown in the chart. Only other advanced industrial countries are included in the calculation of the ISSP median, including Australia, Austria, Denmark, Finland, France, Germany, Great Britain, Iceland, Japan, New Zealand, Norway, Portugal, Spain, Sweden, Switzerland and the United States)

work is essential or very important in getting ahead. This is, predictably, greater than the median among advanced industrial countries, which is nonetheless quite high itself at 73 %. On the other hand, there is a little known countervailing tendency: Americans are generally as or more likely to believe in the role of social factors in getting ahead, such as having well-educated parents, coming from a wealthy family, and knowing the right people. And the American public at large is also at least twice as likely to express these views as the top 1 percenters are. In fact, only 1 percent of the top 1 percenters said that coming from a wealthy family was very important, whereas 31 % of the public did. The American public therefore emerges as significantly more cognizant of social barriers to getting ahead than economic elites do.

Although these particular data also suggest that recognition of barriers to upward mobility is increasing over time (not shown), a few more frequently repeated questions give us greater purchase on this trend. Perhaps the single best question asks whether "people like me and my family have a good chance of improving our standard of living" (see Fig. 12.4). Interestingly, when concerns about inequality are at their highest in the early and mid-1990s, and again in the most recent survey years (see Fig. 12.1), Americans are *less* likely to agree that their standard of living will improve. For instance, the low points of such agreement are in 1992 and 2012 when

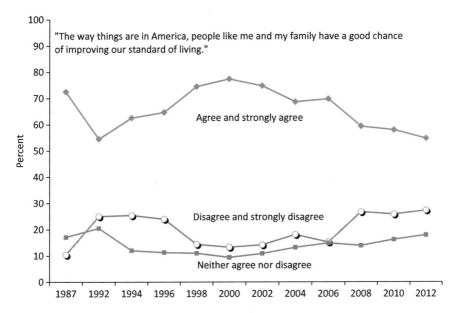

Fig. 12.4 Changes in perceptions of economic opportunity, 1987–2012 (Source: Author's analysis of the General Social Survey)

55 % were optimistic about their chances for upward mobility. This is more than 20 percentage points off the high point of optimism in 2000, when 77 % agreed. (Agreement was also high, at 73 %, at the start of our time series in 1987.) Similarly, Gallup began asking a question in 2001 about the degree to which people are satisfied with "the opportunity for a person in this nation to get ahead by working hard." As shown in Fig. 12.5, they found that satisfaction has been falling ever since this question was launched, from 76 % in 2001 to 53 % in 2012.

The fact that heightened concerns about inequality coincide with greater pessimism about the possibility for upward mobility can be further seen in Fig. 12.6, which helps to illuminate how the various strands of public opinion that we have been discussing fit together.

On the left side, the figure charts the trend in an index of concerns about inequality that includes all three questions in Fig. 12.1 (income differences are too large; inequality continues to exist to benefit the rich and powerful; large income differences are unnecessary for property) scaled from 0 to 1, so that the y-axis indicates the proportionate increase from 1987 in concerns about inequality after controlling for a wide range of factors. When the vertical lines for each year are above the line at 0, it means that concerns are significantly greater than they were in 1987. The red squares show the shift in concerns when not controlling for the trend in concerns about upward mobility from Fig. 12.4; the blue diamonds show the trend when controlling for it.

What we find is that the blue diamonds are almost always below the red squares, indicating that concerns about inequality would not have climbed as much if con-

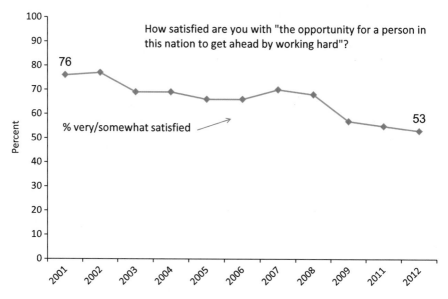

Fig. 12.5 Changes in perceptions of economic opportunity, 2001–2012 (Source: Gallup. Notes: Response categories also include "somewhat dissatisfied" and "very dissatisfied")

cerns about upward mobility had not done so. That is because the two trends are correlated: rising concerns about upward mobility help to "explain" rising concerns about inequality. Except for measures of political ideology and partisanship, no other single variable has as large an effect.

And as can be seen with a similar exercise on the right side of chart, the effect of the trend in political orientation is in the opposite direction: concerns about inequality would have risen even more (as shown by the blue triangles above the red squares) had the trend in political orientation not veered in a more conservative direction over this period, inhibiting the rise in concerns about inequality. In other words, concerns about both inequality and opportunity rose substantially over time, in a coordinated fashion, against the tide of the more remarked-upon trend toward political conservatism, which slowed the rise in concerns to only a minor degree relative to the largely unexplained portion of the shifts.

This conclusion is reinforced by an analysis of other trends that fail to coincide with heightened desires for less inequality. Take, for example, two factors often assumed to be associated with rising concerns about inequality: the growing trend in inequality itself and the business cycle. From both Figs. 12.1 and 12.6, we can see that concerns about inequality do not peak during the trough of a business cycle and then taper off; instead, they stabilize or rise during the initial years of recovery from a recession—in the mid-1990s and in 2012. This is the case even though other public opinion data (e.g., from the American National Election Studies) clearly show an upswing in Americans' assessments of how the national economy is performing during the expansions (and thus Americans are not misrecognizing macroeconomic

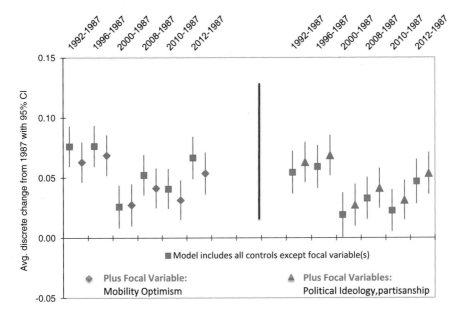

Fig. 12.6 Adjusted trend in index of concerns about inequality (scaled 0–1) (Source: Author's analysis of the General Social Survey. Notes: The outcome is an index of the three questions in Fig. 12.1, scaled to range from 0 to 1 (income differences are too large; inequality continues to exist to benefit the rich and powerful; large income differences are unnecessary for prosperity). All models include controls for factors that were found to affect beliefs about inequality, including age (and age squared), household size and whether the respondent has children under 18, marital status (married/nonmarried), region (South/non-South), race (White/non-White), employment status (employed/nonemployed), subjective social class, family income, and education. Mobility optimism is measured by the variable presented in Fig. 12.4. Political orientation is measured with two variables on a seven-point scale: political ideology (liberal to conservative) and partisanship (Democrat to Republican). These are also interacted with year where appropriate (in 1996, 2010, and 2012))

shifts).[6] Similarly, concerns about both inequality and opportunities for upward mobility subsided during the boom years of the late 1990s, despite most measures of inequality not falling in lockstep, or even continuing to rise.[7]

Taking these and other considerations into account, I find that the peaks of concern about inequality emerge with perceptions of the negative *consequences* of inequality—its practical impact on economic opportunity—rather than with

---

[6] According to the American National Election Studies (ANES), in 2008, 90 % of respondents said the economy was worse than the year before, whereas 36 % said so in 2012. Most Americans are aware that the economy is improving or at least not getting any worse. The diverging pattern of views about the economy and distribution of income are also apparent in the aftermath of the early 2000s recession (McCall 2013, 170–172, based on ANES data).

[7] The trend in inequality is complex and depends on the part of the distribution in which it is measured; thus we need to examine both the actual trends and the trends that the public is most likely to be aware of (McCall 2013, 119–125).

perceptions of the *level* of inequality itself. The fact that perceptions of restricted opportunities endure past the official end of recessions, as is evident in both the early 1990s and late 2000s, suggests that Americans are seeking something more than mere economic growth to alleviate their economic anxieties. During the "jobless" recoveries of late, in which wages have also stagnated, Americans are reacting against patterns of inequitable growth, in which only the top is experiencing gains and the American Dream of shared prosperity is thrown into question. Put somewhat differently, I am suggesting that if the economy were doing well today for everyone—if all boats were lifted and economic opportunity abounded—concerns about inequality would decline despite what some consider to be stratospheric levels of inequality. In my discussion of media coverage, political campaigns, and policy preferences in the next section, I provide additional evidence of this dynamic and further flesh out its details and policy implications.

To sum up, most Americans desire less inequality and have for at least a quarter of a century. Also, by some measures, intolerance of inequality is increasing and is significantly higher today than it was 25 years ago. Regarding matters of opportunity, many Americans recognize that social barriers to opportunity are important, even more so than in similar countries, and much more so than the top 1 percenters do. And, again, by some measures, such perceptions of limited opportunities have increased over the past decade. Lastly, and, most centrally, concerns about restricted opportunities appear to coincide with desires for less inequality. This blending of perceptions of inequalities of opportunity and outcomes recalls the discussion of the middle-ground "equalize outcomes to equalize opportunity" approach at the end of the previous section.

Elite Discourses of Inequality and Opportunity

Although both the content and overall sophistication of public views may be surprising, what is perhaps even more surprising are repeated allusions to the "equalize outcomes to equalize opportunity" approach at several junctures throughout the period of rising inequality by journalists and politicians. In addition to the quotations appearing at the top of this section—pinpointing the central role of inequality in the 1996 presidential election—journalists were linking news about growing economic inequality to the potential eclipse of the American Dream as early as the 1980s. Although these formulations and slogans may not have been as frequent or as well articulated in political platforms as they are today, they nonetheless offer insight into the tacit ways in which Americans, including elites, fuse their practical understandings of opportunity and inequality.

In this section, I first briefly illustrate how this fusion of ideas is depicted in media coverage. For our purposes, the widespread prevalence of this particular framing is less significant than the almost commonsensical appeal of the framing itself across partisan perspectives. Then, for the remainder of the section, I focus on the current political scene, including a discussion of the political and economic strategies for reducing inequality and expanding opportunity that have surfaced in recent political debates and the policy orientation of the public at large.

For close to three decades, editorialists Mortimer Zuckerman of *U.S. News & World Report* and Robert Samuelson of *Newsweek* have been two of the most stalwart commentators on issues of inequality and opportunity from the liberal and conservative perspectives, respectively. Already in 1988, Zuckerman had written a column in response to a report on inequality released by the Congressional Budget Office (July 25). Bemoaning the effects of inequality, in which "most of our citizens have not benefitted from recent U.S. prosperity," Zuckerman related the new developments to the upcoming presidential election, arguing that "the crucial judgment is who can reverse the trends toward inequality and bring more of our people closer to the American dream." According to Zuckerman, growth was no longer a guarantor of the kinds of economic opportunities Americans had come to expect, and widening inequality was the reason why. Fast-forwarding almost two decades ahead, in a 2006 column titled "Trickle-Up Economics" (October 2), Samuelson similarly castigated the skewed nature of economic growth as "un-American" and a threat to "America's social compact, which depends on a shared sense of well-being." As an indication of just how routinely journalists had been covering these issues, Justin Fox of *Time* complained in an article written in 2008 that the income gap is "an issue that's been danced around for too long. It's time to address it" (May 26).

Thus issue fatigue among journalists had already arrived some six months before Barack Obama's victory in the presidential election of that year and a full 3½ years before his first major speech on the subject in December 2011—in Osawatamie, Kansas—itself just a few months after the eruption of the Occupy Wall Street movement. The issue had long been percolating in the media as well as in prior electoral campaigns (in the 1990s) by the time it was the focus of a major social movement and then elevated to the highest level of political expression in the words of the president himself.

Despite this, Obama's emphasis on inequality in the first major domestic policy speech of his 2012 reelection campaign (in Osawatamie), and then again in his 2012 State of the Union address, was not wholeheartedly embraced by independents or pundits and strategists within the wider fold of the Democratic Party. The dispute was nicely encapsulated in an op-ed by the nonpartisan head of the Pew Opinion Research Center, Andrew Kohut, who warned that "what the public wants is not a war on the rich but more politics that promote opportunity." Another analyst argued that "a campaign emphasizing growth and opportunity is more likely to yield a Democratic victory than is a campaign focused on inequality. While the latter will thrill the party's base, only the former can forge a majority."[8] In short, the "equal opportunities" approach was not only very much alive, but it appealed to opinion leaders across the political spectrum, to the center and left as well as to the more predictable right.

---

[8] Andrew Kohut, "Don't Mind the Gap," *New York Times*, January 27, 2012; William Galston, "Why Obama's New Populism May Sink His Campaign," *New Republic*, December 17, 2011.

Yet, in truth, Obama was careful to embed his comments on inequality within a more expansive rhetoric about the need to repair and rebuild the American Dream. His diagnosis followed in the vein of journalists like Zuckerman and Samuelson, who saw inequality as a barrier to opportunity in the form of shared prosperity and equitable growth. Given the obligation of journalists to have their finger on the pulse of ordinary Americans, this rendering echoed public views, in which heightened concerns about inequality coincided with growing pessimism about the chances for upward mobility (as discussed above). That is, the president's vision was more consistent with the "equalize outcomes to equalize opportunities" approach, where both inequality and opportunity took center stage, than it was with another approach—an exclusively "equal outcomes" approach—that *substituted* an emphasis on inequality for one on opportunity, as those reacting against the president's speeches had claimed. The misinterpretation was understandable, however, in that attention to "equal outcomes" has a venerable history among liberals and still enjoys substantial backing, for example, in frequent calls to increase taxes on the affluent as the centerpiece of an anti-inequality agenda (Piketty 2014).

This brings us to a key question: How do these various approaches translate into policy prescriptions? It is one thing for various publics and leaders to coalesce around the definition of the problem but quite another to find common ground on the solution. After briefly describing the advantages and disadvantages of the policies associated with the more familiar "equal opportunities" and "equal outcomes" approaches, I focus on the policies that have evolved in response to the perspective that, in the public's mind, I argue, best characterizes our era of rising inequality, that is, the "equalizing outcomes to equalize opportunities" perspective. Although these policies overlap in several respects with those of the other two approaches, they are also venturing into largely uncharted territory.

As should be transparent by now, the key strength of the "equal opportunities" approach is its emphasis on equalizing opportunities, whereas its key weakness is its rejection of any attempt to *directly* reduce inequalities of outcomes. On the one hand, the prescription of pro-business reforms to accelerate economic growth in conjunction with educational reforms to reward individual responsibility is a winning combination. It reassures the public in its promise to create precisely the kinds of job opportunities required to lift oneself up by the bootstraps to achieve the American Dream of upward mobility, and, in doing so, it harkens back to the Golden Age of postwar prosperity and educational expansion. To the extent that Republicans are more closely identified with this message than Democrats are, they reap the political benefits of an economic opportunity platform (Smith 2007).

On the other hand, in our own post-postwar era, a prescription of economic growth alone does little to correct the skew toward the top in the availability of good employment opportunities. This weakness in the "equal opportunities" approach may become even more salient as *household* incomes in the middle of the distribution continue their historic slide from peaks at the turn of the twenty-first century. The last business cycle (2000–2007) was the first in which median household income and female earnings both failed to post significant gains (whereas median male earnings stopped growing in the 1970s) (DeNavas-Walt and Proctor 2014).

Long the country with the "richest" middle class, the U.S. now lags Canada in median after-tax income levels.[9]

The resulting dynamic could parallel that of the 1960s and 1970s, when anti-discrimination policies were insufficient in reducing inequality in the face of resistance to gender and racial integration by White workers and employers, which then provoked the more proactive approach of "equalizing outcomes to equalize opportunities" (i.e., affirmative action). Indeed, some in the "equal opportunities" camp are afraid that a populist backlash against inequality could usher forth a more drastic leveling of incomes than proactive initiatives. And this has led to a reconsideration of the implicit ban on advocacy of outcomes-based policies, such as raising the minimum wage and the earned income tax credit. To be sure, a resuscitation of the "compassionate conservative" in the present day may entail more attention to equalizing opportunities than equalizing outcomes, but the latter is beginning to be acknowledged in the process.[10]

Although most Democrats endorse an economic growth strategy (there is little reason for anyone not to), and Democratic administrations are in fact more likely to implement policies that deliver middle-income growth, they are more closely identified with the "equal outcomes" than with the "equal opportunities" approach, for the simple reason that they do indeed advocate for more equal outcomes (Bartels 2008; Kelly 2009). As is well known, this approach traditionally focuses on increased taxes on the affluent as the principal method of ameliorating economic hardship and mitigating economic inequality.

On the one hand, the prescription of increased taxes on the wealthy is reassuring to the public in its emphasis on diverting funds from those who do not need them to those who do. On the other hand, there's a fairly severe transparency problem that handicaps this strategy: exactly how are higher taxes on the rich going to translate into greater educational and job opportunities for the rest of the population? On the basis of what history are Americans to put their trust in taxing the rich as the solution to declining opportunities? While in principle popular support for progressive taxes is often fairly high—above the 50 % mark—such support is fickle in the moment, when it comes to specific pieces of legislation, because the benefits are often not clearly conveyed. As Larry Bartels has shown, the public will opt for a small tax cut for themselves even if they perceive the well off as receiving an unfair and disproportionate share of the gains from tax-cut legislation, as was the case in 2001 for support of the Bush tax cuts (Bartels 2005; Lupia et al. 2007).

Interestingly, the middle-ground "equalize outcomes to equalize opportunities" approach offers a potential solution to this transparency problem by diverting the

---

[9] David Leonhardt, "The American Middle Class No Longer the World's Richest." *New York Times*, April 14, 2014.

[10] This includes support among some Republicans for minimum wage increases, at least at the state level (Reid J. Epstein, "Some Republicans Back State Minimum-Wage Increases." *Wall Street Journal*, September 15, 2014), and enhancements of the earned income tax credit (e.g., Reihan Salam, "The Battle of EITC Ideas," *National Review Online,* March 28, 2014). On the new meanings of compassionate conservatism, see Thomas Edsall, "The Republic Discovery of the Poor," *New York Times*, February 11, 2015.

emphasis from equalizing outcomes and redirecting it to equalizing opportunities without losing sight of either objective. Again, such a solution was well underway before the Occupy Wall Street movement got off the ground, underscoring its rootedness in local conditions and political orientations. Beginning in the 2000s, for instance, several states passed measures to raise taxes on high-income households in order to fund popular services, such as education, health care, and public safety. The measures often incorporated an explicit tradeoff between raising taxes—only on the affluent—and funding opportunity-enhancing programs.

In early 2010, to take one example, voters passed a highly contested ballot measure in Oregon by a 54 % majority that, according to the official summary of the measure, would:

> Raise taxes on household income at and above $250,000 (and $125,000 for individual filers). Reduce income taxes on unemployment benefits in 2009. Provide funds currently budgeted for education, health care, public safety, other services.

In a similar fashion, the state of California passed Proposition 30 by a 55 % majority in November 2012. The tradeoff was advertised in the very title of the proposition: "Temporary Taxes to Fund Education. Guaranteed Local Public Safety Funding. Initiative Constitutional Amendment." The temporary nature of the tax hike may be as important as the commitment to funding opportunity-enhancing policies. A similar ballot measure failed in Washington state in part because, it is speculated, the measure left open the possibility that the legislature could vote in the future to increase taxes lower down in the income distribution (Franko et al. 2013). A later and more widely publicized example of an "equalize outcomes to equalize opportunities" approach came with Bill de Blasio's successful 2013 mayoral campaign in New York City, the centerpiece of which was a promise to raise income taxes on the wealthy in order to fund universal preschool education.[11]

Although these initiatives sound commonsensical, their novelty should not be underestimated. As far as I am aware, electoral campaigns in recent political history have advocated for progressive taxes (with reticence), and they have advocated for educational reforms (with gusto), but they have not advocated forthrightly for a progressive tax that would be targeted both in terms of who pays it (the affluent) and which programs benefit from it (education). In a more scholarly vein, educational programs have tended to fall outside the purview of conventional welfare state research and the corresponding "equal outcomes" approach, which focus on transfers of income to fund safety net programs.[12] Nonetheless, education is emerging as

---

[11] It may be argued that these are liberal states, but each also has a history of electing Republican governors and/or passing conservative ballot measures. Young and Varner (2011) provide an analysis of the impact of so-called "millionaire" taxes on the outmigration of millionaires and find little support for the pattern.

[12] In fact, public funding of higher education in particular has been seen as inequality enhancing (Ansell 2010).

a central theme in the everyday politics of redistribution as well as in contemporary research.[13]

Moreover, in some prominent instances, a general call for shoring up educational resources is giving way to a more specific emphasis on creating a more equal educational starting gate for children from diverging socioeconomic backgrounds. Here, politicians are seizing on an academic argument about the negative relationship between income inequality and intergenerational mobility, famously referred to as the Great Gatsby Curve by President Obama's former chief of economic advisors, Alan Krueger (Krueger 2012). In the final section, I will discuss the potential of this strategy further and the scholarly evidence underlying it.

Another emerging prong of the "equalize outcomes to equalize opportunities" approach concerns employment rather than educational opportunities. It too has been missing from the dominant models of income redistribution because its emphasis is on redistribution in the labor market rather than on redistribution "after the fact" in post-transfer and post-tax income.[14] Labor market redistribution simply refers to any action that reduces disparities in pay and earnings in the labor market. Momentum has been building over many years to lift wages at the bottom, for instance, through popular and successful campaigns to raise the minimum wage at the local and state levels, sometimes to a living wage standard. Indeed, in the 2014 midterm elections, one of the most remarked-upon patterns was the simultaneous election of Republican candidates on the one hand and passage of minimum wage increases on the other.[15] Some other notable developments to augment worker pay and facilitate access to good jobs include fast-food worker strikes and anti-wage-theft, anti-deunionization, anti-Walmart, ban-the-box and paid family leave campaigns; these mostly have occurred at the local and state levels, a theme that characterizes the drive for greater and more equitable spending on education as well (Ingram et al. 2010; Bernhardt 2012; Milkman and Appelbaum 2013).

Finally, in an era of soaring top-end pay and stock market returns, and keeping in mind the public's desire for radically reduced executive pay, there is the alternative strategy of reducing earnings at the top in the hopes of redistributing the proceeds to the middle and bottom. The most far-reaching examples in recent years come from overseas: the European Union's 2013 rule to cap banker bonuses at two times salary levels and a binding say-on-executive-pay referendum applying to publicly

---

[13] For example, Ansell 2010; Busemeyer 2012. In research with Lane Kenworthy (McCall and Kenworthy 2009), we show that most traditional redistributive policies that tax and transfer income have not risen in support relative to 1987, controlling for a wide range of factors. By contrast, the only policy that has enjoyed consistent support over time is increased spending on education. Moreover, this issue is now significantly tied to beliefs about inequality, whereas it was not at the beginning of the period in 1987. If we look further back than 1987, we find an even more striking increase in support for educational spending over time.

[14] Again, see McCall and Kenworthy (2009, 460, 470–472) and McCall (2013, Chap. 5).

[15] For instance, in Alaska (69 %), Arkansas (65 %), Nebraska (59 %), South Dakota (53 %), and Illinois (68 %), where the measure was advisory. In January 2015, 26 states will have higher minimum wages than the federal level. Several Republican candidates are backing higher minimum wages if initiated at the state level but are opposed to a higher federal level.

held companies in Switzerland. The latter was launched in 2008 as a response to excessive executive pay packages at major corporations such as Novartis and was passed by a comfortable margin in 2013. Similar proposals have been floated in Germany and France. Although far weaker and less publicized, the Dodd-Frank Wall Street Reform Act of 2010 did mandate and finally implement the disclosure of executive pay and executive-to-median pay ratios in publicly held companies. In each of these cases, employers mounted major opposition to the proposed laws and then to the regulatory bodies that oversee their implementation.

Importantly, however, some efforts to curb inequality have emanated from the corporate sector itself. Though still a relatively small-scale movement, a group of entrepreneurs is promoting the establishment of B-Corporations, which challenge the primacy of shareholder value as the sole responsibility of the corporation and place social as well as profit motives at the heart of their corporate charters. Similarly, the corporate social responsibility movement has been active for decades around issues such as ecological sustainability and equal employment opportunity but is now beginning to organize around the problem of pay inequality. More generally, what is emerging here are various ways to reintroduce "equity norms" directly into an increasingly dominant institution of contemporary society: the corporation (Edmans 2012; King and Pearce 2010). These and other efforts are coalescing around the new concept of "inclusive capitalism" (Freeland 2014a; Summers and Balls 2015).

In sum, although the popular backlash against executive pay may ultimately lead to unintended and counterproductive consequences—such as higher banker base salaries or even executive pay—and may not therefore be ideal from an economist's perspective, the broader lesson for our purposes is that the political and policy response to rising inequality and declining opportunities has been extended outside the traditional bounds of redistributive politics. The objective in many instances is to intervene in the pay-setting process itself. In this respect, advocates are following in the footsteps of the civil rights movement's crusade against pay and employment discrimination. The current thrust—to reduce economic inequality as a path to enhanced labor market opportunities—is almost directly analogous to the historic and ongoing fight to reduce racial and gender earnings inequalities as an equal employment opportunity strategy. Both initiatives are forced by circumstances into an "equalize outcomes to equalize opportunities" approach, with an eye trained first and foremost on the prize of equal opportunity.

The Future Politics of Inequality and Opportunity

As political scientists have long observed, American public opinion is best understood through the lens of pragmatism rather than ideology (Free and Cantril 1967; Walsh 2012; Bartels 2013). In that spirit, I have examined the politics of inequality and opportunity from the point of view of the American public at large, as told through public opinion surveys, media coverage, and the fashioning of new political opportunities, primarily but not exclusively at the local and state levels. What has emerged from this examination is a portrait of a politics in formation, one that conforms to neither of the two dominant political traditions in this country concerning the contentious issue of inequality.

To be sure, both the "equal opportunities" and "equal outcomes" approaches will continue to have an enduring grip on the American mind, but they also fall short in crucial respects. The former's prioritizing of economic opportunity—principally through the rhetoric of educational reform and economic growth—aligns with the public's clear preference for this route to achieving a fair and equitable society, but it does so at the cost of misrecognizing the role that economic inequality now plays in restricting opportunities for economic security and upward mobility. As a result, the latter "equal outcomes" approach strikes a chord with the American public, too, as most want to see a reversal of the growing divide in outcomes, and have for at least the past quarter of a century. The problem with this approach, however, is that income redistribution is too often portrayed as an end in itself, or alternatively, as a source of tax revenues for a diffuse set of social and public goods. Yet Americans appear to be less agitated by the absolute scale of inequality as such than by the consequences of inequality for their prospects of earning a good living. In short, neither approach connects the problem of inequality to the problem of opportunity.

Into this vacuum step a variety of initiatives that I have grouped under the "equalize outcomes to equalize opportunities" banner, whose lineage can be traced back to the civil rights movement. These initiatives fall into one of two categories. In the first, the focus is on the skewed pattern of economic growth and, specifically, the need to redistribute earnings in the labor market in order to lift absolute living standards at the bottom and middle of the distribution. In the second, the focus is on the shift from generic taxing and spending models of redistribution to "taxing for opportunity" models that explicitly target educational opportunity as one of the central goals. Owing to the pragmatic origins of these initiatives, however, they have thus far been launched in a piecemeal and inchoate fashion. Does the future promise something more bold and holistic? Building on the discussion in the previous sections, I conclude with a guiding principle upon which to orient future conversations and then offer two specific directions for further action.

First, the foregoing discussion suggests an absence of political and economic innovation and leadership as the primary obstacle to reducing inequality and expanding opportunity, not public views or public ignorance. The politics and economics of these issues are not by any means straightforward or conflict free, but, with public support, they can reach beyond conventional strategies. I have purposefully presented examples of how this is already happening in which the *majority* of the public is on board, as expressed in public opinion surveys, votes cast for local and statewide referenda, or media coverage across the political spectrum.

This is not to deny the worrisome polarization in political views that is often seen as the most serious obstacle to progress. But it is a reminder that the evidence on polarization among the public—as opposed to among politicians—is far from conclusive and is, more importantly for our purposes, often dependent on the issue at hand.[16] This is why it is necessary to train our attention on particular issues and to recognize the other form of polarization—between the policy views of economic elites and those of the public at large—as of perhaps equal consequence. Indeed, one of the most significant advances of late in political science research is the identification of a "representation gap," in which the policy views of economic elites disproportionately influence the ultimate passage of legislation. In order for this to occur, there must first be differences in preferences by income, and it's these differences that are often at the heart of debates over reducing inequality and expanding opportunity.[17]

Second, with this guiding principle in mind, I suggest two possible avenues for future action; each would enjoy public backing and significantly advance the prospects for holistic and effective change. In keeping with the two-pronged nature of current initiatives, one focuses more directly on expanding and equalizing educational opportunities and the other on doing so for employment opportunities.

Regarding the former, in a somewhat ironic turn of events, the cutting edge of policy innovation in Europe has taken a noteworthy shift in recent years from an outcomes-based agenda to an opportunity-based one, tying the two objectives more explicitly together than in the past. In contrast to the broadly redistributive thrust of traditional welfare state policies, the new so-called "social investment" strategies seek first and foremost to harness the human capital potential of the entire population, regardless of social background or stage over the course of life. This involves, among other things, the development of programs to educate children from disadvantaged backgrounds, retrain unemployed and displaced adult workers for gainful employment, and smooth the transition from home care to paid work for family caretakers. Crucially, such strategies also include "wage progression" or "intragenerational" wage mobility targets for low-income adults and not just educational initiatives for low-income children (see Chap. 13; also Morel et al. 2012; Larsen 2013; Reeves 2014).

---

[16] For instance, with respect to views about the economy and views about inequality, I find far more partisan polarization about the former than about the latter (McCall 2013, 172–74).

[17] Gilens 2012; Gilens and Page 2014. Note that Gilens (2012) shows that there are differences in representation only when there are differences in opinion, which do not occur on every issue. The Appendix provides a list of differences in policy preferences on economic and educational issues between the top 1 % and the general public, as well as some areas of agreement, particularly on education, taken from Page et al. (2013).

In addition to the representation gap by income, Solt (2010) finds that turnout in gubernatorial elections is lower in states with higher inequality, and that the overrepresentation of high-income voters relative to low-income voters is greater as well. And a number of scholars have noted the declining presence of powerful organizations that can lobby on behalf of middle-income and low-income interests (Skocpol 2003; Strolovitch 2007; Hacker and Pierson 2010; Gilens 2012).

In one way or another, the aim of these policies is to eliminate the transmission of "class" advantage and disadvantage from one generation to the next. Though long a goal of social democracy, it also resembles an attempt to shore up the American-style dream, so that achievement is more dependent on individual effort than on family income and cultural capital. That Europe should be leading the charge in this respect, and that it should be the region with lower levels of inequality *and* higher rates of social mobility, is eye opening. Although recent evidence in the U.S. suggests that intergenerational mobility has not, in fact, declined alongside the increase in income inequality, the longer distance to travel from bottom to top has no doubt made upward strides more formidable (Bloome 2014; Chetty et al. 2014). In contrast to conventional wisdom, Americans grasp this reality: They are at least as likely to recognize the unfair influence of social factors in getting ahead as Europeans, and their faith in the ability of hard work to prevail has been falling steadily over the past decade. Thus restoring opportunity in America, in an expansive way, would have wide appeal.

This is where the second avenue of future action comes into play. It entails the involvement, indeed partnership, of the business community, which has "evolved to be the dominant social institution of our age … and yet has fallen short in its potential to serve global society" (Blount 2014; Freeland 2014b). Above, I described several attempts to intervene in the labor market itself: to reduce executive pay, increase minimum wages, and the like. But, arguably, these only scratch the surface. Recalibrating pay incentives and reintroducing equity norms and a more "inclusive capitalism" throughout the economy is perhaps the most daunting challenge lying ahead. Political rhetoric far exceeds concrete action, and our comprehension of exactly *how* (or even whether) corporations can help to restore opportunity in America, in a meaningful way, is extremely limited (Freeland 2014a; also see Chaps. 6 and 10 in this volume; Blasi et al. 2013; Summers and Balls 2015).

Yet we can rely once again on public wisdom to motivate the charge. In preliminary research, my colleagues and I conducted surveys in 2014 and 2015 of roughly 1500 Americans on Amazon Mechanical Turk, a service that crowd sources to provide survey data.[18] We asked respondents a forced choice question about who has the greatest responsibility for reducing income differences: low-income individuals themselves, private charities, high-income individuals themselves, government, or

---

[18] These come from survey experiments and new survey questions that I am developing with a number of collaborators in the U.S. (Jennifer Richeson, Department of Psychology, Northwestern University) and abroad (Jonus Edlund and Arvid Lindh, Department of Sociology, Umea University, Sweden). The results are broken down by partisanship because the mTurk data are not representative. Nonetheless, for related questions that we adapted from the GSS, we found that the results from the mTurk survey are comparable to those from the GSS in the case of Republicans, and not too far off for Independents. Thus we can get a reasonable estimate from the mTurk data of how the public views the role of major companies in reducing pay disparities.

major companies. Respondents could also select an option at the end indicating that income differences do not need to be reduced. Except for this last option, the response categories were randomly ordered across respondents.

What we found is that only 21 % of Republicans and 9 % of Independents say that inequality does not need to be reduced, and for both Republicans and Independents, major companies were viewed as having the greatest responsibility for reducing inequality (33 % of Republicans and 35 % of Independents). Another 33 % of Independents chose government as the most responsible, for a total of 68 % who placed responsibility at the feet of either government or business. For Republicans, the total came in just shy of 50 % (15 % selected government for a total of 48 %). Despite the fact that only 15 % of Republicans selected government as having the most responsibility, however, we suspect that respondents of all political hues would support government regulation of business as part of what is necessary to coax major companies into the conversation over reducing inequality and expanding opportunity (see the uneven but notably high levels of support of government regulation of business by the general public under some circumstances, provided in the Appendix, and also Lipset and Schneider 1987). Finally, the majority of Democrats selected government as the most responsible (54 %), but, surprisingly, over a quarter selected major companies (28 %). Although trust in both government and business institutions has fallen precipitously in the past decade, most Americans still look to them for leadership.[19]

Conclusion

The way forward, in sum, is to eschew a one-sided focus on *either* equal outcomes *or* equal opportunities; to harness the resources and competitive advantages of all major institutions in society, from government, to education, to business; and to build on the pragmatic consensus of local initiatives to forge a national commitment to ensure that our future is as lofty and inclusive in reality as it is in our dreams.

---

[19] Data on trust in business, finance and banks, and government can be found here: "Following the Public on Inequality: IPR Sociologist's Book Scrutinizes U.S. Beliefs on Inequality," posting on Northwestern University Institute for Policy Research website, http://www.ipr.northwestern.edu/about/news/2013/mccall-undeserving-rich.html

Appendix

Table 12A.1 Support of selected policies related to inequality and opportunity

Policy	% wealthy favors	% general public favors
Jobs and pay		
Minimum wage high enough so that no family with a full-time worker falls below official poverty line	43 %	78 %
The government in Washington ought to see to it that everyone who wants to work can find a job	19 %	68 %
The federal government should provide jobs for everyone able and willing to work who cannot find a job in private employment	8 %	53 %
Economic regulation and macroeconomic policy		
The government has an essential role to play in regulating the market	55 %	71 %
Would like to live in a society where the government does nothing except provide national defense and police protection, so that people would be left alone to earn whatever they could	19 %	27 %
The federal government has gone too far in regulating business and interfering with the free enterprise system	69 %	65 %
The following need more [minus less] federal government regulation ["about the same as now" omitted]:		
Wall Street firms	+18	+45
Oil industry	+6	+50
Health insurance industry	+4	+26
Big corporations	−20	+33
Small business	−70	−42
The government should run a deficit if necessary when the country is in a recession and is at war [vs. The government should balance the budget even when the country is in a recession and is at war]	73 %	31 %
Favor cuts in spending on domestic programs like Medicare, education, and highways in order to cut federal budget deficits	58 %	27 %
Willing to pay more taxes in order to reduce federal budget deficits	65 %	34 %
Education		
The federal government should make sure that everyone who wants to go to college can do so	28 %	78 %
The federal government should spend whatever is necessary to ensure that all children have really good public schools they can go to	35 %	87 %
The federal government should invest more in worker retraining and education to help workers adapt to changes in the economy [vs. Such efforts just create big government programs that do not work very well]	30 %	50 %

Source: Page et al. (2013, Tables 5, 7, and 8)
Note: Several areas of agreement on education policy include paying more taxes for early childhood education, the idea of merit pay for teachers, charter schools, tax-funded vouchers for private schools

References

Ansell, Ben. 2010. *From the ballot to the blackboard*. New York: Cambridge University Press.

Bartels, Larry M. 2005. Homer gets a tax cut: Inequality and public policy in the American mind. *Perspectives on Politics* 3(1): 15–31.

Bartels, Larry M. 2008. *Unequal democracy*. Princeton: Princeton University Press.

Bartels, Larry M. 2013. The political effects of the great recession. *Annals of the American Academy of Political and Social Science* 650: 47–75.

Bell, Daniel. 1973. *The coming of post-industrial society: A venture in social forecasting*. New York: Basic Books.

Bernhardt, Annette. 2012. The role of labor market regulations in rebuilding employment opportunity in the U.S. *Work and Occupations* 39(4): 354–375.

Blasi, Joseph R., Richard B. Freeman, and Douglas L. Kruse. 2013. *The citizen's share: Reducing inequality in the 21st century*. New Haven: Yale University Press.

Bloome, Deirdre. 2014. Income inequality and intergenerational income mobility in the United States. *Social Forces*. doi:10.1093/sf/sou092.

Blount, Sally. 2014. "Yes, the world needs more MBA's. Here's why." *Bloomberg Businessweek*, May 5.

Busemeyer, Marius. 2012. Inequality and the political economy of education: An analysis of individual preferences in OECD countries. *Journal of European Social Policy* 22(3): 219–240.

Chetty, Raj, Nathanial Hendren, Patrick Kline, Emmanuel Saez, and Nicholas Turner. 2014. *Is the United States still the land of opportunity? Recent trends in intergenerational mobility*, NBER Working Paper 19844. Cambridge, MA: National Bureau of Economic Research.

DeNavas-Walt, Carmen, and Bernadette Proctor. 2014. *Income and poverty in the United States: 2013*. Washington, DC: U.S. Census Bureau.

Edmans, Alex. 2012. The link between job satisfaction and firm value, with implications for corporate social responsibility. *Academy of Management Perspectives* 26: 1–19.

Franko, William, Carol J. Tolbert, and Christopher Witko. 2013. Inequality, self-interest, and public support for Robin Hood tax policies. *Political Research Quarterly*, April.

Free, Lloyd A., and Hadley Cantril. 1967. *The political beliefs of Americans: A study of public opinion*. New Brunswick: Rutgers University Press.

Freeland, Chrystia. 2014a, *Presentation to Opportunity in America panel* (June).

Freeland, Chrystia. 2014b. It's not just George Soros anymore. *Politico*, June 8.

Gilens, Martin. 2012. *Affluence and influence*. Princeton: Princeton University Press.

Gilens, Martin, and Benjamin Page. 2014. Testing theories of American politics. *Perspectives on Politics* 12(3): 564–581.

Goldin, Claudia, and Lawrence Katz. 2008. *The race between education and technology*. Cambridge, MA: Harvard University Press.

Hacker, Jacob, and Paul Pierson. 2010. *Winner-take-all politics*. New York: Simon & Schuster.

Hochschild, Jennifer. 1981. *What's fair? American beliefs about distributive justice*. Cambridge: Harvard University Press.

Hochschild, Jennifer. 1995. *Facing up to the American dream*. Princeton: Princeton University Press.

Howard, Christopher. 1997. *The hidden welfare state*. Princeton: Princeton University Press.

Ingram, Paul, Lori Qingyuan Yue, and Hayagreeva Rao. 2010. Trouble in store: Probes, protests, and store openings by Wal-Mart, 1998–2007. *American Journal of Sociology* 116(1): 53–92.

Jacoby, Sanford. 1997. *Modern manors: Welfare capitalism since the New Deal*. Princeton: Princeton University Press.

Kelly, Nathan. 2009. *The politics of income inequality in the U.S.*. New York: Cambridge University Press.

King, Brayden, and Nicholas Pearce. 2010. The contentiousness of markets: Politics, social movements and institutional change in markets. *Annual Review of Sociology* 36: 249–267.

Kluegel, James R., and Eliot R. Smith. 1986. *Beliefs about inequality: Americans' views about what is and what ought to be*. New York: Aldine De Gruyter.

Krueger, Alan. 2012. *The rise and consequences of inequality in the United States*. Washington, DC: Center for American Progress.

Ladd, Everett Carll, and Karlyn H. Bowman. 1998. *Attitudes toward economic inequality*. Washington, DC: American Enterprise Institute.

Larsen, Christian Albrekt. 2013. *The rise and fall of social cohesion*. Oxford: Oxford University Press.

Levy, Frank. 1987. *Dollars and dreams*. New York: Russell Sage.

Lipset, Seymour Martin. 1996. *American exceptionalism: A double edged sword*. New York: W.W. Norton.

Lipset, Seymour Martin, and William Schneider. 1987. *The confidence gap: Business, labor, and government in the public mind*. Baltimore: Johns Hopkins University Press.

Lupia, Arthur, Adam Seth Levine, Jesse Menning, and Gisela Sin. 2007. Were bush tax cut supporters 'Simply Ignorant?' A second look at conservatives and liberals in 'Homer Gets a Tax Cut'. *Perspectives on Politics* 5(4): 773–784.

MacLean, Nancy. 2006. *Freedom is not enough: The opening of the American workplace*. Cambridge, MA/New York: Harvard University Press/Russell Sage Foundation.

McCall, Leslie. 2013. *The undeserving rich: American beliefs about inequality, opportunity, and redistribution*. New York: Cambridge University Press.

McCall, Leslie, and Fiona Chin. 2013. *Does knowledge of inequality affect beliefs about inequality?* Paper presented at the Midwest Political Science Association meetings, Chicago.

McCall, Leslie, and Lane Kenworthy. 2009. Americans' social policy preferences in the era of rising inequality. *Perspectives on Politics* 7(3): 459–484.

Milkman, Ruth, and Eileen Appelbaum. 2013. *Unfinished business: Paid family leave in California and the future of U.S. work-family policy*. Ithaca: Cornell University Press.

Morel, Natalie, Bruno Palier, and Joakim Palme (eds.). 2012. *Toward a social investment welfare state?* Chicago: The Policy Press.

Page, Benjamin I., Larry M. Bartels, and Jason Seawright. 2013. Democracy and the policy preferences of wealthy Americans. *Perspectives on Politics* 11(1): 51–73.

Piketty, Thomas. 2014. *Capital in the twenty-first century*. Cambridge, MA: Harvard University Press.

Reeves, Richard. 2014. *Planning the American dream: The case for an office of opportunity*, Center on Children and Families Brief 53. Washington, DC: The Brookings Institution.

Roemer, John E. 1998. *Equality of opportunity*. Cambridge, MA: Harvard University Press.

Rosenbaum, James. 2001. *Beyond college for all: Career paths for the forgotten half*. New York: Russell Sage.

Skocpol, Theda. 2003. *Diminished democracy*. Norman: University of Oklahoma Press.

Smith, Mark A. 2007. *The right talk*. Princeton: Princeton University Press.

Solt, Frederick. 2010. Does economic inequality depress electoral participation? Testing the Schattschneider hypothesis. *Political Behavior* 32: 285–301.

Strasser, Susan, Charles McGovern, and Matthias Judt (eds.). 1998. *Getting and spending: European and American consumer society in the twentieth century*. New York: Cambridge University Press.

Strolovitch, Dara. 2007. *Affirmative advocacy*. Chicago: University of Chicago Press.

Summers, Lawrence, and Ed Balls. 2015. *Report of the commission of inclusive prosperity*. Washington, DC: Center for American Progress.

Vanneman, Reeve, and Lynn Weber Cannon. 1987. *The American perception of class*. Philadelphia: Temple University Press.

Walsh, Katherine Cramer. 2012. Putting inequality in its place: Rural consciousness and the power of perspective. *American Political Science Review* 106(3): 517–532.

Young, Michael. 1958. *The rise of meritocracy 1870–2033: An essay on education and equality*. London: Thames and Hudson.

Young, Cristobal, and Charles Varner. 2011. Millionaire migration and state taxation of top incomes: Evidence from a natural experiment. *National Tax Journal* 64((2, Part 1)): 255–284.

Chapter 13
How Will We Know? The Case for Opportunity Indicators

Richard V. Reeves

Abstract While the U.S. is a world leader in opportunity rhetoric, it is something of a laggard for opportunity metrics. Indicators are necessary to guide policy, drive data collection strategies, and measure progress. We need clear concepts and credible indicators of opportunity to have an idea of whether we have "restored" it or if we are even headed in the right direction. Right now, indicators are the poor relation of the policy-making process, lacking either the immediacy of strong rhetoric or the tangibility of policies and programs. Indicators are the missing link in our attempts to promote equal opportunity, which is unavoidably an American vision of fairness. This chapter argues for a definition of opportunity based on intergenerational relative mobility and describes current levels of mobility, as well as the relationships between mobility patterns and family structure, education, and race. It also provides a brief history of the social indicators movement in the U.S. and outlines some of the theoretical terrain of indicator development. The chapter goes on to describe two current examples of indicator frameworks—from the United Kingdom and Colorado. Finally, it proposes four specific reforms to elevate the role of indicators in the promotion of opportunity: setting a long-term Goal for Intergenerational Mobility; a "dashboard" of Annual Opportunity Indicators; an American Opportunity Survey; and a Federal Office of Opportunity.

Keywords Social indicators • Dashboard of indicators • Intergenerational mobility • Absolute mobility • Relative mobility • Meritocracy • Equal opportunity • Inequalities of birth • Social genome model

R.V. Reeves (✉)
Economic Studies, Center on Children and Families, Brookings Institution,
Washington, DC, USA

© Educational Testing Service 2016   443
I. Kirsch, H. Braun (eds.), *The Dynamics of Opportunity in America*,
DOI 10.1007/978-3-319-25991-8_13

Introduction

The rhetorical attraction of opportunity is irresistible. Every politician in the land sings its praises, laments its absence, or promises its restoration. Opportunity is a leitmotif not only of American political discourse but of American culture: Horatio Alger, the frontier, the land of opportunity, the American Dream … you know the drill.

Take these two quotes—one from President Obama, a Democrat: "Opportunity is who we are … but upward mobility has stalled"—and the other from U.S. Representative Paul Ryan, a Republican and now Speaker of the House: "Upward mobility is the central promise of life in America, but right now, America's engines of upward mobility aren't working the way they should."

Rhetorical agreement that America ought to be a land of opportunity is, of course, hardly news. But it is significant that most senior political figures now agree that we are falling far short of this ideal. Mounting empirical evidence that rates of intergenerational social mobility in the U.S. are low and flat has finally penetrated the American political consciousness. A chance for some bipartisan work to address social mobility has presented itself, a precious moment that ought to be seized.

But while the U.S. is a world leader in opportunity rhetoric, it is something of a laggard for opportunity metrics. Indicators are necessary to guide policy, drive data collection strategies, and measure progress. There are clear summary statistics of economic growth, poverty, and productivity, Why not opportunity? We need clear concepts and credible indicators of opportunity to have an idea of whether we are even headed in the right direction. Right now, indicators are the poor relation of the social policy world, lacking either the immediacy of strong rhetoric or the tangibility of policies and programs. Indicators are the missing link in our attempts to promote opportunity.

Indicators can act as the point of contact between goals, initiatives, and data. First, of course, the overall goal has to be established and given a clear conceptual basis. Then indicators can be drawn together or developed to show long-run progress toward that goal. In addition, shorter-term "leading indicators" can also be defined. Initiatives—a deliberately broad term encompassing government policies and programs, but also work by nongovernmental organizations or even corporations—can then be judged against these indicators.

Evidence-based policy is obviously preferable to what we often get, which is policy-based evidence making. But evidence *of what* is the important question—to which indicators provide an answer. Last but not least, the generation of indicators can shape and promote new approaches to data collection.

In the remainder of this chapter, I will:

(a) Position equal opportunity as the unavoidably American vision of fairness;
(b) Argue for a definition of opportunity based on intergenerational relative mobility;
(c) Describe current levels of mobility, and the relationships between mobility patterns and family structure, education, and race;

(d) Provide a brief history of the social indicators movement in the U.S.;
(e) Outline some of the theoretical terrain of indicator development;
(f) Describe two current examples of indicator frameworks—from the United Kingdom and Colorado—and;
(g) Propose four specific reforms to elevate the role of indicators in the promotion of opportunity: setting a long-term Goal for Intergenerational Mobility; a "dashboard" of Annual Opportunity Indicators; an American Opportunity Survey; and a Federal Office of Opportunity.

All-American: Equal Opportunity as Egalitarian Individualism

The volume in your hands (or perhaps, more likely on your screen) is one of thousands with the word "opportunity" in its title. Especially in America, opportunity is a term redolent of optimism, progress, and freedom. It is, in short, impossible to be against. The danger is that opportunity becomes a protean term, meaning almost anything, or something different to different people in different contexts. Some specificity is therefore required in order to move beyond rhetoric and into action.

I will shortly argue for a specific concept of opportunity, namely relative intergenerational income mobility. But first I will attempt to define equal opportunity as a distinctly American kind of fairness. In his second inaugural address in 2013, Obama declared: "We are true to our creed when a little girl born into the bleakest poverty knows that she has the same chance to succeed as anybody else, because she is an American; she is free, and she is equal, not just in the eyes of God but also in our own."

So: the "same chance to succeed," even though "born into the bleakest poverty." This is the utopian ideal of American fairness, in which the inequalities of birth do not dictate the inequalities of life. While Obama, like most politicians, focused on upward mobility out of poverty, the equal opportunity ideal reaches all the way up the distribution. It is about the chance for a middle class kid to join the elite, as well as for a poor kid to join the middle class. The ideal also goes deeper than political rhetoric. Equality of opportunity is in America's DNA. The moral claim that each individual has the right to succeed is even implicit in the proclamation of Declaration of Independence that "All men are created equal." In his first draft of that historic document, Thomas Jefferson in fact wrote that all were created "equal and independent." This is the distinctly American formula—equality plus independence adds up to the promise of upward mobility. Equal opportunity reconciles individual liberty—the freedom to get ahead and "make something of yourself"—with societal equality. It is how the ideal of natural equality—"born equal" is fused with the ideal of individualism—"born independent." It is a philosophy of egalitarian individualism.[1]

---

[1] I expand on this argument in my Brookings essay *Saving Horatio Alger* (2014). See http://www.brookings.edu/research/essays/2014/saving-horatio-alger.

Chris Hayes writes of social mobility in his book *Twilight of the Elites*: "Those on the bottom who make it to the top rise from their class rather than with it. It is a fundamentally individualistic model of achievement" (Hayes 2013, 23). Hayes wishes it could be different. But that is wishful thinking. Individualism is hard-wired into the very idea of America. The challenge is to ensure that it is genuinely combined with equality of opportunity. Hayes laments, "[T]he meritocratic creed finds purchase on both the left and the right because it draws from each…. It is 'liberal' in the classical sense." Indeed it is—just like America.

Opportunity Equals Intergenerational Relative Mobility

Even the term "equality of opportunity" is, of course, very broad. The philosopher Bertrand Russell, asked what he actually did all day, replied: "[Y]ou clarify a few concepts, make a few distinctions. It's a living." Concepts and distinctions will be important, too, for the motivating project of this volume. We have to be crystal clear what we mean when we talk or write about "opportunity" and equally clear about the distinctions being made between different variants. Amartya Sen, the Nobel Prize-winning economist, famously argued that because everyone favors equality of one sort or another, the key question is: "Equality of what?" (Sen 1979, 1). So, in the spirit of Sen, what do we mean by "equality of opportunity?"

In particular, is our main concern with *absolute* mobility or *relative* mobility? Relative mobility is, as Scott Winship puts it, "a measure of how the ranking of adults against their peers is (or is not) tied to the ranking of their parents against their peers. That is to say, ignoring dollar amounts, did adults who rank high or low in the income distribution also have parents who ranked high or low?" (Economic Policies for the 21st Century 2014). By contrast, absolute mobility rates are all about dollar amounts. In Winship's terms: "absolute mobility ignores rankings and simply considers whether adults tend to have higher, size-adjusted incomes than their parents did at the same age, after taking into account increases in the cost of living."

Most people are upwardly mobile in the absolute sense: 84 % of U.S. adults, according to the latest estimates (Economic Mobility Project 2012). People raised in families toward the bottom of the income distribution are the most likely to over-take their parents' income status, as Fig. 13.1 shows. It is hard, then, from an abso-lute basis, to see that the "engines" of upward mobility have "stalled."

The two key drivers of absolute mobility are the rates of economic growth and the distribution of that growth. Policy should therefore attempt to maximize real income growth for as wide a swath of the population as possible. Relative mobility, which tracks movement up and down the income ladder, captures a different idea of fairness, closer to the ideal of meritocracy. Which kind of mobility to focus on—or rather, what balance to strike between the two—is a normative, rather than empiri-cal, question. But relative mobility gets closer to the ideal of "*equality* of opportu-nity." Even if everyone is richer than his or her parents, we would be a deeply unfair

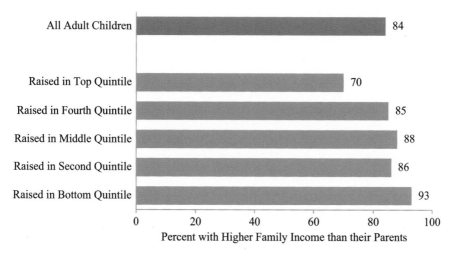

Fig. 13.1 Absolute mobility: share of Americans who exceed their parents' family income (Copyright © July 2012 The Pew Charitable Trusts)

society if everyone was also stuck on exactly the same point on the income ladder. We want growth and more prosperity, but we also want fluidity and more fairness. A common way to present this intergenerational relative mobility is to examine the relationship between the income quintile (one-fifth of the income distribution) that people end up in as adults compared to the quintile they were born or raised in. Alternative approaches include a measure of the correlation between the income rank of parents and their child, used in particular by Raj Chetty, and rank direction mobility (RDM), which tracks an individual's position on the whole income rank compared to their parents' rank—developed in particular by Bhashkar Mazumder (Mazumder 2011, 2014).

Three more questions of definition should be briefly addressed. First, there is an important distinction to be made between *inter*generational and *intra*generational mobility, which is a measure of how far individuals will move up and down the income ladder during their own lifetime, especially during the prime working age years. While these kinds of mobility are related, my primary focus is on the former.

Second, the choice of outcome is important. Most studies of mobility focus on income. But there are, of course, many other possibilities, including wages, education, well-being, and occupational status. Many of these will provide important information about the capabilities and opportunities enjoyed by individuals, but I focus here on income. Income is important in itself and is strongly correlated with other goods. It is also a yardstick that is reasonably easy to measure and compare over time

Third, the presumption underlying this approach to measuring equal opportunity presumes that an outcome—in this case of income—is a good enough proxy for opportunity. They are not the same thing, of course, because there is a difference between an opportunity being available and somebody seizing it (Swift 2004). But for the moment, patterns of outcomes appear to suffice as an accurate reflection of patterns of opportunities.

Mobility: The Current Picture

The current picture in terms of relative intergenerational income mobility (RIIM) is not the main focus of this chapter (see Chap. 8). But a brief overview will provide a context for my broader argument on the need for strong indicators to guide data collection strategies, policy development, and evaluation.

The top line is: Rates of RIIM in the U.S. are low and flat and vary significantly by family structure, education, race, and geography. The U.S. suffers from a high degree of intergenerational income "stickiness," especially at the top and bottom of the income distribution as Fig. 13.2, using the dataset constructed from the National Longitudinal Survey of Youth (NLSY) for the Social Genome Model, shows. There is more than a twofold difference in the odds of a child born in the top quintile remaining in the top income quintiles (the "comfortable middle class"), compared to one born in the bottom quintile (56 % versus 23 %).

Has this picture worsened over time? It seems not. In a comprehensive series of recent studies, making innovative use of administrative records of income, Chetty et al. (2014, 10) investigate geographical variations in mobility (see below) and long-term trends. Their conclusion: "children entering the labor market today have

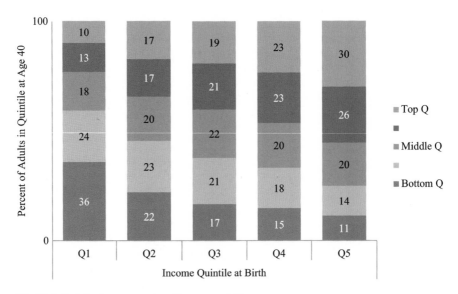

Fig. 13.2 Relative intergenerational income mobility

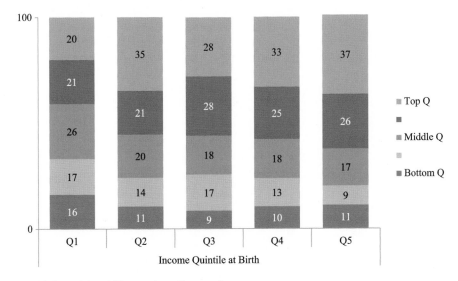

Fig. 13.3   Social mobility matrix: college graduate

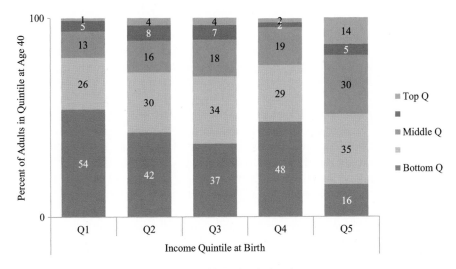

Fig. 13.4   Social mobility matrix: less than high school education

the same chances of moving up in the income distribution relative to their parents as children born in the 1970s."

There are, however, stark differences in mobility patterns at different levels of education. Children with a college degree are more likely to be upwardly mobile. A comparison of Figs. 13.3 and 13.4 shows that among children raised in the poorest quintile, those with a college degree are 20 times more likely than their high school dropout counterparts to make it to the top (20 % versus 1 %).

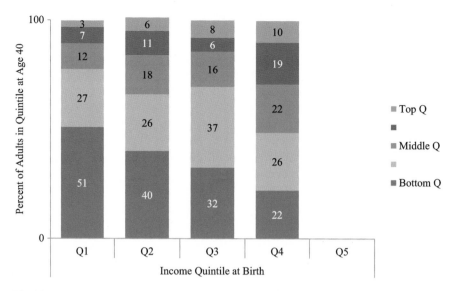

Fig. 13.5 Social mobility matrix: Black Americans. Note: Sample size too small for those born in top quintile

Even top-income children receive a boost by receiving a college degree—37 % of them stay at the top, far more than their high school dropout and graduate peers, as seen in Fig. 13.3. So college degrees can be a double-edged sword in terms of relative mobility, helping improve the economic situation of poor children who go on to get a bachelor's degree but also preserving the economic situation of the affluent.

At the other end of the spectrum, failing to receive a high school diploma damages upward mobility rates. Bottom-income children without a diploma have a 54 % probability of remaining on the bottom rung as adults, as seen in Fig. 13.4. Rates of downward mobility from the middle three quintiles are also very high for those without a diploma (42 % at the second quintile, 37 % at the third, and 48 % at the fourth).

There are striking differences in mobility by race, especially between Black Americans (Fig. 13.5) and White Americans (Fig. 13.6). One in two Black children born into the bottom quintile will remain there in adulthood, compared to just one in four Whites, and only 3 % of Black children rise to the top income quintile. Also, Black children are more likely to be downwardly mobile from the middle: of Black children born to parents in the middle-income quintile, 69 % move downward.

There are also big differences in terms of the mobility patterns of children born in different kinds. As shown in Fig. 13.7, children with never-married mothers face a roughly 50–50 chance of remaining in the bottom quintile, while as Fig. 13.8 shows, children raised by continuously married parents have high upward mobility rates. The two biggest factors behind the "marriage effect" appear to be higher income, even within income quintiles, and more engaged parenting (Reeves and Howard 2014).

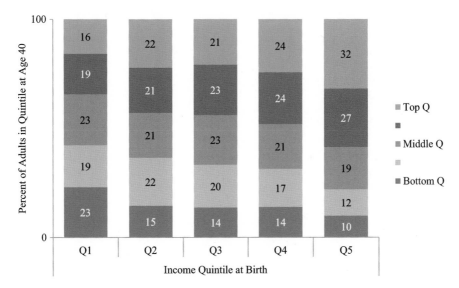

Fig. 13.6 Social mobility matrix: White Americans

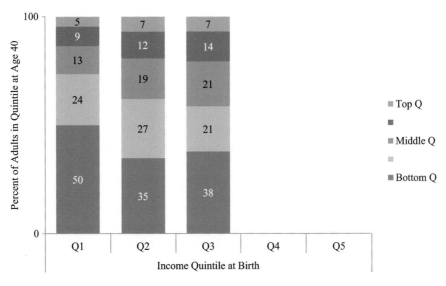

Fig. 13.7 Social mobility matrix: children of never-married mothers. Note: Sample size too small for those born in top two quintiles

Last, there are variations in mobility patterns by geography. Chetty et al. (2014, 26) estimate, for example, that "the probability that a child from the lowest quintile of parental income rises to the top quintile is 10.8 % in Salt Lake City (Utah), compared with 4.4 % in Charlotte (North Carolina)." Five factors correlate strongly with

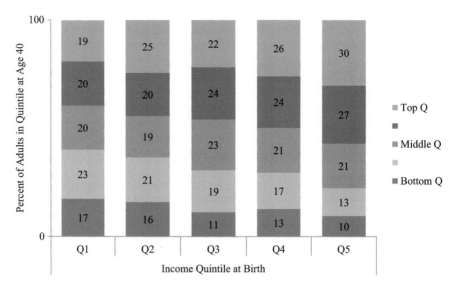

Fig. 13.8 Social mobility matrix: children of continuously married mothers

intergenerational mobility by geography: racial and economic segregation, school quality, income inequality, social capital, and family structure, together "explaining" 76 % of the variation in upward mobility.

This brief discussion of the shape of U.S. intergenerational mobility is intended to motivate the remainder of this chapter, which focuses on the role of indicators to frame and focus strategies to promote greater opportunity. I begin with a brief history of social indicators and an even briefer theoretical overview.

A Very Brief History of Social Indicators

The U.S. has had an on-off relationship with social indicators. Interest began with the 19th century temperance movement, when campaigners began to collect data showing the deleterious social effects of alcohol. The alcohol industry responded with data on how much employment and revenue it generated: The result was a loosely fact-based debate about alcohol in the 1830s. But the measurements of trends began in earnest with the establishment of the Massachusetts Bureau of Statistics of Labor in 1869. But it was far from objective. First, it was run by pro-union officials, leading to biased reports; then it was taken over by pro-business staffing and swung the other way. But it was nonetheless an attempt to give data some official grounding and status.

The Community Indicators Movement was kick-started by the Pittsburgh Study funded by the Russell Sage Foundation in 1910, which inspired similar studies in towns around the U.S., with measures of health, income, jobs and so on. This was a time of great optimism about the potential of social indicators to effect change, as Cohen writes: "They relayed the findings of the technical experts to the public, who, enlightened by the facts, were expected to mobilize public opinion and press for appropriate reforms" (Cohen, quoted in Cobb and Rixford 1998, 7). The idea was that facts could change the world, through a process of enlightenment. In 1933, *Recent Social Trends* was published, under the Hoover administration. At 1,500 pages long, it was a compendium of every piece of social data the authors could get hold of. It also had no impact. The burst of interest in the 1930s did help to create the conditions for a significant widening in the collection of data on social trends. The U.S. Census Bureau, in particular, has captured increasingly rich data on demographic and social trends, especially through the Current Population Survey, which replaced the Monthly Report on the Labor Force in 1948.

Social indicators were out of political fashion until the late 1960s and early 1970s when a series of major studies were undertaken, including *Indicators of Social Change* (Sheldon and Moore 1968) and *Towards a Social Report* (HEW 1969). Across a range of policy areas, including defense, there was a renewed emphasis on the role of indicators in supporting cost-benefit analysis. This helps to explain why a good deal of funding was provided by NASA, which wanted to look at the impact of the space program on American society. (Many reviews of this work said that the links between the space program and the social indicators work were "somewhat tenuous," which seems kind.)

The Office of Management and Budget (OMB) and Census Bureau picked up the baton, issuing a series of *Social Indicators* reports in the 1970s and into the 1980s (U.S. Office of Management and Budget 1974; U.S. Bureau of the Census 1977, 1981). A Center for the Coordination on Social Indicators was established in 1972. Between 1967 and 1973, Senator Walter Mondale submitted a number of bills to create a Council of Social Advisers (to mirror the Council of Economic Advisers) and institutionalize an annual social indicators report.

The movement was largely halted during the Nixon administration, as the role of social indicators lost any normative force. As Clifford Cobb and Craig Rixford write: "Some had envisioned these as the beginning of institutionalized social reporting, but their hopes were quickly dashed as political pressure within the Nixon Administration turned them into *neutral chartbooks, replete with facts but void of interpretation* … the social indicators movement in the United States was effectively over by the early 1980s" (Ibid., 11, my emphasis).

At the same time, many international organizations, such as the Organisation for Economic Co-operation and Development, the United Nations, and the European Union started to get very interested in social indicators, and in the 1990s, surveys and indices of well-being began to gain some traction, partly inspired by the environmental movement. In more recent years in the U.S., there has been a modest renaissance of community indicators, led by the Community Indicators Consortium, Healthy Cities movement, and so on. In one sense, this takes us back a century to where Russell Sage started in 1910, with metro-based approaches to community indicators rather than at a national or federal level. Efforts to improve the quality and increase the salience of indicators at the national level have been led by the National Academy of Science under its Key National Indicator Initiative, resulting in a series of publications, notably an important 2012 report, *Using Science as Evidence in Public Policy* (Prewitt et al. 2012). In 2010, President Obama signed legislation intended to create a Key National Indicators System, following advice from a commission of experts. A budget of $70 million was set aside. The commission was appointed in 2010 but never convened. The money—which was included in a provision of the Affordable Care Act—was never appropriated.

Theory: Conceptual Issues

The selection of indicators is not a straightforward matter. Indicators come in a wide variety of forms. Borrowing heavily from Cobb and Rixford (Ibid.), indicators can be distinguished and defined on a number of axes: inductive or deductive; "pseudo-objective" or "partisan"; descriptive or prescriptive; "local" or national; broad or narrow; and indirect or direct. The choice of indicator is inescapably connected to the purpose of the indicator—this is why they can only even be "pseudo" objective. Indicators of progress toward greater social mobility ought to be deductive (based on a clear theory about what promotes and predicts mobility); as objective as possible; prescriptive (intended to guide policy); narrow (provide as much focus as possible); and direct (getting as close as possible to the causal connection to mobility). But in terms of the choice between national and subnational indicators, the answer can legitimately be "both." Many leading indicators may work in most localities. But especially in a nation as large and diverse as the U.S., there may be some localities in which a particular indicator is more powerful than elsewhere.

In their review of the role of indicators, Cobb and Rixford (Ibid.) offer a number of important lessons, of which I would highlight the following:

(a) A clear conceptual basis is needed for indicators—otherwise you end up with a forest of numbers but no path;
(b) A number is not necessarily a good indicator—just because a number is available does not mean it is "getting at" the trend or factor you are interested in;
(c) There is no such thing as a "value-free" indicator—the simple selection of a particular indicator is a value judgment. It is better to be clear and upfront about the purpose of the indicator;
(d) Comprehensiveness is the enemy of effectiveness—five strong indicators are better than 105 indicators in terms of focusing political energy; and
(e) Indicators should attempt to reveal causes, not symptoms—especially in terms of promoting social mobility, indicators that get close to causal relationships are the most valuable.

Indicators and the U.K.'s Social Mobility Strategy

I served in the U.K. Coalition Government from 2010 to 2012, as Director of Strategy to the Deputy Prime Minister, who was leader of the junior party, the Liberal Democrats. At the time, Prime Minister David Cameron was in favor of what he had labeled the "big society"—a deliberate contrast to both the idea of the "big state" and Margaret Thatcher's claim that there "is no such thing as society." But Cameron and his team refused to define their term clearly or apply any metrics. So my questions to them were always along the following lines: "How will you know when society is bigger? How big is it now? What are your measures?" In the end they stopped inviting me to the meetings. But the truth is they had no way to answer the questions. The "big society" was just a rhetorical device.

Of course "opportunity" is at least as nebulous a term as "big society." But when the U.K. government made a strong commitment to promoting social mobility as its overarching social policy goal, that commitment was buttressed by indicators and institutions. In April 2011, the U.K. government issued a social mobility strategy, declaring: "A fair society is an open society, one in which every individual is free to succeed. That is why improving social mobility is the principal goal of the Government's social policy" (Cabinet Office, HM Government 2012, 5).

The definition of social mobility guiding the U.K. efforts is fairly tight, with a declared focus on intergenerational relative mobility by both income and occupation. Deciding on this definition was a vitally important step, laying the foundations for the selection of key "leading indicators" that are—based on the best available evidence—predictive of long-term trends in mobility. These indicators are shown in Table 13.1 and include income gaps in low birth weight, school readiness, educational attainment at ages 11, 16, and 19, postsecondary education, access to the professions, and early-career wage progression. An independent analysis of the indicators suggests that together they should capture more than half of the likely trends in intergenerational mobility (Gregg et al. 2014). The U.K. government also took steps to institutionalize the social mobility commitment with the creation of a Cabinet committee and a new, independent statutory Commission on Social Mobility and Child Poverty that reports annually to Parliament and the administration.

Indicators and the Colorado Opportunity Project

The State of Colorado has also created an evidence-based indicator framework for opportunity, based in part on the Social Genome Model (Winship and Owen 2013). The overall goal is to help as many Colorado residents as possible become "middle class by middle age" (i.e., a household income of 300 % of the federal poverty line by age 40). Following a yearlong project involving multiple state agencies and key stakeholders, a series of indicators at key life stages have been developed, as shown

Table 13.1 Dashboard of opportunity "Leading Indicators" in United Kingdom

Indicator	Sub-indicators	Department
1. Low birth weight	Low birth weight (disadvantage gap)	DH
2. Child development	Child development at age 2½ (measure still under development)	DH
	Gap in school readiness at age 5	DfE
3. School attainment	Attainment of Level 4 at KS2 (FSM gap)	DfE
	Attainment of "the basics" at GCSE (FSM gap)	DfE
	Attainment of "the basics" at GCSE (deprived school gap)	DfE
	Attainment by 19 of children in state and independent schools (AAB at A level)	DfE
4. Employ-ment and participation in education (age 18–24)	18–24 year olds participating in (full or part-time) education or training (disadvantage gap)	BIS
	18–24 year olds not in full-time education or training who are workless (disadvantage gap)	DWP
5. Further education	Percentage achieving a level 3 qualification by age 19 (FSM gap)	DfE
6. Higher education	Progression of pupils aged 15 to HE at age 19 (FSM gap)	BIS
	Progression of pupils to the 33% most selective HE institutions (state/independent school gap)	BIS
	Destinations from higher education (disadvantage gap)	BIS
7. Social mobility in adulthood	Access to the professions (disadvantage gap)	BIS/DWP
	Progression in the labour market (wage progression)	BIS/DWP
	Second chances in the labour market (post-19 basic skills)	BIS/DWP

Abbreviations: *BIS* Department for Business, Innovation & Skills, *DfE* Department for Education, *DH* Department of Health; *DWP* Department for Work and Pensions, *FSM* free school meals, *GCSE* General Certificate of Secondary Education, *HE* Higher Education

in Table 13.2. These indicators, making use of data available at a state level, will be used to help identify the most effective programs and initiatives. The project is still evolving, but speaking at a stakeholder summit on the project in March 2015, Gov. John Hickenlooper set the bar high: "The Colorado Opportunity Project is going to make history."

The U.K. and Colorado are just two examples of the operationalization of opportunity goals and indicators: They are offered here not as definitive or comprehensive but as illustrations of the potential for such an approach of which I have firsthand knowledge. Are there any lessons here for the U.S. more broadly?

Table 13.2 The Colorado opportunity framework

Model/Goal	Life stage & social genome indicators	Opportunity indicators
Colorado opportunity project goal: *Increasing the proportion of adults – particularly from disadvantaged circumstances – who are middle class by middle age* *(Family Income of 300%* *FPL or higher at age 40)*	**Family formation** (from conception through childbirth) *Born at a normal birth weight, to a non-poor, married mother with at least a high school diploma*	Rate of low birth weight % FPL/ Family income Feeling down, depressed, or sad (maternal depression) Single or dual household parenting Unintended pregnancy (intendedness vs unintendedness)
	Early childhood (0–5) *Acceptable pre-reading and math skills AND behavior generally socially appropriate*	% of parents with concerns about child's emotions, concentration, behavior or ability to get along with others (ages 0-8) % of families relying on low cost food (ages 0-8) Children ages 1 to 5 whose family members read to them less than 3 days per week [SCHOOL READINESS]
	Middle childhood (5-12) *Basic reading and math skills AND social-emotional skills*	Standardized test math scores Standardized test reading scores % of parents with concerns about child's emotions, concentration, behavior or ability to get along with others (9-14)
	Adolescence (12–19) *Graduates from high school with a GPA > 2.5 AND has not been convicted of a crime nor become a parent*	High school graduation status (on time or not) Juvenile property and crime data (violent arrest rate and property arrest rate) Became a teen parent? % of 6th-8th and 9th-12th grade students who report ever feeling so sad or hopeless; % of 6th-8th and 9th-12th grade students who have considered suicide; % of young adults ages 18-25 who are currently depressed

(continued)

Table 13.2 (continued)

	Transition to adulthood (19–29) *Lives independently AND receives a college degree or has a family income of > 250% of the federal poverty level*	Employed status of population (by race, sex and age -16-19)
		% FPL/ Family income
		Attending post-secondary training or education
		Average number of days poor physical or mental health prevented usual activities, such as self-care, work, or recreation
	Adulthood (29–40) *Reaches Middle Class (300 % FPL)*	Average number of days poor physical or mental health prevented usual activities, such as self-care, work, or recreation
		% FPL/ Family income at age 29
		Employment status of the population (by education level age 25+)

Abbreviation: *FPL* federal poverty level

Opportunity Indicators for the U.S.: Four Proposals

Indicators can provide a powerful infrastructure for policy making. This is an established fact in economics but has yet to become so for social policy. The current bipartisan interest in opportunity and mobility, however, could allow for operationalization of key indicators of progress, with potentially long-term benefits. In particular, four reforms should be considered.

Invest in Data for Opportunity

Data is gold, especially in the field of opportunity. Without data, policy decisions are arbitrary, claims are untested, and progress is virtually impossible. Indicators amount, in policy terms, to a weaponized data point. But the data they are based on has to be good.

This is an area where the U.S. can do much, much better, especially given the national commitment to opportunity. There are some hopeful signs of bipartisan activity here, too. House Speaker Paul Ryan (R-WI) and Sen. Patty Murray (D-WA) are together pushing for the creation of an independent Evidence-Based Policymaking Commission to "expand the use of data to evaluate the effectiveness of federal programs and tax expenditures." In particular, the commission, if approved by Congress and the President, will:

(a) study the federal government's data inventory, data infrastructure, and statistical protocols in order to facilitate program evaluation and policy-relevant research;

(b) make recommendations on how best to incorporate outcomes measurement, institutionalize randomized controlled trials, and rigorous impact analysis into program design; and

(c) explore how to create a clearinghouse of program and survey data.

This may not sound very exciting to most people (it is intended not to, so as to avoid stoking unfounded fears about individual privacy). But it is thrilling for policy. The Obama administration has also led a renewed charge for evidence-based policy, as recounted by my colleague Ron Haskins (2015) in his book *Show Me the Evidence: Obama's Fight for Rigor and Results in Social Policy*.

There is, however, a basic data issue too. Progress in terms of understanding trends in and prospects for intergenerational mobility is limited by what Kenneth (Prewitt (2015), 272), former director of the Census Bureau, describes as "a serious gap in the nation's statistics." One promising proposal is the creation of an American Opportunity Survey by linking together various administrative datasets, including the Census, American Community Survey, Survey of Income and Program Participation, as well as data from the IRS and Social Security Administration. As Grusky et al. (2015) argue, this approach would "provide a high-quality infrastructure for monitoring mobility without the cost of mounting a new mobility survey."

Right now, as they point out, the technical infrastructure for measuring mobility in the U.S. is in disrepair. This makes the formulation of policy difficult: It is rather like, as they put it, "formulating monetary and labor market policy without knowing whether unemployment is increasing or decreasing."

Getting better data is not a huge undertaking. The key is to be clear what the data is for. As Isabel Sawhill put it in 1969: "The principal barrier to quantification, in the long run at least, is *not a lack of meaningful data but a failure to define what is meaningful* … to give operational content to our ideals."

Set a Long-Term Goal for Intergenerational Mobility

Indicators are most valuable when an overall goal has been established: in other words, when it is clear what they are indicating toward. Goals can act as powerful policy commitment devices, helping to sustain a consistent focus on long-term objectives (Reeves 2015). In terms of promoting or restoring opportunity, a high-profile bipartisan commitment to a long-term goal could galvanize action on a number of important fronts. Such a goal would sit alongside existing goals for economic growth, monetary policy, employment, education, health, and so on. Because upward relative mobility is the primary concern for most policy makers, the goal should relate to progress on that front. For the purposes of illustration, I propose the following goal: increase the proportion of people born in the bottom income quintile who make it to the middle quintile or higher.

Right now, that number lies at around 40 % (or less, according to numbers generated by the Panel Study of Income Dynamics). In a perfectly mobile society, it would be 60 %. So, without further justification, 50 % seems like a reasonable goal. There are, of course, a host of other possibilities. A weakness of this goal is that it focuses attention on mobility from one specific part of the income distribution—the bottom—whereas equal opportunity ought to apply all the way up. I offer the goal principally in order to generate debate and illustrate the point. But this headline goal does have the advantage of being noncontroversial (at any rate it is hard to see why somebody would oppose it); simple (even if tracking it would be highly technical and controversial); and proximate to the goal of greater relative mobility. Operationalizing a goal like this would, needless to say, require a considerable number of technical specifications, including (but not restricted to): choice of dataset; household size equivalence; income definition; and inflation adjustments.

While the headline goal would apply to the whole population, it could also be used to track progress toward closing opportunity gaps and thereby help to focus policy attention. For example, the proportion of Black and White individuals could be compared in terms of the overall goal. Data from the NLSY suggests that the proportion of Black Americans making the journey is 22 %, compared to 58 % for Whites.

The key point is that the overall goal would act as a "north star," guiding the direction of policy and other activities. We would at least be able to see, over the longer term, if we were making progress. A vitally important caveat, however: Setting such a goal should not precede the establishment of reliable data from which to measure it (see the first proposal above). Of course, there are other strong candidates for a "north star" summary goal, including an improvement in rank-rank mobility (the association between parents' rank in earnings as compared to that of their children's rank as adults), or in occupational mobility, or perhaps in relation to another nation, such as Canada. Each approach will have strengths and weaknesses; each will fail to capture some dimensions of opportunity. But these concerns apply to almost all summary statistics, including those for GDP growth, productivity, and poverty.

Develop a 'Dashboard' of Annual Opportunity Indicators

It takes a generation to track intergenerational mobility: an obvious point, but an important one. It will also be valuable to develop "leading indicators" that can be tracked over a much shorter time horizon but are empirically proven to predict progress against the long-term goal. This is the approach taken in the Social Genome Model, where progress toward the long-term goal—"middle class by middle age"— is measured and predicted by a series of success measures for each crucial life stage. It is also a central part of both the U.K. and Colorado examples described earlier. A dashboard should contain shorter-term data points and trends that—based on the best available evidence—will likely lead to more upward mobility in the long run. As in the U.K. and Colorado, these leading indicators would be best organized around key life stages. The indicators should also emphasize the relative picture, rather than the absolute one: in other words, not just overall rates for each indicator, but the gap between different groups. Increasing college graduation rates will not improve mobility rates if most of the increase is made up of students from affluent backgrounds. For relative mobility, then, the mantra is always: mind the gap. The particular gap ought to be determined in large part by the long-term goal. So if the agreed focus was indeed on movement from the bottom quintile, the most appropriate short-term indicators for the annual dashboard should compare, say, rates of low birth weight births, school readiness, test scores, or postsecondary education between those in the bottom income quintile and those in the top two quintiles.

The point here is not to argue for specific elements of a dashboard—that will require a good deal of investigation—but for its creation. It should also be stressed that many of the indicators become valuable over time, with repeated measurement and reporting, rather than as snapshots at a particular moment in time.

For the purposes of illustration, Table 13.3 combines the indicators used in the U.K., Colorado, the Social Genome Model, and my own paper on "five strong starts." The overlaps are clear. The opportunity dashboard should have as many indicators as are useful but no more. In policy, parsimony is power. Continuous analysis of the predictive capability of the overall dashboard, and the contribution of each of the indicators, should be carried out. If after a period of time a specific indicator appears to be adding little value to the overall predictive power of the dashboard, it can be safely removed.

Create a Federal Office of Opportunity

Better data, a clear long-term goal, and a near-term dashboard are all key elements of a new policy architecture for social mobility. But there is also a strong case for giving social mobility an institutional anchor, in the form of an Office of Opportunity. I've argued elsewhere for such an institution at a federal level, but there is just as strong a case for state or city versions (Reeves 2014). The office would be charged with producing regular reports on progress in terms of both the long-term goal and the shorter-term indicators; for overseeing and advising on data collection; and for generating independent advice on the mobility-enhancing potential of various policy proposals. The office could be established as an executive body, a congressional one, or a hybrid.

Scott Winship has made a more ambitious institutional proposal, an Opportunity, Evidence and Innovation Office (OEIO), based in the White House. His OEIO would bring together a number of existing agencies and fund and evaluate programs and initiatives that "seek to promote upward mobility" (Winship 2015, 36).

Note that none of these proposals are in themselves about policy: rather they are about the generation of reliable data and clear indicators and strong institutional grounding for a focus on intergenerational mobility. They amount to a policy *architecture* rather than a policy. Which policies or programs will work toward the goal— and by association the leading indicators—is a second-order question, and one that should be settled empirically. We should be evangelical about the ends but agnostic about the means.

Table 13.3 Indicators used in the U.K., Colorado, the Social Genome Model, and Reeves' paper on "Five Strong Starts"

Life stages	U.K.	Colorado	SGM	5 strong starts
Family formation	Born at a normal birth weight	Planned pregnancy, born at a healthy weight to a dual-parent household with no history of maternal depression	Born at a normal birth weight to a nonpoor, married mother with at least a high school diploma	Born to mother with at least a high school diploma; born to capable parents
Early childhood	Development indicator not yet defined; school readiness (children achieve "good level of development"; meet standard in phonics screening	Acceptable level of school readiness, adequate social-emotional skills, and parent's ability to provide food to family	Acceptable pre-reading and math skills and behavior generally school-appropriate	Acceptable pre-reading and math skills and behavior generally school-appropriate
Middle childhood	Achieve level 4 in reading, writing, and math	Basic math, reading, and social-emotional skills	Basic reading and math skills and social-emotional skills	N/A
Adolescence	Achieve A to C in English and math at GCSE at 16; achieve level 3 qualifications by 19 or high A-level attainment (at least AAB)	Graduates from high school on time, has developed adequate social-emotional skills, and has not been convicted of a crime nor become a teen parent	Graduates from high school with GPA ≥ 2.5 and has not been convicted of a crime nor become a parent	Graduate high school with acceptable grades; enroll in college
Transition to adulthood	Participate in full or part-time higher education and/or training OR employed	Attended post-secondary education, is currently employed, and has good physical and mental health	Lives independently and receives a college degree or has a family income ≥ 250 % of the poverty level	Receives a postsecondary degree and is without a criminal conviction
Adulthood	Employed in managerial or professional positions or experience wage progression over course of a decade; achievement of level 2 and 3 qualifications if not already	Employed, has good physical and mental health, and reaches middle class (family income at least 300 % of the poverty level)	Reaches middle class (family income at least 300 % of the poverty level)	Married before first child; working before first child is born

Conclusion

The development of key indicators, collection of data, and establishment of technical bodies lack the glamour and immediacy of new policies or programs. But it is partly for that reason that they are more likely to gain crucial bipartisan political support. Even if both sides agree there is a problem, there is very little agreement in terms of specific solutions. Efforts to gain bipartisan support for specific policy programs are likely to be unsuccessful. But there is space for bipartisanship in the creation of an institutional framework designed to track the nation's progress toward greater opportunity, keep the attention of policy-makers on this long-term task, drive the collection and dissemination of higher quality data, and dispassionately assess initiatives intended to improve rates of intergenerational mobility.

Right now, political discussions of opportunity are replete with anecdote and soaring speeches about American exceptionalism. But in the end, the restoration of opportunity is not a matter of opinion or rhetoric. It is a matter of fact. If we are serious about a project to restore opportunity, we need to know when we've arrived.

References

Cabinet Office, HM Government. 2012. *Opening doors, breaking barriers: A strategy for social mobility.* London: Author.

Chetty, Raj, Nathaniel Hendren, Patrick Kline, Emmanuel Saez, and Nicholas Turner. 2014. Is the United States still a land of opportunity? Recent trends in intergenerational mobility. *American Economic Review* 104: 141–147.

Cobb, Clifford, and Craig Rixford. 1998. *Lessons learned from the history of social indicators.* San Francisco: Redefining Progress.

Economic Mobility Project. 2012. *Pursuing the American dream: Economic mobility across generations.* Washington, DC: Pew Charitable Trusts.

Economic Policies for the 21st Century. 2014. *Income inequality in America: Fact and fiction.* New York: Manhattan Institute.

Gregg, Paul, Lindsey Macmillan, and Claudia Vittori. 2014. Moving towards estimation lifetime intergenerational economic mobility in the UK. In *Working paper 14/332.* Bristol: University of Bristol.

Grusky, David B., Timothy M. Smeeding, and C. Matthew Snipp. 2015. A new infrastructure for monitoring social mobility in the United States. *Annals* 657: 63–82.

Haskins, Ron. 2015. *Show me the evidence: Obama's fight for rigor and results in social policy.* Washington, DC: Brookings Institution Press.

Hayes, Chris. 2013. *Twilight of the elites: American after meritocracy.* New York: Broadway Books.

Mazumder, Bhashkar. 2011. *Black-White differences in intergenerational economic mobility in the United States.* Chicago: Federal Reserve Bank of Chicago.

Mazumder, Bhashkar. 2014. *Upward intergenerational mobility in the United States.* Washington, DC: The Pew Charitable Trusts.

Prewitt, Kenneth. 2015. Who is listening? When scholars think they are talking to Congress. *Annals* 657: 265–272.

Prewitt, Kenneth, Thomas A. Schwandt, and Miron L. Straf. 2012. *Using science as evidence in public policy*. Washington: National Academies Press.

Reeves, Richard V. 2014. *Planning the American dream: The case for an office of opportunity*. Washington, DC: Brookings Institution.

Reeves, Richard V. 2015. *Ulysses goes to Washington: Policy commitment devices and political myopia*. Washington, DC: Brookings Institution.

Reeves, Richard V., and Kimberly Howard. 2014. *The marriage effect: Money or parenting?* Washington, DC: Brookings Institution.

Sawhill, Isabel. 1969. The role of social indicators and social reporting in public expenditure decisions. In *The analysis and evaluation of public expenditures: The PPB system, by the U.S. Joint Economic Committee*. Washington, DC: U.S. Government Printing Office.

Sen, Amartya. 1979. *"Equality of what?" The Tanner lecture on human values*. Stanford: Stanford University.

Sheldon, Eleanor Bernert, and Wilbert E. Moore (eds.). 1968. *Indicators of social change*. New York: Russell Sage Foundation.

Swift, Adam. 2004. Would perfect mobility be perfect? *European Sociological Review* 20: 1–11.

U.S. Bureau of the Census. 1977. *Social indicators, 1976: Selected data on social conditions and trends in the United States*. Washington, DC: U.S. Government Printing Office.

U.S. Bureau of the Census. 1981. *Social indicators III: Selected data on social conditions and trends in the United States*. Washington, DC: U.S. Government Printing Office.

U.S. Department of Health, Education and Welfare. 1969. *Towards a social report*. Washington, DC: U.S. Government Printing Office.

U.S. Office of Management and Budget. 1975. *Social indicators, 1974*. Washington, DC: U.S. Government Printing Office.

Winship, Scott, and Stephanie Owen. 2013. *Guide to the Brookings Social Genome Model*. Washington, DC: Brookings Institution.

Winship, Scott. 2015. Up: Expanding opportunity in America. In *Policy options for improving economic opportunity*, 31–57. New York: Peter G. Peterson Foundation. http://pgpf.org/sites/default/files/grant_cbpp_manhattaninst_economic_mobility.pdf.

Epilogue: Can Capitalists Reform Themselves?

Chrystia Freeland

Abstract After spending a decade as a journalist writing about rising income inequality and 2 years as an elected politician trying to do something about it, the author is convinced that the best chance that progressives have of bending the arc of the twenty-first century economy is with a message of inclusive prosperity. That means wholeheartedly embracing capitalism while ensuring that the wealth it creates is broadly shared. It also means embracing capitalists and convincing them that they, too, will benefit when others get a bigger slice of the pie. The moment is ripe for action. But a confrontational strategy of framing the plight of the twenty-first century middle class as a zero-sum political battle, one where the plutocrats have been winning at everyone else's expense, is not the answer. The stunning 2015 election failure of Great Britain's Labour Party serves as evidence to that effect. Most Americans understand that capitalism works as an economic system—just not as a social one—and that many of our most successful capitalists are the people responsible for its effectiveness. Thus the key is for plutocrats to realize it is in their best interest—and everyone else's—to participate in the solution by paying higher taxes. Such a stance has precedent. In the post-World War II era, civic-minded American business leaders were willing to advocate and pay increased taxes even though rates were much higher than they are now.

Keywords Capitalism, Inclusive prosperity, Income inequality, Progressivism, Plutocrats, American Dream

One summer day in 2015, I stood on an elegant stone deck overlooking a swimming pool on one side and a lush well-tended garden on the other. Behind me was a three-story brick mansion, easily worth $10 million, and in front of me was a group of Toronto's 1 %, including a couple of Canada's wealthiest businessmen. My job was to persuade them to vote for me, and for my party, which was promising to raise taxes on the rich to pay for a tax cut and more benefits for the middle class and the poor.

I won't pretend it was an easy sell. But after spending a decade as a journalist writing about rising income inequality and 2 years as an elected politician trying to do something about it, I'm convinced that the best chance that progressives have of bending the arc of the twenty-first century economy is with a message of inclusive

C. Freeland
Canada's Minister of International Trade and a Member of Parliament
for University-Rosedale, Toronto, Canada

© Educational Testing Service 2016
I. Kirsch, H. Braun (eds.), *The Dynamics of Opportunity in America*,
DOI 10.1007/978-3-319-25991-8

465

prosperity. That means wholeheartedly embracing capitalism while ensuring that the wealth it creates is broadly shared. And it means embracing capitalists and convincing them that they, too, will benefit when others get a bigger slice of the pie.

For many on the left, this approach seems worse than a crime; it seems to be a mistake. After all, what the nineteenth-century socialists used to call "objective conditions" today seem to be lining up on the side of a pugnacious, progressive agenda.

Income inequality is surging worldwide—as Oxfam notoriously pointed out in 2014,[1] the combined wealth of the world's 85 richest people that year was equal to the wealth of the globe's bottom 50 %. CEO salaries are escalating—in 2012, the average CEO of a U.S. Fortune 500 company earned 350 times the salary of the average worker, compared to a ratio of 20 to 1 in the 1950s.[2] Meanwhile, middle class incomes have been stagnant or worse for the past three decades, and the economies of the western industrialized countries are barely growing.

There isn't much trickling down and, crucially for progressives, public opinion seems to be noticing. The financial crisis and the recession that followed it have made crony capitalism, especially where Wall Street is involved, an unavoidable issue for the right as well as the left. The hollowing out of middle class incomes, which had been masked by the pre-2008 credit bubble, was the starting point for both Jeb Bush and Hillary Clinton when they launched their presidential campaigns. A 600-page tome by a French economist whose title evokes Marx is a best seller (Thomas Piketty's *Capital in the Twenty-First Century*), and subpar growth across the western world has brought Keynes back into vogue.

Just as the stagflation of the 1970s set the stage for the Reagan and Thatcher revolution, now seems to be the moment for progressives to seize and reshape how we think about the political economy. The temptation is to go nuclear—to frame the plight of the twenty-first century middle class as a zero-sum political battle the plutocrats have been winning but whose outcome can now be reversed, to do to highly paid CEOs and billionaire hedge fund managers what Reagan and Thatcher did to unions and welfare recipients. Even Clinton, she of the $250,000 speeches to Goldman Sachs, is now calling for the "toppling" of the 1 %.[3]

But there's one big problem with this strategy. It isn't working. The most recent example is Britain, where the Labour Party this spring suffered its greatest defeat in three decades. Peter Mandelson, the former Labour cabinet minister and a leading

---

[1] Oxfam International, "Even It Up: Time to End Extreme Inequality," https://www.oxfam.org/en/campaigns/even-it-up

[2] Gretchen Gavett, "CEOs Get Paid Too Much, According to Pretty Much Everyone in the World," *Harvard Business Review*, September 23, 2014, https://hbr.org/2014/09/ceos-get-paid-too-much-according-to-pretty-much-everyone-in-the-world/

[3] Amy Chozick, "Campaign Casts Hillary Clinton as the Populist It Insists She Has Always Been," *New York Times,* April 21, 2015, http://www.nytimes.com/2015/04/22/us/politics/hillary-clintons-quest-to-prove-her-populist-edge-is-as-strong-as-elizabeth-warrens.html

strategist in Tony Blair's three successful elections, argues that the defeat happened because Labour misplayed the issue of rising income inequality.[4]

The mistake wasn't emphasizing Labour's egalitarian values and its belief in government's mission to "lean against inequality." In fact, Mandelson has praised Ed Miliband, the former Labour leader, for identifying the winner-take-all economy as a central issue for our time and spotting the essential fact that "since the global financial crisis, the public's intolerance for inequality has turned to outright anger about the polarization of incomes between the very rich and the rest."

But Mandelson believes Miliband struck the wrong note in his response to rising income inequality: "The bigger reason Labour lost the argument is that the British, on the whole, do not like income disparities being turned into class war. Earlier in his leadership, Mr. Miliband fought on a platform of social justice and fairness, using the language of 'one nation.' In the campaign, he seemed intent on pitting one half of the nation against the other."

There are good reasons to think Americans are equally averse to an eat-the-rich political response to income inequality. A growing body of research suggests that the connection between rising income inequality and public support for redistribution in the United States is a lot more tenuous than progressive common sense might suggest.

"Numerous political theorists suggest that rising inequality and the shift in the distribution of income to those at the top should lead to increasing support for liberal policies," Matthew Luttig, of the University of Minnesota, argues in a 2013 paper. "But recent evidence contradicts these theories. I empirically evaluate a number of competing theoretical predictions about the relationship between inequality and public preferences. In general, the evidence supports the claim that rising inequality has been a force promoting conservatism in the American public."

A separate study, by a group of scholars including Emmanuel Saez, Piketty's long-time collaborator and a leading income inequality researcher, confirmed that finding: "The median-voter theorem predicts that an increase in the demand for redistribution would accompany this rise in income concentration (Meltzer and Richard 1981). However, time-series evidence from survey data does not support this prediction. If anything, the General Social Survey shows there has been a slight decrease in stated support for redistribution in the U.S. since the 1970s, even among those who self-identify as having below-average income" (Kuziemko et al. 2013).

That's a terrible paradox for liberals. Rising income inequality, which makes progressive policies—including more redistribution—more urgent than ever, does not seem to be shifting public opinion in favor of such measures. The changing income distribution may even be making people more conservative.

There's now a lively and agonized debate among liberals about why that may be the case. One cause is surely the extent to which, over the past four decades, conservatives have shaped the ways in which all of us think about the economy. While the left was fighting—and winning—the culture war on values, the right was fighting—

---

[4] Peter Mandelson, "Why Labour Lost the Election," op-ed, *New York Times,* May 19, 2015, http://www.nytimes.com/2015/05/20/opinion/peter-mandelson-why-labour-lost-the-election.html

and winning—the culture war on the economy. From "Tax Freedom Day," to the "death tax," to debt and deficits, since the Reagan and Thatcher revolution, the right has defined and dominated the economic debate in the western industrialized world.

But another factor may be a new economic reality that progressive critics of surging income inequality can find difficult to acknowledge. Crony capitalism—that rigged economic game Elizabeth Warren speaks of so powerfully—is only one of the drivers of surging incomes at the top. Another is the "winner-take-all"[5] structure of the twenty-first century globalized knowledge economy, and the undeniable fact that at least some of the winners are succeeding because they are transforming our lives in valuable ways: Being a Steve Jobs delivers better returns than ever before for the particular genius entrepreneur, but it also happens to offer less employment for everyone else. Consider this—in the 1950s, when Detroit was America's engine of innovation, General Motors employed over 600,000 people. Today, when Silicon Valley is at the forefront of the technology revolution, two of its leading companies, Facebook and Google, employ jointly just 60,000.

Intuitively, Americans understand what is happening—they know that their wages and their jobs are being hollowed out, but they also realize that Silicon Valley whiz kids are driving the process just as surely as Wall Street banksters are. And they know that while the technology revolution that the late Jobs had led with his peers is threatening their incomes and security as workers, it is also vastly improving their experience as consumers. Like the early industrial revolution, today's wave of technological change is having a contradictory impact on those of us in the 99%—enriching our material lives even as it hollows out our jobs and wages. That's why, even in an age of rising income inequality and increasing middle class insecurity, the technology giants who are in the vanguard of the transformation are more likely to be lionized than reviled—witness the spontaneous iPad- and iPhone-lit vigils after Jobs' death.

The temptation for progressives is to view this sympathy for the plutocrats as what Marxists used to call "false consciousness": Bedazzled by the conservative message machine, unfortunate Americans are simply failing to recognize their true self-interest. That's the implicit view, for instance, of a recent scholarly study that concludes that middle class Americans who don't support redistribution are "prisoners of the American Dream" (Manza and Brooks Forthcoming).

Jeff Manza, of New York University, and Clem Brooks, of Indiana University, take as their starting point the contradiction identified by Luttig and Saez—that, despite rising income inequality, "Americans have not increased their hostility to either inequality or the rich, nor have they increased support for redistributive taxes in recent decades." Their answer is belief in the American dream, which, they conclude, "is associated with significantly lower support for taxes and equality" (Ibid.).

But telling people they are brainwashed is rarely a good political strategy, and in this case it isn't even entirely true. In fact, the American Dream, in its narrow, hyper-meritocratic manifestation, is very much alive and well: In 1982, just 40 % of

---

[5] Alan Krueger, "Land of Hope and Dreams: Rock and Roll, Economics, and Rebuilding the Middle Class" (remarks, Rock and Roll Hall of Fame, Cleveland, June 12, 2013).

those on the Forbes 400 list of the richest Americans were self-made—they had built the businesses from which they derived their fortunes, not inherited them; by 2011, that figure had risen to 69 % (Kaplan and Rauh 2013).

The problem isn't rewards for the very best and the very brightest—lucky and smart and hard-working meritocrats are more richly compensated than ever in today's winner-take-all economy. What's going wrong in today's political economy is that jobs for those in the middle, and future opportunities for their children, are vanishing.

In a recent essay lamenting the lack of "sustained resistance to wealth inequality" in the United States, my compatriot Naomi Klein suggests this passivity is because, unlike leftist activists during the original Gilded Age, today we are "fully in capitalism's matrix" and are therefore unable to believe "in something else entirely."[6]

That's true—and most of us don't think it is a bad thing. We've tried the communist alternative, after all, and it didn't work out so well. The dominant concern about capitalism today isn't that it is failing as an economic engine—most goods and many services are getting ever cheaper and more abundant. Our complaint is that our political economy is doing a poor job of sharing the fruits of this twenty-first century capitalist cornucopia.

That's why income inequality is an essential issue for progressives, but also a complicated one. Most Americans understand that capitalism works as an economic system—just not as a social one—and that many of our most successful capitalists are the people responsible for its effectiveness.

This meritocratic effectiveness of the 1% is why the right wins when it succeeds in casting calls for more redistribution as a punishment of success. As former President Bill Clinton put it at his flagship conference last September, "I don't think most Americans resent someone doing well. They resent it if they're not getting a fair deal, too."[7] That's why eating the rich isn't the best way of making the case for more redistributive economic policy. We need to persuade the plutocrats themselves to embrace the idea, too. (For discussion on how Americans overall view inequality and approaches to address it, see Chap. 12.)

This is less of a paradox than you may think. Warren Buffett is right when he quips that there is a class war today—and that his class is winning. But the smartest plutocrats are starting to understand that mass democracy and an economic order skewed so strongly in favor of the 0.1 % won't be compatible for long. That's why socially minded pursuits like impact investing, corporate social responsibility, and inclusive capitalism are the high-status hobbies of many of today's plutocrats.

And warning that capitalism needs to do a better job of serving the middle class or it is doomed has become something of a mini-trend among the super-rich. Nick

---

[6] Naomi Klein, review of *The Age of Acquiescence* by Steve Fraser, *New York Times,* March 16, 2015, http://www.nytimes.com/2015/03/22/books/review/the-age-of-acquiescence-by-steve-fraser.html

[7] Associated Press, "Bill Clinton Defends Wife's Commitment to Poor, *Politico,* June 24, 2014, http://www.politico.com/story/2014/06/bill-clinton-hillary-clinton-poor-108249.html

Hanauer, a billionaire Seattle entrepreneur and tech investor, has written an open letter to his fellow "zillionaires," cautioning that: "If we don't do something to fix the glaring inequities in this economy, the pitchforks are going to come for us. No society can sustain this kind of rising inequality. In fact, there is no example in human history where wealth accumulated like this and the pitchforks didn't eventually come out. You show me a highly unequal society, and I will show you a police state. Or an uprising. There are no counterexamples. None. It's not if, it's when."[8]

Paul Tudor Jones, a Connecticut billionaire hedge fund manager who started his career trading cotton futures in New Orleans, sounded a similar warning in a TED talk in March 2015, predicting that "that gap between the wealthiest and the poorest, it will get closed. History always does it," but predicting that history's unwelcome tool might be war or revolution.[9] A better approach, Jones argued, was to build a fairer version of capitalism: "Capitalism has to be based on justice. It has to be, and now more than ever, with economic divisions growing wider every day. It's estimated that 47 % of American workers can be displaced in the next 20 years. I'm not against progress. I want the driverless car and the jet pack just like everyone else. But I'm pleading for recognition that with increased wealth and profits has to come greater corporate social responsibility (Ibid.)."

Of course, it is one thing to support inclusive capitalism in theory, or a few charter schools, or some women entrepreneurs in Africa, or, in the case of Goldman Sachs, 10,000 small businesses. It's quite another to tolerate higher taxes on your own income bracket. As Larry Summers, the former Secretary of the Treasury and chair of a recent *Center for American Progress* report called *Inclusive Capitalism* (Summers and Balls 2015), put it— "A lot of CEOs ask me how they can help build a more inclusive capitalism. I tell them there is a simple place to start—pay more taxes."[10]

It is time to remember that this is something civic-minded American business leaders were actually willing to do and to support in the postwar era. In 1950, to pay for the Korean War, America's two main business organizations proposed a package of tax increases including raising the corporate tax to 50%, a special additional tax on the defense industry (which would profit from war spending) and a temporary increase in the income tax rate. In 1956, America's leading business group called for a fuel tax to pay for highway building.

These and a dozen other similar episodes of pro-tax lobbying by American corporate chiefs, carefully documented by University of Michigan sociologist Mark Mizruchi in a 2013 book, seem almost fantastical today.

---

[8] Nick Hanauer, "The Pitchforks Are Coming … for Us Plutocrats," *Politico Magazine,* July/August 2014, http://www.politico.com/magazine/story/2014/06/the-pitchforks-are-coming-for-us-plutocrats-108014.html

[9] See TED website at https://www.ted.com/talks/paul_tudor_jones_ii_why_we_need_to_rethink_capitalism

[10] Larry Summers, personal communication, April 2015.

The willingness of postwar American business leaders to advocate higher taxes is even more astonishing because both companies and their bosses paid taxes at a much higher rate at the time than they do now. Corporate taxes accounted for around a quarter of all federal tax revenues in 1965. Today, companies pay around 10% of total revenue, and their share is dropping.[11] Personal tax rates on the wealthy used to be unthinkably high by today's standards, too—in 1963, the top tax rate was 91%.

There's a reason we called them the Greatest Generation—the elites of yesteryear were paid less and taxed more, yet they were much more willing to support further tax increases than their equivalents are today.

Progressives should call on the grandchildren of those postwar elites to do the same today. Even if only a fraction of the plutocrats are persuaded, middle class Americans will respond better to arguments that seek to include the winners of twenty-first century capitalism rather than demonize them.

On that balmy June evening speaking to the 1% gathered poolside in Toronto, I described going skating with my three children a few months earlier at the local public rink, just a few blocks away. As we made our way on to the ice, the richest man in Canada and his youngest daughter whizzed past. I had worked for his companies in the past, and we stopped to chat. He was enthusiastic about the rink—in his opinion, the nicest in town.

I had moved back to Canada just a couple of years earlier. I had been living in Moscow, London, and New York and writing a book about plutocrats, describing how they were forming a global community of peers, walled off from everyone else—a sort of virtual Galt's Gulch, Ayn Rand's fantasy valley to which her supermen retreated to escape the parasitic proletarians. The billionaire at the public skating rink, I told my 1% listeners, was illustrative of an inclusive society that had vanished in much of the world and was under threat even in Canada, where income inequality has increased over the past three decades but the chasm is still smaller than in the United States (TD Economics 2014; Corak 2013).[12]

All of us have a stake in preserving, building, or recovering inclusive prosperity—not least the plutocrats. Because, ultimately, there can be no Galt's Gulch. What Ben Franklin said at the signing of the Declaration of Independence is true of capitalist democracies today writ large: "We must hang together or, assuredly, we shall hang separately."

---

[11] David Wessel, "How to Read Obama's New Budget," Brookings Institution website, February 26, 2014, http://www.brookings.edu/research/opinions/2014/02/26-how-to-read-obamas-new-budget-wessel

[12] In 1982, the top 1 % accounted for 7.1 % of the national income in Canada. By 2012, that share had increased to 10.3 %. Over the same span, the share of national income going to the top 0.1 % in Canada doubled from 2.5 to 5 %. This a big shift, but Canada is still much less unequal than the United States—the share of income going to the 1 % in Canada today is roughly the same as the share taken by the 0.1 % in the United States.

References

Corak, Miles. 2013. Income inequality, equality of opportunity, and intergenerational mobility. *Journal of Economic Perspectives* 27(3): 79–102.

Kaplan, Steven N., and Joshua D. Rauh. 2013. Family, education, and sources of wealth among the richest Americans, 1982–2012. *American Economic Review* 103(3): 158–162.

Kuziemko, Ilyana, Michael I. Norton, Emmanuel Saez, and Stefanie Santcheva. 2013. *How elastic are preferences for redistribution? Evidence from randomized survey experiments,* NBER Working Paper 18865. Cambridge, MA: National Bureau of Economic Research. http://www.nber.org/papers/w18865.

Luttig, Matthew. 2013. The structure of inequality and Americans' attitudes toward redistribution. *Public Opinion Quarterly* 77. doi:10.1093/poq/nft025.

Manza, Jeff, and Clem Brooks. Forthcoming. *Prisoners of the American dream? Americans' Attitudes towards taxes and inequality in a new gilded age*, working paper, NYU Department of Sociology, New York. http://sociology.as.nyu.edu/docs/IO/3858/PrisonersoftheAmericanDream.pdf.

Meltzer, Allan H., and Scott F. Richard. 1981. A rational theory of the size of government. *Journal of Political Economy* 89(5): 914–27.

Mizruchi, Mark S. 2013. *The fracturing of the American corporate elite.* Cambridge, MA: Harvard University Press.

Summers, Lawrence H., and Ed Balls. 2015. *Inclusive prosperity.* Washington, DC: Center for American Progress.

TD Economics. 2014. *The case for leaning against income inequality in Canada*, November 24. http://www.td.com/document/PDF/economics/special/income_inequality.pdf.

Appendix: Members of the Opportunity in America Advisory Panel

Contributing authors **Chrystia Freeland, Douglas S. Massey, David G. Sciarra, Timothy M. (Tim) Smeeding,** *and* **Marshall S. Smith** *also serve on the Advisory Panel for ETS's Opportunity in America initiative. The other panel members are as follows:*

Bo Cutter is a Senior Fellow and Director of the Next American Economy Project at the Roosevelt Institute.

Ron Ferguson has taught at Harvard's Kennedy School of Government for over 30 years. He is creator of the Tripod Project for School Improvement, faculty co-chair and director of the Achievement Gap Initiative at Harvard University, and was formerly the faculty co-director of the Pathways to Prosperity Project at the Harvard Graduate School of Education.

Mark Gerzon is President of Mediators Foundation, which works to increase citizen engagement and civility in politics. He is the author of several books, including the forthcoming *The Reunited States of America: How We Can Bridge the Partisan Divide.*

Peter Gould is Executive Vice President of District 1199C, National Union of Hospital and Health Care Employees, National Union of Hospital and Health Care Employees (NUHHCE), AFSCME, AFL-CIO and Vice President of NUHHE.

Wade Henderson is President and CEO of The Leadership Conference on Civil and Human Rights and the Leadership Conference Education Fund. He is also a member of the ETS Board of Trustees.

Frederick M. Hess is Director of Education Policy Studies at the American Enterprise Institute.

Kurt M. Landgraf is former President and Chief Executive Officer of Educational Testing Service.

Reynaldo F. Macías is professor of Chicana/o Studies, Education and Applied Linguistics, and a former department chair of Chicana/o studies and acting Dean of Social Sciences at UCLA.

Isabel V. Sawhill is a Senior Fellow in Economic Studies at the Brookings Institution.

© Educational Testing Service 2016
I. Kirsch, H. Braun (eds.), *The Dynamics of Opportunity in America*,
DOI 10.1007/978-3-319-25991-8

Index

© Educational Testing Service 2016
I. Kirsch, H. Braun (eds.), *The Dynamics of Opportunity in America*,
DOI 10.1007/978-3-319-25991-8

Printed by Printforce, the Netherlands